NIETZSCHE: *An Introduction to the Understanding of His Philosophical Activity*

NIETZSCHE

An Introduction to the Understanding
of His Philosophical Activity

Karl Jaspers

Translated by CHARLES F. WALLRAFF
and FREDERICK J. SCHMITZ

THE UNIVERSITY OF ARIZONA PRESS   TUCSON

The text of NIETZSCHE was set in Linotype Times
Roman, printed from type on Warren's Olde Style
Antique Wove paper, and bound into books by
Kingsport Press, Inc., Kingsport, Tenn. Gary Gore
of Kingsport was the designer of the pages, jacket,
and the binding.

L. C. Catalogue Card No. 65–12660

TRANSLATORS' NOTE

When the present book first appeared in Nazi Germany thirty years ago, Anglo-American philosophers were barely aware of existentialism and all but oblivious of its forerunners. Typical texts on the history of philosophy never so much as mentioned Pascal and Kierkegaard, and philosophers were inclined to regard Nietzsche as a poet and seer and turn him over to the literati (or, in some cases, to the Nazis). Jaspers was scarcely more than a name, and Heidegger was perhaps first called to our attention by those members of the *Wiener Kreis* who saw fit to make merry over what they regarded as the patent nonsensicality of his much ado about "nothing."

While, figuratively speaking, it would seem to be as true today as it was in the seventeenth century that the English Channel is a greater barrier to the communication of ideas than the Atlantic Ocean, the present climate of opinion in the English-speaking countries is certainly more favorable to this new kind of philosophizing than formerly. Since Kierkegaard's works have become available in English, and Nietzsche has been absolved from his guilt by posthumous association with the Nazis and presented in improved translations, existentialism, as introduced by its various contemporary exponents, appears as the chief alternative to analytic and linguistic philosophies.

While those interested in existentialism can ill afford to ignore Nietzsche, it is still true that the nature of Nietzsche's thought is so intricate and the manner of its communication so ambiguous that it is not easy for most readers to discover what he believed, why he believed it, in what respects his thinking concerns us, and how it leads to existentialism. The present volume by a prominent exponent of the philosophy of *Existenz* presents the life and thought of Nietzsche in such a way as to provide answers to these questions.

Although no adequate exposition of Jaspers' philosophy can be offered here, perhaps this much should be said: Anglo-American readers who find it difficult to get their bearings within *Existenzphilosophie* may do well to note at the outset that if Jaspers seems credulous where others are skeptical (his defense of philosophical faith is a case in point), he is also skeptical where others are credulous. Although few philosophers have practiced science better or esteemed it more highly than this author of an authoritative treatise on psychopathology, he never ceases to insist that one of the chief rewards of the practice of the scientific method is direct acquaintance with the limits of science. Knowledge of these limits and awareness of a beyond discloses the area belonging to philosophy.

As opposed to both rationalists and empiricists, who have stressed clarity as a fundamental philosophic criterion (and frequently even offered to show us how ideas can be made clear), Jaspers insists that clarity is a scientific ideal relating to objects within the world and unattainable in the realm of the things that matter most. He agrees with Kant that where determinate knowledge is impossible, indeterminate thought must take over: to have clear and distinct ideas of the world as a whole, of spirit, or of God is manifestly impossible. Here the Cartesian criterion is simply inapplicable, and other standards must prevail.

Consistency also occupies a curious position here. Much as F. H. Bradley in Part I of *Appearance and Reality* develops at length the innumerable contradictions that crop up in our thinking about the everyday world, Jaspers, taking his cue from the Kantian antinomies, delights in the manifold contradictions that, by revealing the limits of the "understanding," invite us to employ "reason" in order to transcend the given, and the "Ideas" of reason to comprehend what the scientific understanding can never grasp. This may help us to understand how his admiration for Nietzsche can be compatible with his discovery of innumerable contradictions in Nietzsche's thought.

Finally it should be emphasized that neither Jaspers nor Nietzsche takes any interest in the sort of academic philosophy that preserves an inane correctness by avoiding the serious problems that confront existing individuals and by refusing to acknowledge an obligation to live in accordance with one's own philosophy. Philosophy, as they see it, is not an accomplishment to be worked up by students faced with examinations, or practiced by professors who prefer this way of making a living while their real interests lie elsewhere. It is not as though life and a set of facts and meanings were already given, needing only to be accepted at face value and dealt with *ad libitum*. Rather, as the ancients believed, philosophy is a matter of the utmost seriousness: It is a vision that one lives by, in the sense in which Socrates lived by his when, at the cost of his life, he refused to violate the principles he had always honored. Philosophical knowledge is not a mere acquisition—something that one may or may not *have*. It is not a property, for, being internal to the knower, it transforms him basically. A man's philosophy, so to speak, is constitutive as well as regulative: it determines the nature of his experienced world and, in doing so, determines his nature as well as his reaction patterns. Thus for both Nietzsche and Jaspers, philosophical thinking supplies the ground of our being—that out of which we live. The experientialistic interpretationism involved in this (see Book Two, Chapter 5) needs to be kept in mind throughout.

This translation of Jaspers' work attempts chiefly to state the author's meaning as clearly as possible. During the pursuit of their task, however, the translators became vividly aware of the special and rather formidable problem involved. On the one hand, Jaspers' concept of the nature and purpose of true philosophy in general and his approach to Nietzsche in particular seemed to demand, with respect to his own work, what he himself requires for a genuine assimilation of Nietzsche when he speaks (on p. 453 of this book) of the need of "a thinking feeling" (*ein denkendes Empfinden*) on the part of the interpreter. Bringing out the meaning implied thus more than a mere literal rendition; rather it involved considerable interpretation with the aid of all available linguistic means, especially in view of the many virtually untranslatable expressions used by the author. On the other hand, the translators felt compelled to preserve as much as possible of the author's own unique and extremely forceful style as well as of the directness and concreteness (*Anschaulichkeit*) of Nietzsche's language (presented in countless quotations throughout the book) in order to preserve the flavor of the original and the impact and force of its meaning. If the translation can lay any claim at all to literary merit, it is to the extent to which it succeeded in this respect, even though it certainly cannot be a satisfactory substitute for the original.

After some discussion it was decided to omit the frequent parenthetical references through which quotations from Nietzsche are located within the edition of Nietzsche's works prepared many years ago by his sister. Such omissions were made partly for the sake of attractive typography, partly because the author himself seems to sanction this procedure by deliberately omitting such references from his recent *The Great Philosophers* (see p. 101 of the original and p. 10 of Mannheim's translation), but above all because no one who needs a translation could possibly make any use of these references.

The material in fine print in the original is seldom in any sense an *excursus*—sometimes it is even introduced by a colon and treated as an integral part of the presentation (see, for example, p. 338 and p. 351 of the German version). Hence we have simply incorporated it within the body of the text where, according to the conventions followed in England and America, it would seem to belong.

We are of course greatly indebted to other translators. To mention only a few: Following Professor L. B. Lefebre, we have rendered *Dasein* as "existence" and left *Existenz* untranslated, even though this practice led once or twice to the awkwardness of including both terms in the same sentence. Professor Mannheim's version of *The Great Philosophers* has served as both an example and an inspiration. And Mr. E. B. Ashton's exceptionally clear and forceful recreation of *Nietzsche and Christianity* (not to mention his other outstanding translations) is to us more nearly an ideal to be pursued than a goal to be reached.

The work of translating was divided as follows: C. F. Wallraff, who studied under Professor Jaspers in Heidelberg in 1934–35 and is at present a professor of philosophy at the University of Arizona, translated and assumes primary responsibility for the more philosophical parts (Book Two, Chapters 1, 2, and 5, and all of Book Three). F. J. Schmitz, a native German who received his early education and part of his undergraduate as well as postgraduate training in Germany and is now a professor of German at the same institution, translated and assumes primary responsibility for the remainder. However, each translator carefully checked and revised the other's work and shares responsibility for the book in its entirety.

We are most grateful to Dr. Jack Cross, editor, and Mrs. Elizabeth Shaw, associate editor, of the University of Arizona Press for the advice, cooperation, and encouragement which they so generously provided as we struggled with the difficulties intrinsic to the project. And very especial thanks go to Professor Babette Luz who not only read and emended the entire typescript, but also undertook the gargantuan task of translating and renumbering the page references of the original index compiled by Dr. Maria Salditt.

Tucson   CHARLES F. WALLRAFF
August, 1964   FREDERICK J. SCHMITZ

CONTENTS

PREFACE TO THE FIRST EDITION

To many people reading Nietzsche seems easy: Whatever passage one happens upon can be understood immediately, almost every page that he has written is interesting, his judgments are fascinating, his language is intoxicating, and even the briefest reading is rewarding. But anyone who is led by such impressions to read extensively soon becomes disturbed, and his enthusiasm for the directness of Nietzsche's appeal is replaced by an aversion to the great variety of judgments that are seemingly binding upon no one. One finds it insufferable that Nietzsche says first this, then that, and then something entirely different. To proceed in this way is to fail to gain a true understanding or even to discover the real underlying difficulties.

We must abandon mere reading of Nietzsche for a study that amounts to an appropriation achieved by occupying ourselves with the totality of the intellectual experiences which make him so representative of our age. He then becomes symbolic of the destiny of humanity itself as it presses onwards toward its limits and its sources.

Every philosopher of rank requires such study as is commensurate with his stature. Nothing less than this can provide the soil for the inner activity that is the essence of true understanding. Books about a philosopher are intended to promote this inner activity. Instead of providing mere superficial contact, passive enjoyment of linguistic felicities, and an initial misunderstanding that leads to arbitrary emphases, they should afford direct access and point the way. What concerns the philosopher in question should be brought out so clearly that we learn what is involved by dealing with the very thoughts that he had in mind.

Heidelberg, December, 1935   KARL JASPERS

PREFACE TO THE SECOND AND THIRD EDITIONS

The present edition is an unaltered reprint of the first.

This book undertakes, by bringing out the substance of Nietzsche's philosophy, to combat a series of misunderstandings on the part of the generations that have come under his influence and to counteract the aberrations in the writings of a man on the verge of insanity. Nietzsche is perhaps the last of the great philosophers of the past, and it is hoped that his prophetic earnestness will prevail over mere semblance.

I tried to prepare this book in complete independence of the situation at the time and thus to offer an objective and timelessly valid interpretation. But in the years 1934 and 1935, I also intended to marshal against the National Socialists the world of thought of the man whom they had proclaimed as their own philosopher. The book grew out of lectures in the course of which many listeners understood what I meant when I quoted Nietzsche's statement: "We are emigrants. . . ." This quotation, together with his sympathetic comments about the Jews, has been omitted from the book itself and will not be added now, since it is not pertinent to my main concerns. I do not intend to alter the documentary material in the book.

The original plan called for a chapter made up of quotations from Nietzsche's mistaken naturalistic and extremist pronouncements, collected as evidence of his aberrations. The result was devastating, and I omitted it out of respect for Nietzsche. When one reaches the kind of understanding which this book is intended to provide, such aberrations are seen to amount to nothing. Anyone who takes these passages seriously, points them out, or even goes so far as to be ensnared and guided by them has neither the maturity nor the right to read Nietzsche. The essence of his life and thought is so utterly magnificent that he who is able to participate in it is proof against the errors to which Nietzsche

momentarily fell victim and which at a later date could provide phrase-
ological materials to be used by the National Socialists in support of
their inhuman deeds. Since Nietzsche could not really become the philosopher of the National Socialists, they eventually abandoned him without further ado.

My book was planned with a view to unity. Its purpose is such that
it could easily be expanded and enriched. But this would be hazardous
since a work as extensive as this one might well lose its form. A new,
supplementary work, or one that would, in an original fashion, bring
all available materials into a complete whole, would be better than a
revision of an old book.

Heidelberg, February, 1946
Basel, February, 1949   KARL   JASPERS

INTRODUCTION

INTRODUCTION

Essays, a mass of fragments, letters, poems—all this partly in finished literary form, partly as a mighty legacy accumulated during two decades—that is the form in which Nietzsche's thinking is available to us.

His thinking is neither *aphoristic* in the manner of the famous aphorists, with whom Nietzsche intentionally allied himself on one occasion, nor is it *systematic* in the sense of constituting a deliberately planned philosophical system.

In contrast to the aphorists, he is an integral whole: a philosophical life energized to communicate itself by the awareness of a task, an experiencing of thoughts as creative forces.

In contrast to the systematists, he did not build a complete logical structure of thought; his plans for systematic works are either ways of organizing his thoughts for presentation, which always admit of other possibilities, or they are constructs required by particular objectives, each envisioned in accordance with a particular investigative insight or an intended effect of his philosophizing.

The appearance which Nietzsche's work presents can be expressed figuratively: it is as though a mountain wall had been dynamited; the rocks, already more or less shaped, convey the idea of a whole. But the building for the sake of which the dynamiting seems to have been done has not been erected. However, the fact that the work lies about like a heap of ruins does not appear to conceal its spirit from the one who happens to have found the key to the possibilities of construction; for him, many fragments fit together. But not unambiguously; many functionally suitable pieces are present in numerous, only slightly varied repetitions, others reveal themselves as precious and unique forms, as though each were meant to furnish a cornerstone somewhere or a keystone for an arch. One understands them only when guided by the idea of

3

the structure as a whole. But neither can the latter, in turn, be known with certainty to be single and unequivocal: it is as though a number of structural possibilities cut across one another; at times one is in doubt whether the form of a piece was misconstructed or whether it conforms to another architectural idea.

The task seems to demand a search throughout the ruins for the building, even though the latter will not reveal itself to anybody as a complete, single, and unambiguous whole. The search for what is thus hidden can succeed only if the searcher proceeds as though he himself had to erect the structure which fell to pieces while Nietzsche was working on it. It is imperative that we should not become confused by the vast multiplicity of fragments, yield to the fascination of the almost countless details, or capriciously and fortuitously select this or that item. We must, rather, understand Nietzsche in his entirety through Nietzsche himself by giving serious attention to each word without allowing any word, considered separately, to limit our vision. But we would also do violence to Nietzsche if, to continue the figure, we were to impose an entire archeological reconstruction upon the fragments. In his case we must experience both the systematic possibilities and their collapse. Only then do we become aware of the powerful incentive which Nietzsche provides for posterity, not by offering them a place of refuge but by awakening them and indicating the path they should follow, viz., participation in the elevation of human existence which he made possible. No one will envisage the quintessential in Nietzsche unless he achieves it himself.

Concealed within the vast heap of fragments lies the enigma of the dark depths of Nietzsche's being and thinking. It is as though an unknown power had exploded the substance and, at the same time, had attempted to force the fragmented rocks to form a building, though without any prospect of success, so that now fragments of rock and building blocks lie all around. Or again it is as though a substance which could no longer control itself had broken forth; as though the inherent vital force were constantly pressing toward a totality in which nothing would be lost or forgotten, without ever being or becoming this totality.

To simplify matters with a view to ready comprehension, people ask for Nietzsche's *masterpiece* and raise questions concerning the comparative rank and importance of his writings. One person regards *The Birth of Tragedy* as his most charming composition; another places the chief emphasis on the brilliant, clear, varied, and balanced books of aphorisms, from *Human, All-Too-Human* to *The Gay Science;* a third sees the quintessence and climax in Nietzsche's final philosophy. Then again, one takes *Zarathustra* to be the consummation, another the philosophy of *The Will to Power* expressed in his posthumous works. Some consistently prefer the writings published by Nietzsche himself while others, on the contrary, look upon the posthumous material as the soil which nourishes the specific publications, no one of which would be sufficiently intelligible by itself. Accordingly the former distrust the spontaneous jottings of the posthumous materials, which were not re-examined by Nietzsche and, hence, cannot be said to be more definitive than, for instance, his letter-drafts with their radical self-contradictions in regard to his entire attitude toward those persons closest to him; the latter will be inclined to distrust, in his published writings, a phraseology that was developed with regard for literary style and intensified for the sake of effect.

Each one of these people is right in arguing against the other, no one of them is right when taken by himself. Each restriction, as expressed in these evaluations, seems to make Nietzsche less equivocal, but Nietzsche himself is intelligible only when we gather everything together so that the original philosophical movements of his nature, as seen in the variety of his reflections, can finally be comprehended through his own thinking.

It must also be realized that none of Nietzsche's forms of communication has a privileged character. Inherent in the nature of his thinking is an inability to arrive at an encompassing and pre-eminent form to which all the others would have to be subordinated. The form of the essays, which, conceived as wholes, develop calmly and proceed with clarity, is abandoned in the last one of the *Untimely Meditations,* only to recur in the *Genealogy of Morals* and the *Antichrist.* Aphorism dominates the writings of the middle period; it is not given up until the very end, and it already hovers secretly in the background of the earlier essays. Discernible in the posthumous material is a fragmentary kind of thinking which constantly brings forth something new from inexhaustible wealth. This is basic to all the publications of that period. His last writings as well as the first two parts of the *Untimely Meditations* are predominantly polemical in form; *Zarathustra* and the third and fourth parts of *Untimely Meditations* sketch an ideal and are full of promise. Nowhere is Nietzsche's work truly centralized: there is no *magnum opus.* On the other hand, what is essential to his thought is also discernible particularly in what seems incidental and secondary.

Understanding Nietzsche's Work

The Typical Methods Used in Interpreting Nietzsche. The literary interpretations of Nietzsche undertaken so far have, as a rule, one basic flaw: they place him within some general class, as though they unquestionably knew all the possibilities open to existence and to man. In doing so, they subsume him as a whole. Above all it was a mistake to admire Nietzsche as a poet and writer at the cost of not taking him seriously as a philosopher. Again it was a mistake to regard him as simply a philosopher like one of the earlier philosophers and to measure him by their measure. Genuine interpretation, however, does not subsume but penetrates; it does not claim to know with finality; but, while always taking cognizance of what has just been apprehended, it proceeds by a method of questioning and answering. It thereby begins a process of assimilation, the conditions and limits of which it determines for itself. While the above-mentioned false interpretation provides the pleasurable illusion of a general survey by placing its object at a distance and viewing it *ab extra* as an exotic specimen, the true interpretation is a means to the possibility of self-involvement.

The following methods, which are justified in their self-limitation but incorrect in their absoluteness, are often found in connection with misleading interpretations:

1. *Specific doctrines* of Nietzsche are isolated, systematized, and expounded as his real achievements. Accordingly the unifying central thought of the system can be seen, for instance, in the *will to power* which, when used as a starting point, leads to the inevitable exclusion of Nietzsche's mystical raptures and the doctrine of eternal recurrence. Some see the truth in Nietzsche's conception of *life* and in the disclosures of the masked will to power which destroys life (and, as a result, they are at a loss to understand how Nietzsche can annihilate his own conception by taking this will to power to be life itself). Or again, some see the truth in Nietzsche's universal *unmasking psychology* and reject the notion of any positive tendency in him. Each of these approaches certainly discloses some coherence in Nietzsche's thinking but not his thinking per se in its entirety.

2. Nietzsche's *personality* is condensed into a picture (or figure) to be viewed esthetically as an internally coherent and already completed destiny that has no claims upon us. One person will see the charm of his personal subjectivity, the *fate of a genius' soul in its progressive isolation*. Another sees him as representing an objective fate, viz., the destiny of a true man at the transition between two ages when the present is already hollow and the future is not yet real; Nietzsche becomes *Europe's crisis compressed into a human figure* that must be shattered by the prevailing situation, even while he describes with keen insight what now is and what may come. The one emphasizes what is interesting psychologically, the other is too knowing, as though he, the interpreter, were a godlike

spectator observing human history in its entirety and the position occupied in it by Nietzsche. While both suppose that their interpretations apply to Nietzsche, the façades of fake grandiosity which they have erected prevent them from being touched by him. As a result they never experience the powerful personal impetus which Nietzsche makes possible.

3. Nietzsche, considered as a whole, is illumined through *mythical symbols* which endow him with everlasting significance and provide him with a firm historical basis. Some are impressed, for instance, by the Judas symbol standing for Nietzsche's thorough dialectical negativity, by the picture of the Knight between Death and the Devil representing his courage in the face of disillusionment, and so forth.[1] But these symbols become insincere as soon as they purport to be more than a pleasant and ingenious game: they oversimplify, nullify the movement, make Nietzsche into a rigid being, and subject him to an acknowledged all-embracing necessity instead of following him as he actually is. We occasionally find Nietzsche himself using symbols of this type as clarifying means, but only as one means among others.

4. Nietzsche's thoughts and modes of conduct are *psychologically explained*. Showing how he arrived at them is said to be decisive for their value and truth. Nietzsche himself seems to suggest this method when he emphasizes the unity of life and cognition and insists that philosophical systems are to be considered as personal documents of their authors. Nevertheless, he declares: "Where my critics are concerned, I am often under the impression that they are scoundrels. Not *what* is said, but that *I say it* and what should have made *me* in particular arrive at it—only that seems to interest them. . . . They judge me in order to ignore my work: they explain its genesis, and thereby consider it adequately *disposed of.*" This is no contradiction in Nietzsche, but a resolute refusal to confuse a loving grasp of the substance of his thought, attained through an intuitive awareness that illumines *Existenz,* with a capricious psychological understanding that is blind to his true being. For psychology as such falls short of the illumination of *Existenz.* For example, one does not come closer to Nietzsche's nature by interpreting his thinking on the basis of his resentment as an ailing professor (being delicate and nervous, he is said to have glorified the beast) or in terms of a struggle for power and influence presumed to underlie such things as his attitude towards Bismarck and the German people, his strident polemic, and his readiness to become effective by means of sensationalistic writing. This method involves more disparagement than understanding. In any case, what it

---

[1] Cf. E. Bertram, *Nietzsche: Versuch einer Mythologie,* Berlin, 1918.

comes to grips with is scarcely relevant, for even when it is not false and worthless but contributes something to the understanding of Nietzsche, it remains without illuminating force for Nietzsche's true nature.

The question is whether, for the purpose of appropriation, it is possible to devise a method of interpreting Nietzsche which uses these four ways not as ends in themselves but as means of presenting the authentic Nietzsche. In contrast to a dogmatic system, a character sketch, a mythical symbolism, or a psychologically understood clarification, it would keep our view unobstructed so that we could come in contact with the true substance itself and, in partaking of it, realize ourselves. Instead of merely dealing with the philosophical, literary, and biographical material produced by Nietzsche, instead of knowing him as just another person, we would enter into the movement of the authentic Nietzsche.

The real difficulty lies in finding the starting point of this genuine appropriation. For such an appropriation, Nietzsche stands at the level where sources and boundaries become articulate; here, thought and image, dialectical system and poetry find commensurate expression. Then Nietzsche would appear as the man who, because his entire self was at stake, could communicate his grasp of being and his self-understanding truly and essentially.

How Nietzsche Should Be Read. While it is to be feared that the writings of most philosophers will be neglected in favor of books about them, Nietzsche's writings are in danger of being read carelessly because they seem so readily comprehensible.

One would completely miss the path that leads to Nietzsche if he were to give the reader, for instance, the advice that he ought to open Nietzsche here and there, let himself be stimulated, and seize what happens to give him pleasure: "The worst readers are those who behave like looting soldiers: they pick out what little they can use, soil and confuse the rest, and slander the whole." "I hate the reading idlers."

If, on the other hand, one were to suppose that he ought to read a great deal—even everything—hurriedly in order to encompass the whole, then he would again be mistaken. Nietzsche is "a teacher of slow reading. Now it suits my taste . . . no longer to write anything but that which will drive the sort of person who 'is in a hurry' to desperation." In praise of philology he writes: "It teaches people to read well, that is, slowly, profoundly, looking forward and backward, with mental reservations, with doors left ajar, and with tender fingers and eyes."

It is not sufficient, however, for the reader to exercise this "goldsmith's art and connoisseurship of words"; rather he must, through word, sen-

tence, and assertion, arrive at the
partake of the real impetus. A
Venice: "When the copy of *The*
one more favor: take it to the Li
to make a whole of it for yoursel
23, '81).

The reader first becomes awa
when he compares utterances wl
tory. A meaningful study of Nie
later, such contact with the source is made, since the "passionate state"
required by Nietzsche is the source, not the goal. It is at this point that the
reader's task begins. The following means are available:

Principles of Interpretation. Once the thinking of an author has assumed absolute importance, it is not permissible to pick out the passages
which agree with one's opinion and ignore the rest; on the contrary, every
word is to be taken seriously. This is not to say that all the utterances
have the same value. They stand in an order of rank which is not to be
arrived at by means of any preconceived criterion but which derives from
the unattained whole of his thought.

The task of interpretation itself is carried out by relating basic propositions to each other. This procedure gradually initiates a general orientation which, whether confirmed or transformed as the interpretation
proceeds, will always guide the questioning mind of the reader toward a
definitive and basic conception. This applies to Nietzsche more than to
any other philosopher, partly because of the fragmentary form of his
work but, above all, because of the indirectness with which every single
one of Nietzsche's thoughts moves between what appear to be absolutely
positive and absolutely negative poles.

What leads to a true understanding of Nietzsche is precisely the
opposite of that which the seductive allurements of his writings appear to
promise: not the acceptance of definitive pronouncements, taken to
convey the final and indefeasible truth, but rather the sustained effort in
which we continue to question, listen to other contentions, and maintain
the tension of possibilities. What Nietzsche means can never be assimilated by a will to possess the truth in fixed and final form but only by a
will to truth which rises from the depths and strives toward the depths,
which is prepared to encounter all that is questionable, is not closed to
anything, and is able to wait.

The interpretative study of Nietzsche's thinking thus always requires
the gathering together of *all* utterances that relate to a given topic. The

discovery of statements that interpret, reinforce, qualify, and join each other to form a common context is not accomplished through mere compilation of passages which belong together because of the use of the same word (even though this is to some extent helpful as a preparation for the convenient index method); it can be accomplished conclusively only through impartial interrelating, aided by a good memory for what is read.

A sustained effort at such a systematic integration shows the following to be applicable throughout:

1. All statements seem to be annulled by other statements. *Self-contradiction* is the fundamental ingredient in Nietzsche's thought. For nearly every single one of Nietzsche's judgments, one can also find an opposite. He gives the impression of having two opinions about everything. Consequently it is possible to quote Nietzsche at will in support of anything one happens to have in mind. Most parties have been able, at some opportune moment, to invoke Nietzsche: conservatives and revolutionaries, socialists and individualists (as well as those who are indifferent to politics), methodical scientists and idealistic dreamers, atheists and believers, freethinkers and fanatics. Consequently many have concluded that Nietzsche is full of confusion, is never in earnest, abandons himself to his own whims, and that it does not pay to take his inconsequential chatter seriously.

But it could also be that we have here to do with contradictions that are necessary and inescapable. Perhaps the contradictories, presented as alternatives and appearing reasonable and familiar to the reader when considered singly, actually are misleading simplifications of being. If the understanding (*Verstand*) per se is condemned, as it were, to remain on the surface of being, then being may have to become manifest through self-contradiction. This would certainly seem to be true for those who search passionately for the final truth but think only with the understanding and are limited to what is accessible to it. A contradiction arising in this way would be necessitated by the subject-matter; it would be a sign of truthfulness rather than of incompetent thinking.

In any case, it is the task of the interpreter to be forever dissatisfied until he has *also* found the contradiction, to search out contradictions in all their forms, and then, if possible, to gain direct experience of their necessity. Instead of being occasionally provoked by contradiction, one should pursue contradictoriness to its source.

2. One encounters endless *repetitions*. Since all that Nietzsche ever wrote must be published if his thinking is to be accessible, repetition is unavoidable. One must seek to rid the underlying thought of the tedious

inflexibility which it assumes in certain of its specific statements by tracing its various modifications. It is especially important to discover both what makes possible the hundred quotations relating to one topic and also what other topics become important as a result of only one single passage. Only explicit knowledge of the repetitions enables us to notice such single statements.

3. Annoyance with his contradictions and impatience with the capriciousness that Nietzsche's thoughts at first seem to possess furnish the provocation that leads us to bring his thoughts into juxtaposition and enter into the *real dialectic* through which alone his intention becomes clear. We realize how Nietzsche, without conscious mastery over the possibilities presented by the realms of thought and being, still manages to take the necessary routes through these realms. Dialectical clarification occurs to the extent to which we can discover what passages in the different texts belong together. But it cannot be attained simply through logical insight alone; it really occurs only insofar as an expansion and illumination of the realm of possible *Existenz* takes place. Whoever lacks the patience to labor over logical and substantive connections and has no leeway in his soul for the abundance of possibilities cannot read Nietzsche with comprehension.

4. A *whole* emerges, not one already attained but one that impels us to persevere by raising the increasingly incisive question concerning the central axis of Nietzsche's entire thinking in all of its phases. This whole is not a concept, a world-view, or a system; it is the passion of the quest for being, together with its constant overcoming through relentless criticism, as it rises to the level of genuine truth. While we are engaged in discovering statements which, when taken together, provide the necessary foundation for a proper understanding of something further, we must keep in mind the essential difference between the systematic wholeness of mere doctrines, which are themselves only functions of an encompassing whole, and the existential encompassing itself which is a basic incentive, but not a basic doctrine. Both are to be elucidated by so coordinating the various statements that the wealth of particulars becomes suitably related to what is crucial and decisive. This study, which seeks the whole but still must proceed from the whole as it raises questions and assimilates concepts and objects, is inexhaustible.

Only by employing the sort of interpretation that proceeds toward the whole can we derive from Nietzsche himself the criterion that we need in order to place his statements in an order of rank corresponding to their import, to judge how essential each is, and to distinguish the pertinent versions from those that are extraneous and misleading. Inevitably the decisiveness of his awareness of essentials varies from time to time. Still one can arrive at standpoints from which it is possible to apply Nietzsche's own kind of criticism to the movements of his thought. Two paths must be consciously followed:

In the first place, Nietzsche's thoughts can be organized, without any regard for the order of their occurrence, in an existing *whole composed of intelligible ideas necessarily related to each other*. In the second place, since they belong to a development that occupied several decades, they are to be viewed in their *temporal form* as the whole of a life. In the first case, the idea of a *timeless systematic whole* becomes our guide as we search for the timeless position of each thought and for the architechtonic of the system itself. In the second case, the *development* of his life, his knowledge, and his illness becomes the guiding principle as we seek to discover the temporal position of every thought within the totality of the process. On the one hand, each of Nietzsche's thoughts is understood to the extent to which its modifications, contradictions, and possibilities of movement are seen within an objectively related whole; on the other hand, it can be fully understood only in relation to the point in time at which it was entertained: the reader must always know just *when* everything that he reads was written.

These two ways would seem to be mutually exclusive. The demand that we envisage a systematic whole composed of interrelated parts, each apprehensible in its own extra-temporal position, contradicts the demand that we view this whole as a biographical sequence and understand everything in terms of its temporal location within the course of a life.

There are indeed certain basic thoughts of Nietzsche, thoughts of a dominant nature, which appear from early youth on and remain more or less constant in spite of radical modifications. Such thoughts, which outnumber all the others, permeate his entire life in astounding fashion. There are others which appear for the first time as the result of a sudden break in the developmental process. Then, too, there are the rare cases of thoughts which seem to be soon forgotten after a brief period in the foreground. They too are to be assimilated within the one great process which is at once systematic and biographical, for it pertains to the reality of man that the deepest and truest system of his thought must appear in temporal form. This form may be natural and congruent with its object, or it can, so to speak, be biographically obscured or ruined through causal connections which are alien to the object and distort the empirical reality of the specific individual in question. In Nietzsche's case both possibilities were realized in a manner that is profoundly stirring.

Thus *in the first place,* the study of Nietzsche's thinking (unlike that of most great philosophers) requires that we constantly remain in touch with the realities of *Nietzsche's life*. We must concern ourselves with his experiences and his conduct in various situations in order to discover the philosophic content which constitutes the indissoluble unity of his life and thought. The interrelatedness of the two can even be discovered in the external appearance of certain thoughts and images in his works. We must concern ourselves with the course of his life in order to apprehend the process within which everything that he wrote has its proper place.

On the other hand, no biographical study of Nietzsche can be meaningful so long as the events of his life are not integrated with the world of his thoughts. When the two sides are separated, either psychological curiosity is gratified by collecting the all-too-human facts of the case and by enjoying a real-life epic, or the thoughts, abstracted from the personality, are labeled as eternally valid truths—or sheer folly.

In the second place, Nietzsche's thoughts demand an investigation of their *systematic interrelations.* However, the system that derives from Nietzsche—unlike the great systems of philosophy—appears only as a phase or function within an encompassing whole that can no longer be presented in systematic fashion. Instead, interpretation, having gathered together the widely scattered variations on a given theme, must explore them in detail, together with all their contradictions, with a view to traversing all the possibilities, as though the whole were nevertheless attainable. While in the end everything does indeed belong together, it falls back into the temporal extension of a veritable skein of ways of thinking that is by no means systematic.

In the study of Nietzsche the unity of the whole, i.e., of life and thought, of temporal development and timeless system, can only be the guiding *idea,* for Nietzsche's thinking will always elude all attempts at a well-ordered presentation. It is impossible to foresee how far one will get, objectively speaking, in an attempt to obtain a definite and well-substantiated conception of the whole. As the study proceeds, one unavoidably devotes himself completely to the empirically given series of actual occurrences in Nietzsche's life. But one must in addition to this explore his thoughts at length without regard to the time in which they were first entertained. What provides the irresistibly compelling agitation in the study of Nietzsche is precisely this ever-recurring difficulty: neither of these ways makes sense when taken separately while both, taken together, cannot be brought into complete harmony.

Our Presentation and Its Main Parts. A presentation, unlike a mere critical evaluation, undertakes to present the subject itself, and, unlike a narration, it aims at bringing out its essential features. A presentation attempts to efface its own thinking in favor of that which is presented; it must not use its subject as an occasion for any philosophizing of its own. Such thinking is a constant endeavor to yield completely to the thinking of the other person; it is thinking which seeks simply to present what someone else has thought.

Not all the products of the human spirit require a presentation but only those which are creative and live on creatively, those whose infinitely ramified roots receive further renewal and timely articulation as they are inherited and cultivated by succeeding generations. While a new and original understanding of such achievements must be attained time and again through up-to-date presentation, there is no sense in presenting what is terminated, definitive, and therefore entirely finished. One need only report its results.

One cannot present Nietzsche with a view to enabling the reader to gain exhaustive knowledge of him. Because he never attains static finality, either by emerging as a concisely delineated personality or by attaining a finished philosophical system, one can lay hold only upon detached constellations of his thoughts and specific aspects of his existence. The effort to comprehend him is bound to miscarry so long as one attempts to hold him, *in toto,* to a fixed position. Because Nietzsche indirectly reveals himself only through movement, access to him is achieved, not through *perusal* of something formal and systematic, but through a *movement* on one's own part. It is not possible to learn what he really is by merely assimilating thoughts and facts; on the contrary, one can bring forth, through Nietzsche, the meaning that Nietzsche is to have for him only through his own exertions and critical questions.

It follows that a presentation of Nietzsche resulting from such an activity cannot relieve anyone else from having to carry out this activity on his own part. It can at best merely prepare the way for what every student of Nietzsche must achieve for himself through Nietzsche. The point is to provide the conditions that may make it possible to appropriate him more decisively than before—whether by way of participation in his thinking or by way of rejection. Of course the result will not be a mere disclosure of the magic that emerges from Nietzsche's figure with demonic irresistibility; rather, the goal is to purify and transform it into an impulse that gives a deeper meaning to life. Furthermore it will not simply annihilate the Nietzschean sophistry which first becomes fully evident after his thoughts have been transformed by others, although the dissolution of this sophistry is clearly incumbent upon us.

There is no way of presenting Nietzsche that goes directly to the central point. If we presumed to exhibit such a central point, we would fail to be challenged and stimulated by his greatness. That is why we must follow several ways in succession. However, the several ways that lead into Nietzsche's presence culminate, not in a synthesis, but rather in an illumination of the profound depths which are indirectly disclosed by the many vistas with which he, intentionally or unintentionally, confronts us.

The ways that we follow proceed to the same goal and derive from the same source: all are intended to increase our readiness for a comprehensive appropriation of Nietzsche by providing clear knowledge of particulars, and all derive from the awareness of a basis that is beyond actual comprehension because it never appears the same twice. The goal and the source are not directly communicable, but without them the different ways in their isolation and their objectifying clarity would be meaningless. Nietzsche is inexhaustible. Considered *in toto,* he is not a problem to be solved. For what he is has yet to be made evident, partly at least, through the way in which future generations will appropriate him.

We have made *three divisions* involving, first, his *life,* as the indispensable basis of any authentic experience with Nietzsche; second, those *basic thoughts* which, within a great variety of particular subjects, express his original impulses; and third, a quest for *his whole way of thinking* throughout his *Existenz.* In each case the foundation consists of facts which, I believe, must be recognized if Nietzsche is to be understood. But each task is dominated by a different point of view:

In the account of his *life,* the radicalism of the extremist is stressed. Instead of being overwhelmed by an accumulation of facts (although no one who has ever actually encountered Nietzsche can set any limit to his desire to know them), we should, without concealment or exaggeration of what has actually occurred, reveal the empirical conditions of his status as an exceptional man: the reality of a life that constantly sacrificed itself and was sacrificed.

The presentation of his *basic thoughts* must show, by a detailed arrangement of his effective primary motives, how each thought is so self-critical that none in the end remains unchanged. Nietzsche's formulations of his cosmic visions are to be investigated until the point is reached at which they are shattered. In this connection it is up to us constantly to avoid becoming stranded on grounds that are either radically positive or radically negative.

Interpretation *of the whole,* which Nietzsche accomplishes through his self-understanding and which we can attain through our own understanding, should throw light upon the existential significance of his life and his thought. Our task is to remain receptive to his influence by avoiding a static view that restricts him to a specific standpoint and by gaining a conception of the lofty demands which he makes. Nietzsche finally proves to be the incomprehensible exception which, without being a model for imitation, exerts an absolutely irreplaceable quickening influence upon others who are not exceptional. In the end one cannot help but ask how a man who is by no means representative can still become as overwhelmingly significant as though he spoke for humanity itself.

The Method of Presentation. Presenting Nietzsche's thinking is a matter of bringing out the really basic *philosophical* thoughts. Although he did not think in a methodical and systematic manner, still for purposes of presentation his thoughts must be placed within some sort of framework. While no leading role is assigned to any single thought or concept, still the exuberance of Nietzsche's language, musical and even plastic as it often is, conceals a basic conceptual structure which must be laid bare. Merely repeating his language with its far-ranging immediacy would of course be senseless since Nietzsche himself is to be read in any case. Rather it is a matter of disclosing the skeleton, so to speak, so that we can the better comprehend, as we read Nietzsche, the logical relations and cognitive limits which he observes and thus lay the groundwork for a kind of thinking on our own part in the form of genuine (i.e., creative) criticism.

Furthermore, the presentation should be *well-documented* throughout. It is of course more convenient to give Nietzsche's thoughts the appearance of being coherent and complete within themselves. But this would be to lose precisely the resistance, furnished by their inconsistency, which seekers after truth find so stimulating: the bringing together of thoughts so that they complement, contradict, and incite one another is all the more effective for an understanding of Nietzsche when every single step is supported by a direct quotation (a procedure unavoidably limited, in every case, by our restriction to bare essentials).

Thus virtually all Nietzsche-literature justifiably abounds in *quotations.* It is essential, however, that these citations *bring out something new,* instead of presenting a mere chrestomathy of beautiful passages, ingeniously establishing chance relations, arbitrarily isolating special tendencies of thought, or presenting a collection of sensational aphorisms. Thoughts are to be placed within their own proper contexts, even when their essential relations have not been explicitly emphasized by Nietzsche. For, while Nietzsche's brilliance as a writer is evident to the reader on every page, the self-generating illumination that accompanies his philosophizing tends to be largely concealed. This is why quotations or constructions arbitarily chosen for a special purpose only dazzle without clarifying and are philosophically misleading. Compiling passages in an illuminating way is only possible as a result of an interpretative endeavor to use a knowledge of the whole in order to bring out those decisive fundamental thoughts which we must know if we are to read Nietzsche for ourselves with insight (this being our main goal) and, above all, if we wish to enter into serious work with and on Nietzsche. Selection based upon personal preference must cease to the extent to which knowledge of the whole dictates a presentation in which this whole is to become in the highest degree palpable.

Ideally, the art of quoting should resemble that of a goldsmith: it should be a matter of properly setting the gems of philosophic thought and then arranging them so that they not only appear to good advantage when viewed singly but also mutually enhance each other, making the whole superior to the component parts or any mere congeries thereof. The gems may shine with new lights when arranged differently,[2] and they cannot be made to shine from all angles at once. What counts is the brilliance arising when the undistorted quintessence of what Nietzsche said and meant is revealed.

Moreover, when Nietzsche's thoughts are brought together, friction also is bound to ensue, and this in turn reveals the self-criticism contained in this thinking. One may argue forever about the right and wrong of his specific utterances, but this is not to become acquainted with him but only to use him as a topic for conversation. It is not until the dissonances, boundaries, and abysses emerge within the entire movement of his thinking that critique becomes possible. Basically this is carried out by Nietzsche himself, for critique belongs to the very essence of his kind of

---

[2] One difficulty must be openly acknowledged: quoting involves removal of sentences from their contexts, which means that they are withdrawn from certain meaningful relationships and placed in others. Thus to quote is to commit an act of violence. What is important is that arbitrary relations be avoided and that each single violation lead to a more adequate acquaintance with the totality of Nietzsche's thought. Anyone who is accustomed to become so absorbed in texts that, in his own thinking, he supplies or extracts meanings virtually without limit on every page, or who seeks to gain an understanding based on a particular text as such, may view with revulsion the procedure of relating statements taken from the widest possible variety of source materials. A detailed discussion of this would never end. But the limitation to be placed upon this sort of violence (a limitation which I hope I have never inadvertently transgressed) is simply this: no marring of the sense, transformation into the opposite, or obvious falsification is to be tolerated. At the same time it is unavoidable and to be expected that either an impoverishment or an expansion of meaning is a possible outcome when a given quotation is judged within the context of an entire edition of his works instead of that of a single work taken by itself.

truth—a truth that constantly endeavors to surpass itself and drive itself onward.

The Dependence of Understanding on the Nature of the Interpreter

It accords with Nietzsche's intentions and concept of truth that the way in which an individual understands reveals what kind of person he is. That is why Nietzsche is not simply looking for readers as such, but for readers who belong to him.

Philosophical Truth. The manner in which I gain philosophical truth differs basically from that in which I acquire new scientific knowledge. Everyone recognizes that the latter is a kind of understanding which is sharable [3] and which can be acquired through mere training and industry. But in the process of understanding philosophical truth (and in all science insofar as it is philosophically inspired), self-realization becomes possible, an awakening takes place, and I discover myself as a result of the very way in which I discover being.

If truth, however, is not all on one level and is not the same for everyone, if access to it depends upon a condition existing in the truth-seeker, and if laying hold upon truth is self-realization, then we cannot escape the age-old question of what this entails in connection with the *communication* of truth, a question that jeopardizes the very possibility of any unequivocal communication and, in the end, truth itself. For since truth exists only in communication and is unavoidably as public as the language by which alone it is conveyed, it is inevitable that the clash of irreconcilable presuppositions will, at the very least, produce a state of affairs in which truth becomes misunderstood, perverted, abused, and even open to question.

When this point is reached, two fundamental interpretations are open to us: first, the doctrine of *stages of truth* corresponding to stages of human *Existenz* (the Pythagorean typology); and second, the doctrine of the inescapable *ambiguity of truth* and the consequences thereof (which Nietzsche pushed to its limits).

The doctrine of stages leads to intentional concealment and to a course of education intended to develop sufficient maturity for understanding to occur. It assumes that no one should learn the truth before he is ade-

---

[3] The "understanding" (*Verstand*) is here regarded as operating at the level of the Kantian "consciousness in general" (*Bewusstsein überhaupt*), which is identical in all rational minds and whose contents are duplicable, interchangeable, or sharable (*vertretbar*). —Trs.

quately prepared to come to grips with esoteric matters that are hidden from the novices. This, however, would be an extrinsic regulation resting upon the assumption that the educators already know the stages of *Existenz* and the stages of truth corresponding to them. Like gods, they would have to grasp and possess all truth. Also required is a method of selection based, not upon acquired knowledge of facts and capacity for practical work, but rather upon the very being of man, his nobility, and his potentialities. This too calls for a superhuman capacity for discrimination in matters pertaining to the human spirit. Finally this would presuppose a mode of appearance of truth which conceals it without making it an overpowering authority, that is, one that allows it to remain true even when it is deliberately concealed.

Nietzsche will have none of this; he takes the second approach. No one knows the stages, no one is gifted with the ability to make differentiations in accordance with the absolute meaning of being itself; there is no concealment affecting the truth itself apart from its capacity for being misunderstood precisely when it is most obvious. It is through ambiguity that the truth is protected from appropriation by the unqualified. That is why Nietzsche enters the public forum where he is ostensibly audible to all. He wishes to encounter the one who is capable of facing up to his truth and to unmask the one who has no right to it and of whose reaction to the misunderstood truth it might be said: "A little fit of rage makes him expose his innermost and most ridiculous self."

What Is Required for Genuine Interpretation. The foregoing explains the demand which Nietzsche repeatedly makes upon the innermost being of anyone who wishes to understand him. He finds it "impossible to teach the truth whenever the way of thinking is base." Whoever feels opposed to him fails to understand his position and, consequently, his arguments. He cannot understand unless he is "the victim of the same passion" and has experienced "brightness and fire and dawnings of day" within his own soul; "I can but recall and remind; I can do no more."

Nietzsche speaks of the ability to understand him as "a mark of distinction which has to be earned." He wants his thoughts to be fenced in "so that pigs and dreamers will not break into my gardens." He foresees grave dangers through "intrusive admirers," sends away the intruders and strangers, and derides "Zarathustra's ape." His first experiences of being misunderstood lead him to express his "horror at the thought of the totally unqualified persons who will in time rest their illegitimate claims on my authority" (to his sister, June, '84).

It follows from this that *one has the right* to Nietzsche's thoughts only insofar as he is of the same rank. "The opposite way of thinking is that of the newspapers: namely that evaluations as such are things which anyone may claim as his own property. This is simply to assume that everyone is of the same rank." The fact that "value judgments are taken over like garments" is due to the "belief that everything is subject to the judgment of everyone." "Today, thanks to the presumptuous spirit of our age, we have . . . arrived at the point where we no longer believe in spiritual privileges and in the incommunicability of final insights." All of Nietzsche's thinking rests upon his awareness of these privileges, his knowledge of the incommunicability of what is final, and the sensitive heed which he pays to the autonomous existence of others of his own rank.

But if truth is intrinsically comprehensible only to persons of corresponding rank, then every single individual must ask: Who am I? Can I understand? Do I have a right to participate? There are no answers to these questions. And there is only one way: through association with Nietzsche to attain to a kind of elevation of soul that cannot be planned, foreseen, or put in concrete terms, even though, when realized, it will show me for the first time what being is and what I am.

Why One Hesitates to Communicate the Real Truth: the Danger Involved. Nietzsche is aware of the danger unavoidably connected with the revelation of the truth: "There are books which have opposite effects upon a person's soul and general well-being, depending upon the rank of the soul that makes use of them: in the case of a base soul they are dangerous, devastating, corrupting; to the lofty soul they are the heraldic challenge which arouses the bravest to courageous deeds." Since communicated truth is inevitably ambiguous, Nietzsche may well insist that "our noblest insights must—and should!—sound like follies, and under certain circumstances even like crimes, when they surreptitiously reach the ears of those who are neither suited nor predestined for them." When Widmann, speaking before the Bernese Alliance (*Berner Bund*), called Nietzsche's books dangerous and compared them to dynamite, Nietzsche let it pass.

This danger is necessary and no one should be deprived of it, since it is impossible to tell in advance on whom it will act creatively and who will find it devastating. What is called for is not concealment of the truth but rather something far more difficult: the courage to acknowledge, to think through, and to say openly what we really know.

The ambiguity of truth has nothing to do with the kind of dishonesty that practices concealment or deliberately preserves recognized ambiguities. It is an unintentional ambiguity that inheres in the communication of the truth just because the recipients are essentially so different. Courageous truthfulness means *risking* ambiguity rather than willing it.

Hesitation, however, is understandable. The thinker is inclined to restrain himself when he sees how destructive an idea may be and recognizes the perversions and abuses which may spring from it. Hence Nietzsche could, on one occasion, ask the great men of the past whether they "were profound enough to refrain from writing what they knew"; he could write, even in his youth: "The roots of our thoughts and intentions should never be exposed to the bright light" (hence "to be capable of silence about such things at the proper time is a noble art. The word is a dangerous thing. . . . How much we must leave unsaid! And it is precisely the fundamental insights of religion and philosophy that belong to the *pudenda"* [—to von Gersdorff, Sept. 18, '71]); and when subsequently he experienced hesitation again and again, he still demanded of himself forthright and fearless pursuit of the truth in both thought and word, knowing that—in opposition to any intentional concealment in the interest of the presumed well-being of mankind—strength resides solely in a sort of openness that has nothing in common with the undisciplined and unscrupulous idle chatter that poses as the vehicle of truth. It is said of Zarathustra: "Even the least little evasion by means of silence is completely enervating to him. He feels that he has avoided a thought. . . . The least reservation, the slightest omission, prevents any outstanding success."

Nietzsche Does Not Want Believers. Since Nietzsche's thoughts are to be considered as neither vindicated by authority nor as absolutely valid truths, it would be wrong to become his "disciple." It is inherent in the very nature of this kind of truth that it is communicated only insofar as it awakens an appropriate personal response. Hence, from beginning to end, Nietzsche is the "prophet" who, unlike all prophets, *refers everyone to himself:*

"Faithfully follow your own path; in this way you will follow me." "He who climbs by his own might, will bear my image to a brighter light." " 'Now this is *my* way. Where is yours?' Thus I answered those who asked me for 'the way.' *The* way? There is no such thing!" Nietzsche longs for the independent other person: "I should like to consort only with men who have their own model and do not pattern themselves after me, thus making me responsible for them and enslaving me."

Hence Nietzsche's constant effort to repel: "I want to arouse the greatest distrust against myself." "It is inherent in a master's humanity to warn his disciples against himself." Zarathustra leaves his disciples with the words: "Go away from me and be on your guard against Zarathustra." These words are emphasized through repetition in *Ecce Homo,* together with the addition: "Here no fanatic is speaking, no one preaches, and no faith is required."

Even Nietzsche's appearance in the guise of the "Lawgiver" is but one of his ways of being indirect. It means: "I am a law only to those who belong to me; I am not a law to everyone"; but it also signifies the resistance which enables the other who really belongs with Nietzsche to find himself: "I shall not give the other the rights that I have won for myself; on the contrary, he shall have to take them—as I did—by force! . . . If it is necessary for me to promulgate a law, as though all were to be made in my image, it can only be for the purpose of enabling the individual to discover and strengthen himself by contradicting it."

It is in harmony with this attitude that Nietzsche wishes neither to rule nor to be canonized: "Rule? Impose my type upon others? Monstrous! Does not my happiness consist precisely in beholding many others?" And finally: "There is in me nothing of the founder of a religion. I do not want 'believers,' and it seems to me that I am too wicked to believe in myself. I never talk to the masses. . . . I am terribly afraid that some day I may be canonized. . . . This book is intended as a preventive against any mischief that might be perpetrated on me."

The Intention of Nietzsche's Communication. What is Nietzsche's real intention in this conflict between prophetic proclamation and rejection of blind followers, between pedagogue and iconoclast, and in all the interplay of statements that cancel each other out while they yet strike at the heart of things? What will replace the religious founder for him and what does he wish to be for others? A hint of an answer to these questions is contained in a sketch entitled "Genius of the Heart." "The genius of the heart, . . . whose voice is capable of reaching down into the depths of each soul, whose adeptness is such that he is capable of presenting what to his followers is an added compulsion to follow him more and more profoundly and completely: the genius of the heart, who silences all that is loud and complacent and teaches how to listen, who smooths the rough souls and lets them taste a new desire—to lie quietly like a mirror so that they may reflect the deep sky; the genius of the heart who divines the hidden and forgotten treasure . . . underneath the turbid ice and is a divining-rod for every grain of gold; . . . the genius of the heart whose touch sends everyone away richer, richer of himself, . . . burst open, caressed by a warm wind, sounded out, less certain perhaps, but full of hopes that have as yet no name, full of a new will."

Did Nietzsche Find the Sort of Readers He Wanted? When he was young himself, he still had faith in *young people:* "I know that these hopeful ones will understand all these generalities as they encounter them and will draw upon their own intimate experiences in translating them into a doctrine of personal significance." But before long he wishes to warn the "over-fervid, conviction-thirsty youths not to regard his doctrines straightway as guiding lines for life, but rather as theses that should be weighed well. . . ." And in the end the young men who admire his literature become a burden to him, "for it is obvious that this is no literature for young people" (to Overbeck, May 13, '87).

Disillusioned, he then seeks *the companion:* he thinks of his writings as baited hooks for catching the right people. But the true readers fail to arrive. Refusing to compromise and continuing to unmask all hollow pretences, Nietzsche clings to his truthfulness and finds himself more and more abandoned. While passionately searching, he deliberately renounces the only measures that could make him understood in his own time.

The fame that Nietzsche foresaw with certainty arrived, but he experienced little more than the first beginnings of it. Has Nietzsche been understood since as he wanted to be? We are as yet scarcely in a position to answer this question with a flat affirmation or denial. *Our task* is to become ourselves by appropriating Nietzsche. Instead of yielding to the temptation to take the apparent univocality of doctrines and laws as proof of their universal validity, each of us should respond to his challenge by attaining individually the highest rank of which his nature is capable. We should not subordinate ourselves to oversimplified principles and imperatives but, rather, through him find the way to the genuine simplicity of truth.

Book One

NIETZSCHE'S LIFE

Surveys

Since a study of Nietzsche's thoughts can lead to genuine understanding only when accompanied by an explicit awareness of the course of his life, we shall begin by mentioning in brief summaries that which is factual.[1]

[1] *Source materials dealing with his life.* Only the study of Nietzsche's books and letters is really essential. Passing beyond that, we find that knowledge of his empirical existence cannot be gained from a single definitive work but must be taken from all the sources in their entirety since no clear and comprehensive report of the facts based entirely upon primary materials has ever come forth. Available reports are marred by deliberate omissions on the one hand and opinions and viewpoints on the other. Thus we have no recourse but to read back and forth and arrive here and there at something essential, at the cost of having to witness quarrels and having to share in evaluations that are hardly characteristic of Nietzsche even though they are part of his fate. At any rate, no one should read all these things unless he has already formed his own conception of Nietzsche's true nature on the basis of his books and letters, for only thus can one avoid being led away from Nietzsche's own niveau either by palliating embellishments or by a mass of objective stipulations.

The two main works are: Elisabeth Förster-Nietzsche, *Das Leben Friedrich Nietzsches*, Leipzig, 1895–1904; abbreviated and altered in two small volumes: *Der junge Nietzsche* and *Der einsame Nietzsche;* and C. A. Bernoulli, *Franz Overbeck und Friedrich Nietzsche, Eine Freundschaft,* Jena, 1908.

The sister's work creates a mood indispensable for an understanding of his personality, especially in the first volume which deals with his childhood. Without Overbeck, the Basel reports and Bernoulli, the real Nietzsche would have remained indistinct. Here speaks a feeling for facts which deserves enduring gratitude, even though one may not always accept the conceptions and criteria that prevail.

From the literature concerning the quarrel between Weimar and Basel: C. A. Bernoulli, "Zuschrift" (documents reported in connection with the suit to prevent the publication of Gast's letters to Overbeck): *Das literarische Echo* X, 1907; also the reply in the *Nietzsche-Archiv*, pp. 1325–30. Josef Hofmiller, "Nietzsche und seine Schwester"; *Süddeutsche Monatshefte* VI, 2, 1909, pp. 395–403.

In addition to the two extensive main works, the following communications convey to the reader both gripping facts and inconsequential minutiae:

Paul Deussen, *Erinnerungen an Friedrich Nietzsche*, Leipzig, 1901.—J. Mähli, "Erinnerungen an Friedrich Nietzsche"; *Die Gegenwart* LVIII, Berlin, 1900, pp. 246 ff.—Malvida von Meysenbug, *Individualitäten*, Berlin, 1901 (especially pp. 1–41 which concern her relations to Nietzsche).—Meta von Salis-Marschlins,

The External Course of his Life.[2] Nietzsche was born in the parsonage in Röcken. There were pastors among the ancestors of both of his parents. When he was five years old, he lost his father, and his mother moved to Naumburg where Nietzsche, surrounded by female relatives, grew up with his sister, two years his junior. At the age of ten he entered the Naumburg grammar school, and at the age of fourteen (1858) he was given a stipend (*Freistelle:* a scholarship covering room, board, and tuition) at Schulpforta, that venerable boarding school celebrated for its uncommonly outstanding humanistic teachers. At twenty (1864) he began his university studies with two semesters at Bonn, where he joined the Frankonia fraternity (*Burschenschaft*), only to withdraw in 1865 when he found that in practice it did not agree with what it meant to him as an ideal. With Ritschl, his teacher, he went from Bonn to Leipzig where he and Erwin Rohde became the most brilliant disciples of this master of philology. Here he founded the Philological Society, published philological studies and, even before he completed his degree, was offered a position as professor at Basel on the recommendation of Ritschl. The latter had written to Basel: "Numerous as are the young spirits who have developed under my own eyes for upwards of thirty-nine years, I have never known a young man . . . to become so mature so quickly and at such an early age . . . as this Nietzsche. . . . I predict that if he lives for a long time (and my God grant that he will!), he will eventually stand in the foremost ranks of German philologists. He is now twenty-four years old: strong, robust, healthy, and brave in body and soul. . . . He is the idol of the entire world of young philologists here in Leipzig. You will say I am describing some sort of prodigy. Well, that is what he actually is, and, at the same time, amiable and modest. . . . He will accomplish anything he puts his mind to." [3]

Next came the two decades preceding the outbreak of insanity. From 1869 to 1879 Nietzsche was a *professor* at the University of Basel and,

Philosoph und Edelmensch, Leipzig, 1897.—Arthur Egidi, "Gespräche mit Nietzsche, 1892," in: *Die Musik.* Erster Jahrgang, 1902, pp. 1892 ff.—Julius Kaftan, *Aus der Werkstatt des Übermenschen,* Heilbronn, 1906.—Avenarius concerning Nietzsche's relations to the *Kunstwart: Andler,* IV, 564–67.—Carl Spitteler, *Meine Beziehungen zu Nietzsche,* München, 1908.

Important *documents* are contained in the following publications:

O. F. Scheuer, *Friedrich Nietzsche als Student,* Bonn, 1923.—Johannes Stroux, *Nietzsches Professur in Basel,* Jena, 1925.—Gottfried Bohnenblust, "Nietzsches Genferliebe"; *Annalen* II, Zürich, 1928, pp. 1 ff.—E. F. Podach, *Nietzsches Zusammenbruch,* Heidelberg, 1930.—E. F. Podach, *Gestalten um Nietzsche,* Weimar, 1932.

[2] Cf. the chronological table in the Appendix.
[3] Stroux, op. cit., pp. 32–36.

like J. Burckhardt, also taught six hours at the Pedagogical Institute. The patrician homes of Basel were open to him. He established more or less intimate relation with the outstanding minds of the University: J. Burckhardt, Bachofen, Heusler, and Rütimeyer. A close bond sprang up between him and Overbeck, a friend with whom he shared a house. The high point of his association with people—of his whole life in fact, and remembered as such to the very end—was his series of visits with Richard and Cosima Wagner between 1869 and 1872 in Tribschen, near Lucerne. After his book, *The Birth of Tragedy,* appeared, he was banished from philological circles, and von Wilamowitz was given precedence. Consequently the philology students in Basel stayed away from him. In 1873 began those spells of sickness which forced him to take a leave of absence for the year 1876–77, a great part of which he spent in Sorrento with P. Rée at the home of Malvida von Meysenbug. In 1879, at the age of thirty-five, he was compelled to resign from his position because of illness.

During the second decade (1879–89), Nietzsche traveled from place to place in search of a climate that would relieve his painful afflictions, never remaining anywhere for more than a few months on account of seasonal changes. For the most part he sojourned in the Engadine and on the Riviera, occasionally in Venice, and finally in Turin. The winter was most frequently spent in Nice, the summer in Sils-Maria. As *"fugitivus errans"* he lived on modest means in plain and simple rooms, wandering during the day through the country, with his eyes protected from the light by a green sun visor, and coming in contact with all manner of travelers.

While his earlier publications—*The Birth of Tragedy* and the first part of *Untimely Meditations* (against Strauss)—had caused a sensation and were either enthusiastically applauded or bluntly rejected, his later writings were unsuccessful. The books of aphorisms scarcely sold at all, and Nietzsche sank into oblivion. Special circumstances involved him in nerve-racking difficulties with his publishers, and he finally published his writings at his own expense. Only during the last months of unclouded consciousness did he perceive the first signs of the approaching fame about which he had not entertained a moment's doubt.

Excluded from his profession, entirely devoted to his real and acknowledged mission, and living, as it were, outside of the world, he began to wish for renewed contact with reality when his health took a turn for the better. In 1883 he made plans for lectures at the University of Leipzig, but within university circles such lectures were considered impossible because of the questionable content of his writings. Nietzsche remained outside of the world and became increasingly tense as he continued to devote himself to his work.

In January, 1889, when he was forty-five years old, an organic brain disorder caused his collapse, and in 1900 death terminated his long illness.

Nietzsche's World. The world in which Nietzsche moved and in which he could observe, think, and express his thoughts, was conveyed to him—first during his youth—by the German culture, with its humanistic schools, its poets, and its patriotic traditions.

Nietzsche took up the study of classical philology. This not only provided him, throughout his life, with the great ideas of antiquity, but it also led to a fortunate meeting, while he was still a student, with a genuine man of research. Ritschl's seminar of classical philology was unique in its technique of philosophical interpretation; various non-philologists, including even numerous medical men, participated in it with a view to learning "method." In the skill and attitude which Ritschl promoted, there was something basic which all the sciences share: the art of distinguishing the real from the unreal, the factual from the fictitious, demonstrable knowledge from mere opinions, and objective certainty from subjective conviction. One can attain a clear concept of the nature of scientific knowledge only by focusing attention on what is common to all of the sciences. Here Nietzsche became aware of the essential nature of the scholarly investigator: his incorruptibility, his ceaseless critical struggle with his own thinking, his simple and guileless passion.

Nietzsche's pronounced *pedagogical* impulses found only scant realization. He performed his tasks as a university professor and his duties as a teacher at the Pedagogical Institute [4] most conscientiously but with growing dislike. During the entire decade of his professorship he lived in a state of tension, striving, while performing his rigorous professional duties, to preserve as much energy as possible to devote to the as yet indefinite calling which attracted and agitated him.

In 1867–68 Nietzsche served with the mounted *field artillery* in Naumburg. However his service came to a premature end when, in jumping on his horse, he incurred an injury that resulted in suppuration and an illness that lasted for months. During the war of 1870 he volunteered to serve as a *nurse*. His loyalty to the neutral country in which he

---

[4] For reports concerning Nietzsche as a teacher see Bernoulli, I, pp. 66 ff.

was a professor would not allow him to serve as a combatant. He became afflicted with dysentery and, even before the end of the war, returned to his post as a teacher.

The fact that Nietzsche lived in foreign countries from his twenty-fifth year until the end of his life—that, for twenty whole years, he saw Germany from the outside—made a profound difference in his world-view. His position on the outside enabled him (as life on the border, so to speak, commonly does) to sharpen his critical outlook and to recognize the commonplace, especially during the later period, when he ran the risk of becoming uprooted as a result of his constant traveling. Change produces constantly renewed stimulation of the sensibilities, enables one to live within a horizon that is ever expanding to embrace whatever acquires true substance, and heightens one's love and one's hatred for his native land since the feeling for the latter is intensified by its remoteness.

As a result of Nietzsche's estrangement from the world, from his profession, associates, and pedagogical activities, he had to derive new experiences from a program of *reading* that covered a very extensive range of topics, although the amount had to be limited because of his eyes. While we know which books he borrowed from the Basel library between the years 1869 and 1879 and know of most of the books in his own library,[5] we are of course not in a position to say that he read them all, though they did pass through his hands and, in some way, did attract his attention. He had weekly lists of new books sent to him (to Overbeck, Apr. 11, '80), and he consistently planned to stay in cities with large libraries (to Overbeck, May 2, '84, and Sept. 17, '87), but nothing of all this could develop beyond a mere beginning.

Especially conspicuous is the large number of books dealing with natural science and ethnography, as though he wished to make up for having neglected factual knowledge while studying philology. Cursory reading of these books may have stimulated him, but for the most part they are below his level and must be regarded simply as a substitute for an actual first-hand acquaintance with matters pertaining to the biological and physical sciences.

That Nietzsche can discover so much through relatively little reading is quite astonishing. He immediately grasps the essential. As he reads, he visualizes the authors of the books and intuitively senses what their thinking and writing really amount to and what they signify existentially.

---

[5] Lists of books borrowed by Nietzsche from the Basel library from 1869 to 1879 appear in Albert Levy, *Stirner et Nietzsche,* Paris, 1904, pp. 93–113. Concerning Friedrich Nietzsche's library, see Arthur Berthold, *Bücher und Wege zu Büchern,* Stuttgart, 1900, pp. 429–56.

He is conscious not only of their subject matter, but also of the substance of the thought which takes this subject matter for its theme.

Words and thoughts often pass directly from the reading matter to Nietzsche, a fact that is of less significance for the intent of his philosophizing than for the actual origin of his means of expression. That the term "superman" [6] is found in Goethe and the term "cultural philistine" (*Bildungsphilister*) in Haym, is no more essential than his taking the expressions "perspectivism" and "decadence" from Bourget. Such receptivity as Nietzsche's—spontaneous, directly operative and all-absorbing—is indispensable to all creative work.

Nietzsche *philosophizes* even as a boy. Schopenhauer becomes *the* philosopher for the young man, while F. A. Lange, Spir, Teichmüller, Dühring, and E. v. Hartmann supply him with the traditional concepts. Of the great philosophers, he has read only Plato with some thoroughness, and then as a philologist (at a later date he is "appalled when he realizes *how little* he knows of Plato." [to Overbeck, Oct. 22, '83]). The substance of his philosophizing does not come to him primarily through the study of these works; rather it develops out of his contemplation of the Greek world of the pre-Socratic period: the pre-Socratic philosophers above all, then Theognis, then the tragic poets, and, finally, Thucydides. His study of Diogenes Laertius, undertaken as a result of his philological interest, provides him with some knowledge of the history of philosophy. Nietzsche, who has almost never studied the great philosophers thoroughly, and who relies upon secondary materials for most of his knowledge, is still capable of penetrating to the primary sources beyond the dry husks of thought handed down by tradition. Impelled by his own nature, he becomes each year more decisively concerned to lay hold upon the genuine philosophical problems.

As a result of his way of philosophizing, he is attracted by the poets quite as much as those who, strictly speaking, may be called philosophers. During his youth, he is transported by Hölderlin, especially his *Empedocles* and *Hyperion,* at a later date by Byron's *Manfred.* During the last years he also comes under the influence of Dostoevski.

Perhaps his interest in music is even more deeply rooted and fateful. No other philosopher has ever been so completely imbued with music or

---

[6] While Walter Kaufmann presents some good reasons for translating the term *Übermensch* as "overman," we have retained the more generally accepted expression "superman," as it seems to convey Nietzsche's meaning somewhat more directly and forcefully. What the comic strips have done to this and other words should be of no concern here.—Trs.

has found it so overwhelming. Even as a boy he is quite transported by it, during his youth he is prepared to devote his life to the music of R. Wagner to whom he is unconditionally attached, and late in life he confesses: "And in the end I am an old musician who can find no consolation except in tones" (to Gast, June 22, '87). In 1888 his attachment to music is even further intensified: "Music now brings me experiences as really never before. It sobers me and detaches me from myself . . . , and in doing so it strengthens me. Every evening of music is followed by a morning filled with resolute insights and ideas. . . . Life without music is simply a mistake, a hardship, an exile" (to Gast, Jan. 15, '88). To him nothing under the sun "could be of more concern than the fate of music" (to Gast, March 21, '88).

Yet this same Nietzsche turned away from music with equal passion. In 1886 he wrote of the years after 1876: "I began by denying myself, explicitly and on principle, all romantic music—that ambiguous, pretentious, and sultry art which robs the spirit of its strength and joyousness and induces the proliferation of all sorts of vague yearnings and bloated lusts. 'Cave musicam' is to this day my advice to all those who are manly enough to insist on cleanliness in matters of the spirit." Accordingly his judgments about music are in agreement with the age-old anti-musical philosophical tradition: "Music has no sounds to express the raptures of the spirit: in endeavoring to represent the psychic states of Faust, Hamlet, and Manfred, it omits the spirit and conveys emotional states." "The poet stands higher than the musician, for in appealing to the whole man he makes higher demands, and the thinker makes still higher demands: he requires one's freshest energies, concentrated and entire, and summons us, not to enjoyment, but to a combat involving the fullest renunciation of all self-centered impulses." Nietzsche is of the opinion that "the faulty and even fanatical development of the understanding and the lack of restraint of hatred and vilification were probably brought about partly by that non-discipline known as music." Music is "dangerous": "Its debauchery and its penchant to provoke Christian situations . . . go hand in hand with a lack of cleanliness of the mind and riotous dreams of the heart." Somewhat more favorable, at least, is the view of music which sees it as articulating something which is eventually to find superior expression in thought: "Music is my precursor . . . So much has not yet been said or thought."

Nietzsche appears to find an escape from so contradictory an approach to music when he distinguishes between *genuine music* and *romantic music,* which he calls dangerous, voluptuous and beclouding. To the music of Richard Wagner he wishes to oppose the former, which he believes he has found in the works of Peter Gast. As early as 1881 he conceives of Gast as "his master of the first order" whose music is related to his own philosophy (to Overbeck, May 18, '81); and this music signifies "the justification in sound of all my new practice and rebirth" (to Overbeck, Oct., '82). Nietzsche, in following this path, finally demands that music "be serene and deep like an afternoon in October; that it be self-willed, uninhibited and tender; a sweet little woman full of meanness and charm." While on this path, he also exalts Bizet's *Carmen* as a singular paragon, something which he did not really mean, however: "You must not take seriously what I say about Bizet; since I am what I am, there are a thousand reasons why I cannot consider him. But he is most effective as an ironical antithesis to Wagner" (to Fuchs, Dec. 27, '88).

If one sees how completely Nietzsche is overwhelmed by music, if one takes account of his dubious judgments—especially those very erroneous but stoutly maintained evaluations of Peter Gast's compositions—and considers his own compositions, he realizes that music cannot be his forte (Nietzsche acknowledged, in writing, the following judgment of Hans von Bülow in 1872: "Your Manfred-meditation is the most phantastic extravagance, the most disagreeable and anti-musical piece that I have laid eyes on in quite some time. . . . Is the whole thing a joke, and did you perhaps intend to write a parody of the so-called music of the future? . . . Despite all aberration, one can sense in the product of your musical fever a spirit that is unusual and distinguished. . . ."). Nietzsche's nervous system—indeed, the very substance of his being—is musical to the point of defenselessness. But music is, as it were, the antagonist of his philosophy: his thinking becomes more philosophical as it becomes less musical. Nietzsche's philosophizing is wrested from the musical and achieved in a struggle against it. Not only his thought-processes, but even his mystical experiences of being are unmusical as well as anti-musical.

New materials for his philosophizing come, in a manner peculiar to him, from still another source. For quite some time he has held a number of French writers in extraordinarily high esteem: [7] La Rochefoucauld, Fontenelle, Chamfort, and, above all, Montaigne, Pascal and Stendhal. Psychological analysis becomes the medium of his philosophizing—not the analysis of empirical psychology proceeding causally, but that of

[7] Fritz Kröbel, *Europas Selbstbesinnung durch Nietzsche: Ihre Vorbereitung bei den französischen Moralisten*, München, 1929.

sociological and historical psychology using the method of *Verstehen*.[8]
He wishes his experience to be a "voluntary reliving of all the evaluative
standpoints of the past and of their opposites as well." He wants co-
workers to join him on the path of research that he envisages: "Where is
there a history of love, avarice, envy, conscience, piety, or cruelty?
. . . Have researches ever been carried out concerning the various divisions of the day, and the consequences of regulating the times to be
devoted to work, rest, and festivals? Have the experiences involved in
living together in groups—in monasteries, for instance—ever been
recorded?"

Nothing in the world is as significant to Nietzsche as the *great men*
whom he deifies or devilizes. In Goethe, Napoleon, Heraclitus, he sees
unequivocal and indubitable greatness. He finds Socrates, Plato, and
Pascal to be great men, but so highly ambiguous that they must be
evaluated in opposite ways, depending on the circumstances in which
they appear. St. Paul and Rousseau he always rejects, Luther almost
always. He admires Thucydides and Machiavelli for their pellucid truthfulness and realistic incorruptibility.

Nietzsche attains to his most profound historical consciousness when
he sees the relation of his thinking and his innermost nature to those great
ones who shared his problems and concerns and who lived with him in
the realm of the spirit: "This is my pride: that I have a lineage. . . .
That which moved Zarathustra, Moses, Mohammed, Jesus, Plato, Brutus,
Spinoza, and Mirabeau is the medium in which I live. . . ." "When I
speak of Plato, Pascal, Spinoza, and Goethe, I know that their blood
flows in my veins." And he speaks of "my ancestors, Heraclitus,
Empedocles, Spinoza, and Goethe." [9]

The Portrait of Nietzsche. The reports about Nietzsche by contemporaries always seem to distort his portrait somewhat. He is regarded from
an inappropriate point of view, assimilated to the ideals or counter-
ideals of the time, or judged by spurious criteria, as though viewed in a
distorting mirror.

The idealized portrait provided by his sister, magnificent as it is in its
own way, is as far from the truth as the more realistic, disconnected,

[8] This psychological term which, like *Gestalt* and *Prägnanz*, has been adopted
without alteration by some English-speaking psychologists, has been used by
German philosophers since Dilthey to refer to our *ab intra* knowledge of others
when we "understand" them in the sense of being directly aware of their feelings,
attitudes, and thought-contents. —Trs.

[9] For very detailed descriptions of everything that influenced Nietzsche, what
he read, what he knew, and what he used, cf. Charles Andler, *Nietzsche. Sa
vie et sa pensée,* Paris, 1920–1931.

agitated, but questionable account furnished by Overbeck. We may well be grateful to both, especially for the factual material which they offer, but their deficiencies leave one eager to hear even the most trivial reports of everyone who saw and talked with Nietzsche. To be sure, these copious though confusing descriptions do provide us with the beginnings of a portrait. But the portrait fails to take final shape: too much remains incomplete and even ambiguous. Contemporary accounts have to be corrected through personal documents (his letters, works, and notes) and viewed in connection with the unforgettable tone of everything which he himself provided, including the last traces and incidentals of his writings. In what follows, some of the testimony of his contemporaries is given:

Reporting on Nietzsche as a *schoolboy,* Deussen writes: "All forms of histrionic simulation, whether for the sake of praising or blaming someone, were totally foreign to his nature. . . . I have heard him utter many an ingenious remark, but I have seldom heard him tell a good joke. . . . He disliked gymnastics, and while still young he already tended to be plump and to suffer from congestions in the head. . . . A simple stunt, performed in a jiffy by a skilled gymnast, was a difficult task for him; while performing it he would turn very red, become breathless, and break into a sweat. . . ."

A report of 1871 states: "The glasses he wears remind one of a scholar, while his fastidious attire, his almost military posture, and his bright, clear voice contradict this impression." [10] In the same year Deussen writes: "Long after eleven o'clock, Nietzsche, who had been a guest at Jacob Burckhard's, appeared. He was animated, fiery, resilient, and self-confident, like a young lion."

This is the way his colleagues see him: "Nietzsche enjoyed the good will of all the colleagues who knew him, as he was thoroughly inoffensive by nature." [11] Eucken remarks: "I still remember vividly Nietzsche's amiable attitude toward the doctoral candidates: he was never unfriendly or irritated but held conferences in a kind, though superior, manner. . . ."

Scheffler [12] characterizes the lecturer as follows: "In appearance modest and indeed almost humble. . . of small rather than medium stature. His head set deep between the shoulders on a stocky but frail body. . . . Nietzsche adopted the fashion of the day. He wore light-colored trousers, together with a short jacket, and a neatly tied cravat that

[10] Elisabeth Förster-Nietzsche, *Wagner und Nietzsche,* p. 83.
[11] Mähly, *op. cit.,* p. 249.
[12] Quoted in: Bernoulli I, 252.

fluttered around his neck . . . long hair, the strands of which framed his pale face. . . . Of heavy, almost tired gait. . . . Nietzsche's speech, soft and unaffected . . . had but one thing in its favor: it came from his soul . . . the magic of this voice. . . ."

In 1891 a Pole described from memory the Nietzsche whom he had met in the mid-seventies as "a tall man with long thin arms and a round, mighty head crowned by a bristly crest of hair. . . . His mustache, which was a deep black, fell below his chin on both sides of his mouth. His preternaturally large black eyes shone like balls of fire behind his spectacles. I thought I was seeing a wildcat. My companion wagered that he was a Russian poet taking a trip to rest his nerves." [13] This description is especially questionable, for according to Lou Salomé's statements, Nietzsche was of medium height and had brown hair.

Ungern-Sternberg in 1876 reports: "Expression of pride, subdued, to be sure, by weariness and a certain hesitancy in movement brought on by his nearsightedness. Very obliging, pleasant social manners, simplicity, and dignity."

Lou Salomé writes in 1882: "Something concealed, an intimation of an unspoken loneliness—that was the first strong impression that gave Nietzsche's appearance its captivating power. It offered nothing striking to the casual observer; the medium-sized man in extremely simple and extremely neat clothes, with serene features and brown hair, smoothly brushed back, could easily be overlooked. He had a light laugh, a quiet way of speaking, and a cautious, pensive way of walking with his shoulders slightly stooped; it was difficult to imagine this figure in the midst of a crowd, for it bore the stamp of one who stands apart and alone. His hands were nobly formed and incomparably beautiful—so much so that one could not help looking at them. . . . His eyes, too, spoke a revealing language. Though half blind, they nevertheless had nothing of the spying, blinking, unintentionally intrusive way of many near-sighted persons; rather they seemed like guardians and keepers of inner treasures and mute secrets. . . . Faulty vision endowed his features with a very special kind of charm by causing them to reflect his innermost psychic processes rather than fleeting external impressions. These eyes looked inward and, at the same time, into the distance or, better still: inward as if into a distance. Whenever, under the spell of a stimulating conversation with one other person, he revealed his true self, an inspiring light would come into his eyes; but when he was in a dark mood, his loneliness spoke from them, ominously, almost threateningly, as if from monstrous

[13] Quoted from: Harry Graf Kessler in *Die neue Rundschau,* 1935, p. 407.

depths. Nietzsche's overt behavior, too, conveyed the impression of things concealed and unspoken. In everyday life he showed great courtesy and an almost feminine gentleness—a constant, goodhearted equanimity. He took pleasure in the refined forms of social intercourse. . . . But in it all lay a penchant for disguise. . . . I recall that when I spoke to him for the first time, his deliberately formal manner shocked and deceived me. But I was not deceived for long by this lonesome man who only wore his mask as unalterably as someone coming from the desert and mountains wears the cloak of the worldly-wise. . . ."

Deussen says in 1887: "This was no longer the proud bearing, the resilient step, and the fluent speech of former days. He seemed to drag himself with effort, inclined to one side, and his talk often became clumsy and halting. . . . We retired for an hour in the Hotel Alpenrose to get some rest. Scarcely had the hour passed when our friend came to our door, inquired with tender solicitude whether we were still tired, and begged our pardon in case he should have come too early. I mention this because such exaggerated care and consideration had not been part of Nietzsche's character. . . . When we parted, his eyes were filled with tears."

The impression of ambiguity which Nietzsche's nature conveys, receives further confirmation from extant photographs: every single picture of him is, at first sight, disappointing; they too are distorting mirrors. They do, of course, reveal something when contemplated long and often, and with a perceptive mind. The mustache can be viewed as an eloquent token of his penchant for concealment and reticence. His visionary gaze suggests the possession of an aggressiveness that leads to clarity. But it is not easy to catch sight, even momentarily, of anything of Nietzsche himself. Artistic portraits, especially, are unreliable masks reflecting the tastes of the time. Finally, Olde's etching, showing the paralytic, is certainly a truthful picture, but it is an agonizing one to those who can truly see.

If available accounts of Nietzsche's appearance and behavior beget uncertainty and the photographs leave us in doubt, a glance at Nietzsche's handwriting seems to bring Nietzsche's personality directly before us again.[14] We are indebted to Klages for an analysis from which we quote a few statements:

---

[14] Isabelle von Ungern-Sternberg's *Nietzsche im Spiegelbilde seiner Schrift*, Leipzig o.J., is of especial importance because of the numerous samples of his handwriting taken from every period of Nietzsche's life. Ludwig Klages, "Nietzsche und seine Handschrift," *Gesammelte Abhandlungen*, Heidelberg, 1927.

Klages knows "of no single handwriting by any outstanding personality who lived during the entire period between our classic days and the turn of the last century that even remotely resembles that of Nietzsche." To him it seems that they all resemble each other more closely than any one of them resembles the writing of Nietzsche. In the latter he finds "something extraordinarily luminous and bright . . . together with a pronounced lack of warmth; . . . something transparent, immaterial, crystalline—the extreme opposite of cloudiness, fluidity, and undulation . . . something remarkably hard, sharp, and of glasslike brittleness . . . something formed, finished, and even chiseled in its every detail." Klages sees the sublime sensitivity and irritability and the emotional life that is rich "although incapsulated within the organism of its possessor," in the sense that his experiences are his experiences alone. He sees the severity, the self-control, and the relentless self-judgment as well as the "powerful urge for self-esteem." The handwriting attains the clearest possible organization, it reveals that sort of simplification which automatically projects a virtually naked framework of letters; it betrays "an impetus striking ever anew in a thrustlike movement." One feels "the spirit of fencing . . . in the realm of thought"; "despite its having a profile that seems cut out of stone, the handwriting has about it something disquietingly unbounded, unforeseeable, and sudden." But, according to Klages, it certainly is not the handwriting of a man of action: compared with the calligraphy of a Napoleon or a Bismarck, for instance, that of Nietzsche appears "in the light of an almost fragilely delicate structure." It expresses an extreme spirituality and a "creative capacity of almost unimaginable scope": "We have never before encountered an unstylized handwriting which exhibited such sharpness and acuteness of angle together with an equally perfect rhythmic distribution of the writing masses and an almost pearl-like sequence!"

If, taking all this together, we were to ask about Nietzsche's empirical appearance, we would also have to ask: How is a man bound to appear, who, because of his truthfulness, his scale of values and conception of rank, finds himself in awkward positions and condemned to wear masks, or is quickly disillusioned and even overcome by revulsion? A man who develops something within himself that is not yet shared by others, who sees and wills what as yet no one else sees and wills, who consequently can never find confirmation in the world of men nor even be content with himself since all life and experience appear to him first as a trial and then as a failure?

Even today the picture of Nietzsche does not assume tangible form; he withdraws into shapes with which he cannot be identified. And yet we do see him, the wanderer, as he walks ever onward; we behold him, so to speak, ascending to inaccessible mountains. Even as he moves and vanishes he remains visible, for he was capable of living autonomously and of communicating his own inner life.

Nietzsche's Fundamental Trait: Being an Exception. Detached from all actual existence—from vocation and society—Nietzsche finds neither marriage nor pupils and followers, he creates no sphere of activity for himself within the world, and, losing his firm abode, he wanders aimlessly from place to place as though seeking what he can never find. But being thus an exception is itself substantive and positive: it characterizes all of Nietzsche's philosophizing.

It was in Bonn in 1865 that he first experienced a distinct crisis. While it was yet of vague import and involved only a change in his way of life, still it induced him to set out resolutely on his destined path. He became aware that the sort of student existence he was leading, his varied activities, his participation in fraternity-life (*Leben in der Burschenschaft*), self-development through the acquisition of knowledge, and the possibility of an academic career could never provide true fulfillment for him. Life to Nietzsche was neither a pastime nor a matter of following pre-established rules; and, while being thus distracted, he realized that he had given himself over to a mode of existence that could not be reconciled with the demands of a seriously conducted life. Spiritually he had indeed lived on a high level, but that was not sufficient for him. He was confronted by an Either/Or: either to drift with life or to accept the extraordinary as having claims that are valid for every day. Now for the first time his innermost attitude became suitably concentrated, though without his knowing as yet *what* provided the concentration and made demands upon him. This process was quite inconspicuous, although it can now be clearly discerned through his letters and his behavior-patterns. It was without pathetic accent and without catastrophe (since his resignation from the fraternity can scarcely be called catastrophic). Naturally his fraternity brothers accused him of arrogance or regarded him as lacking in *camaraderie,* for no one really knew what went on within him. But during this year the course that his life was to take became relatively certain and determinate: mere possibility gave way to an actuality that would drive him, through ever new transformations, into his *Existenz* as an exceptional being, by means of an insatiable urge that would constantly require him to surpass himself and never give him any peace.

An exposition of his life, guided by a philosophic interest, stresses this *Existenz* as an exception which actually underlies all changing appearances, even though none of them reveals it directly. The problem may be approached in three ways: we may study the course of his *spiritual development, his friendships,* and his *illness.*

The Course of Nietzsche's Development

On the one hand, Nietzsche's work is a single whole; on the other, each one of his writings has its characteristic place within a developmental process that extends over two decades. In the course of this process the most extraordinary transformations appear, making it all the more surprising that the new seems to be rooted in tendencies that are present even from the beginning. Knowledge of the course of his development makes possible a more profound understanding of his work, since it enables us to advance from the temporal location of each specific utterance to a view of the development as a whole.

The Development of His Work. A compendious survey of his writings provides a preliminary characterization of the stages through which Nietzsche's thought passed.[15]

Nietzsche's *youthful writings* are of no great importance intrinsically, although we can, in retrospect, discern in them the seeds of most of his later thoughts and impulses as we come to know them. The *Philologika* (three volumes) offers an impressive picture of Nietzsche's scientific work, interspersed with numerous viewpoints which constitute the beginning of his philosophizing. However, what may properly be considered his "works" falls in the following groups:

1. His *earlier writings* include *The Birth of Tragedy, Untimely Meditations* (1871–76), and, from the posthumous material, the fragments of a book about the Greeks, the addresses *Concerning the Future of our Educational Institutions,* and the notes for a planned part of *Untimely Meditations,* entitled "We Philologists." All of these writings are in the

---

[15] Cf. the chronologically arranged list of his works in the Appendix.

42

form of treatises intended to be read consecutively. They still express faith in genius and in the impending German culture that is to be created directly out of the present disorder.

2. *Works appearing between 1876 and 1882: Human, All-Too-Human, Mixed Opinions and Maxims, The Wanderer and his Shadow* (the last two combined to constitute Vol. II of *Human, All-Too-Human*), *The Dawn,* and *The Gay Science* (Books I–IV) are basically aphorisms. In these succinct discussions a multidimensional abundance is expressed, largely without tendentiousness. Here is presented, in the form of frigid, totally detached, disillusioned, and highly critical observations, what ultimately was to unfold in gradual growth following *The Dawn:*

3. *Nietzsche's final philosophy:*

a. *Thus Spake Zarathustra* (1883–85) is basically a series of addresses by Zarathustra to crowds, companions, the "higher men," his animals, and himself, within a frame of situations and actions of this fictitious figure. What Nietzsche regarded as his *magnum opus* resists all traditional means of classification: it is to be taken as poetry as well as prophecy and philosophy, and still it cannot be viewed as precisely any one of these.

b. The course of his thought after 1876 appears in considerably shorter fragments in the posthumous material of volumes XI–XVI. The mental processes expressed in volumes XIII–XVI are involved with thoughts that are later to become basic (will to power, transvaluation, decadence, eternal recurrence, superman, etc.) but reach beyond them almost without limit. The quiet recording of thoughts in a sharp, concise form that strives for maximal clarity without having as yet a definite literary purpose is characteristic of these fragments. Retentive and coherent thinking that probes systematically is by no means lacking, though it is submerged by an abundance of striking impressions. Direct and promising grasp of the immediate and concrete is more important than a logically developed system of thought.

c. Between 1886 and 1887 Nietzsche writes and publishes *Beyond Good and Evil* and, in connection with it, the fifth book of *The Gay Science.* Although he here returns to the sort of book that is composed of aphorisms, he now shows a stronger tendency toward coherent presentation and provocative pathos. *Toward a Genealogy of Morals* contains essays in the form of systematic investigations. Prefaces written by Nietzsche for earlier works reveal his impressive retrospective self-knowledge.

d. In 1888 appears a last interconnected group of writings that contains the concluding expression of self-knowledge: *The Wagner Case,*

The Twilight of the Idols, the *Antichrist, Ecce Homo, Nietzsche contra Wagner.* Written at a frenzied tempo, they are intensified to the limit, unspeakably aggressive, and aimed at an irresistible effect.

Thus the course of his thought is usually divided into *three periods:* (1) up to 1876, a time of veneration, resting upon faith in culture and genius; (2) from then until 1881, a period of *positivistic faith in science* combined with dissecting criticism; and (3) the era of *the new philosophy* which lasted until the end of 1888. In other words, a process of gradual though radical estrangement leads him away from his *youthful faith* in friendship and discipleship and from a life of confidence in the future of his people; drives him forcefully through a period spent in a "barren wilderness" in which all things are seen contemplatively and "put on ice"; and terminates in a new faith, born of the passionate tension of a consummate loneliness which knows practically no bond with individuals or with his own people and expresses itself only symbolically and in a visionary manner. The number of periods can be increased through further subdivision, especially of the third part. To characterize the middle period as merely positivistic and scientific is false. But still, the threefold division itself coincides with the decisive transformations and, in fact, rests upon Nietzsche's own view of himself.

Nietzsche's Own View of his Course. The two radical steps that lead from the first to the second period and from the second to the third were *at one and the same time* consciously seen and deliberately chosen. These transformations in his thinking are discernible in everything from his literary style to the setting of his goal. As he looked back upon his life, he never denied these changes but emphasized and interpreted them. The extent to which he understood himself has impressed all his readers. Roughly speaking, the first change occurred between 1876 and 1878, the second between 1880 and 1882.

Looking back from the third phase, Nietzsche could see his entire path as a meaningful whole. To him the three phases appeared, not as a simple succession of different events that might well have been otherwise, but as an over-powering necessity, the dialectic of which required precisely *these* three phases. Nietzsche's interpretation of these three phases as the "Way to Wisdom" follows:

"*The first path:* Worshipping (and obeying and learning) better than anyone else. Assimilating all things that are venerable and letting them struggle with one another. Putting up with every difficulty. . . . Courage, time of fellowship. (Overcoming wicked and petty inclinations. The most receptive heart: One cannot conquer without love.)"

This was the time when Nietzsche infected his friends with his enthusiasm for Wagner and Schopenhauer, when he subjected himself to the discipline of his philological studies and worshipped his teacher Ritschl with a trusting heart. And all the while he allowed the objects of his veneration to contend for mastery within himself (Wagner and Schopenhauer with the philologists, philosophy with science). He not only enjoyed personal freindships but still shared in the life, first of the fraternity, and then of the philological society which he had founded. He educated himself strictly and cast off forever any petty feeling—if such ever existed. Wherever he went, he assumed that all whom he encountered were kind and amiable, and he met them with an open heart. It is in such terms as these that Nietzsche describes the attitudes of his youth.

"*The second path:* Breaking the heart of the worshipper when he is most strongly committed. The free spirit. Independence. The time of the wasteland. Critique of all that is venerated (with idealization of all that is not venerated). The attempted reversal of evaluations (. . . natures such as Dühring, Wagner, and Schopenhauer have not even attained this level!)."

When Nietzsche, from 1876 on, assumed his new position, friends were shocked by the contrast, for this position appeared to deny everything that had gone before. It was the time of his "detachments" and "overcomings." To the very end of his days he was scarcely able to recover from the most difficult task of all: shattering his overpowering and loving devotion to Richard Wagner, to whom he had been most closely attached. With the disintegration of all that he had revered, existence, to him, had to become a desert in which only one thing remained, namely that which had relentlessly forced him into this path: truthfulness that knows no limits and is not subject to any condition. Heeding its challenge, he subjected himself to the new discipline of reversing all his previous value-judgments and, as an experiment, of accepting as positive (of idolizing) all that he hitherto had esteemed lightly (anything anti-artistic, anything naturalistic, the exact sciences, the skeptics). It is this attempt at utter truthfulness that he finds lacking in the previously highly regarded men, in Wagner, in Schopenhauer, and likewise in Dühring (who in his criticism of contemporary values is only seemingly related to him); they all are content to remain in a state of believing-without-questioning, of worshipping, and of accepting-things-as-true, as though there were no other possibility.

"*The third path:* Great decision whether suitable for positive attitude, for affirmation. No longer any God or man above me! The instinct of the creative person who knows where to set to work. The great responsibility and the innocence. . . . (Only for a few: most people will perish even on the second path. Perhaps Plato and Spinoza succeeded?)." [16]

The attempt at reversal and negation could not be the end. It is a question of whether the creative source of directive life which dared this extreme step is capable of bringing forth the affirmation—the genuine positiveness which stands the test under all questioning. This positiveness no longer comes from another, not from God, not from a venerated person, and not from someone "above me," but solely from his own creativeness. Now the extreme must be attained, but in the positive and no longer in the negative sense: "To grant one's self the right to act. Beyond good and evil. He does not feel humiliated by fate: he is fate. He . . . holds the lot of mankind in his hand."

This self-analysis, expressed retrospectively in numerous variations by Nietzsche, clearly agrees with the self-analysis uttered *simultaneously* with the two great transformations of 1876 and 1880:

(1) During the years after 1876, Nietzsche declares that he has given up the metaphysically artistic views which dominated his earlier writings. He rejects his "superstitious belief in genius." "Now for the first time I could attain the simple view of real human life." And in a letter: "This metaphysical beclouding of everything true and simple, the battle with reason against reason, . . . this it was that finally made me sick and sicker. . . . *Now* I shake off what does not belong to *me,* men as friends and enemies, habits, comforts, books" (to Mathilde Maier, July 15, '78).

Basic to Nietzsche's attitude is his belief that he is now *actually finding his own self.* While he formerly talked *about* philosophy and philosophers, he now begins to philosophize from his own being. "Now I dare to pursue wisdom itself and to *be* myself a philosopher; formerly I worshipped the philosophers" (to Fuchs, June, '78). He sees himself a hundred paces closer to the Greeks: "as I now *myself live,* in every detail, striving for wisdom, while I formerly merely worshipped and idolized the wise" (to Mathilde Maier, July 16, '78).

(2) The second step (1880 ff.), which was to lead out of the "desert" of negation to the creation of the new positiveness, naturally had to have a more profound effect and be at first still obscure in regard to the nature of the new ideas proclaiming themselves. The manner in which Nietzsche simultaneously becomes conscious of this and soon gains a

[16] Concerning Nietzsche's retrospective self-analysis cf. also: the *Vorreden,* 1, pp. 1 ff., 2, pp. 3 ff., and *Ecce Homo,* 15, pp. 1 ff.

definite self-understanding, develops between 1880 and 1883. It can be traced chronologically from its faint beginnings to the clear conception of the new:

Nietzsche's self-awareness and therewith his awareness of his task was always in evidence. He had already written to Gersdorff (Feb. 4, '72) concerning the *Birth of Tragedy:* "I count on a slow quiet stroll—through the centuries, as I tell you with deepest conviction. For certain eternal things have been uttered here for the first time: this must ring on." But these words—if measured by his later self-awareness—do at the same time express acquiescence, something like naturalness and moderation, insofar as he imagines himself as belonging in the circle of historically effective personalities on the basis of a single great achievement. This acquiescence was even more dominant after *Human, All-Too-Human;* at that time he remarked: "I had no notion that I had a right to entertain *universal* ideas of my own and even to declaim them. Even now the feeling of having been the most miserable novice comes over me; my loneliness and my illness have accustomed me somewhat to the 'brazenness' of my literary endeavors" (to Gast, Oct. 5, '79). But now, since the middle of 1880, the change—beginning faintly—suddenly becomes extraordinary. The still obscure task, the accomplishment of which will not be one spiritual creation among others but which, according to his later self-analysis, will split the history of the world into two halves, is thus proclaimed: "It now *seems* to me as though I had meanwhile discovered the right path and the way out; nevertheless, something like this must be believed and rejected a hundred times" (to Gast, July 18, '80). Then from Marienbad the first sentences sounding a new note of confidence that he is at the source: "Certainly there has not been so much thinking here since Goethe, and even Goethe probably did not let such fundamental things go through his head" (to Gast, Aug. 20, '80). And then we read: "I often do not know how I could bear my weakness (in spirit, health and other things) together with my strength (in visualizing prospects and tasks)" (to Overbeck, Oct. 31, '80); and it becomes clear that this strength is the novelty which overwhelms and almost confounds him: "Without great counterweights to balance very broad, very soaring urges that dominate me," I should "turn into a fool" (he means without his illness which incapacitates him again and again and reminds him of man's finiteness). . . . "Scarcely have I shaken off the misery of two days, when once more my folly pursues the most unbelievable things. . . . I live as though the centuries were a mere nothing. . . ." (to Overbeck, Nov., '80). The evaluation of his new activity corresponds to this. This no longer is literary labor. Of *The Dawn* he writes: "Do you think that you are dealing with a *book?* Do you, too, still consider me a writer? My hour has come" (to his sister, June 19, '91). "It is one of the strongest spiritual drinks. . . . It is a beginning of my beginnings—what still lies ahead of me! . . . I am at the summit of my life, i.e., of my tasks. . . ." (to Overbeck, Sept. '81). What Nietzsche was later to consider the third phase had now arrived in the form of the fate which claimed him completely and which he knew he was destined to carry out.

In July and August came the time which he was to remember until the end as having given birth to the one of his ideas that he considered the most profound (eternal recurrence) and the essence of which was brought out at that time in his letters: "Thoughts have arisen on my horizon the likes of which I have never yet seen. I probably will have to live a *few* more years" (to Gast, July 14, '81).

Since 1881 Nietzsche thus knew definitely, even with regard to content, that something entirely new was emerging. It is subsequently expressed with alarm, with the realization of its overwhelming seriousness. "When you have read the Sanctus Januarius" (from *The Gay Science*), he writes to Overbeck, Sept., '82, "you will have noticed that I have entered a new *sphere.* Everything ahead of me is new, and it will not be long until I get a glimpse of the *frightful* countenance of the future task of my life." This new element makes its first appearance in "*Zarathustra*" after the earliest traces have already been revealed in *The Dawn,* with definite beginnings in *The Gay Science.* In view of this new element—even before the appearance of *Zarathustra*—Nietzsche considers *The Gay Science,* at the very moment of its conclusion, as belonging to the second period and therefore past; with it, "the work of 6 years (1876–1882), all my 'free-thinking' has come to an end" (to Lou, 1882). When the first book of *Zarathustra* appears, on the other hand, Nietzsche is immediately conscious of its extraordinary incisiveness for his work:

"Meanwhile I have written my best book and taken that decisive step for which I did not have the courage last year" (to Overbeck, Feb. 3, '83). "The time of silence is past: let my Zarathustra . . . divulge to you to what heights my will has taken flight. . . . Behind all the plain and strange words stand my *most serious intention* and my *whole philosophy.* It is the beginning of a process of revealing myself—nothing more!" (to Gersdorff, June 28, '83). "It is a matter of a tremendous synthesis which I believe never yet to have been in any man's head and soul" (to Overbeck, Nov. 11, '83). "I have discovered my new land, totally unknown to everyone so far; now of course I still have to conquer it step by step" (to Overbeck, Dec. 8, '83).

Neither after 1876 nor after 1880 was Nietzsche's transformation a mere mental process producing a new insight; both times it was an existential event which he subsequently interpreted through his dialectical scheme and to which he gave an appropriate structure. In order to indicate the profound importance of this event, he spoke in each instance of a change of "taste" that had taken place in him. "Taste" is conceived by Nietzsche as something which substantially precedes any thought, any insight, any value-judgment: "I have a taste, but it rests upon no reasons, no logic, and no imperative" (to Gast, Nov. 19, '86). But this taste is for him the final authority that speaks from the depths of *Existenz*:

After 1876 he notices, for the first time and irrespective of any content, a change in his "taste"; he sees and wills the "difference in style": he strives to attain the highest possible precision in the relationship and resilience of all movements, and the most cautious moderation in the use of any pathetic and ironical devices, in place of the "somewhat pompous and uncertain gait and sound" characteristic of his earlier writings. He finds these earlier writings unbearable because they speak "the language of fanaticism."

Corresponding statements concerning his new taste now evident appear after 1880. Of the *Birth of Tragedy* and *Human, All-Too-Human* he says: "I can no longer stand all this stuff. I hope that I shall yet outgrow the 'writer and thinker' Nietzsche" (to Gast, Oct. 31, '86); and during the last year (1888), looking back to the time of his conception of the idea of recurrence, he writes: "When I think back a few months from this day, I find as an omen a sudden and most decisive change in my taste. . . ."

The Third Period in Particular. The arrangement could lead one to suppose that, during the third period beginning with the second step, Nietzsche possesses the whole truth and succeeds in expressing it in his work. However, this period too is in constant flux. Nietzsche makes the highest demands upon himself and ventures the utmost. What is exciting at this time is the way in which the task takes shape as Nietzsche works toward its impending fulfillment. Far from being content with his attainments, he becomes increasingly aware that everything is yet to be done. His conscious planning and his own evaluation of what he has accomplished must once more be gathered and understood in chronological sequence from his own statements.

Twice more, in 1884 and 1887, Nietzsche feels that he is breaking with the old and making an essentially new start:

(1) When *Zarathustra* is left uncompleted, a new plan for the con-

struction of his real philosophy arises. Insofar as he designs a systematic pattern of work to be produced, it is a sketch. Insofar as it calls for new studies, it is a program:

Nietzsche wishes to undertake a "revision" of his "metaphysical and epistemological views." "I must now go step by step through a whole series of disciplines, for I have resolved to spend the next five years in perfecting the philosophy for which I have built myself a vestibule through my *Zarathustra*" (to Overbeck, Apr. 7, '84). In accordance with this intention, Nietzsche writes two months later: "Now that I have built this *vestibule* of my philosophy, I must get to work again . . . until the *main structure* also stands completed before me. . . . During these coming months I intend to draw up a pattern for my philosophy and a program for the next six years" (to his sister, June, '84). After three more months he has succeeded in working out this program: "I have . . . *finished* with the main task of this summer; the next six years will be devoted to elaborating a sketch in which I have outlined my philosophy" (to Gast, Sept. 2, '84).

But for the time being, there is no progress beyond the sketch and the program. Instead something new and dark is seeking expression. The distance from everything so far brought forth by him, even from *Zarathustra,* is to be radical: "All that I have written so far is *foreground; . . .* I am occupied with things of a dangerous nature. At one time I *meanwhile* recommend, in a *popular* manner, *Schopenhauer* and *Wagner* to the Germans, and at other times I am *thinking Zarathustra through;* to me these are experiences, but above all they are also *hiding places* in which I can again sit still for a while" (to his sister, May 20, '85). Nietzsche is constantly filled to overflowing with thoughts and is entirely overcome by the basic impulse uniting these thoughts and the awareness of the unprecedented newness of it all; but he must ask himself whether it is at all possible to express its real essence: "Almost every day I have dictated for two to three hours, but my 'philosophy,' if I have the right to give this name to that which maltreats me down to the roots of my being, is *no longer* communicable, at least not in print . . ." (to Overbeck, July 2, '85).

Now, however, Nietzsche does not limit himself to working out the "main structure" of his philosophy, and he does not wait six years. On the contrary, he next writes and publishes *Beyond Good and Evil* and the *Genealogy of Morals,* those writings which reveal the nature of his philosophizing—insofar as he himself presented it to the public—most completely but without system. They are a provisional substitute for the main work, not the ultimate goal; he counts these writings among his "preparatory" ones. Indeed, Nietzsche does not for a moment deceive himself about this; their completion only leaves him with a keener awareness of his task. For a second time (1887), there is an accumulation of statements showing that Nietzsche was aware of standing at the conclusion of something and at the beginning of the new.

(2) In part they are sketches and schedules resembling those of 1884. But it seems as though, in 1887, he once again experiences a tremendous crisis, although his concern, as seen by us, is simply the same great philosophy with which he is occupied during the entire third period. His statements, taken in chronological order, are as follows:

The first is reminiscent of 1884: "The compulsion to erect a connected structure of my thoughts during the next years lies on me with the pressure of a hundred hundredweights" (to Overbeck, March 24, '87). But something incisive must have taken place again: "I feel that there must be a new chapter in my life—and that the whole great task now lies before me!" (to Gast, Apr. 19, '87). This incisive event does not, as in 1884, simply require the learning of many new things: I "now need profound isolation even more urgently than inquiring and learning more about 5000 isolated problems" (to Gast, Sept. 15, '87). This resolve again expresses a view of the future: "Now nothing more will be printed for a number of years,—I absolutely have to withdraw and wait until I can shake the last fruit from my tree" (to Overbeck, Aug. 30, '87). Of the *Genealogy of Morals* he writes: "With this work, incidentally, my preparatory activity has come to an end" (to Overbeck, Sept. 17, '87). He is quite aware of the whole situation: "It seems that a sort of epoch is ending for me" (to Overbeck, Nov. 12, '87). This awareness deepens: "I am . . . in the midst of taking account of men and things for myself and of storing away my whole 'hitherto.' Nearly everything I do at the present amounts to writing *finis* to it. . . . Now that I must go on to a new form, I need first of all a new estrangement . . ." (to Fuchs, Dec. 14, '87). This knowledge of the conclusion of everything done so far is final: "My life now stands at high noon in a significant sense: one door closes, another opens. . . . I have now finished with men and things and have written *finis* to it. Who and what is to be left for me, now that I must go on to what is actually the main purpose of my existence . . . that is now a vital question . . ." (to Gersdorff, Dec. 20, '87). "Now my task is to collect my thoughts as thoroughly as possible so that the *fruit of my life* may slowly ripen and become sweet" (to his sister, Dec. 26, '87).

But Nietzsche does not pursue the new path he had resolved to follow. Something else takes hold of him. Instead of avoiding publication for years, instead of letting his fruit ripen in a contemplative atmosphere, he begins, a few months later, the series of writings of the year 1888. In the forced tempo of this year, he casts into the world these aggressive writings (*The Wagner Case, Twilight of the Idols, Antichrist*, and his *Ecce Homo*). He is no longer constructing his complete philosophy; rather he evinces the totally new intention of taking a hand at once, of making history, and of bringing the crisis of Europe immediately to a climax. So his voice, already at the point of breaking, is raised to a shout, shortly before his brain disorder causes him to be swallowed up by silence.

We must ask whether, according to Nietzsche's personal testimony and measured by his own criterion, his work attained completion, even if this consisted in no more than an objective and clear presentation, in the sum total of the notes found posthumously, of the quintessence of what he meant to express.

The *first indication* that this was not attained is given by Nietzsche himself; for he states again and again, from 1884 on until far into 1888, and often in similar words, that he has momentary inner visions of the whole, but that he also sees the actual execution still ahead of him. What was supposed to come, according to his awareness and his intention, ever since 1884, never actually took shape. To be sure, he visualizes what he wants: "There have been . . . hours when an immense all-inclusive philosophy (and something that has been called philosophy since time immemorial!) spreads out before my eyes . . ." (to Overbeck, Aug. 20, '84). In 1888 he is still in the same situation, seeing the whole before him without having realized its actuality: "The contours of this undoubtedly tremendous task before me rise ever more clearly out of the fog" (to Overbeck, Febr. 3, '88). "Nearly every day for one or two hours, I have mustered the energy required to see my whole conception from top to bottom . . ." (to Brandes, May 2, '88). He is glad that Peter Gast seems to sense the whole, even though only fragmentary writings appear: "You realize that it will develop into a whole. Something that *grows*, as it seems to me, into the earth (down!) *and* at the same time out into the blue sky!" (to Gast, Apr. 12, '87). But Nietzsche knows that it does not yet exist.

Nietzsche is no longer thinking of the projected main structure of his philosophy when, during his last months of sanity, he is certain of success and, in *Ecce Homo*, surveys his whole work with deep satisfaction. His writings of the year 1888 indicate that he has already abandoned his previously intended path. What appears now as an imperative task is accompanied by a feeling of complete success such as he has scarcely known before (a feeling possibly comparable to, but by no means identical with, that of the days of the Zarathustra-inspiration): "In the main, I feel more than ever the great serenity and certainty of being on my way and even close to a great goal" (to Overbeck, Sept., '88). "I am now the most grateful person in the world—in an *autumnal mood* in every good sense of the word; it is my great *harvest time.* Everything is easy for me, I succeed in everything, although scarcely anybody has ever dealt with such great things" (to Overbeck, Oct. 18, '88). This is the beginning of that subjective fulfillment of the last weeks which Nietzsche spent in a feeling of constant bliss before the outbreak of insanity.

A *second clue* concerning Nietzsche's failure to realize his planned creation is furnished by the last expressions of his understanding of his own work prior to the eruption of the new vehemence of 1888. When at the end of 1887 he writes *finis* to everything done so far, he adds: "Of course, precisely therewith this previous *Existenz* has been exposed for what it is—a mere *promise*" (to Gast, Dec. 20, '87). And shortly before the end when he desires only several years of peace and forgetfulness "for something that seeks to ripen," he speaks to Deussen of that which is yet to come as the "belated sanction and justification of my whole being (a being that otherwise and for a hundred reasons would be eternally problematical!)" (Jan. 3, '88). To be sure, he is certain of having "achieved a great deal, in spite of everything," but still, in the end he must admit: "I myself never got beyond attempts and ventures, never beyond prologues and promises" (to Gast, Febr. 13, '88). He was not granted the chance to go further. Instead of being allowed to fulfill his promises, he was seized by the overwhelming aggressive impulse that led to the writings of the last half of 1888.

The Constant Element in the Unfolding of the Whole. In our review of the course of his development, the third period stands out: it alone reveals his later way of philosophizing at its best and in all its originality; on the other hand it also shows the greatest dogmatic solidification. The other periods seem like preparations and preliminary stages. Still we must raise the question whether Nietzsche expresses something constant at all times and whether in his case the first two periods, precisely because they are preparatory stages for him, are not different from the early stages of the kind of person who does not experience them as a preparation but finds their spiritual tenor and outlook altogether congenial to his own nature.

A relation between all periods is indeed discernible; for that which is to reach its full proportions much later is always present, even when hardly noticeable, and that which appeared previously is retained as well. When Nietzsche, for example, develops the idea of the *"free spirit"* during the *second period,* this is by no means a break with his former self nor a transition to the contemporary "free spirit." He is not thinking at all of the free spirit as a libertine or as a person with a pathetic belief in freedom. He has no intention of hanging up a "caricature or a distorted picture of spiritual freedom to be worshipped." On the contrary, he wants methodically to isolate and push to the limit the severity of a venturesome way of thinking that is not bound to any faith. His thinking, rooted as it is in the need to shatter idols, seeks the meaningful freedom in which he lives. Even in this second period we can see that he is by no means concerned to think at random but wishes to "stretch an electric bond over a century, from a death chamber into the birth chamber of new liberties of the spirit." When the Nietzsche of this period insists above all on *science* and glorifies it, he does so consistently, even though he has questioned it radically and will do so again. At this time he simply accentuates it and, as though awakening from a dream, "finds it necessary for one to assimilate positivism in its entirety." By this he means realistic knowledge, and he immediately adds that he does not want positivism as such, but only as a foundation for idealism."

The posthumous writings allow us to observe that Nietzsche often thinks things that he is *not yet* ready to mention publicly and will not express until later—if at all. What seems most contradictory in the publicly uttered statements is thus more clearly shown to be intrinsically connected. The critical notes on R. Wagner of the year 1874 are perhaps the most impressive example of this: they contain all the essential viewpoints of the annihilating polemic of 1888, although *Richard Wagner in Bayreuth* was written with the enthusiastic approval of the master as late as 1876. In agreement with this, Nietzsche confesses in 1886 that during the time of his publications dealing with Schopenhauer and Wagner (of the first period) he believed "no longer in anything at all, as the popular saying goes, not even in Schopenhauer." It was during this time that a piece of writing was produced that he kept secret: "The Amoral Aspect of Truth and Falsehood." In fact, this already contains the profound interpretation of truth that belongs to his later philosophizing.

While incisive *crises* appear but twice during the course of his development, closer examination shows that the third period does not provide serenity but reveals a new way of thinking that is forever in crisis. Just as Nietzsche's entire life exhibits a soaring enthusiasm which finds only the most indirect expression during the first period, so his life is also pervaded by a negativity which in the second period appears as an objective analysis and in the third as an overwhelming awareness of crisis. Even though the years 1880 and 1881 seem to inaugurate a period of fulfillment, he experiences each crisis as actually an abandonment occasioned by a concentrated if indefinite demand for something still to come; he relinquishes before having gained new ground; he abandons every harbor in order to confront infinity on the open sea. The fulfillment of the Zarathustra period proves insufficient; the task is still before him. It is as though all affirmation is presented to him through negation, indeed *as* negation. The positive appeals to him as attractive and comprehensible, but it at once turns into something other than what he sought. Thus the negation becomes most potent precisely at the time when Nietzsche is actually struck—one might even say stricken—by his failure to attain to the full truth of being. It is as though whenever Nietzsche actually lays hold upon the mere *positive aspect* of something, he is seized by something *totally positive* which mercilessly knocks the factually apprehended out of his hands. That Nietzsche repeatedly experiences this and consciously accepts the limitless challenge, constitutes the incessant crisis of his spiritual life. Only the peaks of the few decisivie crises are clearly visible to us.

Furthermore we become aware of an unchanging ingredient when Nietzsche, while engaging in retrospective interpretation, maintains persuasively that his first efforts are basically identical with his final philosophy. When in 1886 he criticizes his *Birth of Tragedy* (whose "artist's metaphysics," "romanticism," and metaphysical "consolation" he now rejects), he recognizes nevertheless in its substance, as expressed in the rebirth of Dionysus, his unchanging intent. He claims that he always arrives at the same decisions: "They have already been written down, as concealed and obscured as possible, in my *Birth of Tragedy,* and all I have subsequently learned has fused with it and become a part of it" (to Overbeck, July, '85). He notices in his early writings the same impulses that still move him late in life: "In reading through my literature, . . . I discovered, much to my satisfaction, that I am still in possession of all the strong impulses of will that are articulated there. . . . Moreover, I have *lived* in accordance with my original plan (namely in *Schopenhauer as Educator*)" (to Overbeck, summer, '84). Of his writings about Schopenhauer and Wagner, he says finally: "Both works speak only of myself, *anticipando.* . . . Neither Wagner nor Schopenhauer is psychologically presented in them" (to Gast, Dec. 9, '88).

Conversely, Nietzsche had at an early age anticipated and expressed what he was actually to become as well as what he intended to become. Even before 1876, he wrote out what sounds like a presentiment of his own end: "Terrible loneliness of the last philosopher! Rigid nature surrounds him, vultures hover over him." At that time he composed the "talks of the last philosopher with himself": "I call myself the last philosopher because I am the last man. Nobody talks to me but myself, and my voice comes to me like that of a dying person! . . . Through you I conceal my loneliness from myself and make my way into the multitude and into love by lies, for my heart . . . cannot bear the terror of the loneliest loneliness and compels me to talk as if I were two." Nietzsche writes this as a professor in Basel, surrounded by friends, in the time of his enthusiasm for Wagner, during the success of his *Birth of Tragedy,* when no *Zarathustra* had yet appeared on his horizon.

Finally it is quite amazing that, as we learn from the writings of his youth (1858–68), he expressed, even as a boy, impulses and thoughts belonging to his later philosophy:

As early as this, *Christianity* has ceased to be just a form that provides assurance of profound depths and has become the object of a question: "Great revolutions are in the offing, once the masses understand that all Christianity is based on assumptions; the *existence of God,* the authority of the Bible, immortality, and inspiration will remain problems forever. *I have tried to deny everything:* Oh, it is easy to tear down, but to build up!" He speaks of the *"break with everything that exists,"* of the "doubt whether humanity has not been misled for two thousand years by a phantom picture."

Furthermore the concept of the man who becomes *more than man* is already emerging: "Only full, profound natures can dedicate themselves with a terrible passion so completely that they almost seem to step out of their humanity." The more-than-human is even now, in an evolutionary sense, mentally projected into the empty horizon of a *limitless* future and related to the idea of *eternal becoming:* "After all, we scarcely know whether humanity itself . . . is not merely a stage, a period in the universal whole, in the process of becoming. . . . Is there no end to this eternal becoming?"

Also positivistic reflections, taken over from the contemporary period, already appear, as when, for example, he asks what could draw the souls of many people down to the level of the ordinary and then gives the answer: "A fatal structure of skull and backbone, the station and nature of their parents, the ordinary in their environment. . . ."

As if anticipating his own last intention of the year 1888, he plays with the thought that "by resolutely *overthrowing,* as soon as possible, *the entire past of the world,* we should at once join the ranks of independent gods"; but he immediately realizes that "world history would then be nothing for us but a dreamlike trance; the curtain falls, and man once more finds himself, . . . like a child waking up in the glow of the morning and laughingly wiping the frightful dream from his forehead."

It is uncanny, and yet characteristic of Nietzsche's destiny, that even the fifteen-year-old (1859) with his groping and still indecisive thought-processes expresses the emancipation that leads to radical independence:

> None so bold be ever
> To ask with rash endeavor
> Where I might have my home.
> Ne'er by space I'm captured
> Nor by fleeting hours enraptured,
> Free like the eagle I roam.

Friends and Loneliness

That Nietzsche's passionate desire to communicate did not prevent his loneliness from increasing throughout his life is a fundamental fact. His letters, being intrinsic to his work and therefore inseparable from his life, provide documentation.

His friends included people of high rank. He came in contact with the foremost spirits of his time. He was surrounded by unusual men. But he could neither captivate nor be captivated for very long.

A study of his friendships—the special way in which each one reaches fruition, the expression of their real essence, the phases of their development, and their final breakdown—provides an irreplaceable insight into Nietzsche's being as well as an unparalleled experience of the possibilities of friendship. This wealth is not to be measured by the number of people with whom he was intimate; it is to be considered in terms of the essentially different directions in which these possibilities were clearly realized. Our task is adequately to comprehend, first, these possibilities and then the resulting loneliness. Our investigation discloses the following facts:

Nietzsche was profoundly attached to two friends, *Erwin Rohde* and *Richard Wagner*. These friendships were not permanent, but despite their external course, both men became companions of his soul for the rest of his life. As long as he was with them, he was not yet really alone. Immediately after his separation from them, his radical loneliness began.

In his loneliness he attempted to win new friends (Paul Rée, Lou Salomé, H. v. Stein). While they were not of the same caliber as the two he had lost, they were by no means insignificant or devoid of rank. As before, however, each of them brought further disappointment and failure. Throughout this period one man stands in the background: Peter Gast, not of equal stature, but enshrouded in Nietzsche's illusions and

58

providing a surrogate for all that the latter had been deprived of. Some human relationships, in contrast to the portentous flux of these ill-fated friendships, are sufficiently enduring to provide support for his life. But what endures in them has no existential effect on the deeper reaches of his nature and his task. Indispensable as security (*Geborgenheit*) may be to him as a human being, he simply cannot find it in anything permanent: it is not to be found among the members of his own family or in the quasi-permanence of a social intercourse sustained by individuals who, in all their repeated comings and goings, can have no deep and lasting effect upon him. It is lacking in his many social and intellectual contacts with outstanding men of his time and even in the constant support of the faithful Overbeck.

The result is always increased loneliness. We must ask how this became necessary to Nietzsche's *Existenz* as an exception. Since it may seem as though he lacked the basic conditions of all communication throughout his entire lifetime, it is important to understand that his task, as it were, consumed both him and his potentialities for friendship. While his own view of his loneliness may not furnish an answer to our question, it is bound to prove illuminating.

Rohde and Wagner. Only two of his friends were of really fateful significance for Nietzsche: Erwin Rohde, the friend of his youth, and Richard Wagner, the only creative artist whom Nietzsche, thirty years younger, approached with boundless adoration.

The climax of the enthusiastic friendship *inter pares,* between Nietzsche and *Rohde*,[17] was reached in 1867. When they came to the lecture "radiating spirit, health, and youthful bravado, in their equestrian garb, with riding whips still in their hands, they were admired by the others like two young gods." [18] They were called the Dioscuri. They themselves felt toward all people as if they were together "on a separate pedestal" (Rohde to Nietzsche, Oct. 10, '67). They were bound to each other by an earnestly ethical-philosophical partnership: as soon as their "conversation turned to profound matters, a quiet and full harmony sounded forth." [19] Their exchange of views continued through the correspondence that began in this year. They had in common their rejection of the "present age," their love for Schopenhauer and Wagner, their notion of

---

[17] Correspondence between the two in *Briefe,* II.—O. Crusius, *Erwin Rohde,* Tübingen, 1902.—Bernoulli, I, pp. 259 ff.; II, pp. 149–167.—Podach, *Gestalen um Nietzsche,* Weimar, 1932, pp. 34 ff.
[18] Elisabeth Förster-Nietzsche, *op. cit.,* I, 190.
[19] *Ibid.,* p. 243.

philological studies, and their assimilation of the spirit of Greece. Not until 1876, when Rohde married, did the exchange of letters suddenly become less frequent. Thereafter it ceased for prolonged periods, flared up in occasional communications and greetings, and then ended with a break in 1887.

The letters between 1867–1876 constitute an incomparable document of a youthful student friendship on a high spiritual plane. The fact that this friendship did not remain constant was of fateful decisiveness for Nietzsche; but it became, at the same time, almost symbolic of the fact that Nietzsche, driven by the absolute demand of his existential truthfulness, could not abide the bourgeois world, even when its representative had human nobility. What brought about the separation?

Keeping subsequent failures in mind, we can discern in the letters between 1867 and 1876 the following specific traits which adumbrate the danger to come:

Rohde considers himself as the receiver, Nietzsche as the giver. Toward the superior one he assumes the position of the pupil, toward the creative one that of the unproductive one: "To me it seems at times like a defection that I am unable to join you in fishing for pearls in those ocean depths and must instead amuse myself and take a childish delight in gudgeons and other philological vermin. . . ."[20] But during all my better hours, my thoughts are with you. . . . Let us thus always remain united, dear friend, even though the one chisel statues of sublime gods while I must content myself with carving miniatures" (Dec. 22, '71).

Rohde's elemental yearning for his only friend is stronger than Nietzsche's, since the latter's friendship is basically motivated by his task. The general tone of the letters expresses a more devoted love on the part of Rohde. It is as though Rohde concentrated all his feelings on his friend. His are the frequent pleas for a letter, for a single line; it is he who is concerned about whether Nietzsche is loyal and well-disposed toward him.

Thus everything really revolved around Nietzsche. Rohde had nothing to offer that corresponded to Nietzsche's writings and plans. His purely technical assistance was often called for and willingly given. This assistance was at its height in their "comradeship-in-arms" against Wilamowitz, even though it expressed friendship rather than philological unanimity. When Nietzsche had been ostracized by the philologists, it was a courageous act for Rohde to come to his assistance with a publication that endangered his own academic career.

---

[20] The mixed metaphor (gudgeons—vermin) is Rohde's own—Trs.

By disposition, Rohde was prudent in his approach to all that was extreme and extravagant in Nietzsche's ideas and plans: for example, to the idea of giving up the whole wretched academic world to form a secular monastic community; to Nietzsche's plan to transfer his professorship to Rohde with a view to devoting his own life to publicizing Wagner's work (through lecture tours and the like); and finally to Nietzsche's most extravagant cultural designs as long as the "chain of related duties," essential for this culture from its foundations to its highest pretensions, was not clearly worked out. This defensive moderation was instinctive and expressed neither rejection nor a sense of superiority.

Without anything specific being done or said, this friendship had to die when Rohde's prudence turned into conscious respectability, his elemental feeling for the friend of his youth—a feeling to which the latter never responded in kind—died away, and he ceased to receive his inspiration from Nietzsche and have him for his model. Something had happened without either of them having consciously intervened. An imperceptible change of attitude occurred in the case of Rohde, while Nietzsche's feelings for Rohde, attended by an increased yearning for his friend, remained unchanged throughout all the transformations of his thinking. In the letters since 1876, Rohde became artificial while Nietzsche expressed the feeling of the old friendship in a simple and most touching manner.

The reasons for the estrangement are obvious. It probably is no accident that Rohde's marriage coincided with the cessation of regular correspondence. Rohde's elemental need for love and communion had been satisfied by his friendship to such a degree that this friendship was bound to become neutralized from the moment that his feelings found gratification in another manner. The strength of Nietzsche's feelings was such that they did not lead to youthful exuberance but lasted throughout his lifetime. After his marriage, furthermore, Rohde became more and more firmly bound to the *bourgeois world,* its institutions and accepted opinions, and to the rules of the philological profession.

The contrast between the two natures makes Rohde and Nietzsche exemplary *representatives of two distinctive worlds.* In their youth they both live in the realm of boundless possibilities and feel an affinity through the exuberance of their noble aspirations. Subsequently they go in opposite directions. Nietzsche remains young, leaving concrete reality as his faith in his task assumes existential import. Rohde grows old, bourgeois, stable, and skeptical. Hence courage is a fundamental trait in Nietzsche, plaintive self-irony in Rohde.

The sense of suffering constantly, occasionally indicated during his youth by his skepticism and yearning, attains dominance as a basic trait in Rohde's nature in a way that is at once touching and pitiable: "If I were only a complete scholar! a complete Wagner! This way I am only half of one and, in addition, something of a one-twentieth of a Faust" (June 2, '76). Rohde himself knows whither his path will lead him, but this knowledge does not save him. In complete uncertainty he wavers to and fro, once he has taken the decisive step which comes between the two following utterances:

Jan. 3, '69 (24 years old): "The real *definitivum* is the land of the philistines, of the healthy people, of Freytag's model professors, of the national-liberal smart alecks. We other weak souls can exist only in the *provisorium,* as a fish only in running water." Feb. 15, '78 (33 years old): "In the end it is probably a salutary stupor which permits one to live on like that. . . . My marriage has been the final step in making my clockwork run with unfailing regularity. . . . As for the rest, the state of matrimony is a thing to be pondered; it is unbelievable how it makes one *age*; for, in a way, one has reached a summit, with nothing beyond it."

Rohde retained the interests but not the attitudes of his youth; he looked to the world of the Greeks for the object of his contemplation rather than the norm of obligation; he sought in Bayreuth hours of forgetfulness in romantic feelings; and he submitted completely to the law of philology. By 1878, therefore, he could no longer understand Nietzsche and defiantly said of himself: "I on my part simply cannot jump out of my skin" (to Nietzsche, June 16, '78). For a while Rohde, despite his rejection, still seemed to retain his awareness of Nietzsche's superior nature: "And so I feel again as I always did when I was together with you: for a while I am elevated into a higher rank, as though I were spiritually ennobled" (Dec. 22, '79). Nietzsche, however, soon perceived the great distance between them; perplexed by a letter from Rohde, he wrote to Overbeck: "Friend Rohde wrote a long letter about himself, in which two things, however, almost *hurt* me, 1st the sort of thoughtlessness with respect to the *direction* of life with such a man! and 2nd the abundance of poor taste in word and phrase (perhaps it's called 'wit' in German universities—may heaven protect us from it)" (Apr. 28, '81). He ceased to feel any relation between Rohde and himself: "Rohde wrote; I do not think that his picture of me is correct. . . . He is incapable of learning anything from me—he has no sympathy for my passion and suffering" (to Overbeck, Mar., '82). Rohde still managed to maintain an exaggerated esteem that at once put a distance between them: "You, dear friend, live on a different level of moods and thoughts: it is as though you had lifted yourself above the atmospheric layer of haze in which we all stagger about and gasp for air. . . ." (Dec. 22, '83). But this esteem was even then basically forced rather than felt, and it changed into the most unkind and vexed rejection, which he expressed to Overbeck after the reading of *Beyond Good and Evil:*

"I read most of it with great displeasure. . . . [It is] full of a repulsive debasement of everything and everybody. The truly philosophical in it is as paltry and juvenile as the political is silly and unrealistic. . . . Nothing goes beyond whimsical notions. . . . I am no longer capable of taking these endless metamorphoses seriously. . . . Expression of a gifted *ingenium* incapable, however, of accomplishing what he really would like to. . . . I find it quite right that this sort of thing is without effect. . . . Especially, and above all else, quite annoyed by the gigantic conceit of the author . . . in view of the sterility which in the end peeks out everywhere with this imitative and eclectic mind. . . . After all is said and done, Nietzsche is and will ever be a critic. . . . We others are not satisfied with ourselves either, but neither do we expect any particular veneration for our defectiveness. What he needs is to work quite honestly and in workmanlike fashion for a change. . . . I am reading Ludwig Richter's autobiography in order to cool off (1886)." [21]

Finally Rohde denied, to Overbeck, his comradeship-in-arms with Nietzsche against Wilamowitz by calling it a youthful folly.[22] In his *Psyche* (1893), which treated of the subjects they had in common during their youth, he never mentioned Nietzsche; thus he even banished him from the study of classical antiquity.

The *difference in nature* between Rohde and Nietzsche, because of its sharp contrast, throws much light upon Nietzsche. From the very start Rohde is by nature the rootless skeptic inclined to be resigned and to seize upon any support that is offered him. Nietzsche on the other hand is at an early age, and always remains, the very opposite: "Not one step toward accommodation, not for anything in the world! Great success can be gained only by remaining faithful to one's self. . . . I should harm or destroy many evolving individuals along with myself if I were to weaken and become skeptical" (to Gersdorff, Apr. 15, '76). But by 1869 Rohde is able to say: "And so it happens to me here as elsewhere that I, after angrily rebelling inwardly, gradually become resigned and plod along in the sand like the others. . . ." He is ready for "resignation, the goddess

[21] Bernoulli, II, p. 162 ff.
[22] *Ibid.,* p. 115.

with the leaden wings and the dizzy poppystalk . . . called contentment by men." He does not, like Nietzsche, turn every disappointment into an ingredient of his own education, every stage into something to be overcome, but he "seeks consolation, or rather stupefaction, in work" (Feb. 15, '70). For Rohde, the consequence is on the one hand his "achievement" in scholarship and, on the other, the overburdening of his soul with unassimilated things; hence he frequently laments: "I am of unfree spirit." External disappointments make him "see everything in the most hopeless light for weeks and months" (Dec. 23, '73). Rohde possesses a devastating honesty toward himself and, being aware of his method, become increasingly displeased with himself. He loses his verve because he cannot shake off the after-effects of all the trivial everyday experiences; but his good intention to retain at least what he possesses stays with him and suffices, in his world, to make of his philological work more than a philologist generally accomplishes. But it is precisely for this reason that his relation to Nietzsche becomes ever more uncertain. He wants to do everything as correctly and well as he possibly can but staggers from affirmation to negation and back again. He is no longer bound to Nietzsche by anything more than a romantic remembrance.

The two friends saw each other for the last time in Leipzig in 1886, after an interval of ten years. Rohde, because of "really trivial disagreements, was very ill-humored, which was typical of him." [23] Nietzsche was taken aback over finding his friend ensnared "in paltry disagreements, constantly nagging and displeased with everything and everybody." [24] And Rohde wrote about Nietzsche: "He was surrounded by an indescribably strange atmosphere, something that seemed really weird to me at that time . . . as though he came from a land where nobody else dwells." [25] Nietzsche did not enter Rohde's home then, and he never met his wife and children. The following year a rupture came in their correspondence because of a haughtily deprecating utterance by Rohde about Taine. Both tried to heal the rupture, but without result. After Nietzsche had become insane, Rohde destroyed those last letters that had so aroused Nietzsche's profound anger; but he did not destroy Nietzsche's letters. When the ailing Nietzsche was told of Rohde's death by his sister, he looked at her "with large, sad eyes: 'Rohde dead? Oh!' he said softly . . . a big tear slowly rolled over his cheek." [26]

[23] *Briefe,* II, XXIII.
[24] *Ibid.,* XXIV.
[25] *Ibid.,* XXV.
[26] *Ibid.,* XXVII.

The friendship between Nietzsche and *Richard Wagner*[27] seems to present a simple picture: the enthusiastic veneration of the younger man was placed in the service of the master: he began the interpretation of the latter's work with *The Birth of Tragedy* (1871) and continued it through *Richard Wagner in Bayreuth* (1876). But thereafter Nietzsche changed his judgment about Wagner. First he withdrew quietly and went his own philosophical way, but in 1880 he wrote the pamphlet against Wagner's art in which his former attitude was turned into its opposite. Nietzsche seems to have abandoned the celebrity whom he formerly worshipped and to have changed his opinion incomprehensibly. Some accuse Nietzsche of perfidy and see its roots in his emerging sickness which, in their opinion, begins with the writing of *Human, All-Too-Human;* others, on the contrary, see Nietzsche as discovering himself and—on the basis of their agreement with Nietzsche's criticism of Wagner—consider the previous friendship a temporary desertion of his own self for Wagner. Either interpretation of the facts underlying this friendship is too one-sided.

In the first place, Nietzsche's criticism exists implicitly even from the very beginning; in fact its quintessence was written down as early as January, 1874. For the retrospective reader it is clearly recognizable even in the publication *R. Wagner in Bayreuth* (1876). Although this criticism seems devastating at first glance, it has to be of the sort that is compatible with the closest of ties with the one criticized.

Secondly, Nietzsche from first to last regarded Wagner as the one incomparable genius of the age. His criticism of Wagner is his criticism of the age. As long as Nietzsche still has faith in his age and believes in the possible realization of a new culture within it, he stands by Wagner; the moment he sees his age as a whole going down to ruin and seeks the

---

[27] Nietzsche about Wagner: *Richard Wagner in Bayreuth*, 1876. *Der Fall Wagner*, 1888. *Nietzsche contra Wagner*, 1888.

E. Förster-Nietzsche, *Wagner und Nietzsche zur Zeit ihrer Freundschaft*, München, 1915.

The two publications by Wagner from the period of his contact with Nietzsche are to be compared: *Beethoven*, 1870, and *Über die Bestimmung der Oper;* his open rejection of Nietzsche (without mention of his name) in *Publikum und Popularität* (Part 3).

Nietzsche-Wagner literature: Ludwig Klages, "Der Fall Nietzsche-Wagner in graphologischer Beleuchtung," 1904; in *Gesammelte Abhandlungen*, Heidelberg, 1927.—Kurt Hildebrandt, *Wagner und Nietzsche. Ihr Kampf gegen das neunzehnte Jahrhundert*, Breslau, 1924.—Bernhard Diebold, *Der Fall Wagner. Eine Revision*, Frankfurt, 1928.

About Wagner: Carl Fr. Glasenapp, *Das Leben Richard Wagners*, Leipzig, 1908 ff., Vol. IV, V, VI.—Guy de Pourtales, *Wagner als Mensch und Meister.*—About Cosima: Graf Du Moulin-Eckardt, *Cosima Wagner.*

rebirth of man from altogether different depths than those presented by works of art and the theater, he opposes him. Insofar as Nietzsche thinks of himself as belonging to his age, his criticism of Wagner is also a criticism of himself as Wagner's adherent.

For both of these reasons, and in spite of his vehemently expressed opposition to Wagner, Nietzsche turns against those who would like to appropriate his critique of Wagner, with its sharp, relentlessly revealing formulations. Since they are not moved by the profundity of the question about man's being but grasp only the psychological import of his direct and chiding words, they fail to understand it and regard it as a mere pamphlet. "It is obvious," he says, "that I will not easily give anyone the right to appropriate my own evaluation, and no irreverent riffraff . . . shall be permitted to use their coarse tongues even to utter as great a name as that of Richard Wagner, whether it be in praise or in disagreement."

Nietzsche's veneration and criticism are bound to the cause of the potential creativeness of living man. It is through Wagner as the genius of his time that Nietzsche realizes what this time itself represents. As long as he sees in Wagner a new Aeschylus and thus has before his eyes the highest attainment possible on earth, his faith in his age remains. But as soon as his standards of truth, genuineness, and substance call Wagner in question, the entire world of his contemporaries disintegrates.

The unity of man and cause, of friendship and matters of greatest concern to the age, made of Nietzsche's love for Wagner an experience of lofty humanity. It was his only attempt at direct and active cooperation in making greatness a reality in this world: the new culture was to arise on the basis of Wagner's genius, the heritage of antiquity, and a philosophizing that proceeded from man's very essence. When he measured the Bayreuth enterprise and the phenomenon that Wagner presented by his standards of truth and reality and human culture, he saw them, in spite of their grandeur, as mere theater that failed to express being. These standards not only destroyed the values that he had formerly found in contemporary reality and separated him from all human beings, but they even deprived him of the opportunity for *any* action in the world as thus perceived. For a while he had wished to work, build, and create with Wagner within this world; afterwards he did nothing but think and write down his thoughts. Himself forgotten, lonesome and ignored, hopeless in relation to all contemporary possibilities, he then set about to work for a future that he would not see. The task that Wagner had set for himself— raising man to his highest level—Nietzsche also recognized as his own to the very end; but the solution had become radically different. And so he could, even at a late date, agree with those who "know that I believe, even today as much as formerly, in the ideal in which Wagner believed,—what difference does it make that I stumbled over so much of the human, all-too-human that R. W. himself put in the path of his ideal?" (to Overbeck, Oct. 29, '86).

Thus it is understandable that in spite of all hostility Nietzsche remained permanently attached to Wagner. Nietzsche found no one among his contemporaries who shared his concern with the problem of man's being as did the Wagner he had come to understand and love. Even toward the end of his life, after hearing the Prelude to *Parsival,* he wrote: "It so moved and elevated me that I am profoundly shaken when I think of it. It is as though after many years someone finally spoke to me about the problems that trouble me, though of course not by giving the answers that I may have ready for them. . . ." (to his sister, Febr. 22, '87). Having devoted himself entirely to opposition, he can suddenly feel that "with a real shock I have become aware of how closely *related I* actually am to Wagner" (to Gast, July 25, '82).

What Nietzsche loved in Wagner was the unity of person and cause, as though the task itself had found its human incarnation: "Wagner was by far the *most complete* man I have met" (to Overbeck, Mar. 22, '83). "I loved him and nobody else. He was a man after my own heart. . . ." His association with Wagner, as revealed through the testimonies of that time, must have been a singular and extraordinary source of happiness for him; the human proximity and the consciousness of the task produced a climax compared with which all later relationships established by Nietzsche were bound to appear insipid. "Except for Wagner, no one so far has met me with one thousandth the passion and suffering necessary to understand me" (to Overbeck, Nov. 12, '87). "At that time we loved each other and hoped for everything *for one another*—it really was a profound *love,* without ulterior motives" (to Gast, Apr. 27, '83). And at the end of *Ecce Homo:* "The rest of my human associations I count lightly; but for no price would I omit from my life the days of Tribschen, days of trust, gladness, and sublime incidents—the *profound* moments. . . ."

Only by keeping this situation in mind can we gain any intimation of the excruciating and self-rending internal conflict which Nietzsche's unrelenting will to truth made inevitable. This struggle, however, was originally not intended as a separation from Wagner but as a preparation for the struggle on behalf of Wagner. After Nietzsche had become totally dedicated to Wagner and, for instance, had even mutilated and supplemented his writing concerning the *Birth of Tragedy* in this service, he began to hope that he might have an effect on him: he was ready for and intent on communication expressed through struggle. Toward other people, such as Deussen, Nietzsche was didactic, he kept at a distance, was kind and friendly, made indictments, and broke off. There was nothing of the kind this time: Nietzsche held on to this friendship with all his love and in the knowledge that everything was at stake; he clung to it with his uncompromising truthfulness as much as with a humble readiness to suffer and sacrifice for the venerated genius. Nietzsche sought unobtrusively to overlook or ignore Wagner's lack of interest in things that would not directly promote his own work and to put out of his mind his discovery, as early as 1873, that this work contained dangerous potentialities and actual flaws. He forced himself to write about Richard Wagner in Bayreuth and ventured his loving criticism in the hope of being able to influence Wagner's innermost self. He was understandably concerned over the possibility of its complete rejection. But Wagner failed to understand and heard nothing in it but his own apotheosis.

At the opening of the festival plays in 1876, Nietzsche was appalled by the mass attendance, the traits exhibited by the well-to-do bourgeois audience, and the pomp and circumstance. To him this was no regeneration of German culture. Finally he saw himself as the victim of a delusion from which he must liberate himself. But even now—as Nietzsche suddenly departed from Bayreuth in order to reflect in solitude—he hoped that the friendship could be preserved. He omitted from *Human, All-Too-Human* whatever might prove too painful, sent verses pleading for loyalty and love with the work, and lived in the high-minded belief in the possibility of friendship with mutual acknowledgement of the difference in ways: "Friends, nothing unites us, but we take pleasure in one another, up to the point where the one furthers the direction of the other, even though it should run directly contrary to his own. . . . Thus we shall grow up next to each other like trees, bold upright and straight, precisely because we rear ourselves one through the other." Nietzsche's hope proved to be vain. Icy silence of Wagner—something which Nietzsche considered a "deadly insult" (to Overbeck, Mar. 22, '83)—that was the end.

Wagner had not noticed Nietzsche's struggles and his unobtrusive attempts at authentic communication with him. Like later observers, he found the break sudden and unheralded (he had, in a manner of speaking, taken possession of Nietzsche, and he dropped him when *Human, All-Too-Human* appeared). To Wagner, the friendship with Nietzsche appeared as an episode. Older by thirty years, he had attained full maturity in his work; Nietzsche joined him to serve this work. Still

Wagner, too, found this episode unique. In 1871, upon receiving the *Birth of Tragedy,* he wrote to Nietzsche: "I have never yet read anything more beautiful than your book! . . . I told Cosima that you come right next to her: then nobody else for quite a stretch. . . ." In 1872: "In all honesty, next to my wife you are the only boon that life has brought me." In 1873: "I read in it again and I swear to you by God that I consider you the only one who knows what I try to do." In 1876, regarding the publication *Richard Wagner in Bayreuth:* "Friend! your book is tremendous! Whence did you learn so much about me?" Afterwards there is no sign, on the part of Wagner, of any understanding of Nietzsche. All he did was to express himself disdainfully.

The separation was a fateful event of the most decisive kind for Nietzsche, though not for Wagner. Nietzsche's works and letters abound to the end in direct and indirect utterances about Wagner, their friendship, and about his own privation. The memory of it never leaves him alone: "Nothing can compensate me for the fact that I lost Wagner's good will during the past years. . . . Not a single disagreeable word was ever spoken between us, not even in my dreams, but very many encouraging and happy ones, and perhaps I never did laugh so much in anybody's company. That's all over now—and what is the use of being in the right against him in many points! As though one could in this way wipe this lost friendship from memory!" (to Gast, Aug. 20, '80). The separation, which Nietzsche senses in the last talks between himself and Wagner in Sorrento (1876), seems strikingly expressed in these words: "Such a leave-taking, when at last one separates for good because feeling and judgment no longer can be made to harmonize, brings us closest to a person, and we beat violently against the divisive wall which nature has erected." Nietzsche never regretted his association with Wagner. His remembrance was always positive: "Let it suffice that my error—including my belief in a common and interwoven destiny—brought dishonor neither to him nor to me and at that time was no small comfort and blessing to both of us as two people having grown lonely in two very different ways."

Wagner's image remained something for which he had to struggle within himself, as he had already done during the years of proximity. "This has been my most severe test, as regards justice toward men—this whole association and no-further-association with Wagner" (to Gast, Apr. 27, '83). Even in the most devastating outbursts of criticism we seem to hear, alongside the profound earnestness over the destiny of man's being, the love which can only temporarily disguise itself as hatred because of the strange potentialities of the human soul.

The Period of Increasing Loneliness. The most profound breaks in Nietzsche's friendships occur during the years after 1876 and mark the turning in the way of his human associations.

1876 is not only the year of his ultimate disillusionment over Bayreuth and his final spiritual separation from Wagner. In the same year, Overbeck married, and the five years of living together in the same house came to an end. Rohde also married. In 1878, *Human, All-Too-Human* appeared with the consequence that Wagner publicly rejected the work with disdain and Rohde was taken aback: "Can anyone *so* divest himself of his soul and take on another one in its place?" (to Nietzsche, May 16, '78). Nearly the whole circle of people around Nietzsche, who together with him had looked up to Wagner, assumed a distant position toward him.

Nietzsche's resolve to shoulder his task, together with the necessity for completely dissolving all previously valid ties, won out. As a human being desirous of finding the actuality of his private world to be in agreement with the world in general, he certainly might have wished for another way. The negative experiences encountered when he attempted to seize upon general possibilities only made him conscious of his own nature as an exception incapable of actualizing itself and finding happiness by going the way of others. Expressions of his decision run the gamut from natural pain to the awareness of his entirely different task and from touching, simple utterances of human resignation to proud self-assurance concerning his calling. On the whole the decision is made with unheard-of conviction even though it is occasionally veiled in particulars. Rohde's announcement of his engagement became the occasion for a poem which he enclosed with his letter to Rohde: a bird sings in the night, calling his mate, a lonely wanderer stops and listens:

> No, wanderer, no! Not *thee* I hail,
> With loud display . . .
> But thou shalt ever onward stray
> And never understand my lay! . . .

Nietzsche writes: "Perhaps I have a bad flaw in me. My longing and my need are of a different kind: I can scarcely express and explain it" (to Rohde, July 18, '76).

Nietzsche's path into loneliness begins. Henceforth he is aware of it. On this new path he tries associating with new people; it is like a struggle for friendship at the abyss of ultimate forlornness. Three more times he offers his innermost self to another human being: to Rée, Lou Salomé, H. v. Stein; three times he experiences disappointment.

Paul Rée,[28] a medical man and author of publications concerning the origin of moral feelings, five years younger than Nietzsche, drew close to him—especially during the winter of 1876–77 spent in Sorrento with Malvida von Meysenbug—in conversations concerning their common interest in a non-transcendental investigation of the origin and empirical reality of morality. To be sure, Nietzsche later placed himself in definite opposition to him (because Rée's analysis of morality, resting on English prototypes, was in essence totally different in source and goal from his own). To be sure, Nietzsche scarcely learned anything from Rée (since prior to their acquaintance his own positions were already decisive); nevertheless, the actual occurrence of these talks with Rée must have been a source of great happiness to him: he was encouraged by the opportunity to speak freely with at least one single person about problems that at the time he regarded as ultimate. The cold consistency of radical analyses was comforting to him (in return, he overlooked their insipidity for a while). In this clean atmosphere without illusions he could breathe. His admiration and liking for Rée must have been great for a time, but it gave rise to no high-spirited friendship and was no substitute at all for the unequalled fullness in the association with Wagner.

Through M. von Meysenbug and Paul Rée, Lou Salomé [29] became acquainted with Nietzsche in Rome in the spring of 1882. Their final parting took place in the autumn of the same year. It had been hoped that Nietzsche might find in this uncommonly intelligent girl a pupil who would adhere to his philosophy. Nietzsche, overwhelmed by the impression her spirit made on him, passionately—without any erotic overtones—seized upon the opportunity to teach his philosophy to another human being. Having hitherto divorced his thinking completely from all human beings (although in the depths of his nature he had not wanted this separation), he now tried to make of Lou the pupil who was to understand the most secret thoughts of his philosophy: "I no longer want to be lonely and wish to learn again to become a human being. Ah, in this

[28] Kurt Kolle, "Notizen über Paul Rée," *Zeitschrift für Menschenkunde,* Jahrgang 3, 1927, p. 168. *Mitteilungen aus dem Nietzsche-Archiv,* Weimar, 1908 privately printed.
[29] The book by Lou Andreas-Salomé, *Friedrich Nietzsche in seinen Werken,* Wien, 1894, contains no reports about personal relationships beyond a few reprinted Nietzsche letters. Other sources: the reports by Nietzsche's sister contained in her biography (in the chapter "Bittere Erfahrungen") and in the exchange of letters between Nietzsche and his mother and sister (1st ed. 1909, pp. 486–506). *Mitteilungen aus dem Nietzsche-Archiv* (Weimar, 1908). Also indispensable is Bernoulli's work on Overbeck. Further: Bernoulli, "Nietzsches Lou-Erlebnis," *Raschers Jahrbuch,* I, p. 257. Podach, *Nietzsches Zusammenbruch,* Heidelberg, 1930.

subject I still have to learn almost everything!" (to Lou, 1882). The relationship did not involve him and Lou exclusively: Rée and Nietzsche's sister played decisive roles. It ended in disappointment and became subsequently involved and encumbered, through repetition of utterances, a letter of which Nietzsche accidentally gained knowledge, etc. Finally things came to such a pass that Nietzsche insisted on a duel with Rée and felt himself insulted and degraded to the limit of his endurance. Even today only insufficient information about the real situation has been made public.

What is essential is the fact that, at first, Nietzsche experienced a sort of instability such as he had never known before. It was not merely the magnitude of his disappointment after being certain of having found a person who shared "exactly the same task" with him: "Without this premature belief I would not . . . have suffered . . . to such a degree from the feeling of loneliness. . . . As soon as I had merely dreamed this dream of not being alone, the danger was frightful. Even now there are hours when I do not know how to endure myself" (to Overbeck, Dec. 8, '83). In addition he was oppressed by feelings that were totally foreign to his nature. He complained of becoming himself "finally the victim of a savage feeling of revenge" despite the very fact that his "innermost way of thinking had rejected all revenge and punishment" (to Overbeck, Aug. 28, '83).

The difference is striking when comparison is made with the fateful immensity and profound suffering occasioned by the break with Wagner. To be sure, what Nietzsche says of himself in 1883 may apply to both separations: "I am too concentrated a nature, and whatever strikes me, goes to the center of my being." But there is this difference: in his break with Wagner, his own task compelled and bore him up; in the break with Lou and Rée, even the goal and task which he thought he had in common with them could waver for a moment: "I was and am terribly *doubtful* about my right to set myself such a goal—*the feeling of weakness* overcame me, in a moment when everything, everything, everything should have given me courage!" (to Overbeck, summer, '83).

Nietzsche reveals his own self by the way in which he masters what he regards as weakness. Instead of giving in to a resentment that is foreign to his nature, he utilizes his experiences to form a just picture of the people involved, especially of Lou, while effecting a complete inner separation from them. "Lou is by far the *most intelligent* person I have become acquainted with" (to Overbeck, Feb. 24, '82). He does not wish to fight with these people: "Every disdainful word that is written against

Rée or Miss L. makes my heart bleed; it seems that I am not well-made for hostility" (to Overbeck, summer, '83). He would like to untangle and clarify everything without the slightest intent of a new approach: "Dr. Rée and Miss Salomé to whom I should like to make some amends . . ." (to Overbeck, Apr. 7, '84).

He totally despaired of the possibility of an objective-philosophical intimacy with any person. Never again did he attempt it with the same expectations. Therewith his awareness of his loneliness became even more intense and profound. To be sure, he continued to search for new friends (to Gast, May 10, '83), but without real hope as he found it to be impossible on purely human grounds: "And I realize more and more that I no longer fit among human beings—I commit nothing but follies . . . so that I always seem to be in the wrong" (to Overbeck, Jan. 22, '83).

Heinrich von Stein [30] came to Sils-Maria in August of 1884 for a three-day visit with Nietzsche. They had never met before, and they never saw each other afterwards. They had known of each other for some time, and an exchange of publications which began in 1882 was followed by an intermittent exchange of letters. At first Stein was interested in Nietzsche and sensed his greatness, though without feeling himself bound to him or even receiving a decisively new impulse; he experienced—like so many before him—an indefinable intensification of his own self while talking with him: "My sense of being is increased when I speak with you" (to Nietzsche, Dec. 1, '85). "The definite inner freedom which I at once feel in conversation with you was a remarkable experience for me" (to Nietzsche, Oct. 7, '85); but this did not imply any agreement with Nietzsche's philosophizing. For Nietzsche, on the other hand, because of the prospect of a philosophical friendship, this visit produced a last, gentle tremor.

Several weeks after the visit, he reports to Overbeck (Sept. 14, '84): Baron Stein "came directly from Germany to Sils for three days and journeyed directly again to his father—a way of giving *emphasis* to a visit that impressed me. He is a splendid example of humanity and manhood completely understandable and agreeable to me because of his basic heroic attitude. Finally, a new person who is of my kind and instinctively respects me!" To Peter Gast (Sept. 20, '84): "In his vicinity I felt like that Philoctetes on his island during the visit by Neoptolemus—I mean

[30] Correspondence between Nietzsche and Baron von Stein: *Briefe,* III, pp. 219–264.

that he too sensed something of my *Philoctetes-faith* "without *my* bow *no* Ilion will be conquered!' " Later Nietzsche recalls in *Ecce Homo:* "This excellent man . . . was as if transformed through a windstorm of freedom during these three days, like one who suddenly is lifted to *his own* height and grows wings."

Stein writes to Nietzsche, apparently in the same tone and with the same feeling (Sept. 24, '84): "The days of Sils are a great memory for me, an important, hallowed part of life. Only by faithfully clinging to such events do I find it possible to confront the frightfulness of existence and, more than that, to find it worthwhile." Nietzsche thereupon (Nov., '84) sends him a poem (dealing with friends, his forlornness, and his kingdom up above in the regions of ice) that was later entitled "From High Mountains" and attached to *Beyond Good and Evil:*

> For friends I'm waiting, ready night and day:
> *New* friends! 'Tis late! Do not delay!

"This is for you, my dear friend, as a remembrance of Sils-Maria and in gratitude for your letter, *such* a letter." Stein answers by proposing to Nietzsche that he participate, in writing, in a discussion undertaken by Stein and several friends concerning the content of several articles in the *Wagner-Lexicon.* Nietzsche is taken aback: "What a strange letter Stein wrote me! And this as an answer to such a poem! Nobody knows how to behave anymore" (to his sister, Dec., '84). To the poem he added these verses before its publication: *"This* song is over,—the sweet outcry of yearning died on my lips."

Nietzsche was resigned: this disappointment was no longer a shock, and his love remained unchanged. When Stein died in 1887 at the age of thirty, Nietzsche wrote: "I am still quite beside myself about it. I was so fond of him, for he belonged among the few people whose *existence* as such gave me pleasure. Nor did I have any doubts that, in a manner of speaking, he was *reserved* for me" (to Overbeck, June 30, '87). "It hurt me, like a personal deprivation" (to his sister, Oct. 15, '87).

The avowal of his loneliness goes through all these years. He acknowledges it, laments it, and calls to his old friends from it as if in despair. As late as 1884 he wants to turn to them again; however: "The idea . . . of *declaring* myself, so to speak, through a very personal kind of message 'to my friends'. . . was an idea born of discouragement" (to Overbeck, July 10, '84). A few weeks later he composes that moving farewell to his old friends ("From High Mountains") with a faint hope for Stein. He yearns for pupils: "The problems confronting me seem to be of such radical importance that several times each year I conceived the presumptuous notion that the intellectuals to whom I revealed them would have to put aside their own work in order to devote themselves for the time being entirely to my affairs. What happened then each time was, in an odd and uncanny way, the opposite of what I had expected." [31] Here, too, he renounces: "Too much in me tries to mature and grow together; the time for 'pupils and school' *et hoc genus omne* has not yet come." (to Overbeck, Feb. 20, '85).

One single person had to serve as a substitute for all that he was deprived of during the years of loneliness. Indeed it was only during that period that he was interested in *Peter Gast,*[32] who remained unalterably devoted to him from their first acquaintance in 1875 to the end. Gast's kind understanding, his ability to express Nietzsche's ways and aims might seem to the latter like a magic meeting of his own self in another person; but these characteristics remained without weight because Gast's individual being could not come under serious consideration. That Nietzsche asked to be addressed as "Herr Professor" indicates a preservation of distance. Gast ably assisted Nietzsche in copying and proofreading, and right up to the end sent him those gladdening, completely affirmative letters that comforted him and bolstered his often wavering self-confidence.

For example, Gast writes upon receiving the *Zarathustra:* "There is nothing like it in existence—because the goals that you assign have never been and *could* never be assigned to mankind by anyone. One could wish that this book had the circulation of the Bible, as well as its canonical authority and its staff of commentators. . . ." Nietzsche answers: "A feeling of awe came over me while reading your letter. Supposing that you are right—then my life would not be a failure after all? And least of all just now when I was most convinced of it?" (to Gast, Apr. 6, '83).

Nietzsche admits repeatedly what this friend means to him: "I am at times completely beside myself for being unable to say an honest and unconditional word to anybody—I have absolutely nobody for this except Mr. Peter Gast" (to Gast, Nov. 26, '88).

Nietzsche heaps his illusions upon Gast. He regards him as the creative musician who overcomes Wagner, by bringing forth a new, no longer romantic music appropriate to Nietzsche's philosophy. He is incessantly concerned, in his activity on behalf of Gast's compositions, to have them

---

[31] *Briefe*, III, 249.
[32] Nietzsche's letters to Gast: *Briefe*, IV.—*Die Briefe Peter Gasts an Friedrich Nietzsche*, 2 Bde., München, 1923–1924.—Josef Hofmiller, "Nietzsches Briefe an Gast," *Süddeutsche Monatshefte* VI, 2, 1909, pp. 300–310.—Hofmiller, "Nietzsche." *Süddeutsche Monatshefte*, 29. Jahrgang 1931, pp. 84 ff.—Podach, *Gestalten*, pp. 68 ff.

performed and to interest directors in them. Above and beyond that, in his dealings with Gast, he gives free rein to his capacity for kindness and helpfulness.

The way in which Gast becomes for the lonely Nietzsche the constant, reliable medium for the incarnation of all that reality has denied him serves to bring out and intensify, through contrast, the significance of Nietzsche's problem: the impossibility, repeatedly experienced during these years, of an enduring friendship founded on essentials and penetrating to the core.

The Permanent Element in Nietzsche's Human Relations. Whatever in his relations with other human beings Nietzsche found to be philosophically substantial and existentially of absolute importance always proved to be elusive: it disappeared within the movement of his own being. And whatever endured in a friendship would seem to bear the stamp of slight significance for him precisely because of its endurance. The all-consuming tempo of his experience of being manifests itself in the unworldliness of his exceptional nature. But exceptional as he may be, his human nature reaches out for what is naturally and universally human. While this latter is never decisive, he does not wish to dispense with it, and, reaching for a little natural happiness, he seeks to grasp it just as it is (so long as it does not interfere with his task!), much as he would like to preserve everything abandoned and lost.

He always felt a natural closeness to the *members of his family.*[33] His mother and his sister accompanied him through life: they served him as a child, nursed him when he was sick, and tended to his wants. He always felt closely bound to them; a passage from *The Wanderer and his Shadow* (1879) sounds as if it were meant for them: "About two persons I never thought deeply: that is the root of my love for them." In 1882 this relationship was exposed to a serious strain in connection with his experience with Lou, and the consequences never seem to have entirely disappeared. His letters reveal the violent force of the climactic events.[34]

Monstrous contradictions also appear among the utterances made to and about Lou Salomé. They seem to reflect an attitude that characterizes all of Nietzsche's conceptions and intellectual formulations: he is so receptive to the manifold possibilities of things that he is invariably

---

[33] *Briefe,* V.—Podach, *Gestalten,* p. 7 ff., p. 125 ff. Luise Marelli, *Die Schwester Elisabeth Förster-Nietzsche,* Berlin, 1933.

[34] The negative utterances: to Overbeck, Sept., '82, Febr. 11, '83, and Mar., '83; to his mother, Aug., '83; to Overbeck, Febr. 5, '84. Henceforth thoroughly positive ones: to Overbeck, Sept. 14, '84, Oct., '84; to his sister, Mar., '84, Dec., '85, Dec. 26, '87, Mar. 31, '88, Dec.. '88.

captivated first by one set of possibilities, and then, almost immediately afterwards, by another. Thus, in his excitable mood, he allows expressions to escape him that he would soon like to call back. He writes to his sister as early as July 10, '65, that he is inclined to see "everything—things and persons, angels and men and devils—as very dark and completely ugly during some discontented moments," and on one occasion he confesses: "I am very glad that I tore up several letters to you—creatures of the night. However, a letter to our mother that still is of the same species did escape me" (to his sister, Aug., '83). He recognizes his own contradictoriness and sees it to be rooted in a strength of his nature: "But anyone who is so much alone with himself . . . and, in addition, sees all things not merely from two, but three, four sides . . . judges even his own experiences quite differently" (to his sister, Mar., '85).

For purposes of cognition and preparation it makes good sense to entertain and explore various possibilities, but in active life it is necessary to decide between them. Nietzsche seems to decide only when his task as a creative thinker is concerned, and then he brooks no interference. In human affairs he behaves very nearly like one who simply allows others to decide for him while confining his own activity to their breakup. This appears, for example, to be the case at the time of his attachment to Lou. When finally he appears as the one who is guilty and forsaken by all, the one who feels in the depths of his being that he really is of no importance to anybody, then he clings to his natural ties: the members of his family somehow remain for him the most reliable people. To be sure, one senses occasionally, like a shadow over his life, that his mother meant little to him in his heart. His sister is not bound closely to him in a philosophical partnership. But he never permanently gave up his mother and sister in situations of conflict (whatever he may have done temporarily); rather he preferred them to all other people out of a certain feeling of natural trust: they were to remain with him when all others left, and he did not wish to break with them. The blood tie and a recollection going back to the beginning of his childhood proved to be not only invincible but precious, humanly irreplaceable possessions.

His sister's solicitude was also of benefit to posterity. A well-documented knowledge of all sides of Nietzsche is possible only because, from his boyhood on, his sister kept all manuscripts, including the posthumous materials, which she collected and preserved when they seemed to be of no importance to anyone. Of course only their future publication will reveal Nietzsche's full scope.

Right up to the end Nietzsche's sociability permitted him to enter into vital relations with a considerable circle of people. Some met with him and then departed, to return occasionally or stand in the background where they could again be addressed at an appropriate time. While none of these people was indispensable to him, still this social situation as a whole—involving occasional affectionate contacts, considerable good-will and human interest, and Nietzsche's pleasure in the existence and gaiety [35] of others combined with his readiness to help them—provided an atmosphere that was indispensable to him. Now and then one of them would come into prominence for a while through correspondence.

Of his schoolmates, *Deussen, Krug,* and *v. Gersdorff* remained close to him. New acquaintances were added later: *Carl Fuchs* (1872), *Malvida von Meysenbug* (1872), *v. Seydlitz* (1876), and others. During the last decade, traveling companions begin to play an increasing role without attaining real importance.

Deussen [36] occupies a peculiar place. Nowhere else in his correspondence is Nietzsche so extremely and ruthlessly didactic. His awareness of his superior status is combined with a serious interest in Deussen's intellectual development, which is to be genuine and directed toward something essential. Thus Nietzsche spurs him on with appreciative applause for excellent accomplishments. In this association, Nietzsche's fairness is just as impressive as the admirable truthfulness which later enabled Deussen to present the whole affair to the public without reservation. It is as though each personality attains a typical greatness through contact with Nietzsche, each on his own level and according to his potentialities. The more one concerns himself with each particular relationship and studies the individuality of each single person involved, the more clearly one will see a circle of plastic personalities that belong with Nietzsche, are illumined in his vicinity, and stand out more clearly than he himself in his unfathomableness.

For some personalities of European prominence, Nietzsche professed an unwonted reverence, e.g., *Jacob Burckhardt* [37] and *Karl Hillebrand*.[38] He virtually pleaded for their good-will, watched every nuance of their judgment, felt as one of them, and was not aware of the silent reserve they observed toward him.

[35] Cf., for example, his letter to Overbeck, Nov. 15, '84.

[36] Cf. Paul Deussen, *Erinnerungen an Friedrich Nietzsche,* Leipzig, 1901 (in it also the letters). Also: Paul Deussen, *Mein Leben,* Leipzig, 1922.

[37] Cf., besides *Briefe,* III: Bernoulli I, 51 ff.

[38] "Briefwechsel" (edited by O. Crusius), *Süddeutsche Monatshefte* VI, 2., 1909. Hillebrand reviewed the first three parts of *Untimely Meditations* immediately after their publication and, while expressing agreement, urged a return to moderation and reality. The reviews were reprinted in: Hillebrand, *Zeiten, Völker und Menschen,* Bd. II, 2. Aufl., Strassburg, 1892: 1. "Einiges über den Verfall der deutschen Sprache und der deutschen Gesinnung."—2. "Über historisches Wissen und historischen Sinn."—3. "Schopenhauer und das deutsche Publikum."

It is part of his fate that other high-ranking personalities to whom he paid much respect finally ignored him as being of no consequence: *Cosima Wagner* and *Hans von Bülow*.

One friend stands out: the church historian, Franz Overbeck.[39] From 1870 on he was at Nietzsche's side, first as a housemate, colleague, and friend to the young man, then as a constant helpmate in practical matters when Nietzsche matured, and finally as a truly loyal companion for life. His family was *provided* by nature; the permanence of this friendship simply came *as a gift*. The reliability of Overbeck's conduct was manifested in an uncommon way: for decades his constant inner readiness to help issued in ever-repeated small, unobtrusive acts of assistance.

The friendship between Nietzsche and Overbeck never became clouded because there was no real intimacy in matters that truly concerned Nietzsche: he did not expect to meet Overbeck in the high regions of his actual task. Overbeck was like a firm foothold in the fluctuating waves of people and things.

Nietzsche respects Overbeck's capacity and accomplishment; he likes his steadfastness. This is expressed in some passages in his letters: "It always makes me feel so good when I think of you in your work, it is as though a healthy natural force were *blindly* working through you, and yet it is an *intelligence* that is working with the finest and most critical material. . . . I owe you so much, dear friend, for being allowed to watch the drama of your life from such close range" (to Overbeck, Nov., '80). "Every time we met, I experienced the deepest pleasure from your calmness and gentle firmness" (to Overbeck, Nov. 11, '83). "Admittedly it is getting more and more bothersome to associate with me, but I know that, thanks to your natural *equanimity,* our friendship will also keep its two feet on the ground" (to Overbeck, Nov. 15, '84).

The quiet stability of Overbeck's nature, his intelligence and clarity, afford Nietzsche so much comfort that he expresses himself in his letters to him as to a friend with whom he shares his innermost being, although he does not expect, as he ordinarily would in such a case, any understanding of the last impulses of his own *Existenz*. His trust in Overbeck is almost unlimited. Only very rarely, and not until the last years of increasing irritability, does he manage to write ironically, as on one occasion: "It really put my mind at *rest* to know that such a fine and well-meaning reader as *you* is still in doubt about my real *intent*" (to Overbeck, Oct. 12, '86).

---

[39] *Der Briefwechsel Nietzsches und Overbeck,* Leipzig, 1916.—The work of Bernoulli about both.—Walter Nigg, *Franz Overbeck,* München, 1931.

Towards Nietzsche, Overbeck was independent, and not merely because he was older. While he ranked below Nietzsche—something he knew and admitted—he nevertheless had his place in Nietzsche's world by virtue of his own special intellectual achievement. A radical truthfulness that can be compared to that of Nietzsche, an unbiased way of observing, a readiness to permit the realization of every possibility: this did not lead him, like Nietzsche, to extremes but caused him to end up, as he grew older, in a style full of stipulations and reservations, in which no longer anything of consequence was said, and in contradictions which dialectically remained unresolved (as, for instance, in a notation that begins: "Nietzsche was not a great man in the true sense of the word" and then continues: "whether Nietzsche really may be a great man—something that I least of all can doubt").[40] He had some awareness of Nietzsche's nature, but his objectivity developed in a direction that virtually blocked his access to Nietzsche's ways. His lack of passion resulted in a peculiar erudition, not wholly lacking in greatness, that enabled him, as an unbeliever, to solve, in an awkward but consciously undertaken and thus honest manner, the problem inherent in the teaching of theology (i.e., never to speak before students of his convictions but to limit himself to historical-scientific statements). His erudition kept his soul closed to Nietzsche's questions and visions without preventing him from being solicitous both as a friend and in a practical way. He did all that one could possibly do in confronting a genius-like exception: he helped him with humility, received him with awe and respect though without real understanding, and—without allowing his feelings to be hurt—coped patiently with difficulties in order to fulfill the task of being a friend. Neither curiosity nor obtrusiveness nor self-surrendering service but unsentimental, manly loyalty held fast here. It was the depth of the loyalty rather than the depth of a destiny finding fulfillment in friendship that bound the two together.

The Limits of Nietzsche's Capacity for Friendship and His Loneliness. It is distressing—so much so that one is inclined to doubt Nietzsche—to see him in awkward situations: to see how he attaches himself to people at random and expresses his closeness to them,[41] how he invites a scarcely known young student on a trip and receives an open refusal,[42] how he makes a marriage proposal out of the blue and then, on another occasion,

---

[40] Bernoulli I, 268, 270.
[41] Cf. Egidi, *loc. cit.,* and about Bungert: letters to Gast, Mar. 7, '83 to Apr. 2, '83.
[42] Cf. Bernoulli I, 256 ff. (Scheffler).

has somebody look for a wife for him,[43] how he approaches Rée and Lou. Nietzsche knows "the sudden madness of those hours when the lonesome person embraces anyone indiscriminately and treats him as a friend and gift of heaven, only to push him away an hour later in disgust—disgust with himself (to his sister, July 8, '86); and he is burdened by "the shameful memory of the kind of humanity that I have so far treated as my equals" (*ibid.*). But he is able to deal with these and other cases: his manner of overcoming them is more characteristic of him than his getting involved.

The picture of Nietzsche as a hero of steel-like hardness, who relies on himself and moves through the world untouched and unshaken, is false. Nietzsche's heroism is of another kind. He has to suffer a human fate from which all forms of natural human fulfillment are withheld. Driven by human impulses, he has to deviate again and again from the course of his task (*Aufgabe*) with a view to simplifying it. He must, for example, find ways of becoming more effective, seek an outlet for his urge to teach, and believe in his friends: always his heroism consists in his return after failure. That is why his decisions relating to worldly activity become more and more negative. The magnificent development of his special and virtually unbounded intellectual experience is made possible by the fact that he does not become involved in the impenetrable opaqueness of his age and does not cling to any illusion.

Nietzsche's loneliness can be discussed on two levels: (1) from a *psychological standpoint* one can criticize his lonely nature, judging it by an absolute standard for possible human *Existenz* in general; this is to do him an injustice, since the method employed inevitably yields pejorative conclusions; or (2), one may sense the never wholly comprehensible *task* that consumes him, gain from it some insight into his *Existenz* as an exception, and thus arrive at an understanding of Nietzsche himself.

(1) The *psychological* critique, proceeding as it does on a superficial level, might well present something like the following picture: the independence which Nietzsche attains through his will to truth gives him neither self-assurance nor certainty in the world, but rather makes him sensitive beyond measure to his own inadequacy and to the baseness of other types: he can live only among the nobility. But since he himself does not always remain noble and since he must so frequently endure blindness and baseness and untruthfulness in others, he is repeatedly overcome by alarm and finally reaches the state of disillusionment in

---

[43] Cf. concerning the marriage proposal, spring, 1876: Bohnenblust, *loc. cit.,* and also: H. W. Brann, *Nietzsche und die Frauen,* Leipzig, 1931.

which he breaks with everything. Hence his ever-growing estrangement wherever he turns: he is satisfied with no one—not even himself. When insight comes to fill the place of his missing instincts, his truthfulness brings everything to wrack and ruin by applying absolute standards. He must constantly call everyone in question since his urge to communicate, like the rest of his nature, is intolerant of every form of imposture. Whatever is allotted to him contains the seeds of failure, for deceitful accommodation is foreign to his nature. While this is rooted in his honesty, his sense of responsibility for a present spiritual reality, which is never perfect and never wholly noble, does not gain any force in the depths of his soul. Nietzsche severs relationships without effecting anything positive; he teaches only by challenging without entering into the fray on equal terms. He seems to possess something of an unreadiness to communicate in the sphere of concrete historicity (though this latter could lead, even without accommodation, to a fruitful enhancement and general elevation in the world as it develops, through illumination, into an overcoming, rather than annihilating, force). It is possible that Nietzsche on occasions suffered more from hurt pride than from a failure of communication; and, from a psychological standpoint, this might seem to indicate an unwillingness for such communication. Genuine communication can succeed only when people are unmoved by insults because they continue to be *what* they are and remain *where* they are, refusing to abandon the real world in favor of an imagined state of independence outside of it. Only in this way can they remain ready to free other persons and themselves from entanglements, and only in this way can they really question others and answer them. People of this kind may wish to intrude, but they are modest and hesitant precisely in situations in which Nietzsche abandons these restraints: for instance when he on one occasion breaks off all communication with cheap candor and in an insulting and censorious manner; when he again, in his loneliness, throws himself prematurely at a stranger; or when he proposes marriage at random. The reason for this failure could be that Nietzsche's will to communicate, in the last analysis, is without ties to the autonomous being of the other and hence is not really a will to communicate at all. Nietzsche is uncommonly amiable, he takes the initiative, is helpful and unusually ready to offer assistance, but he always seems to love only himself while he loves the other person only as a vessel for his own self; he lacks real devotion to a human being. He yearns for love, but he fails to seize the moment of spontaneous response of the soul itself which is the condition of a realization of love. Therefore, though he expresses genuine gratitude for everything that life gives him, he seems capable of becoming downright ungrateful and disloyal in communication (as shown by his occasional comments to others on Overbeck and even on his mother and sister). He is able to hold fast, but only in his need for human contact, when the other person is patient and remains ready (Overbeck, his sister) or when the other is a faithful disciple and helper (Gast). He is actually attracted only by independence and loftiness; in his own mind, he does not deceive himself about those patient people close to him to whom he usually writes with uncommonly tactful consideration, even caution, and constant expressions of gratitude. He strives for the utmost and judges correctly by this criterion; but he leaves all others in their confusion or constriction, unwilling to enter a dynamic union with anyone and to achieve mutual self-realization through a loving struggle with and for one another. He remains constantly censorious or enthusiastic (when he, in an intensified expression of friendship, glorifies the other with apparently total devotion). We must ask: did Nietzsche not love with the kind of love that springs from the bottom of the soul, a love which produces communication and keeps it alive because it embraces existential reality itself rather than merely absolute standards and rapturously imagined idols? Did he, in the last analysis, suffer from loneliness even more because he did not love than because he was not loved?

(2) Only one who does not believe in Nietzsche's *task* and his *awareness* of this task can accept such a psychological discussion of Nietzsche. If Nietzsche loves himself and loves the other person only as a vessel of what is his own, then this latter is indeed the all-consuming and all-demanding task which forces him to become an *exceptional being*. Nietzsche can give himself to the other person when he sees in him the realization of the presently necessary task (thus he gives himself to Wagner), or he can surrender himself to the still undetermined task not yet brought out of the shadow of thinking; but he cannot yield to human communication as such. This existential inadequacy results from the existential positivity that inheres in the task of the exceptional man.

Hence the decisive reason for his loneliness cannot be sufficiently determined in a psychological manner. The essence of his mental *Existenz* compels him, against his will, to separate himself as an exception. His thoughts, when openly expressed, are bound to frighten others away. Nietzsche endures the sacrifice which he must make only with great reluctance: "Even now, after an hour of agreeable conversation with total strangers, my whole philosophy is wavering: it seems so foolish to insist on being right at the price of love, and to be unable to communicate the best in me without destroying the feeling of fellowship" (to Gast, Aug. 20, '80).

Throughout Nietzsche's life there runs an inescapable contradiction between what he desires as a *human being* and what he wishes to do as the *bearer* of his *task*. Thus he laments his loneliness and yet welcomes it; he suffers from the lack of anything humanly normal, seems to try to remedy it, and yet chooses consciously an exceptional existence. "The antinomy of my . . . situation and form of *Existenz* consists in the fact that I feel that all the things which I *need* as a *philosophus radicalis*—freedom from profession, wife, child, fatherland, creed, etc. etc.—are just so many *deprivations,* insofar as I fortunately am a living being and not merely an analyzing machine" (to Overbeck, Nov. 14, '86; similarly to his sister, July, '87).

One must sense the destiny in Nietzsche's task if one is not to take what is remarkable in Nietzsche's life as a mere psychological fact but, instead, hear the note in it which belongs to him alone and to nobody else. This note, as an expression of the relentlessness of his own destiny, can already be heard when the young student writes to his mother: "There can be no question of influence since I first would have to become acquainted with persons whom I could regard as being above me" (Dec., '62). The force of this destiny goes through his life: it parts him from Wagner, whom *he* leaves, and from Rohde, who leaves *him.* This destiny becomes increasingly clear to him until his last years when he writes: "My whole life has broken apart before my eyes: this entire, weirdly concealed life which takes a step forward every six years and actually desires nothing further except this step while all other things, including my human relations, are only concerned with a mask of myself so that I have always to be the victim of the necessity of leading an entirely concealed life" (to Overbeck, Febr. 11, '83). "One actually becomes a very exacting type of person if one's life is sanctioned by his work: that is, one therewith loses the knack of pleasing people. One is too *serious,* and they feel it: there is a diabolical seriousness behind a person who *insists on respect* for his work. . . ." (to Gast, Apr. 7, '88).

Insofar as Nietzsche's life is dedicated to the realization of a task, the latter produces a *new* will to communication—communication with people who know the *same need,* the same thought, the same task, and communication with *disciples.* Nietzsche was possessed with an extraordinary yearning for both.

(a) In spite of everything, he again and again scrutinizes his friends, wondering whether they do not experience the same shock that tore him loose from his very roots, whether they, too, do not know what he already knows:

It was so difficult to give up Lou and Rée because with them he "could talk of the things" that he was "interested in" without a mask (to his sister, Mar., '85). He complains that he "lacks a person with whom I can ponder over the future of men" (to Overbeck, Nov. 11, '83). "At times I long for a secret conference with you and Jacob Burckhardt, more in order to ask how you get around this distressing need than to tell you any news" (to Overbeck, July 2, '85). "J. Burckhardt's letter . . . depressed me, despite the fact that it was full of the highest respect for me. But what does *that* matter now! I wanted to hear 'that is *my* distress! That made *me* grow silent!' . . . I have no lack of people except those with whom I can share my concern, my concern" (to Overbeck, Oct. 12, '86). "From childhood on until now, I have found *nobody* who could have the same distress of heart and conscience that I have" (to his sister, May 20, '85).

(b) The will to communication that springs from the task seeks *pupils* and *disciples:*

His writings, in the form in which he published them, were to be "fishing hooks," "nets," attempts to lure: "I need disciples *while I am still alive,* and if the books that I have written so far are not effective as fishing hooks, then they have 'missed their calling.' The best and most essential can be communicated only *from man to man,* it cannot and should not be made 'public' " (to Overbeck, Nov., '84). He listens and wonders who hears him: "I found nobody, but again and again some odd form of that type of 'raging stupidity' which is so eager to be worshipped as virtue." "My yearning for pupils and heirs makes me impatient now and then and even seems to have led me to do some foolish things during the last years. . . ." (to Overbeck, Aug. 31, '85). "Perhaps I always secretly believed that I would no longer be alone at the point of my life *at which I have arrived:* that here I would receive vows and oaths, that I would have something to found and organize. . . ." (to Overbeck, July 10, '84). Concerning *Zarathustra* he remarks: "Not to hear the sound of an answer after such an appeal from my innermost soul, that is a *terrible* experience. . . . It lifted me out of all bonds with living men" (to Overbeck, June 17, '87). "It has already gone on for ten years: not a sound reaches me anymore." In 1887 he writes to Overbeck that it *"hurts* frightfully that in these fifteen years not one single person has 'discovered' me, has needed me, has loved me."

Nietzsche had sacrificed the necessities of general human *Existenz* to his task; the communication which his task required and which he so passionately desired completely failed to materialize. Nietzsche explains this to himself as follows:

The *nature of cognition* is such that it inevitably involves loneliness whenever it becomes the whole of life: "Should one assume the right to see the meaning of life in cognition," then "estrangement, separation, and perhaps even frigidity" are necessarily involved (to Overbeck, Oct. 17, '85). This estrangement could not but be exacerbated by Nietzsche's way of cognizing: "In my relentless and underground battle against everything that men hitherto have venerated and loved . . . I myself have unwittingly turned into something like a cave—something hidden that could no longer be found even if one went out to look for it" (to v. Seydlitz, Febr. 12, '88).

Nietzsche sees a further basic reason for this loneliness in the fact that *genuine communication* is only possible between people who occupy *the same niveau*. It can take place neither with those who stand higher nor with those who stand lower: "There certainly are much finer minds and stronger and nobler hearts than I possess, but they are of no avail to me except insofar as I attain equality with them and we can help each other." "As a result of having frequently *concocted* some friendship or scientific kinship in order to escape the anxieties of loneliness," he confesses, "many disappointments and contradictions" came into his life, though "of course, much happiness and radiance as well" (to his sister, July, '87).

With all his passion he longs for people of *highest* rank: "Why do I not find among the living those people whose glance reaches out higher than mine and who must see in me one of their kind? I yearn so much for just such people!" But, they do not appear, and Nietzsche experiences despair instead: "Gnashing I beat against the shore of your shallowness, gnashing like a wild wave as it bites, with repugnance, into the sand."

Never does he meet his equal in kind or in rank; hence, in the end he is forced to say: "I am too proud to think that a human being could love *me*. This would presuppose that he knows who I am. Just as little do I believe that I shall ever love anyone: this would presuppose that I would, for once, find a human being of my rank. . . . I never had a confidant and friend with whom I could share what occupies me, distresses me, or elevates me" (to his sister, Mar., '85). Nietzsche may well shudder at the fact that with inequality of rank, communication ceases at the decisive point: "Incommunicability is in truth the most terrible of all forms of loneliness, and difference is the mask that is more iron-like than any iron mask. Perfect friendship can exist only *inter pares. Inter pares!* An intoxicating expression . . ." (to his sister, July 8, '86). But he must shoulder the consequences of inequality: "The eternal distance between man and man drives me into loneliness." "Whoever stands as I do loses, to speak with Goethe, one of the greatest human rights, namely the right to be judged by his peers." "There is nobody alive who has the right to praise me." "I no longer find anyone whom I could obey or whom I should like to command."

When Nietzsche looks back upon his life, he feels that it could not have been otherwise, loneliness having been indissolubly blended with his nature from early childhood on: "Even as a child I was alone this way. Today, in the 44th year of my life, I am still alone" (to Overbeck, Nov. 12, '87).

This loneliness, thus shown to be a part of his life, cannot be avoided: "I yearned for human beings, and I searched for them. I always found only *myself,*—and I am no longer yearning for myself!" "Nobody comes to me any more. And as for myself, I went to all, but I *reached* nobody!"

The result is expressed by Nietzsche during the last decade with ever increasing intensity, in a manner that is unspeakably sad and sometimes nearly *despairing:*

"Now there is no longer anybody alive who loves me; how can I still love life!" "There you sit at the shore, freezing and hungry: it is not enough to save one's life." "You complain that I use screaming colors? . . . perhaps I have a nature which *screams,* 'like the stag for fresh water.' If you yourselves were this fresh water, how pleasant my voice would sound to you." "For the lonely one, even noise is a consolation." "If I could give you an idea of my feeling of *loneliness!* I have nobody, among the living or among the *dead,* to whom I feel related. This is indescribably horrible. . . ." (to Overbeck, Aug. 5, '86). "It is so seldom that a friendly voice reaches me. I am now alone, absurdly alone. . . . And for years no refreshment, not a drop of humaneness, not a breath of love" (to v. Seydlitz, Febr. 12, '88).

The real miracle is that Nietzsche became capable of renunciation at all. Actually, words like the following rarely occur: "What have I learned to this day? To give myself pleasure in all situations and to have no need for others."

It was not until the transformation of the last months that Nietzsche could cease suffering and seemingly forget all that had gone before: "Even *suffering* from loneliness is a pretext. I have always suffered only from manifoldness. . . . At an absurdly early period—at the age of seven—I already knew that no human word would ever reach me: has anyone ever seen me sad about that?"

Illness

Nietzsche's work abounds in questions concerning the significance of illness. He himself suffered almost continuously from various illnesses during the last two decades of a creative life that ended in insanity. For an understanding of Nietzsche, acquaintance with the facts of his illness, a clear differentiation between these facts and their possible significance, and a knowledge of Nietzsche's own attitude toward sickness are prerequisites.[44]

The Illnesses. On Jan. 8, 1889, Overbeck arrived in Turin to take his mentally ill friend home. Letters indicative of insanity (to A. Heusler and J. Burckhardt) had induced Wille, the psychiatrist who had been consulted in Basel, to request urgently that immediate steps be taken. Nietzsche had indeed deteriorated. On the previous day he had fallen down in the street. Now Overbeck found him "cowering in the corner of a sofa"; "he rushes toward me, embraces me violently, and then sinks, in twitches, back onto the sofa." He launched forth in loud songs, ragings on the piano, scurrilous dances and leaps, and then uttered, "in an indescribably soft tone, sublime, wonderfully clairvoyant, and inexpressibly awesome things about himself as the successor to the dead God." [45] Nietzsche became increasingly demented until his death in 1900.

---

[44] Literature dealing with Nietzsche's sicknesses: P. J. Möbius, *Nietzsche,* 2. Aufl., Leipzig, 1904.—Ottokar Fischer, "Eine psychologische Grundlage des Wiederkunftsgedankens." *Zeitschr. f. angew. Psychologie* 5, p. 487, 1911.— Ernst Benda, "Nietzsches Krankheit," *Monatsschr, f. Psychiatrie und Neur.* Bd. 60, p. 65, 1925.—Kurt Hildebrandt, *Gesundheit und Krankheit in Neitzsches Leben und Werk,* Berlin, 1926.—E. F. Podach, *Nietzsches Zusammenbruch,* Heidelberg, 1930.—Paul Cohn, *Um Nietzsches Untergang, mit vier Briefen von El. Förster-Nietzsche,* Hannover, Morris-Verlag o.J. (1931).—E. F. Podach, "Nietzsches Krankengeschichte (Abdruck der vollständigen Jenaer Krankengeschichte)," in: *Die medizinische Welt,* vierter Jahrgang; p. 1452, 1930.
[45] Bernoulli, II, 22 ff.

We are bound to ask when his illness began. The letters show that no ravings indicative of insanity appear prior to Dec. 27, '88. On this day he writes a clear letter to Fuchs, but on the same day he writes to Overbeck: "I myself am just now working on a *promemoria* for the European courts with a view to an anti-German league. I intend to constrict the 'Reich' in an iron shirt and provoke a war of desperation." The succeeding days are filled with changing, deteriorating, and yet spiritually permeated and stirring illusory thoughts which he announces in letters and on painstakingly inscribed slips of handmade paper. Nietzsche becomes God, becomes Dionysus and the Crucified one; both become one; Nietzsche is everyman, all men, every dead and living person. His friends are assigned roles. Cosima Wagner becomes Ariadne, Rohde is placed among the gods, Burckhardt becomes the great teacher. Creation and world history are in Nietzsche's hand. It is essential to realize that *no indication of such madness* can be discovered *prior to Dec. 27, '88.* To search his writings for any madness before this date has been shown to be futile.

For an illness of this description to begin so suddenly indicates psychosis. What is involved is an *organic* brain disorder, probably progressive paralysis, but in any case a process of degeneration brought about by *accidental external causes* in the form of infection or misuse of toxins (though this latter is improbable and unproven); there is no question of an inherited constitutional predisposition to such a disease.

It is not possible to use present-day means to determine how long before Dec. 27, '88, this process of destruction had started. The present methods of physical examination (especially lumbar puncture), which must be employed along with psychopathological data if one is to make certain of his diagnosis and discover the date of onset of the paralysis, were not available at that time. The fact is that Nietzsche was *constantly ill in some way after 1873,* but not mentally ill. The mental illness, as the final state, throws its shadow backward and suggests to many people that its symptoms are discoverable throughout this long period. This assumption, however, obscures the facts just as does the opposite view that Nietzsche's mind was completely sound until the end of 1888. The diagnosis of Nietzsche's illnesses, dependent as it is on the medical lore of the period with its classificatory schemes, nowhere attains complete certainty. In order to find even a hypothetical answer to the question about all that might be connected with the brain disorder that finally appeared, one would have to compare it, first, with the progress of cases of paralysis observed in great numbers in institutions. But this comparison remains inadequate since it can only in a superficial manner provide the psychological data needed to discern the intellectual endeavors during the decade preceding the obvious breaking out of the illness.[46] Second, his case can be compared with those of outstanding men who are known to have suffered from paralysis or may have done so: for instance, Rethel, Lenau, Maupassant, Hugo Wolf, Schumann.[47] Although the biographies of significant personalities, because of the wealth of utterances, could teach us more than the case histories of uncreative people, *no decisive result* has been obtained so far through a comparison of these men with Nietzsche.

And such comparisons do not show us what may precede, possibly for decades, an acute outbreak of paralysis, or what, if it occurred, would *not* be a part of the symptomatology of the preliminary stage. Since we cannot know for sure, even today, we are left, in Nietzsche's case, with the simple task of recognizing, *through description,* the course of the illnesses and those psychologically ascertainable mental states that certainly cannot be considered illnesses, without learning which things constitute *one* illness and which are distinctly *different* illnesses that merely happen to attack the same person at the same time.

Of interest in this description are essentially the *breaks in the total state* of his psycho-physical existence that produce changes from which there is no complete recovery. These breaks are as follows:

1. After a serious attack of dysentery contracted as a nurse during the war, Nietzsche soon made a seemingly good recovery, but stomach disorders recurred at intervals thereafter. The disturbances began gradually but became frequent from 1873 on. Above all, attacks of violent headaches, together with sensitivity to light, vomiting, a general paralysis-like feeling, and conditions such as those experienced in seasickness, more and more often caused him to be bedridden. Several times he was unconscious for prolonged periods (to Eiser, Jan., '80). The near-sightedness from which he suffered since his youth was aggravated by permanent eye trouble; in addition to acute attacks there was constant pain and pressure in his head (to Eiser, Feb., '80). More and more his intellectual existence came to depend upon having others read to him and take his dictation.

These illnesses afflicted him throughout his *entire* life in varying degrees of severity; improvements and exacerbations alternated irregularly. Thus in 1885 he wrote again of a "rapid diminution of eyesight." On the one hand, the year 1879 was the worst according to his letters ("I experienced 118 days of serious attacks; I did not count the milder ones,"

---

[46] For material, cf. Arndt and Junius, *Archiv f. Psychiatrie,* Bd. 44.
[47] Unfortunately I did not have access to the publication by Gaston Vorberg, *Zusammenbruch: Lenau, Nietzsche, Maupassant, Hugo Wolf,* München, 1922.

to Eiser, Febr., '80); on the other hand, improvements occurred ("and now this remarkable improvement! To be sure, it has lasted only five weeks so far," [to Marie Baumgartner, Oct. 20, '79]).

In spite of the severity of the disorders, the long duration of this illness, and the consequent profound change in Nietzsche's existence, a medical diagnosis that would combine the symptoms into an unequivocal, clearly recognizable picture of the illness is not available. There has been talk of migraine, of a psycho-neurotic process in connection with his estrangement from Wagner, of an organic process of disease of the nervous system, but the results are not clear.

In May of 1879, Nietzsche, forced by illness to give up his professorship, began his itinerant life. However, *The Wanderer and his Shadow* appeared during the summer of that year. During the following winter, spent in Naumburg with his mother, his condition became so poor that he expected his life to end (farewell letter to Malvida von Meysenbug, Jan. 14, '80).

2. However, by February, 1880, Nietzsche is again in the south where he begins to make new notes which lead to the publication within the year of *The Dawn*. Spiritually a development now takes place which gradually reveals a reformulation of his thoughts, a truly genuine awareness of his task, and an accompanying self-assurance. We can see this transformation develop from August, 1880, until its climax in July–August, 1881, and even up to his inspired states of mind during the years 1882 and 1883.

Anyone who reads his letters and other writings in chronological order, keeping both past and future in mind and thus consciously observing the temporal relations of the utterances to each other, cannot escape an extraordinarily strong impression that Nietzsche underwent at this time the most profound change that he had ever experienced. It is revealed not only in the contents of his thinking and in new creations, but also in the forms which his experience assumes; Nietzsche submerges himself, as it were, in a new atmosphere; what he says takes on a different tone; and the mood that permeates everything is something for which there are no harbingers and indications prior to 1880.

We do not now ask whether the self-analysis of his spiritual development [48] is valid; we do not doubt its truth. We ask no questions concerning the meaning of the spiritual contents and the existential import seized upon by Nietzsche; we do not doubt their inner connection as revealed by the total presentation of this book. But we do ask whether

[48] Cf. pp. 28 ff.

something existing in and by itself does not appear in such a way as to reveal within Nietzsche's life an ingredient that is of no spiritual or existential necessity and that lends to the new a color that is not necessarily part of it; or, in other words, whether there may not be some elements entering the service of these spiritual impulses and aims whose origin points to what we vaguely call a "biological factor."

The *method* employed in considering the incisive experience of the year 1880 and of those that followed does not subsume under medical categories or look for "symptoms" that are "suspect"; rather it is nothing but a mere *chronological comparison*. It is not a matter of observing the phenomena *as such* but of finding out whether they are new, of singling out those which did not exist before, and of determining the extent to which they remain psychically and spiritually *incomprehensible* on the basis of what preceded.

This presentation starts from that *total impression* which is attained through exact chronological reading. Its purpose is to produce such an impression in the reader, insofar as he is confronted by the same question during his own study of Nietzsche, by guiding him toward it through presenting individual utterances and facts. At the same time, no proof is offered which, by arguing from details, would lead inevitably to the conclusion that we are dealing with the effects of an illness. For us, this total impression is significant in that it directs us to that which, in the present state of our knowledge, cannot be proved but is still possible if not probable. The question which agitates the student of Nietzsche and which is basic for the comprehension of his life is the question concerning the significance of this incisive experience (1880–1883): whether it is a purely immanent spiritual development or whether, under the influence of extra-spiritual, biological factors (i.e., factors recognizable, in principle, as belonging in the realm of the natural sciences), something takes place here which leads to the climax of Nietzsche's creative work, something which produces results for which his previous disposition cannot account and which thus prevents his being fully understandable and causes a strangeness that places him at an unbridgeable distance.[49] From the profusion of the utterances that must serve as factual material, some are given below for purposes of comparison.

While a feeling of the end still predominated during January, 1880,

---

[49] What we shall merely indicate here through a methodical observation of chronologically arranged material from posthumous writings and letters is in need of a methodical execution which cannot be accomplished with complete success until the new great complete edition provides the posthumous material and the complete correspondence (in chronological arrangement).

("I believe that I have completed my life's work, though of course like one who has not been allotted sufficient time. I should still have so much to say, and I feel myself so rich during every hour free from pain!" [to his sister, Jan. 16, '80]), the quality of his self-confidence, his experience of existence, and the actualities of his all-encompassing basic mood undergo a tremendous transformation:

From Marienbad: "Constantly in boundless high spirits of late!" (to Gast, Aug. 2, '80). "I was quite beyond myself. Once, in the forest, a gentleman stared very sharply at me as he passed: at that moment I felt that my face must express radiant happiness. . . ." (to Gast, Aug. 20, '80). From Genoa: "I am ill much of the time, but in incomparably better spirits than in other years at this same time" (to his sister, Dec. 25, '80). From Sils-Maria: "There never was a human being whom the word 'depressed' would have suited less. My friends, who sense more about my life's task, are of the opinion that I am, if not the happiest, then at any rate the most courageous of mortals. . . . My appearance is moreover excellent, my muscular system almost like that of a soldier due to my incessant hiking; stomach and abdomen are in good shape. My nervous system is splendid, very keen and strong, considering the immense activity in which it must engage!" (to his sister, middle of July, '81). "The intensity of my feelings makes me shudder and laugh. . . . On my hikes I wept . . . tears of jubilation; meanwhile I sang and talked nonsense, filled with a new vision that puts me ahead of all men" (to Gast, Aug. 14, '81). From Genoa: "Here in Genoa I am proud and happy, completely *principe Doria!* —or Columbus? I walk, as I did in the Engadine, over the heights with shouts of happiness and with a glance into the future that nobody before me has yet dared. Whether or not I succeed in accomplishing my great task depends on conditions which are not within my power, but belong to the 'nature of things.' Believe me: the peak of all moral contemplation and work in Europe and of a great deal else is now with me. Perhaps the time will yet come when even the eagles will have to look up to me with awe" (to his sister, Nov. 29, '81).

Bad days and weeks intrude between elevated moments. But the contrast is quite different from what it formerly was. The wonted attacks are not absent, but his physical suffering is less severe than in 1879. He remarks to Eisler, during a favorable moment in 1882: "On the whole, I may consider myself as one who has recuperated or is, at least, recuperating." His complaints about attacks and eye-trouble, especially in view of his painful dependence on the weather, never completely cease throughout the following years. But the contrast between the attacks and the periods free from them is henceforth overshadowed by the more incisive new contrast between the *intensified states* of a creative experience of being and the terrible melancholy of weeks and months of *depression*. In accordance with this is the fact that Nietzsche, while going through his mental "desert" between 1876 and 1880, remains spiritually sovereign and in no way feels that he has lost ground: only physically does he feel hopeless, expecting the end (during these years he is conscious of possessing a sense of vast distance, serene simplicity, and intentional avoidance of fanaticism; he is conscious of breathing deeply). Not until after 1881 does he come to know the sudden changes from nothing to something and the relapse into nothingness; thereafter, he not only seizes upon the great affirmation with jubilation, but he experiences its necessity with despair during periods when it does not arise. A dependable, even state never occurs. The ups and downs are extraordinary. While looking back on these years he writes: "The vehemence of my mood-swings was frightful during the past years" (to Fuchs, Dec. 14, '87).

Letters written at the time verify what Nietzsche later reports: that each of the first three books of *Zarathustra* was written in about ten days, in a state which intensified his total natural condition in an unheard-of manner, days which were afterwards followed by much longer states of hopeless emptiness and melancholy. When these states became perspicuous and communicable, he spoke of them as "inspiration" and described their profoundly enigmatic nature as follows:

"It would indeed be difficult to reject the idea of being mere incarnation, mere mouthpiece, mere medium of overwhelming forces as long as one harbors the slightest remnant of superstition. The term revelation, in the sense that suddenly, with indescribable certainty and delicacy, something becomes visible and audible—something that shakes one most profoundly and overthrows one—simply describes the actual situation. One listens but seeks not; one takes but does not ask who gives; a thought flashes forth like lightning, with necessity and without hesitation—I never was able to choose. A rapture whose tremendous tension occasionally finds release in a flow of tears, during which one's pace unintentionally grows first stormy and then slow; a state of being completely beside oneself, together with the most distinct awareness of countless delicate shudders and tremblings down to the toes of one's feet; such depths of happiness in which what is most painful and gloomy does not appear as contrast but as something necessary, something demanded, as a needed color with such a superfluity of light; all happens completely involuntarily but as in a storm of a feeling of freedom, of absoluteness, of power, of divinity. . . . Most remarkable is the involuntariness of the image, of the simile; one has no longer any concept of what is image, what is simile."

Alongside the days of actively creative inspiration during these years appear *states of experiencing being* which are abysmal in their terrifying depth. They are now boundary experiences that make him shudder, now mystical heights of perfect clarity. Nietzsche reports them rarely, but decisively.

"I was in a real *abyss* of feelings, but I raised myself fairly perpendicularly from this depth to my height" (to Overbeck, Feb. 3, '83), and later again: "It is night again around me; I feel as though there had been lightning—for a brief span of time I *was entirely* in my element and in my light" (to Overbeck, Mar. 11, '83). Nietzsche presents the unspeakable through a magnificently persuasive simile: "I stand still, I am suddenly tired. Ahead . . . abyss everywhere. Behind me . . . the mountains. Trembling I reach for a hold. . . . Here the shrubbery—it crumbles in my hand. . . . I shudder, and I close my eyes. Where am I? I look into a purple night, it draws me and beckons me. What feeling is this? What happened that your voice suddenly fails and *you feel as if buried, under a burden of drunken and opaque feelings?* From what are you suffering now! yes, *suffering*—that is the right word! What serpent has bitten your heart?"

The various states of mystical light, dangerous shuddering at the boundary, and creative inspiration are limited to the years 1881–1884. From 1885 on there is no longer any mention of such feelings, experiences of being, and revelations. When Nietzsche on a later occasion writes that he is "without hold" and "can easily be blown away overnight through a storm" and that his situation is "one of being unable to climb up or down, very high, but constantly near danger, without any answer to the question, Whither?" (to Gast, '87), this is now said without reference to experienced states but rather out of concern for his task, while those earlier utterances proclaim the boundary experience he actually lived through. Now Nietzsche is simply "tortured day and night by" his "problems" (to Overbeck, spring of '86). When he writes once more: "During the past weeks I was inspired in the strangest manner," it is merely a question of sudden thoughts which compelled him "to jot something down" even at night (to Fuchs, Sept. 9, '88).

The intensified states are accompanied by a feeling of extraordinary *menace*. The emotional intensity is not natural: "At times, the premonition runs through my head that I am actually living a highly dangerous life since I am one of those machines that may *explode!*" (to Gast, Aug. 14, '81). He later considers the whole of *Zarathustra* as "an explosion of forces accumulated over a period of decades": "In such explosions the author himself may easily be blown up. I often have that feeling. . . ." (to Overbeck, Feb. 8, '84). Even when annihilation is not threatening, Nietzsche's total condition is so unstable that a more intensive experience again and again makes him ill immediately: "My feelings undergo such violent explosions that one single moment literally suffices to produce a change . . . that makes me thoroughly ill (this happens about twelve hours afterwards, and it lasts two to three days)" (to Overbeck, July 11, '83). "Of what avail is the most sensible way of living if at any moment the vehemence of feeling may strike into it like lightning and upset the order of all bodily functions?" (to Overbeck, Dec. 26, '83).

In what has been reported above, there appears an inseparable fusion of the spirituality of Nietzsche's creativity with experiences that seem to come out of nowhere to assail and overcome him. One who does not become absorbed by the totality of these experiences and by the complete transformation of the atmosphere might indeed say of each particular instance that it is the way in which creativity always reveals itself. Even though the following arguments are not proofs, they nevertheless indicate that Nietzsche's creative processes, whose purpose is the fulfillment of the preceding phases of his philosophizing, have for their foundation something that cannot be regarded as simply an attribute of the creative person in the absence of an added "biological factor":

a. That the exulting feelings and rapturous states assume the form of *seizures* or *attacks* leads one to think that they are brought about by non-psychical causes. In relation to their spiritual import and their productiveness in creating this import, the times at which they occur and their chronological sequences are accidental. Furthermore they reveal a peculiar character only from 1881 till 1884.

b. The sheer number of the states whose relations defy understanding, as well as their incoherent variety, their antecedence to periods of creation, their gradual diminution since 1884, and their coincidence with phenomena that go beyond a spiritual process of creation and its consequences—all these things suggest a process that affected Nietzsche's entire constitution while it became a helpful factor in his creative work.

c. Nietzsche is *36 years old* when, for *the first time* in his life, he has these intensified experiences which carry him beyond the realm of ordinary human events. Creative persons are acquainted with exalted moods, profound insights, and fruitful inspirations, but these things are as essentially different from what Nietzsche experiences as, for instance, the notion of warmth is different from that of real fire. What in the case of the creative person is natural and generally expected is hardly comparable to the strange experiences that Nietzsche suffers as psycho-physical realities. Something new seems to emerge from his biological constitution in its entirety. The question concerning the nature of this biological factor cannot be answered. What happened to Nietzsche since 1880 must for the present remain uncertain. But the unbiased observer who has carefully studied the letters and writings in their entirety and in chronological sequence can, in my opinion, scarcely doubt that something incisive took place. There is no justification for considering this occurrence as the first phase of paralysis as long as experience with paralysis does not show, through a comparison of cases, that these preliminary stages are part of it; and even then they would not, in themselves, be identical with the paralysis as a destructive process. To designate the process as schizophrenia or as schizoid seems futile to me, since such diagnostic categories are, at their very best, ill-defined and etiologically meaningless; and they become meaningless in every respect when they are applied without evidence of tangible, i.e., psychotic, symptoms (such as appear in the cases of van Gogh and Strindberg). My observations of the two "physiognomies" of Nietzsche, separated as if by a break in spite of the unity of Nietzsche's nature, have nevertheless convinced me that, even in the absence of diagnosis, we must speak here of a biological factor which eventually may come to be recognized as psychiatry advances.

3. A *final* decisive change clearly begins toward the end of 1887. It in turn leads to new phenomena which totally dominate everything after September, 1888. He now becomes for the first time confident that his activity will determine the entire course of world-history—so confident that in the end his insanity assumes the appearance of a meaningful leap into the actualization of an illusion that takes the place of reality. Next he undertakes to secure his own immediate success (an enterprise to which he was unaccustomed), then appears a new polemical style, and finally he yields to an all-absorbing euphoria.

The *new note* expressing an extreme further intensified is heard in these strange but perhaps true statements: "It is not impossible that I am the foremost philosopher of this age, indeed perhaps even a little more, something decisive and fateful that stands between two millenniums" (to Seydlitz, Febr. 12, '88). This runs through the whole year. He speaks of his "decisive task which . . . splits the history of mankind into two halves" (to Fuchs, Sept. 14, '88) and says: "Concerning the *conse-quences,* I now occasionally look at my hand with some distrust because it seems to me that I hold the destiny of mankind 'in my hand' " (to Gast, Oct. 30, '88).

While his self-confidence, especially with respect to its theme, remains understandable throughout, since it is part of his mode of thinking and has been repeatedly expressed during the years since 1880, Nietzsche now undertakes a *new activity* which is foreign to his former nature. Although he has repeatedly rejected, during previous years, the idea of someone writing about him (for example Paneth, to Overbeck, Dec. 22, '84)—in spite of his desire to escape from the agony of loneliness and gain a genuine disciple (though not to propagandize)—he now engages in *enterprises:* he promotes translations and establishes connections with the *Kunstwart,* with Spitteler, with Brandes, and with Strindberg.

As late as June, 1888, he is still able to write once more "that my . . . entire position as an 'immoralist' is still much too premature at present, still much too unprepared. The thought of propaganda is totally foreign to me; I haven't stirred a finger in that direction yet" (to Knortz, June 21, '88). But in July he gives Fuchs detailed advice on how to write something about him if the opportunity should arise. In August, when Fuchs has failed to react, he does not wish his "literary recipe" to be taken seriously, but in December he approaches Fuchs anew: "Perhaps you are in a warlike mood? I should find it extremely agreeable if a gifted musician would now side with me publicly as an anti-Wagnerian. . . . A little brochure. . . . The moment is propitious. One can still say true things about me that could almost become silly trifles within a couple of years" (Dec. 11, '88). He is enraptured over the lectures that Brandes delivered about him; a *vita* written at the request of Brandes (Apr. 10, '88) is in itself a clever and undignified piece of propaganda when measured by Nietzsche's earlier general attitude. Soon he presents his publisher with an unrequested blurb intended to call the readers' attention to Brandes' lectures about him; he reports this to Gast as follows: "I left it up to Fritsch to announce something in the press about my Copenhagen success" (to Gast, June 14, '88). The publisher did not comply with his wish. Furthermore, he induces Gast to write in the *Kunstwart* about *The Wagner Case* (to Gast, Sept. 16, '88) and, after this has been done, insists on issuing a special publication in which Gast's article is to be combined with one by Fuchs ("The Nietzsche Case. Marginal Notes by Two Musicians." [to Gast, Dec. 27, '88]). Nietzsche's last writings are meant to be effective immediately—at this very moment—and consequently are written according to plan and designed for publication in a definite sequence.

Another indication is provided by the *blunt letters* through which he breaks with people close to him or venerated by him: a still somewhat restrained harbinger of this is the letter to Rohde of May 21, '87. Then comes the break with Bülow on Oct. 9, '88: "Honored Sir, you did not reply to my letter. I shall never again molest you, that I promise you. I am sure you have an idea that *the foremost spirit of this age* expressed a wish to you. Friedrich Nietzsche." This is followed by the break with Malvida von Meysenbug on Oct. 18, '88, and the farewell letter to his sister in Dec., '88.

If one compares the excited years of the Zarathustra period with the excitement of 1888, the latter shows an increase in aggressiveness, drastic harshness, and extravagance of rational utterance, in the absence of vision and serenity. The will to action dominates.

But the decisive symptom of the new condition is a *euphoria* which appears only occasionally in the course of the year but is constant during the last months.

This tone is softly heard first in letters to Seydlitz (Febr. 12, '88): "The days here come along with an impudent beauty; there never was a more perfect winter." To Gast he writes (Sept. 27, '88): *"Marvelous clarity, autumnal colors, an exquisite feeling of well-being on all things."* Later on: "I am now the most grateful person in the world—of an *autumnal* mood in every good sense of the word: this is my great *harvest time.* Everything is easy for me, everything turns out well for me. . . ." (to Overbeck, Oct. 18, '88). "I looked at myself in the mirror. Never before have I looked like that: in exemplarily fine spirits, well-nourished, and ten years younger than permissible. . . . I rejoice in having an excellent tailor and value being considered everywhere as a distinguished foreigner. I am convinced that in my *trattoria* I am served the best food they have to offer. . . . Between the two of us, I have never known, until this day, what it means to eat with appetite. . . . Here day comes after day with the same unrestrained perfection and flood of sunlight. . . . The coffee in the first-class cafés, a small pot, of remarkable quality, even prime quality, such as I have never yet found. . . ." (to Gast, Oct. 30, '88). The tone of happiness is never again interrupted. "On and on it goes, in a *tempo fortissimo* of work and good mood. Furthermore, everybody here treats me *comme il faut,* like an extremely distinguished being; they have a way of opening the door for me that I have never experienced anywhere else" (to Overbeck, Nov. 13, '88). "I carry on such tomfoolery with myself and have such private-harlequin-ideas that I occasionally *grin* (I cannot think of another word) for half an hour on the open street" (to Gast, Nov. 26, '88). "Exuberantly beautiful autumn day. Just came back from a great concert which, in the last analysis, is the most powerful concert-impression of my life; my spirit continually made grimaces in order to cope with an extreme pleasure. . . ." (to Gast, Dec. 2, '88). "For some days I have been leafing through my literature, and I feel, for the first time, that I can cope with it. . . . I did everything very well, but I never had any idea of it" (to Gast, Dec. 9, '88). "All who have any dealings with me, down to the peddler woman who selects delicious grapes for me, are without exception perfect human specimens, very polite, cheerful, a little fat,—even the waiters" (to Gast, Dec. 16, '88). "I discovered this paper, the first on which I can write. Likewise pen. . . . Likewise ink, the latter, however, from New York, expensive, excellent. . . . Four weeks ago, I began to understand my own writings, and what is more, I treasure them. . . . I am now of the absolute conviction that all has turned out well, from the very beginning; all is one and has one purpose" (to Gast, Dec. 22, '88). To Overbeck on Christmas: "What is so remarkable here in Turin is the perfect fascination I have for others. . . . When I enter a large store, every face changes. . . . I get the choicest in choicest preparation. . . . I never had a notion of it, neither what meat, nor what vegetables, nor what all these really Italian dishes *could* be. . . . My waiters beam with politeness and kindness. . . ."

A few days later Nietzsche is in a state of insanity in which he continues to live for another decade in an apathetic twilight.

The understanding of Nietzsche does not depend upon possession of a medical diagnosis. But it is essential to know, first, that the mental illness at the end of 1888 is an organic brain disease, which derives from an external cause and not from an inner disposition; second, that in the mid-1880s Nietzsche's entire spiritual constitution is probably transformed by a biological factor; and third, that the year 1888 immediately precedes the mental illness with its direct effect of profound disintegration and reveals changes in his mood and behavior that are unlike anything previously found.

So far as diagnoses are concerned, probability definitely favors the view that the mental disease at the end of 1888 was a paralysis. In addition, a severe "rheumatism" of 1865 extending to arms and teeth has been diagnosed as meningitis caused by infection; the attacks, as migraine (which doubtless they partly are, as a complex of symptoms; but the question is whether as a whole they are a symptom of another illness); the appearances of illness since 1873, as a psychoneurotic process occasioned by his inner separation from R. Wagner; the transformation from 1880 to 1882 as the first indications of the later paralysis; the many sensations of intoxication of the later period and even the collapse itself as the consequence of toxins (particularly hashish). If we were to accept the principle of explaining, as far as possible, symptoms of illness from a single cause, we would conclude that all illnesses after 1866 were stages on the path to paralysis. This is however entirely open to question. Medical categories are of significance to a philosophically relevant conception of Nietzsche only if they need not be doubted. Except for the fact that the concluding mental disease was almost certainly a paralysis, these diagnoses are dubious.

Illness and Work. There are those who regard the topic of Nietzsche's illness as degrading. They think that to relate the characteristics of his work to his illness is to disparage him. "They are the works of a paralytic," says the one; "Nietzsche was not mentally ill prior to the end of 1888," says the other. The indolent mind claims the right to choose the simple alternative: either Nietzsche was ill, or he was of world-historical greatness. It is denied that he could have been both at the same time. We must oppose these unqualified and final, absolute annihilations as well as the false attempts at rescue, since neither the one nor the other reveals any understanding of Nietzsche's thinking or any comprehension of the actuality of his life. In both cases dogmatic assertion is used to impede inquiry and stifle investigation.

Generally speaking, the value of a creation may be regarded and judged only in terms of its spiritual substance; the underlying causal factors are irrelevant to the value of the product. A speech will not be regarded as either worse or better when it becomes known that the speaker customarily drinks a bottle of wine beforehand in order to free himself from inhibitions. The intrinsically incomprehensible causality of the natural process, in which all of us are involved, tells us nothing concerning the intelligibility, the meaning, and the value of the spiritual events to which it gives rise; it can only reveal—if our knowledge extends that far—an incomprehensibility on a totally different level. But this general delimitation is not enough.

When a pathological process or other biological factor exerts an influence on a psychical event, various questions arise: Was this influence beneficial, harmful, or indifferent? Did a spiritual possibility assume a peculiar guise under the new conditions? If so, in what ascertainable directions? These questions cannot be dealt with by *a priori* methods but only empirically—preferably through comparative studies of patients. To the extent that any empirical knowledge is obtained, the first question is: What singular and irreplaceable creations would *not* have come into being *without sickness* (an answer asserting that they would have would be a stunning proclamation of the spiritual actualities in the world [50])? Next we must ask what *flaws,* discernable to the critic without reference to any sickness, must be *related to the sickness* and which flaws might be expected due to the *type of sickness?* (In this case the answer may save the purity of the work because a way has been found to differentiate between flaws that are foreign to the spirit and the questionable elements intrinsic to this spiritual movement as such.)

Such pathographical observation is not without danger, however, for the one who employs it. Instead of providing a vision of the sheer brilliance of the created work, its incompetent use may simply serve to obscure the greatness of both creation and creator. A supposedly critical judgment that merely maintains that this or that is pathological can never, by proceeding from the meaning and content of a spiritual work, determine whether or not something in it should be attributed to sickness. It is unscientific and dishonest first to reject as pathological the work before us and then present the rejection as the result of an objective ascertainment of damning facts by way of a psychopathological investigation.

Only a few points of departure are available for answering the question as to the relation between Nietzsche's sickness and his work. Generally we are left with open questions which must be kept in mind as questions if we are to study Nietzsche properly. The *method* of empirically ascertaining connections between mental illness and work can only proceed indirectly. We follow two ways:

1. We may search for temporal coincidences. When changes in style, in ways of thinking, and in basic ideas *coincide* with a transformation of physical or psychical reality, a connection is then probable, unless the spiritual alteration can be understood in the same way as other spiritual transformations in the person under consideration. This method, because of its diagnostic indefiniteness, does not lead to an obvious result but to a total aspect of connections in which at the same time something is left open. Nietzsche's life does in fact exhibit parallels between the spiritual development of his work and the biographically ascertainable or presumed psychophysical changes.

a. The development of the various bodily illnesses since 1873 runs parallel to Nietzsche's spiritual "separations." But his illnesses during those years do not attain the character of a psychic change, their relation to any spiritual alteration being external and incidental. Although the

---

[50] Concerning this cf. my essay: *Strindberg und van Gogh* . . . Zürich, 1922, 2nd ed., Berlin, 1926.

fact that he never recovered is of extraordinarily incisive importance in Nietzsche's life, it is not of substantial incisiveness for the manner of his spiritual experiences. On the other hand, an indirect influence makes itself felt through the serious limitation of his ability to work and through the eye affliction which hinders his reading and writing. This is a contributing though not decisive reason for the aphoristic style which prevails in his publications after 1876. The process of dissociation, which understandably proceeds from causes within his development, is surely promoted by his invalidism but not conditioned by it.

b. Since 1880 the course of events and a different way of viewing it run parallel to a change in his entire work:

A new *style* is manifested by the forcefulness of his images, his increasingly mythical similes, the plasticity of his visions, the ring that his words now have, the impelling force of his diction, and the compactness of his language. Nature and landscape become more charged with life, more laden with destiny; it is as though he were united with them, and they became like his own self. Friends notice the new element: "You . . . have begun to find your form. Your *language,* too, is now really finding its fullest sounds" (Rohde, Dec. 22, '83).

A new and gradually increasing *activity* replaces mere contemplation and questioning and serves his determination to undermine Christianity, morality, and traditional philosophy, and substitute a new synthesis. Of course the direction of this determination was evident even during his childhood.

New *basic thoughts*—the idea of eternal recurrence, the metaphysics of the will to power, the radical thinking through of nihilism, the concept of the superman—now have for Nietzsche an extraordinary importance and mystery formerly unknown to him. Now they rest on original philosophical boundary experiences that overwhelm him for the first time. Many of these thoughts, including that of eternal recurrence, appeared in his earlier writings. But what previously seemed merely possible has become substantive; it now possesses the overpowering force of consuming truth.

For not only does Nietzsche possess consummate philosophic sensibility for the first time, but he now is moved and pervaded by original experiences of being to such an extent that everything previous—whether judicious or visionary, venerating or disparaging—can only appear as mere intellectual contemplation. Nietzsche now seems to speak from a new world.

The new retains an astonishing tension through the *fixation* of thoughts and symbols which now begins. What had formerly, as particular, been taken up and annulled in a process is now given absolute significance, without precluding the possibility that it will be loosened again in an intensified, violent movement. The most extreme nihilism is combined with an unconditional affirmation. The coexistence of sudden emptiness with forced symbols can produce a chilling mood in the reader, while in the very next moment precisely that which constitutes Nietzsche's most original philosophizing is expressed.

c. The resumption of the systematic creation of his main philosophical edifice during the year 1884 coincides with the diminution of the abrupt and overwhelming mystical experiences that, during the years 1881 to 1884, provided inspiration for his creations. The atmosphere becomes more rational. The incisive change during the years 1884 to 1885 is profound: Nietzsche's mental states and creations occur prior to it; after it, his systematically constructive and aggressive experiments predominate. "Revaluation" holds the stage. Reinhardt made the observation— surprising at first, then plausible even though not directly proven so far—"that not a single one of his poems originated during his last years. Even the poem 'Venice: At the Bridge . . . ,' so fondly thought of as testimony of a final bursting into song, had already come into being." [51]

Toward the end of 1887 and again of 1888, a repetition of the crisis of 1884 seems to occur that points toward the creation of the "main edifice," but in the place of work on the latter, the wholly unexpected forced tempo starts, together with the neglect of the task which up to this moment has been of paramount importance. The harbingers of the pending mental illness run parallel to the new writings. What is striking in these writings, however, is a change, not in the spiritual substance or in the significance of his thinking, but rather in his form of communication.

2. We examine Nietzsche for phenomena that are expected to occur as a result of organic processes. Since a reliable diagnosis that might relate to their occurrence before 1888 is lacking, we are not at present in a position to look for symptoms of a definite disease. In Nietzsche's case, the method of proceeding from a knowledge of pathological processes and their causes to what is known to belong to such processes is useless. All we can do is to assume the existence of an infra-mental biological factor, even of a diagnostically undefined type, and ask what changes in the appearance of his mental activity would be analogous to those which characterize *all* organic mental illnesses.

Nietzsche's work is not of the kind that could fill us with unqualified admiration. He has a capacity for stirring us deeply, awakening our most

[51] Reinhardt, *Die Antike* XI, 1935, p. 197.

essential impulses, intensifying our earnestness, and illuminating our insights; but that does not prevent him from repeatedly giving the impression of failing, of plunging into a void, as it were, or of having an oppressive effect through narrowness, immoderation, and absurdity. Perhaps this imperfection cannot be explained simply as the result of a movement that must remain open in accordance with the nature of his philosophical objectives; it cannot be regarded as a mere result of the dependence of the thought-contents on our own compelling readiness to appropriate them; nor can it be accounted for by saying that incompleteness belongs to the essence of all philosophizing. On the contrary, it would seem that something enters here that is not appropriate to this essence, something which, to be sure, did not become disturbing until 1881. It is of course not possible to differentiate with finality and complete objectivity between genuine openness demanded by the cause pursued and downright failure; but to raise the question is to become aware of our task: we must understand the disturbances in order to enter more decisively into the movement of Nietzsche's philosophizing. To put it briefly, there are three disturbances:

a. There is a lack of restraint which, because of Nietzsche's excessive fluctuations of mood, permits extremes, and which, by narrowing his view, allows him to present exaggerations in simplified form by expressing them in dogmatic antitheses. A decrease in wonted tactfulness and occasionally an uncritical attitude (previously impossible in their present form and never permanently dominant since the old impulses always regain control) lead to heedless polemics and increasing indiscriminate vituperation; but even in this there is a profundity which leads the reader astray by causing him to take even the blunders equally seriously—a source of bafflement and confusion until he learns to be discriminating in his appropriation. Nietzsche intentionally goes to extremes: on the one hand he tries to go to the utmost limit, not in order to remain fixated there, but rather to effect a dialectical union with the opposite. He also seeks the "magic of the extreme" which always has the advantage in the struggle. These two aspects of the extreme are clearly recognizable only when they are distinct from the extreme as it occurs unconsciously as a result of mere lack of restraint.

b. While the lack of restraint merely leads to immoderation or narrowness and distorts the true substance, though without obliterating it, Nietzsche's *estrangement* contains a second element: the period after 1881 with its new agitations brings him mystical experiences which are unlike anything that we can undergo, even though the limits which they attain and the beauty which their presentation reveals stir us profoundly.

Their "strangeness" moreover struck his contemporaries; after his last meeting with Rohde (1886) the latter wrote: "He was surrounded by an indescribable atmosphere of *strangeness* that at the time I found quite uncanny. There was something in him that I had not known before, while much that used to distinguish him was no longer present. It was as though he came from a land where nobody else lives." [52] Nietzsche himself refers to "the unspeakable strangeness of all my problems and illuminations" and states that several times during this summer people have testified to his strangeness (to Overbeck, Sept. 14, '84).

c. A third and indeed radical disturbance is occasioned at the end of 1888 through the *premature breaking off* of his spiritual progress by the paralysing illness. As a result of this, the development of Nietzsche's thinking remains in an incomplete state which is anything but characteristic of him. His work does not mature, as he himself confesses shortly before his unforeseen end. The place of this work is taken by the polemical writings of the last period—writings which are unparalleled in their raging tension, clairvoyance regarding specific matters, injustice, and overpowering diction. Thus Nietzsche's being, as he expresses it during the last year, does indeed forever remain problematical because of its premature termination. It is as though the most incisive, or rather the most decisive, spiritual event of the last century has been ruined from ambush by the indifferent causality of nature and thus prevented from attaining its inherent clear grandeur.

Now that we have followed the two paths to knowledge of the relation between Nietzsche's sickness and his work, we must pause to reflect upon the meaning and significance of our objective.

A question which may not be substantially decisive but which is of momentous significance for the whole understanding of Nietzsche is the one concerning the spiritual *transformation since 1880* and the possibility of its coincidence with a newly arising biological event. About this there exists at present no thorough investigation which is based upon and puts in order the entire material; this is the most urgent requisite for a Nietzsche biography. Möbius was the first one to recognize the incisive nature of the break, but he encumbered his insight with so much absurdity that he rightly did not gain any approval. The break as such, indistinct as its nature (or even its medical diagnosis) still is, becomes the more obvious to me, the more frequently I scrutinize the correspondence and posthumous material that is so far known to us.

It seems as though the transformation in Nietzsche's thinking and experiencing, beginning in 1880 and continuing into the year 1888, is

---

[52] O. Crusius, *Erwin Rohde*, p. 150.

such that the effect of the biological factor, the immediacy of vision in his new manner of experiencing, and the new philosophical substance stand to each other in a relation of undeniable identity. It is confusing for us to be suddenly asked to consider as illness or an unknown biological factor just that which Nietzsche rightly understood as a necessary development of his thinking, that which constituted the spiritual greatness and existential depth of his nature, or that which signified the enigma of his exceptional nature with its growing universal relevance. Our presentation might appear as an equivocation which—though with the proper stipulations—secretly overthrows and debases, to the point of inconsequentiality, the very subject that it purports to represent as irreplaceably significant within the whole. It might be said that this would reveal a spiritual creation and then immediately dismiss it as mere illness.

In answer to this we may reply that we nowhere assert such "identity" but, rather, that all we *know* of a person is always a particular aspect seen from one point of view and never the whole man; furthermore that the seeming and ever-puzzling change from one aspect to another, as though both were one and the same, points to the dark chasm into which we cannot penetrate. The fact that Nietzsche first attained his true stature with the break of 1880 does indeed belong among the mysteries of coming into existence and of being an exception—analogous to Hölderlin and van Gogh and yet again so different. The "sick" factors— if we can so designate the unknown biological factor, since it might be on a level with causalities of later recognized disease processes—*not only were of a disturbing nature* but may even have made possible what otherwise would not have eventuated. Now for the first time Nietzsche arrives at the sources with the immediacy of one who stands at the first beginnings. His nature, because of its wealth of possibilities for reflection and its basic characteristic of complete originality, is such that it calls to mind the pre-Socratic thinkers—but it does not do so before 1880. The stylistic blunders seem to spring from the same ground as that on which the unheard-of became expressible. It cannot be doubted that his poetic power increases. Omnipresent, as though the overcoming of difficulties were mere play, is above all the unperturbed assurance of success which is expressed in every syllable, together with the burning consciousness of being, as it rises from the depths of its source and becomes immediate language without the bleaching mediation of reflection. What at first impresses one as accidental and strange may suddenly appear as the most profound truth or the meaningful strangeness of the exceptional. The spirit imparts meaning even to the insanity, and so permeates the insane notes that they become indispensable to the work.

Thus Nietzsche's experience of the world crisis, an experience that really attains its full depth after 1880—his immense terror in the face of his visions of the future, his being consumed by the task of gaining a foothold in this moment in the history of the world when the horrible danger of dissolution is present and everything depends on man—coincides with the painful, intensified, and depressive states of an altogether different origin; the self-confidence which at times seems pathologically conditioned is also understandable and justified. Whoever desires to decide here with a clear Either/Or turns the enigmatic reality into something unequivocal, at the expense of possible truth which here requires that the enigma be acknowledged and the discoverable pursued in every possible way.

A threefold approach to the relation of Nietzsche's sickness to his work is therefore indispensable: first, that of the empirical investigation of the facts; second, after the criticism of his work, one that permits the removal from his work of those flaws which can be regarded as accidental disturbances resulting from illness, with a view to arriving at a pure conception of Nietzsche's way of philosophizing; third, the increasingly mythical envisioning of a total reality in which the illness seems to become a moment of positive meaning, of consummate expression of being, of unmediated revelation of something that otherwise would remain inaccessible.

Of primary importance for the first approach is the method of empirical science which never reaches the boundary of a knowledge that ultimately is all-encompassing. This is the condition for a self-restraining realization of the other two approaches; without it, the one—the critical one—would become an unmethodical and hence unrestrained criticism with the verdict "sick"; the other—the mythical view—would turn into unrealistic enthusiasm. An approach searching for the pure truth of Nietzsche will never be able to separate with finality from this truth everything that is not pertinent and should be eliminated for being *faux pas* or something meant to add color and tone for the sake of appeal. The mythical view of Nietzsche's total reality cannot be given communicable expression on our part. It is not possible to substitute, one for the other, the meaning of empirically ascertaining and critically cleansing utterances on the one hand and the mythical ones on the other; nor must they be confused.

Nietzsche's Attitude toward Illness. It is imperative that we distinguish between the two totally different questions concerning, first, Nietzsche's attitude toward his *medically* ascertainable or surmisable illnesses and, second, his way of speaking in an *existentially interpretative* manner of "being ill" and the function of illness within the totality of his life.

In asking first how Nietzsche reacted to his illnesses and interpreted and judged them medically, we must again differentiate: (1), the physical afflictions and violent disturbances since 1873; (2) the psychic changes since 1880, resulting from the "biological factor" that cannot be diagnosed medically; and (3) the psychosis at the end of 1888 and its prodromes during the previous year. These questions are raised with a view to ascertaining the attitude of the patient toward his illness (a factor that plays an important role in all therapy) and discovering what kind of insight he has into his illness (this being, for the psychiatrist, indicative of the nature of the affliction). It is always a question of how the patient himself sees his illness from the medical point of view—a viewpoint which, as a human being, he will be able to assume unless he is prevented from doing so by the disease itself. Our questions about Nietzsche take these three directions:

(1) Nietzsche's ways of dealing with those illnesses that appeared as physical afflictions (paroxysms, disturbances of vision, headaches, etc.) were at first in accordance with contemporary custom: he consulted physicians, specialists, and authorities, expecting them to prescribe only on the basis of rational knowledge. Nietzsche, however, was subjected to numerous ineffective treatments since many physicians apply therapeutic measures even when there is no rational basis for them, assuming that there is invariably—and not merely in particular, outstanding instances —a sensible, i.e., causally effective treatment. Going beyond the counsels of physicians, Nietzsche applied his own therapy on the basis of observations made on himself and of the hints which he came across in his reading. Not unlike physicians of positivistic persuasion and faith in scientific authority, he occasionally confused rational, empirically proven methods with positivistic notions of possibility. He probably succeeded to a certain extent in the methodical choice—using precise meteorological data—of the climate that was at least most suitable for him. For the rest, his life was fraught with necessarily uncertain experimental attempts: "All sorts of mixtures with which he treated himself stood on Nietzsche's stove in Basel," Overbeck reports concerning the period from 1875 on.[53] Later he employed all sorts of medicaments, salts, and, above all, rationally effective soporifics (considerable quantities of chloral hydrate), although the effectiveness of soporifics when used routinely is extremely questionable, and finally a tincture containing hashish which he probably had obtained from a Dutchman. Occasionally he showed

[53] Bernoulli, I, p. 167.

pride in his medical "invention": "I felt a sense of triumph when Dr. Breiting prescribed again for me the phosphoric potassium first used medicinally by myself; he has become fully satisfied concerning its effectiveness. I am thus the inventor of my own medicament. I am likewise proud of my rational typhoid treatment last winter. . . ." (to Overbeck, Oct. 27, '83).

However, this tribute to medical illusions does not constitute Nietzsche's accomplishment, for on the whole the illusions remain secondary and unimportant to him. His accomplishment lies in the fact that in spite of everything he liberated himself from constant consultation, occupation, and guidance through physicians. This liberation was a part of the self-treatment which prevented him, even during the gravest states of illness, from thinking and acting as though his illness were the crux of his life. While unable to escape destruction through an organic process, he could in the long run escape all the possibilities for hysteria, neurosis, anxiety, and busyness.

From a *medical* point of view, Nietzsche was mistaken in his prognosis. During the time (1880) when an improvement of physical sufferings was soon to begin and the great development in Nietzsche's thinking was about to start, he wrote in a farewell spirit to M. v. Meysenbug (Jan. 14, '80): "After several symptoms, the relieving cerebral stroke is close enough to me." He also wrote to others of his approaching end.

(2) The biological factor, noticeable in Nietzsche, we believe, since 1880, naturally could not be explicitly recognized by him, though he noted with astonishment the change in "taste" that *preceded* the new thought. But Nietzsche, as a cool observer, did occasionally focus his attention on the possible connection between spiritual creation and physical and biological processes. It was natural for him to be interested in this, though what he found was accidental. Thus for example: "Yesterday I figured out that the crucial climaxes in my 'thinking and poetizing' (*Birth of Tragedy* and *Zarathustra*) coincide with a maximum of magnetic solar influence while, on the other hand, my choice of philology (and Schopenhauer) (a kind of self-confusion) and likewise *Human, All-Too-Human* (simultaneously the worst crisis of my health) coincide with a minimum" (to Gast, Sept. 20, '84).

3) Nietzsche did not recognize his mental illness (scarcely ever does a person afflicted with paralysis have insight into his illness) and did not expect it. In the year 1888, when the changes in his emotional life and extreme tension already appeared as harbingers of the insanity that would soon overwhelm him, he possessed an unshakable confidence concerning his health. Nietzsche never considered the possibility of

becoming insane but very frequently, on the other hand, that of sudden death, cerebral stroke, or the like. He once wrote to Overbeck (May 4, '85): "I occasionally had a suspicion that you might be inclined to consider the author of *Zarathustra* whacky. My danger is indeed very great, but it is not of *this* kind."

Insofar as Nietzsche establishes the *significance* of illness in his *life*, the fact that every illness can also bring *advantages* is only of secondary importance. His illness procured for Nietzsche the desired liberation from his office through retirement; and in his situation it served to ease the strain of separation from human beings and things from which he had become estranged: "It spared me any break, any violent and offensive step." But in no way does this make Nietzsche's illness anything like a "neurosis of expediency": since it was deep-seated and rooted in the physical, its external consequences were merely incidental.

The interpretative method which Nietzsche uses in assigning to his illness a role in the totality of his spiritual creation does not derive from considerations of expediency or from empirically verifiable knowledge of causal relations gained through detailed observations: "I simply am not mere spirit or mere body, but still a third thing. I always suffer from the whole and within the whole. . . . *My self-conquest* is basically my greatest strength" (to Overbeck, Dec. 31, '82). It is on the basis of this third thing, his *Existenz,* which supports and directs both spirit and body and which is manifest in the all-absorbing movement of self-control, that Nietzsche's magnificent interpretation of his illness and his attitude towards it is elaborated. This existential interpretation transcends the categories of utility as well as the medical and therapeutic categories. In the following way it adds new dimensions to the concepts of illness and health:

Nietzsche's concepts of illness and health possess a peculiar ambiguity: Illness which derives from and serves true health—the health of *Existenz* which comes from within—is actually an indication of this health. Health in the medical sense, which typically belongs to a being without substance, becomes a sign of true illness. This interchangeability of the words "healthy" and "ill" produces an appearance of contradiction, for Nietzsche's pronouncements are as decisively in favor of illness and opposed to the self-satisfaction which comes of being in good health, as they are appreciative of health and contemptuous of illness. Repeatedly he turns with disdain against the inanity of those who, conscious of their own health, turn away from anything strange to them: "The poor creatures of course do not realize how cadaverous in color and how ghost-like their health looks." He stigmatizes the methods of the educated Philistine who invents, "for his habits, his viewpoints, his rejections and patronage, the universally effective term *health"* and gets rid of "any inconvenient disturber of the peace by suspecting him of being sick or eccentric." In opposition to this, Nietzsche asserts: "Actually it is an annoying fact that 'the spirit' is in the habit of descending with particular sympathy upon the 'unhealthy and unprofitable' ones." These formulations cannot conceal the fact that all Nietzsche's philosophizing favors health, disparages illness, and seeks to overcome all that is ill. Again it is the difference in the concept of health that makes this contradiction possible.

This concept, as Nietzsche realizes, is not ambiguous by accident. "Health as such does not exist. It is your goal that determines what health ought to mean even for your body. . . . The concept of normal health . . . must be given up. . . . Of course, health might appear, in one case, like the opposite of health in another." "Health and sickness are not essentially different. . . . We must not make distinct principles or entities of them. . . . Actually there are only differences in degree between these two kinds of existence. . . ."

What is thus determining in Nietzsche's existential interpretation is an idea of health that is not founded on biological or medical facts but considers the *worth* of man *in the totality of his existential rank.* Only when seen in this light do the strange discussions in which Nietzsche, as it were, appropriates his illness to himself gain their meaning: he relinquishes himself to it, he heeds, and he overcomes it. This process can be followed in detail:

Illness as a *natural happening* is, in accordance with such an interpretation, not of personal but only natural origin. Pursuing this path of interpretation requires a quite different level of thinking from that of causal insight. An existential meaning is injected into the meaninglessness of mere natural happening, without insisting, however, on the validity of a universal causality, which in this case would be of a magical, superstitious nature. Accordingly, something that wishes to communicate with *Existenz* brings forth the illness in order to be existentially effective through it. Nietzsche is grateful to his illness for its vitally decisive *contribution* to his spiritual growth. As he views the complex of situations in retrospect, he sees that, without being aware of it, he had wished to escape his real *task* through philology, professorial career, veneration for R. Wagner and Schopenhauer, and through his whole idealistic-romantic attitude: "My sickness alone brought me to my senses." "Sickness is the answer each time when we are inclined to doubt our right to *our* task, when we begin to make it easier for ourselves in some way.

. . . It is our alleviations for which we must pay most dearly!" But when sickness called Nietzsche back to his task, it did not disappear again. In accordance with his interpretation, however, Nietzsche expected until the very end that it would be overcome: "I have a task. . . . This task has made me ill, it will also make me well again. . . ." (to Overbeck, Nov. 12, '87).

Illness, no matter how it may have come about, is for Nietzsche still undetermined in its meaning. It depends upon what *Existenz* makes of it: "Illness is a clumsy attempt to attain health: we must come to nature's aid with our spirit." Thus Nietzsche reinterprets his continuing illness, and he does so, in fact, by the way in which he overcomes it: he enlists its service, so to speak; he recognizes its dangers and becomes master, if not of the sickness itself, at least of the dangers.

The illness, employed *in his service,* makes possible for him, as he believes, the peculiar nature of his new thinking: "My illness gave me the right to a complete reversion of my habits . . . it presented me with the *necessity* for lying still, for idleness, for waiting and being patient. . . . But that really means thinking!" And it also becomes a *means for experiencing and observing.* He reports to his doctor that he "made . . . the most instructive tests and experiments in the spiritual-ethical field particularly in this state of suffering—this joyous thirsting for knowledge lifts me to heights where I am victorious over all torment and all hopelessness" (to Eiser); and in *Ecce Homo* he recalls: "In the midst of torments which accompany an uninterrupted, three-day cranial pain together with troublesome vomiting of phlegm, I possessed a dialectician's clarity *par excellence* and very deliberately thought things through for which I am not enough of an acrobat, not cunning and not cool enough under healthier conditions." He interprets his illness finally as the impetus through which he, free of all external supports and all falsely idealistic triteness, without need for religion and art, is driven forward on the path of genuine self-reliance: "Concerning torture and denial, my life during my last years may be matched with that of the ascetic of any time; . . . only my complete loneliness made me discover *my own resources"* (to Malvida von Meysenbug, Jan. 14, '80).

At the same time however, sickness brings its new existential *risks.* Above all it can produce, according to Nietzsche's interpretation of his experiences, an arrogance that withdraws from all things and expresses itself in an insight that unmasks everything: When the states of illness teach one to look "out on things with a terrible coldness," when all the "little, deceitful enchantments" of life disappear, then the suffering person thinks "with contempt of the . . . nebulous world in which the healthy person moves without hesitation; he thinks with contempt of the noblest and dearest illusions . . . and with frightening clairvoyance . . . he admonishes himself: dare to be your own accuser . . . enjoy your superiority as judge. Rise above your suffering." Then as never before the pride of one who at least understands while being ill rears up "in veritable contortions of arrogance." But when the first dim rays of alleviation and recuperation appear, "the first effect is that we struggle against the dominance of our arrogance. . . . Away, away with this pride, we cry, it was a sickness and one more contortion! . . . We look again with longing eyes on people and nature. . . . We are not angry when the enchantments of health again come into play."

Illness, as Nietzsche interprets its existentially dangerous effect, can also mean that the content of thinking is inspired through *life,* i.e., through the *type of states* from which the patient thinks. Instead of urging the thinking on beyond itself, illness draws the thinking, so to speak, into itself. Nietzsche thus asks of *all* philosophizing whether it was not illness which brought it forth.

To free himself from the danger of having his thinking exhaust itself in the service of a dominant state of illness, Nietzsche tries to experience these states in such a way that, to be sure, he gives himself to them momentarily but does so only in order to oppose them more decisively through knowledge of them. He allows every state to speak within himself, but to none does he concede victory. He not only experiences the arrogance of cool clairvoyance, but also the intoxication of recuperation; and in this manner he views the healthy from the perspectives of illness, the sick from those of health. At one time he exposes his thoughts to the pressure of illness in order to see what will become of them, and at another time he subjects the sick thoughts to the criticism of health. Nietzsche thus becomes grateful to the illness that will not heal: "I [am] sufficiently aware of the advantage I generally have, in my changeable health, over all the stocky intellectuals. A philosopher who has made his way through many states of health and makes it again and again, has also gone through just as many philosophies; he simply cannot help but constantly transmute his condition into the most spiritual form and distance; philosophy is just this art of transfiguration." Sickness points "the way to many and opposing sorts of thinking." It becomes "the teacher of the great suspicion."

Gaining mastery over illness by finally making all forms of it indispensable to the promotion of knowledge and, in addition, overcoming the nihilistic thinking that appears during illness, presupposes, as Nietzsche implies, *real health;* the kind of health which "temporarily relinquishes itself body and soul to illness" and which "will not do without illness itself as a means and fishing hook of knowledge." "He whose soul thirsts [to] experience the entire scope of all prevailing values and desirable things [is] in need of the *great health:* the kind that one does not merely possess but repeatedly acquires at will and must acquire, because one gives it up again and again, and must give it up." This health has, in a manner of speaking, incorporated illness; it cannot become sick at all except as a means to its own end. The measure of this health of the spirit is "how much of sickness it can assume and overcome—make healthy." Because the road to real health can only lead through illness, Nietzsche is of the opinion that "precisely the sickly writers—unfortunately almost all the great ones are among them—usually have a much surer and more even tone of health in their writings because they are more skilled in the philosophy of mental health and recuperation than are the physically robust ones."

These principles of interpretation show that Nietzsche comprehends *his own illness* as a symptom of the very great health which vanquishes everything.

This becomes evident to him through his constant *will to health.* "If anything at all has to be said against being ill, against being weak, then it is this: that the actual instinct for getting well, i.e., the militant instinct in man, is softened up in it." But in taking hold of his illness, Nietzsche is conscious of his "tenacious will to health": " 'Forward!' I said to myself, 'tomorrow you will be well; today it suffices that you act healthy.' . . . The will to health itself, the pretending to be healthy, was my remedy."

In addition, however, Nietzsche is decidedly conscious of his *nature* as a *healthy* being. To be sure, he constantly laments his illness in his letters: "The element of uneasiness, helplessness, discouragement that is the consequence of my state of health" (to Overbeck, Dec., '85); in the end he even calls his earlier years "years of decadence" (to Gast, Apr. 7, '88). But in spite of all sickness he holds the basic conviction: "I took myself in hand, I made myself well again"; the condition for this is *"being basically healthy.* A typically morbid nature cannot become healthy and, even less, make itself healthy; conversely, for a typically healthy person, illness can even be an energetic stimulant to living." "My way of being ill and healthy is a good part of my character." "I lack any morbid trace in me; even in times of grave illness I did not become pathological."

The End

Each of the three parts in which we presented Nietzsche's life revealed a kind of ruin. His spiritual development could not reach fruition through his work; uncompleted, it remained a heap of ruins; Nietzsche's life was "for a hundred reasons an eternally problematic existence." His friendships led to the experience of a loneliness that is perhaps without parallel. Nietzsche's sickness not only terminated his life in a ruinous way, but as it gradually developed, it became so much a part of him that we can scarcely imagine him as living and working without it.

Above and beyond this, the extraordinary in the form of the immoderate is found everywhere in Nietzsche's life: the all-too-early call to a professorship, his difficulties with publishers compounded to the point of grotesqueness, his existence as a *fugitivus errans*. In his complete loneliness, Nietzsche's dialectic rose, in 1888, to boundless negations without providing any answer to the radical No but an indefinite Yes. This path could lead no further.

But previously, during the last decade, even mystical experience attained the perfect certainty of being: Nietzsche, in the Dionysian dithyramb "The Sun Sets," saw the day of his life ending:

> Thou shalt not thirst much longer,
> my scorched heart!
> From unknown mouths I feel a breeze,
> —the coolness great descends . . .

He speaks to himself:

> Stay strong, brave heart of mine.
> Do not ask: why?

116

His longing: "O gladness golden, come! Of death most secret, sweetest foretaste!" becomes fulfillment: "Round about only waves and play. What was too heavy, sank into blue forgetfulness"; he finds his way into boundless being:

> Silvery, light, a fish,
> my boat is swimming out.

Book Two

THE BASIC THOUGHTS OF NIETZSCHE

There is scarcely a vital subject that Nietzsche has not commented on. From his writings one may prepare compilations dealing with virtually everything, great and small: with the state, religion, morals, science, art, and music; with nature, life and illness; with work, man and woman, love, marriage, and family; with peoples, eras, history, historical personalities and contemporaries; and with the last problems of philosophizing. Taken singly, each one of these writings may be more or less weighty; but always the correct understanding of a specific utterance depends upon a grasp of the *characteristic aspects* of the movements of his thought and a knowledge of the *issues* that govern his thinking.

One arrives at the *characteristic aspects* of his thought in two ways: by following his limitless *negations* and by laying hold upon what is *positive*. Even in Nietzsche's negations, there are always present positive sources of an encompassing nature that express themselves indirectly through negation. On the other hand, the direct communication of the truth always contains implicitly the contradiction that again integrates the positions that seem most absolute into the all-encompassing movement —except when Nietzsche, contrary to his nature, becomes momentarily snared within a dogmatic fixation (something that produces a break in his thought and, in fact, is never carried to extremes).

To the very end, Nietzsche's problem as he sees it is to proceed from the negative to the positive. It is not to be supposed that after a merely critical period he suddenly comes into possession of a new faith. Always the hazard of not-being and the awareness of being are simultaneously present to him. Even at the very last he counts himself, with Burckhardt and Taine, among the radical nihilists, "although I myself have never despaired of finding the way out—the hole through which one arrives at the 'something' " (to Rohde, May 23, '87).

Right up to the time of his breakdown, negative and positive statements stand in sharp contradiction to each other. On the one hand: "I do not establish any new *idols*. . . . The *overthrowing* of idols (my word for 'ideals') is a part of my trade." And on the other hand: "After long years . . . I proceed to do again, even in public, what by myself I always do and always have done, namely, to paint images of *new* ideals on the wall."

In his view such contradiction expresses the only procedure that is absolutely necessary after "God is dead." He calls ideals "idols" when they are past, but they signify truth to him when they belong to the future. "He who no longer finds greatness in God does not find it at all—he must deny it or create it." Nietzsche intends to create it: "You call it the self-destruction of God; but He is only shedding His outer covering. . . . You shall see Him again soon, beyond good and evil."

What appears dual within Nietzsche's consciousness and in his actual conduct—denial and assertion, dissolution and creation, annihilation and generation—gives rise to a false problem when we expect an affirmative answer on the plane on which the negating judgment is valid: that of rational comprehension, expressible in terms which can be understood by everyone. At this point everything depends upon an original philosophic insight:

The rationally conceived universal as such is critical and negative, that is to say, the understanding (*Verstand*) by itself is dissective. Only the historical reality (*Geschichtlichkeit*) of the irreplaceable being that is not universal, that stands on its own and is one with its source, is positive. Such a being, however, remains not merely concealed, but even insubstantial until it gains illumination through the mediation of the understanding. Nietzsche did not possess, but unconsciously followed, this deep insight which led Schelling, its originator, to distinguish his negative from his positive philosophy. Denial, as the mode of appearance of rational comprehension, is itself affirmation in the service of historical reality. This latter, again, in expressing itself, enters the sphere of the rational and disintegrates when the movement is expressed in words. The rational always exists only as conditioned by something else, and its validity depends upon relations; the historical is a self-sufficient reality that fuses with the communications of self-becoming.

Without the scope of negative philosophy no positive philosophy is possible. Only in the purgatory of the rational can man truly become aware of his positive historicity. The latter becomes articulate only through the rational, by virtue of which it can, indirectly at least, lay hold upon its historical roots. Hence the positive, as the basis of the historicity of *Existenz*, employs all modes of rationality, surrendering itself wholly to them and yet guiding and uniting them on the basis of its own historical source. While the source cannot know itself, it illumines itself immeasurably within the universality of the knowable and its products.

When the positive appears in the form of direct statements, it becomes rational-universal and enters the area of limitless dissolution. For the positive must inevitably assume verbal form and become cognitive when it is absorbed within rationality—though within a rationality that is false because it does not understand its own nature. In the form of a universally cognizable doctrine, the positive is destroyed at its roots since the mere understanding makes it universal and abstract. This occurs in the most radical manner when the doctrine of the distinction between negative and positive (or rational and historical) philosophy is used to exclude the understanding, after which all rational tests are rejected in statements of an actually rational nature.

These considerations point the way to the issues that most deeply concern Nietzsche. Insofar as he expresses the positive directly, the content becomes questionable. Insofar as he searches and experiments, he establishes an extraordinary claim to possible *Existenz*. Nietzsche philosophizes in a new philosophical situation created during the centuries preceding him:

A *naïve* philosophy, capable of representing God and the world and man in it, is blind to the distinction between rationality and historicity; it can communicate its values through images and concepts with serene directness without necessarily falling into existential error. Later, after the collapse of naïveté, it can still provide retrospective esthetic satisfaction because of the simplicity and completeness of its work, and it can still appeal as a result of the *Existenz* that upholds it. But when, due to the collapse of the unquestioned totality of God, soul, and world, the distinction between rational universality and existential historicity finally becomes felt and known, then disturbing skeptical questions come to the fore within the sphere of the rational. To Nietzsche, these were: What is man? (Chapter I), What is truth? (Chapter II), and What do history and the present age signify? (Chapter III). Thereafter, being also is present in its historicity and even searched for in the will to the future (Chapter IV), as interpretation of the world at this instant (Chapter V), and as mystical unity of being (Chapter VI).

For Nietzsche these disturbing skeptical questions themselves contain an impulse that leads to positive results: a love of the nobility of man, condemned as that nobility is to despair of every realization; the inexorable earnestness of a truthfulness that calls the truth itself in question; and a comprehension of historical figures that comes to grief upon the senselessness and purposelessness of history.

Among his *positive* apprehensions we find the will to the future, expressed as a sketch of the "great politics," which is rooted in his always indeterminate concept of creativity (*Schaffen*). We also find a universal doctrine of the will to power—a doctrine that offers an inspiring view to those who lead the counter-offensive against nihilism, although it defeats itself by moving in a circle. And we find in mystical states an experience of being, expressed above all in the doctrine of eternal recurrence, which founders in paradoxes.

Nietzsche's contributions are by their very nature capable of being grasped only by those who can respond in kind. Hence Nietzsche's thought can sometimes appear empty while, on other occasions, it can be profoundly moving. It is indeed empty to those who are looking for something that is valid for all times; it comes as a fulfillment to those who can participate in the movement. When one's own feelings are inspired by Nietzsche's original motives, the negative developments of thought convey more than the positive statements which, in their false rationality, soon seem like empty husks. On the other hand the positive sayings may carry one away momentarily whenever it is possible to approach them symbolically and take them as *signa*. Finally the negative sayings can become tedious whenever no picture, creative thought, or symbol seems to remain within them.

In contrast to the greatest philosophers of the past, Nietzsche characteristically appears more truly himself in his negations than in his affirmations. The *ultimate goal* towards which the genuine, original driving force proceeds is not clear, although no serious reader can fail to be aware of the nature of this force: Nietzsche destroys confining horizons and offers unlimited space; he teaches us to raise critical questions, but his criticism, unlike that of Kant, does not set bounds to our inquiry; he presents a plethora of possibilities and awakens the powers that animate our innermost selves.

1

MAN

When all that has been generally accepted as true begins to seem untenable, Nietzsche becomes the more decisively concerned about man. From first to last he is spurred on by his discontent with man as he now is and by his longing for the realization of genuine human possibilities. Hence a fundamental feature of Nietzsche's thought is the movement of his love that, when disillusioned, expresses itself as a most frightful denial of human existence, only to reappear in the guise of a passionate affirmation of the essential nature of man:

Boundless and constantly recurring is Nietzsche's sorrow over men as they really are: "What arouses our repugnance today? . . . That such vermin as human beings can predominate and multiply. . . ." "There they stand, unaware of their wretchedness. And now as I proceed through their midst, revulsion devours my heart." Not one of them is a complete being: "It is always the same: fragments and limbs and revolting monstrosities—but no men!" They ruin everything with their talk and betray everything. "I should even refuse to inhale their breath." The paroxysm of disgust with man receives symbolic expression in the frightful sentence: "It is doubtful that a world-traveler has anywhere in the world discovered an uglier region than the human face." That love of man, however, is the genuine basis of this sorrow over man is expressed in the following memorandum: "As Chamfort used to say, he who does not become a misanthrope in forty years has never *loved* mankind."

Even the Saint (in *Zarathustra*) once loved mankind but now loves God instead: "I do not love man; to me he is too incomplete a thing. Love for man would be the death of me." Nietzsche, unlike the Saint, wishes to remain in the world in order to serve man. He believes that the Saint's love of the Godhead can be understood as a consequence of the same dissatisfaction with mankind that torments him. But he finds it objectionable that saints "wished to flee into a beyond instead of building

125

for the future." "Religiosity was a misunderstanding on the part of those higher natures who were tormented by the ugly image of mankind." Hence disgust with man is the great danger. When deeply moved, he must repeatedly go through whole days afflicted by "a feeling blacker than the blackest melancholy, contempt for man." This contempt itself is a transition, for "the great despisers are the great worshippers."

Consequently, Nietzsche *resists his own disgust:* "My disgust with man had become too great, as had the accompanying disgust with the moral arrogance of my own idealism. I drew closer to him whom I held in contempt, and I sought within myself all that of which I was contemptuous. . . . I took sides against all the accusers of mankind." At this point he imposes a demand upon himself: "For me there shall be no man who arouses my disgust or hatred." "Was not the one who was most contemptuous of man, for that very reason, man's foremost benefactor?" Furthermore, he finds that clearly "I love man, and I love him most when I oppose this propensity."

Nietzsche's *longing* for the genuine man, while giving rise to his contempt, is nevertheless the force that moves and consumes him: "How does it come about that I am forever *hungering* for men that do not become small at the sight of nature or at the thought of a walk over the fortified hills of Genoa? Is it just that I don't know how to find them?" Zarathustra is puzzled to discover that such sorrow as this is never shared by others: "You are sorry for yourselves but not for mankind. . . . None of you is grieved by that which grieves me." The complaint almost takes the form of abhorrence, and then of adjuration: "What is it that I in particular find totally unbearable? . . . That I must smell the guts of a poorly fashioned soul! Basically everything else can be dealt with. . . . But from time to time, if there are any heavenly patronesses, may I be granted a glance—only one glance—at something perfect, something that has attained its end, something happy, powerful, triumphant, . . . a glance at a man who justifies mankind, a complementary and redeeming fortunate instance of a man for whose sake one can stoutly maintain his belief in mankind."

In spite of the above, Nietzsche's final position involves *affirmation of man just as he is* with all his possibilities. His previous attitude—"I have thoroughly searched among men without finding my ideal"—is overcome. In the end, the mere wish is contrary to his nature; he finds man admirable and venerable. He is contemptuous of "man as we wish him to be, and, generally speaking, of all ideals of man." "What justifies man is his reality." The actual man is far superior to some man or other who is merely wished for or dreamed about—some possible ideal man. Questions of desirability in relation to man are "absurd digressions." Still such affirmation does not mean contentment and passivity: "The unwarped man delights in the fact of man and the ways of man, but still continues onwards!"

The fact that everything which we find to be actual, lovable and honorable, or even contemptible is, in the last instance, accessible to us only in human form, and only in the fashion in which men can experience being, leads Nietzsche to the basic question: *What is man?* This question does not relate to a clearly demarcated and fully determinate object, but to the encompassing that we are (*das Umgreifende, das wir sind*). Still, to answer it, I must seize upon something determinate. This may be the empirically observable existence of man, in which case I objectify his subjective states. It may be what human beings have believed to be objectively valid (reason, morality, and God), in which case I take these beliefs for my objects, thus objectifying them, even while, by regarding them as mere opinions of men, I relativize them. Or I may seize upon an ideal of man, though always the ideal in determinate form is unreal and untruthful.

I may thus investigate man psychologically or interpretatively, but I never stand apart from him as though he were observably alien to myself in the sense in which a mere thing within the world is alien. On the contrary, I am what I investigate, either actually or potentially. Hence the knowledge of the existence of man, of his place in the world, and of his boundless variability involves, explicitly or implicitly, a relation to the possibilities of my own behavior. Thinking is no longer simply a search for knowledge: it becomes an *appeal to my freedom*. The question of the nature of man relates to a number of further questions: What does man *will* to make of himself, and what *can* he make of himself? What *purpose* is his transformation to serve? Consequently man has two profoundly different attitudes toward himself: He can *observe and investigate himself* as an existence that simply is of such and such a nature and that undergoes alterations in accordance with discoverable laws, and he can also submit to criteria and *impose upon himself demands* which must honestly be acknowledged if he is to insure his own regeneration. He cannot actually do the one without the other, for a complete and final separation would cripple or impoverish his attitudes. However a methodological separation is unavoidable as a temporary expedient. We call the observation of man's existence "anthropology" and "psychology," while the making of demands upon his innermost nature we call "philosophy." Psychology investigates, makes discoveries, and predicts. Philosophy appeals, projects possibilities, and prepares the way for decision.

But tacitly present in all human psychology is an interest in possibilities and an appeal for further self-development, just as, in all philosophy, psychology continues to function as a means of expression as well as a condition without which the philosophical appeal would remain thin and insubstantial.

For purposes of exposition it is necessary to separate, when possible, what really belongs inseparably together within the whole: First of all Nietzsche undertakes an objective study of the *existence* of man as it undergoes constant psychological change within the larger theater of the world. In the second place, he seizes upon the *freedom* of man as the way in which he realizes himself. And finally, turning away from human actuality, he sees in the *symbol of the superman* a creed which expresses in an indefinite manner what man will become when he conquers himself. The range of Nietzsche's knowledge of man becomes for the first time evident in this thoroughly devastating development of a kind of thinking that proceeds through contradictions.

The Existence of Man

When man lays hold upon his source, he is more than mere existence (*Dasein*): He is a being that changes and realizes himself by his own efforts. But throughout all ramifications of his being he continues, *in addition to* everything else, to live at the level of existence.

Insofar as Nietzsche (with the purpose of his philosophizing always in mind) considers existence, he attempts, first, by the use of comparisons, to determine *the position which man really occupies within the world* and, second, to investigate man in all his psychological *variability*.

What Man Is in the World. Nietzsche looks out upon the world, asking what the presence of man in it signifies.

The age-old experience of *the vanishingly small importance of man* in relation to the universe is expressed when Nietzsche finds it to be true of the organic "that the mere drop of life within the world is insignificant in relation to the whole character of the monstrous ocean of all that comes into being and passes away." "Life upon the earth is an instant, a brief episode, an exception without consequence"; man is only "a small over-strained kind of animal whose days are numbered."

In order forceably to convey the impression of the contrast between man's nullity and his presumption, Nietzsche toys with the following thought: "If God created the world, then He made man His ape to provide constant amusement during His overlong eternities." But the curious self-consciousness of man stands in contrast to his role: "What is the vanity of the vainest of us in comparison with that of the most modest, in view of the fact that the latter feels himself to be a 'man' within nature and the world!"

In view of the immeasurable extent of the universe, these considerations lead Nietzsche to a paradoxical thought-experiment (*Gedankenversuch*): *Inorganic nature* is genuine being. Its unlimited becoming is devoid of deception; hence to flow into a unity with this nature is the proper consummation of man: "To be redeemed from life and to return to dead nature can be an occasion for celebration." "We become wholly true. . . . Death must be reinterpreted! Through it we become reconciled with the actual, that is to say, with the inanimate world!"

Within the world of the animate, *man is comparable to an animal.* Indeed it is as though "we, together with all nature, press onward toward man as toward something that stands high above us." But with a shudder we find that "here is where the refined beasts of prey are in action, and we are right in their midst. . . . Their founding of states, their warmaking, . . . their ways of deceiving and trampling on each other, their screams when in distress and howls of joy when in victory—all this is a continuation of bestiality." Hence the many phrases in which Nietzsche calls man a beast: "Man is the foremost beast of prey," and when "this mad melancholy beast known as man . . . is to some degree prevented from being bestial in his acts, at once the bestiality of his ideas breaks out." "Man is the most cruel animal"; what is more, he is "the most courageous animal," and, "when he thinks, he is an animal that judges."

But in fact, *man is not an animal.* It is only because he distinguishes himself from the animals that it is so frightful to him to be like an animal, or even to be able to be so. What is decisive is the source of his fright—the nature of the difference between man and animal. The very fact that man was victorious in his struggle with all the animals gives him a special status. But the essential difference, marked by a sharp break in the series rather than a movement along a continuum, is due to the capacity of man's *self-consciousness* to distinguish itself—whatever else it may be capable of doing. Man, according to Nietzsche, knows himself to be different from the animals in having memory, for example. Erroneously, according to Nietzsche, man believes himself to be distinguished by his freedom. Becoming conscious of himself, he has a self-contradictory attitude toward the animal: he can envy it on account of what appears to be its fortunate condition, or he can observe the accursedness of bestial life: "One can imagine no blacker lot than that of the beast of prey."

In the second place, the essential difference is brought out by Nietzsche when he considers man as the source of as yet undetermined possibilities: In contrast to the animals, every one of which behaves in accordance with the laws of his species, man is "the animal that is *still not fixated* (*das noch nicht festgestellte Tier*)." That is to say that man is indeed no longer merely an animal, but a being whose nature is still to be determined. The indeterminacy of his boundless possibilities carries with it the threat of disorder, with the result that he appears as a sickness with which existence is infected: "That which has brought man victory in his struggle with the brutes has also brought about his perilous pathological development." Consequently "there is a basic flaw in man." The metaphorical assertion that man is a sickness is recurrent: "The earth has a skin, and this skin is diseased. One of its diseases is called man." But when Nietzsche speaks of man as the animal of a still undetermined nature, he has a double sense in mind. In the first place, the evolution of this sickness called man is a *fundamental error,* but, in the second place, it is precisely this sickness that constitutes his *true worth.*

Man's "sickness" is shown by the fact that human development rests upon radical errors. Man became "human" only through illusion and folly: "The beast within us insists upon being lied to. . . . Without erroneous moral assumptions man would have remained a beast." The errors that were indispensable to the development of humanity are reducible to the "basic view that man alone is free in a world of the unfree; that he is the eternal miracle-worker, the super-animal, the demi-god, the meaning of creation, the one whose non-existence is unthinkable, and who furnished the key to the riddle of the cosmos." Consequently, man is "a highly mendacious, artificial, and opaque animal." The disease of humanity, "in contrast to the condition of the animals, all of whose instincts are adapted to very specific tasks," is expressed by the fact that man, being a mere bundle of unfulfilled possibilities of "indeterminate nature," "abounds in contradictory evaluations and, consequently, in contradictory desires."

What makes man sick is precisely that which constitutes his value. The sickness itself becomes the *bearer of value.* For example, in connection with the specific disorder of humanity which the priestly type represents to Nietzsche and which he so radically rejects, he adds that it was first as a result of this essentially dangerous priestly type of human existence that "man could become an interesting animal at all and that here for the first time the human soul, in a higher sense of the words, gained *depth* and became *evil*—the two basic forms in which, up to the present, human superiority to the other animals has appeared!" And, above all, the reason for the sickness is the greatness of man. For how does it come about that man, more than any other animal, is sick, insecure, variable, indeterminate, and undecided? "Surely he has ventured, innovated, challenged, and defied fate more than all the other animals together: man, the great experimenter with his own self, the discontented and never-satisfied one who contends with animals, nature, and the gods for final dominion; man, who has not yet been vanquished and who is ever of the future."

Hence when Nietzsche can say on one occasion that "man represents no progress beyond the animals," what really concerns him, in connection with the man who is not truly a man, is that he is becoming like an animal (i.e., that he conforms to a definite, fixated type of existence); that the "diminution of the human type—his approach to mediocrity—" occurs; that while he imagines himself to be rising within civilization, he is really sinking; and that "cultivation of all the virtues by means of which a herd prospers simply develops the herd-animal in man," with the possible result that the animal "man" will thus become set in a conventional form.

What Nietzsche means by these characterizations of man is sometimes ambiguous. While seeming to speak objectively about an existence that distinguishes man from the animals, he touches upon just that *boundary of existence* (*Daseinsgrenze*) that belongs only to man as such. All the indeterminacy, untruth, and sickness that appear as a loss in man are actually the possibility of a genuine source (*Ursprung*) that eludes all inflexibly objective observations. Since Nietzsche's philosophy, however, is directed toward this source, it employs knowing and psychologizing only as means.

Man as Basically Alterable. That man is the animal "that is still not fixated" signifies his nearly boundless alterability. The primary propulsion back of this has its source in man, who wishes to project himself into existence. But this source and the humanity that proceeds from it first become psychologically visible as existence in specific actual opinions, evaluations, and purposes, and in the orderliness of the psychical events and transformations that derive from them. A number of different possibilities are open to the latter. Man's lack of fixation permits one drive to be concealed by another and even to be transformed into its opposite. It is at this point that Nietzsche develops his magnificent psychology—the *unmasking* psychology in the use of which he was a master, and which, together with the psychology of Kierkegaard, gave rise to all subsequent psychology of this type (which often, being sundered from the extensive mental context in which Nietzsche places it, amounts to little more than a series of superficialities, banal repetitions, and pragmatic applications). A survey of the basic features of this psychology should relate the wealth of Nietzsche's thought to the underlying decisive concepts:

The framework within which Nietzsche's psychological understanding (*Verstehen*) occurs is composed of (1) *the fundamental relation of man to himself* when he sees and evaluates himself, deceives himself about himself, and proceeds to mould himself; and (2) *the operation and transformation of drives.*

(1) *Reflexive behavior.* It is next to impossible to see one's self. It seems unavoidable that we have a better view of external things than of our own natures and internal processes. That men know what they really intend and what they have done, Nietzsche calls the "primordial delusion." The view we have of other selves is scarcely better: "One always stands a few steps too close to himself, and a few steps too far from his neighbor. That is why one judges his neighbor in too wholesale a fashion, and himself in the light of specific features and happenings that are trivial and incidental." The views we take of ourselves depend only to a slight extent upon what we actually are and do; for the most part they are suggested to us by others. "The poets and artists were the first" to provide "frameworks for this purpose."

In spite of our lack of self-knowledge, we *evaluate ourselves* constantly. Our judgments may be located, first, on a scale between the extremes of self-confidence and self-distrust. Only a few have "faith in themselves." Some of these simply possess it as "a useful blindness," while "the others are forced to acquire it. They use all their accomplishments primarily as an argument against the indwelling skeptic. They are the great self-detractors," i.e., they are constantly at pains to justify faith in themselves because they live by high standards. But such things are rare. What is common everywhere is rather "inner mistrust"; this lies deep "in the hearts of all dependent men and herd-animals." It can be conquered only through affirmations that come from without: "through the luster of an untarnished name and corroboration of all kinds." One should not be deceived by the fact that the self-distrust of the majority of men does not produce hesitation and modest conduct, but rather an exalted self-consciousness: "It has intoxicated itself in order to avoid trembling."

Second, self-evaluation is carried out between the poles of self-respect and self-contempt. The *self-contemptuous man* is ashamed to the depths of his being; his auto-intoxication produces a habitual state of hostility: He who "is discontented with himself is always prepared to avenge himself: we others will be his victims." Hence "one thing is necessary" for the community of mankind: "that man become self-satisfied." At the same time a certain remnant of self-respect is always present: "He who despises himself still respects himself as a despiser." But genuine self-respect is the cardinal trait of the aristocrat. The self-respect of the majority—as opposed to the consciousness of the aristocrat, rooted as it is in being—does not refer to one's entire existence, but only to one's possibilities: "Everyone has his good day when he finds his higher self." Men deal differently with this higher self: many of them "become their own play-actors" and "many fear the higher self because it makes claims upon them." Finally, self-admiration, the perversion of self-respect, means the loss of true self-being: "The most highly endowed person no longer has anything to offer when he admires himself. . . . In looking up to himself he becomes his own servant and worshipper; he can only obey, that is, imitate himself."

Our inability to see ourselves, along with those propensities to self-evaluation that parade as self-knowledge, causes us to live in constant *self-deception.* What we really are is concealed from us in a number of ways: (a) The framework within which we view ourselves is determined by *language.* Since words are usually names of extreme states, and since, where words leave off, what exists for us usually leaves off as well, the appearance of the self conveyed by those few states which have names and are present to awareness is bound to be discrepant with what we really are. (b) Unconsciously we seek out the *principles* which conform to our temperaments: "Our thought and judgment are subsequently taken to be causes of our nature." We interpret ourselves intellectualistically. (c) *Success* leads to falsification: "Success often satisfies the conscience by glorifying the deed, but failure casts the shadow of remorse over the most honorable act." At the start "the motives and intentions are seldom clear and simple enough, and at times even the memory would appear to be obscured by the success achieved." (d) The *image of our past* must be agreeable to us. "One forgets much of his past and deliberately excludes it from his memory. . . . We are always actively engaged in this kind of self-deception." (e) We are contaminated by *the views which others take of us:* "What we know of ourselves is not decisive for our happiness. . . . At times we are suddenly overwhelmed by what others know of us (or think they know of us), and we realize that their opinions can overpower our own."

If follows from the above that the self for which we consciously live is by no means our actual self: the vast majority live their whole lives "only for the phantom of an ego. . . . Consequently all of them together reside in a cloud of impersonal opinions and arbitrary or, one might say, fictitious, evaluations. This cloud of opinions comes very close to having a life of its own, independent of the people that it envelops: from it derives the enormous effect of universal judgments about 'man.' "

Man, though blind to himself and captivated by his own self-deceptions, still manages—in spite of the self-evaluations by which he lives—*to mould his own nature*. To mould himself would appear to be the highest possibility open to man: "In man, creature and creator are united." The first step is *self-control* of the most familiar kind: "When self-control is lacking in small things, the ability to apply it to matters of importance withers away. Every day in which one does not at least *deny* himself some trifle is badly spent and a threat to the day following." Impetuosity always tends to overpower self-control, and Nietzsche develops methods for resisting it. If self-control is to be accomplished, one must know what has happened and plan everything that he undertakes. Speaking figuratively: "You must eat not only with your mouth but also with your head, or your mouth's gluttony will destroy you." One must pursue a kind of self-control that involves liberation and release if he is to avoid the hazard of being unable to trust the free beat of his own wings and of constantly having to take up arms against himself: "For one must at times be able to lose himself if he intends to learn something from what is alien to us." Self-control is ruinous when it becomes *self-assault*. It is then an expression of the cruelty of the will to power that torments itself from sheer delight in the production of suffering. In contrast to this, the Greeks with their reasonable and moderate regulations were wise: "They accepted the all-too-human as unavoidable and, instead of denouncing it, preferred to give it a sort of second-class justification by incorporating it in the rites of society and the cult. It was usual to provide a moderate release for evil and questionable impulses instead of attempting to annihilate them completely. . . . The Greeks were content to accept evil in moderate doses that were neither fatal nor thoroughly contaminating to everything affected."

(2) *Drives and Their Transformations*. Man scarcely knows the drives that constantly propel him. He has names only for the grosser ones. Their number and strength, their ebb and flow, their play and counterplay, and, above all, the laws governing their nourishment remain unknown to him. Thus it comes about that the nourishment of drives is a matter of luck: daily events toss their booty now to this and now to that drive. Our experiences are a food scattered before us by a blind hand. Each drive views the events of the day as possible means to the achievement of its purposes; hungrily it manipulates, as it were, every state of affairs in which man finds himself.

Insofar as possible, drives avoid whatever might prove resistant. But usually their satisfaction is frustrated by the actualities of the situation, for circumstances induce or force men to inhibit (*hemmen*) or suppress (*unterdrücken*) their drives. Unsatisfied drives, however, find various means of release.

The suppression of drives alters the condition and essence of human beings. "All instincts *turn inward* when deprived of outward discharge. This is how what is later called the 'soul' develops within man. The entire inner world, originally as thin as though pressed between two taut skins, expands and becomes distended—attains depth, width, and height—to the extent to which outward release has been inhibited."

Because inhibition is the source of the growth of the soul and the products of the spirit, as well as of perversions and falsifications, it is characteristic of it to work sometimes affirmatively and exhortingly and, at other times, negatively and with intent to conceal: [1]

Abandonment of the urge to believe in God, of the God-founding instinct, and of the need for this guardian and friend is for Nietzsche an example of the *positive* influence of drive-inhibition: "There is a lake that one day resisted the urge to be drained and erected a dam at its outlet. Since that day the lake has risen higher and higher. . . . Perhaps man will climb ever upward when he no longer *pours forth his soul into a God* (*in einen Gott ausfliesst*)." An example of a *negative* result: "To think of revenge and carrry it out is a brief affair like an attack of high fever; to think of revenge without the power and courage to carry it out is to go about poisoned in body and soul." Inhibition is, on the one hand, the source of the development of the human soul and, on the other, the source of the soul's deceptions, degenerations, illnesses, and infections, since all of these proceed from transformations caused by the inhibitions of drives. In all these psychological observations, the negative side predominates. Nietzsche exposes above all the feeling of power in its various disguises, as well as the resentment of the powerless who embrace ideals only to employ them as an indirect way of attaining superiority. Nietzsche distinguishes especially the following general psychological types of transformation:

(a) *Gaining satisfaction from the unreal.* While hunger cannot be satisfied by delights that are merely dreamed of, most drives can. It is not only our dreams that have the tendency "to compensate, within limits, for that unfortunate failure to find nourishment," but our waking life also has the capacity—although without the freedom of interpretation that is

---

[1] Reading *verschleiernd* for *entschleiernd.*—Trs.

found in dreams—to read meanings into things: "The significance that an occasion has for us depends upon which one of our drives happens to be in the ascendency." And it is also true that any event will be radically different according to the type of person one is. Our experiences are "much more what we put into them than what they originally contain": Lived experience is a fabrication. An elaborate world of symbols, which depends upon the kind of "delights dreamed of," unfolds before us: Whatever things and ideas symbolize within experience becomes their misleading actuality.

(b) *The release of tensions in inappropriate ways.* Whenever a normal outlet for a man's drives is lacking and, in addition, he is too weak and powerless to obtain what he wants and become what he would like to be, a poisonous tension arises within his soul. It seeks to find release through some substituted tangible reality, be it only indignant scolding or destructive activity: "Even the soul must have certain swamps for draining off its filth. This purpose is served by persons, situations, social classes, the fatherland, the world—or even the dear Lord himself." This stream, in the form of never-ending slander, may be harmless: "The slanderous talk of other people is often not really meant for us but is simply an expression of vexation or ill humor that springs from some entirely different source." However the release can easily become more active: "A man who has failed in some task would rather blame his failure on the evil will of someone else than on accident, . . . for one can *avenge* himself upon persons, but he must simply swallow accidental hardships." Nietzsche sees in Pauline Christianity an example of the way in which this psychological transformation and the subsequent need for release can take charge of the whole man: "Even Paul believed that a sacrifice was necessary in order that God's profound displeasure with sin could be overcome. Since that time Christians have never ceased to look for a victim on whom they could vent their discontent with themselves. Some good thing or other must die for their sins, whether it be the world, or history, or reason, or joy, or the peaceful contentment of other men."

Nietzsche also applies this psychology of release through substitute activity directed towards substitute objectives to the understanding of many criminals: Either the criminal himself fails to comprehend his intentions and his actions, or whatever comprehension he has is falsified by misunderstanding.

Finally, Nietzsche's psychology regards the simple method of talking-out as the most essential, wholesome, and safe kind of release. People have good reason to be grateful to the priests "upon whom they could unload their secrets, their cares, and even worse things (for he who expresses himself is freed from himself; and he who has 'confessed' forgets). Here is a compulsion of great urgency." Still this relief through confession is equivocal. For it is precisely as the result of confession that people of certain temperaments become thoroughly embittered.

(c) *Sublimation* is what Nietzsche calls the transformation of coarse drives into refined ones. "When a drive becomes more intellectual, it acquires a new name, a new stimulus, and a new value. It is often contrasted with the previous state of the drive as a sort of contradiction." To Nietzsche, for example, there is, "strictly speaking, neither such a thing as unselfish behavior nor completely disinterested contemplation. These are simply sublimations in which the essential element would appear to be so volatilized that it is discoverable only through the most refined observation." Thus Nietzsche speaks of "men with sublimated sexuality." For the sex-drive is capable of "great refinement through the intellect (love of mankind, worship of Mary and the saints. . . . Plato took love of knowledge and philosophy to be a sublimated sex-drive). Meanwhile its old direct effectiveness prevails." "The degree and kind of a man's sexuality penetrates to the highest reaches of his spirit." Furthermore, when esthetic experience makes its appearance, sensuality is not dethroned but merely transformed.

Sublimation can take place only as a result of *inhibition*. During "periodic intervals of restraint and fasting" the drive learns how to "knuckle under and grovel, but also how to purify and intensify itself. . . . This provides a clue to the explanation of the paradox that precisely in Europe's Christian period . . . the sex drive became love (*amour-passion*) as a result of sublimation."

For the most part Nietzsche regards sublimation simply as an alteration of the old drive, without expressly acknowledging that the spiritual has a new source of its own. At the same time this source is tacitly presupposed in the following: "The man who has conquered his passions has come into possession of a fertile field. To sow the seed of good spiritual works on the soil of subdued passions is the thing that must be done next. The conquest is a means rather than a goal: unless this is realized, all manner of weeds and other devilish things will grow up on the rich soil that has just been abandoned, and soon the goings-on will be madder and lustier than ever before."

(d) *Forgetting* is not simply an automatic memory-process, but a requirement of life for the success of psychic absorption of experiences: "Forgetfulness is no mere *vis inertiae*. . . . Rather it is an active and, in the strictest sense, positive inhibitory power which is responsible for the fact that whatever we live through, experience, and ingest, no more enters our consciousness during the process of digestion (one might even call it in-soul-ization) than does bodily nourishment (incorporation). . . . Anyone in whom this inhibitory apparatus is damaged accomplishes nothing." Memory, furthermore, is effected by those drives that are intent upon retention: "Memory takes account only of facts that the drives acknowledge; it learns only what has been transformed into the object of a drive! Our knowledge is the weakest form of our conative life; that is why it is so powerless to oppose strong drives." On the other hand, transformed drives are entirely capable of inhibiting and falsifying our memories. "My memory says: 'I have done this.' My pride, remaining obstinate, says: 'I cannot have done it.' In the end my memory gives in."

Nietzsche observes that psychologically causal mechanisms play a role in these transformations (*association, habit, fatigue*). Spontaneously and without express intention, he employs most of the possible theoretical concepts of extra-conscious mechanisms, but he does not develop them methodically.

Drives are not only transformed by the restraints imposed upon them; they may also be *subdued* or even *obliterated*. "A people's culture" is revealed to Nietzsche on a large scale "in the uniform restraint of their drives." Each man's strength is the natural and unperverted integration of his drives in the pursuit of a goal. But Nietzsche also recognizes the possibility of forcing drives to disappear entirely and without residue when he shows how, in the end, the passions themselves can be rendered powerless through suppression of their appropriate speech and gestures, or when he calls for the weakening and extirpating of the needs which were formerly satisfied by religion and are now to be satisfied by philosophy.

Nietzsche distinguishes the *types of drives* in many ways: some derive from a surplus of energy, others from a void; some are continuous, others periodic; some are unchanging needs requiring repeated satisfaction, while others grow apace, will settle for nothing, become increasingly hungry as they are fed, and undergo essential changes as they develop. There are countless names for drives: the desire for pleasure and for struggle, the will to power, the desire to excel (*agonales Bedürfnis*), the will to truth, the craving for knowledge, the need for rest, the herd-instinct, etc. Nietzsche recognizes that every psychology of motivation is also an indication of the nature of the psychologist who accepts it— especially when there is a tendency to recognize only one drive as genuine: "Whenever anyone constantly seeks, sees, and cares to see only hunger, the sex-drive, and vanity, as though these were the only possible genuine motives . . . any true lover of knowledge should listen diligently," for he will here receive instruction about facts "from a scientific head on the body of an ape, an exceptionally fine intellect grafted onto an ordinary soul—no rare occurrence among physicians and moral physiologists." Subsequently Nietzsche himself reduces all drives to a single one: the will to power. Thus he offers not only an account of a *multiplicity* of drives, but also a doctrine of *one single* basic force.

The above brief sketch of Nietzsche's psychological formulations refers to an extensive area of Nietzschean thought that is unusually self-sufficient and complete. But while the average man is inclined to regard this portrait of himself as an adequate likeness, Nietzsche sees in it only a perspective on a plane that he cultivated extensively but was quick to transcend. At any rate these thoughts belong to the small portion of Nietzsche's world that has been added to our climate of opinion by the popular representatives of an unmasking psychology.

This clarification of the self, articulated as a psychology of motivation, is actually for Nietzsche only a moment in the whole development that man's attitude toward himself undergoes. Though in the absence of such a clarification man remains bewildered and unclear, he does not become free as a result of it, but rather founders by simply surrendering himself to his psychological cognizability. Man comes to himself by passing through this phase, already guided by a new goal, and sustained by an impulse that immediately transforms the realm of the knowable into the realm of freedom and changes psychological observation into an inner activity. It is with these further advances that Nietzsche is genuinely concerned. Only for their sake is the unveiling psychology—this "school of suspicion"—needed. The distrust that it generates is intended only as a stage through which one must pass.

Whatever man may be, he is *not* the presumed existence and set of events which is comprehended by the psychology of motivation. His true being is not apparent from his momentary condition, subject as it is only to the rules which govern psychological variability.

Man as His Own Creator (Morality)

Man's "freedom" means that his alterability involves more than changes in accordance with those natural laws that apply to all existence: he is responsible for his own transformation.

During the entire course of history this transformation has been brought about by *morality*. We apply the term "moral" to those laws to which human conduct and attitudes have been subjected in order that men may thereby for the first time become what they are. The contemporary world claims to acknowledge Christian morality. When one's faith wavers, he still regards "morality" as self-evident. As modernism becomes godless, it regards morality as a solid ground upon which it still stands and by whose laws it lives.

Nietzsche attacks morality in every contemporary form in which he finds it, not in order to remove men's chains, but rather to force men, under a heavier burden, to attain to a higher rank. He becomes aware that the *value* of morality poses a significant problem. In all the stages of philosophy (even the skeptical), morality was considered to possess the highest value. All creeds were very much alike in this respect. "He who is willing to dismiss God clings all the more firmly to the belief in morality." Consequently, once the problem of morality is posed, it becomes, in Nietzsche's opinion, so radical as to call in question what for thousands of years has been too obvious to be challenged.

By assailing and disavowing the moral law and freedom, both of which have been vital realities within human experience, he hopes to issue *a new challenge* which will arouse what is genuinely and distinctively human. What was called freedom becomes *"creation"* (*Schaffen*). He wishes to substitute *"nature"* for duty, the *"innocence of becoming"* (*Unschuld des Werdens*) for what the Christians call grace and redemption from sin, and *the historical reality of the individual* (*die geschichtliche Individualität*) for what is accepted as universally valid by men in general.

Nietzsche's Attack on Morality. At any given time his attack depends upon what aspect of morality is under consideration. First of all he takes as his object the fact of the *plurality of moralities* and the possibility of investigating their *origins,* then he passes on to the *claim to absoluteness* which is advanced by moral demands.

The plurality of moralities and their origins: The fact of moral pluralism appears to rob every kind of morality of its supposed universal validity. The singularity and exclusiveness of each kind signifies that no group of moral judgments is to be explained in terms of the existence of the human species, but "rather in terms of the existence of peoples, races, etc., and, in fact, of peoples that have had to assert themselves *in opposition* to other peoples and *classes* which wished to be set off sharply from those in the lower ranks." Hence every distinct kind of morality is historically separate as one historically actualized possibility among others.

Still this argument need not lead Nietzsche to reject morality in its entirety, for a moral demand in its historical singularity might possess compelling and warranted obligatoriness for specific men at specific moments. And it is not necessary to renounce the universal validity of a law for man as man, but only the timeless universal validity of definite contents of that law. The demand for lawfulness in general, understood as agreement with the source of man as such, may remain indefeasible, even though its content is inexpressible and the possibilities that it opens to us are numerous.

One should distinguish between moral conduct and moral *judgment* concerning conduct. Nietzsche rejects the truth of moral judgments without qualification. His psychological observations concerning the origin and development of such judgments are inexhaustible. Among other things, he unmasks the pleasure taken in causing pain, the release of impotent instincts for revenge, the habit of furtive self-aggrandizement, the joy in feelings of power, and the mendacity of all moral indignation and the presumptuous judgment in all moral pathos. His magnificent "ridicule of all the moralizing of the present day" is conclusive.

This psychology of the usual moral judgment, instructive as its truth may be to everyone, need not by any means be taken to impugn morality itself. Even though moral judgment—especially judgment passed upon others—may be impossible insofar as it lays claim to dogmatic finality, morality itself may still, in consequence, remain an even more decisive intelligible actuality.

According to Nietzsche it is the *Socratic* and *Judaeo-Christian* morality (which he regards as identical) that is accepted as valid in Europe. He attacks this morality by exposing its origin and development. He refers to it as the "sum of the conditions of survival of an impoverished and partly or wholly ill-grown sort of man." He calls it "slave-morality." The powerless, too, have their will to power: it is "the instinct of the *herd* opposed to the strong and independent, the instinct of the *sorrowful* and poorly endowed opposed to the fortunate, the instinct of the *mediocre* opposed to the exceptional." In spite of their impotence, all of them find in morality the means to mastery and to the creation of an internal (and eventually an external) power. For these moral values are fundamentally evaluations, by inferior people, of behavior patterns that afford them protection; and wherever these values prevail, the existence of their creators and bearers, namely the inferior people, attains increased value while that of the intrinsically powerful and radiant people is depreciated. "The slave-insurrection of morality begins when *resentment* itself becomes creative and gives birth to values." Insofar as the strong and successful ones, who are always in the minority, accept the evaluations of the crowd, the powerful are subjugated to the congenitally weak and infirm.

Still, insofar as such arguments from *origin and development* appear *in every sense* to annul the validity of morality, Nietzsche counters with the statement: "He who has gained insight into the conditions under which a moral judgment has arisen has not thereby even touched upon its value." This value "remains unknown even when one is well aware of the conditions under which it arises."

Such assertions by no means re-establish the view that, in spite of everything, there is an absolutely valid morality; they only show that *some other consideration* must prove decisive in connection with the question of the *value* of any given moral system. For if "no morality is intrinsically valuable," and the concept of morality "is not even so much as relevant to man's worth," still this adverse judgment passed upon morality would be impossible unless *some positive value were presupposed* to provide the standard of judgment. The question is: What is the intention and purpose of Nietzsche's dissolution of morals? He tells us that he wishes to attain "the greatest power, depth, and splendor of which the human type is capable." But when this demand is stated with such earnestness as that of Nietzsche, it is as decisive and absolute as any moral demand. Consequently his attack is not aimed at morality in general; it is directed at one specific morality from the standpoint of another.

So far as the derivation particularly of *Christian* morality from resentment is concerned, it should be made clear that, on the one hand, many specific occurrences within Christendom are indeed understandable in these terms, while, on the other hand, the moral evaluations that are perverted through resentment are subject to these perversions only because they derive from some other source. Nietzsche himself stopped short (an astonishing fact!) before the figure of Jesus. Here he finds the actualization of a way of life in which everything is genuine and without pretense or falsehood. "Basically there was only one Christian, and he died on the cross." It is an "irony of world-history" that "mankind prostrates itself before the very opposite of the source, significance, and justification of the gospels."

In other words, Nietzsche's attack upon morality first presupposes an *indefeasible value* that is above every special morality (i.e., it presupposes the source of Nietzsche's own morality), and, second, it leaves open the possibility that a spurious morality may have originally come from a genuine *source*.

Moral claims as unconditional: Nietzsche is confronted with versions of morality—both religious and philosophical—whose demands are *unconditional* and whose contents are taken to be *universally binding.* *Christianity* bases its morality upon the law of God: "Christianity assumes from the outset that man does not and can not know what is good and what is bad for him. Man believes in God who alone knows these things. Christian morality is a command issuing from a transcendent source. It is beyond all criticism; it has truth only if God is the truth. It stands or falls with the belief in God." *Philosophically* morality depends upon itself as a capacity of reason. It does not rest its case upon derivation from anything external, but upon a growing mental awareness of its source in the supersensuous nature of man. It heeds the law, not as a divine command, but as its own demand in which it is at one with itself and with every rational being. What is revealed in morality is not simply the existence of man as a being that is determined in its type by nature, but rather man's transcendent origin.

Nietzsche does not merely deny that moral acts are objectively discoverable (which Kant also denies, since he holds that the rightness of an act does not necessarily attest to its moral character but merely its legality); he also denies the sense and validity of the inner moral demand to act in conformity with the moral law. (Whether this ever really happens or not, i.e., whether morality is actual or simply springs from motives of utility, inclination, and concern with extraneous ends, can, according to Kant, never be objectively settled by empirical means:) Nietzsche goes on to deny not only the universal validity of specific contents of moral demands, but the law of the lawfulness of conduct as being identical with moral conduct itself. He impugns the *unconditionality* of morality— whether in self-sufficient original philosophic form or in the form of its religious derivative—on the following bases:

(1) *Morality as alien to reality.* If morality is *unconditional,* then its demands possess *absolute* validity. Its content must be *discovered* or *heard,* not as an empirical but as an intelligible fact. In opposition to this, Nietzsche asserts: There are no moral facts. Morality is simply a *construction* placed upon certain phenomena; more precisely speaking, it is a misconstruction. In other words: "There are no moral phenomena, but only moral interpretations of phenomena." Moral matters have nothing to do with things "in themselves"; they are simply matters of opinion. They are part of the world of appearance.

Now if morality is nothing but interpretation, there must be *something* to be interpreted. *What* could it be that is thus morally interpreted? One of Nietzsche's answers is: "Morality is a sign-language of the feelings," and these feelings in their turn are a sign-language of the functions of everything organic. Early in his career Nietzsche asks whether, like dreams and other psychological phenomena, "our moral judgments and evaluations are only images and phantasies of a physiological process unknown to us." At a later date he provides the answer by saying that he has accustomed himself "to see in all moral judgments a bungling kind of sign-language by means of which certain physiological facts might be communicated."

In this way, Nietzsche expresses in concise biological terms what he calls in the broadest sense *reality, actuality,* or *nature.* It is of these that morality provides a sort of *interpretation.* In his attack, he arrives at the conclusion that moral judgments make us falsify ourselves and become less real because they *pass reality by* and, consequently, lead us astray. Instead of letting us master nature in a natural fashion, morality ensnares us in vain imaginings and thereby makes us fall victim to an unseen and undesired actuality. As a result, so long as we act morally, we, in fact, miss the possibilities that are real to us and thus allow "chance to become a law unto us."

Since morality is alien to the actual and is bound to remain unreal because of the very principle on which it rests, Nietzsche views moral philosophy as nothing more than a creature of the imagination occupying itself with vain conceits: "In the whole history of moral development, truth does not once make its appearance: all its conceptual components . . . are fictions, all its psychological interpretations . . . are falsifications, all the logical formulations which are dragged into this kingdom of lies are sophisms. The badge of the moral philosopher himself is a complete absence of any kind of cleanliness."

In the first place, this attack presupposes that it is possible to know what reality is and also to know that this reality exists in such a way that I can deal with it as something simply given. But still, throughout the whole of Nietzsche's philosophy, *all reality is itself only interpretation* [2]—a kind of exegetical construction beyond whose limitless variations nothing else exists. I have only *one kind* of consciousness of reality; I do *not* know reality as an independent existent outside of myself.

In the second place, Nietzsche presupposes the *absolute value* of this reality which he calls nature. But he cannot maintain this either, insofar as to him every value can be only the value of *one* single reality as a way of interpreting this very reality.

Certain specific aspects of Nietzsche's attack, based upon the irrele-

[2] Cf. pp. 184 ff., 287 ff.

vance of morals to reality, appear plausible: he hits upon the psychological truth about certain ways of behaving that pretend to be "moral," points out the ever present disparity in all human conduct between what is intended and willed and what actually occurs as a consequence of the deed, or strikes at the irresponsible practice of acting on principle and producing evil in a blind urge to sacrifice while finding comfort in leaving the successful outcome to God. But the root of the import of the absoluteness that moves men to act is not reached by Nietzsche. In Nietzsche's thought, then, one must always distinguish between the psychological truth that relates to the specific phenomena of human existence, and philosophic expressions of the truth that concern the source itself, for this latter alone is in question when we wish to come to grips with the roots of morality.

(2) *Morality as contrary to nature.* For morality to be "unconditional" means that it ought to exist only for its own sake. It need not justify itself by reference to something external to which it is a means; rather it is itself the measure of all existing things—the measure by which they are to be accepted or rejected. But to rest the case for the ultimate value of morality upon the formula "morality for morality's sake" is, according to Nietzsche, not only to accept its complete lack of realism, but also to pay the price of devaluating actuality itself. Nowhere does actuality pass the test of morality; adjudged by this test it is simply immoral and opposed to value and, consequently, something which ought not to exist. Like "beauty for beauty's sake" and "truth for truth's sake," "the good for its own sake" is a "form of the evil eye for the actual," "for since life is essentially something immoral, it must constantly and unavoidably be in the wrong from the standpoint of morality (especially Christian, i.e., unconditional, morality)."

Nietzsche concedes that the value-distinctions and rank-orders which morality provides are defensible—but only as rank-orders of that which is actually living and, in this capacity, as indicators of the conditions underlying the existence and progression of some particular form of life. But as revelations of a higher world—which they have to be if they are to be unconditioned—they turn into the very opposite of life and acquire a life-destroying character. To insist that everything become moral "would mean to rob existence of its *greatness,* and to castrate mankind and reduce it to a miserable mass of nondescript Chinamen."

This attack, which claims that morality is "contrary to nature," is annulled however when Nietzsche, reversing himself, also speaks of *morality* as *"part and parcel of nature."* Everything belongs to nature— even that which appears to be opposed to it. The modifications of nature's existence are very numerous. Of any moral system one can say: "It is a fruit that betrays the soil from which it grew." Morality is thus changed into a mere set of opinions held by one or the other type of man. It is not a source but a consequence—it is itself a product of nature. As such a consequence of the development of a particular type of man, morality in every one of its forms should be viewed as a natural phenomenon. These two ways of viewing morality—both as contrary to nature and as itself perfectly natural—thus appear to annul one another.

Nietzsche, in seeking to reject any *"unconditionality,"* can do this only on the basis of a new unconditionality. He himself knows this to be unavoidable. Whenever we value something unconditionally our experience is moral, and, contrariwise, whenever our experience is moral in nature, we are dealing with something unconditional. It is "simply not possible to relativize a moral experience; it is essentially unconditioned." Hence, in unconditionally opposing the value accorded to "nature" to the unconditionality of morality, Nietzsche himself does precisely what he condemns: he pronounces an absolute value-judgment. The basis for "absolutistic morality" expressed in such words as "my evaluation is final" is also the basis on which Nietzsche involuntarily—though knowingly—proceeds.

The Double Circle. The unambiguous arguments against morality can thus all be robbed of their decisive effect by an appeal to certain of Nietzsche's other tenets. He has a new way of raising critical questions—more ambiguous ones—by moving in inescapable circles. First he asserts that morality is itself a product of immorality, and then he urges that the criticism of morality itself derives from the highest kind of morality.

(1) *Morality as a product of immorality.* Nietzsche believes that, from the very beginning, the moral has come from something immoral, viz., the will to power. Morality "is a special case of actual immorality." For him this is psychologically discernible in individual cases: "One does not become moral *because* he is moral! Subordination to morality can be slavish, or proud, or selfish, or thoughtless, but intrinsically there is nothing moral about it." On the contrary "our morality rests on the same foundation of lies and misrepresentation as our wickedness and selfishness." Historically this can be seen on a grand scale: "All the means by which mankind up to now was to be made moral were fundamentally immoral." An indication of this is "the *pia fraus,* that heirloom of all philosophers and priests who 'improved' mankind. Neither Manu, nor Plato, nor Confucius, nor the Jewish and Christian teachers have ever

doubted their *right* to lie." Consequently "to *create* morality one must have the unswerving will to the very opposite." "Morality has remained in good standing for so long only thanks to immorality."

Even if the contentions here argued for were correct in their entirety and not merely to a large extent, they would still not be convincing, since it is true, here as elsewhere, that the manner in which something develops and reaches fruition is not decisive for the significance and value of the finished product. But insofar as it is asserted that all morality in its entirety is a product of development rather than a matter of individual developmental relations, the very meaning of morality as something specific, with a source of its own, is obliterated by a reduction of all being to *one* kind of being (nature, reality). It is not the moral that is unconditioned but rather actual nature.

(2) *The derivation of the critique of morality from the highest morality.* That Nietzsche's radical rejection of morality is itself a consequence of his moral involvement is consciously asserted in the following circle: Moral development is bound to have the result that the truthfulness demanded by *morality* finally calls in question the very morality in which it is rooted; morality becomes suspect for purely moral reasons. Judged by the truthfulness which morality itself demands, morality is reduced to mere semblance, and it therewith forfeits its right to condemn pretence. Thus this "self-overcoming of morality" occurs only in moral men: "The critique of morality represents a high stage of morality." "In us morality achieves its own self-destruction." Just because "one of the highest and most potent efflorescences of the moral sense is the sense for truth itself," morality, by insisting on truthfulness, has "placed around its own neck the noose with which it can be strangled—its own last moral demand is the suicide of morality."

But in these circles the self-assertion as well as the suicide of morality appears. For just as we are left, in the first case, with self-assertive immorality within the circle that reduced morality to a special case of immorality, so, in the second, *morality* becomes the basis for the circle that derives the destruction of morality from *morality itself*. In neither case does the negation strike the heart of the matter, though it presents origins and lines of descent concretely. Without such concrete presentation the circles are merely formal. Their consequence—not logical but rather derived from existential grounds—can be self-sufficiency in self-assertion as well as self-negation through the suicide of morality.

Because Nietzsche's critique of morality transcends the specific and penetrates to the outermost limits, he is in fact compelled either to annul his statements in consciously constructed *circles* or to leave them standing in unrecognized *contradictory* opposition to each other.

At the start, Nietzsche had intended the two *circles* as attacks whose results would be final: the first by reducing morality itself to its opposite; the second by demanding the rejection of morality on the highest moral grounds. But when Nietzsche views reality (nature) as neither moral nor immoral, but rather as the encompassing being, he is, as a consequence, driven to reject in turn his own condemnation of morality: Moral condemnation is in itself simply a fact within nature; when I now condemn one single thing within nature, I condemn the whole of it, since everything is involved with everything else. It follows that when I condemn this condemnation, as I do, I am doing precisely the thing for which I just reproached those who play the moral judge: I am condemning the whole. I can and must say Yes to nature by affirming even the moral condemnation that I just now rejected. In this circle all positions annul one another, and there is no escape.

But if one retains these positions, they remain in inescapable *contradiction,* so that while one is being expressed the other has to be left out of consideration. We hear that "it is not possible to live outside of morality," as well as the contrary, that "one can live only with an absolutely immoral way of thinking." Or again, morality "is the only interpretative scheme with which man can endure" and, on the other hand, "the world, morally interpreted, is unbearable."

Nietzsche's Demands. If we place before us the *fundamental meaning* of Nietzsche's total attack on morality (something that cannot be comprehended from any single argument), we find that it involves more than the attack on the Christian interpretation, which regards human conduct as sinful, and more than the attack on the codification of ethics accepted by philosophers or on the moral conventions within society. The attack proceeds victoriously against *all* fixated and derived phenomena of generally accepted morality and points beyond to the source of morality itself in a universally valid *ought.* Only thus can we understand how Nietzsche is aware of the awesome implication of his position (because of him "the history of mankind is broken in two"): "The lightning flash of truth has struck precisely that which stood highest up to the present. He who understands what was thus annihilated can see whether or not he has anything at all to cling to. . . . He who exposes morality thereby brings to light the worthlessness of all the values in which men believe or have believed." Nietzsche's critical questioning is extraordinary, but it is not the culmination of his thinking and experiencing: the questioning cannot be understood unless we sense the *genuine positive demands* that struggle within it for recognition. Nietzsche's reflections upon morality are far from being exhaustively expressed in a series of aggressive statements which formally refute each other. On the contrary, his formalism contains hints of a depth of intention whose existential significance we must bring into focus.

Nietzsche's *demands* cannot be of the sort that set up definite prescriptions and proscriptions which could guide the purposeful will. He starts much deeper because he wishes to reach the possible *Existenz* of man through indirect illumination of those *modes of existential actualization* which he envisages. This appeal of Nietzsche, which seems to express the very substance of his being, will be elucidated in four direction:

(1) *He champions the individual in opposition to the universal.* The morality which he opposes is founded upon a substance common to all men, upon the Deity, or upon reason. Nietzsche counters by saying: "My morality would consist of decreasing man's universality more and more and making him more specialized . . . and less understandable to others." As it is so essential to Nietzsche "that there is no single morality that alone can make us moral," he wishes to place the individual ahead of all moral and rational universals. But he does not intend to give the isolated individual as such free scope for his self-centered caprice. Rather he reaches into the depths of existential historical reality (*existentielle Geschichtlichkeit*) to make us aware of the law in the form in which it becomes audible in the concrete situation of *Existenz*. Thus by the word "individual" he means, not the isolated private person, but the single human being who always knows that "we are more than individuals; we are also the entire chain and charged with the tasks of all the futures of the chain." It may be said of this potentially existing single being that "each individual is an attempt to reach a species that is higher than man."

Still Nietzsche's statements abound in individualistic phrases which, when taken by themselves, lose their existential sense.

(2) *The innocence of becoming.* From his attacks on morality Nietzsche draws the following conclusion: If it is true that insofar as we believe in morality we condemn life, then we must "annihilate morality in order to liberate life" and "attempt to be as amoral as nature." If man, when his powers are fullest and noblest, is part and parcel of nature, then the important thing is to *bring him back* to nature and the truths that she contains. Nietzsche speaks of this demand as his "assault against two millennia of perversion of nature and of desecration of man."

Still, if everything is nature and even morality is a product of a certain kind of nature, then all demands are nonsensical. When whatever exists and occurs must belong to nature, nothing may ever properly be commanded to rise above nature, and there is nothing that we can stigmatize as unnatural with a view to its rectification.

Nietzsche does in fact arrive at this last conclusion when he revokes every demand and *demands that all demanding cease.* Here he succeeds for the first time in regaining complete innocence and effecting a great liberation for all human behavior: "The opposition has been taken out of things; the homogeneity of all events is preserved." He no longer needs to exclude anything and is simply concerned to unite opposites. As a result of this liberation, he has no desire to annihilate even what he attacks. While the will to one single morality would amount to the tyranny of its adherents over all other types of men, Nietzsche concedes that he has "not declared war against the anaemic ideal of Christians with a view to annihilating it. . . . The continuation of the Christian ideal is one of the most desirable things there is. . . . We immoralists thus need the power of morality: our instinct of self-preservation demands that our opponent remain strong."

In this way Nietzsche gains insight into what he calls the "innocence of becoming" (*Unschuld des Werdens*)—an insight that conquers all other moralities with their dichotomy of good and bad or good and evil.

Wherever indignation and the urge to discover the guilty party predominate—wherever attempts are made to fix responsibilities—there "existence is robbed of its innocence." We need not blame others—neither God nor society nor parents and ancestors; we need not succumb to our instinct for revenge, to our urge to shift the blame for all our discomforts to a scapegoat, or to any other stultifying impulses. Rather we have the right to an absolutely affirmative view that embraces everything—even what we momentarily reject—within the total chain of events.

Whenever we blame ourselves, we are succumbing to the bigotry of moral narrowness. Nietzsche wishes to achieve a consciousness of innocence. Why does he take such pains to prove in every possible way the complete innocence of becoming? "Was it not simply in order to create for myself the feeling of complete irresponsibility—to place myself beyond every kind of praise and blame, to make myself independent of everything connected with yesterday and today—so that I could pursue my goal in my own way?" The seal of the attainment of freedom is "being no longer ashamed of one's self." When knowledge of the innocence of becoming is gained, then for the first time the highest possibilities present themselves: "It is the innocence of becoming alone that gives us the greatest courage and the greatest freedom."

Nevertheless, when Nietzsche attempts to reconcile all opposites, to see nature merely *as* nature and all things as natural, and to acquire the innocence of becoming, he cannot but discover that nothing follows from mere contemplation: no demand, to be sure, but also no impulse. Thus he returns to the thesis: "No impulse can be derived from nature as known." A "beyond good and evil," maintained merely as such, would in fact be just as empty a beyond as any known to metaphysics. Man must will something, move toward its realization, and receive guidance from its direction. This direction is not provided by becoming per se; it is always contained *within* becoming in the form of a real act through which one shows what he is and what he wills and through which he immediately becomes again subject to demands in the face of opposites and able either to hearken to the law or to turn a deaf ear to it.

Nietzsche's philosophizing is not intended to allow thinking man to sink peacefully into the undisturbed innocence of becoming. On the contrary, he should be able, by listening to the source of the possible, to learn what is historically called for by his own specific situation. Insofar as Nietzsche's thinking is intended to lead us through these self-destructive antitheses into the clarity of the audible, where the concrete and determinate law gives way before the encompassing law that becomes known only historically, this thinking must itself lose all definiteness. Hence Nietzsche is not content with such final statements as "the innocence of becoming has been restored," or "all is necessity—all is innocence"; rather he wishes to hit upon the productive factor in this extreme freedom. He calls it "creation."

(3) *Creation (Schaffen)*. Creation is the highest demand; it is authentic being, the ground of all essential activity:

Creation is *evaluation:* "Without evaluation the nut of existence would be hollow!" "Change of values—that is change of the creators." "As yet no one knows what is good and bad—except the creator!—He is the one who creates the goal for mankind and gives the earth its meaning and its future: the one whose *creativity* makes it possible for something to be good or bad."

Creation is *faith (Glaube)*. The sterile lack faith. "But he who was driven to create always had his prophetic dreams and astrological portents—and had faith in faith!"

Creation is *love:* "All great love . . . still wishes to create—the object of its love!"

In creation is *annihilation:* "It is only as creators that we can annihilate." All creators are hard. "To my love I sacrifice myself, and my fellow-men as well—this is the language of all creators." The will to create is the will to become, to grow, and to shape, . . . but destruction too is involved in creation." Together with the *creative* good, which is *the highest good of all,* "goes the greatest evil."

"All creation is *communication (Mitteilen).*" The moments of greatest creation are those of increased capacity for communication and understanding. "Creation: that means to give of ourselves, leaving ourselves emptier, poorer, and more loving."

Still, all aspects of creation together form a *unity:* "The knower, the creator, and the lover are one." The unity is "the great synthesis of the knower, lover, and annihilator" or, again, it is called "the unity, in power, of the creator, the lover, and the knower."

The *condition* of creation is great pain and lack of knowledge. "Creation—that is the great deliverance from suffering. . . . But if the creator is to exist, suffering itself is needed." "To see right through the perishable net and the last veil—that would be the greatest tedium and the end of all creators."

In creation *authentic being is attained.* "*Freedom* appears only in creation." "Our only happiness consists in creating." "As a creator you transcend yourself—you cease to be your own contemporary."

The high value of the creator is *unconditional* for Nietzsche: "Even the most trivial creative act is better than talking about what has been created." "Our salvation does not lie in knowing but in creating." "You should learn only for the sake of creating": "One even *ought* not to know more of a thing than what one can create. Furthermore the only way to *know* a thing truly is to attempt to make it."

But it is as though the creator were *invisible:* "The people have little conception of the great, that is, the creator. But they have an appreciation for all agitators and imitators of great things."

Just what creation is remains *necessarily* indefinite. It is one of those *signa* of Nietzsche's philosophizing that, like "life," "will to power," and "eternal recurrence," is never conceptualized. Our thinking runs aground on them, either negatively, through becoming lost in a void or through misunderstanding due to simplification, or positively, by being translated into an actual impulse. In every kind of philosophizing we find these ultimate inconceivables that are aptly expressed but never conquered by words. Nietzsche always treats creation as though it were self-evident, but virtually never takes it directly as his theme. He does not develop and explain its nature. It is never a possible goal of the will. But his formulations have all the power of an as yet indefinite appeal to recall and to come to grips with authentic being.

Creation is absolutely primordial, but it is not a first beginning, as though nothing had ever been before. If, after the annihilation of morality, creation is the new morality, then it is precisely the creator who does *the preserving within the annihilation.* Consequently Nietzsche maintains throughout his thinking the position that he in no way intends to destroy morality by denying it.

Nietzsche is not simply hesitant: we must "guard against rushing violently head over heels to exchange our customary morality for a new evaluation of things." Rather he explicitly demands the preservation of traditional morality: "We will be the inheritors of morality when we have destroyed the moral." We possess "the moral sense as a great legacy of previous generations." "We should not underestimate what a couple of millennia of morality have bred into our spirit!" Precisely in the case of the creative path-finder, "a kind of wealth in moral inheritance must be presupposed." "We wish to be the heirs of all previous morality and *not* to begin anew. All our actions are simply morality reacting against its previous form."

In the end Nietzsche bases the possibility of creativity of the heirs themselves on *the struggle against the pressure which Christianity has exerted* for thousands of years: through this struggle the thorough-going Christian morality has "created in Europe a splendid spiritual tension. . . . With so tense a bow one can now shoot to the most distant goals." Twice the attempt has been made on a grand scale "to relax the bow: once by the Jesuit Movement and again by the democratic enlightenment." But Nietzsche, sure of still having the full tension of his own bow, wishes to preserve and increase the tension in the world as the source of a creation that will far outstrip all previous creation. What, in the critique of morality, is creatively destructive, must after all—since this is not the end of all things—assert itself in a new way as creative morality.

For *himself,* Nietzsche is aware that he lives on "a rich moral heritage" and that he is in a position to treat morality as an illusion just because to him it "has become instinctive and unavoidable" (to Fuchs, July 29, '88). To be sure, the morality that governs him and that enables him to reject morality, does not derive from a timeless conscience but from a positive attitude that is at once original with him and historically inherited. As an immoralist he feels himself to be "still related to the age-old German integrity and piety." Being what he is, he would not be able to apply the conclusions that could conceivably be drawn from his own doctrine: "It is all very well to talk about all kinds of immorality; but to live by them is another matter! For example, I could not bear to break my word or even to commit murder. It would be my lot to pine away for a shorter or longer time and then perish!"

(4) *Man as his own creator.* Nietzsche views man as more than a being that passively undergoes alterations: he never doubts that man is free and that he develops himself. His criticism of morality is intent upon making precisely this genuine freedom again possible. But man's freedom has its own specific meaning: the freedom of self-realization is simply creation. How man the creator is also the self-developer has been formulated by Nietzsche in three different ways:

(a) Since man is a creative being, in that he *appreciates, measures, and evaluates,* there are no absolute values that simply subsist as realities needing only to be discovered. Rather values are the form in which man, in a unique moment of historical actuality, lays hold not only upon the conditions of his existence but even those of his own self-being. Values are never final; at any given time they must be created. That is why Nietzsche, in the present moment of world history, assumes the task of a "transvaluation of all values."

(b) Change, furthermore, comes about in connection with the fundamental relation that man assumes toward himself by seeing himself, evaluatiɪg himself, being deceived about himself, and giving form to himself. In this occurs, in addition to what is open to psychological investigation, something that is forever psychologically unobservable, although for self-being it constitutes the genuine assurance of its actuality: what I myself really am comes to me from without as though I were given as a present to myself. Hence Nietzsche tells us that behind every psychologically analyzable effect that man can have upon himself lies the incomprehensible riddle of a genuine depth which makes possible self-organization without repression and self-mastery without self-violation. As fundamental impulses emerge, I am carried, beyond all mere psychological actuality, to that from which the latter first acquires its meaning and its form. It is not a question here of grasping a psychologically discoverable measure and a mean between extremes, for what Nietzsche means by these words transcends the psychological. But self-being is far better attuned to it than to anything psychologically knowable: "It is best never to speak *of two very great things: measure and mean.* Very few people know the powers and omens that come to them from *the mysterious paths and inner experiences* and conversions. They revere them as something divine and avoid noisy proclamations."

(c) Finally the change derived from the evaluative impulses within the medium of reflexive behavior can only be realized through a capacity for *motion within one's own nature* that does not exist as an entity, but has its being in the process of becoming through which it realizes itself. This is what Nietzsche regards as the phenomenon of the procreation of that which I already am in the sense of existential possibility, a phenomenon that transcends all psychologically visible conversions and all biologically knowable processes. Man as creator changes with the new evaluations that he assumes and at the same time becomes that which he really is. Thus Nietzsche makes Pindar's demand his own: *Become what you are!*

Nietzsche's stern earnestness paralyzes every sort of moral pathos. His kind of thinking can not rest content with, or even find edification in, any proposition, demand, law, or specific content. It proceeds indirectly by demanding that one take seriously those profound inner depths that would simply be obstructed by appeal to any derived law and any fixed standard.

When one gives up the moral universal that makes its demands with logically inflexible unconditionality, no return is possible. One is threatened by the possibility of sinking into a limitless void. The loss of the resistance afforded by immutable moral laws may as easily be followed by abandonment to caprice and accident as by emergence from the source of an authentic and historically unique possibility.

In the end, the contradictory elements and circles in the movements of Nietzsche's thought are simply the means to touch indirectly upon what lies beyond form, law, and the expressible. Nothing can be at this boundary, and yet everything must be there. This thinking must always end with allusions to a ground from which my being will come toward me: allusions like "the mysterious paths of inner conversions," the "belief in ourselves," "creation," the actuality of life as the lightness of the "dance." But all formulae remain ambiguous and self-discrepant when they are involved with belief in a being whose becoming does not derive from what it is. In connection with what we ourselves basically are, this amounts to saying: "Belief in ourselves is the strongest bond, the most compelling whiplash—and the strongest wing."

Creation as Freedom without Transcendence. We must now examine in greater detail Nietzsche's idea that creation takes the place of freedom, or, in other words, *is* freedom. In the sense employed by the philosophy of *Existenz*,[3] freedom, whether Christian or Kantian, exists in relation to transcendence. Freedom is the potentiality of a finite being; it is limited by transcendence, and it depends on an incomprehensible source lying at this limit (whether this be called "grace" or "being-

---

[3] Jaspers uses the term *Existenzphilosophie* to characterize his own view (*Philosophie*, III, p. 217; *Von der Wahrheit*, p. 165), while he prefers to use the word *Existentialismus* to signify a view which he rejects (*Philosophie*, I, xxiii).—Trs.

given-to-oneself"). The decision as to what has eternal significance is made through freedom. That is, freedom exists historically as the union of the temporal and the eternal and as the decision that is itself merely an appearance of eternal being.

Nietzsche rejects this freedom. He professes to follow Spinoza because the latter denies the freedom of the will, the moral order in the world, and genuine evil (to Overbeck, July 30, '80). The freedom that Nietzsche acknowledges and asserts amounts to being rooted in one's self and having the source of life within one's self without transcendence. Such freedom is both *negative* and *positive*. The way of freedom is *negative* insofar as it discards, breaks through, and denies what has been real and binding: "To cut oneself off from his past (from fatherland, belief, parents, companions), to associate with *outcasts* (in history and in society); to topple what is most revered and affirm what is most strongly forbidden. . . ." On the *positive* side, the fruits of freedom are of the nature of "creation." The positive cannot occur without the negative, because it can be attained only by traversing the negative way. The dialectic of the first discourse of Zarathustra shows that this way leads from service through the rejection of service to creation. But were the negative to detach itself from the positive and remain negative merely, it would amount to an empty and therefore spurious freedom. All negation is justified only by the creative positing to which it is preparatory and which it conditions or follows. By itself it is inferior to obedient service in accordance with tradition. That is why Zarathustra asks of all liberators who wish to remove man's chains for the sake of freedom as such: "Free for what?" He is indifferent to "freedom from" and expresses the opinion that "there are many who discarded their last vestige of worth in throwing off their servitude."

Since *negative* freedom is entirely inadequate, it is of paramount importance that negation should be carried out from the standpoint of *positive,* creative freedom. If positive creating were not the genuine ground of the annulment of existing obligations (and it is here the existential rather than the argumentative ground that is in question), then one could well exclaim in fear: "Your wild dogs clamor to be set free." By the same token, mere restraint of one's own unbridled impulses is not enough, when this springs from the inane denial of anything having instinctive existence and not from the sense of positive creative substance: "You have conquered yourself. But why do you behave solely as the vanquished? I want to behold the victorious one. . . ." This latter is the creator.

Thus Nietzsche's freedom without transcendence is by no means intent upon simply returning to mere life; it aspires to the life of authentic creation. Just as Nietzsche's denial of morals does not mean the annulment of all morality but a laying hold upon what is *more than merely moral,* so here his sole intention is to stimulate man to higher achievement. To be sure, without God, Nietzsche's purpose seems to lead to the radical loss of all bonds: what remains is just to live as before and to allow life to continue as always. But this is to turn Nietzsche's idea into its very opposite. Its challenge is tremendous, for the entire burden is laid upon the individual. He requires each of us to follow the insecure and thus dangerous new path of the individual who is not yet sustained within a stratified society and who must find the source of his ties within himself. Nietzsche is asking those who abandon morality to bind themselves by still higher and more inexorable bonds. After all, morality is no longer real; it is only an empty and deceptive show. Threateningly, he exclaims: "If you are too weak to give laws to yourselves, then let a tyrant lay his yoke upon you and say: 'Obey! Gnash and obey!' and all good and evil will be drowned in obedience to him."

One can find decisive evidence for this interpretation of his doctrine. In a moment that led to his later, lonely, existence, he found it unbearable that his "immoralism" could be confused with the "less than moral" by a person whom he had believed to share his conception of a philosophy that lives through creation at a level above morality. "You have within you," he wrote, "that impulse to a sacred selfishness which is the impulse to obey the highest commandment. You must at first have confused it, under the spell of some curse, with its opposite: the selfishness and delight in plunder of a cat that *desires nothing beyond being alive. . . .*" But the meaning of this mere life is simply "feeling for life in a void; . . . something I find extremely repugnant in man" (correspondence with Lou, Nov. 1, '82). Nietzsche expresses the contrast even more tersely: "She told me herself that she had no morals—and I supposed that hers, like mine, were stricter than anyone's" (correspondence with Rée, '82). This high claim that no one can fully live up to does not exist, to be sure, as a definable duty, and it cannot be fulfilled by acting in accordance with a specific law. Still the expression of this new morality clearly intends the very opposite of mere amoral living.

To be sure, Nietzsche characterizes the new, higher, and still wholly indeterminate morality as "that of the creating ones," but he does not express it in terms of any definite contents. The creative transvaluation of all values must bring forth his new "morality:" "Who will create the *goal* that stands high over all humanity as well as over the individual?" The path can no longer be that of previous morality which intended merely to "preserve." Now that there is no goal for all, "an *experimental* morality is called for: *setting* one's self a goal." What is meant is "a substitute for morality through the will to our goal and consequently to the means to this goal." It is the substance of the future that is to become free: "They will call you the destroyers of morality, but you are really only the finders of yourselves." Everyone is made to rely on himself. A new self-sufficiency must develop: "We must free ourselves of morality in order to be able to live morally," or again: "I had to invalidate morality in order to realize my moral will."

When Nietzsche makes his magnificent claim on a deeper unattained source, he believes that *it can be reached only without God.* "To rule and no longer be God's vassal—this is the means left to us for ennobling man."

Because Nietzsche wishes to define, circumscribe, and interpret the creative source apart from transcendence, it constantly comes about that, in spite of his will to something more-than-life, he suddenly finds in his hands mere nature in the sense of what is biologically knowable, or he is left with only the corresponding mere psychological or sociological actualities. The new morality is to be a "natural" morality, and this is affirmed in spite of all the thoughts that should render it untenable when he says: "Every naturalism in morality, that is, every *sound* morality, is governed by an instinct for life."

For example, the demand, *"Become what you are!"* illustrates the way in which Nietzsche's formulations lead him involuntarily from the *appeal to an existential source* to the mere assertion of *natural facts* (and hence of particular investigable existents within the world). In seeming correspondence with the above exhortation, Nietzsche, by ascertaining the nature of this developing being instead of demanding a certain nature of him, is able to say: "One becomes a decent man just because he *is* a decent man, i.e., because he is born with a capital of good instincts and favorable conditions. . . . Today we know better than to regard moral degeneracy as something separate from the physiological." Now it is certainly impossible at the level of existence to separate the physiological or causal (to say nothing of the psychological and sociological) from *Existenz:* whatever we come to know about ourselves through scientific investigation is so intimately bound up with us that we could not exist without it. But, inseparable from this observable existence that we know ourselves to be, there is also something else: the source of man himself, which transcends science. Only the clarity of conceptual distinction removes the ambiguity of a being that allows existential possibility and physiologically and psychologically investigable actuality to appear as identical rather than merely as involved with each other: (1) The being that I "ought" to become may simply have the significance of *just-being-that-way* (with the consequence of withholding oneself on the basis of the principle that is really born of despair: I just happen to be that way); *ought* then no longer has any real meaning but is an inexorable *must*. Or (2) the being that I ought to become means as well the *encompassing force of possibility* (*das Umgreifende der Möglichkeit*) which I can never know as something fixed and determinate and which no one else can know. This possibility remains open and reveals again and again what I am (while self-witholding only leads to ever-recurring confirmation of the same inferiority or imagined excellence). On the plane of psychological facts, Nietzsche himself denies "unchangeability of character" and condemns the "average man's belief in himself as in a fully developed and completed state of affairs." Psychologically, "we are free" to choose among possibilities. But this source from which it is decided "what we are free" to do—this being that cannot be identified by objective procedures of characterology but which we ourselves most truly are—is that to which the demand "Become what you are!" is directed. This demand, which would be meaningless if it referred merely to an innate just-being-so as a psychological state of affairs, becomes "dangerous" when taken seriously because it is directed at the still indeterminate source of my being and is exposed to all kinds of misunderstanding. For it is not a definite law and an objectively derivable obligation that decides, but rather reliance on the "creative" source in me, and this may be lacking. Hence when Nietzsche says, "Become what you are: that is a challenge which is permissible in the case of only a few men but is superfluous in the case of only the very fewest of those few," even this challenge may become meaningless when one reverts to the view that man has an objectively identifiable nature. But the meaning of that true and willed existential danger that creativity may never come forth—a danger present to Nietzsche's consciousness with extraordinary urgency and persistence—is audibly conveyed.

Immanence Reverses Itself. Whenever anyone has been sure of possessing the kind of freedom that Nietzsche denies, he has viewed it as inseparable from himself, and, in being thus free, he has experienced both nullification and security in confronting transcendence. But creation, which Nietzsche substitutes for existential freedom as the sole immanent actualization of his kind of freedom, ends within itself or is lost, since it has only itself to depend on. The creating individual, whether he runs into obstacles or is able to continue on his way, has, according to Nietzsche's philosophy, an awareness of destiny rather than a relation to transcendence. In the place of transcendence Nietzsche puts "necessity," [4] metaphysically so conceived that every accident that happens to me and every impulse that stirs within me appears as meaningful in relation to the totality of my development as a *creator*. Necessity, thus conceived, is not wholly unlike the freedom which he denies, though it differs essentially from the causally interpreted necessity of a psychical and biological order of occurrences. In spite of everything, the one affords Nietzsche a transcending consciousness of being within the whole, while the other offers merely a relative knowledge of particular relations within the world.

Creation without transcendence, or self-being without God, must lead to two conclusions that Nietzsche actually draws. When human finiteness ceases to be evident *as* finiteness because it is no longer enclosed by any infinity, i.e., when creative freedom faces nothingness instead of transcendence (for that which has nothing outside of itself is everything, with the result that its finiteness cannot be taken seriously), then either (1) creation is *absolutized as a temporal actuality* to which no valid standard applies, or (2) it is *deified*. Naturalizations express the first conclusion, hybris the second. Neither of these relates to transcendence; each is, instead, a way in which confidence becomes evident at the boundary which is no longer a boundary but a fulfillment. Nietzsche has expressed both consequences in a singularly daring language in which all logical thinking reverses itself:

(1) In assuming a position outside of morality, Nietzsche believed that he was *in agreement with Jesus*. "Jesus took sides against those who judge: he wished to be the destroyer of morality." "Jesus said: . . . Of what concern is morality to us who are sons of God!" Nietzsche saw in Jesus the anticipated realization of his own idea (blurred in the process of deification) of what is more than morality and, hence, what he himself desired to be: "God, conceived as the state of being liberated from morality, compressing within Himself all the fullness of life's contrasts, redeeming and justifying them in divine agony: God as beyond . . . good and evil." It is in accord with the nature of this conclusion that Nietzsche in the early stages of insanity signed himself "The Crucified" as well as Dionysus.

(2) Essentially the same self-confidence in transgressing all determinate morality appears as if reversed in its nature when aimed not at the source (there being nothing but nature and actuality) but *at triumphant effectiveness* within the world: "We immoralists are today the strongest

[4] *Vide infra,* pp. 356 ff.

power: the other great powers need us. We construe the world in our own image." Whatever has the appearance of validity seems to have gone by the boards when there is nothing left but mere brutal actuality in its immediacy, in which such self-confidence seeks nothing but victory for itself. Then one begins to wonder whether we are left, not with the more-than-moral, but rather with the less-than-moral—the mere existence of the forces of nature. This self-confidence does indeed become inseparable from demonic triumph in these awesome statements: "We immoralists are today the only power that needs no allies in order to attain victory. . . . We do not even need the lie. . . . Even without the truth we would come to power. . . . The magic that fights for us is that of the extreme."

Neither of the above expresses any longer the ethos of finite beings that go their way in tension with transcendence and bound by historical reality. Because these last demands of Nietzsche leave no room for the spirit who feels himself bound because of his knowledge of finiteness, both deification and sinking into the extremes (as an overpowering efficacy) are possible. Where finitude, confinement of the finite, and possible *Existenz* appear eliminated in this manner, finite creatures like ourselves are shut out. It is as though freedom in Nietzsche's thinking becomes transformed into creation, which, in its ambiguous indeterminacy, offers us no solid ground to stand on, while creation in turn is consumed in an explosion which leaves only a phantom deity or nothingness behind.

Finally it is always like a return from deification and devilization to find determinacy and concrete range of application in Nietzsche's thinking. Then, in opposition to deification and the immoderation of the extreme, he seems always prepared to come back to his acceptance of the statement: it is essential for manliness "that we do not deceive ourselves about our *human* position: rather let us proceed strictly according to *our measure.*" But man must find his own limitation in the world by following *a way of life.* In seeking to find a way, Nietzsche accomplishes man's task of setting limits to himself.

To be sure there are times when he finds this way hopeless. His situation, which does not permit him either to live with morality or to live without it, he characterizes as follows: "Perhaps a devil invented morality in order to torture men through pride, and a second devil at some time took it away from them to make them suffer from self-contempt." The impossibility of escape from this makes it seem that "perhaps man must simply perish as a result of his morality."

But actually the way remains open to Nietzsche: "We who again dare to live in an *amoralized* world—we pagans— . . . realize what heathen belief is: to have to conceive of beings higher than man." Nietzsche believes that these beings that transcend humanity *can only be expected to emerge from the man* who transforms himself within the world. In place of the deity and of all morality, it is the *image of man* that becomes significant in propelling us upward.

Nietzsche's Conception of Man as a Driving Force

Conceptions of man are either descriptions of *actual* types, or they are projections of human *possibilities*. Those drawn by Nietzsche lie on both levels. The first level presents a great multiplicity of *existing forms:* sociological types such as the merchant, the politician, the priest, the scholar, and, in addition, various characterological types. It is not necessary to rearrange these amply rewarding psychological studies and report on them. What is essential is to note that even his psychological representations always convey a vague discontent that leads one to search for the *"superior man."* Accordingly the second level shows various ways in which men *transcend* their mere existence. Either these superior men appear to have turned out well but are in such peril that they founder against the reality of life, or they are consumed with a self-dissatisfaction which miscarries and needs to be overcome. Hence Nietzsche finally looks beyond all "superior men" to a last possibility and finds the *superman* on a third level—the only one on which the true goal of man is to be found.

Conceptions of man that are not mere representations of human reality but are self-evident forms that man will assume upon realizing his possibilities are either *ideal types* through which I orient myself, *anti-types* which I shun, or *guiding types* that direct my course. These conceptions are imaginative functions which I use to promote my own development, as I look to ideal types, contrast myself with the anti-types, and become aware of the driving force of guiding types in their formless indeterminacy. Nietzsche's "superior men" are at once ideal types and anti-types. It is as though every *determinate* ideal of man has to be destroyed, for it at once becomes a perversion of itself when regarded as completed. On the other hand, the formless indeterminacy of the superman is like a guiding ideal which serves to prevent me from foundering and atrophying while embracing a determinate ideal.

Nietzsche's *projections* of men also signify *a way of struggling* for the genuine man. The *inequality* among men means not only that there are innumerable ways of conceiving of their *factual* existence, but also that the various conceptions of human *possibilities* cannot be gathered together within *one single* valid ideal. When I find hovering before me a conception of man that, unlike an object of mere contemplation, effectively impresses and takes hold of me, then all my utterances, demands, and volitions become a silent *struggle for this conception.* Nietzsche challenges the mendacious "good and just ones" who proceed as though the one universally right way were the true way: "You are not struggling for justice, all you just ones, but rather you are struggling to win a victory for *your* conception of man. Behold! This is Zarathustra's will to justice: that all your conceptions of man shall be shattered on *his* conception of the superman."

Nietzsche struggled for his conception of man. His task—to see it truly and to render it effective—was already clear to him in his youth when he asked: "Who will now dedicate himself as guardian and knight to the service of humanity—that inviolable sacred treasury in which wealth has gradually been deposited by the most heterogeneous races? Who will set up the *picture of man?*" What Nietzsche saw in all morality, he himself performed: "Morality can do nothing but erect pictures of man. . . . Perhaps they will influence someone or other."

In presenting and characterizing Nietzsche's conception of man, we may well overlook the extensive material of the first level, with its sketches from actual life, magnificent as it is. His picture of man becomes truly *dynamic* on the second level—that of the "superior men." The third stage will present the superman, but so abstractly that he almost fades away into nothingness.

The Superior Man. Nietzsche originally placed his faith in the conception of the superior man. Until the superman as the shatterer of all ideals took a strong hold upon him, he regarded the superior man as a sufficient consummation. Thus he is able to describe him as the man who can lay aside his chains—"those grave and significant misconceptions in religion, morality, and metaphysics"—and as the one who has finally attained his first great goal: "the separation of man from the brutes." But this kind of creative freedom is not open to mere man as such, for freedom of the spirit may be given "only to the ennobled man." "He is the first one who may say that he lives for the sake of joyousness," and only individuals succeed in this: "It is still the time of individuals."

As Nietzsche sees it, superior men do actually exist, even though they are constantly threatened and are forever coming to grief. They are in extreme *danger,* both *from without* and from *within.* Being extraordinary, they come to ruin in a society that is in bondage to the ordinary; they are made submissive, melancholy, and sick. Only "those with iron constitutions, like Beethoven and Goethe," were able to stand firm. But "even they show the effect of the most fatiguing struggle and tension: they breathe more heavily and their manner easily becomes too violent." Society is the relentless enemy of these great ones. "People hate the idea of a higher kind of man." Their isolation is charged up to them as a fault. Granted that "there is continuous success, in individual cases, in many various places on earth . . . through which a higher type finds expression," still the "downfall of superior men is the rule." It is exceptional for them to have the good fortune to "be able to act at the right time"; their general mode of existence is that of "people who sit waiting in all corners of the earth, knowing scarcely that they are waiting, and knowing even less that they are waiting in vain."

When Nietzsche's loss of faith in man comes to include all of those who have been recognized and honored by the world, he begins to believe that the conception of a truly noble humanity will never attain concrete form. The noble man is covert and enigmatic. Disenchanted with everything visible, Nietzsche places his faith in the following possibility: "Perhaps that which is supremely beautiful is still brought forth in darkness and is scarcely born before it disappears into endless night. . . . The great man, precisely in those matters that command the greatest veneration, is still invisible like a too distant star: His victory over force remains without witness and consequently without song and singer." The following would also seem relevant at this point: "Up to now no artist has risen to the task of representing the supreme man, i.e., the one who is at once simplest and most complete. But it may be that the Greeks, in the ideal of Athena, have seen the farthest of anyone up to the present."

Noble men, both as actualities and as developing possibilities, lose significance for Nietzsche. He becomes increasingly discontented with superior men in every possible form in which they become manifest.

To Nietzsche every form of human greatness is already suspect because of the true reason for its ascent. He asks: "Are you climbing, you higher men? Or are you not . . . *pushed* upward by what is basest in you? . . . Are you not *fleeing* from yourself, you rising ones?" He contrasts them with the one whose very nature might be considered of high rank from the start: "This one *is* from above!" But Nietzsche seems to subject such "being" to doubt wherever he encounters it.

The "psychologist" in Nietzsche is well aware of the forgery that is generally perpetrated in the veneration of great men: "What a torment superior men are to the one who has recognized them for what they are!" Thus he considers the poets as "men moved by the moment, inspired, sensuous, childish, frivolous and precipitate in trust and mistrust, usually attempting to hide some injury in their souls, often using their writings to avenge themselves for some inner defilement, and seeking forgetful escape from an all-too-accurate memory through their poetic flights. . . ."

But Nietzsche does not find the inadequacy of man merely in his innumerable obvious perversions; in studying the highest forms of mankind he discovers an insufficiency in his very essence. When, for instance, he regards the *heroic* existence as the highest, still another more distant possibility appears to him: not content that the hero whom he loves should possess "the neck of a bull," he wishes him to display "the eye of an angel as well." Hence this demand is made upon the hero: "He has yet to unlearn his will to the heroic. . . . His rushing passion has not yet passed into serene beauty. The beautiful is unattainable by any violent will. . . ." Even genuine heroism exhibits the constant insufficiency of man. The hero is not the consummation, for he, too, still has within him what is characteristic of man as man, i.e., all the overcoming, sacrificing, and being in transition: "This is the secret of the soul, that only after the hero has abandoned her does a dream bring her—the super-hero."

Nietzsche always suspects *histrionics* when one simply fabricates a picture of the superior man, for using the ideal as a model is a sign of a dishonest life. The philosophy of the ancients is a case in point: They "found it necessary to invent (in the abstract) the perfect man—good, just, wise, a dialectician—in short, the scarecrow of the antique philosophers: a plant torn loose from any soil, a humanity devoid of all definite regulating instincts, a virtue that rests upon merely logical grounds."

All of Nietzsche's critical questioning of the noble man leads to the same conclusion: that Nietzsche, who constantly presses on to something higher, can never rest content with any figure, whether real or imagined. It is precisely where his love is the greatest that he experiences the deepest pain: "When I was most deeply troubled about man, it was his perfection and not his sins and great follies that made me suffer most."

Nietzsche's love for the superior man, as well as his discontent with him, finds its profound and stirring expression in the fourth part of *Thus Spake Zarathustra.* Superior men seem to understand Zarathustra, they seek him out and expect him to save them from the distress of their discontent with the world, with men, and with themselves. Each of them reveals a trait of greatness in his very inadequacy. The kings show their dislike for ruling over a mob; the "spiritually conscientious one" shows self-sacrificing thoroughness in the investigation of his chosen object; the "magician" is aware that his wealth of showmanship does not constitute greatness; the "last pope" is unusually enlightened in matters pertaining to God; "the ugliest man" despises himself and cannot tolerate pity; the "voluntary beggar" is radical in his renunciation; the shadow of the "free-thinker" shows ruthlessness in his skepticism of all words, values, and great names. All of them say and do something that is true. For a moment Zarathustra can give his love to each of them as though he sees in them something of his own kind. But not only is each one wanting in some particular respect; each shows a basic blindness when he tries to understand Zarathustra's idea. Thoroughly and deeply disillusioned, Zarathustra addresses all higher men as follows: "You may verily all be superior men, but you are simply not lofty and strong enough—for me. By 'for me' I mean for that which is inexorable but silent within me." His rejection assumes many forms. He does not care for "men with great longing, great disgust, and great ennui." The basis of their lives is non-being. That is why in all their needs there is a fear that causes them to avoid the risk of decisive action and the danger of failure: "Of course all those who, like yourselves, stand on infirm and delicate legs wish above all, whether they know it or conceal it from themselves, to be treated with indulgence." Consequently he finds them questionable to the very roots of their beings: "You superior men here, have you not all turned out to be failures?" Failures can still acquire value through sacrifice, but they fail in that also: "You superior men, none of you learned to dance on beyond yourself! What does it matter that you turned out failures!" The way in which they fail and reveal their failures through misunderstanding is pitilessly symbolized within the poem when, in the presence of Zarathustra, they become gay, cast off their distress, and joyously abandon themselves to noise and laughter: "With me they have forgotten how to cry out in distress, but, unfortunately, they still cry out." Zarathustra "has not yet seen a great man."

Opposition to Hero-Worship. No actual man can meet the final test if perfection is required. Anyone who makes some particular man the object of a cult, as though this man were perfect, debases his own human potentialities. On both grounds Nietzsche condemns men's unconditional subordination of their very souls to any man. History offers the most frightful examples: "Men of this ilk surrounded Napoleon . . . , who imbued the spirit of our century with romantic prostration before the hero." These fanatics of "an ideal with flesh and blood" are, according to Nietzsche, usually in the right so long as they are negative, for they themselves have their origins in what they deny and are well acquainted with it. But as soon as they absolutely and unquestioningly affirm their ideal in this physical individual, they become dishonest, for they must place the heroized person at such a distance that he is no longer clearly visible. Still their intellectual conscience secretly knows how that came about. When finally the deified one even "betrays himself openly in a loathsome manner as a Non-God who is Much-Too-Human," then these fanatical hero-worshippers arrive at a new self-deception: they take issue with themselves and as interpreters experience something in the nature of martyrdom.

The Superman. That Nietzsche abandons every kind of "superior man" and rejects every sort of deification of a specific individual is due to an impulse that never permits him to rest content with anything limited. If the high fails us, there must be something higher. If man appears as a failure even in the "superior man," then the question arises: How is man himself to be surpassed? The idea of the superman is intended to supply the answer. Facing the universal failure shown by every kind of human being, Zarathustra exclaims: "Since man is a failure, let us continue onward and upward!" Zarathustra's vision goes into the distance from which emerges what to him is all-important: "The superman lies close to my heart; he is my first and sole concern—not man: not my neighbor, not the poorest, the most sorrowful, not the best. . . . What I can love in man is this, that he is a transition and a decline." Nietzsche cares neither for what is visible in man nor for what is concealed, but rather for the future that lies beyond man and is to be reached through him.

To bring forth the superman is our task: "It lies within *our* nature to create a being higher than ourselves. *To create beyond ourselves!* That is what drives us to procreate, and that is the urge behind our activities and our achievements. Just as all volition presupposes a goal, man presupposes a being which, while not existing, gives purpose to his existence." Beings are to be created which "in their sublimity stand far above the entire species of men."

It is Nietzsche's *faith* that creates for itself the idea of the superman. Expectantly he says: "In spite of all, he must come to us sometime, this *redeeming* man . . . who gives the earth its purpose, . . . this victor over God and nothingness." In fact what is meant here is a substitute for the Godhead, like the doctrine of eternal recurrence which plays that role at a later date: "God has died. Our desire is now that the superman live."

The image of the superman, as Nietzsche sees it, remains indeterminate. The weight of his thought lies in the task which he assigns. But this, too, remains indeterminate:

He asks man to fix his gaze entirely on these heights. Speaking to those who want nothing more than to understand great men, he exhorts: "Your strength should be great enough to see beings that stand another hundred miles *above* them!"

But of course conception as such would be merely contemplative. What counts is the activity that makes it possible to actualize what one sees. Nietzsche strives to promote the task of bringing forth the superman with his whole thinking, through the movement that he generates, and especially through "intensification of all contrasts and chasms, elimination of uniformity, and the creative efforts of those of superior power." Inevitably the possibility of the superman is bound to increase the danger which is conceived in its most extreme form when it gives rise to the question: "How could the development of mankind be sacrificed in order to help a superhuman being to come into existence?" The truly basic attitude calls for self-sacrifice so that a greater being may emerge: our humanity has value only as a transition and a decline. It is required of us that we "dance beyond our own selves."

But Nietzsche is never able to say how such a thing could actually come about. He develops the idea of a self-sacrificing, out-going, and all-conquering attitude. But his infinitely general idea that all genuine human activity should have an upward propelling effect is inadvertently transformed into the biological conception of a method of breeding and cultivation from which we could expect that a new being would arise at the boundary between the existing species of man and a higher one.

Since Nietzsche constantly submits all positions to honest critical questioning, it is quite understandable that he nullifies even this abstract "higher and higher" which the thought of the superman involves (just as he nullifies the thought of God): "We are always drawn upward even to the realm of the clouds. On these we place our gaily-colored balloons and then call them gods and supermen. They are after all just light enough for these thrones!—all these gods and supermen. Oh, how tired I am of all insufficiency. . . ."

2

TRUTH

Nietzsche's attempt to formulate a true conception of human nature ended with the dissolution of man. His passionate will to truth dared to draw the most extreme conclusions. Man having become lost, so to speak, and all specific value-judgments having become questionable, Nietzsche is now concerned to find out *what being true consists in.* The result is that even the general concept of truth becomes dubious, and the possibility of truth and reason appears to vanish. When truth now is scrutinized, traditional philosophy falls apart into its various historical manifestations, much as morality crumbled when man was examined.

At the same time, when we think Nietzsche's thoughts with him, it seems as though every negating process reveals a being without which the negation would be impossible. It is not merely that something must be experienced before it can be negated but also that, in a sense, the negated is repeatedly encountered as the subject of Nietzsche's affirmations. That is why every penetrating presentation of his negative philosophy receives an impetus from a positive source. His rejection of historical substance becomes, when actualized, a new kind of mastery of it.

Nietzsche's various reflections as he seeks to discover *what it means to be true* can scarcely be brought into a single systematic order. Although they are actually fused with each other, we shall trace them from three independent sources indicated by Nietzsche himself: (1) *methodical science.* (2) *the theory that truth has its being in a construction* devised by living existents, and (3) *a boundless passion for truth.* In all cases we arrive at intelligible positions located on a route that seems to end in failure: Nietzsche is intent on the *dissolution of reason.* Finally, all of these reflections on truth lead to a *transcending breakthrough.*

Scientific and Philosophic Truth

Nietzsche treats of truth in science as though it were an immediate source. If this source is later seen as derived and thus called in question,

171

still its independence on its own proper level is not lost nor is it challenged at this point. He decisively takes his stand on scientific ground, and it may at first appear that this ground is sufficiently firm to satisfy the passion for truth.

The Methodical Attitude. In his view it is the *method* that is definitive of science. Not only are "the most valuable insights" methodological, but "the scientific spirit rests upon insight into methods." The mere factual *results* of science are, as such, not characteristic: "If the methods were lost, the results could not prevent a renewed prevalence of superstition and nonsense." True knowledge is a matter of method.

It is true that Nietzsche did not discover any new method of natural science and did not even take one single step toward the logical clarification of scientific methods. Taking the validity of scientific insight for granted, he concerned himself rather with evaluation. His theme was not the methods as such, but *the methodical attitude*.

This latter brings a singular security into the world: "It is a source of deep and abiding satisfaction that scientific findings are *indefeasible* and capable of providing the means to new discoveries. It could well be otherwise! Indeed we are so thoroughly persuaded of the eternal change of all human laws and concepts that the extreme reliability of scientific results actually is a cause for astonishment!" Method leads to a level of truth that provides all who employ it with a unique and indispensable experience of one mode of being: "How grand to discover something that is calculable and determinate! There are laws whose truth remains beyond the reach of any individual!"

The methodical attitude seeks *certainty* rather than persuasion, the cogency of well-founded truth rather than the content of knowledge. Thus it accepts even the "unpretentious truths" and regards "the tedious, sure, and enduring truths as superior because of their important consequences in the attainment of further knowledge."

The methodical attitude destroys every kind of absolute knowledge in order to replace it by the unchallenged possession of a determinate knowledge of particulars with which it can accomplish something within the world: "Knowledge is valuable in that it . . . impugns so-called absolute knowledge"; "the 'belief in final and ultimate truths' begins to wane." Science permits "a mastery of nature" without requiring any final insight into cause and effect. When this attitude definitely and methodically gains control over the relationships that can be known, it does not lose itself in absolute knowledge or in the negativity of a nonknowledge that is skeptical of everything.

Thanks to his thorough grasp of the fact that true knowledge consists in method, Nietzsche recognizes further that the methodical attitude is not simply an idiosyncrasy of some specialized science that stands apart from life but is a genuine possibility open to man in all of his thought about and interpretation of the empirical data affecting him. He characterizes the scientific spirit (i.e., the spirit of method) as a property of human rationality by contrasting it with its opposite as follows: "No matter how much merely clever people learn of scientific findings, one quickly discovers from their conversations . . . that they lack the true scientific spirit in that they do not have the necessary instinctive distrust of the aberrations of thought. . . . Merely arriving at some hypothesis or other about a thing suffices to fire them with enthusiasm. . . . Merely having an opinion involves becoming fanatical." As opposed to this tumult of opining and asserting, the mastery of the scientific method is a constant quiet struggle. "Men of a scientific turn of mind" know above all "that the capacity to entertain all manner of idle conceits must be kept under strict surveillance by the scientific spirit." Because of the unfortunate consequences of a lack of method in all areas of life, he urges that "at present every man should have a thorough acquaintance with *at least one science:* he would then know what method is and see the necessity of the most extreme circumspection." To have worked hard for a while at one of the more strict and demanding sciences "increases one's energy, his capacity for drawing conclusions, his tenacity, and his persistence; it teaches one to attain his goal in a deliberate manner. Thus in relation to all that one later undertakes, it is very helpful to have once been a man of science."

Nietzsche's demand for instruction in the scientific method is all the more insistent because, in addition to his awareness of the *irreplaceable* value of the kind of certainty that only this method can yield, he recognizes the extraordinary hazards that accompany its progress in the course of human history. Even during his last year, when he saw that the whole scientific labor of the ancient world had been performed in vain, he commented: "All things necessary for a culture founded on learning—all scientific *methods*—were already there. They had already discovered the great and even incomparable skill of reading with discrimination—this *sine qua non* of a cultural tradition and of the unity of science; natural science, in league with mathematics and mechanics, was making progress in the best possible way—the sense for facts, the last and most valuable of all senses, had its schools. . . . Everything necessary for proceeding with the work had been discovered. Methods (one must say this ten times over!) are the essential things as well as the most difficult; and for the longest time they have to struggle against habituation and laziness. What today we have reconquered with indescribable self-discipline—an unbiased approach to reality, circumspect procedure, patience and dogged earnestness in connection with smallest matters, all that pertains to cognitive *integrity*—these things were present already! Present more than two thousand years ago!"

The Origin and Life of Methods. Methods are not to be applied mechanically, for the truths of science are no more disposed to reveal themselves to frigid indifference than are other truths. There is no such thing as a disinterested process through which truths may automatically be discovered. By representing the origin and development of scientific methods psychologically, Nietzsche shows that they constantly receive their animation from a substratum that in itself is foreign or even hostile to the truth. Methods can no longer be taken seriously and relied upon when they develop into routine calculation by means of an intellectual machinery that has a merely external trustworthiness in the service of a finite purpose.

That which is alien to the truth (and is consequently alogical and unreasonable) but none the less provides the basis and essence of all cognition is many-sided. There are such incitements as delettantism, boredom, and habituation, but these lead to superficial knowledge. A fruitful source of genuine insight, however, is necessity, even though a compelling awareness of the necessity may cloud the insight. We should make good use of our perilous times, for knowledge first becomes inescapable and inexorable when the issue is: Acquire knowledge or perish! "Until truths are inscribed upon our flesh with knives, we secretly reserve a tendency to disparage them."

Furthermore, methods actually develop everywhere as a result of experiencing and employing the very opposite of scientific procedure, viz., of yielding to all the aspects in which things may appear as a result of various possible ways of dealing with them: "We must try out different ways of dealing with things, being now mean and now kind to them, and alternately treating them with justice, passion, and coldness. One man talks to things like a policeman, another like a father confessor, and still a third like a wanderer and curiosity-seeker. They will yield, now to sympathy, and now to assault." But genuine knowledge cannot be gained until the most manifold powers within us are brought together in a "higher organic system." Within scientific thought these powers, when isolated, are fatal to knowledge though when they join forces they limit each other reciprocally, thus holding each other in check. So it is with "the urge to doubt, to deny, to wait-and-see, to collect, and to analyse." "The means to knowledge, the states and operations that in human beings prepare the way for knowledge . . . —phantasy, rapture, abstraction, desensualization, discovery, intuition, induction, dialectic, deduction, critique, gathering of material, objective thinking, contemplation— . . . all these means taken individually have . . . at one time or another been regarded as the alpha and omega—as constituting the content, the gold, and the final sum of cognitive values." But they do not become incitements to the scientific method unless they promote and limit each other.

The essence of the scientific insight that is possible as a result of the cooperation of various forces is *"objectivity."* But considering the incitements that are the starting point and condition of knowledge, this can "not be understood as a disinterested awareness—which is nonsense— but as the capacity to keep one's own pros and cons under control and to bring them into play or keep them out." The only way to promote objectivity is "to know how to make cognitive use of the variations in perspective and emotive meaning." Hence we should not be ungrateful "for the resolute transformations of accustomed values with which the human spirit has inveighed against itself. . . . The *more* feelings about a thing we express in words and the *more* eyes we can direct upon it, the more complete our concept of the thing and the greater our objectivity becomes." "Occasionally we promote the truth through a double injustice . . . when we view two aspects of a thing one after the other, always disavowing the concealed side, in the false belief that the side we confront contains the truth in its entirety."

So *struggle* is always the source of insight: The objectivity of methodical investigation is the result of forces struggling to impose limitations upon each other; it is rooted in life itself and is real only insofar as it is part of life. Furthermore this critical procedure of working things out in the light of the idea of valid and reliable knowledge is substantially safeguarded by the struggle between individual investigators. "Were not each individual so deeply concerned about *his* truth, that is, about *his* being in the right, then there would be no research method at all. . . . The personal struggles between thinkers finally produced such a refinement of method that it was actually possible for truths to be discovered." It is the very violence of the struggle that makes possible a state of affairs that promotes the progress of all science; the individual for instance need not be so mistrustful as to test every assertion relating to some field distant from his own, since this comprehensive testing that the individual could never possibly carry out for himself comes about simply "because each one has competitors in his own field who are extremely mistrustful and who watch every move he makes."

The Limits of Science. When Nietzsche finds methods to be the authentic basis of the compelling validity of scientific knowledge and then catches sight of the conditions under which they can be employed in the service of life (as well as the infrequency of their successful realization and the speed of their decline), it seems as though he has discovered an absolute value in methodical science. Through personal experience he had become well acquainted with the will to knowledge that consumes itself in passionate work on an object, as though science were an end in itself. But it was Nietzsche above all who, in an era that prided itself upon science, saw how man erred in seeking to formulate *all* truth scientifically. In the course of his own scientific work, he became clearly aware of certain limits of science expressed in the following basic principles:

1. *Factual scientific knowledge is not knowledge of being.* Only with reservations can he on one occasion express the opinion that we approach "the actual essence of our world" more closely by means of science. Even before he wrote this, he considered the notion "that thought, following the threads of causality, reaches into the most profound depths of being" to be an "insidious illusion" that leads science again and again to its limit. Accordingly the erudite "do not even come in sight of the really great problems and interrogation marks." While they deal "in a purely factual manner with small isolated areas within science," the universe as a whole remains a closed book to them. But if scientific knowledge, properly understood, never arrives at what most truly *is,* it still, precisely for that reason, does make possible an inkling of it: "In the end science paves the way for a sovereign *absence of knowledge*—a feeling that 'knowledge' simply does not occur . . . , and that the idea of knowledge is itself contradictory." From the depths that are beyond the reach of science, something foreign to science comes into existence: "There are frightful powers that confront 'the scientific truth' with truths of an entirely different kind."

2. *It is not the possession of the truth but the quest for it that is satisfying.* This is the significance of the methodical pursuit of certainty. Anyone who were to rejoice in the possession of scientific truth would show a ridiculous pride "in being authority and master" over a small object chosen more or less at random, while discarding everything else and being indifferent to the abysmal ignorance with which his knowledge is surrounded. "It was for this reason that Lessing, the most honest of all theorists, to the great embarrassment and annoyance of the scientifically

minded, laid bare the profoundest secret underlying all science by hazarding the remark that he was more concerned about the search for truth than about the truth itself."

3. *Scientific certainty provides no security in connection with the things that really matter most.* Such certainty relates to methodically acquired knowledge of the determinate and relative, while the sort of security generally desired is confidence in the whole of things. Nietzsche's remark that it is a "prejudice that certainty is better than uncertainty and the open seas" is not directed against the methodical certainty of science but against the will to security within the whole. It is the "spiritually overconscientious one" who seeks "more security" to whom Zarathustra recommends instead "courage and adventure and delight in the uncertain and the untried."

4. *Scientific knowledge simply cannot give purpose to life.* "It cannot . . . point the way; rather it can be useful only when the direction is already known." It is not bound to be useful, it only may be so. Clearly science cannot guarantee salvation through science. There is "no preestablished harmony between service to the truth and the well-being of mankind."

5. *Science cannot answer the question concerning its own meaning.* Scientific work would not be done, were there not some reason which, in itself, eludes scientific justification and evaluation. "Had we not to some extent continued to be unscientific men, just what could science mean to us? . . . To a merely cognizing being, cognition would be a matter of complete indifference!" Whether the will to science is supported by practical purposes (utility), the morality of truthfulness, the enjoyment of a merely contemplative awareness, or the goals posited by philosophy, in any case, it is always something extra-scientific that gives rise to science and provides its significance.

Through exposing these limitations, Nietzsche becomes fully aware of the *baselessness of the claim that science is an end in itself*—a thesis which he takes to be of modern origin. Science has indeed always been cultivated, but as a means. During the ascendancy of the Christian view that "science is a secondary matter, not final and unconditioned, and not an object of passion," science was not cultivated from a love of knowledge; it was simply "a condition and an ethos," a noble employment in fortune and misfortune. When this enterprise became a kind of end in itself, it was regarded as something "inoffensive, self-sufficient, and truly innocent." It dealt with truth in accordance with tradition and by way of leisurely investigation of the palpable, subject to the stipulations imposed by religious belief. It would seem to hold generally of this sort of search for truth—whether supported by Christian belief or by some other unquestioned attitude toward life—that the "truth as a coherent whole exists only for souls that are at once powerful and inoffensive, peaceful and joyful (as Aristotle was), just as it is only such people who are in a position to search for truth."

The modern thesis of *science for science's sake* has another source. Basically the peaceful occupation with science described above involved a denial of the radical will to pursue and possess knowledge. But the tacitly accepted conditions which maintained control over it were eventually assailed by a spontaneous and unrestrained passion for truth. An "unconditioned bent and urge" to know—"so seldom observed today, to be sure"—came to possess science. As long as this passion proceeds by its own light, it permeates science, preserves its methods and supports the inexorable truth-criteria of a sort of knowledge that knows no limits within the realm of particulars, defends it against every kind of obscurity, but sets its sights upon the sort of truth that can no longer be regarded as merely scientific. In fact it remains unconditioned, and, in discovering the limits of science, it passes beyond the scientific methods which it has mastered to new experiences in philosophical thinking. But if this passion takes itself to be identical with methodical scientific investigation, it will inevitably lead to perversions. Nietzsche characterized the *factual presuppositions of these perversions* in the following manner when he saw how very questionable the doctrine of science for science's sake was:

1. When science "is still something like passion, love, ardor, or suffering," it is the latest and most refined form of the *"ascetic ideal."* Such science is founded upon morality; it is the will to truth "at any cost." But in actual practice this will changes into the "disquietude of estrangement from ideals" and into a new self-deception: "How often, after all, the real meaning of the proficiency of our most learned men, their unfailing assiduity, their burning of the midnight oil, even their craftsmanship, is the concealment of something or other from themselves!" Nietzsche does not wish to spoil the pleasure which honest scientific workers derive from the exercise of their craft; on the contrary, he is delighted with what they are doing. But still, "the fact that scientific work is today carried on as a stern discipline does not show that contemporary science as a whole has a goal, a will, an ideal, and the passionate fervor of a great faith." As the ascetic ideal declines, this sort of science loses its meaning. At present, though this is not openly avowed, "science has absolutely no belief in itself." It preserves itself still by means of the ghostly force of the ascetic ideal, by virtue of which its essential task may be seen "in examining the

most common and ordinary occurrences for their own sakes." This involves "a will to come to a halt before the factual" that forbids both negation and affirmation and ends by "renouncing all interpretation."

2. Nietzsche notes the present loss of confidence in religion. Since science has now accomplished numerous specific useful things, people place their trust in *it,* and they tend to submit to it just as completely as they formerly submitted to religion. At this point the *urge for security* comes into play: What is involved here is "that penchant for truth that is essentially a penchant for safety." This "will to truth and certainty derives from fear engendered by uncertainty"; it is "simply the longing for an enduring world." *Weakness* seeks persuasion and now hopes to find it in the form of scientific certainty (which however, is definitely not what is wanted, since constant questioning and an incapacity to encounter the whole of things are essential to science). In scientific knowledge, weakness seeks increase of strength, not the satisfaction of an interest in things or of a boundless passion for truth. Thus, scientific certainty is perverted into a reassuring kind of practical truth that is preserved with anxious tenacity.

That this perverted form of science takes the place of religion and then serves to satisfy mere animalian wants is expressed with biting irony as follows: "The goal of modern science is the least possible amount of pain and the longest possible life—thus a kind of eternal bliss, though a very modest kind compared with what the various religions have promised."

3. When science is not pursued with methodical strictness within its own proper limits, and when more is inadvertently demanded of it than it can possibly accomplish, then the typical errors of a purported *knowledge of being* appear, and, as a result, the certainty that science can achieve is lost, together with the philosophical truth that could proceed from a genuine source. When the man of science finds that he can no longer endure the vacuity of his subject, he discovers, in the wasteland of his ascetic explorations, "those shimmering mirages, known as philosophic systems, which, with all the deceptive force of magic, provide the solution to every riddle." Anyone who succumbs to this is lost to science. Again, one may "embellish" science: one may seek to provide entertainment and present "a digest of science containing all manner of remarkable and striking illustrations." Or the sciences may assume a personal unity in special "natures for whose sake science exists—at least it seems so to them. . . . It is people of this ilk who are responsible for the delusion that a science is now complete and has attained its goal" and thereby

create the sort of enchantment that "has been disastrous for science and misleading to the genuinely qualified workers of the spirit. . . . Such people are usually referred to as philosophers."

If the presumed intrinsic value of science leads to such perversions, it is because the authentic source of the passionate will to know, which previously supplied the pathos, has been lost. It was this source that brought into existence our modern science, of which it is true to say: "It is something new in history that knowledge should undertake to be more than a means." But Nietzsche's critical questioning goes beyond all those perversions to the source itself. Here at the source, the matrix of the unbounded and unconditional will to know proves not to be something known, but rather something which underlies and supports the will to know, namely, a *faith* in the value of knowledge: "Even science derives its support from a faith; there just is no science that does not take something for granted." At the root of modern science lies the assumption that "nothing is more necessary than truth, and all else is secondary to it." The sense in which this faith came to seem questionable to Nietzsche will be explained in the latter part of this chapter. But first let us examine the train of thought that, while viewing science within its proper limits, still relates it closely to the meaning and purpose of philosophy.

Science and Philosophy. It is essential that Nietzsche recognized a kind of truth inhering in the scientific method and equally essential that, being aware of the limits of scientific truth, he did not regard such truth as final and absolute. The question of the limits of science is raised, not with destructive intent, but with a view to penetrating to the very essence of science itself. "What is involved is the *mastery,* not the annihilation of science." When science is viewed in the clearest possible light, it is seen to have originated in philosophy. In the end science presupposes the passion for knowledge. This is philosophizing, and the scientific methods are its instruments. *True science and true philosophy are one:* "Philosophy does not exist per se and apart from science; the same sort of thinking is pursued in both areas." Since "all sciences" rest "only upon the general foundation of philosophy," ideally "the *one* philosopher is identical with all scientific endeavor. . . . It is well to point out the gigantic unity in all the cognitive drives"—the unity which has deserted "the fragmented man of learning."

Thus the truth is to be found in that which unites science and philosophy, and neither the savant who ceases to be a philosopher nor the philosopher who abandons science stands in an authentic relation to it. But it is still possible to view scientific methods and philosophizing as the

wo poles of a unified whole, and Nietzsche constantly *isolates* these
extremes as he comments on them:

He sets sharp bounds to science, expressing them first of all in posi-
ivistic terms: "We are scientific precisely to the extent to which we are
esolved to accept the testimony of the *senses*. . . . The remainder is
abortive and prescientific, that is to say, it is metaphysics, theology,
osychology, and epistemology." Again, science is *"formal* science, a
science of signs, as is logic and that applied logic, mathematics."

A further boundary appears in that the truth with which the man of
science is concerned is not consciously regarded as his own creation.
Existence is presupposed, and, in "unveiling" it, the man of science
oelieves that he is *finding* the truth. That existence is thus comprehensible
s from the outset tacitly taken to be its justification.

Finally there is the limitation inherent in the fact that any scientific
work is always performed within an isolated and specialized field and
that, if it is to be pursued for its own sake, it necessarily presupposes an
attitude that considers life as a whole: viz., the belief "in a bond and a
continuity between all scientific work so that the individual may investigate as small an area as he pleases and still be confident that his work is
not in vain."

The fact that science can become largely independent of philosophy
and still occupy the lives of scholars and investigators who, having been
forced to specialize, may perform their specific tasks with complete
mastery without thinking any longer about the meaning of their activities,
leads Nietzsche to the question of the traits, motives, and *Existenz* of
these men. Drawing upon personal knowledge gained from his life in the
academic world, he describes, both reverently and disparagingly, a
wealth of characteristics belonging to various learned men and scientific
investigators:

Whatever else he may be, "the ideal savant . . . is surely one of the
most valuable tools there is." Nietzsche explains "why the savant is more
noble than the artist: he must be simpler, less ambitious, more temperate,
quieter . . . and lose himself completely in matters that seldom appear
to be worthy of such a sacrifice of personality." The magnificence and the
poverty of such an existence is presented in *Zarathustra* through the
"spiritually conscientious one" who is nothing more than a superlative
authority on the brain of the leech. He characterizes himself as an
investigator: "I should rather know nothing than to have half-knowledge
of many things! . . . I proceed to the foundation. What difference
does it make whether it is large or small? Or whether it is called
swamp or sky. . . . Wherever my integrity leaves off I am blind,

and I want to be blind. But wherever I want to know, there I want to be honest, i.e., hard, stern, cruel, relentless."

Philosophy, which occupies the opposite pole, is described no less decisively. Of paramount importance is that which does not have its being through science but still achieves cognizability and communicability—that through which science is first aroused to activity. Such philosophy becomes for Nietzsche infinitely more than just one pole of the sphere of knowledge. To clarify the nature of philosophy, Nietzsche presents a portrait of the philosopher in which his conception of his own nature and task is indissolubly blended with what could be achieved by philosophy in general:

The philosopher discovers his task where *being in its entirety* emerges, whereas science offers methodical certainty about *particulars*. His own self serves him as a "reproduction and abbreviation of the whole world." The philosopher must, at one time or another, have traversed every stage, have risked every attitude and experience, have occupied every standpoint, and have availed himself of every expression. "But all these things are mere preliminaries. It is his job to create values." In addition, he is also "the man of unlimited responsibility who has the entire development of mankind on his conscience."

Philosophers are experimenters willing to involve their own selves. They feel "the burden and obligation of a hundred of life's attempts and temptations," they "hazard themselves constantly," and their delight in trials avails itself of "experiments of a dangerous sort." They may even "feel themselves to be disagreeable fools and dangerous question marks." Their thoughts are always questions, and their answers are never final. They are "in every respect philosophers of the hazardous perhaps."

They are always at loggerheads with the present—with the world of their contemporaries. As a result of their insight into the whole of things, philosophers know enough to exclaim: "Indeed! When a couple of generations have passed away, no one will hold to the prevalent opinions that threaten to enslave you today." But this knowledge is not merely negative; their opposition to their own era rests upon their secret capacity to "know about man's new greatness and about a new and untrodden path to his exaltation."

Philosophers are self-sufficient; they do not have to look to anything else for support. They have no need for firm anchorage in a creed. Their skepticism is "boldly masculine. . . . This kind of skepticism despises without rending itself; it undermines but gains possession; it does not believe, but it avoids losing itself in unbelief; it promotes a perilous freedom of the spirit, but it keeps the heart in check." The skepticism of he philosopher provides much more than skepticism: "reliable standards of value, the intelligent application of a uniform method, and the shrewd courage which characterizes men who can stand alone and bear the burden of their own responsibilities. . . . They will not consort with truth in order to find it 'pleasing' or 'edifying' or 'inspiring.' "

Only comprehensive experience and whole-hearted dedication of one's entire being will enable a man, in lonely opposition to the *de facto* world and drawing upon a positive skepticism that penetrates to the most profound truths, to become the sort of philosopher of whom it may be said that he "commands," that he creates values, organizes them, and determines their orders of rank. Nietzsche, when still a young man, remarked: "All great thinkers laid down laws concerning the measure, coinage, and weight of things."

Insofar as philosophy and science stand at opposite poles, philosophy should have the leadership. For all science depends upon philosophical insight for its goal and its meaning; even its procedures (methods) have their source in philosophy. "Some trace of philosophical thinking is to be found at the heart of all scientific thinking."

In every respect philosophy takes precedence. It should "sustain spiritual advance throughout the centuries and thus provide for the eternal fruitfulness of all that is great." For mere science, "great and small do not exist." Philosophy differs from science in that it "chooses and extracts the uncommon, the astonishing, the difficult, and the divine" and that it "calls attention to what is vain and superfluous." It follows "the path that leads to things worth knowing," while science tackles, without discrimination, everything that can be known and used. Since the concept of greatness is changeable, "philosophy begins by providing laws for greatness."

When the distinction between the two becomes a final separation and all unity is lost, then the leadership of philosophy as well as the meaningfulness of science (and consequently truth and truthfulness) ceases. This can occur in many ways:

In pathetically mistaking itself for science, philosophy actually turned against science. Almost all of philosophy since Socrates has waged "a battle against science." "It is the same battle that was later waged by the church": "People wished to remain free to pursue their own 'path.' . . . They hated the step-by-step procedure and the tempo of science. They hated the unwillingness to conform, the wait-and-see attitude, and the personal indifference of the scientific man." "The entire history of philosophy is permeated by falsehood and forgery. Apart from the truly respectable but rare skeptics, an instinct for intellectual integrity fails to appear." Indeed the poverty of today's "mishmash-philosophers, who consider themselves realistic or positivistic" and of "philosophy reduced to epistemology" is, he thinks, sufficient reason why a first-rate man of science, who otherwise would have to obey the philosophers, may be forgiven for feeling superior. For these contemporary philosophers "have been brought back under the jurisdiction of science," although scientifically they are unproductive. Nothing at all remains to them of the true meaning of philosophy.

Science on its own part has in recent times brought about so "inappropriate an exchange of ranks" with respect to science and philosophy that men who are merely learned now try to play the role of philosophers. "The declaration of independence of the scientific man, his emancipation from philosophy," expresses fundamentally a "plebeian instinct": "Full of arrogance and devoid of good sense, he sets out to lay down laws to philosophy and, for once, play the master—what am I saying?—the *philosopher.*" The specialist instinctively turns against all attempts at synthesis, the industrious laborer against genteel leisure, while the utilitarian rejects philosophy as a succession of refuted systems from which no one derives any benefit.

As described by Nietzsche, philosophizing (in spite of its "commands") is a search right up to the end. One cannot but ask how it is possible for philosophy to assume the leadership over science when it "is" not the absolute truth. Nietzsche has scarcely shown how this leadership is actually to be exercised, and the reassuring formulae that we have encountered do not always tell us what philosophy is. Rather, philosophy as a conceptual structure, as a complete and final work, as a rational body of internally consistent thoughts—virtually the entire history of philosophy—is found to be dubious. It is certainly not to this that he looks for a secure and definite ground for truth.

The Theory of Exegesis: Truth and Life

Truth has been regarded as a timeless subsistent known to those who draw near to it: an unalterable and incontestable being that has only to be discovered.

Nietzsche's insight into the limits of science, whose presumed absence of presuppositions proved to be an evasive delusion, and his experience with a boundlessly moving impulse inherent in creative philosophy made him skeptical of any subsisting realm of truth. In the course of his searching skepticism he developed the following theory of truth: All knowledge is an interpretation of being provided by a living and cognizing subject; there is no truth that is not entertained in thought and believed, that is, that is not found within that encompassing being that we are (*das Umgreifende des Seins das wir sind*),[1] and that is possibly all the being there is. Thus conceived, truth is not something independent, unconditioned, and absolutely universal. Rather it is inextricably involved with the being of a living subject and the world that he has constructed. But this world as it appears to us is, like ourselves, in a constant process of temporal change.

This theory develops out of the kind of doubting that expresses a determination not to be deceived by what appears obvious and unquestionable. Nietzsche intends, by demolishing all that was prematurely established as eternal truth, to proceed to the authentic truth that is one with the source and illumines the path of living *Existenz* itself. The thoughts here involved constantly vacillate between the denial of every possibility of a subsisting realm of truth and the encounter with a truth not yet fully grasped; such thoughts could not receive articulate expression apart from a theory of *being* to the effect that to be is to be interpreted.[2] In turn, this theory of truth unavoidably leads to the question of its own truth or, in any case, of the sense in which it can be said to count as true when judged by its own criteria. Accordingly a critically oriented presentation of this theory of truth will be attempted in the following pages.

Truth as Illusion. Nietzsche believes that the essence of man—the sole form of cognitive life with which we are acquainted—has emerged in the course of universal becoming as a unique way of interpreting being: "The general phenomenon of intellect is unknown to us; we only are acquainted with special cases." The way in which we see, think about, and apprehend the world is a result of the sort of intellect we have. By the same token, however, "every single kind of intellect must have its own way of understanding the world."

Our human way of interpreting the world, like that of any existence that cognizes in time, must transform everything that it takes to be true and, consequently, actual. It is only "because we have viewed the world for thousands of years with moral, esthetic, and religious pretensions and with blind inclinations, passions, and fears" that it has "gradually become

---

[1] The author is accustomed to distinguish between what might be called the subjective and the objective poles of being: the being that we are, and the being that surrounds us. The former includes existence (*Dasein*), consciousness in general (*Bewusstsein überhaupt*), spirit (*Geist*), and *Existenz;* the latter, the world and transcendence.—Trs.

[2] For the fundamental significance of this doctrine and for Nietzsche's own world-interpretation, see Book II, Chap. V.

so wondrously colorful, frightful, significant, and animated. . . . The human intellect has permitted the appearances to shine forth and has infused all things with its own basic misconceptions. . . . That which we now call the world is the result of a host of errors and phantasies which have gradually accumulated in the course of organic development. . . ."

What a cognizing living being calls truth is the way in which he conceives of his world. But the truth that is bound up with life Nietzsche calls "error": "Truth is the kind of error without which a definite species of living being cannot live." Still, insofar as this life is the *sine qua non* of the mode of being of everything else and, as the sole existence (*Dasein*), is the one thing that has authentic value, this error is not to be rejected: "We do not regard the falsity of a judgment as an objection to it," for repudiating false judgments would amount to repudiating life itself. One must "allow untruth as a condition of life." The error that is a promoter of life is, as such, "truth."

The truth believed by living beings is called error, not merely because it develops and undergoes change, but also because it is as various as the modes of human life: "There are many kinds of eyes . . . and hence many kinds of 'truths.' It follows that there is no truth."

Such utterances can surely be meaningful only from the standpoint of a kind of truth—unattainable as it may be from the level of life—that can detect the erroneousness of the knowledge that serves life. This involves two distinct concepts of truth: To begin with, truth appears as the kind of error that supports life. But again it appears as remote from life, as though one must abandon life in order to arrive at the criterion through which life's errors can be recognized.

Nietzsche has in mind a way of thinking calculated to overcome this duality: What is called life-promoting error is the only entire truth, though it cannot properly be called either truth or error. "The concept of truth is nonsensical. The whole realm of the 'true-false' has to do only with relations between living beings, not with the self-existent. There is no self-existent living being." On this view truth signifies "not necessarily the opposite of error but, in the basic cases, only the relation of different errors to each other." That is why Nietzsche asks: "What forces us anyway to assume that there is an essential opposition between the true and the false? Does it not suffice to grant that illusoriness differs in degree and that there are, as it were, brighter and darker shadows and tonal qualities of the illusory?"

But still we cannot escape the necessity of having to distinguish between truth and error. For without such a distinction it would not be possible to speak meaningfully of truth. It is only by means of this distinction that one can make the paradoxical attempt to remove the antithesis by maintaining that truth and error differ merely in degree of illusoriness but do not differ in kind. When Nietzsche actually occupies this standpoint, everything intrinsically valid disappears in the constantly changing, insubstantial, and ephemeral appearance which is to be equated with being itself. "Truth," then, "is not something present all along that needs merely to be discovered and disclosed; it has to be created. The word 'truth' is the name of a process . . . that in itself is never final: not a process of becoming aware of the truth as something initially independent, fixed, and determinate but of conferring and actively deciding the truth."

The thoughts about the illusoriness of truth just sketched acquire a twofold meaning when they are explicated. First of all, they constitute a theory that can be applied in the socio-psychological clarification of the circumstances under which things are taken to be true. This is to forget what it means for the theory itself to be true and to be concerned, instead, merely with the empirical truth involved in specific relations between human behavior-patterns. But in the second place, the theory itself is a means of expressing a philosophical awareness of a limit and therewith an existential claim and a principal feature of the consciousness of being as such.

The Application of the Theory. Nietzsche intends to explain socio-psychological actuality by means of a theory concerning the univeral errors of an existence made possible by these very errors. The application of the theory, according to which all knowledge (i.e., opinions about what is true) is an involuntary self-limitation of life to that which is suitable for it in a given instant and under the circumstances attending it, may be illustrated as follows:

The truth that binds living beings together must be *communicable.* The statement: "There are many kinds of eyes . . . and hence many kinds of truth" is limited by that which makes society possible. For any community and for those living in it, only that is true which can be communicated to all. Hence universal communicability is unconsciously accepted as the source and criterion of those truths that promote life through communal means. Truth is that which our conventional social code accepts as effective in promoting the purposes of the group. Verbal truth is "a mobile army of metaphors" that after long use have come to seem definitive to a community of men. This community will condemn as a "liar" the person who misuses its unconsciously accepted, and therefore valid, metaphors with a view to hypostatizing what everyone considers to be unreal. Community members are obliged to "lie" in accordance with fixed convention. To put it otherwise, they must be truthful by playing the group's game with the conventionally marked dice. To fail to pay in the coin of the realm is to tell forbidden lies, for, on this view, whatever transcends conventional truth is falsehood. To tell lies of this kind is to sacrifice the world of meanings upon which the endurance of his community rests. Conversely, there are *forbidden truths:* This same threat to the continuance of the community is also counteracted by relentlessly preventing anyone from thinking and uttering unconventional but authentic truths.

What Nietzsche wishes to come to grips with is clearly a sociopsychological entity that may well exist without ever becoming aware of the real problem of truth. What occurs here is an unconscious self-limitation. Nietzsche sets such wide boundaries around the kind of truth that consists in life-promoting errors and draws its strength from its indubitability that he even includes what is pre-eminently communicable, namely, the rational. It is precisely because of its universal communicability that the rational seems to him questionable: "Whatever is demonstrable is true—this is an arbitrary definition of the concept 'true.' . . . Lurking in the background is the utility of such an accepted meaning of the word 'true,' for the demonstrable appeals to what, more than anything else, all our heads have in common (i.e., to logic). This quite naturally shows it to be nothing more than a utility criterion in the interest of the majority." Hence the self-evident validity of rational conclusions that are universally communicable is a matter of the unconscious self-limitation of the truth to the requirements of civilization.

When a theory is to be employed in this way, it is first of all essential to recognize that the degree of validity of the knowledge it provides remains undetermined, for it would be unwarranted to assert that it is valid for all human existence. Only when it is possible to show empirically and *in concreto* what the limits of its proper application are, does it have any meaning in relation to human knowledge. In the second place, it is characteristic of this sort of theory concerning knowledge that its results are not of the kind that can be attained through disinterested observation by an unconcerned and passively cognizing faculty. While such presentations as those sketched above may seem to be mere applications of a theory, their real crux is an appeal: whether we entertain them reluctantly or find them illuminating, we consider them with a view to altering something in ourselves.

Speaking generally, such thoughts as the above move in two essentially different directions and pursue two different goals. At times Nietzsche points out the limitations of the awareness of being achieved from the standpoint of actual existence. This he does by enacting in thought a theoretical approach to life as an interpreting existence whose developing truth is constantly being created and is never fixed and final. Then again, psychologizing and sociologizing with the same concepts, he appeals to possible *Existenz* (the life of the elite with its exaltation). In both cases he philosophizes, but the concepts that arise are inclined to degenerate into the merely theoretical thoughts of the research worker, for the different ways of coming to grips with truth, when seen as symptoms of different modes of life, appear as objective facts to be investigated. This leads to an "application" which threatens to deprive the theory of its philosophic character. The latter first comes decisively to the fore when we carefully follow out the logical circle which underlies this thinking, for it is this that enables us to feel the philosophic source.

The Circle. Within life's process of becoming, all truth concerning the truth of life must be in process, i.e., it must be a kind of error. Even what we are now saying about what is true must itself be dubious. Here Nietzsche's thought finds itself in a situation that shows us a necessary characteristic of all thinking that takes place on the boundary:

When knowledge undertakes to know knowledge, or the truth about truth is sought, thought proceeds in a circle. When this is the simple self-assertion of self-illumining truth, there is no difficulty. But when the circle consists in the overcoming of truth by itself, then either the self-overcoming is final and the truth founders, or a new mediated self-assertion arises insofar as a new source of truth appears within the circle. Such thinking of the truth through truth is neither helped nor hindered by any externals. There are two possibilities for the disappearance of the circle in the substratum to which it refers. How is one to decide between them?

Let us assume first that the self-overcoming of truth is necessitated by an absolutely valid truth, viz., by knowledge about the life-process of a constantly specious truth. But then (1) this valid truth about truth includes a fixed point of undoubted truth (the logical inexpugnability of self-relatedness is involved) and the question arises how I, proceeding from the fixed point now attained (even if this is merely negative), can go on to further truths. Or (2) one may proceed to ask whether the consequences of this insightful self-overcoming of truth must mean the end of the search, so that a long historical process during which men looked in vain for truth is to be put as completely out of mind as though it had never occurred.

Nietzsche undoubtedly would have rejected both possibilities, i.e., (1) the establishment of a new system of truth on the basis of a newly gained indubitably fixed point (somewhat in the manner of Descartes), and (2) an end to all bother about truth. He did *not* mean either of these.

Now let us assume instead that all thought of truth is carried on within a thinking substratum, which is *Existenz,* and that this substratum is the life of truth which, as life, announces itself through these thoughts. Then, proceeding from "the life of truth," the choice between the two circles turns in favor of the self-assertion of truth. The truth, in illuminating the sources of being, proceeds through a movement of self-reflection to *Existenz,* which does not destroy but confirms it and turns against the vacuity of the lifeless rationalistic formalism of the first of the above-mentioned possibilities. Such formalism cannot maintain itself; it is blind to genuine truth and even destructive of such truth as inheres in its own correctness.

It is this second view that Nietzsche accepts. His thoughts about truth, since they deny what is required for their formulation, must run into incessant contradictions. Such thoughts would be nothing more than a nonsensical confusion, did they not enable us to experience limits that can be revealed only indirectly. When the concepts which his theory of truth generates attain these limits, we experience the fulfillment of the kind of thinking that unavoidably uses even contradictions as indirect indicators. His theory is not a theory about a given state of affairs; it is a philosophical means of expressing first the existential appeal to the essential truth born by essential life and, second, the possibility of a life-transcending intimate awareness of being.

Truth and Existenz. When Nietzsche, for example, characterizes the mendacity of the idealists (whom he usually calls "the good and the just") as "the unwillingness at any price to see how ultimate reality is constituted . . . ," what he is saying is true of all life: that untruth is a condition of its existence. What in other connections is but an interpretation of vital existence here becomes an attack. Thus it appears that *this* lie is not identical with the sort of illusoriness which constitutes the truth of life itself. He distinguishes between the universal illusion that is an entirely indispensable condition of life and the illusion that conditions a specific kind of life (and only *appears* to improve a particular situation). To recognize the latter illusion is psychologically to understand, unveil, reject, and thus existentially decide (insofar as the thinking involved is an inner activity rather than a merely contemplative judgment).

In fact Nietzsche's will to discriminate is decisive at this point. He does not find the illusoriness of truth to be of one kind; there are as many varieties of it as of life itself. Life is not homogeneous, for there are essential differences in rank. That Nietzsche at once ascertains, affirms, and attacks what is formally the same (untruth as a condition of life), means that he appeals to the life of higher rank and rejects the inferior life. As appearance confronts appearance, the one may be taken to be untrue in relation to the other. The reality that "the good and the just" of our example veil with their lies is nothing other than universal illusoriness. At this point, the lie and the truth confront each other as false and true illusoriness.

In the sort of thinking that appeals to the life of high rank (which basically is nothing other than possible *Existenz*), further contradictions appear when things formally the same but materially different are judged in opposite ways. Thus there is no mystery about the contradictions that arise when the will to a permanent, fixed, and discoverable truth is, on one occasion, affirmed as a condition of life and, on another occasion, rejected as stultifying.

Nietzsche holds that a known world is a condition of life. Within this world the "will to truth is a stabilizing factor that makes for truth and permanence . . . a translation into being." It is in this vein that Zarathustra says: "The will to truth is the will to the intelligibility of all being. . . . First of all you shall make being intelligible." Life wants and needs unchanging subsistent truth. But that which, in the form of permanent truth, is a condition required by life for the sake of its own permanence, has, from another point of view, the opposite effect on life, namely a paralyzing one: "The assertion that the truth is simply there is one of the most seductive doctrines that there is. When this is believed, the will to test, investigate, exercise foresight, and perform experiments is paralyzed. . . . Here the feeling of laziness pleads the cause of truth. . . . It is more comfortable to conform than to test." [3]

Another apparent verbal contradiction appears when he rejects as a sign of an impotent life the belief that the world is fundamentally as it

[3] When Nietzsche goes on to say that "consequently the truth is more portentous than error," it must be remembered that in the philosophically hortatory context here provided, the words "truth" and "error" can exchange meanings: Truth as subsistent is indeed for him always "error"; when error is a condition of life, i.e., of the life of high rank, then it can be called truth in the sense of life-promoting error; when it is detrimental to life, then it can be called truth in the sense of the inferior or declining life of a laziness that finds it convenient.

ought to be, only to require it again as a necessity of the creative life. He rejects it when he writes: "Belief that the world that ought to be now *is*, that it actually *exists*, is a belief of the unproductive ones who do not wish to create a world as it ought to be. They presuppose it as present. . . . 'The will to truth' as the weakness of the will to create." But there must be a difference between the belief in an enduring being that derives from the unproductive life, a belief which Nietzsche thus existentially rejects by means of psychological clarification, and the belief in being which belongs to life as such and must be philosophically illuminated. This becomes obvious when Nietzsche seemingly says of the creators, what he has said of the impotent, but now in an affirming and exhorting way: "Man projects his drive to truth beyond himself in the form of a world that is already at hand. His need as a creator invents the very world on which he is working—he anticipates it. Such anticipation (such 'belief' in the truth) provides his support."

The life-process within which truth has its being in constantly changing illusion does indeed seem to Nietzsche to be an endless movement that always accepts a fixed and final truth only to bring about its dissolution. But essentially its philosophic significance is determined by what man becomes as a result of it. If all truths that belong to being and can be incorporated in life are undergoing alteration, then truth is never an independent reality with which we can rest content. On the contrary: "To be true means to be capable of exalting the human race."

Truth in Relation to Life-Forces That Both Condition and Destroy It. Psychological clarification of *de facto* relations and existential incitement to the exaltation of vital truths interpenetrate each other in Nietzsche's numerous presentations of inescapable circles within which neither truth nor life (here conceived as opposites) can stand independently. Nietzsche stresses three directions in which the development of truth must come about in relation to other life-forces that threaten to destroy it and, at the same time, supply its indispensable conditions:

(1) If truth is to receive expression, then it must *take effect* within the world; ineffective truth might as well not exist. In the absence of the will to communication, and thus to effectiveness, no enduring will to truth is possible. (2) Truth is involved in the constellations of *power* that make possible the existence of those thinkers who entertain the truth. (3) Without the impetus to knowledge provided by *belief*, the search for truth would never take place. But all these conditions can also become destructive: the extinction of truth may result from (1) the independence assumed by its effects, (2) a conflict with power, and (3) the absolutiza-

tion of the belief that inspires it. The following reflections may serve to bring these three tendencies before us:

(1) Men must inevitably undertake to secure the *effectiveness* of truth—if only by speaking out. This, to Nietzsche, is of portentous significance, for "effectiveness" as such is ambiguous: the effective can continue to be true only insofar as it is understood and is convincing. However it turns into its own opposite whenever it is merely persuasive, i.e., when it is promulgated through suggestion and leads to thoughtlessness.

An attitude of indifference to the effects, assumed by one who, for the sake of the truth, wishes to say nothing but what is true, is itself untruth, for it is blindness to the significance of the effects: "Simply to demand that only the truth be spoken is to presuppose that one already possesses the truth. If this, however, only means that one should say what he *takes* to be true, then there are surely cases in which it is *important* that this should be conveyed in such a way that it will *influence* the other person so that he also will accept it as true."

If what I am after is the effect as such, then I no longer pursue the truth but only the effective means. It is not merely that the truth of a statement uttered for the sake of effect is now inconsequential; from the standpoint of one concerned only with the effect, it can even be said that "whatever is to have the effect of truth must not itself be true." How that which is originally true can lose its truth as a result of arrangements made for its effective propagation Nietzsche demonstrates historically when he lays before us the means and methods employed by "a veritable school of the means of seduction."

Nietzsche sees the inescapable necessity of effectiveness. But when he recognizes it, one almost always notes a tone of irony—an affirmation that is also a negation. He writes: "To make propaganda is not respectable, but it is clever." Today it is especially necessary at least "to use uncouth speech in conformity with the times": "Delicacy and reticence are no longer understood, not even by those who are like ourselves. That about which one does not raise his voice and shout simply does not exist."

Whatever forms the effects may assume, they turn out to be discrepant with the authentic truth, no matter how inseparable from the process of general dissemination they seem to be when viewed within the context of Nietzsche's realistic considerations. Nietzsche recognizes not only the necessity of communication but also the self-sufficiency of truth: "The proposition: 'This thought cannot be true!' is shocking. 'It will not be accepted as true!' leaves me cold, for I take that for granted."

(2) Wherever truth is grasped at all, it is involved with *power:* Within the objective world, it is dependent upon an established and authoritative power that permits or hinders its communication; within the subjectivity of the individual, it relies upon the provocative will to power of the thinker.

Intrinsically and taken by itself, truth is not a force. "Rather it must attract force to its side or join the ranks of the forceful if it is not to perish again and again!" This danger appears, for example, when the thoughtlessness constantly displayed by the average man becomes a determining factor: "As a result of sheer habituation, human beings subordinate themselves to everything that purports to be powerful" and in so doing become enemies of the truth. Man prefers not to think and not to be enlightened: "Enlightenment arouses indignation: the slave wants something categorical and understands only the tyrannical."

As long as each creative thinker's will to power prevails—and without it creative thinking cannot so much as get started—all criticism is annulled. For evidence of the truth already appears in his heightened feeling of power.

(3) Truth is not at first pursued merely for the sake of the objective validity that it acquires in science; its pursuit is incited by *belief:* "All actual striving for truth has entered the world as a result of the struggle for a sacred assurance. Apart from the pathos of the struggle, men would take no interest in logical derivation." "There can be no basic drive for truth, i.e., for pure truth apart from consequences and emotional involvement." At the very least there must be belief in the truth, through which (even if the belief itself is false) the truth can become worth the struggle to us: "Even skepticism involves belief—the belief in logic." Hence there really is "no such thing as a drive to knowledge and truth, there is only a drive to belief in the truth. Pure knowledge is unmotivated."

If belief, belief in the truth, and the desire to believe in the truth are original conditions without which no search for truth could ever get under way, these very factors also develop into a threat to the truth. This occurs when belief or its perversion into a desire for unbelief, i.e., the drives as such, set themselves up as the criterion of truth. Every form of belief takes itself to be true, but the truth-criterion it employs differs essentially from the criterion of objective, methodical, and universally valid, well-grounded truth. For the criterion of the truth of belief is the "evidence of strength" which it provides to those who rely on it. Methodical, objective truth, on the contrary, can "be throughout painful, pernicious, and fatal." Generally speaking, "belief is fashioned by means diametrically opposed to and, in fact, exclusive of the methodical prin-

ciples of scientific investigation." Those false truth-criteria, whose application in matters of proof spells the demolition of truth, are, according to
Nietzsche, such "tests of strength" as (a) the *will to happiness,* (b)
martyrdom, and (c) *virtuous behavior.*

(a) Experiencing *pleasure* in connection with a truth and finding
happiness in it are never cogent proofs. Quite the contrary: the history of
the conquest of truth shows that men "have had to struggle for truth
every step of the way; for its sake they have had to renounce almost
everything they normally set their hearts upon, everything they love, and
everything that permits them to trust in life. For this, greatness of soul is
required: the service of the truth is the most difficult and demanding
service." While, according to Nietzsche, belief claims that "because it
makes us happy it is true," the scientific search for objective truth
concludes from its experience that "just because belief makes us happy, it
follows that it lies." Truth is always lost when the will to happiness
assumes control. So philosophy, itself a kind of belief, took its deceitful
departure from those sciences that pursued the truth as such when it
raised the question: "Which way of cognizing the world and life enables
man to live most happily?" The one who wants only his happiness is
necessarily "indifferent to all unproductive knowledge and downright
hostile to dangerous and destructive truths." But, on the other hand, the
inexorable demands of truth are indifferent to happiness: "There is no
pre-established harmony between the furtherance of truth and the well-
being of humanity."

(b) Throughout the course of history, belief has often been attested
by *martyrdom.* When Nietzsche speaks about truth per se as if it were
fixed and immutable and could be insightfully grasped in its pristine
purity through the colorless medium of timeless meditation, he rules out
the testimony furnished by the sacrificed blood of the martyrs: "Blood is
the worst possible witness to the truth; it poisons even the purest doctrine
and turns it into madness and hatred in our hearts." Above all, scientific
truth, by its very nature, is incapable of being either confirmed or refuted
by martyrdom. The researcher himself comes to seem dubious to Nietzsche when he proceeds at this level: Whenever the truth (i.e., the
scientific method) was seized upon and promoted by those who sensed in
it an implement of warfare, they proclaimed, precisely through the battle
they waged, "the concept of truth quite as unconditionally as their
opponents—they became fanatics, at least as far as their attitudes were
concerned." The words "persuasion" and "belief," which are the pride of
martyrdom, are names for the most unfavorable state of scientific knowledge. Insofar as genuine investigators assumed, in their battle, the atti-

tude of their opponents, i.e., the believers, and sought to decide questions of truth "through sacrifices and heroic resolutions," they directly promoted the hegemony of the anti-scientific methods: "In the role of martyrs they compromised their own achievement." Hence the demand which Nietzsche makes in this connection: "Beware of martyrdom and of 'suffering for the truth's sake'! Even of putting up your own defense as though 'the truth' were a person so inoffensive and awkward that it needed to be defended! Go into hiding! And take your masks and your refined manners with you so that you will not be recognized! . . . The martyrdom of the philosopher, his 'sacrificing himself for the truth,' brings to light the agitator and play-actor hidden in him."

(c) "Virtuous conduct" is no criterion of truth; it says nothing either for or against it: "Truth is not proven in the same way as is truthfulness, and the latter is surely no argument for the former."

If the criteria of the certainty of belief—the evidences of strength variously expressed as the will to happiness, martyrdom, and virtuous conduct—are substituted for the criteria of truth, then the truth is bound to be eradicated. Truth "demands criticism, not adoration." In connection with such truth, Nietzsche maintains that "we 'knowers' are especially mistrustful of all kinds of believers."

But still, not only does the principle hold that "neither man nor beast would be able to live without the extraordinary security provided by belief," but we are also *dependent upon belief as a source* for all the richness and fullness of our being: "We have Christianity, the philosophers, the poets, and the musicians to thank for a superabundance of profoundly moving experiences." If Nietzsche also insists that to prevent these experiences from proliferating too wildly "we must invoke the scientific spirit, which . . . cools belief's passionate longing for final and unshakeable truths," still he will never renounce this ground of all knowledge.

Furthermore when Nietzsche calls belief in question by applying the standard of objective truth, this does not prevent him from *claiming belief as his own* and finding it to be a fountainhead of truth. It is not merely that he speaks of "my belief . . ." and of "those of us who hold to another belief. . . ." He also says: "Because you are barren, you are lacking in belief. But he who was ever impelled to create . . . believed in belief!" And again: "It is not works, it is belief that is decisive here and sets up an order of rank at this point . . . , some fundamental certainty or other." But in connection with his own belief he claims that he does not possess the criterion that normally strengthens all belief: "If there is a belief that leads to blessedness, well now, there is also a belief that doesn't."

Whether it is a matter of effect, of power, or of belief, in every case that which endangers, veils, or demolishes the truth is itself a fountainhead from which the search for truth springs. This alone makes Nietzsche's contradictory statements not only comprehensible but even inescapable. In the struggle for truth there is always an impetus directed against its very conditions that must not be entirely eliminated if truth is to remain within the world.

Awareness of Being Attained at the Boundary. The basic idea of the universal illusoriness of truth gives rise to a view of being that moves in three steps as though in a circle: (1) To begin with, the pure truth, as *distinguished* from the entire realm of illusory appearances, is to be assimilated; then (2) the question of the *compatibility* of this truth with inescapable illusion makes life problematic; and finally (3) all existence, with its universal illusoriness, is grasped and reinstated through philosophic transformation by *the good will to illusion.*

(1) The first step hazards the following argument: If the fundamental vital process that changes within and together with a changing world of its own construction can, by its very nature, only know being as an illusion which, like enduring being itself, must be regarded as the underlying condition of life, then the question faced by a living being engaged in philosophizing is no longer Descartes' question about the possibility of error, but the very reverse: "How is any kind of truth possible at all if knowledge is founded upon falsity?" Here the *truth,* as insight into the vital process of which error is a necessary condition, is actually attained in Nietzsche's thinking. Nietzsche expects scientific investigation to come to the same insight: "Some day the scientific process will celebrate its highest triumph through a History of the Origin of Thinking." It is true that this insight can only to a slight extent free us from the world of appearances which, through the process of life, has become a necessary part of us, "but at least it can momentarily elevate us above the whole process." When Nietzsche, translating his philosophical awareness of a boundary into a project for scientific research, claims that it is a task of science "to measure the degree of falsity and investigate the necessity of basic error as a life-condition of a sentient being," he occupies a standpoint from which it seems easily possible to arrive at the pure truth about the whole.

Still this truth would have to have a radically different character from the truths of life which must appear as error when viewed from this standpoint. Man rises for a brief instant above life. Insofar as this elevation is the transcending awareness of the phenomenality of all existence, it is the Kantian consciousness of being. But insofar as it amounts to a scientific study of the psychology and sociology of the historical development of knowledge, he misunderstands this philosophic transcending and believes that he possesses knowledge about the whole of things from a study of particulars within the world.

In either case thinking can only proceed as it becomes identical with life. Hence such thinking is subordinated to the necessities of life, and these are recognized as error when it is discovered that the truth is unsuitable to our vital purposes and that life is conditioned "by perspectivistic illusion."

(2) Here the second step begins. "The final question concerning the condition of life is posed. . . . To what extent can the truth be incorporated?" To this question, which amounts to asking how knowledge and error can be reconciled with one another, the young Nietzsche answers: "The will to know and the will to err are the ebb and the flow." We can and we must gratify both in turn, just as we experience day and night. But mere contiguity of the two is no solution. Perhaps Nietzsche's recommendation of "a free, fearless hovering above men, customs, laws, and traditional evaluations of things" provides a clue. The nature of philosophic insight into the truth itself—an insight that is no longer erroneous —is, consequently, not meant to spring from life itself, for it is a philosophical suspension over life. What from this elevation is seen to be true is not the truth of life, and what is true within life is, from this point of view, illusion. If within life it is necessary "that something should *count* as true—not that something should *be* true," then what is important about these elevated truths is that they never appear as life, but have meaning only in a realm above life. If philosophic insight into the vital process as a whole is to have any sense, its own conception of the truth about the truth of life must differ markedly from the errors that are intrinsic to life. Life itself can of course never attain to and incorporate the former without invalidating its own truth and destroying itself.

Thus we are left with the duplicity of a truth that appears first as life-supporting error and then as true knowledge of this necessary true-to-life error. The argument proceeds endlessly back and forth: "Life is the condition of knowledge. But error is the condition of life—error of the most profound kind. Error is not eliminated by being seen for what it is. . . . We must love and cultivate error, for it is the matrix of knowledge. To love and promote life for the sake of knowledge; to love and promote error for the sake of life . . . —these are the basic conditions of all passion for knowledge."

(3) The final step proceeds from this untenable cleavage of truth: on the one hand, erring life; on the other, and elevated beyond this, lifeless but true ideas. Insight into the vital necessity of error, the illusoriness of truth, and the bottomless depths to be traversed in the unending search for truth is the reason for Nietzsche's demand that we consciously and deliberately lay hold upon the truth in the limited form that it always assumes within actual life; we are always within and still always beyond; we have nothing but the illusory, but when we experience it *as* illusory, it constitutes for us a cipher of being. If being is simply the illusory, still the fact that, at the boundary, its illusoriness is apparent *transforms my entire consciousness of being*. Consequently philosophizing of this kind forces us to approach true being within the bounds of existence and thus "remain loyal to the earth."

Nietzsche demands, first of all, that we consciously limit ourselves to the present. Truth resides in that which can be embodied in the here-and-now. Nothing in the beyond is to be allowed to cheat us of the contemporaneous. We may well remain "indifferent" to the questions concerning last things, and we need not wait to hear "what science will eventually discover" about them. It is not necessary for human beings to be certain about the most distant horizons in order to live fully and purposively. . . . "We must again become good neighbors of the nearest things." It is in this connection that he outlines the principles governing a self-controlled and fruitful life: One is no longer to take as a guide what appears on the horizon—the things that are most distant, indeterminate and cloud-like: "One ought to ascertain things with respect to their degree of nearness before giving final direction to his life." In the place "of basic truths, basic probabilities" are enough "to live and think by." Nietzsche complains of a lack of capacity for observation: "What, for so many, makes the earth into a field of ill-fortune is ignorance about the most trivial and common things, and failure to look sharply. . . ." What lies near at hand is incomparably important because it involves necessities upon which our lives are entirely dependent. We simply must be thoroughly at home in this area if our existence is to retain the freedom to choose among its possibilities: "We take seriously the most humble things that have been despised and neglected in all times. . . . We have discovered that the 'smallest world' is always the most decisive." In the daring language of his last years, he can say: "The little things—food, place, climate, recreation and all the casuistry of self-seeking—are incomparably more important than everything that has been regarded as important up to now."

It is futile to gaze into the most distant regions; all beginnings and sources of actual appearances are either inaccessible or of no consequence: "The insignificance of the source grows apace with insight into it. But the nearest things that are around us and in us gradually begin to show color and splendor, mystery and richness of meaning beyond anything dreamed of in the past."

In calling us back to things that are nearby, Nietzsche is not concerned with mere utility. Rather a second self-limitation of the truth appears when he asks us to affirm the illusory for what it is, to will it, and to place our trust in it. If the passion for knowledge begins with the unmasking of all the illusory, it can, as a consequence, grasp the meaning and necessity of illusion instead of dispensing with it. It is as though the will to truth held itself in suspension by willing illusion while refusing to succumb to it, for it recognizes the illusoriness while yielding to it: "This belief in the truth proceeds to its last conclusion, namely that, if it is to worship at all, it must worship illusion and that it is the lie that is divine—not the truth!" With this the truth becomes unapproachable: "We can no longer believe that the truth continues to be the truth when the veil is removed. . . . One should have more respect for the modest way in which nature has hidden herself behind riddles and multi-colored uncertainties. . . . Oh, these Greeks! They knew how to live accordingly: to do so, it was necessary to stop courageously at the surface, the draping, the skin and to worship appearance. . . . The Greeks were superficial—because profound!"

The will to illusion in philosophizing is indeed always opposed by "that sublime tendency in the knower who takes, and *prefers* to take, things deeply, thoroughly, and variously—a kind of cruelty in the intellectual conscience. . . ." But such philosophizing is also aware that, "if anything were to unveil the essence of the world before our eyes, it would disillusion us most disagreeably. It is not the world as a thing in itself but the world as our idea (as error) that is so rich in significance, profound, and wonderful." Thus the philosopher returns to illusion.

The unconscious limitation of life ties us to error; the conscious limitation and the humble acceptance of illusion keeps an open mind. But still the truth that was to be excluded by these limits continues to hover threateningly in the background. Inexorably it makes itself known, for man, when he philosophizes, does not cease questioning, in spite of all good intentions with regard to boundaries, horizons, and illusoriness. In thinking he experiences more than an idle play of the intellect; rather he experiences a sort of breakthrough of something further that never allows him to come to rest at any boundary or fixed horizon.

Consequently Nietzsche's will to truth, indefinite as it may be, not only persistently reasserts itself in spite of his critical questioning, but is in fact always passionately real to him. His struggle for the truth constantly presupposes truth as something self-evident, and then time and again allows it to reach a precipice.

Nietzsche's Passionate Longing for Unlimited Truth

Nietzsche sought methodical certainty within the sciences, but he did so only with a view to demarcating the limits of science more decisively. He developed a theory of truth as the interpretation provided by living beings in order to actualize the circle of thought. He was impelled, not by a destructive will, but by an insatiable passionate longing for truth that is not content to know the mere particulars or to arrive at some kind of certainty or other, but that forces its way beyond the determinate and conceptually knowable to the source and the limit. Nietzsche often acknowledged such a passion for the truth: "What are good-heartedness, delicacy, and genius to me if the possessor of these virtues is lukewarm about his beliefs and judgments and his longing for certainty is anything less than his innermost desire and deepest need. . . . To be surrounded by the whole wonderful uncertainty and ambiguity of existence and not to ask questions . . . —that is what I find to be contemptible." "The passion for what is 'true' regardless of all considerations is the highest— and hence the rarest—passion so far known!" Nietzsche is prepared to resign himself unreservedly to this passion; he is able to silence all objections springing from consideration of what is necessary or condu- cive to life: "My philosophy—to rescue men from illusion at any cost!" For "our knowledge has become a passion that does not draw back from any kind of sacrifice." Nothing is going to conquer it: "A joyful shout for knowledge—your last cry."

Seized by a passion for truth, he embraces honesty (*Redlichkeit*) as the new virtue and regards justice (*Gerechtigkeit*) as the most venerable of human attitudes. Neither of these two kinds of truthfulness can be identified by signs that are rationally unambiguous; and neither of them is regarded as a plastic ideal. Rather, that in which truthfulness consists becomes a threat to the truth, which now enters upon a struggle with itself. The passionate demand for unlimited truth first attains to its full stature when it turns on itself and calls itself in question.

Honesty. When all determinate forms of truth seem to disappear, honesty remains as our last resort. In the dissolution of knowledge, it is present as a possible new beginning; it is indestructible so long as the self remains. Nietzsche embraces it warmly, for, as the expression of a truthfulness that inheres in man and interpenetrates everything, it amounts to "intellectual integrity."

Honesty is the presupposition of *Existenz* and, unlike justice, is consequently not expressly praised any further. "I do not mean that honesty per se is something absolutely high and pure: with me it is like the *demand* for purity. Be one what he will—genius or actor—let him only be pure!" Honesty, however, is demanded without any limitation: "It is impossible for me to recognize any great man who is not honest with himself."

The most important kind of honesty is "honesty with ourselves." It is primarily through this that self-development becomes possible. First of all, the "development of honesty makes us increasingly independent of the inspiration of the drives," and, in the second place, the extent of my capacity to know depends upon my honesty: "It is not because your eyes cease to discern, but because your honesty leaves off that your eyes no longer see anything." Thus "honesty with respect to anything actual could well become a matter of decency, with the result that the unrealistic dreamer would be simply left out of account as ill-behaved."

Nietzsche speaks of honesty as *his* virtue, *our* virtue, the *new* virtue: "In all other matters we are merely the heirs and perhaps the squanderers of virtues." According to him honesty does not appear among either the Socratic or the Christian virtues: "This is one of the youngest virtues, not yet mature, still frequently unrecognized and mistaken for another, scarcely conscious of itself—still in the process of development." "We are the first to have that instinctual and passionate integrity which fights more fiercely against the 'sacred lie' than against any other kind of untruth."

Why has this virtue continued right up to the present time to be so rare? Nietzsche answers: Because there are so many reasons for being untruthful with a good conscience. When, for example, people believed something *in majorem dei gloriam* or declared things to be true because they wished them to be, but in circumstances in which they could feel selfless, they experienced no pangs of conscience because of the untruthfulness involved, for "when they can feel selfless, it seems to them permissible to have little concern for the truth." Even among philosophers nothing is more rare than intellectual integrity. They concede only certain truths, for "they know what they have to prove." Their "love of the good" destroys their integrity, and their "fine feelings" are presented as arguments. The masses above all will have nothing to do with honesty:

"In their blind fury they hate the knower and that youngest of the virtues which is called honesty."

Honesty, however, sets its own limits. In one and the same breath Nietzsche can appeal to us with his demand for limitless honesty and then set limits to it. He can say, for example: "When one day our honesty becomes tired . . . we shall remain hard, we, the last Stoics!" And subsequently he demands: "Let us free spirits see to it that our honesty does not become our vanity, our snobbishness and ostentation, our limit and our stupidity! Every virtue tends towards stupidity, and every kind of stupidity toward virtue. Let us be careful to avoid becoming saints and bores as a result of honesty."

The self-limitation of honesty has a double meaning: (1) Life forces upon us a distinction between honesty with *myself* and honesty with *others*. One may have to learn to be dishonest with others if he is to be true to himself: "Intentional dissimulation derives from . . . a feeling for honesty with oneself." But again (2) to the honest person, being honest with oneself becomes doubtful.

(1) Proceeding in the one direction, Nietzsche finds that honesty must be limited first of all (a) as a result of a tolerance that is willing to make allowances: "Let us proceed humanly with respect to our sense for honesty, even though we have in it the thumb-screw that will draw blood from all those grand egotists who even now wish to subject the whole world to their own faith."

The self-limitation of honesty derives also (b) from a sincere appraisal of the real possibilities: In this world it is not possible to live without lies. The problem of authentic truthfulness, he believes, has never been really faced by anyone. "The things that are said against lying express the naïveté of the schoolmaster." Strangely enough, when truthfulness is demanded through the command "thou shalt not lie," it is precisely "the *liars* who always have recognized actuality and have had the honest view (the refusal to be deceived) to the highest degree, for they were also well aware of the incompatibility of this popular truthfulness with the facts." Truthfulness is only possible under very special circumstances. "The whole human sphere involved must be small, neat, and worthy of respect, and the advantage throughout must be on the side of truthfulness." Actually, the situation is as follows: "One says what he thinks and is 'truthful' only *in certain conditions,* namely when he can be understood (*inter pares*) and, furthermore, when the understanding accorded him is cordial (again *inter pares*). In strange situations one conceals himself, and anyone who has an aim in view expresses what he wishes to have thought about himself rather than what he really thinks."

(2) Since a boundless honesty would probably be impossible, because self-defeating, Nietzsche, transcending the world of human realities to a metaphysics of the world as illusion, points out the inherent self-limitations of honesty. The assertion that "truthfulness would be an unnatural tendency in a world that is essentially false" may still be taken to refer to outward dissimulation, but it can also be seen to hit upon something that inheres in the nature of truthfulness itself. Even when he was a youth he saw only the illusoriness of art as a path to the truth. "To be entirely truthful—a splendid heroic urge of man encompassed by a mendacious nature! Possible only in a very relative sense. . . . As for the truthfulness of art: it alone is honest today." But in the end truthfulness is meaningful to Nietzsche only "as a means to a special higher potency of falsehood," while with respect to knowledge he holds that "truthfulness is only one of the means to knowledge; it is *a* ladder but not *the* ladder." So in the end it becomes meaningful to assert: "He who is truthful finally ends up realizing that he always lies," and Nietzsche can say of himself: "What do you know about how much falsity is necessary for me if I am repeatedly to permit myself the luxury of my truthfulness?"

Justice. According to Nietzsche, truthfulness and honesty first receive their proper meaning from justice, which they have made possible. It corresponds to Nietzsche's practical, voluntaristic, and didactic attitude that he finds honesty to be simply a matter of purity, but justice to be a matter of pathos. He acknowledges this as follows: "We heterogeneous beings, now glowing with fire and now chilled by spirit, wish to bow down to justice as the sole goddess which we recognize as standing above us." "In truth no one has more of a claim upon our veneration than the one who possesses the drive and the force of justice. For in it the highest and rarest virtues are united, preserved, and concealed as in an unfathomably deep sea." When justice seems to be unattainable, the older Nietzsche says: "I was late in discovering that I was entirely wanting in something, namely, justice. 'What is justice and how is it possible? And if it is not possible, how is life to be borne?' I am constantly asking myself these things." At all times his attitude is: "Be things as they may, we wish to be just and to go as far in this as is possible for us." The search for truth itself is here justified for the first time: "Only insofar as a truthful man is categorically determined to be just is there anything great about the striving for truth that is everywhere glorified so thoughtlessly."

But what justice really is first becomes evident in the progression of its meanings through Nietzsche's seemingly incompatible statements.

The just man wants truth "not in the form of cold, ineffective knowledge, but in that of a judge who orders and punishes; not as an egotistical possession of the individual but as the sacred right to rearrange all the boundary stones of individual possessions." Since truth is the condition and the essence of justice, it is typical of justice "to turn away with indignation from anything that will dazzle and confuse our judgment about things; consequently it is an opponent of convictions, for it intends to give to everything, living or dead, actual or imaginary, what is truly its own, and this calls for a clear and unbiased view. In the last instance, it will even concede to blind or short-sighted 'conviction' what belongs to conviction, thus yielding to its opponent for the sake of the truth." This will to be just—to give to every kind of existence what is its own—is boundless. Since each individual kind needs a general philosophical justification of its way of living and thinking, Nietzsche insists that "even the evil, the unfortunate, or the exceptional man should be granted his philosophy, his rights, and his place in the sun! . . . A new kind of justice is required! . . . Even the moral earth is round! It has its antipodes, and they too have their right to exist." This is to insist that "we must banish all the false grandeur from the world again because it is in opposition to justice, to which all the things surrounding us may rightly lay claim!"

But does such a thing as justice exist? Scarcely among average men, for among them "the virtue of justice is seldom in evidence, even more seldom recognized, and it is almost always met with deadly hatred. . . . Few truly serve the truth, for only a few really wish to be just, and of these latter again only the very fewest have the strength that would enable them to be just."

Insofar as there is such a thing as justice, one must carefully avoid confusion if he is to see it in its true light. The word is constantly misused: In hatred, envy, malice, and desire for revenge, the resentment of the impotent person speaks of justice that he himself does not possess: "Secretly his soul exults in the fact that even revenge is carried out with full justice." Nietzsche adds: "And mine rejoices in this, that in all revenge at least a spark is struck from the anvil of justice."

True justice derives from an *active* feeling and not, like its perversion, from a *reactive* one. Reactive feelings employ justice as a façade in order to procure for the impotent a spurious feeling of power through something seemingly as intrinsically valid or unreal as the demands of justice. Or again reactive feelings will turn justice into mere affect: "Generally a little dose of assault, meanness, or insinuation suffices" to "force blood into the eyes and eliminate fairness from the view" of men.

On the other hand, in the exceptional case of unusual personal strength, the active feeling of justice may be possible even when an individual is physically powerless: "When it actually happens that the just man continues to be just (and not simply cold, moderate, distant, indifferent; for being just is always a positive mode of behavior) even toward those who wrong him—when the view of the just and judging eye, with its lofty, clear, profoundly penetrating, and yet charitable objectivity, remains unclouded even under the impact of personal injury, vilification, and suspicion—that is a bit of perfection and highest mastery in the world, in fact something that one would be wise not to expect and, in any case, should not *believe* in too readily."

It is only this *active* justice that arrives at true judgment: "Only superior strength can judge, weakness must tolerate if it is not to simulate strength and turn the tribunal of justice into a stage."

From the standpoint of active justice, Nietzsche finds that even knowledge—though it must initially question and deny and hence pronounce negative judgments—becomes affirmative in the end, for it finally concedes the truthfulness of all things: "We understand and experience all things, and there is no more hostile feeling left in us. . . . 'All is well'—we find it difficult to deny. We suffer whenever we become so unintelligent as to oppose anything."

It might thus appear that justice is an unambiguous ideal or even that men could become just, but Nietzsche sees the impossibility. So long as justice is practiced only by "man as he tries to ascend from pardonable doubt to apodictic certainty . . . and from the rare virtue of magnanimity to the rarest virtue of all which is justice" and not by a being that, like a "frigid cognizing demon," spreads about himself "an icy atmosphere of superhuman majesty," this virtue will not be realized. Resembling the demon while being "nothing but a humble man," man must "constantly atone in his very being for his humanity and tragically waste his substance in his striving for an impossible virtue." Since we can never possess complete knowledge and still are unable to live without pronouncing value judgments, i.e., since we must evaluate in the absence of adequate knowledge, it is impossible for us to become just: "He who thinks more deeply knows that he is always in the wrong, no matter how he behaves and judges."

Still, in this necessarily unjust world, Nietzsche continues to strive for justice and to require it of man. But whatever the form in which this striving is expressed, it must repeatedly call itself in question both (1) in relation to its own intrinsic nature and (2) in relation to reality.

(1) Justice per se becomes questionable when it is devoid of or

destructive of love. "Nothing can be given to men who are actually just: they return everything. Hence the just are anathema to lovers." Nietzsche certainly does not wish to overrate the kind of love that is *blind:* love is evidently more obtuse than justice and precisely for that reason more agreeable to all. It is as impartial as the rain. But Zarathustra, having a vision of truly *substantial* love, says: "I do not care for your cold justice. . . . Tell me where to find justice that loves with discerning eyes." To be entirely self-sufficient, justice would have to lose the substance that comes only from clear-sighted love. While Nietzsche finds justice to be primary and superlative, he may nevertheless say: "Justice appeared before me, and I smashed my idols and was ashamed . . . and forced my eye to look at what it was unwilling to see and thither to take my love." But when justice is self-sufficient, love cannot be forced, and a lack of love is evident in the following: "I am painfully just in order to preserve distance." To Nietzsche clear-sighted love that is naturally just is an ideal which is never realized through justice as such. Hence as a result of his knowledge of love, Nietzsche must call justice in question.

(2) Justice is also questionable when viewed in relation to actual existence:

To begin with, injustice is inseparable from life as such, for all life is conditioned by perspectivity with its inescapable falsehoods. Injustice is indeed always greatest "wherever life, though least developed, and most narrow, poor, and inchoate, still cannot avoid regarding itself as the measure and the end of all things and cannot desist from calling in question and undermining, in a stealthy, mean, and persistent way, whatever is higher, greater, and richer." But even the richest and fullest life requires some injustice. Were this superior life to judge itself, without compromise, from a historical perspective, it would destroy itself. "Justice, as pronounced from a historical standpoint . . . is a frightful virtue. Its judgment always amounts to annihilation. . . . When justice alone is in control, the creative instinct is weakened and discouraged."

The actualities of human existence are responsible for a kind of "justice" that, unlike the existential justice of clear-sighted love, is juristic in nature. It does not have the validity of a natural law but depends instead upon constellations of power which it, in turn, calls in question. Such "justice" arises only "among those of approximately equal power. . . . Where there is no clearly recognizable higher power and a struggle could only result in senseless damage for all concerned, mutual agreement is sought. . . . Consequently justice is requital and exchange engaged in by nearly equal powers."

But Nietzsche himself concedes the inadequacy of the kind of justice described above. It is abstract and devoid of love and creative efficacy; it is a fixed and static state of affairs possible under certain transient conditions of power. Even at the sociological level, justice is something more than mere exchange when it develops out of a comprehensive activity. The whole matter now appears to Nietzsche under an entirely different aspect, as though it had turned into the very opposite of what it was before: "What is first and most powerful is precisely the will and strength to achieve superior power. It is the ruler who then first establishes 'justice,' that is, measures things according to his own measure." As seen from this standpoint, "giving everyone his due would be to will injustice and attain chaos." Justice has become a "function of a far reaching power" which looks beyond the limited perspectives of good and evil and consequently has the advantage of a broader horizon, namely, the intention of preserving something more than this or that person." The power alluded to is the creative life: "Justice as a mode of thought that, from considerations of value, constructs, eliminates, and annihilates—*the highest representative of life itself*." *Zarathustra* becomes the "grandiose" form and revelation of the sort of justice that forms and constructs and, as a result, must annihilate."

Justice as a metaphysical actuality: Just one more step in the direction of the indeterminacy of the creative life, and the standpoint is reached where justice no longer concerns the problem of human truth but attains transcendence. When it becomes doubtful as a human possibility, Nietzsche reinstates it in metaphysical form. It is no longer the justice that men know, strive for, and fight over, but rather "eternal justice," "regnant justice"; no longer the essence of the search for truth but the essence of things as they happen.

He does indeed reject the thought of justice as measured by *guilt* and *expiation:* "That rewards and punishments lie in the consequences of our deeds—this thought of an immanent justice is thoroughly false." But he is acquainted with another kind of metaphysical justice that is not possible without "transgression." He encounters it in connection with Aeschylus who "places the Olympian world on his scale of justice" and "sees Moira enthroned as eternal justice." Both the suffering of Prometheus, the bold blasphemous "individual," and the anticipation of a twilight among the gods on threatened Olympus necessitate a conciliation amounting to the realization of justice in which both are judged and reinstated. "Through transgression men win the highest and best things in which they can participate and then must accept the consequences": Active sin is itself the authentic Promethean virtue. It is the basic contradiction in which both gods and men have right on their side.

Nietzsche believes that he finds in the thought of Heraclitus a conception of *authentic justice* that does not involve transgression and its consequences: "The world itself is a mixing bowl that must be stirred constantly. All becoming derives from the war of opposites. . . . The struggle goes on eternally. Strife governs everything, and it is precisely this strife that reveals eternal justice. It is a wonderful . . . conception which takes strife to be the continuous rule of a uniform and strict justice in accordance with eternal laws. . . . It is Hesiod's good Eris transfigured into a universal principle. . . . Just as every Greek fights as though he alone were in the right while an infinitely secure measure of forensic judgment decides at each instant which side is to be victorious,—just so the qualities strive with one another. . . . Things themselves do not really exist; they are merely the flash and the flying sparks of drawn swords; they are the brilliant glitter of victory in the war of opposed qualities." Heraclitus "could no longer view the warring pairs and the judges as separate from one another; the judges themselves appeared to fight, and the fighters themselves to judge. Indeed, since in the end he only saw eternally reigning justice, he dared to proclaim that it is simply the strife of the many that constitutes eternal justice." In other words: "Everything existing is both right and wrong, and it is each of these with equal justification."

To Nietzsche also, the human will to justice appears to assume a modest role before the justice that lies beyond. The struggle of the truth with itself, as a result of which justice continues to be an unconditional requirement (expressed philosophically as the increasingly clear appeal to the inner activity of the individual) even while it is called in question, becomes transferred to a metaphysical level; here, in pure contemplation, it ceases as an active philosophic procedure and turns over the struggle to the being of things, so that it can be truthfully stated: "It is delightful to observe things; frightful to be them."

How the Will to Truth Overcomes Itself. The will to truth developed on the soil of morality: "The sense of truth is itself one of the most refined and powerful efflorescences of the moral sense." Nietzsche is aware that his own life is based on this highest of all moral drives—the boundless will to truth—when he says "that even we knowers of today, we godless and anti-metaphysical ones, still take our fire from the torch which has been kindled by a belief held through thousands of years." Not until Nietzsche subjects to critical questioning even the unlimited will to truth into which this traditional belief has developed, is the cognitive passion that derives from truthfulness forced, in turn, to become skeptical of itself. The circle, now involved in the passion for truth, is once again carried to its extreme. If "belief in the truth *begins* with doubt about all previously accepted truths" and if this belief will tolerate no other gods besides it, then the passion for truth must end with a question to which the belief must itself be subjected. A bottomless abyss stands revealed. The doubt thus reached has two forms:

(1) The hostility of truth to life is (in connection with the theory that illusion is a vital necessity) a reason for rejecting it: "Unconditional knowledge is a chimera that belongs to the age of virtue; it would destroy life. We must *sanctify* lying, and the delusions of belief as well as injustice." Consequently "we have taken a dislike to this will to truth, to 'truth at any price,' this delirium of youth in love with the truth."

(2) Thought, proceeding along the road to knowledge, must itself suffer a reversal. The first condition of the kind of knowledge that does not draw back in fear before anything is belief in nothing: "As long as you still feel the stars as something 'above you,' you lack the clear vision of the knower." But then truth too must cease to be something "above you": "Truthful! That is what I call the one who, having crushed his adoring heart, enters a godless wasteland." So-called free spirits are not free: "It is precisely their belief in the truth that makes them more firm and categorical than anyone else." It is against them that the radical questioning of the truth must hazard the decisive step: "Nothing is true, all is permitted. . . . *That* was freedom of spirit, *therewith* belief was withheld from truth itself."

Nietzsche finds that this reversal, in which everything seems destined to vanish as a result of the self-destruction of the will to truth, arises at the turning-point of history, i.e., in the present age. This reversal is identical with the self-annulment of morality and the death of God. When "the awe-inspiring catastrophe of a two-thousand year training for truth . . . concludes by forbidding a mendacious belief in God," it must at once take the following step: after Christian truthfulness has drawn a series of conclusions, it must finally draw its *strongest conclusion*—the one directed against itself. This occurs when it poses the question: "What does all will to truth signify?" Nietzsche is in a position to say that this is what must happen: "All great things destroy themselves through an act of self-annulment."

But still this collapse of the circle in which the will to truth reduces itself to a mere nothing is only a boundary of Nietzsche's thought. Either the circle once more receives substance through a circular movement which revives the struggle on behalf of a truth that is again taken for granted, or a transcending breakthrough reveals something further at this boundary of thought.

Unlimited Doubt. The movement of Nietzsche's thinking seems to become stranded whenever, as frequently occurs, the will to truth requires its own surrender. But always a new progression begins; for the goal is authentic being rather than nothingness. It is authentic being toward which the passionate will to truth, in the form of an ineradicable skepticism, strives with ever renewed insistence. Nietzsche refuses to set limits to his "mistrust," regards his philosophizing as a "school of suspicion," and, following the path of the "perilous perhaps," ventures every possible thought in purely "experimental" fashion. His passion for truth always reasserts itself when it has been called in question, but it fails to establish itself on any solid ground. As though driven by fate, he seems compelled to expose every intellectual triumph immediately to unlimited skepticism. He does not relapse into the nothingness of the theory of truth that annihilates itself by moving in a circle, but he fills the circle with ever new developments through which his will to truth reasserts itself. He does not get bogged down on any purportedly definitive correct insight into the nature of truth but draws all such insights back into the whirlpool of his thoughts.

The Dissolution of Reason

It is not Nietzsche's insight into the limits of science, but rather his account of truth as illusoriness and the suicidal annulment of all truth (as it were) within a constantly recurring circle of ever-changing aspects that lead him to a skeptical questioning of reason in general. Whether he deals with morality, truth, or the death of God, he seems always to become lost in nothingness. But what Nietzsche intends is to pass by means of these extremes to a being that cannot be rationally apprehended. He seeks to reach this being by dissolving or breaking through reason.

Nietzsche's *attack on reason* assumes four forms:

1. Opposed to the assertion that truth is found in thought stands his theory of exegesis (*Auslegung*) supplemented by the view that all products of thought are illusory. Taken together these constitute the logic peculiar to Nietzsche: The categories of thought are illusions necessary for life; they are useful, and they are instruments of control. Failure to believe in them would mean the end of the human race. But still they are not true; they are fictitious. They do not derive from being but from the condition that alone makes thought possible, viz., that something remain

identical with itself. Only things that remain the same (e.g., identical instances and static entities) have true being for thought. This assumption of self-identical being "is necessary if we are to think and to draw inferences, for the formulae of logic are applicable only to what remains the same." Nietzsche develops this theme step by step as follows:

Thinking in terms of identity requires the law of contradiction. But this is simply another fiction within the deceptive horizon of an intellect *intent upon being*. That "we fail in trying to affirm and deny one and the same thing" is only a subjective empirical judgment, expressing an incapacity of our cognitive faculties and not an inescapable "necessity" for being itself. "This law does not provide a criterion of the truth, but only an injunction concerning what is to count as true."

Identity and incapacity for self-contradiction are, according to Nietzsche, ultimately rooted in an "ego" that posits itself as self-identical and constant. Apart from this posit there is no ego. Nietzsche uses as an instrument of attack what German Idealism had thought through in its logic of the ego as a thinking consciousness in general. Since the basic presupposition underlying all rational processes is our "belief in the ego," we are faced with this limitation: "Our thinking itself involves that belief. . . . To abandon it is to be able to think no longer."

That ego, identity, and impossibility of contradiction reciprocally support each other provides the circle in which thinking can proceed in the form of an invariably fictitious exegesis of being necessary for a living organism.

Now since it is also the case that all categories (thing, substance, subject, object, predicate, as well as causality, mechanism, etc.) concern only ways of being identical and being different without contradiction, they are all posited by the intellect in the service of a mode of life that requires permanence as its necessary condition: i.e., they are all fabricated by a living being. From Nietzsche's fragments it is possible to put together an elaborately developed doctrine of categories that shows in tediously repetitive fashion that every single category involves these aspects of identity and so forth and stands in the service of life and the will to power.

The upshot of this Nietzschean "logic," which can be repeatedly verified, is that while the intellect is a means to life, still it cannot grasp what most truly *is,* namely, constant becoming: "Our intellect is not contrived to understand becoming; it strives to demonstrate the universal cold inflexibility of everything." But "the character of the world of becoming" is "incapable of being expressed in formulae"; it is "false," "self-contradictory," and incommensurable with logic. "Knowledge and becoming are mutually exclusive. . . . A kind of becoming must itself create the delusion of being," that is, of constant self-identity. This delusion is only possible as a result of the self-enclosing circle of thought. What in the end is meant by these expositions, founded as they are upon the theory that all the thought of living beings consists in interpretation, is that reason is limited to intellect and that its pretension to truth must be annulled in favor of another kind of claim made on a wholly different level.

2. In *the life of man* reason is unnecessary, hazardous, and impossible. It is *unnecessary:* "The irrationality of a thing is no argument against its existence; rather it is its underlying condition." It is *hazardous:* When reason purports to provide knowledge of all things, it becomes ruinous; to the question "whether reason with its presumed omniscience has done more to preserve than to destroy," Nietzsche answers: "If humanity had actually behaved in accordance with its reason, i.e., in accordance with its opinion and its knowledge, it would long since have perished." It is *impossible:* There is no single all-supporting truth of reason enabling human beings everywhere to come to an understanding with each other. When, for instance, tolerant apostles of reason choose to rest their entire case upon rational insight, it always turns out that exception is made of a few "fundamental truths" in regard to which there *can be no tolerance.* "To cleave to reason would be fine if only there were *one* reason! But the tolerant man must depend upon *his* reason with all its weaknesses." There is in fact no *one* reason to serve as a basis for human existence.

What do such attacks upon the *belief in reason* signify? Insofar as reason, claiming independent existence, purports to give rise to the truth of our existential awareness of being and, as the one universally valid truth, to be intelligible and available to anybody and hence capable of providing the common foundation of communal life, Nietzsche must call reason in question because it obscures the really sustaining truth of *Existenz.* Nietzsche's philosophizing probes into this deep truth. When he finds in it only life-conditioning errors that go by the name of "fundamental truths," this discovery is simply a *sign* to which thought is momentarily limited, but with which he cannot rest content.

3. To the *metaphysical question* as to whether reason is supreme within the world, philosophical thought has always given affirmative, though extremely various, replies. Nietzsche, contrariwise, flatly denies that a metaphysical reason permeates the whole: "The only rationality known to us is the tiny bit that belongs to man." The maelstrom of forces in the world is devoid of reason. "That the world is *not* the epitome of eternal rationality is conclusively shown by the fact that the particle of

the world with which we are acquainted—our human rationality—is not any too reasonable." For "even in the wisest, reason is the exception: chaos and necessity and swirling stars—*that* is the rule." "Taking everything into consideration, one thing is impossible: rationality. A little bit of reason indeed, scattered among the stars,—this sourdough has been stirred into everything." He finds it astonishing that there is such a thing as reason at all. How did it enter into the world? "How befitting that it should have entered in a non-rational manner—through an accident. It is like a riddle, we can know about it only through guessing."

The traditional metaphysical belief in the thoroughgoing rationality of the world either accompanied belief in God or it was simply identical with it. In Nietzsche's view both are finished. Belief in the truth was simply a consequence of the belief that "God is the truth and that the truth is divine. . . . But what if precisely *this* becomes increasingly incredible and nothing any longer proves to be divine except error and blindness and lies—when God himself proves to be only our most persistent lie?"

Nietzsche's aim, in this attack, is the rejection of the belief and trust in the objective rationality of the whole as something in principle conceivable and discernible. To posit reason, thus understood, as the Absolute would prevent him from catching sight of being itself. His aggressiveness conceals an appeal to the source in man, who should attain to genuine self-certainty instead of taking refuge behind a supposedly universal rationality of an existence which includes himself.

4. The substance of Nietzsche's attacks, *viewed historically,* amounts to a rejection of traditional philosophy. Insofar as philosophers sought the truth and being itself in reason, construed as the totality of logically stabilizing forms, Nietzsche cannot but repudiate them. Consequently, traditional philosophy, almost in its entirety, must lose its meaning. The attack is directed against the very first great representative of the opposition: "Parmenides said: 'One does not think non-being.' Standing at the opposite extreme, we say: 'Whatever can be thought must surely be fictitious.' " When logicians regard "*their* boundaries as the boundaries of things," Nietzsche replies: "I have declared war upon such logical optimism." His refusal to trust any philosophy that asserts the absolute validity of reason affects, above all, Descartes, the representative of a more recent period, and his "*belief in the immediate certainty of thought.*" He is determined to be a better doubter than Descartes, who disbelieved in everything but reason itself and regarded the clarity and distinctness of knowledge as a reliable basis for truth. Nietzsche finds "the very reverse, namely a revolution against the absolute authority of

the goddess reason wherever men of a more profound nature are to be found." He rejects as "Gothic titanism" Hegel's "attempt to inject a kind of reason into evolution": "Standing at the opposite pole, I find even in logic a kind of irrationality and accident." The verdict applies generally: "For thousands of years, philosophers have manipulated mummified concepts. . . . They regard death, change, and age, as well as procreation and growth, as objections—even refutations. What *is* does not *become,* and what becomes *is* not. . . . Now we all believe in being, to the point of despair."

Nietzsche's standpoint vis-à-vis reason as the bearer of our consciousness of being, though of inestimable historical effectiveness within the stream of modern thought which moves towards the elimination of all values (discoverable as an undercurrent in every chapter in which we present Nietzsche's basic thoughts), never attains to adequate clarification of what it involves and what it makes possible for philosophical thinking.

First of all, Nietzsche's struggle with reason is not thoroughgoing. We have yet to see what he means when he uses the word "reason" to endorse something: In human life, reason is *necessary.* Man's "little bit of reason" must be "exerted to the utmost, and it always spells ruin for him when, for instance, he gives himself over to 'providence.'" Thus Nietzsche requires us to follow our reason in taking things vigorously in hand, instead of conveniently acquiescing in events which we call by the name of "providence." Human reason can certainly not deal with everything, and it cannot grasp the universe as a whole (reason becomes ruinous when human conduct is guided by such opinions). Still reason must continue to operate according to standards that Nietzsche has never undertaken critically to define.

Furthermore Nietzsche pleads the cause of reason against those of its enemies whose *motives* he rejects: "Among certain pious ones I discovered a hatred of reason. . . . Thus a bad intellectual conscience does at least betray itself." Furthermore, he refuses to be identified with philosophers who depreciate reason whenever within them "the ascetic self-contempt and self-scorn of reason decrees: There *is* a realm of truth and a realm of being, but it is precisely reason that is excluded from it!"

And above all, Nietzsche himself is capable of *accepting reason.* Then reason appears, not as the individuating procedure of the understanding and not even as thinking consciousness but rather, encompassing everything, as "the great reason" of the "body," while the "little reason" which goes by the name of spirit (*Geist*) is only an instrument of the body. Or again, in connection with those aspects of our behavior which at present are still incomprehensible and seemingly accidental, he speaks of the "higher reason of our future task." With this concept of "great reason" he lays hold upon a far-reaching meaning that again dissolves all hostility to reason, even though this concept, symbolized by the body, remains completely indeterminate. Such a statement as the following can only apply to this great reason: "Our sole happiness lies in reason; everything else in the world is *triste*. But I find the highest reason of all in the work of the artist."

The contradictoriness of Nietzsche's positive and negative formulations gives his dissolution of reason the appearance of an ambiguity involving mutually exclusive meanings:

His negative pronouncements, taken alone, tend to promote an indifference to reason. It may well appear that, whenever Nietzsche himself becomes indifferent to reason, his logical demands are accordingly vitiated. Hence contradictions in his statements are apt to stand mutely side by side as though, for an instant, he did not experience the sting of their opposition. The contradictions then become undialectical and cannot, as they stand, be brought into fruitful movement. Further, the fact that Nietzsche says now one thing and now another may seem to the reader to signify an indecisiveness equally receptive to all possibilities. Finally, in this connection, it must be noted that his penchant for true systematization and organization appears capable of being replaced by a desire for mere intellectual orderliness.

But not all of Nietzsche's pronouncements are equally germane to what he really means. The deviations (*Abgleitungen*) are almost unavoidable insofar as he uses the words "reason," "understanding," and "intellect" without methodically defining and elaborating upon their meanings. His statements, while directed against those who take reason for granted as something all-too-obvious, themselves often presuppose some self-evident notion of what reason is. Then Nietzsche's "reason" usually becomes sufficiently indeterminate to overlap with thinking or opining, while knowledge overlaps with identity, order, and law, and these latter overlap with vitally necessary interpretations of being, as well as with intellect and understanding for the sake of expediency.

Thus what Nietzsche really intends to accomplish philosophically with his dissolution of reason often bogs down temporarily. Actually he is passionately striving for something superior to reason, something that constitutes his "great reason." His attack on "reason" is really waged by the great reason against the little reason of an understanding that already takes itself to be fully knowledgeable. But from a Kantian viewpoint the attack is uncritical since the great reason in its entirety is never thoroughly elucidated. Thus whenever the great reason is not positively present to him to furnish reliable guidance, Nietzsche becomes the skeptic who again abandons both his positive and his negative assertions. Such relentless abandonment, however, is itself one of the phenomena that show how his thought derives from a source in the encompassing that is not merely interpretative life of a given kind but the "life" of truth from which, in spite of everything, the self-assertion of truth proceeds. In his formulations, this life of truth is not present with the quiet clarity and cogent peace characteristic of Kant. But it may well be that Nietzsche in the end simply means this: The life of truth is the encompassing within which reason and *Existenz* have their source, although this source as such is not knowable. It is only through the unfolding of factual knowledge and practically effective activity that this life can recognize itself as a constant process of clarification that never attains its final goal. This is not life as a biological, psychological, or sociological existence (for as such it would be an object within the world, subject to empirical investigation), rather it is life as a source that comprehends both the object and the act of investigation. It is this which Nietzsche constantly appears to touch upon but never succeeds in grasping in a philosophically decisive manner; this is the moving force that gives to his philosophizing the impetus to vanquish all that is known.

Because the encompassing is discernible in all of Nietzsche's thinking about truth (although it never becomes objectified), his thought remains philosophical and does not become lost in the objectivities of disciplines like psychology, bogged down once and for all in the blind alleys of logic, or stranded in unyielding positions.

Philosophizing must use as its medium a reason that grasps its source (though its essence derives from the extra-rational). When reason is methodically present in its encompassing, illumining, and propelling inevitability, when it is not confused with mere understanding, fixating intellect, and purposeful finitude, when in the articulated whole of its functions it is known through philosophical logic—then and then only can philosophizing remain true to itself within the one great current of its history. Reason is powerful only to the extent to which its philosophical self-penetration is accomplished even in a logical sense. When reason is thus understood, Nietzsche's own philosophizing becomes a singularly great achievement of reason, though one that fails to push logical clarity concerning itself to its limit.[4]

But however decisive the task emerging from Nietzsche's thought may

---

[4] In connection with Nietzsche's understanding of himself, cf. pp. 383 ff.

appear *to us* to be, we have no direct assurance that it could have appeared so to Nietzsche. Not only does the truth for him lie beyond reason (though this truth is always found and heard and made communicable on the path of reason), but apparently "truth" without and in opposition to reason appears as a monstrous, bewitching, and terrifying darkness. How, in his transcending breakthrough, he speaks of this, necessarily concealing much and revealing little, will be explained in the following section.

With his "dissolution of reason" Nietzsche has created a new beginning: the way is to be found to a more profound reason; a new gigantomachy must arise within philosophizing. Within every soul awake in this age, this battle must be fought. It has, however, a double aspect: Reason, now becoming sure of itself, struggles together with the substance of night, which belongs to it and apart from which it would lose its own nature, and at the same time it struggles against its enemy in the guise of radical nonsense and anti-reason.

The process of living and thinking within an encompassing reason that is ever present while still in search of itself and that is always limiting itself critically with a view to illumining and taking up into its own movement what lies beyond the limit, comes face to face with that being which it is not, but through which it is. But it is as though in this battle, reason and its opponent were also allies, as it were, since each of the two sides grows and thrives upon the other.

However, this same reason finds itself confronting a radically opposing will that refuses to be enlightened by any sort of movement and that, on its part, uses the intellect as a mere means, robs all reason's pronouncements of the ground of their vitality and assimilates them to the caprice of irresponsible chatter. This contrary will, having joined the chaos of night, can converse deceitfully with reason and engross it within itself by concealing the chaos behind a semblance of order.

This struggle involves the most radical trials. In all three directions (the great reason, the darkness of night, and the opposition of anti-reason), Nietzsche appears to make extreme statements. In the course of the struggle, reason must become what it possibly already is, even though it does not know itself to be such: it must break through all the bounds that it has acknowledged and, in the end, fall back upon itself again. If Nietzsche's life has been the decisive event, then the starting point of the philosophy of the future is to be found right here.

Nietzsche's statements can seemingly signify anything and everything; we find that in the end they belong together in a progression of the "great reason." This must be clearly brought out, at its very darkest if possible

—even when he appears to surrender the truth while accomplishing a transcending breakthrough.

A Transcending Breakthrough to the Truth

The *limitations of science* made room for a philosophizing that seeks its own basis. The *theory that truth has its being within life* allowed the truth either to come to nothing with life or to amount to just a kind of error necessary to a given organic form. The *passionate will to truth* understood itself, but in such a way that it constantly had to see itself disappear into something alien to truth. Science seemed to sink back into philosophizing, truth into life, and the will to truth into the darkness of its conditions. Always the question of truth led to a precipice: at every point a leap had to be made. In the end, Nietzsche breaks the circle by accomplishing a transcending breakthrough, the ambiguous expression of which, whether in extreme formulations or in silence, will for the first time reveal or conceal the real basis of his thoughts concerning truth.

The question of truth is the question of all questions; its meaning is identical with the question of being for us. It aims to arrive at the inescapable presupposition of all thoughts and deeds that lay claim to validity. The question cuts the ground out from under the questioner: it simply renders every determinate appearance dubious and, in widening the questioner's horizon to the utmost, it detaches him from any and every specific logical ground.

The question departs from its original meaning as soon as it narrows itself by taking some presupposition for granted as though it were self-evident. But since thought cannot take a single step forward without determinacy, i.e., without taking a certain degree of narrowness into the bargain, it comes about that, as soon as truth is spoken of, it ceases to be *the* truth since it becomes a *special* truth with distinct limitations. In the last analysis, it is impossible to ask what it really is, for the question is too indeterminate to admit of an objective answer. But still this indeterminacy is not nothing, and to operate with it belongs to the philosophically transcending ascertainment of what constitutes the truth.

Nietzsche's philosophical strength is shown by his constant overcoming of every form of truth that momentarily purports to be the truth itself. In all cases the presumed truth turns out to be a mere representative rather than the truth *in propria persona*.

While up to this point our theme has been Nietzsche's elucidation of all the modes through which truth is represented, we must now see how Nietzsche philosophizes on the basis of a truth that remains completely indeterminate—a boundless truth within which everything seems reduced to nothing. For when, instead of calling in question every determinate form of truth, we focus upon the truth itself directly, it disappears in a vast indeterminacy unbounded by any horizon. Only by speaking negatively can one transcend to it. According to Nietzsche, it is incommunicable, and it only reveals itself indirectly: it is danger; it is death; it is even the source of the saying that, within the world, *nothing is true and all is permitted.*

The Incommunicability of Truth. What constitutes the incommunicability of authentic truth is the fact that it ceases to be such whenever its existence assumes any sort of determinate form. This is touched upon in a dialogue which Nietzsche presents as being carried on between Pyrrho, the skeptic, and an old man. Pyrrho, undertaking to teach men indirectly and without fanaticism says: "I intend to warn people against myself." He wishes to become a teacher of mistrust, "such mistrust as has never before appeared in the world, mistrust of everything and everybody." To the objection that his words too are those of a fanatic who asserts the truth with dogmatic finality—in this case the truth of this mistrust— Pyrrho replies: "You are right! I intend to distrust all words." The old fellow answers: "Then you will have to be silent." Later in the discourse, becoming doubtful, he asks: "Do we now still understand each other completely?" When Pyrrho laughs, he asks: "Are silence and laughter now your entire philosophy?" The skeptic replies: "It would not be the worst."

To Nietzsche laughter is an expression of this truth that cannot be communicated: "Learn to laugh at yourself the way one must laugh!" "I myself placed the crown upon my own head, I personally canonized my laughter." The rank of a philosopher is determined by the rank of his laughter. Consequently one can say both: "The commonness of a person who roars with laughter surpasses that of any beast," and (of Zarathustra): "A man transformed, transfigured, who laughed! Never in the world has anyone laughed as he did!" In connection with his writings, Nietzsche warns us: "He who cannot laugh over them should not read them." Out of the anguish of man comes this truth for which there are no words: "The most sorrowful animal on the earth invented for himself—laughter." "Those who have been deeply hurt laugh like the Olympians."

Sanctification of laughter, the lightness of the dance, and victory over the spirit of heaviness belong together. Nietzsche is pressing onwards toward the "truths to which we can dance," and he is well acquainted with the objection to all determinate, fixated truths that, in their finality, purport to be absolute: "No feet can dance to such truths, and that is why they are by no means truths for us." "I do not know what more the spirit of a philosopher could wish beyond being a good dancer. Surely the dance is, so to speak, . . . his sole piety, his divine service." In his exaltation Zarathustra says: "Now I am light, now I fly, now I look down upon myself, now a god dances within me." [5]

The Danger Presented by Truth. The truth that Nietzsche calls dangerous is sometimes *determinate knowledge* and sometimes the *indeterminate being* of the truth itself merely appearing in the form of determinate knowledge. In his writings these two are inseparable.

Truth in the form of *insight into the illusoriness of all truth* remains negative. The previously discussed Nietzschean antinomy of truth as a *semblance* necessary to life and truth as *insight into this semblance* poses a problem that he came quite early to regard as a threat to life itself: "We are from the very outset illogical and consequently unrighteous beings, and we are capable of recognizing it. This is one of the greatest discords of existence, and one of the hardest to resolve." How this is best tolerated and how it is possible to live with it at all is expressed by the question "whether one can deliberately cleave to untruth or, assuming that one cannot avoid doing so, whether death would not be preferable." But the whole of human life is deeply submerged in untruth, and the individual "cannot draw it from this well without developing a most profound grudge against his past." But this leads to the danger that there "would remain only one way of thinking which, as a personal experience, would lead to despair and, as a theoretical matter, to a philosophy of dissolution." Nietzsche chooses to face up to this: "Admitting that untruth is the condition of life . . . at this point more than anywhere else, one must resolve not to 'bleed to death' over this 'recognized truth.' In this greatest of all dangers one must at once summon the fundamental creative instincts in man which are stronger than all feelings of value."

When Nietzsche views truth in its determinacy as error required by life, always and inevitably the idea of a *truth per se* stands in the background, not only as the negation of all determinate truth, but as the possibility of making contact with being itself. This truth that is at once negative and positive, insofar as it lies beyond all determinacy and is simply itself, and insofar as it also can appear as knowledge of being, must in every form prove dangerous to life, i.e., to existence that is bound up with error. Consequently from the standpoint of life itself, the will to

[5] Cf. p. 407 and pp. 410 ff., in the chapter entitled "How Nietzsche Understands Himself and his Own Thought."

truth is questionable: "What is there in us that really wills the truth? . . . Why not rather untruth? Why not uncertainty? Or even ignorance?"

Thus it seems fortunate that man knows so little of himself. Nature is silent concerning the wisest things and confines him within a proud illusory consciousness: "Woe," therefore, "to the fatal curiosity that would wish for once to peer out and down through a crack and then realize that mankind depends upon what is pitiless, covetous, insatiable, and even murderous." He can live only in the indifference of his ignorance, "clinging to the back of a tiger while enveloped in dreams." In this state of affairs the truth-instinct is ruinous. It was naïve "to assume without further ado that knowledge could arrive at nothing but what is salutary and useful to man and that indeed nothing else whatsoever could—or even must—exist."

If, then, life depends upon mere semblance, truth is "a destructive principle, inimical to life," both in its entirety and in every last individual manifestation. This relates especially to living beings who are still developing: If "every man who strives to mature needs to be enveloped by an illusion, by a protective, veiling cloud," then truth that dispels the cloud would amount to destruction of the germ and the withering of life.

Hence we realize that something in Nietzsche urges him away from the truth when he tells us how indifferent he always has been toward it and when he speaks out against the tyranny of the "true": "I do not see why the absolute rule of the truth should be desirable; it was quite enough for me that truth should have great power. But it must have a chance to fight and have an opposition, and one must be able now and then to *relax* from it by consorting with untruth." One becomes disenchanted with the truth, for "all knowledge of truth is unproductive."

However Nietzsche does not regard the danger involved as a decisive objection to the truth. He willingly accepts the possibility of damage: "To be injurious and to destroy belong as much to the tasks of the philosopher as to be useful and constructive." Still his knowledge of the danger enables him to understand both the *will to ignorance* and the *courage to face the truth.*

The danger is the ground which supports a *radical will to ignorance:* "There are times when blindness is necessary and some of our errors and articles of faith must be left intact—at least so long as they keep us alive." That is why it is reasonable to say: "Once and for all, there is much that I choose *not* to know. Wisdom even places limits upon knowledge." "That one becomes what he is presupposes that he does not have the least idea what he is." Even science itself rests upon a will to refuse to know certain things: "From the very beginning we have known how to preserve our lack of knowledge. . . . Up to now science has been able to arise only upon the . . . granite foundation of ignorance, and the will to know upon the basis of a much stronger will: the will not to know, the will to uncertainty and to untruth."

Because of the danger, a genuine will to knowledge requires courage: "All of us are afraid of the truth." But "error is cowardice." "One approximates to the truth . . . exactly to the extent to which he has the courage to move forward." One's spiritual power is "measured by the extent to which he can endure the truth, or more precisely, the extent to which he needs it in diluted or veiled form." But even the most courageous among us seldom has the courage to accept what he really *knows.*" Nietzsche acknowledges (in the fragments to *Zarathustra*) that "there is such a thing as an unconscious self-defense, caution, concealment, and guardedness when we confront the most difficult knowledge. . . . There is something of which I did not tell myself anything. . . . We find that our sole means of enduring the truth is the creation of a being that can *endure* it; i.e., unless we voluntarily become blind to it and deceive ourselves again."

Truth and Death. The danger of truth is more than danger. The whole truth is death—thus Nietzsche seems to regard the matter. He tries to capture what he means with various symbols, though he never attains clarity.

At an early age, he appears, by means of a mythological symbol, to catch sight of the union of ultimate knowledge with a gruesome sinking into the abyss of a *fatal unnaturalness:* "Oedipus, the murderer of his father, the husband of his mother, Oedipus who solved the riddle of the Sphinx! What does this mysterious triad have to tell us? . . . That wherever the true magic of nature is destroyed by oracular powers, a monstrous contravention of nature must be assumed as its cause. For how could one possibly force nature to give up its secrets except through successful opposition—i.e., through the unnatural? . . . He who . . . solves the riddle of nature must also, as murderer of his father and spouse of his mother, violate the most sacred of nature's laws. Indeed, the myth appears concerned to insinuate that wisdom is an unnatural abomination and that anyone who flings nature into the abyss through his wisdom will have to experience the dissolution of nature within himself."

In the form of a utopia Nietzsche envisages the decline of man as a "tragic finale of knowledge." Knowledge of the truth could finally remain as man's single monstrous goal, and this could become so absolute as to require the sacrifice of all humanity. The problem would be: "Which cognitive drive could become so powerful as to cause man *to offer himself up* in order to *die* with the light of prophetic wisdom in his eyes? Perhaps when fraternization with the dwellers on other stars is once attained for the sake of knowledge and men have conveyed their wisdom from star to star for a few thousand years—perhaps then the glowing enthusiasm for knowledge will reach such a flood-height!"

To the question as to whether mankind as a whole wills death along with the truth, the answer in terms of this utopia must be that it could be hazarded but not directly willed. "It is possible that humanity will be destroyed by a passion for the truth! . . . Our cognitive instinct is too strong to permit us to prize happiness without knowledge or the happiness that comes of strong and securely intrenched delusions. . . . All of us would prefer the destruction of man to the retreat of knowledge."

When it is further asked whether "it is *permissible* to sacrifice humanity to the truth," Nietzsche as a young man answers: "It is scarcely possible. . . . If it were possible, it would be a good death and an escape from life. But no one can, without some degree of illusion, be so sure of possessing the truth. . . . The question whether it is permissible to sacrifice mankind to a delusion must be answered in the negative." Later on, after the radical leap in his thinking, the answer is: "We are experimenting with the truth! Perhaps mankind will perish from it! Be it so!"

Abandoning the form of utopia, Nietzsche investigates the thought of incompatibility of existence and truth: "It may even follow from the basic constitution of existence that man may be destroyed by his complete knowledge." In that case truth would be the annihilation of illusions—"the great means of overcoming mankind (its self-destruction!)." Truth as unconditional duty would be a hostile, world-destructive force. If it is correct to say that "truth kills—indeed it kills itself (insofar as it knows that it is based upon error)"—then it must also follow that "the will to truth—could be a concealed will to death."

But Nietzsche has sought to convey his own most profound experience of the sort of knowledge that would prove fatal if brought to completion, not through such preponderantly intellectual expositions, but through songs that provide sudden illumination and isolated statements that strike one with the instantaneous force of lightning flashes:

Paradoxically he finds that it belongs to the very essence of knowledge to emerge from love and then, in its successful advance, destroy this love: "The knower seeks union with things and sees himself as estranged—this is his passion." But this leads to two processes that are fatal to him or the objects of his knowledge. Either he wants *"everything to be resolved into knowledge"* ("a striving to spiritualize everything"), or "he loses himself in things" ("his death and its pathos").

The first possibility (everything resolved into knowledge) is experienced most fully in the "Night Song." This "song of one who loves" is Nietzsche's stirring lament expressing the loneliness of one who has come to identify himself with pure truth. As such he cannot be loved and he can no longer love; he consumes himself in the readiness of the will to love and in an indeterminate, unworldly, and friendless love: "I am light; Oh that I were night! I live in my own light, and I drink back the flames that burst from me. I am ignorant of the happiness of those who receive! It is night: Woe to me that I must be light! And suffer thirst for nightly things and endure loneliness!" An extraordinary experience that overpowered Nietzsche has here found expression: "As a result of a superfluity of light and a sun-like nature, to be condemned not to love." That would be truth, sufficient unto itself and attaining fulfillment in itself. It is the torment of truth as the consuming light, as though being, in becoming pure spirit, were not transfigured but rather became congealed in a ghostly existence of being-no-longer.

In the same connection Nietzsche touched symbolically upon the *second possibility* (losing oneself in things—death). He says of the "Night Song": "The answer to any such dithyramb of sun-like isolation in the midst of light would be Ariadne. . . . Who, beside myself, knows what Ariadne is!"

Ariadne, the Labyrinth, the Minotaur, Theseus, and Dionysus—this whole area of mythology is repeatedly alluded to with all its mysterious ambiguity when he wishes to suggest the last secret of the truth: that the truth is death, or that it is something else desired with the passion for truth that will, in turn, end in death:

The Labyrinth, from whose devious windings there is no escape and within which annihilation by the Minotaur is imminent, is the goal and the fate of the knower. Hence anyone who seeks the complete independence of knowledge, "without having to do so, proves thereby that he is daring to the point of wantonness. He enters a labyrinth, and he multiplies a thousandfold the dangers which life itself inevitably entails and among which must be counted, as by no means the least, the fact that no one can clearly see how and where he goes astray, isolates himself, and is consumed little by little by the cave-dwelling Minotaur of his conscience. Granted that a person of this ilk perishes, this occurrence is so incapable of being understood by others that no one has any pity or sympathy for it. And he can no longer turn back!" Contemptuously this new independent philosopher turns on the philosophers of old who taught the way to happiness and virtue: "Why does one like us turn aside to become a philosopher . . . or a ghost? Is it not to *get rid of* virtue and happiness? We are by nature much too happy and much too virtuous to fail to be tempted a little by the prospect of becoming philosophers— i.e., immoralists and adventurers. . . . We have *a peculiar curiosity about the Labyrinth,* and we are taking pains to make the acquaintance of Mr. Minotaur." The philosopher sits "in his cave, year in and year out, day and night, alone with his soul, in intimate dispute and dialogue. It can be a labyrinth, but it can also be a goldmine."

Such is the truth; it leads us into the Labyrinth and into the power of the Minotaur. Consequently the knower has still another entirely different goal: "Whatever he may tell us, a labyrinthine man never seeks the truth but always only his Ariadne." The search for the truth leads on to something other than the truth—something that resembles it but is not among those truths that can be grasped *as* truths. Nietzsche has never told us what Ariadne is; perhaps he could not.

In turn she comes to represent death. Just as she provided, up to this point, the answer to the "sun-like isolation in the midst of light," i.e., to pure spirituality estranged from being, by holding out the prospect of fusion with her being or of salvation from the labyrinth of truth, so now she becomes instead the undoing of Theseus' search for truth: " 'Ariadne,' says Dionysus, 'you are a labyrinth. Theseus has become lost in you, he has no more thread. What does it profit him not to be devoured by the Minotaur? What now consumes him is worse than the Minotaur.' " Ariadne answers: "That is my last love to Theseus: I destroy him."

But even this is not Nietzsche's final word. Rather Dionysus is the new truth when Theseus becomes "absurd," i.e., becomes a fanatic who seeks the truth at any cost. Nietzsche as Theseus is indeed lost in the labyrinth of Ariadne, but as Dionysus he becomes the truth that transcends both death and life. From this last standpoint he can say to Ariadne: "I am your labyrinth." [6]

Is Dionysus the truth where darkness, as belonging to the truth itself,

---

[6] I do not wish to enter into the biographical discussions that try to prove that Ariadne is Cosima Wagner. There can be no doubt that at times remembrances of Cosima play a role when Nietzsche speaks of Ariadne, especially in the insane note to her: "Ariadne, I love thee.—Dionysus." But these clues contribute absolutely nothing to an understanding of the philosophical meaning of this symbolism. This latter remains essentially a boundary, untranslatable into rational or psychological conceptualizations and incapable of being expounded at all except in terms of the existential boundary-experiences that proceed from Nietzsche's passion for the truth.

redeems and overcomes it, because the paradoxical turning-points of the search for truth within the realm of the living arrive at the being that now for the first time—in Dionysus—is the truth? All comprehension—indeed all actual experience—of that which Nietzsche here can no longer expressly say ceases. Ariadne, as the "answer to the sun-like isolation in the light," as the helper in the labyrinth of truth, as the labyrinth itself, Ariadne for whom Dionysus becomes the labyrinth—these are the positions in which Ariadne remains as an enigmatic symbol.

In the end Nietzsche's position is that the final truth *is* death. Zarathustra is the symbol; for the proclamation of his highest truth, the culmination of his being, and the fate of necessity is at once his *decline*. Does man will death insofar as it is the truth, and does he shun it only insofar as it is untruth? In Nietzsche's thought the abysmal ambiguity of death in truth and truth in death remains inexplicable.

"Nothing Is True, Everything Is Permitted." When all determinate truth within the world is called in question and no representation of truth is the truth itself, this formulation, which appears to deny all truth, must become possible. When removed from context, such a statement—often repeated by Nietzsche—is unintelligible. Taken by itself it expresses complete lack of obligation; it is an invitation to individual caprice, sophistry, and criminality. But to Nietzsche it represents the emancipation of the deepest and therefore truest of human motives, unimpeded by any of those forms of so-called truth which, being fixed and final, are actually untrue. The passion for truth, in the guise of radical and incessant doubt, causes all determinate appearances to perish. While truth as transcendence—as the completely indeterminate and indeterminable truth itself—cannot lie, yet every specific truth within the world can. Only the concrete historicity of *Existenz,* indubitably present though uncognizable, is then true. What sets a limit to doubt is not some truth or other, not the thought of an absolute truth, but this *Existenz.* In Hamlet's words: "Doubt truth to be a liar, but never doubt my love."

By calling in question any and every kind of fixation of the truth, Nietzsche makes a most extraordinary demand: "By 'freedom of the spirit' I mean something very specific: surpassing the philosophers and other disciples of the 'truth' a hundredfold in severity with oneself, in integrity and in courage. . . . I treat previous philosophers as despicable libertines hiding under the hood of a woman: truth. . . ." Only this attitude of unlimited openness to the possible under the strict leadership of something unknown, *Existenz* itself, can truly say: "Nothing is true." The meaning of the statement is then not unbridled caprice but rather: "Now you must give the highest proof of being of a noble kind."

Only inborn nobility would be able to give content to the enormous negativity of this proposition by drawing upon the historical positivity of its love and its creative will. For nobility possesses the drives and powers that can call all existence of determinate truth in question for the sake of something higher which they are ushering in. Now that nothing "is" any longer true, "everything" is permitted; impalpable being is free. Only where being itself comes forth from the depths of historicity does the statement have the meaning that Nietzsche meant it to have. But even here it is soon annulled: it has sense only as the punctual expression of a decisive moment.

Even in the context of Nietzsche's philosophizing, the statement can only remain true when it carries with it the whole of the truth entertained by Nietzsche. As a short formula it is of ruinous ambiguity, for the convictions which it directly conveys are precisely the opposite of what Nietzsche intends it to say indirectly. As an expression of radical licentiousness it is intrinsically incapable of providing any guidance whatsoever. Then it immediately signifies the sinking into the nothingness of indeterminate possibility that accompanies the end of all truth. In this form it obliterates the distinction between the truth of an appearance which promotes life and the capricious lie of an individual, as well as that between historicity and chaos. All existence would then be uniform and on the same level; everything would be the appearance of the same becoming that struggles with itself internally in the guise of a multiplicity of wills to power. The final boundary would be empty meaninglessness and futility.

As decisive as this aspect may appear, still within the broader context of Nietzsche's thought it cannot be the last word. This statement stands at the very summit of his thinking about truth as it seeks to express, in the form of a crushing negation, a more profound affirmation of the truth than any general formulation can convey. But instead of supplying a hortatory symbol, it provides a belligerent polemical formula which conveys more nearly an expression of despair than an awareness of the source.

As we deliberately go through the dialectical movements in which the truth never attains its goal (since it can never be possessed but in the end even denies itself), we are forced back to find fulfillment in our own historically present *Existenz*. Through our knowledge of this movement we become aware of not possessing the truth. Only perseverance in this movement can overcome the danger of deception which will result if we thoughtlessly use Nietzsche's isolated and isolating formulae as dead-sure dicta and, with the aid of these dialectical thoughts, arbitrarily justify or condemn everything.

3

HISTORY AND THE PRESENT AGE

Man is not static and unchanging: his existence is not simply repeated from one generation to another. He is what his history makes him. History keeps him in constant movement, and it has long been one of the tasks of philosophy to make him conscious of this movement. The way in which this takes place profoundly determines man's awareness of his existence. When accomplished within the framework of an all-encompassing philosophy of history, we feel secure in the source from which we grow, the substance in which we live, the ground on which we stand, the time in which we find ourselves, and the task which confronts our age. But in Nietzsche's case, this totality is disrupted, and such total views as he presents are mere trial perspectives to be relativized immediately. As a result, his historical thinking is broken up, so to speak. We can observe three directions in which he proceeds. First, Nietzsche is a *spectator of the actual historical process:* in sharing the awareness of world-history achieved by his "historical" century, he seeks to discover the essential realities and the underlying causal connections. Second, in place of history itself, the *actuality of this historical consciousness* and its significance for life become the objects of his inquiry and consequent doubt. Now he deals with historical remembrance, its motives, forms, and eventual results. Third, his glance is directed to *his own age,* for his historical thinking is concerned above all to fathom it. He wishes to comprehend the world-historical moment in which he participates, with a view to knowing what is really being decided now. Although, unlike the Christian philosophers and Hegel and his descendants as well, he is unable to determine precisely, from a knowledge of the totality of world history, where we are today, he is actually moved, as they were, by the same pathos of a total historical consciousness. Standing at a historical turning point, he is intent upon fathoming its meaning so that his thoughts may provide a direction.

The Forms through Which History Reveals Itself to Nietzsche

Nietzsche is not a research specialist who pursues methodical investigations (except for the short span of his youth when he consciously submitted to discipline and served the cause of science as a classical philologist) nor is he the constructive philosopher of history who develops a completely cohesive, compact whole to express his present historical consciousness. He is rather a seer who presents us with a prodigal abundance of observations as he gives utterance to his vision of the various aspects of things. To be sure, he is occasionally overcome by esthetic delight in the appearances of things, and at times he is victimized by meretricious grandiosity. But his fundamental impulse is the will to understand: he looks to knowledge of the historical process for the basis of an evaluation of human affairs.

The Universal Basic Features of History. Understanding the prevailing laws of the historic process as well as sociological necessities and psychological types of behavior, Nietzsche seeks to discover the basic course of events concealed behind the endless abundance of phenomena in the historical foreground. This endeavor gives rise to groups of comments exemplifying the directions that his views of history take:

1. The first quest is for the widest horizon: When does history begin, and what is the factor which initiates its movement? Nietzsche answers that it does not begin until the individual's creative urge for liberation asserts itself; history is the movement in the tension between individuals and the inflexible invariability of a totality that keeps them in subjection.

Prehistoric ages, as Nietzsche constructs them, are exclusively determined by a tradition that is universally binding and absolutely beyond question. Nothing actually happens. The most frightful thing of all, for people of such an age, is the feeling of isolation. To be considered an individual is not a pleasure but a punishment. Every misery and every fear has something to do with being alone. The more an individual's act expresses the "herd instinct" rather than his private inclination, the more moral he is in his own eyes.

World history is preceded by aeons of such "morality of custom." These immense periods—in comparison with which "world history" is only "a ridiculously small segment of human existence"—comprise "the real and decisive fundamental history which determined the character of humanity."

Change during the *historical* period always has come about through breaking with tradition: "It is free-thinking that makes history." But the "free spirit" is invariably weak compared with tradition. To ask how it might nevertheless realize itself is to ask about the "genesis of genius" and thus about the recurrent beginning of actual history.

Nietzsche's formulations derive from the dependence of the individual on the universally binding whole and the reciprocal dependence of this whole on the individual (so that both human existence and human enhancement, both social permanence and historical change, may be possible). His defense of the individual, the genius, the free spirit is passionate. This is not contradicted but complemented by his statement that "nothing is more detrimental to a good insight into culture than consideration of genius and nothing else." He intends in this way to use the "cult of culture" as an antidote to the cult of genius. For the reverberation of everything human—man's ant-like performances along with the work of genius—must not become lost again: "How could we dare to dispense with the common, deep, and often awesome thorough-bass without which melody really cannot be melody?"

This reciprocal play, when viewed as a whole, reveals a stern inevitability. Insistence on free choice is opposed by "an omnipresent and universally binding belief, in brief, by the absence of free individual decision. Up to this time, man has labored hardest to come to an agreement concerning a large number of things and promulgate a self-imposed *law of conformity.*" It is precisely when the choicest spirits fight against this binding conformity in matters of general agreement, with the searchers for the truth in the vanguard, that there is need of *"virtuous stupidity* and of the imperturbable time-beaters of the *slow* spirit, so that the adherents to the great universal faith may stay together." On the one hand, action guided by individual choice leads to social chaos, and any relaxation of obligation deriving from personality differences is dangerous; on the other hand, the group best able to preserve itself—the one "in which most members possess a vital community spirit in consequence of generally accepted principles, sanctioned by custom and not open to discussion (i.e., in consequence of a common belief)"—is threatened by the other danger: "a gradual increase of stupidity as a result of inheritance." Nietzsche recognizes the antinomy of the historical movement, and, while he is aware that he is a creative exception, he acknowledges the demands of history. *"We others are the exception and the danger.* We are eternally in need of defense! Well, something can really be said in favor of the exception, as long as he does not attempt to become the rule." Hence he calls "the hatred of mediocrity unworthy of a philosopher": precisely because the philosopher "is the exception, he has to protect the rule; he has to maintain the confidence of the average man in himself."

2. To Nietzsche the course of history is the process of *taming man*

through the agency of metaphysical, religious, and moral errors. The starting point of the development is man as a wild and lawless natural force. This is something we now have almost forgotten. Our age is, in a manner of speaking, a mild climate compared with earlier tropical periods: "When we see how the most furious passions were once overpowered and broken with awesome force through metaphysical concepts, we feel as though before our eyes wild tigers in the tropics were crushed in the coils of monstrous serpents. . . . Even in dreams we are not confronted by anything like what the peoples of the past saw while awake." But what happened then is the condition of our existence. Our being grew out of the transformation of these events. "It seems that all great things must first pass over the earth as monstrous and frightening distortions in order to engrave their eternal demands on the heart of humanity. Such a distortion was dogmatic philosophy: the Vedanta doctrine in Asia, for example, or Platonism in Europe. . . . Now we are the heirs of all the strength which the struggle against this error has fostered." "If one deducts the effects of these errors, then one deducts humanity, humaneness, and 'human dignity' as well."

3. History reveals the perennial *dreadful powers* which man conceals behind a veil but does not destroy. They are indispensable to his existence. "Culture is only a thin apple peel over a fiery chaos." Everywhere these powers are seen to supply the first impetus: "The wildest forces are trail breakers, initially destructive, although their activity was necessary. . . . The terrible energies—those which we call evil—were the cyclopic architects and road builders of humanity." Every superior culture began with barbarians. In this beginning "a great many things are veiled." But the horrible continues to occur at all times; it is simply more veiled because nobody seems to commit it: "Pluralities have been invented to do things for which the individual lacks the courage. For this reason, all commonwealths are a hundred times more honest and instructive concerning the nature of man than the individual." Means of accomplishing many things to which the individual would never agree are available to the state: division of responsibility, of command, and of execution; the interspersion of the virtues of obedience, of duty, of love for country and ruler, the maintenance of pride, sternness, strength, hatred, and revenge.

Eras, Peoples, and Men. General types of events provide one perspective for Nietzsche's historical thinking. His view of eras, peoples, and great men provides the other. He contemplates and tersely characterizes primitive ages, the world of antiquity, India, Christianity, the Renaissance and Reformation, the Enlightenment, and the peoples of the present era. But the figures that adorn the surface of history do not seem to him to be alike in value. However extensively he may survey the huge area of world-historic realities, his evaluation is always sharply focused: Existentially, Nietzsche is constantly connected with his subject-matter only at one single point in history: the golden age of Greece. While occasional statements about phenomena of the Renaissance, of the pre-historic Germanic period, and of the Roman world may reveal similar relationships, they are born of the moment and are never developed. Only the Greek world, in which he was absorbed, receives extensive exposition. Throughout his entire life, he spontaneously identifies his own potentialities with those of the Greeks. This is united with his will to realize the lofty German nature which he views as analogous. But while he regards the Greek world as definitive and takes it to be unques-tionably [1] the focal point of history (much as was the figure of Christ to the believing Christian), he projects the Germanic world entirely into the future and finds it to be in terrible danger because of itself. Consequently his love for what is truly German—that on which he bases all his hopes for the future in a decaying world—takes the form of a passionate criticism which grows in intensity during the course of his life.

The Greek is the "man who has achieved the most," the Greek people are "the only people of genius in the history of the world," "the Greeks surely have never been overestimated."

Greek antiquity is "the only true home of culture," and "the Greek world is seen as the one truly profound possibility of life." That is why Nietzsche asserts: "Up to this point, I recognize the highest culture merely as a reawakening of Hellenism." Hence if we were to approach antiquity merely from a historical point of view, we should lose its culture-producing force. Mere knowledge of the Greeks would, as such, be an empty knowledge about culture; it is a question of the "decision for culture." On the basis of the latter, Nietzsche can hope that "we are becoming more Greek from day to day; at first, as is proper, in concepts and evaluation . . . but eventually, it is to be hoped, also with our bodies! Therein lies (and has ever lain) my hope for things German."

Nietzsche is convinced that "the knowledge of the great Greeks edu-cated me." Only through its Greek source did he comprehend the defects of his own time: "Only to the extent that I am a pupil of former ages, particularly of the Greek, do I acquire such untimely experiences *via* myself as a child of this present age."

---

[1] That Nietzsche calls the Greeks in question implies that he is thinking of the Greeks since Socrates. He regards the pre-Socratic world as sacrosanct.

However one cannot, "through denial of the German spirit, jump directly, so to speak, and without a bridge into the Hellenic world which has become foreign to us." The goal is rather "the rebirth of Greece out of the renewal of the German spirit." "Of course one must first know how to search out this German spirit in its hiding places."

Only when all contemplation comes to an end and the knowledge of things Greek enters our bloodstream, can our own blood bring the Greek shadows to life. How strongly Nietzsche felt within his real historical self that the identity of his own source with the renewal of the ancient source ought to transcend any difference between Greek and German is evident when, even as a youth, he did not wish to remain a "pupil of sinking antiquity," but preferred to seek his models "by looking courageously into the primal world of greatness, naturalness, and humanity of ancient Greece." This can also be seen when, at the end of his life, he puts into words what had actually motivated him in the beginning, namely "that the real dignity of all German philosophizing consists in being a reconquest, step by step, of the soil of antiquity, and that any claim to originality sounds petty beside that higher claim of the Germans to have repaired the bond that seemed torn—that with the Greeks, the most highly developed type of man up to the present."

The Vital Significance of Historical Consciousness

Nietzsche is deeply impressed by the fundamental fact that the nature of man, unlike that of the brutes, is a product of history, i.e., of unconscious tradition and conscious remembrance. Without history man would cease to be man. He attains each new manifestation by laying hold of the past and pushing himself away from it in his knowledge that there is a future. Hence, as Nietzsche shows, he needs history in order to gain, from great examples of what man can do, courage for his present activity, elevation of his nature, and consolation in despair (in monumental history); he needs it in order to view his own individual origin with loving piety (in the history of antiquity); and he needs it in order to overcome, through the productive impulses of his present being, what has merely existed (in critical history).

Historical science turns historical remembrance into knowledge. Nietzsche became acquainted with it in an age that boasted of being uniquely historical. And he was the first to subject all historical science to critical questioning.

The Fundamental Errors of Historical Science. Historical science is not timelessly valid knowledge of a finished and unchanging state of affairs; rather history (*Historie*) *as knowledge* changes with history (*Geschichte*) understood as *a series of actual occurrences within the world*. Nothing past is unalterably dead: Whatever issued from an authentic source lives on beyond a new present to undergo unforeseeable transformations. It is forgotten and again revived, it is discovered after seemingly having been known for some time, and it provides a new impulse after it has long been regarded as insignificant. Within the vitally creative knowledge that constitutes true history we can never know with certainty what actually occurred. The past depends on the nature of those living at any given time; impulses rooted in that nature make history a matter of concern to them: a propelling force, a standard, an ideal or counter-ideal. That is why, on the one hand, genuine history (*Historie*) can never become strictly scientific, while on the other, it cannot preserve its truthfulness without exact investigation. Exact investigation, however, applies to materials, presuppositions, and all the things that every human understanding (*Verstand*) alike recognizes and is forced to accept as factual and as precisely what it always has meant. In contradistinction to this, historical memory (*die geschichtliche Erinnerung*), as it proceeds within the fully apprehended medium of this factual material, sees with the historical eyes of a being whose reach exceeds that of the understanding and that is capable of realizing itself through the very memory that it makes possible.

Above all, a total knowledge of anything past is impossible, not because the materials are too extensive to be surveyed or have been handed down in defective form, but because of the infinite possibility of each living *Existenz* which can become known only by a memory that generates itself within its own world. To know the past in which I am rooted is not to become identical with it, or even to penetrate it. Any presumed total knowledge would have to destroy the genuine appropriating remembrance through a scientifically incorrect and existentially false semblance of knowledge. To combat this, Nietzsche calls contemporary, i.e., "unhistorical," life to his aid. In doing so, however, he seemingly fails to mark the distinction between an unhistorical existence whose brutal indifference, like that of an animal, derives from sheer ignorance and forgetfulness, and the very different unhistorical being that is truly human, i.e., original being in and of the present and, as such, the very source of historical vision.

Nietzsche does not vent his wrath on the scientific method as such or on historical remembrance, but rather on those historians who claim to use the *methods of pure science* and thus pretend to a knowledge they do not at all possess. This is evident throughout all their thinking; it is evident, for instance, when they insist that *necessity* governs the course of events and again when, confronted with this necessity, they reject the question that is "cardinal" for Nietzsche's method of gaining historical insight: "What would have happened if this or that had not occurred?" Their glorification of success gives rise to their "historical optimism" and their failure to understand "how brutal and senseless history is." Against them Neitzsche cries out: "Everything that has been suppressed by success will eventually rebel." The historians, in their obsession with science, are producing a history "expressive of the sneers of the victors and of their own servile attitude in the face of the facts."

The Life-Destroying Effect of Historical Science. The erroneous principle which serves as the foundation of all scientific history is not an inconsequential matter. Nietzsche is overwhelmed by the discovery that *history can ruin man.* In a publication of his youth, titled *Concerning the Advantage and Disadvantage of History for Life,* he arrives at the conviction that history in "excess" becomes evil. In the first place, when the historical sense develops into the ability to impersonate, momentarily, every foreign nature, the personality is weakened. Having become insubstantial as the result of such histrionics, the inner being of a person thus obsessed with a knowledge of the past and incapable of understanding the present becomes alienated from his tangible, living reality. In the second place, this approach leads to the notion that objectivity and justice will result. The consequence is that history destroys the instincts. Through premature consciousness it impedes the maturing of the germ of all life. The historian's belief that mankind has reached maturity gives rise to a feeling of decadence and in the end leaves nothing behind but an ironical awareness of our own insignificance and the decay of all things. By these paths history robs man of the value of historical memory. Through it man develops knowledge of greatness but no capacity for it (monumental history); he studies the past merely as past and does not respect it (ancient history); and he condemns what has occurred for no real reason and in a merely deleterious way (critical history).

But what is "excess" in history? Besides *remembrance,* which distinguishes man from the animal, man needs, in Nietzsche's words, *forgetfulness,* which he has in common with the animal. In order to be able to bear historical remembrance without being destroyed by it, one must appropriate it through adaption. *"Plastic energy"* determines the scope of the historical which can be absorbed without disaster. The amount of history that is bearable depends upon the strength of the *personality.*

The two powers of remembrance and forgetfulness Nietzsche calls the *historical* and the *unhistorical* in man. Since both are needed, he can, in a seemingly contradictory manner, proclaim the one or the other as essential according to the context.

Occasionally Nietzsche completely *rejects* history. He can consider "the task of the science of history as solved" "when the entire, intrinsically coherent cycle of past endeavors has been *condemned.*" The science of history then becomes superfluous. "In its place must step the science that deals with the *future.*"

Genuine Historicity (Geschichtlichkeit). In spite of the above, Nietzsche's *positive approach* to the genuinely historical predominates. He reveals a possibility open to the historical sense in the present age, which, as he believes, presents us with the task of going beyond the irrevocably finished original folk-cultures to found a new existence through a comparative study of culture. From this standpoint, Nietzsche can praise our age: "In view of the past, we enjoy all cultures . . . and nourish ourselves from the noblest blood of all ages . . . while previous cultures could enjoy only themselves and nothing beyond." But such "enjoyment" is not passive contemplation. More than that is now open to us: "He who can feel the entire history of mankind as *his own history,* feels, through an immense generalization, all the grief . . . of the hero on the evening of the indecisive battle that brought him only wounds and the loss of his friend. But to bear this immense sum of grief . . . as the man with a horizon of millenniums ahead of him and behind him, as the heir, . . . as the noblest of all ancient nobles and, at the same time, as the first member of a new nobility . . . would after all provide a *happiness* that no man has yet known. . . . This sudden feeling would then be called—humanity!"

Nietzsche can in passing even accord some value to attempts at a *history of life and the universe* reaching beyond man into infinity: "In the striving for knowledge of the entire historical development which . . . for the first time broke down the old walls between man and animal, morality and physics," we must "recognize a striving for the genius of mankind within the whole. History conceived as complete would be cosmic self-awareness."

In spite of his unveiling of the ruinous effects of the self-isolating historical consciousness and in spite of his view which sometimes sees the past as merely a chain, we find a passionate adherence to history at the core of Nietzsche's challenge. He speaks with genuine shock of the possibility of the loss and ruination of the past: "Have you no compassion for the past? Do you not see how in its abandonment it depends

. . . on the mercy, the spirit, the fairness of each generation? Could not, at any moment, a great monster appear who would force us to deny it completely, who would make our ears deaf to it or even hand us a whip to mistreat it?" "Zarathustra does not wish to lose any of mankind's pasts or cast everything in the gutter."

For Nietzsche, the depth of appropriation of the past is the real source of the future. "To impregnate the past and beget the future—let that be the present for me."

The Present Age

If the past is still hidden and awaiting, as it were, the awakening of its highest possibilities, then the present signifies the call to grasp what the moment offers. It is from the consciousness of this present that Nietzsche proceeds to envisage the past and conceive of the future. He wants to know what is actually happening now.

The Image of His Age. Even when he was quite young, Nietzsche was *terrified* by the image of his age. He discovered symptoms of the eradication of culture: "The waters of religion recede and leave behind swamps and ponds; the nations again draw apart in the most hostile manner. . . . The sciences disintegrate and dissolve all that was firmly believed. . . . Everything serves to promote the coming barbarism. . . . Surely forces are present, immense forces, but they are wild, primitive, and wholly merciless. . . . Now everything on earth is determined only by the coarsest and most evil forces, by the egoism of those engaged in acquisitive pursuits and by the military despots." The *Existenz* of modern man reveals "an unspeakable poverty and exhaustion, despite the unspeakable variety borrowed from previous cultures." A knowledge about culture is his substitute for culture. In his inner self, "gray impotence, gnawing dissatisfaction, busiest boredom, and dishonest misery" prevail. "Nothing stands on firm feet with a rugged faith in itself. . . . Everything on our path is smooth and perilous, and, furthermore, the ice which still supports us has become so thin: soon no one will be able to walk where we are now walking."

Nietzsche also has a few things to say *in favor of the present,* though doubt usually asserts itself in the end: "We have outdistanced the Greeks in enlightening the world through natural and human history, and our knowledge is much greater, our judgments are more moderate and just. Moreover a gentler humaneness prevails. . . . The fact that, in the last analysis, we would rather live in this age than any other is essentially to the credit of science, and surely there never existed for any generation such an abundance of noble joys as we have. . . . But with all this 'freedom,' living is good only if we merely wish to understand and not participate—that is the modern fly in the ointment. . . . Thus arises the danger that our knowledge will take its revenge on us, just as ignorance exacted its revenge during the Middle Ages. . . ."

A closer scrutiny of the *origin* of the tremendous world transformation soon reveals some tangible phenomena. The *machine* represents a destiny: it changes the world in which we live; we become indifferent to the objects with which we deal. For the machine is "impersonal in that it removes any basis for pride in a piece of work, removes its individual goodness or faultiness,—and thus its small portion of humanity. In former times, household goods and clothes became symbols of mutual esteem and solidarity, but now we seem to live only in a state of anonymous and impersonal slavery." The machine further effects a change in man through the techniques that it requires. It "does not provide an impulse for rising higher. . . . It causes busyness and monotony." The machine even takes hold of community life. It "furnishes the pattern for party organization and war strategy. But it does not teach individual autonomy: It converts whole groups into machines and every individual into a specialized tool." In summary: "The press, the railroad, and the telegraph are premises the thousand-year conclusion of which nobody has yet dared to draw."

Furthermore Nietzsche regards his age as determined by the *masses:* "This today belongs to the mob." "Great mediocrity is the danger of our age." It is no longer capable of assimilating the knowledge it inherits. "The rapid many-sidedness of modern life" extinguishes man: the noise of the present prevents anything from growing. Everybody talks, but nobody listens to anything. "Everything falls into the water, but nothing falls into deep wells any more." "Everything is talked to pieces"; "everything is betrayed."

The attempt to overcome the feeling of emptiness produced by boredom leads to a search for *intoxication:* "So it comes about that this age is most inventive in producing intoxicants. We know intoxication in the form of music, of blind worship at the feet of individual persons and events; we know the intoxication of the tragic, that is, the horror at the sight of destruction; we know . . . senseless work." Even "the mysticism of belief in nothing with its attendant self-sacrifice" is only another form of intoxication.

An additional, and basic, characteristic is the fact that the world, deprived of its substance, seeks its fulfillment in empty dramatics. What is merely theatrical carries people away as though it were genuine, and everyone tends more and more to play a role instead of living. One basic thought, intended to answer the question: What is going on today "when everything is shaking and the whole earth is trembling"? gives depth and unity to these alarming descriptions of the age: *Unbelief has become a reality*. The fundamental fact of the age is becoming evident:

"God Is Dead." This insight, which dominates all the later writings of Nietzsche, is proclaimed early—even before 1872: "Either we die of this religion, or the religion dies of us. I believe in the primitive Germanic saying: All gods must die." At the same time he said of his age: "The withering will (the dying God) is fragmentized into individualities. Its striving is always toward the lost unity, its telos is always further decay." Toward the end of the seventies he writes: "The loss of faith is notorious, . . . and now follows the cessation of fear, of authority, and of trust." Nothing remains but "living according to the moment, for the coarsest of aims. . . ." The idea of God's death recurs in one new version after another. Nietzsche gives expression to it when, in a parody, he represents men as prisoners and Jesus as the son of a jailer who has just died. The son says: "I shall free everyone who believes in me, as surely as my father is still alive." Another time Nietzsche's passion speaks out directly in his description of the "madman" who seeks God with a lantern on a bright morning in the market place. Among the laughers he cries out: "Whither went God? . . . I will tell you. We killed him, you and I. . . . But how did we do it? How were we able to drink up the ocean? . . . Whither are we moving? . . . Are we not straying as though through an infinite nothing? . . . How are we to console ourselves, murderers of all murderers? A greater deed was never performed, and whoever comes after us belongs, because of this deed, to a higher history than all history hitherto." When all are silent and look puzzled, he throws his lantern on the ground and says: "I have come too soon; . . . it is not yet my time. This monstrous event is still on the way; . . . it has not yet reached the ears of men. . . . This deed is still farther from them than the farthest stars—and yet they have committed it."

Nietzsche does not say, "There is no God," or "I do not believe in God," but "God is dead." He believes that he is ascertaining a fact of present-day reality when he peers clairvoyantly into his age and his own nature.

In answer to the question as to *why* God died, he speaks in parables:

"God died of his pity for men." But "when gods die, they always die many kinds of death." Why is God the victim of murder? "He beheld man's depths and abysses, his hidden shame and ugliness. His pity knew no moderation. . . . Man cannot bear to have such a witness live."

The Origin of European Nihilism. Thus the question: *Why* is God dead? is symbolically answered in a number of ways. In its non-symbolic form it appears as an inquiry into the historical origin of contemporary nihilism. Nietzsche believes that he finds it to be rooted in *Christianity's* very definite (i.e., moral) interpretation of the world. For in the end, "the sense of truthfulness, so highly developed through Christianity, becomes disgusted with the falsity and mendacity of all Christian interpretation of the world." Christianity has created a fictitious world, the mendacity of which is finally recognized through truthful impulses engendered by Christianity itself. As a result nothing is left. Christian existence has depended for all its supports and values upon a fictitious world, and when the fiction is recognized for what it is, it must vanish into such nothingness as no man has ever experienced. The time arrives "when we have to *pay* for having been Christians for two thousand years: We lose the stabilizing force that kept life going, and for a while we are completely at a loss. . . . Now everything is false through and through."

Nietzsche believes that, from a *logical* standpoint, the situation in which such nihilism arose can best be characterized as a result of erroneously believing that such categories as *meaning* and *wholeness* have absolute validity when applied to the world. If I falsely presuppose that this world must have some all-encompassing meaning, then, since no honest man can discover it, the result is bound to be the vacuity of a frightful disillusionment—the torture of the "in-vain." "This meaning could have been . . . the moral world order; the increase of love . . . ; the approach to a universal condition of happiness; or even the advance toward a universal state of nothingness—a goal is still a meaning. The common denominator for all these types of conception is that something is to be attained through the process itself; and now we realize that nothing is obtained, nothing is accomplished by this process"; "disillusionment over the alleged *purpose of becoming"* contains the "cause of nihilism." Nihilism also appears "when one takes wholeness . . . and universal organization for granted" and, with "a profound feeling for coherence and interdependence," believes that "the general welfare demands the devotion of the individual"—only to discover that "anything general in this sense does not exist!" Again the result is nothingness in the form of a loss of all values: "Man actually ceases to believe in his own value when he realizes that there is no infinitely valuable whole working through him."

Once these two insights are gained (that becoming serves no purpose and that it is not controlled by an all-pervasive unity), one last escape for the disillusioned is left: "Condemnation of the entire world of becoming as illusion, and invention of a true world that lies beyond." This, according to Nietzsche, is the great Platonic-Christian fiction, the collapse of which produced the abyss of nihilism. Men "admit the reality of becoming as the *sole* reality, refuse to take any kind of secret path to worlds beyond and to false deities—and are *unable to bear this world, even while refusing to deny it.*" Thus nihilism originates when our consciousness of being is decisively determined by the contrast between a world beyond, created and made worthy and venerable by mere thought, and the actual world that constitutes our own reality. To expose this fiction is to confront the following dilemma: "You must either get rid of your venerations or—get rid of yourself." That is to say, either the invented "true world" is to be dismissed as a fiction, in which case everything of value becomes untenable, or the reality that I in fact am, has to be relinquished, and then I cannot live. Thus no matter what we choose in this situation, nihilism makes its appearance either as a negation of values or as a negation of life: "A nihilist is a man who decides that the world as it is ought not to be, and that the world as it ought to be is nonexistent. Accordingly existence is meaningless. . . ."

In interpreting the Platonic-Christian *Weltanschauung*—which he wishes to expose logically as the absolutization of categorical forms ("the cause of nihilism is belief in the categories of reason")—Nietzsche undertakes to grasp contemporary nihilism historically. But his age does not even know *what* is happening to it, let alone *where* its situation originated. Nietzsche lives with the horror of seeing what no one sees and of knowing what no one else worries about: The event "is so huge . . . that one may scarcely maintain that even intelligence of it has already arrived—to say nothing of a general awareness of its implications and a realization of how much must collapse, once this faith is undermined, because it . . . was built on it."

The Meaning of these Theses. Nietzsche's basic theses having to do with the rise of nihilism, "the death of God," and the movement of man toward an unprecedented revolution are of uncanny urgency. They represent his experience of his age—an experience through which he comes to understand what he himself is. They remove any basis for repose in this world and offer a challenge of irresistible existential earnestness. But they may take on radically different meanings, depending upon the way they are interpreted. He who allows himself to be enchanted esthetically by their dramatic magnificence does not even begin to be touched by them. He who derives from them the determining principle: There is no God, sinks away into a banal godlessness that is not at all what Nietzsche intended. We must critically inquire into the significance of these theses.

They cannot be expected to express a knowledge of the entire course of human events, including the present crisis itself. For historico-philosophical dicta concerning the *whole,* telling us which way the world is going—dicta that have dominated historical thinking concerning mankind from Augustine to Hegel almost as a matter of course—can have no permanent place in the course of Nietzschean thinking:

Nietzsche dismisses the total world-process that these philosophers and their disciples devised in order to explain and vindicate their own age and show the finger of God at work in the forces of history. He rejects it with scorn. In opposition to this he states that "humanity as a whole has *no* goals," and that "man as a species is *not* progressing."

If we are to speak of goals, then "the goal of humanity is not to be seen in its end, but rather in its highest representatives." "Mankind has no goals other than great men and great works." Still the higher forms of man appear only as lucky incidents and are extremely perishable.

The course of history is equivocal: it is neither sheer progression nor regression, but both. Every better future is also a worse future: "It is fatuous to believe that a higher, new stage of mankind would combine all the excellent features of earlier stages." "Perhaps the begetting of gen-iuses is confined to a limited period of human history. Perhaps mankind will come . . . closer to its real goal at the middle of its road than at the end." "No matter to what height humanity may evolve—it may well stand even lower at the end than at the beginning."

The view that the world process and the history of mankind as such constitute a meaning that moves toward its fulfillment would, in a manner of speaking, produce a state of peace within the totality of mankind from a feeling of being secure in its divine origin or its historical ultimate goal. Nietzsche turns against this with his "new fundamental feeling: our unquestionable transitoriness. . . . Why should some little star be exempted from the eternal spectacle (of becoming). . . ?"

But even the total aspect inherent in this basic feeling cannot remain since it would claim absolute validity for a statement about the whole. When the whole origin and goal of history are denied, an annihilating feeling can arise. Nietzsche formulates this as a mere *possibility:* "Feeling ourselves *squandered* as humanity (and not merely as individuals) just as we see individual blossoms squandered by nature, that is a feeling above all feelings." Were someone to succeed in containing in this sense the total consciousness of mankind, he would break down cursing existence: "When we know that it will eventually be all up with mankind, an expression of aimlessness will impose itself on all human endeavor."

Finally, Nietzsche himself is forced to combat this and all other views of the process in its entirety. He knows that, because we are always within the process and not outside of it or above it, we cannot survey it.[2] Hence definitive knowledge of our age, which we would have to accept as universally valid, cannot be intended even when he writes: "God is dead." Such a statement would be without meaning, in spite of the apodictic form which he employs here as elsewhere. To view his thesis as a proclamation of the truth per se would be to oversimplify his meaning, for this would amount to the banality of a "now-we-know" attitude rather than the supreme challenge that he intends. Actually the statement expresses the tension engendered by the realization that it is possible, and also it signifies, like a call in the last hour, an awareness of the uncertain direction that things are taking. Perhaps the actual content of this statement can be realized only by those who dogmatically believe in it (Nietzsche would then become the seducer who instills nihilism through suggestion, but he would agree that it befits this type of human being to succumb to this seduction). It may also be said that this statement initiates a new and higher human reality conceived as a way of thinking that impels man upward, or it may serve to arouse us to do all the more resolutely anything that will refute it and thus gain the assurance that God is *not* dead.

There can be no doubt, however, about the way in which these thoughts live in Nietzsche: they do not constitute knowledge, but persist as an immense tension that has its source in himself. At an early age he remarks: "He who attacks his own time, can only attack himself: what can he see, after all, but himself?" And late in his life he can still say in amazement: "Only recently have I admitted to myself that until now I have been a complete nihilist: the energy, the radical manner with which I proceeded as a nihilist, deceived me about this basic fact." At no time, however, was Nietzsche a nihilist and nothing more; the very pathos in nihilism itself is not nihilistic ("Pathos is the inconsistency of the ni-

---

[2] Cf. Book II, Chapter V.

hilist"). Furthermore, his insight that "God is dead" imposes an inexorable task upon him.

At the very least this task involves a struggle against that which no longer *is* but still *seems* to be—and even exerts world-dominance: the task of active negation. For, though God be dead, his shadow still lives: "Men's nature being what it is, there probably will be caves for thousands of years to come in which His shadow will be shown. And we—we still have to vanquish even His shadow!" But this is, in Nietzsche's view, no easy task that can be accomplished as a matter of course; he compares it with the last sacrifice on the ladder of religious cruelty: once upon a time man sacrificed men to his God; then he sacrificed his strongest instincts to his God; but now "the sacrifice of God to Nothing—this paradoxical mystery of ultimate cruelty—remains for the generation growing up at this moment." Therein lies the radical will to true being, as though he meant to say: the deity must in the end take care of itself, it must proclaim itself; if it does not, then we must also vanquish its shadow.

However, in refusing to consider nothingness as final, Nietzsche proceeds positively to overcome nihilism. He considers his entire later philosophy, including his "great politics," his "world interpretation," and his doctrine of "eternal recurrence," as a counter-movement against it.

Moreover, for anyone who is not deceived by the foreground, Nietzsche's thinking contains an affirmation in every negation. All his questioning conveys an urge toward source, origin, and authenticity. He may not succeed in expressing his affirmation positively; but an affirmative mood at least is always present in his thinking, even when it takes the form of the most radical and devastating analysis of his own age.

4

GREAT POLITICS

Nietzsche's longing for *authentic man* leads him to despair of any specific form in which man is actualized. In the light of the *truth* as he has come to see it, everything is undergoing dissolution. Looking upon *his age,* he sees a universal-historical decline. As though overwhelmed by destiny, he is driven on by a negation that stops at nothing. It is not that he seeks negation as such; rather, he constantly searches for something positive in the situation confronting him. But the positive that he seeks is not a concrete picture of the real man who should soon develop, a direction for improving the age, or an assertion of a newly arisen truth; it must be quite different from any such reformatory measures. He is now too candid to shrink from anything, and consequently he severs all ties previously taken for granted, whether religious, moral, philosophical, scientific, or political; but he does this in order to arrive at the ultimate source of human possibilities in general. And it is with a view to encountering this source that he develops his "great politics," his metaphysic of the "will to power," and his mysticism of "eternal recurrence." All previous thinkers retained a frame within which to attempt their innovations; there had always been a world whose totality remained much the same even though its particular contents, provinces, and tasks underwent noticeable changes. Now it is as though one must again begin at the beginning. Consequently, Nietzsche's will to positiveness is characterized by intangibility: while its expression is easily misunderstood as a particular positiveness, it strives for total inclusion of what has never yet existed.

Nietzsche's "great politics (*grosse Politik*)" does not spring from one concern among others, but from the single concern with the rank and future of mankind that permeates his whole being. The conviction that man must develop until he attains his highest potentialities determines his political thinking. Three paths open up to him:

1. Nietzsche takes stock of the *political actualities* (the state, war and peace, the present situation of European democracy). He does not expect to attain a final level of conclusive knowledge but intends to derive evaluations from his all-inclusive demand for humanity. His values, which are as decisive in origin as they are conceptually indeterminate in scope, become the criterion measured by which the actualities that his knowledge has clarified stand or fall.

2. The great politics is a continuous creation of the *future* in thought, not for the purpose of learning what actually will happen—since no human being can know that—but in order to keep possible eventualities effectively in sight. The future in question, upon which everything depends, is not to be viewed as already determined but as something that we must bring forth. This politically effective future is still completely *undecided*. With this in mind, Nietzsche says: "I love the uncertainty of the future." But visions of future possibilities determine our present will, the more decisively, in fact, the more extensively the totality of possibilities operates: "I want to teach you to soar after me into distant futures." Through the medium of possibilities, the future, as that which we will, affects our present. For "the future is as much a condition of the present as the past. That which should and must become, is the foundation of that which is."

Since the one line of happenings that will actually take place must be obscured by the wide variety of possible occurrences, Nietzsche can no more attain a unified vision of the future than he can draw up a definite plan to be followed. Hence the reader who expects to be guided by a truth expressed in unequivocal terms is bound to be disappointed by Nietzsche's thoughts of the future, plastic as they may be in their details—especially when he sees everything that Nietzsche says dissolve in contradictions and multiplicities. Going beyond the clarity of concisely conceived future possibilities, Nietzsche, not knowing how it will be, wants "to compose the myth of the future."

By a mental projection of the future, "great politics" is led to a *decisive awareness of the present moment* of mankind. When the present is thus understood from a viewpoint that has the most extensive perspective possible, real perspicacity concerning the present age is born. It is this perspicacity that causes him great concern and gives rise to his radically new demand. For him, the present *moment* is precious above all else. All signs proclaim that "our European culture is in motion . . . as if moving toward a catastrophe: like a river that heedlessly rushes toward its end."

3. Such an extreme situation calls for the most extreme measures if the danger is to be staved off. Something new to cope with the decay of

millenniums must be forced into existence from the very depth of man's being. But still nothing is done: "What are we really waiting for? Is it not for a great noise of heralds and trumpets? There is a kind of calm that has a choking effect: we have been listening much too long." Everything is prepared for a complete transformation, "only the great, persuasive men are lacking." Nietzsche envisages these persuasive men in a dreadful wasteland of grandiose conception. Through them the task of great politics must be fulfilled. What is their duty in this moment? They will be the radical *transvaluators of all values* and therewith the *"lawgivers."*

But even though great politics begins with a transvaluation that looks toward the totality of humanity's future, Nietzsche does not wish to begin anew, as if in a void, by *breaking* with the entire past. He does not want to lose *history,* though he must now really subdue it in his attempt to free himself from historical tradition. He believes the new beginning to be possible only through the broadest possible conception of the past as well as the future. That is what he has in mind when he says: "The right to my own values—whence did I take it? From the rights of all the old values and the limits of these values."

Nietzsche's politics (unlike "little politics," concerned as it is with the particular situation of a state, or "immediate politics," involving actual and directly effective political action) has a source that is prior to any definite activity. Nietzsche calls it *"creation."* [1] The conceptuality of Nietzsche's political thinking must be such that it springs from an awareness of the source of its creation within a movement directed against all that merely exists or happens to be and toward a future that is still indefinite. The creative lawgiver will found it.

We shall follow these three intertwined Nietzschean paths—his *clarifying scrutiny* of political reality, his *visions* of future possibilities, and the *task* he sets for the great politics—after indirectly indicating, through a contrasting characterization, the particular nature of his political thinking:

It was *after his estrangements* that Nietzsche became truly concerned about the decisive problem of what he calls his "great politics." In his youth, without thinking about politics, he lived in the active hope of a renewal of German culture through Wagner's art. Afterwards he dreamed of a worldly cloister, of an order of knowledge no longer intent on changing the world but on comprehending being. This dream actually grew out of a withdrawal from politics: "What shall henceforth be the occupation of the nobility, when every day it becomes more apparent that occupation with politics is disreputable?" It is in his loneliness and

[1] Cf. pp. 151–53.

separation fom the world that Nietzsche, pondering the totality of human existence by scanning the present age to its farthest horizon and visualizing its most distant future, begins his search for the goal: the "great politics" is to decide the course of this age and therewith to answer the questions of man's future. He finds the task of this politics to be "of such magnitude that any previous conception of it has been completely lacking"; for "when truth joins battle with the lie of millenniums, we shall witness upheavals that surpass anything heretofore dreamed of. The concept politics has then become entirely absorbed in an ideological war. . . . *Great politics* did not exist on earth before me."

Nietzsche calls himself the "last anti-political German" to contrast his own political position with that of the world around him which, after the success of 1870–71, submitted in bourgeois self-satisfaction to the politics of the day, placed a false value on momentary events, and persistently recognized the significance of factual power alone. Mockingly he maintains that scholars who turn politicians are generally assigned the comic role of providing politics with a good conscience, and he asserts that "any philosophy which holds that the problem of existence is altered or even solved through a political event, is a facetious or a sham philosophy."

Apart from Nietzsche, *all political thinkers* regard politics as precisely delimited. They usually take it to be bounded by God or transcendence or refer it to a specific human actuality. Political thinking can for instance proceed (as in the case of Hegel) within the scheme of existing and developing totalities; then it is a systematic whole expressing the self-awareness of a factual reality; in more specific terms, it provides justification and condemnation and a sense of fulfillment through a substantial awareness of the existence of the encompassing. Or again, it can develop (as in the case of Machiavelli) with a view to particular realities and their significance for the autonomy of power; accordingly, types of situations and rules of behavior are developed either as a political technique or as a direct appeal to those whose actions are not capable of being fully rationalized but spring from will to power, presence of mind, and courage. Nietzsche follows neither course: he provides no constructive whole like Hegel's and no practical political technique like Machiavelli's. Instead, his thinking derives from an all-encompassing concern for the being of man, even though he neither retains nor discovers a substance capable of encompassing everything. He envisages the decisive origin of political events without becoming methodically absorbed in specific concrete realities of political activity as they are revealed daily in the struggle of powers and personalities. He hopes to generate a movement that will quicken the ultimate grounds of humanity's being, and he wishes through his thinking to impel those who hear and understand him to enter into this movement. Still he does not limit or define the content of this movement politically, ethnologically, or sociologically. Rather, as he sees it, that which underlies and determines all judgments is provided by an attitude directed upon the whole of *being*. It is no longer mere politics but philosophy, on the basis of which, within the wealth of possibilities but without rational principle, opposing and contradictory ways can be tried solely under the guidance of the idea of saving and advancing humanity's being.

In comparison with the great traditional constructions of political science and philosophy of history, Nietzsche's political thinking is bound to show an absence of logical unity and of consistent, precise conceptual procedures. The substance of his thinking shuns any attempt at unequivocal expression, but still it generates a wholly uniform atmosphere. Such thinking can sweep through one's soul like a storm; but it cannot be formalized and conceptualized in a clear and conclusive manner. Insofar as Nietzsche intends to produce this atmosphere, he avoids anything that could resemble a doctrine. The most various possibilities are tried with equal vehemence without any attempt to unite them in relation to a clearly stated goal. His conceptuality is not meant to express a truth that is assuming a fixed and final shape; rather it appears to present itself as a means of unlimited flexibility in the hands of a governing will to think that is not bound by anything. In this way its formulation attains a maximum of suggestive power. Only by taking this *power of expression* together with the *capacity for change* can we lay hold of the import of such thinking.

One cannot make a rational system of Nietzsche's politics without falsifying his thought. His voluntaristic thinking, whose direction is determined vitally rather than conceptually, exhibits what is most characteristic only when one seeks out the *antitheses* which it contains.

Nietzsche's View of Political Reality

Nietzsche's thoughts turn upon the fundamental and constant necessities in human relations: first of all, the state and war and peace. Thereafter he considers the contemporary political situation: democracy in Europe. Characteristic of his thinking is the grand view as such; it is this, rather than the concrete delineation of specific subject-matter, from which the direction of his great politics is to emerge.

The Fundamental Necessities in All Human Relations. The need for a sovereign governing authority (the state) and, in addition, the constant possibility of war and peace, provide the boundaries within which and

through which human life exists. Nietzsche rarely speaks of the significance of the state and of war in terms of the specific historical forms they
have assumed and the changes they have undergone or their decisive
effects within the historical constellations, for he focuses his philosophizing essentially on the universally human boundary situation.

The *state:* So far as its origin and its abiding reality is concerned, the
state in Nietzsche's opinion is a destructive, assimilating power that
enslaves the mass of humanity. Without it, on the other hand, there can
be no human society and no creative individuals. "Only by the *iron clamp*
of the state can the larger masses be so pressed together that . . .
stratification of society, with its pyramidal structure, must result." Thus
the state rests on a human necessity. Since this latter exercises an inner
compulsion, the state is accepted as something highly beneficial despite
the force with which it intrudes into life. Not only does all history show
"how little the subjects care about the atrocious origin of the state," but it
also reveals the enthusiastic surrender to it "when the hearts of men,
involuntarily drawn by the magic of the growing state, are filled with the
sense of a profound secret purpose . . . , when even the state is considered with ardor as the goal and summit of the sacrifices and duties of
the individual."

Nietzsche tries to clarify the significance and value of the state by
investigating the effect of this condition of existence on the human
situation. To him the state is the power that gives a characteristic stamp
to the individual, the people, and the culture.

Culture exists through the state alone. Of course, the fact that culture
is impossible without the "contented mass of slaves" and without the
conditions that produce the state is "the vulture that gnaws at the livers
of the Promethean promoters of culture"; but to wish to oppose these
conditions would be to wish to oppose culture itself. Permanence in
human affairs can be achieved only through the state. No culture can
grow when man continually has to start anew. Consequently "the great
aim of statesmanship should be permanence. This outweighs everything
else, being more valuable even than liberty." The situation before him in
which nothing is planned from a long-range view is taken by Nietzsche to
be a symptom of weary government: the fact that "the individual does not
receive any stronger impulses to participate in the building of institutions
planned to last for centuries" constitutes the ruinous difference between
"our agitated ephemeral existence and the sustained serenity of metaphysical ages."

In showing us what the state has to be, Nietzsche also shows us the
danger it represents. When it abandons its creative ground, it becomes

the force that destroys the true being of man through a process of leveling. When this form of the state is glorified, he calls it the "new idol" and sees in it the actual enemy of all that the genuine state should make possible or bring forth: the *people, culture,* and man as the *creating individual:*

In the first place, the perverted state brings about the "death of *peoples.*" The "most unfeeling of all monsters falsely asserts . . . . 'I, the state, am the people.' " If the life of the state is not identified with the people, then the concept of the mass prevails: "Far too many are born; the state has been invented for the superfluous ones!"

Second, the state which falls short of its purpose becomes the enemy of *culture.* Nietzsche contradicts his own glorification of the state which grew out of his contemplation of the state-born culture of Greece when he views the modern state as the non-creative tool of the overpowering force of the mass of "the superfluous ones": "The idea of a culture-state is entirely modern. . . . All great ages have been ages of political decline: whatever is great in the sense of culture was non-political, even anti-political. . . . Goethe opened his heart to the personality of Napoleon; he closed it when the Wars of Liberation came." "Culture owes its highest attainments to politically weakened times."

Third, the state is destructive of the *individual.* It "is a clever arrangement for the protection of individuals against one another, but if its refinement is exaggerated, the individual will in the end be weakened and even dissolved by it; meanwhile the basic purpose of the state is most thoroughly thwarted." "Wherever the state ceases, the man who is not superfluous really begins: there begins the song of the necessary one, the unique and irreplaceable melody." Therefore let us have "as little of 'state' as possible!"

Finally Nietzsche accomplishes the most extreme relativization of the state when he says: "The action of the man who sacrifices the state to avoid betraying his own ideal can be a superlative achievement through which alone the state's entire existence attains its meaning for posterity."

Dubious as any specific state may in fact be, Nietzsche never challenges the supremacy of the state as the boundary of human existence: It has influenced nobler types of men as an expression "of a higher sentiment." Why? Because "the impulse of heroism rather than the standpoint of prudence was dominant in the creation of the state: the belief that there is something superior to individual sovereignty." Involved here is "respect for race and elders . . . respect for the dead . . . homage to something spiritually superior and victorious: the delight of meeting one's ideal face to face."

Nietzsche approves the state when he looks upon the movements of peoples and when he sees culture and individual creativity as possible only in and through it. But he rejects the state as the ruin of man when it functions as a solidifying force in favor of mass and mediocrity and when it is no longer concerned about the unique and unmatched but only about the replaceable "superfluous ones."

Corresponding to this dual aspect of the state, Nietzsche recognizes a twofold conception of *law*. To be sure, law always expresses "the will to perpetuate a prevailing power relationship." But either this relationship represents the dominance of average desires which seek merely to secure their existence through law, in which case the law proliferates into an endless accumulation of statutes; or the power relationship supporting the law is intended to assure the dominance of true nobility. In the latter case, law is viewed as the means for securing a hierarchy of creative men. While in the first case the lawgiver is simply the impersonal legislature, in the second the lawgiver is a person and thus superior to the law. The justification of punishment is also essentially different: in the first case it is a utilitarian act (retribution, deterrence, correction) helpful to society or the criminal; in the second case, punishment would be motivated by the "will of formative power," and the image of the true man would become the standard for law: "It must be the condition of society that it represent the highest type of 'man,' and *from this* condition society derives its legal right to combat as hostile per se everything that is hostile to it."

No matter how Nietzsche looks upon the state, he never glorifies the "state as such" but, leaving all illusions aside, surveys the actual forms in which it appears and then finds its significance in its function of elevating or leveling man. The requirement that it serve the ultimate purpose of man and his creative possibilities becomes the criterion for evaluating actual states.

War and peace: Nietzsche views war in its undeniable reality as the boundary—the annihilation and, at the same time, the condition—of human existence. War is a concern of the state as the final authority deciding the course of things; the state emerges through war and, in turn, brings it about. Without war the state would cease. War and the possibility of war revive the waning sentiment for the state. Even the youthful Nietzsche expresses the idea that "war is as much a necessity for the state as the slave is for society," and late in life Nietzsche repeats: "Life is a result of war, society itself a means to war."

But Nietzsche is not an enemy of peace or a glorifier of war. His honesty does not permit him to assume an absolutely final position, as though any recognized boundary of our existence were subject to our verdict and our legislation.

Hence, Nietzsche dwells on the *idea of peace*. But the peace which he advocates differs in character from that of the pacifists who try to compel peace by force, i.e., through tremendous armies, or who would like to bring it about through gradual disarmament. He opposes his utopia to all others: "And perhaps a great day will come when a people, distinguished . . . through war and victories . . . voluntarily proclaims: 'We break the sword' . . . Disarming oneself, from an *intensity* of feeling, while one is the best armed—that is the means to *real* peace. . . . Our liberal representatives of the people lack, as is well known, the time to think about man's nature, or they would know that they are laboring in vain when they work for a 'gradual lessening of the military burden.' "

This heroic idea of peace differs radically from the pacifistic ideal, for it expresses the quintessence of man's attitude. On the other hand, it has nothing in common with Kant's idea of eternal peace with its elaboration, from rational principles, of definite conditions of possible peace. But both Kant and Nietzsche, rather than construing the immediate possibilities of practical politics, expound their demand for the idea itself. Nietzsche never ceases to champion the idea of peace as at least a possibility. He maintains prophetically that, if it is taken seriously, the idea cannot in *any* form realize itself through force or even survive anywhere in the struggle by employing force. Hence he predicts a "party of peace" that, without sentimentality, would forbid its members and their children to carry on war and would also prohibit any course that could possibly lead to the use of force. It would therefore also "forbid the use of the law courts." This party would simply refuse to fight. Being sincere and having renounced force from the nobility of its nature rather than from impotence, it can be devoid of any resentment and therefore "hostile to any feeling of revenge and vindictiveness." Differing in essence from the usual type of humanity, it is bound to "evoke combat, contradiction, and persecution against itself: a party of the oppressed, at least for some time; but soon the great party."

That Nietzsche immediately sets this "peace party" over against a future "war party" which proceeds in the opposite direction with quite as relentless a consistency—"it honors peace as the means to new wars"— shows again that he neither veils the boundary situation of human existence nor untruthfully ignores present actualities.

He believes that the unavoidability of war is, in the first place, psychologically rooted in man's urge to extremes: "For the present, wars provide the greatest agitation of the imagination after all Christian raptures and horrors have grown stale." Perilous explorations, ocean voyages, and conquests of mountains are unavowed surrogates for war. It seems to him essential that wars should arise from such obscure compulsion if man is to retain his potentialities: "It is pure fancy to expect much of man, once he has forgotten how to conduct war." One can see "that a highly cultured and therefore necessarily weary humanity like that of the present Europeans needs not only wars but the greatest and most terrible of wars—i.e., temporary lapses into barbarism—in order not to lose its culture and its very existence by means of culture."

His basically philosophical *attitude* toward a *life of danger* gives rise to the well-known statements in *Zarathustra:* "And if you cannot be saints of knowledge, then be at least its warriors. . . . You say that it is the just cause that sanctifies even war? I say to you: It is the just war that sanctifies any cause. . . . Therefore live your life of obedience and war. Of what importance is a long life? What warrior wants to be spared!" But he who—like the "saint of knowledge"—does not carry on war must nevertheless "learn from wars: bringing death into the range of interests for which we fight—that makes us venerable."

However, the glorification of war as such cannot be Nietzsche's intention. Like nature, war proceeds "without concern for the worth of the individual." In its disfavor we can say: "It makes the victor stupid and the vanquished malicious; in favor of war: in either of these ways, it makes men more natural by turning them into barbarians; for culture, wartime is wintertime—the time for sleep—and man comes out of it more vigorous for good or evil."

This thinking really amounts to standing at the boundaries without being deceived about the condition and the source of all human existence. Nietzsche follows up the last demands and attitudes without relinquishing the ground from which the opposite possibilities develop. The meaning is lost when particular thoughts are isolated, but it reappears in the exploration of all possibilities. Only the whole reveals the face of existence in such a way as to compel greatness of vision, depth of inspiration, and a surge upward in what Nietzsche calls "great politics."

The Present Political Situation (Democracy). Historically speaking, the state and war and peace are capable of assuming countless diverse forms. The fact that all human relations are constantly undergoing change means that any period is a time of transition. Nietzsche recognizes his own period as a world-historically decisive time lying between millenniums; he regards it as the termination of previous history and the possible beginning of a new era. In contemplating his age and taking an inventory of it, as it were, he finds *democracy* to be the all-embracing and all-determining condition. It alone can provide the soil from which the shapes of the future must grow; it is the political reality in the wake of the French Revolution, the full scope of which was first recognized by de Tocqueville: "The democratization of Europe cannot be stopped." He who resists it can do so only with the means which the democratic idea has provided, and thus he will himself promote the process of democratization. Political actions that oppose it will only contribute to the advancement of democracy. Democracy is the fate that threatens every existing thing from its roots up.

Still, the nature of democracy remains largely undetermined. To begin with, what Nietzsche has in mind is not some particular form of political constitution or specific political theory or doctrine. It is not the theory of the popular will which is supposed to make itself felt through democracy, for this will of the people is itself intangible and indefinable except in terms of the form in which it gains control and is itself controlled and shaped in turn. Responding to those who tend to see, for instance, its commensurate expression in universal suffrage through which the majority decides with finality over the weal and woe of all, Nietzsche says: The majority cannot be the *basis* for this right since by it the rule of the majority is first constituted; rather, the unanimity of all those who proclaim their will to subject themselves to the majority would have to be the basis. "For this reason the opposition of even a very small minority suffices to set this right aside again as unworkable; and non-participation in a vote is just the kind of opposition that causes the whole voting system to break down." These and similar reflections are frequently encountered in Nietzsche's writings, but to him they only touch the surface. The actual democratic process as he understands it is a profound occurrence: In the first place, state and government were, for a millennium and a half, subject to the standards of the *Christian religion*. These continue to determine the nature and the goals of the democratic movement even though their religious nature is now expressly denied. Second, with the waning of the Christian faith, state and government must continue *without religion:*

1. The *Christian origin* of European democracy explains the basic impulse which, in Nietzsche's opinion, can be detected in all the forms through which it manifests itself: while the Greek was the man who achieved most, the abuse of power by Rome led, in Christianity, to the successful rebellion of the impotent, with the result that the history of Europe signifies, in Nietzsche's eyes, an ever renewed victory of the

weak, the continuous "mob and slave rebellion," which in democracy and socialism presses on toward final victory.

2. As the *Christian faith* begins to wither, the democratic movement is set in motion with the masses now insisting on governing and on being governed without religion. This process, which appears to Nietzsche in many varied forms, is sketched as follows:

Since religion appeases the heart in times of need and distrust while absolving the government of blame, and since it protects the uniformity of popular sentiment, it makes government possible and contributes to its permanence. When religion begins to die away, the very foundation of the state is also shaken, and the democratic impulses—representing as they do a secularized Christianity—become dominant. A government that is dominated by these impulses ceases to be a sacred mystery and becomes a mere instrument of the popular will: it no longer enjoys any religious sanction. After repeated changes in attitude and futile experiments, distrust of *all* governments wins out in the end: "The consequence of the democratic concept of the state is the *death of the state* and the setting free of the private person (I take care not to say: the individual)."

By observing and attacking the entire democratic situation from all sides, Nietzsche illumines the condition of the present-day unbelievers who are hampered by Christian ideals that are no longer understood. *Parties,* being essential to democracy, come in for discussion, as do the two main social classes to which the situation gives rise:

As the democratic world grows more irreligious, the significance of castes decreases. Two externally determined groups come increasingly to the fore among the masses of humanity: the possessors and the non-possessors, or the *bourgeoisie* and the *socialists.* Nietzsche's attention is mainly focused on what they have in common. Separated from religion and without a new basis for creative *Existenz,* both lead, in his view, an illusory existence that has no future, however powerful they may be at the moment.

He asserts that the *bourgeoisie* are lacking in real justification: "Only he who has spirit should have possessions; without it, possession is a public danger." Because their *Existenz* is insubstantial, the possessors come to regard the desire to own ever more as the meaning of life; it is their pastime in the struggle with boredom. They masquerade with culture and art and thus arouse the "envy of the poorer and uneducated . . . since gilded crudeness in an alleged 'enjoyment of culture' makes it appear to be only a matter of money." The sole remedy against socialism would be "living a life of moderation and frugality . . . and supporting the state when it imposes taxes on anything superfluous. You do not want these remedies? Then, you rich bourgeois who call yourselves 'liberal,' admit to yourselves that the sentiment of your own heart is that which you find so terrible and threatening in the socialists but which you consider as inevitable within yourselves. . . . If you did not have your wealth . . . this sentiment of yours would turn you into socialists."

His objection to the *socialists* is that they have the same attitude but under different conditions; they too think only of the existence rather than the rank of man. Their intention is to "procure idleness for ordinary natures."

Nietzsche tries to reduce the attitude of *this* "socialism" to a principle and finds it in the fact that socialism *insists on ignoring* "the actual inequality of men." Because, as a consequence, the mass of average men will indeed make the decisions, socialism, conceived in its final form, is the *tyranny of the most inferior* and the most stupid. This tyranny is expressed as "the morals of the herd animal": "Equal rights for all," "equal claims of all," "one herd and no shepherd," "sheep like sheep." With respect to its origin, Nietzsche calls the socialists' ideal "a doltish misunderstanding of the Christian ideal of morality."

Insofar as "socialism" tries to present itself as the answer to the labor question, Nietzsche rejects the question because he regards it as falsely formulated and bluntly declares: "I cannot at all perceive what they intend to do with the European laborer after they have turned him into a question." He can pose the question only in this way: How does man attain harmony and satisfaction with his particular necessary task? How can the order of inequality be justified when the religious sanction is abolished?

What Nietzsche considers the decisive and basic feature of the democratic age emerges when he asks what will become of *man* in it. He sees the masses, the pressure they exert, the "many-too-many," the uniform leveling. Despising the masses, he demands: "Create for yourselves the concept of a people; you can never imagine it noble and high enough." We can easily make allowance for the fact that he often says "people (*Volk*)" when he means "masses (*Masse*)."

The *masses* destroy those who, within a *people,* would achieve their individuality and yet, through their very presence, share in the task of making the people meaningful. In the masses there can be no meaningful fulfillment of the people through individuals. They are "uniformed. . . . Thus the sand of humanity is bound to be generated: all very equal, very small, very rotund, very amenable, very boring." The democratic age rejects any higher type of man. Its citizens no longer see man's rank; it is the age of the little folks who no longer believe in the saints and the great virtuous men; of the bourgeois who no longer believe in the higher nature of the ruling caste; of the scientific craftsmen who no longer believe in the philosopher. In his opinion, the masses seem to deserve attention "only from a triple viewpoint . . . as blurred copies of great men . . . as resistance to the great . . . as tools of the great; as for the rest, let the devil and statistics take them." The masses are everywhere, with the educated and the uneducated; men no longer dare to be themselves, regardless of the camp in which they find themselves; and, above all, they only desire prosperity, comfort, and gratification of the senses. The consequence of this democratic world that Nietzsche is led to expect is that "it will therefore move toward a *spiritual enslavement* the like of which has never before existed."

Visions of the Possible Future

Because of his concern for the human condition, Nietzsche's thoughts are directed so energetically toward the future that his elucidation of general and contemporary politics is easily confused with his all-pervading consideration of what the future will bring forth. He always views the present as containing the germ and the threat of ominous things to come. Hence Nietzsche's visions are not only diverse; they present decisive alternative directions: he sees the decline of man, but he also sees his rise. His great politics requires a voluntaristic kind of thinking within which visions of destruction and visions of new creations are intertwined; its purpose, in fact, is to accomplish a quickening prognosis by means of a contemplative one and thus to prevent or bring about some possible future situation.

Democracy—the irreligious government of the European world since the French Revolution—will, in accordance with Nietzsche's predominant vision, lead to a type of humanity under the *"new masters."* But, in addition, *other possible courses for democracy,* which he rarely or only temporarily investigates, exist in his mind. Furthermore, there are considerations of the future dealing with the *world political developments of the nations* in their relation to one another and visions of possible *changes in man's nature* in general.

The Ways of Democracy. Nietzsche's conception of the future of democracy is most equivocal. Of the various possibilities that he tests from time to time, three are striking, though they point in quite different directions.

One possibility points to a world externally regulated and internally organized, secured through knowledge and prudence, and united in a "league of nations." Even though Nietzsche believes he can detect something dreary and monotonous in the men of his time who "deliberately and conscientiously work for the democratic future," he is nevertheless aware of the extraordinary things that they might bring forth: "It is possible that posterity will think . . . of the democratic work of a number of generations as we do of the building of rock dams and protective walls—as an activity which necessarily spreads much dust on clothes and faces. . . . It seems that the democratization of Europe is a link in the chain of those tremendous prophylactic measures . . . by which we differ from the Middle Ages. Now the age of Cyclopean edifices has arrived! Final security of the foundations so that the entire future can build on them without danger!" He hardly troubles to explain what these foundations are: they include all the spiritual forces and works, the acquisition of knowledge and contrivances which overcome darkness and chaos. On these foundations even a workable peace seems possible to him: "The first practical result of . . . democratization will be a European league of nations in which every single nation, bounded in accordance with practical geographical considerations, represents a political subdivision similar to a canton. The historical remembrances of past nations will scarcely be taken into account any longer since the pious feeling for them . . . will be gradually but radically uprooted." In this new world everything would be decided according to rational principles and shaped with effective intelligence. The diplomats of the future "will have to be students of culture, farmers, and transportation experts and have reasons and considerations of utility instead of armies to back them up." The people attaining absolute power in this democracy have nothing in common with "socialism as a doctrine concerned with the changes affecting property acquisition." But they will regulate the distribution of property; for instance, they will move against the "princes of the stock exchange," and "create a middle class that can safely forget socialism like a sickness that has been overcome." This democracy, of which Nietzsche speaks "as of something to come" (he emphasizes that he does not at all mean the present one) "intends to procure and guarantee independence for as many as possible" by combatting and getting rid of the three great enemies of independence: the have-nots, the rich, and the parties.

A second and, in fact, opposite possibility would be realized if socialism were to gain control of the state. For socialism demands "a political power as total as that ever possessed by any despotism; indeed in striving for the actual annihilation of the individual, it exceeds anything known to the past." According to Nietzsche, this way is dangerous because it cannot lead to anything permanent. For socialism "can no longer even count on religious piety toward the state . . . and can therefore hope to exist for only brief periods, here and there, and through extreme terrorism. Consequently it prepares in secret to rule through terror."

Nietzsche only briefly alludes to a third possibility. If democracy fails to find the rational orderliness of the league of nations and if, instead, the "death of the state" occurs, then a "prospect that is not unfortunate from every point of view" will be the consequence: chaos will not arise, "but an even more expedient invention than the state will overcome the state." Of course Nietzsche does not wish to engage in the dissemination of this notion when nobody can yet point to the seed-grains that are to be sown in that future. "Let us have confidence . . . that *for the time being* the state will endure for quite a while and that the destructive attempts of overzealous and hasty dilettantes will be beaten off!"

The World-Political Development of Nations. The projects for a possible democratic future concern for the most part inner-political conditions; however, these will be essentially determined, as long as a plurality of states exists, by the external political relations between states. The way they develop from within and in relation to each other will in the end decide the development of man. Nietzsche's vision of the future reveals a portentous situation. He foresees "a succession of several martial centuries that have no equal in history" and believes "that we have entered the classical age of war on the largest scale, the age of scientific war with popular national support"; "there will be wars such as have never yet been on earth."

For the first time in history the significance of these wars will be determined by the fact that the issue will be *world rule*. The "age of national wars" therefore is part of the *"whole entr'acte* character typical of present European conditions"; the great possibilities of the future are revealed only when we look at the whole: "The time for little politics is gone: the very next century will already bring the struggle for world rule—the compulsion toward great politics." Political thinking can derive its real meaning only from consideration of this goal. It is a matter of "entering the battle for the government of the earth with good prospects" and, above and beyond this, in everything spiritual—in thinking and writing—of *"making ready* that still distant state of things in which the good Europeans will take hold of their great task: the conduct and guardianship of the entire culture on the earth."

Nietzsche asks himself what significance the *nations* will have on this path of destiny and scrutinizes, as it were, their existential physiognomy. He judges some of them only in passing: "The *Americans* are too quickly depleted,—perhaps they merely appear to be a world power of the future." "Nobody any longer believes that *England* itself will be strong enough to continue playing its old role even for another fifty years. . . . Today one must be a soldier first if he does not wish to lose his credit as a merchant." "In present-day *France,* it is the will that is most seriously diseased." Only Russia and Germany really seem to concern Nietzsche from the standpoint of great politics:

Nietzsche believes that in the physiognomy of *Russia* he can discern signs of extraordinary strength and a singular future: "Signs of the next century: entrance of Russia into culture. A grandiose goal. Proximity of barbarism. Awakening of the arts, magnanimity of youth, and fantastic madness."

What, politically speaking, will become of *Germany?* On the one hand he says, with goading annoyance: "The Germans themselves have no future"; but he also states that "they are of the day before yesterday and of the day after tomorrow,—they have no today." Nietzsche's criticism of the Germans, outdoing itself, springs from a boundless and often disillusioned love. Precisely when he can no longer see in the Germans anything of value, he interprets this as a sign of the future: "The Germans *are* not yet anything, but they are *becoming* something. . . . We Germans *demand* something of ourselves that has not yet been demanded of us—we demand something *more!"*

In Nietzsche's projections of world politics, *two possibilities* play the main role: either the *political disintegration of Europe* expressing Europe's declining destiny in general, together with new combinations for a world government, or the political *unity of Europe and world government through Europe.*

It is the latter possibility that is dominant in Nietzsche's thoughts: "My concern is—One Europe." But in the end, the external fate of Europe in the world is determined by its inner fate; hence Nietzsche's demand: "To compel Europe to decide whether its will to decline is really a 'will.' Prevention of the growth of mediocrity. Destruction rather than that!" Perhaps Europe is this perishing world; but Nietzsche just as decisively sees Europe as the only great chance for man in general. On the one hand, he sees the future European "as the most intelligent slave animal, very industrious, basically very modest, excessively curious, spoiled, weak-willed,—a cosmopolitan chaos of affects and intelligence"; the danger is that "Europe will grow increasingly dull and the European man become increasingly insignificant." On the other hand, he considers the potential European as the "super-race" in comparison with "races" that have arisen in "consequence of a milieu" and through "a firmly imposed role." He favors the "good European" and hopes for him on the basis of "signs from which it is manifest that Europe strives to become united." Nietzsche believes that he can perceive this actual general direction in the mysterious efforts of the souls of all the more profound and more representative men of his century as they "attempt to anticipate the European of the future." Now, as always, Nietzsche pursues this thought to its ultimate conclusion. Viewed in this connection, therefore, the national spirit that manifests itself in his age can actually be a sign of danger "now that everything points to greater common interests": As a dogma, "nationalism, the way it is understood now, actually demands narrowness." He sees Napoleon's greatness in the fact that he conceived of "Europe as a political unity," and he believes there are indications that "the economic union of Europe will necessarily occur as well." He thinks he can even see "what is basically taking place—the disappearance of nationalism and the creation of the European man."

This, however, is not the only possibility. In view of the danger that Europe may perish at the "hands of the mob," Nietzsche on one occasion imagines the salvaging of a remnant: "Remove in good time what must be saved! And designate countries to which, because of a certain inaccessibility, culture can withdraw—Mexico for instance." Another time he thinks of the possibility of a union between Germany and Russia. He wants "an alliance with Russia . . . because the accumulation of will-power seems greatest and least exhausted among the Slavs: a German-Russian world government is by no means one of the greatest improbabilities." "I see a more pronounced trend toward greatness in the feelings of the Russian nihilists than in those of the English Utilitarians. . . . We need the most urgent cooperation with Russia. . . . No American future!" This idea of cooperation comes to nought again in view of the threat posed by an overpowering Russian future. This threat may indeed have dwarfed everything else for a moment: "Russia must become master of Europe and Asia, it must colonize and gain China and India. Europe will be like Greece under the rule of Rome." This is seen as a possibility in the long run; Russia and the Church have an advantage: "They can wait."

Nietzsche thinks quite differently when his European consciousness regains its strength. Then he sees in Russia—with its tremendous reserve of energy and will—not only the greatest danger but also the possibility for awakening Europe through resistance. Then he even wishes for "such an increase in the Russian threat that Europe would have to resolve to become threatening, so to speak, by developing a will . . . , a prolonged terrible will of its own that could set goals for milleniums to come."

While all these conceptions are characterized by a tendency toward the formation of ever larger units—Europe, world government—Nietzsche may have the exact opposite in mind when he considers the extent to which the formations of political union are achieved only through external force in the battle of powers: "The fragmentation into atomic political bodies is the most distant perspective of European politics still imaginable" in case the petty states are swallowed up by the super-states, the latter by the monster state, and "the monster state finally bursts apart because, in the end, it lacks the girdle to encompass its body: the hostility of neighbors."

But all these visions of the future again and again reach a final point where they break apart. None points to future stability in world affairs. Rather they are Nietzsche's way of pursuing to their final consequences all the dangers through which the instability of his contemporary world becomes manifest. He destroys the false sense of security engendered by the belief that the mere setting of universal goals is an assurance that the world is in order. What becomes manifest is the uncertainty of the direction of everything, not the certainty of a clear guidance. Nietzsche's visions of the future are visions of a bottomless world; he would not commit himself to any of these future possibilities.

Looking beyond all internal-political conditions and external-political combinations, Nietzsche finally focuses on the problem of man's development in general.

Spiritual Transformations of Man's Nature. Through a whole series of incidental visions of the future Nietzsche touches upon the nature of man:

Technology for instance produces possibilities of life unknown to the past, with the result that man is able to develop a new consciousness of his being and of himself: "In the new century man's control of nature will probably give him far more energy than he can consume. . . . Aviation alone will overthrow all our cultural concepts. . . . An age of architecture will arrive when man will again build for eternity, as the Romans did." "In the future there will be, first, countless institutions which one enters voluntarily for treatment of one's soul; second, countless remedies against boredom, for at any time one will be able to hear lecturers and the like; and third, festivals in which many individual inventions are combined to attain the total purpose of the festival."

Such changes, which depend on the development of technology, especially in connection with the ever broadened and increased opportunities for knowledge, present the danger that *culture will perish by its own hand.* "Life becomes increasingly burdensome, and we may well ask whether man's inventive capacity will suffice to deal with the highest degrees of burdensomeness." Knowledge especially can become unbearable: "When science becomes less and less pleasurable and takes more and more of the enjoyment out of the comforts of metaphysics, religion, and art," life threatens to fall into despair; then two opposing forces will be needed: "Heat must be produced through illusions, partialities, and passions, while the malignant and dangerous consequences of overheating must be prevented with the aid of diagnostic science." It can be predicted that, unless this twofold requirement is fulfilled, "the interest in truth will cease . . . illusion, error, and fantasy will reconquer step by step . . . the soil formerly held by them; the next consequence is the ruin of the sciences and the sinking back into barbarism; humanity must begin all over again. . . . But who can guarantee that it will always again find the strength for this?"

Furthermore, when Nietzsche sees everything in a process of extremely hazardous transformation or when he thinks of the social revolution that may well come about, he is by no means convinced that the ideas born of his enthusiastic longing for human nobility will be realized by this revolution. Its success "will be less than expected: what man *can* do always falls far short of what he *wills,* as has been shown by the French Revolution. When the grand *effect* and the *intoxication of the thunderstorm* are gone, it becomes evident that one would have to have more *energies* and more *practice* in order to do more." One can only hazard vague guesses as to how man's innermost nature will be affected by the death of God, the ruin of all traditional values, the disappointments over attempted innovations, and various inconceivable catastrophes. During the next centuries "the religious forces might still be vigorous enough for an *atheistic religion* a la Buddha, and science would not object to a new ideal. But it would not be universal love of mankind! A new man must come forth. I myself am far from that and do not desire it *at all!* But it is a probability."

When Nietzsche peers into the most distant future, he conceives—taking up the evolutionary concept of man's origin—the extreme possibility that man, having evolved from the ape, "will turn again into an ape, while nobody will take any interest in this astonishing ending of the comedy."

Nietzsche's concern over the devastating possibilities and his hope for the noble man are expressed in *Zarathustra* in the grandiose symbolism of the two contrasting figures of the despicable "last man" and the "superman" on whom all hope rests.

The New Masters. Nietzsche's view of the possibility of a new leader-ship differs from his vision of an unstable future world. While in the latter case he perceives the world as sliding away, so to speak, in the former he inquires about the new coherence and transformation of a world drifting without guidance. Nietzsche now sees this world, which owes its condi-tion to democracy, as a way of bringing forth a new authority. He accepts democracy as the fate of the Occident and the starting point of the most hopeful possibilities, even though his evaluations run contrary to the form in which it appears. Of Zarathustra he says that "his hatred of the democratic system of leveling is only on the surface" and that he actually is "glad that things have reached that point. Now he can accomplish his task." This is to say that democracy creates the conditions for an un-precedented form of government which will seize the whole earth. The "democratization of Europe" is justified by the results it makes possible, i.e., the fact that it is "at the same time an involuntary arrangement for the breeding of tyrants." For through the undermining of religious faith, through the subsequent disintegration of all hitherto accepted val-ues, through the unprincipled mode of life of nearly all people of all classes, through the transformation of man into "sand," uncertainty will at last become so great that men will grovel in the dust before *any* com-manding strength of will." The same condition under which a mediocre kind of man, "the hard-working herd animal called man," generally de-velops will also give rise to "exceptional men of the most dangerous and most attractive quality." The strong man will probably have to turn out stronger and richer than he ever was before.

Nietzsche's thoughts concerning future politics are summed up in his question regarding the *nature of these new masters.* It is fundamental to his notion of the masters, who will use democracy while destroying its essence, that their nature is determined by the situation:

In the first place, the course of things *can no longer be left to itself.* But it can be guided by a truly *superior type of man* capable of encompassing, in his thoughts, all human possibilities. "A new kind of philosopher and commander is needed."

In the second place, in a godless age these masters must be able to endure without believing in or consulting God and still make their decisions with the same profound sense of responsibility formerly in-duced by a belief in Him. Especially their relationship to the people is entirely new. Popular rule, being the rule of mass-characteristics and expressed through security measures which are democratic but ultimately leveling and destructive, is to be replaced by a rule that will grow out of the fusion of the substance of those governed with the will of the masters.

This will no longer come about through the active insight of those who obey, but through the weakness of the now godless mass clamoring for strength: the masters of the earth "must now take the place of God and gain for themselves the absolute confidence of the ruled." Nietzsche's hope is for "an audacious ruling race resting on the broad expanse of an extremely intelligent herdlike mass."

Hence the fate of humanity rests with the future masters. Nietzsche is alert to both *their possibilities and their perils*. From a psychological point of view, the *sort of masses* which are to be ruled determines what the masters can be. For they are not dictators who command merely on the basis of some abstract truth or as a result of their own superhuman greatness; they must be men who first win the unconditional confidence of the masses in a godless world by being men of the people. There must be effective and intimate interaction between the masters and the people whom they rule. Of decisive importance is: Which people will resist the possibility of turning into a mass? [2]

On the one hand, the nature of the masses is determined *through the nature of the masters*. Nietzsche observed this relationship in his own time: "We complain about the lack of discipline in the masses; . . . they reveal themselves as undisciplined in the degree to which the educated show their lack of discipline; no matter how we behave, we lead the way for the masses; we elevate or ruin them as we elevate or ruin ourselves."

On the other hand, however, the masters depend on the *nature of the masses:* "A first-rate organizing force like Napoleon, for example, must be *in harmony with* the type that is to be organized!" Hence "whoever, in the past, had to deal with man on a large scale judged him in accordance with his basic qualities. . . . That is what Napoleon did. The Christian virtues meant nothing to him, he treated them as non-existent." "Napoleon himself, however, having been corrupted through the means which he had to employ, lost his nobility of character. Asserting himself among men of a different kind, he could have applied different means; accordingly a Caesar would not *necessarily* have to become bad."

In view of the necessity of governing the human masses so that the higher man can develop, and in view of the frightful perils threatening humanity in general in the democratic world, Nietzsche expresses his longing and his concern: "The picture of the kind of leaders that we have in mind, . . . the need for such leaders, the terrible danger that they might

[2] Cf. pp. 423 ff. for Nietzsche's ideas of the people.

fail to come or might turn out to be bad or degenerate—these are the things causing *our* real worry and gloom."

While Nietzsche is unable to give plastic shape to these real *new masters,* their image is everywhere before him. "The masters of the earth" will constitute a new aristocracy of body and spirit that is self-trained and that constantly absorbs new elements. . . ." He visualizes "their new saintliness, their renunciation of happiness and comfort. They grant the claim to happiness to the humblest person but not to themselves." They will take for their foundation the most severe self-legislation "through which permanence for thousands of years will be given to the will of philosophical men of authority and artist-tyrants: a higher type of men who will make use of democratic Europe in order to gain control of the destinies of the earth and to work as artists on the shape of 'man' himself." They will have the attitude expressed "in Plato's *Theages"*: "Each one of us would like to be lord over all men if possible or, even better, be God."

In order to strengthen the relationship between governors and governed and also increase the rank of some individuals as much as possible, the new masters will deliberately undertake *the transformation of man* —something which in the democratic age had proceeded in the direction of leveling. A method of breeding that looks far ahead must furnish the basis for what alone makes possible the "constancy of conditions": the contentment of men within the whole in such a way that the individual is raised to the highest level possible for him in the necessary state of "slavery." For this it is essential that the different types of men should not be measured according to a single standard supposed to apply to all men. The *attitude* characterizing every type of existence needed by the whole must have the chance for self-assertion, and the rulers must assist it in this respect. Since "being average is happiness for the average person, . . . it is unworthy of a more profound mind to consider mediocrity itself objectionable." "Mastery in one field, specialization as a natural instinct," must be promoted as an attitude expressing an appropriate way of affirming life. On the other hand, anything "undermining the worker's instinct, pleasure, and feeling of contentment with his humble being must be rejected."

The basic problem in the transformation of man is the *relationship between worker and employer* and the modification of both. According to Nietzsche, the democratic world has failed completely in this regard: it is not a question of exploiting every opportunity for profit but of focusing one's vision on the "welfare of the worker, his physical and spiritual *contentment."* It was a mistake to utilize only the labor and not to think of the laborer as a complete human being. The wonted practice of "exploiting the laborer was stupid; it was a despoiling process at the expense of the future, a threat to society." Nietzsche foresees a new kind of labor-relationship, the model for which is the military relation: "Soldiers and leaders have a still loftier relationship to one another than workers and employers. . . . It is strange that submission to powerful persons, to tyrants and army leaders, is felt to be far less painful than the submission to unknown and distinterested persons such as all the tycoons of industry represent. . . . So far manufacturers have been devoid of all the characteristics of a higher caste. . . . Perhaps, if they had the dignity of a hereditary aristocracy, there would be no socialism of the masses. For the masses basically are ready to accept slavery of any sort, provided the higher individual constantly gives evidence of being higher, of being born to command through dignity of behavior!" Nietzsche regards the contemporary state of slavery as barbaric since there are no true masters for whom the work is done; the "future of the worker" under genuine masters will be no less "slavery," but still different in essence: then "workers must learn to feel like soldiers. An honorarium, a salary, but no wage! No relationship between payment and achievement! But the placing of the individual, *according to his type,* so that he can reach the *highest level of achievement* that his capacity permits." Then prosperity and daily enjoyment of life are to be the concern of those who serve; a reversal of the roles played now by bourgeois and laborer will be necessary: "Let the workers, for a change, live as the bourgeoisie now do; but above them, distinguished through frugality, the higher caste: thus poorer and simpler, but in possession of the power." Only the true human rank, the master-nature of those in command, takes the sting out of the necessary condition of slavery, makes those who serve content by giving them what they deserve, and provides them with the opportunity to revere those who command them for what they are.

The Task of Great Politics

By philosophizing negatively, Nietzsche breaks with everything that men, by universal acknowledgement, have shared, whether it be God, morality, or reason. He denies that the people who form a society or a state all have something in common. For him men are simply unequal. "There are no human rights." He denies any right per se. Whenever he comes across something claiming absolute validity, he sees it simply as an example of the complete lie that a generally valid "truth" represents for him. Human beings are incapable of meeting on the basis of a valid truth but live by imposing upon themselves "a law of consent" in matters required by existence. Since there is in truth no higher court than men themselves to which questions about the rank and worth of men and about what is to count as true can be referred, such decisions are made by the sort of men who are actually in power. Nietzsche's final instruction with regard to the world is: *Fight for this power*. In a narrowly political sense this would signify a struggle for state power. From the standpoint of great politics it means fighting with the aid of the creative thoughts which invisibly shape and transform men. Truth attains actuality only in the struggle for power; here lies both its source and its limit.

The new masters for whom Nietzsche longs will represent and bring forth the noble man in a world that has become godless; Nietzsche's great politics takes upon itself the task of providing the philosophical inter-pretation these masters need and of making them aware of themselves: "I am writing for a species of men who do not yet exist: the masters of the earth."

The Lawgivers. At the turning point of history, the *"transvaluation of all values"* is the condition of constructive action. The moment has arrived when "the great problem of value is posed for the first time, . . . when spiritual passion of a degree and freedom never before imagined takes hold of the *ultimate* problem of mankind and conjures up the decision about its destiny. . . ." (to Overbeck, Oct. 18, '88). But this transvaluation cannot be accomplished in the form of a momentary and occasional appraisal or from feelings of inclination and aversion, but only from the deepest source. Therefore "before all things can be laid on the scale," the revision of all value-judgments is in need of "the scale itself—I mean that highest kind of fairness of highest intelligence whose mortal enemy is fanaticism." Mere appraisals amounting to little more than substitutions would be worthless superficialities. Creative evaluation must give expression to the very source that is the necessary basis for the development of being. The transvaluation must not serve a singular and conclusive evaluation entertained for its own sake; the reappraiser must have the capacity to serve as a scale in such a manner that he sees the possibilities as a whole and contains within himself the whole breadth of future being. It may seem as though Nietzsche thus intensified his de-mand upon the source of humanity beyond anything humanly possible to the point that, in meeting this demand, any unconditional participation of man in his historical actuality would degenerate into fanaticism; but it is precisely this creative transvaluation which Nietzsche calls *legislation:* It is not the purpose of this encompassing legislative philosophizing to formulate juristic or moral principles since they are, on their part, rather the consequence of total evaluations.

Laws, in their bare formality, work destructively in the end; they are alive and true only when brought forth by creative legislators. "Only when life grows rigid, do the laws pile up," and the situation arises to which the saying of the ancient Chinese is applicable: "When kingdoms are destined to perish, they have many laws." "Alas," Nietzsche cries, "what has become of the respect-commanding countenance of the lawgiver who must mean more than the law, namely the desire to keep it sacred out of love and respect?" Those who cling to laws "are actually searching for a great man before whom the laws are wiped out."

What is most characteristic of Nietzsche's "great politics" is the fact that, in connection with the lawgiver, it does not deal at all with the active politician but with the philosopher—just as it has little to say about the particular politics of any concrete situation but takes up the total world-historical situation of his age. Although, in connection with the men who in the future will move history, he foresees "the essential identity of the conqueror, legislator, and artist," still for him the real movers and lawgivers of the future are the philosophers: "They will really determine the Whither and the Why."

Nietzsche has declared the purpose of philosophical thinking by making a claim probably never heard before. His awareness of the immeasurable *creative effect* of genuine philosophizing—*his* way of philosophizing—is extraordinary. The philosophers "reach for the future with a creative hand." They want to "force the will of millenniums into new paths" and prepare for "great" ventures and wholesale experiments of discipline and breeding." Imbued with the power of his thinking, Nietzsche asserts his superiority: "We, the thinking-sensing ones, are those who actually are always *making* something that does not yet exist: the entire ever-growing world of evaluations, colors, weights, perspectives, stepladders, affirmations, and negations. This poetry that we invent is continually memorized, rehearsed, made flesh, and translated into reality, in fact into commonplace reality, by the so-called practical people (our mimics)." Insofar as the practical doers have the advantage of dealing with concrete reality, Nietzsche responds as follows to any mockery that might be directed against the impotence of his dreamlike irreality: "You fancy yourselves to be free. . . . We, the appraisers, made you what you are by winding you up, you clock-works!" The relation of creative thinking to creative doing—their separation and their identity—changes in Nietzsche's formulations. The politicians of his great politics at one time are the "masters of the earth"; at another time, however, they are called the masters of these masters: "Beyond the rulers, freed from all bonds , live the highest men; and the rulers are their tools." The influence is not exerted through direct or visible deeds, but it is really decisive in the long run: "It is the softest words that bring the storm. Thoughts that come on the feet of doves guide the world." "The world turns about the devisers of new values, not the inventors of new noises; *inaudibly* it turns."

Nietzsche lives in the awareness of this kind of philosophizing at the turn of history: "After all, who can feel with me what it means to feel with every fibre of one's being that the weight of all things must be determined anew!" (to Overbeck, May 21, '84). He expects the coming generation to produce the effect for which he is laboring, the generation "in which the great problems which torment me and through which and for which I am still living must take shape and be translated into deed and will" (to Overbeck, June 20, '87). He strives for his life's purpose: "My task: to urge mankind on to resolves that will decide the *entire* future!"

At the same time, however, terror seizes Nietzsche at the thought of the effect that philosophy, including a philosophizing like his, never before undertaken by anyone, will have: "So far, philosophy has only a short history: it is a beginning; it has not yet conducted any wars. . . . Let us individuals live our precursory existence and leave it to posterity to wage wars over our opinions—we live in the *midst* of human time: the greatest fortune!"

The Way of Great Politics. Nietzsche's first answer to the question of what must be done, politically speaking, is that the *conditions* for his great politics must exist before any action is possible. The creative source of great politics—transvaluation and legislation—just because it is a source, cannot possibly be a goal. Politics can proceed *from* it, *not create* it. This source does not become actual like something that I can deliberately choose as my goal because I find it useful and desirable. In fact two conditions must be fulfilled if transvaluation and legislation are to be realized. First, creative legislation is not merely a matter of common sense or energetic will; it derives solely from the substantiality and breadth of vision *of creative man.* In Nietzsche's opinion, however, "one will today, and probably for a long time yet, look in vain for . . . men of such great creativity." Second, the new evaluations that are to proceed from creative transvaluation must *encounter readiness* in the world; mankind must already have an unconscious urge for that which the creating reappraiser brings it: "Transvaluation of values—what could that mean? The *spontaneous* movements must be there. . . . Any doctrine is useless unless everything in the way of stockpiles of energies and explosives is already at its disposal."

Nietzsche realizes that these decisive conditions for his great politics do not yet exist. To him this stands in shocking contrast to the fact that he also recognizes precisely this age as the world-historical moment in which the *most distant possibilities* and the greatest tasks become visible: "With respect to the future, a tremendous vista of mankind's ecumenical goals extending over the whole inhabited earth lies open before us for the first time in history."

Characteristic of Nietzsche's view of the course to be followed is his visualization of extremes and his conception of an indeterminate whole. Due to his concern for the most remote possibilities and horizons, his thinking scarcely reaches the point of concrete action within the *de facto* world and, as a result, it takes the form of a continuous polemic which is relentlessly realistic but does not actually shape empirical reality. Whether his great politics relates to the past, the future, or the present, it often seems as though everything becomes obscured and virtually obliterated by distance.

The *past* is no longer anything: "There is much more ahead for mankind; how could the ideal ever be found in the past?" The *future* is seen as so extensive that it scarcely touches contemporary man: "It is not surprising that a few millenniums are necessary to find the point of contact again; a few millenniums do not matter!" The *present* is conceived as encompassing mankind in its entirety, so much so that the concrete historicity of the individual and his people (*Volk*) threatens to disappear in consequence of such a demand as the following: "As many international powers as possible in order to become accustomed to the world perspective."

Nietzsche does demand: "Presagings of the future! Celebrate the future, not the past! Live in hope! Blissful moments!" And he concludes these demands by saying: "And then drop the curtain again and *turn your thoughts to definite, immediate goals!*" But taking hold of these immediate goals is not the task of great politics, and consequently they are not pursued.

Consideration of extreme and very distant affairs is actually the essence of this great politics. In Nietzsche's view, Providence no longer guides human destiny; God is dead, and man can place no trust in any power beyond himself. Hence he himself must take his entire destiny in hand. It is the necessary purpose of this intentionally non-transcendent thinking to make man conscious of this very task; man is approaching "the great task and problem: how is the earth as a whole to be governed? And to what purpose shall 'man' in his entirety—and no longer as a people or race—be reared and bred?" "Man himself must take over the government of the earth on a large scale, and his 'omniscience' must guard the future destiny of culture with keen eyes." What must therefore be done? *"Make long-term decisions concerning methods, over centuries! For in times to come the guidance of the future of mankind must fall into our hands!"*

But again this prospect, as grandiose as it is ultimately sterile, is not taken to imply that something of this sort could be accomplished right now and that a suitable resolution could be made. If, like a god, without transcendence, and following methods based on my knowledge, I want to gain control of the whole, I am bound to produce a devastating melee unless I am acquainted with the whole. But, Nietzsche insists, such knowledge as is required for taking up and carrying through our methods exists only in rudimentary form: "At any rate, we must attain a knowledge concerning the conditions of culture that will go beyond anything hitherto and that can serve as a criterion for ecumenical goals if mankind is to avoid destroying itself through planned universal government. Herein consists the tremendous task of the great minds of the next century."

Instead of developing an unambiguous political theory, Nietzsche's thinking reveals the abyss of existence and the ambiguity of all reality. All attempts to draw conclusions relating to concrete action from it must end in failure in the absence of two conditions that Nietzsche himself sees as prerequisite to possible political action: a transvaluation of all values that develops into an effective *belief* and a scientific *knowledge* of causal connections in human affairs that exceeds all previous knowledge. Unless both conditions are present, it will be futile to look to Nietzsche for any conclusions whatsoever concerning concrete action. If, in connection with the first condition, one acts as if he believed in what Nietzsche himself, spurred on by belief, accomplished throughout the whole of his philosophizing, he is still left with the question as to the object of this belief: Nietzsche could be the false prophet who leads astray. As to the second condition, if one plans and acts as though mere knowledge of what lies within the horizon of practical attainment in the world were equivalent to an expert knowledge of the whole, then the intended effect never arrives; misconstruing Nietzsche, we have accepted a cheap positivism in lieu of knowledge. In neither case are we following Nietzsche. It would be a radical error to believe that Nietzsche designed anything that could simply be taken over. This is incontestably shown in the realm of great politics by the fact that Nietzsche does not think for everybody but avowedly only for the "new masters."

Education and Breeding. Throughout his life Nietzsche's views concerning the methods to be applied proceeded in one single direction: the concept of *education,* held during his youth, gave rise to the concept of *breeding* expressed in the philosophy of his later years.

He views education as the source of the development of men yet to come—the field in which the future is growing. "The time will arrive when everyone's thoughts will turn to education." Because man's evolution must ultimately be founded on the type of education he is given, he views education as the boundary of existence. Within this boundary he takes the creation of the highest nobility of which man is capable as the meaning of education. With this in view he even makes concrete proposals, but as such they are neither decisive nor consistently maintained.

For example Nietzsche proposed the idea of an organization for education in a series of early lectures on the future of our educational institutions. The proposed organization is democratic inasmuch as it considers all the people and undertakes to select from all levels; it is aristocratic insofar as it is concerned with the best: "Our goal cannot be the education of the masses but education of the carefully selected individual, who is equipped to produce great works of permanent value." The education of the people must, in his opinion, remain outside of the province of this organization. It "can be managed only in a quite external and crude manner; the authentic, deep regions where the great masses have some contact with education, where the people harbor their religious instincts, expand the fiction of their mythical pictures, and remain loyal to their mores, laws, home soil, and language—all these regions can be reached directly—only through destructive acts of violence. . . . Truly promoting public education implies maintaining that wholesome unconsciousness, that sleeping-one's-way-to-health of the people." He reproaches his age for impairing and weakening education by lowering its standards so that everyone may be educated and advocates the opposite policy of restricting it to a few so that it may be strengthened and rendered self-sufficient. He even conceives of the "ideal of an educational sect": "There must be circles like the former orders of monks, only with a broader content."

Abandoning all definite conceptions, Nietzsche uses the diversity of his thinking to bring out the antinomy that lies in the concept of education:

Everything that we expect to achieve through education is already *pre-supposed as present* in the one who is to be educated.

In our passionate striving upwards, we expect, hope to see materialized, and wish to procreate, in the following generation, what our own generation could not produce. But experiences shows that only what already exists by itself is capable of development. Hence to be beneficial, education must liberate: "Your true educators show you the true essence of your nature, something that cannot be taught at all. . . . Your educators can only be your liberators." One needs educators, for "one must learn to *see,* one must learn to *think,* one must learn to *speak* and *write.*" But when education is inferior, it is "a leveling basically intended to adapt the new being to prevailing habits and mores"; "the educational environment proposes to make every man unfree" as though "he is to become a repetition"; education then is "essentially the means for ruining the exception in favor of the norm."

In pressing on to the limit, Nietzsche in time advances beyond these positions. He yearns for the higher man of the future, and, no longer content merely to hope for him, wishes to bring him into existence. Great politics must not stop at an education that is either a leveling or an unfolding of what already exists. The pedagogical concepts of education do not extend to the ultimate source of human development. An education that imparts thought-contents, conveys bodies of knowledge, develops skills, and presents "worthy objects"—a mere education of emotions and ideas—does not suffice. Fundamental to all education is rather a process that reaches deeper into man, brings forth his very being, and thus provides the basis on which his education can really begin. "Procreation of better men is the task of the future."

This process that reaches into the depths and brings forth man's being is dual. It is either "taming" or "breeding." By *taming* of the beast "man," he means its pacification, i.e., its quietening and weakening according to its *standard of normality. Breeding* on the other hand means a forced heightening of the *rank* of human beings. Nietzsche considers both as necessary, but as he now sees it, "education is breeding."

But how is such education to accomplish the task of breeding? The problem to be solved first is: What "type of man should be bred? What type is most desirable for being of higher value, more worthy of living, and more promising for the future?" Clothing his all-inclusive intention in the language of biological simplification, Nietzsche considers it "decisive for the destiny of a people and of mankind that culture is started in the right place. . . . The right place is the body, the gesture, the diet, the physiology; the rest will follow from that." Also of importance in this connection is the medical report preceding any marriage, plus measures to prevent sick persons from propagating their kind. But Nietzsche's concept of breeding reaches beyond this biological aspect: he regards *creative thinking* itself as a form of breeding, for concepts transform the man who thinks them; hence he teaches that "concepts should be considered as experiments by means of which the durability and permanence of certain kinds of men are bred and tested." His own "experimental" thinking, his philosophizing, is intended to have a breeding effect.

When Nietzsche, however, thinks of the directors of human destinies, i.e., of the men who will apply his ideas about breeding and present their really effective morality to mankind, thereby bringing man forth in accordance with his type, he reserves for them the "great politics of virtue." The problem with which it is concerned is not how to *become* virtuous but how to *make* people virtuous.

Thus in Nietzsche's view, the concept of education presupposes breeding, and his idea of breeding either grows vague and indefinable because it is taken to involve thinking as a means, or it is narrowed down to biological particulars. But here too, as elsewhere, the particular content, even though it may seem to provide the entire solution, is scarcely essential; what counts is rather the unflinching look at the boundaries and the breaking of all traditional prejudices.

Great Politics and Philosophy

The wealth of possibilities in Nietzsche's political thinking does not permit any specific standpoint—whether attractive or repugnant—to be isolated from its larger context. Each utterance needs explication and reinterpretation through other utterances. Even then these conceptions of great politics do not give rise to a complete and independent whole; and nowhere does Nietzsche's great politics lead to a utopia. The indefiniteness of the whole, in contrast with the definiteness of the parts, constitutes its openness. It is this indefinite openness that characterizes both the possible course of things and the path to be taken by action, so long as we do not allow our attention to become fixated by individual visionary aspects of the future. Consequently Nietzsche's great politics is ambiguous: it seems intended to employ judgments and demands of the greatest generality to induce an activity that will take man as the material for creative formation in order to transform him into a different, better, and higher-ranking being. But although the term politics seems to imply something that has to occur here and now, his stipulations do not produce any concrete acts concerned directly with tasks that could be useful. In this respect, "great politics" does not envisage any definite policies relating to a special sphere of human activity, but it awakens, so to speak, an essential political mood which is directed to the possibilities of human existence taken as a whole: it is concerned, through thinking, to bring to light what may even now be pressing toward the surface in the growing germ of living consciousness. But what this is cannot be made clear in the "great politics," apart from the totality of Nietzsche's philosophizing.

It would be easy to pass over Nietzsche's grandiosely exaggerated thoughts, the consequences of which embrace all manner of absurdities; it would also be easy to be carried away by them. But instead of this we must seek to understand the basic force that moves them. We shall attempt to make clear in three directions how Nietzsche's "great politics" flows back into the philosophy from which it derives:

1. In the first place, since the intent of the sort of thinking that touches upon the whole of human existence (and usually seems fantastic to the realist, concerned as he is with the present) is intrinsically philosophical, it can look back upon a long series of ancestors. This intent can briefly be characterized through a comparison. It is normal for youth to demand that everything be changed from the ground up. Ignoring the hard labor called for by concrete actuality and abandoning all historical grounds to rely on the absolute, youth believes that the magnitude of its vision and of the ideal requires it to rebuild existence from the ground up. Philosophizing involves something closely related to this youthful attitude: a passionate longing to proceed from the inner grandeur of an intuition of being (the whole realm of possibility) to its actual realization and fulfillment. In as far as it is a dream, it may be permitted to pass beyond all limits. But it is more than a dream since it certainly anticipates the real through contemplation of what is possible, even if it fails to do so through overt action (in this respect Nietzsche's great politics resembles the political philosophy of Plato and the ideas of Kant). It is a volition banished from reality to the boundless realm of present unreality. Bereft of achievement, the grief thus felt intensifies the imagination and leads to utopian aberrations or, as in Nietzsche's case, ends in the loud cry that tends to sound hollow as he strains his voice in the presence of emptiness. But in fact we owe the communicable ideas through which our darkly pulsating life is believed to attain its meaning to the creative source within a few great thinkers. What was there revealed of the law encompassing all definite laws becomes the basis of our capacity for meaningful volition.

2. Faced by the unpredictability of events, by visions of a future

bound to arouse dread, and by the vagueness of all ideas relating to the particular political actions that ought to be carried out, Nietzsche finds the omnipresent source upon which everything else depends and which, when all becomes chaotic, is thrown back entirely upon itself: *the individual as an autonomous being.* It is as though at this point Nietzsche touches upon the completely unpolitical as the great counter-pole of the political, but in such a way that all creative politics can proceed only from it.

When Nietzsche focuses his attention on this autonomous being of the individual, he is thinking of himself and the way in which he lives in an age that has no use for him and in which he cannot find his world. He writes: "There are even now the sort of people who in former times would have belonged to the ruling classes of priests, aristocrats, and thinkers. Now we behold annihilation." What is left for them to do? "Rejected by falsehood, secret flight back to what is overcome, and nocturnal service in temple ruins! Likewise service in the market halls!" These men "achieve greatest independence through restraint and refuse to be citizens, politicians, and possessors. . . . Mankind perhaps will have need of them in times to come when the ordinary man of anarchy has passed on. Fie on those who now offer themselves blatantly as saviors to the masses! . . . We intend to be prepared! We shall be the mortal enemies of those among us who escape into mendacity and call for reaction!"

Making his demands on the innermost strength of independent being, he calls to those following him: "For the kind of men who mean anything to me, I desire suffering, loneliness, illness, degradation. I wish them to become acquainted with the torture of self-distrust and the misery of the vanquished: I have no compassion for them because I desire for them the only thing which today can prove whether a person has value or not: *that he stand firm.*"

He instills courage: "You self-possessing ones! You autonomous ones! Do not fight against opinions that are charity for slaves! Whatever political or social forms may come forth, all of them will always be mere forms of slavery—and you will be the rulers under all forms—because you alone belong only to yourselves."

In this state of belonging to oneself, Nietzsche finds the only position for creative thinking,[3] in which actual mastery (but of an invisible nature) and insight (which no longer acts practically) become identical. The thinking of "great politics" thus accomplished can have the appear-

---

[3] Cf. pp. 151–53.

ance of purest contemplation: "My goals and tasks are more extensive than anyone's, and what I call great politics provides at least an excellent standpoint, with a bird's-eye view of the things of the present" (to Overbeck, May 2, '84). The "great politics" no longer expresses any will to rule, but its thinking purports to be that which does rule in the end: "The *inclination* to rule has often appeared to me as an inner symptom of weakness. . . . The mightiest natures *rule,* it is a necessity . . . , even though they may bury themselves during their lifetimes in garden cottages!" To Nietzsche, the creative philosophers are the mightiest of all, not as a result of any power over their contemporaries, but because of the way they control themselves and, through the consequences of their thinking, eventually move the world: "The great moral natures arise as self-restrainers . . . during times of disintegration. They are the governing natures (Heraclitus, Plato) in a transformed world where they only have to rule themselves."

Nietzsche thus sees men as individuals. In this he is not prompted by a feeling for humanity which accords to each individual man inalienable rights and an irreplaceable value; he expressly rejects this notion and believes instead that the individual as such is the final source of all creation and, in its creativity, the sole manifestation of being that he can love and respect. He continues his quest until he reaches a point where something can remain unshaken, even though this may appear as simply a victory for inner-worldly composure amidst failures. As the only tangible form that humanity can in the end assume and as the author of great deeds that set up and realize new goals, the independently existing individual is the permanent condition that determines everything else. The autonomous being of the individual is, in Nietzsche's opinion, still "mighty" even on those occasions when the might of the masses triumphs, since the masses, in turn, must ultimately be guided by men who constitute it. Nietzsche is perennially concerned about the way in which the individual autonomous being can and must exist (*existieren*) under all circumstances, so that its existence can document humanity and so that it will be prepared for the tasks to come. Whether by assuming mastery, by appearing in anonymous loneliness, or by assuming some quite unforeseeable form, individual self-being in a time of leveling must somehow generate itself and finally determine the course of events.

Even when the entire future seems hopeless to him, Nietzsche, using a simile, keeps his sight focused on the potential autonomy of the individual: "Hundreds of profound lonelinesses together form the city of Venice—this is its magic. A picture for the men of the future."

3. In the following chapters Nietzsche's basic thoughts are presented

separately. They are experimental possibilities which Nietzsche subjects to constant contradiction and self-nullification. Occasionally they may appear to be little more than a series of fortuitously acquired notions; but Nietzsche, by instinct and intent, gives them a pervading unity. His political and philosophical thoughts are closely related to each other. This can be expressed as follows: his great politics, which is the will to action for the future, signifies the will to the highest type of man: the superman. For this the European master race is the primary requisite. This master race, through its humanity and its will, produces the counter-movement to the nihilism that resulted from all previous evaluations—especially Christian ones. This counter-movement, which is to be initiated through Nietzsche's philosophizing, is rooted in Nietzsche's basic conception of being. Philosophizing, not for all, but for the potential masters, it unites a speculative mysticism (eternal recurrence) and a metaphysical interpretation of being (will to power) with an inspiring vision of the superman of the future. This is not knowledge of something that exists but the impulse to overcome nihilism, which first will be driven to deduce from the concept of incessant becoming the extreme conclusion that the world is without meaning and goal and that all activity is futile. It is this temptation to ultimate negation inhering in this intensified nihilism that will then produce the radical turn to the affirmative that relates neither to a world beyond, nor to God, nor to an ideal, but rather to the totality of actual world-being in the whole and in the individual. In the two following chapters this will be shown to be the encompassing significance of the "great politics."

5

WORLD EXEGESIS

To answer the question of the nature of ultimate reality by providing a picture or conceptual construct of the world in its entirety is, and has always been, a mistake. Nevertheless it is true that all philosophizing is best characterized by the way in which it conceives of the world.

Nietzsche is one of a series of metaphysicians whose conception of being purports to be all-inclusive and thus to comprehend the universe as a whole. His fundamental principle is the *"will to power."* This kind of metaphysical construct places him in conscious relation to the perennial possibilities of world-interpretation in the grand manner.

Still, Nietzsche came after Kant. He took for granted the critical questions handed on to him and could no longer accept a naïve dogmatic metaphysics. Thus the fundamental principles of his metaphysics were fashioned from a transformation of Kant's critical philosophy. In the process of this transformation, he developed the theory that the whole world exists as a mere exegetical construction, that world-knowledge is the *exegesis* entertained at a given time, and that his own philosophy of the "will to power" is but a *new exegesis.*

Finally, Nietzsche's metaphysics is characterized by the fact that it definitely relates to *this world merely, and to no other.* For him there is no transcendent reality. He wishes to do away with the age-old distinction between an underlying reality and its superficial appearances (between the true and the merely phenomenal world). For him there is only the world itself: nothing exists in addition to the "will to power" which alone, in its various forms, constitutes our world. For his metaphysics, the world exists as pure immanence.

The World as Commentary

We come to grief whenever we undertake to think of the world as it is in itself. When we think, we entertain a *meaning,* insofar as this is what we call the notion by means of which we objectify the world. When

Nietzsche asks "whether an existence without exegesis, i.e., without sense, would not simply be 'nonsense' " and, on the other hand, whether "all existence does not naturally involve the practice of exegesis," he answers that this can "not be discovered from a self-examination of the intellect, since in the course of the analysis the human intellect could not avoid viewing itself in, and only in, its own perspectival forms." What existence would be apart from this, i.e., apart from the process and product of exegesis, cannot be discovered through the use of the human intellect, which invariably apprehends itself as well as things by means of its own constructs. In fact the following becomes *his fundamental thesis:* All being is a product of exegesis: "There are no things in themselves and there is no absolute knowledge; the perspectivistic, illusory character belongs to existence." Nor is there such a thing as an "event per se what occurs is a group of phenomena selected and united by an *interpreting being.*" From this Nietzsche concludes (1) that there can be *no true conceptual apprehension* of an enduring self-sufficient reality, and (2) that *epistemology is impossible.*

(1) Comprehension, in the sense of laying hold upon being per se in its fixed state, seems nonsensical to him: "To grasp everything would mean to do away with all perspectivistic relations, it would mean to grasp nothing and to misapprehend the nature of knowledge." Such knowing is exegesis, it is not explanation but an attribution of meanings: "There is no set of facts: everything is fluid, evasive, receding; our opinions are the most enduring things of all." Man finds nothing more in things than what he himself has put there.

(2) Epistemology, conceived as an attempt critically to analyze man's cognitive faculty, is simply an object of Nietzsche's contempt. In agreement with Hegel, he says: "How can an instrument be capable of analysing itself when it has only itself to rely upon for the analysis?" Since it is absurd for a cognitive apparatus to undertake the task of cognizing itself, Nietzsche regards as comical any philosophy that reduces itself to an epistemological enterprise.

But isn't Nietzsche's own thesis concerning knowledge as exegesis itself an epistemology? No, it is an attempt radically to separate our consciousness of being from every determinate and consequently insular provision of an enduring and immutable truth, an attempt to expand our horizon endlessly, to overcome every final fixation of being, and to vindicate the claim of the apparent to be the real and the true.[1] We must now see more specifically what this means.

---

[1] Concerning the effect of the "theory" of exegesis on the meaning of truth, cf. pp. 184 ff.

Exegesis as a Metaphor. The metaphor of "exegesis," used to express the basic relation of human existence to being, is taken by Nietzsche from the relation of interpretation to text in philological work. The text contains a meaning which the interpretation is intended to discover. What is given as factual and unalterable is the text or, in another sense, a meaning to be conveyed by it, which may or may not be properly understood; and an interpretation that goes beyond this is open to question. It is the business of philology to approach the true meaning of old texts by eliminating premature, wildly imaginative, and inventive renderings. In dealing with literary documents, philology expresses its newly won understanding; thus in understanding texts, it creates new texts. The unique movement and dialectic of philological understanding provides Nietzsche with a metaphor suitable for expressing the understanding of being on the part of the existence that construes it. He applies this metaphor to all kinds of knowledge. Two wholly different matters to which it relates may serve as examples. He calls "nature's conformability to law" an exegesis, saying that it is "interpretation, not text." And he characterizes in the same way the activities of the philosophers: "We, the observers of European affairs, whom fate has sought out to confront with an enigmatic and unread text that discloses itself to us more and more . . . while an increasing number of rare things clamor within us . . . demanding light, air, freedom, and verbal expression."

The text of being appears firm and reliable and capable of being correctly construed when he says: "To be able to read a text *as text,* without permitting any interpretation to commingle with it, is the latest kind of inner experience. Perhaps it is scarcely possible." Or again: "Much understanding is required to apply to nature the same sort of disciplined explanatory skill as contemporary philologists have learned to employ in their approach to books of all kinds. It is their intention simply to understand what is written, without sensing or even presupposing a double meaning." But then he maintains the very opposite of this: "The same text admits of countless constructions: there is no such thing as a 'correct exegesis.'" It is this second position that is decisive; it is this aspect of the metaphor that discloses the boundless fluctuation of possible exegeses of being: "The basic presupposition that there is a correct interpretation at all—or rather *one* single correct one—seems to me to be empirically false. . . . What is incorrect can be ascertained in innumerable cases; what is correct is *almost always unascertainable.* . . . In a word, the old philologist says: There is no single beatific interpretation" (to Fuchs, Aug. 26, '88).

All that poets and musicians create, all that consciousness summons in dreams, reveals in feelings, and illumines in thoughts of obscure origin—all these things are themselves only signs, constructions, and possibilities, as is all existence. "Granted that it is senseless, one task unavoidably remains—that of reading sense into it."

"This applies to tones, and to the destinies of peoples as well. They can be interpreted in the most different ways and in terms of very different goals." Thus it is with our exegesis of *consciousness*. In dreams, consciousness goes its way unhindered, but perhaps it is even true that "all our so-called consciousness is a more or less fantastic commentary on an unknown and possibly unknowable but felt text. . . . After all, what are our experiences? Much more that which we read into them than what they contain!" And so it is with our thoughts when, from an indeterminate, felt obscurity, they emerge into the clear light of the intellect: "In the form in which it comes, the thought is a sign with many meanings which has to be recast until its ambiguity is finally overcome. It just makes its appearance within me—whence and how? I don't know. . . . The source of thought remains hidden; it is highly probable that it is only the symptom of a far more encompassing state . . . within which something emerges to express itself by means of signs. Thus it is with every *feeling* which, in itself, signifies nothing. When it arises, we have to interpret it, and how strange our interpretations often are!"

When seen in these connections, the text, precisely because of its multiplicity of meanings, is almost non-existent, and thus there is a tendency to lose sight of it as the standard for the truth of the interpretation. But, in another connection, Nietzsche insists all the more that the genuine text must be preserved from contamination by mistaken exegesis. In this vein he asks that man be sent back into nature. We must "become master of the many vain and fanciful constructions and secondary meanings that up to the present have been scribbled and painted over the eternal, basic text *homo natura.*"

Here, where any unambiguous exposition would fail, Nietzsche's contradictions show us what he is driving at. Existence both provides and is a product of exegesis. It is regarded as a circle that renews itself constantly while seeming to annul itself. It is now objectivity and now subjectivity; it appears first as substance and then as constantly annulled substance; though unquestionably there, it is constantly questioning and questionable; it is both being and not-being, the real and the apparent. We must not simplify these thoughts. Nietzsche does not allude to the ego that posits itself and creates the world, to the world that is merely my idea, to the self-conscious world of idealism that knows and is known, or even to the world as an object of investigation by the critical reason that illumines it. Over against such thoughts as these—thoughts which, with their increasing determinateness, appear together as a consequence of Nietzsche's way of speaking—stands the true fulcrum of his thinking: the claim to pass beyond all these fixed positions to the point where I myself as a unique and inimitable individual must in truth read (i.e., construe) being, since I am as I am. In all pronouncements that seem to be merely general, Nietzsche refers to the *historicity of Existenz.* The limitlessness of the many historically developed exegeses is the basis of our own being which, as an authentic source, now surveying all exegeses and looking through them, is directed upon the text itself. At this point the truth is not experienced as just another mode of interpretation to be tried out as part of a game, as it were; it is experienced as the truth of *Existenz* itself—the absolute truth which is present to *Existenz* when, in the *fullness of historical consciousness,* it reads the world as a cipher. Here general knowledge of the exegetical process and every special exegesis that is knowable *ab extra* is fused within the presence of being itself. Then the truth is "my" truth, but, at the same time, *not mine merely,* for while, in the first place, *it has become historical* as that within which I find myself fused with being, it is, in the second place, being itself—which Nietzsche calls will to power—in the mode in which it becomes existential as my self.

Although, according to this theory of exegesis, all existence is thus construing and construed existence and although the text to be read is both outside of me and within me and I myself am indeed only the text that I can read, still Nietzsche points out a possible boundary. The process does not proceed ad infinitum: although I constantly undergo change as I provide exegeses, I do eventually strike bedrock. There is something firm and constant that is not resolved into interpretation and is not even touched by it: "Basically there is within us, way 'down below,' something unteachable—a granite of spiritual fate. . . . In connection with every cardinal problem, an unchanging 'that is I' speaks. . . . At times one finds certain solutions of problems . . . perhaps one calls them his 'convictions.' Later on he sees in them only . . . road signs pointing to the problem that we are—more correctly, to the great stupidity that we are, and to our spiritual fate and our incorrigibility way 'down deep.' "

The Manifestation of Exegesis. Nietzsche makes clear, both in principle and in application, that exegesis becomes manifest as (1) constant transvaluation, (2) incessant becoming, and finally (3) recognition of its own nature, so that (4) within the realm of possible exegeses each one receives its own proper rank and value:

(1) What he calls "interpretation of existence" is, he believes, not to be separated from *value-interpretation*. The value of the world lies in our interpretation. Exegesis is not disinterested; in itself it constitutes clarification of value through appraisal. That is why the two titles of his projected *magnum opus* concerning the will to power—"A Transvaluation of All Values" and "An Attempt at a New World-Exegesis"—say basically the same thing. Right down to the most abstract distinctions of categories, exegesis is an expression of the will and a means of satisfying a need to judge all being in terms of value to oneself.

(2) Exegesis is never definitive; it is always *in process*. "What is essential to organic beings is *a new exegesis of events:* the perspectival inner multiplicity which in itself is an event." "The world that concerns us is false, i.e., it is not fact but fiction. . . . It is in a state of flux like a constantly shifting falsehood that never even approximates the truth, for—there is no 'truth.' " *Anything construed will itself, as a new construction, be subject to further construction.* Thus "every elevation of man" involves "the overcoming of narrower interpretations," provides new perspectives, and consists in the acceptance of new horizons.

(3) This endless process of interpretation appears to arrive at a sort of consummation in the *self-apprehension of the exegesis,* i.e., in the exegesis of the exegeses. This step, which is deliberately taken by Nietzsche, involves recognizing the exegesis for what it is without neglecting its existential reference.

Before this point was reached, it was necessary that exegeses should be unreservedly believed to be absolutely true. For thousands of years men "had to cling with clenched teeth to a religious interpretation of existence," prompted by "the fear of an instinct which vaguely sensed that it was possible for man to possess the truth too early, at a time when he was not yet strong enough for it."

But now Nietzsche takes the risk of emancipation. Of course, we too "are unable to look around our own corner: it is a hopeless curiosity that would know what other kinds of intellects and perspectives there *might* yet be." But we today are at least far removed from the ridiculous brashness that, viewing things from our corner, would decree that perspectives should be had only from that corner. Rather we find that the world has once again "become endless, insofar as we are unable to dismiss the possibility that it contains endless interpretations. Once again a great shudder comes over us. . . ." Only the man of high rank can bear the "world's endless susceptibility to interpretation." Regarding "the plurality of interpretations as a sign of strength," he "does not wish to deny the unsettling and enigmatic character of the world."

(4) The exegeses are not arbitrary and *not of equal value*. In the first place, beyond merely conceptual reconstructions, there is a higher stage of reinterpretation through *activity*. Furthermore, neither the kind, the sense, nor the content of the interpretations is subject to criticism on the part of the old-fashioned epistemology which unquestioningly operated with the imagined criterion of a single valid truth relating to an absolute being; rather, critique is provided by the vital course of events: "Every interpretation [is] a *symptom* of growth or decline." Casting his critical eye upon the exegeses that are available to him, Nietzsche finds that "the previous exegeses all had a certain relevance to life: they supported it, rendered it tolerable or strange, added refinement, or even separated what was sick and caused it to die off." On the other hand there are regnant exegeses that Nietzsche opposes as enemies of life: e.g., the Christian and most of the philosophical ones. He himself wants to offer a better one: "My new exegesis gives the future philosophers as masters of the earth the impartiality they require."

Nietzsche's New Exegesis (The Will to Power)

We cannot say what the world as a whole is. It is false to change all processes into a familiar world of our own, and then say: "All is will (everything wills); all is pleasure or pain (everything endures); all is motion (everything flows); all is tone (everything sounds); all is spirit (everything thinks); all is number (everything reckons)." Nietzsche warns us against *all* notions of the whole: "Let us guard against thinking that the world is a living being . . . or that the universe is a machine. . . . Let us guard against saying that there are laws of nature. . . . Let us guard against thinking that the world eternally creates novelties." All these "shadows of God" darken actuality. We are within the world, and the whole of the world is, *as a whole, not* accessible to us.

Considering these decisive insights, it is at first astonishing that Nietzsche himself offers his own new exegesis of the world in its entirety as a statement about what actually exists. We shall undertake to discover what he can mean by such an attempt. The being to which he refers cannot be both a special construct and an absolute being. What is it? "It would have to be something that is not subject, not object, not energy, not matter, not spirit, and not soul. But I shall be told that anything of this sort would be virtually indistinguishable from a phantom? That is just what I believe, and it would be sad if it were not the case! Of course, it would have to be indistinguishable from everything else that exists and could exist—and not merely from a phantom! It must have the cardinal family trait by which all things can recognize their kinship with it."

These statements provide a remarkably apt intimation of the scope and meaning of the ontological thinking that Nietzsche demands. He rejects every determinate species of entity that as such is supposed to express the nature of being. Nevertheless, his world-exegesis appears in fact to revive just the sort of specification that he rejects.

To start with, Nietzsche calls that which truly is and which is all-inclusive by the name of *life*. Then he discovers that wherever life is, there is also will to power. Since all life displays will to power, the latter is "to be viewed as a shorthand formula for the whole tendency. Thus will to power becomes a new specification of the concept 'life.' " He then continues: "Life is merely an individual instance of the will to power; it would be entirely arbitrary to assert that everything strives to attain this form of the will to power." Now "the innermost essence of being [is] the will to power," and life, as only one mode of being, is not the end, for "wherever there is decline . . . life sacrifices itself—for power." "Even what is greatest will risk its life for the sake of power." In this way Nietzsche arrives at something determinate as did old-fashioned meta-physics: "The world viewed *ab intra*—the world defined and charac-terized in terms of its intelligible character—would be simply will to power and nothing else."

The nature of being is accessible *to us* only through life and the will to power: "The extent of our feeling for life and power . . . provides us with a measure of being." "Being" is a "generalization of the concept 'life,' . . . , i.e., of 'willing,' 'acting,' and 'becoming.' "

But "life" and "will to power" are expressions that, whether taken in their direct and customary sense or in their definite biological and psychological sense, fail to hit upon what Nietzsche has in mind. Since they are used to refer to being itself, what they really are remains "unfathomable." The breadth of world-exegesis which his starting-point reveals must be retained. His world-exegesis is not really knowledge. The incognizability of being as life and will to power is due to the fact that we only conceive of that which we ourselves have already constructed: "The more knowable a thing, the farther from being, and the closer to a mere concept." Nietzsche's exegesis, which acknowledges that all knowledge is exegesis, will assimilate *this* knowledge to its own exegesis by holding that the will to power itself is the ever operative and infinitely various urge to interpret. Nietzsche's interpretation is actually an interpretation of interpreting, and for that reason different from those of all earlier, comparatively naïve interpretations which were undertaken without awareness of their own interpretative character.

We must now undertake to sketch, in basic outlines, the conceptions which Nietzsche used to elucidate that unfathomable being to which the expressions "life" and "will to power" refer. First we shall examine the *basic exegesis* as such, then we shall turn to the *empirical disciplines* which supply content for his basic ideas, and finally we shall enlarge upon *the interpretation of the entire world* as a manifestation of the will to power which Nietzsche worked out in detail.

The Basic Exegesis. It is a question of bringing together the many determinations (*Bestimmungen*)—widely scattered in Nietzsche's works —in such a way that the profound and far-reaching significance that isolated statements fail to convey is brought out as clearly as possible. No single determination, merely as such, can hit the mark, for what is determinate is particular. But while all thought is determinate, the determinations can, when taken together, express the true meaning that is bound to be lost when they are taken separately.

1. *The basic determination of life as "will to power": Life is evaluating.* "In order to live, one must evaluate." Because life involves appraisal, preference, insulation, wishing to be different, it is a will to be other than nature, for nature is boundlessly extravagant and indifferent. Being is not something standing over against us that we evaluate, it is this evaluation itself: "The evaluation itself is still this being. Even when we say 'No,' we continue to do what we are."

Life, constantly evaluating, attributes to the flux of becoming those values to which it subordinates itself. "To live is to obey." But this deepest instinct in all willing has remained the most hidden, "for in practice we always follow its command because we *are* this command."

"Willing is not craving, striving, demanding: it is distinct from these because of the *feeling of command.*" To will is to will *something,* and it belongs to the nature of willing that something is commanded.

Life, which is valuing and willing, obeying and commanding, has an ever-present criterion of its success: "Life is a fountain of pleasure." Since "the inner essence of being is will to power," "all growth of power [is] pleasure, and all feeling of not being able to withstand and become master is pain." "An act that derives from the life-instinct is shown to be a right act by the pleasure involved."

"But *who* feels pleasure? *Who* desires power? . . . Absurd question! since the will to power, and consequently the feeling of pleasure and displeasure, is basic." "The will to power is the last fact to which we can penetrate"; it is "the inner substance of being," the essence of the world.

2. *Basic determinations through conflict:* No one of these elementary determinations is separable from the existence of conflict. "Opposition, resistance, and thus, relatively, encroaching unities are necessary." When the conflict is examined, it proves to be a struggle with others and within the self; in either case it develops out of a *will to grow* and to increase. ("To have and to want to have more—growth—is life itself.")

In the first place, life is "always *at the expense of other lives*" and is, as a result, "essentially appropriation, overpowering the foreign and the weak, incorporation, and, at the very least, exploitation." This is to say that "life essentially, i.e., in the performance of its basic functions, employs injury, oppression, and annihilation and cannot even be conceived without these characteristics."

In other words, life is a constant process of "ascertaining relations of power. . . . It is a *struggle,* if only we enlarge the meaning of the term sufficiently to see conflict in the relation of the ruler to the ruled, and resistance in the relation of the obedient to his commander." Not content merely to define life as "a continuous form of the various processes for ascertaining strength," Nietzsche looks upon absolute being and sees "*all* events and all processes as tests to ascertain relations of rank and power."

Life is not lived merely at the expense of others; it is lived at one's own expense. It is "that which must always *overcome itself.*" "Life—this means constantly casting off from the self something that is ready to die."

The need for overcoming is due to the fact that life is a *trial* (*ein Versuchen*). To grasp this principle is to attain an intensification of life: to try many things and overcome many things. "Let your life be an hundredfold trial, and let your failures and successes constitute a proof." "One must be willing to perish in order to be able to rise again. . . . One hundred psychic transformations—let that be your life and your fate."

Since this last basic fact of being, the will to power, can express itself only through struggle, "*it seeks for that which opposes it.*" Since opposition produces inhibition, and inhibition gives rise to displeasure, the latter is a necessary moment in all activity. "Dissatisfaction is life's great stimulant." "The will to power seeks displeasure in the form of resistance. At the center of all organic life there is a will to suffer."

The will to power seeks that which life actually is: "Wherever life appears, it appears as pain and contradiction." It is important to realize "that life itself requires enmity and death and the cross of the martyr." "Life—is torture!"

This, therefore, is the fundamental determination of authentic life: In order to appreciate life, you must *stand above it!"* Life's will to power is not the will to mere life as such. Life is subordinate to the authentic being that constitutes the will to power and is to be sacrificed to it. The old truth recurs in Nietzsche's thought: "Love for life is almost the opposite of love for a long life. All love thinks of the instant and of eternity—but never of 'length.' "

Standing-above-life reveals itself decisively in the *will to danger*. Of course "to live at all is to be in danger," but it is something more "to seek instinctively a life that is raised to a higher power: the life of danger." "That one wagers his life in the game is the consequence of an exuberant, lavish will, for every great danger makes us curious about the extent of our power and our courage." And when one gives up his life in battle, then "every victory involves contempt for life." That is why Nietzsche says that "the secret of making existence as fruitful and enjoyable as possible is contained in the words: Live dangerously!"

Nietzsche's view that life is *will to power* (i.e., will to increase and to improve, struggle for growth) is opposed to other determinations that may at first seem related to it. Unlike Spencer, he says: "Life is not an adjustment of inner to outer conditions, but a will to power that draws upon its inner resources to subdue and incorporate more and more of what is 'external' "; it is not primarily reaction but action. In opposition to Darwin: Life is not a struggle for existence, for this is simply an exceptional state of affairs. It is much rather a struggle for power, for something more and better. Against Spinoza: Self-preservation is not the essence: life functions with a view to self-aggrandisement rather than mere self-preservation. Against Schopenhauer: What he calls "will" is merely an empty word, for in characterizing this will, he has omitted the meaning of its goal. There is no will to exist, "for what is not cannot will; and how can that which already possesses existence still will it! There is will only where there is life: not will to life but will to power."

3. *Basic determinations through exegetical perspectives:* When we recall that all existence is exegetical, that all being is perspectivistic, and that, if we were to discount this aspect of the world, nothing would remain, we ask ourselves how this principle of being relates to the will to power.

It is the will to power itself that practices exegesis (interprets). *Qua* life, it is conditioned by the perspectival: "Life is only possible under the guidance of those forces that make for narrowness and create perspectives." The will to power interprets by means of the perspectives that it has provided: "Mere differences in power could not experience themselves as what they are." Entities intent upon growing interpret other similar entities in terms of value. "The truth is that interpretation is a means of gaining mastery over something." While "everything that occurs in the organic world is an overpowering," this overpowering is "a reinterpretation, a rearranging, as a result of which the previous sense and purpose is necessarily obscured." "Every center of power has its perspective for all the rest, i.e., its quite definite evaluation, and its kind of action and reaction. Now there is no other kind of action at all, and 'the world' is but a name for the total play of these actions."

If one inquires *who* acts, provides the matrix, wills power, and interprets, Nietzsche answers: "No subject-atoms"; "the interpretative process itself exists as a form of the will to power"; we are not to posit an interpreter behind the interpretation. "The constant transitoriness and volatility of the subject" has no solid core of being: "The subjective sphere is constantly growing or declining; the central point of the system is constantly shifting." The perspectivistic sphere is not a product of the behavior of antecedently existing subjects that want to preserve themselves: "It is not the particular being, but *the struggle itself that undertakes to continue in existence, to grow, and to become self-conscious by means of an organic being.*"

Being conscious is the same as being interpreted, and Nietzsche characterizes both as spirit (*Geist*); knowledge within the perspective of a given exegesis is spiritual existence (*geistiges Dasein*). This exegetical existence moves in a circle: It serves the will to power of life that produced it, but then again, becoming autonomous, it disengages itself and turns back upon life. Thus it seems identical with life when it is absorbed into it, but appears estranged from life when it opposes it. It is less than life insofar as it is encompassed by it and more than life insofar as it, in turn, determines, forms, inspires, and sacrifices life. Since therefore spirit itself is life, being sometimes life's instrument and sometimes life's master, one may say paradoxically that life is superior to and stronger than knowledge, and that life is a means to knowledge. Or we hear that "when life and knowledge appear to contradict each other, no serious struggle has taken place" and, at the same time, that the struggle between life and knowledge becomes all the more powerful, the stronger the two drives are. If, on one occasion, spirit is called a mere "instrument in the service of the elevation of life," it is also claimed, with equal right, that "spirit is life that cuts into life itself."

When Nietzsche's will to power appears as the essence of absolute being, the question arises how the many wills that result from the fragmentation of being are related to each other. This relation either involves exegetical understanding or it does not, but obedience is possible only where understanding is present: "What sort of compulsion is it that a stronger soul exerts upon a weaker one? It might possibly be that the apparent disobedience of the latter is rooted in a failure to understand what is wanted; e.g., a rock cannot be commanded. . . . Understanding arises only between those who are closely related to one another, and it is this that makes obedience possible." But when Nietzsche applies the will to power metaphysically to absolute being, he uses the term "exegesis" in a correspondingly broad sense. Then *all that is* is regarded as a kind of exegesis, that is, a series of *signs* with an infinite variety of possible meanings: "Everything material is a kind of symptom of the course of unknown events; everything conscious and felt is likewise a symptom. The world that makes itself known to us through these two sides may well have many other symptoms." Basically, however, the unknown is the will to power. Thus he takes all existence to be a kind of *speech* "through which the forces understand one another," but at the same time he finds a radical rent in the fabric of the world due to the disparate ways in which speech and understanding are carried on: "In the inorganic world where *there is no misunderstanding,* communication appears to be perfect. *Error begins* in the organic world"; "what originally gave rise to life was the greatest conceivable error." "One gains the impression that life is disposed to appearance; I mean error, deception, dissimulation, meretricious brilliance, and self-delusion."

4. *Basic determinations through essential differences in kind:* While the will to power, as formulated by Nietzsche, does not inhere in any substratum but is identified with a struggle that is self-dependent and self-sufficient, still the decisive contentions of Nietzsche derive from the fact that the will to power is not of one single invariant kind. This will is rather, as it were, a *what* that wills, and this *what* embraces *essential* differences.

There are, to be sure, many formulations which Nietzsche uses to describe power as a homogeneous something that exhibits merely quantitative differences. The following statement would seem to be unequivocal: "Nothing connected with life has any value apart from the degree of power," and again: "Quantities of power can determine and delineate rank, and nothing else can." "Your rank depends upon the quantity of power that you are." "Value consists in the highest quantum of power that man is able to absorb." On this showing, *quantity of power* would be equivalent to *quantity of value,* and power per se would be rank.

But "power" is ambiguous. The degree of power is by no means in every sense the same as the order of rank, and that is the reason for the many references that appear to disparage power: "One pays dearly for coming to power; power makes one stupid"; "power is tedious." These and similar pronouncements show that power and value are not simply identified by Nietzsche. Consequently he finally abandons the quantity of power as a measure; it is not the quantity but the quality that is decisive: The "mechanistic view accepts only the quantitative, but force resides only in the qualitative." It may even be that quantities are themselves only signs of qualities: "In a purely quantitative world, everything would be dead, rigid, unmoved." But still, quantities of power are not unequivocal signs of quality. Turning to politics for an example, we note that in the life of a state the greater amounts of power do not necessarily coincide with the higher values.

The alienation of *de facto* power from the higher values brings radical evil into the world. If "the soul of the powerful is the true source of elevated feelings," it is by no means the case that high-ranking qualities when devoid of power are high absolutely, for their value is dubious: "Always, when the higher is *not* the more powerful, it is lacking in some respect: as yet it is only a fragment and a shadow." When, on the other hand, *de facto* power is not combined with superior value, the effect is often ruinous: "The Roman emperors' misuse of power" brought about the victory of the morality of the powerless throughout Europe; for the moral concepts of Christianity were the means of allowing weakness to gain the mastery over misused power, the result being that neither the vanquished power of Rome nor the newly constituted power of Christianity could, as power, represent the higher values: Roman power was too crude, while Christian power was wielded by inferiors. In all these thoughts, the preconceived union of power and value appears untenable; the greater power does not *ipso facto* have the higher value. So long as we simply equate the two, such thoughts as those just noted cannot be harmonized. But it is only by tentatively equating them that we can take Mess to be correct in saying : "This is precisely Nietzsche's meaning, that the Greek is incomparably more powerful than the Roman who is a mere 'ruler' but not a 'lawgiver.' " [2]

[2] *Nietzsche der Gesetzgeber,* p. 200.

After recognizing that power and value do not coincide—although, to start with, they were said to be the same—Nietzsche undertakes to glorify as the true acme of being an intuited but unthinkable power, or again, to deal in penetrating fashion with the question as to why the higher existence is not necessarily also the victorious one.

The first way naturally yields no rationally conceivable results. It leads to merely repetitive phrasings which rise from the hymnic characterizations of life to the mystery of being at a point where all opposites are united and where all high degrees of power involve freedom from good and evil as well as from truth and falsity.

The second way, on the other hand, leads to an illumination of the kinds of evaluation, and these, in turn, to the source of an essential difference between those who want power and those who possess it. But instead of investigating the possibly limitless multiplicity that inheres in the essence of the will to power, Nietzsche concludes by recognizing two original drives (there are "two wills in the battle for power"): that of the strong and that of the weak, that of *ascending* and that of *descending* life, the will to life and the will to nothingness, the instinct to rise and the instinct to perish.

If an increase in power per se were the same as an increase in value, the course of events would be unequivocal, and success in winning power would be a proof of rank. But worldly observation shows that the most powerful in terms of rank can be rendered powerless and even annihilated by those who are devoid of rank but possess *de facto* power. "The strongest are weak when they have to contend with the organized instinct of the herd, the faint-heartedness of the weak, and the overwhelming but merely numerical superiority of the masses. . . . One always has to defend the strong from the weak, and the fortunate from the unfortunate. . . . If one expresses reality in terms of morality, this morality would imply that the average men are more valuable than the exceptional ones. . . . Everywhere I see the survival of those who compromise the value of life." "The weak . . . are more clever as well; . . . they have *more intelligence.*" So the situation is this: "We are more liable to be destroyed by our strengths than by our weaknesses." It may be added that the strong decimate each other; for "it is as natural for the strong to repel each other as for the weak to seek unity." The basic question: "Why did life succumb?" is finally answered: This results from a perversion of values that appeared when the powerless devised scales of value that amounted to a defamation of life, of high values, and of authentic power. The will to power of the powerless is an essentially different kind of will, for it disparages power. This impotent will to power that uses spirit simply as a means to triumph over strength unconsciously causes, in turn, a degenerative change in the entire being of man.

Still, because of the nature of those seeking power, the essential difference between the two forms assumed by the will to power is not thought by Nietzsche to imply the adverse and unqualified conclusion that one of them ought not to exist. Both are necessary. He asks whether the victory of the weak and mediocre does not probably offer a better guarantee of the survival of life, i.e., of the species, and whether this victory is not a necessary defense against something still worse: "Suppose that the strong became dominant in every respect—even in the determination of value. . . . This would lead the weak to despise and seek to . . . exterminate themselves. . . . And would we really want a world devoid of the contributions of the weak: their freedom, deference, spirituality, and pliability?" Furthermore, weakness is necessary because the weaker natures, being more tender and refined, are primarily responsible for all "progress." Finally, defection from life is necessary to life itself: "Even decadence is not something to be attacked," it "is not as such deserving of condemnation," rather it is "a necessary consequence of life."

In this context one can understand why Nietzsche's value judgments seem ambiguous throughout: they derive their peculiar meaning from the standpoint from which they are pronounced. The essence of the will to power always betrays itself, for example, when men, in their existence, face an emergency and then are forced to combat danger: "The weaker one feels driven to join the stronger. . . . The greater this urge for unity, the more readily can one infer weakness; the stronger the urge for variety, difference, and internal decay, the stronger the indwelling force." Paradoxically, true power, in the sense of superior being, can realize itself while rejecting direct increase of strength. "It is perfidious to strive for power. Men of the best quality seek diminution."

How Nietzsche, who regards himself as belonging to the genuinely powerful ones in the battle against both brute force and the *de facto* dominance of the weak, gives final expression to the paradox involved in the relation between power and value, is shown in such statements as the following: "I do not speak to the weak; they wish to obey, and everywhere they fervently embrace slavery. . . . I have found force where no one looks for it: in simple, mild men who have not the least desire to rule."

The Observable Facts from Which Nietzsche Proceeds. The problem of power occupied Nietzsche long before he caught sight of the essence of being in the "will to power." His philosophical leap from a grasp of particular facts in the world through a variety of determinate concepts of power to a metaphysics of existence as the indeterminate will to absolute power is clear. But the tangible empirical data remain as the *terminus a quo* of his metaphysics; and, when viewed in retrospect they appear to supply its confirmation. He collected observations and heaped up interpretative formulations in three areas. A few preliminary statements relating to them may serve as an intimation of what his various writings develop *in extenso:*

1. *The psychology of the feeling of power:* Nietzsche's conception of the "will to power" is by no means identical with his conception of the drives that aim to provide a feeling of power. The one relates to genuine being that has become extra-empirical; the other to observable psychological experience. The one involves an abstract will, intent upon determining the course of its own being; the other, the conscious pursuit of the enjoyment attending the feeling of power. But the psychological is nevertheless an experiential point of departure that provides clarity as well as contrast whenever the will to power is spoken of. Nietzsche develops the psychology of the feeling of power in an especially penetrating fashion.[3]

Nietzsche finds the will to power hiding behind the most surprising disguises. The way it transforms and deceives itself with a view to its own self-satisfaction, and constantly crops up in new places is, to him, one of the fundamental facts of psychic actuality: A person will give expression to his power whether it hurts or benefits others. Those who are by nature proud and strong seek out undaunted beings like themselves in order to struggle against them whenever possible; on the other hand, compassion for others is the most agreeable feeling of power known to those who are without prospects of great conquests. A very old means of gaining consolation in the face of adversity consists in making others suffer for it: even the humiliated are able to provide themselves with a feeling of strength by condemning others and hunting for guilty parties. The struggle for distinction is simply a struggle to overcome one's fellowman.

Nietzsche finds the most spiritual will to power in philosophers and ascetics, priests and hermits: Barbarians find "indescribable happiness in the sight of torture" when they torment others; ascetics find their happiness in tormenting themselves: "Happiness, regarded as the most vivid feeling of power, has perhaps never in the world been carried to a higher pitch than in the souls of superstitious ascetics." The impression made by the will to power in the ascetic even conquers those strong men who

[3] Cf. pp. 134 ff.

express their own will to power in basically outward directions. Thus it is quite understandable that "the most powerful men have always reverently bowed down before the saint, as before the enigma of self-mastery. . . . They sensed in him a superior force. . . . It was the 'will to power' that made them stand in awe before the saint."

But if the will to power, constantly intent upon creating a feeling of power in some form or other, is the cardinal psychic drive, why should there be such a thing as submission at all? Nietzsche gives various answers: "Men are in the habit of subordinating themselves to whatever is intent upon power." The use of power involves exertion and requires courage. The thirst for subjection characterizes the downward process of declining life. But submission that, in these cases, implies the ineffectiveness of the will to power is actually a refined form of the feeling of power. The weak may rightly say: "We subordinate ourselves in order to enjoy the feeling of power." And finally a paradoxical reversal may appear among the strongest: "Precisely those who pursue power most desperately find it indescribably agreeable to feel that they are *overpowered*. . . . To be entirely powerless for once! A plaything of primal forces!"

From such starting-points Nietzsche reaches the conclusion that "the whole of psychology up to the present has rested upon moral prejudices: it has not ventured into depths. As yet no one has suggested that we consider it as morphology and a doctrine concerning the evolution of the will to power. But when he goes on to urge "that psychology should again be acknowledged as the mistress of the sciences, and that the other sciences exist to prepare for and serve her," since she "now more than ever provides an approach to the fundamental problems," this approach does not lead to science, but directly to the metaphysics of the will to power.

2. *Basic sociological constellations of power.* The facts of human society exhibit a basic relation in the absence of which human existence would not endure for an instant: that of master to servant. "Exploitation . . . is a consequence of the genuine will to power. . . . Its reality is the prime factor in all history." Within society and the state there is a constant struggle for power. Nietzsche observes the reality, the motive forces, the disguises, and the weapons of the struggle.

(a) *The life of the Greeks* provides him with the most magnificent panorama of all, since it throws the most light upon the nature of man. It is here that he finds the "tiger-like delight in annihilation," which viewed "the cruelty of victory as the very acme of exuberant jubilation." The

Greeks, in contrast to all the religions and philosophies of the world, did not turn in terror from this mode of life; rather "battle and delight in victory were recognized and accepted." However, the typically Hellenic view recognized, in addition to the bad Eris that provokes the death-struggle, the good Eris that provokes contest through jealousy, envy, and rancor. The contest became the vital basis of the Greek states. Through ostracism they removed those rare individuals whose incontestable superiority would have eliminated all competition so that the contest of forces could be revived. If we remove "the contest from Greek life, we find ourselves peering into a pre-Homeric pit of horrible wild hate and joy in annihilation."

(b) A second picture emerges when we confront the difference between *external de facto power and genuine inner force* in the world of the ancients. The state that cannot attain its ultimate goal tends to expand in monstrous fashion; hence Nietzsche finds nothing sublime in the Roman Empire when he compares it with the Athenian city-state. He regards the decline of Greece as the outstanding example of the fact that greater *de facto* power is not per se higher in value: "The political defeat of Greece was the greatest of cultural misfortunes, for it gave rise to the theory that the cultivation of culture is possible only when men are . . . armed to the teeth. There brute force . . . achieved a victory over the aristocratic genius among the peoples." This underlies Nietzsche's requirement that "the *higher* man should stand at the head of the state" and "the highest man should also be the supreme ruler on earth." If this does not come about, what then? "Political dominance without genuine human superiority is the greatest possible desecration." "Human destiny involves no greater misfortune than for the most powerful men on earth to be less than first-rate. Then everything becomes false, distorted, and monstrous."

(c) The modern *greed for money* provides a third picture of the operation of power within society. It is not real need but a frightful impatience that furnishes the motive-force: "The lust for power makes use of different means, but the same volcano continues to glow . . . and what was at one time done for the sake of God is now done for the sake of money. . . . Today all this provides a superlative feeling of power and an untroubled conscience."

(d) The struggle for power is not only waged against our contemporaries but against the past as it comes down to us through *historical tradition*. A fundamental process in all history is the re-interpretation of the materials of tradition, undertaken by the contemporary will to power, with the result that "anything existing, regardless of its origin, is again and again deliberately seized by a superior power, construed, reformed, and put to some new use."

(e) The will to power *disguises itself* routinely. In the political arena the weak begin by requiring justice of those who hold power. When a second stage is reached, they request freedom, i.e., they wish to break away from those who are in authority. Finally they speak of "equal rights," which is to say that so long as they are not dominant, they wish to prevent their rivals from increasing their strength. The impulse to enjoy power activates the lower classes as well as the princes, but, instead of being expressed as such in the process of self-analysis, it prefers to assume the guise of right and virtue: "How mad our moral judgments are! When one enjoys power, he feels and characterizes himself as good, and that is precisely the time when the others . . . call him . . . evil! . . . The greatest conquerors have always expressed themselves in the pathetic language of virtue. They have always been surrounded by masses of people who, finding themselves in a state of exaltation, would only listen to the most exalted language."

(f) The most effective concealment employed at any time in history by the sort of impotence that seeks power was, in Nietzsche's opinion, the guise assumed by that *slave-morality* which, from its very inception, was essentially opposed to the *morality of the aristocrats*. What determines the natures of the men who stand within any social constellation of forces is not so much the conscious choice of weapons as the implements of warfare unconsciously resorted to. Speaking generally, Nietzsche asserts: "The means which man has discovered for giving himself a feeling of power practically constitute most of our cultural history."

3. *The strong and the weak:* This contrast that permeates Nietzsche's basic exegesis of the will to power has its point of departure in the various ambiguous standpoints which he finds to be implicit in current thought —especially that of the medical profession. Often limited to the imaginative products of contemporary positivistic science, he fails expressly to distinguish clearly empirical findings from the obscure meanings conveyed by general notions: illness in the sense of a distinct, scientifically discoverable process (with its many etiologically distinct varieties), and illness in the merely dyslogistic and question-begging sense. Furthermore, he fails to differentiate between types of reflexive behavior that can be called "sick" and "healthy" (with the result that from his standpoint one who is medically ill may show by his behavior that he is existentially sound, while one who is medically sound may turn out to be existentially ill). Systematic conceptual clarity was not his immediate

goal; verbal contradiction does not obscure his existential intuition, but it does stand in the way of the clarity of his expression, especially when the factual findings of empirical science are involved.[4] In addition, his view would seem to confuse what derives from the comprehensive interpretation of humanity in its entirety with the special knowledge of specific facts about human beings that alone are truly scientific. The cultural types of an epoch are brought under the same categories as neurotic syndromes. Physiologico-psychological modes of human existence and existential modes of basic actuality that never are manifest on the same plane merge without differentiation within the descriptions that characterize them. Only in passing does he separate the declining life that he would have die out from the sort of existence that, in spite of its decline, is valuable as a condition of the life of the rest. His extensive presentations of these things may lead the rationalistic understanding to express its subjective resentment in seemingly objective concepts and, with its presumed knowledge of all modes of existence, to sit imperturbably in judgment. But they weary the devotee of clarity by the repetitiveness with which vague and indeterminate ideas find expression.

Neglecting the numerous psychiatric, physiological, biological, characterological, and sociological expositions that one encounters in reading Nietzsche, we shall set forth a few of the categories which he employs in contrasting *two types of life:*

The character structure of the *weak* is chaotic; of the *strong,* synthetic. The former is "the many-sided man, the interesting chaos"; the latter, the one "in whom the different forces are resolutely yoked together in their pursuit of *one* goal." The weak will, devoid of any unifying center, grows out of a multiplicity of impulses; the strong will, with its precision and clarity of direction, results from the co-ordination of the impulses under the dominance of a single impulse. Among the weak, moderation is a consequence of inability, nonentity, and poverty; among the strong, moderation is delight in restraint, the exultation of the rider on a fiery steed.

The weakling is the man of onesidedness or compromise, the middle of the road, and mediocrity. It is the strong one "who represents the antinomian character of existence in the strongest terms."

The weakling has no strength to withstand stimuli; he who is strong transforms them by assimilating them. In contrast to the sudden and uninhibited reactions of the weak, strength shows itself in procrastination and delayed reaction. The weak, being unable to resist stimuli, are

---

[4] Concerning illness, see pp. 111 ff.

"accidentally conditioned," they "coarsen and exaggerate their experiences to the point of enormity"; depersonalization is the consequence. The strong become masters of accident by converting it into destiny. The strong man may well say: "Whatever does not destroy me makes me stronger." "Things which are open only to the strongest natures—leisure, adventure, disbelief, even debauchery—would necessarily prove fatal to weaker natures if made available to them." "The factors which normally contribute to the diminution of man impel the stronger and rarer natures to attain greatness."

The weak are incapable of coping with experiences; the strong are capable of reconstituting and incorporating them. "There are those who possess so little of this strength that they inevitably bleed to death from one single traumatic experience . . . as from a bleeding laceration." (To be sure, he is *not* speaking of strength and weakness when he says: "I love the one whose soul remains deep even when wounded and who can perish as a result of even a trifling experience"; for here he is dealing with the existential illumination of faithfulness and internality, which proceeds on an entirely different level.) At the level of the opposition between strength and weakness, he asserts that "the strong man, powerful in the instincts of his sound constitution, digests his deeds just as he digests his meals; he is able to cope with heavy fare."

The life of the weak is poor and empty, that of the strong is rich and copious. Both suffer: the one from poverty, the other from superfluity.

The weakling wants peace, harmony, freedom, equal rights; he wishes to live where it is not necessary to defend himself; the strong man is partial to doubtful issues and formidable things. "The one avoids all risks, the other seeks them out." The one is vengeful and vindictive, the other has an aggressive pathos.

The World Interpreted as the Appearance of the Will to Power. In every appearance whatsoever Nietzsche finds the will to power. Wherever he probes "to the bottom of things," he strikes upon this will. All world history is nothing but this will in the multiplicity of its forms.

His metaphysics of the will to power, as he develops it, resembles the dogmatic metaphysical systems of the past. To be sure, when we compare it with the view of Leibniz, we find no monads (subject-atoms), but rather growing or diminishing systems of power units. There is indeed no harmony, except for the constant establishment of positions in the struggle between power-quanta that constitute being itself. As in the case of Leibniz, we find here too a greater or lesser degree of clarity with respect to the monads, which now appear as power quanta (of Nietzsche's interpreting will to power). Distributed throughout the world, these constantly changing, greater and smaller quantities of power constitute genuine being. If one tries to bring together all of Nietzsche's definite thoughts on this subject, he arrives at a relatively systematic whole that seems to correspond formally to the great philosophic speculative systems of the seventeenth century.

Thus Nietzsche, who does everything he can to arouse and preserve our awareness of what is possible, to reveal every last perspective, and to discover countless interpretations, appears to conclude by absolutizing something specific. Instead of reacting to the liberating questions that can no longer be answered in general terms by referring back to the historicity of contemporary autonomous *Existenz,* he seems rather to reply in universal terms when he accounts for authentic being by reifying the will to power.

The whole task of metaphysics, thus narrowly conceived, is a "morphology of the will to power." The "transformation of the will to power, its elaborations and specializations" are to be presented as parallel to the visible appearance of the forms of all things. Nietzsche follows out the far-reaching ramifications of this task. Here we can at most convey a few of the chief points which Nietzsche makes with a directness that sometimes is tremendously impressive, but sometimes proves most strange.

Within this metaphysics, two ways are methodically distinct.[5] (1) Following the first way, Nietzsche seeks to understand the various means of structuring the cosmos which we create through exegesis when we experience our world *cognitively, esthetically, religiously,* and *morally.* This way leads to an exegesis of the exegesis: his own exegesis is used to illumine all the others. While exegetical formulation is said always to proceed from the will to power, it is important to see whether it expresses the will of a rising or a declining, a truly powerful or an actually powerless life, for this is symptomatic. Consequently what interpretation offers as truth, beauty, religion, and morality is always ambiguous: it may appear as a symptom of weakness or of strength, and what is apparently the same content (e.g., nihilism, esthetic intoxication, or the moral law) may have two different meanings, depending upon its foundation. (2) Then again, Nietzsche seeks to interpret the world itself, stressing the *inorganic,* the *organic,* and the *conscious.* Proceeding in this way he construes metaphysically what life misconstrued when, in re-

---

[5] The remainder of the present section (largely in fine print in the original) has been altered slightly for the sake of clarity: a sentence has been displaced, two paragraphs have been consolidated, and the outline of topics has been changed in form though not in content.—Trs.

sponse to a momentarily inescapable but deceptive set of underlying conditions, it provided the exegeses described above. A brief sketch of these two ways follows:

(1) *Interpretative formulations of the world.* (a) *Knowledge:* When Nietzsche is concerned with the truth that is involved in life, he finds its criterion "in a heightening of the feeling of power": the intellect is partial to those "hypotheses" that normally give it a feeling of power and security, and it accepts them as true. That is true "which gives thought the greatest feeling of power," i.e., the mastery of what is provided "by touching, seeing, and hearing—for which the greatest resistance is required."

Accordingly, as he explains, "knowledge is employed as an instrument of power"; "the will to truth is developed in the service of the will to power"; "natural science intends to use its formulae to teach us how to subjugate the powers of nature"; "the degree of our feeling for life and power gives us the measure of being, reality, and the non-illusory."

Nietzsche's "logic" is controlled by this interpretation. The law of contradiction "contains no criterion of truth, but only an imperative relating to that which is to count as true." When he expounds the meaning of specific categories, he always holds that "all meaning is will to power." Even the fact that there are identical instances—this presupposition of categorical knowledge—rests upon the same basis: "The will to identity is the will to power."

(b) *Beauty* is form created by art or made visible by observation. "Our love of the beautiful is . . . the formative will. . . . Our pleasure in forming and transforming is elemental." "The will to beauty" signifies "ruthless development of forms: none but the strongest are truly beautiful."

The significance of art, as the form in which the will to power appears, is that it is "the greatest stimulant to life"; it is the redemption of the knower who sees and wants to see the frightful and questionable character of existence; the redemption of the doer who not only sees this frightful character of existence but wills it as a part of life (the hero); the redemption of the sufferer who learns, through art, of states of mind in which suffering is willed, clarified, deified. The will to power speaks through art, which reveals the state of things without fear of its fearfulness.

The differences in both degree and kind within the will to power appear within the different arts: "The supreme feeling of power and assurance gains expression in that which has a *grand style.*" In architecture, "it is the intoxication of the great will that demands artistic expression; the most powerful men have always inspired architects." Art goes beyond the artist and reaches the innermost being of the world. The will to power and to life would have us hold fast to the illusoriness of the beautiful: "The world itself is nothing but art . . . ; in such a world of illusion as this, the categorical will to knowledge . . . appeared to me as a desecration of the primal metaphysical will."

(c) *Religion and morality* are regarded by Nietzsche chiefly, though not entirely, as modes of appearance of the will to power of the powerless. The religious man is "the one who, feeling himself to be unfree, sublimates his states, i.e., his instinctive tendencies to submission." Morality in the guise of slave-morality is the means to dominance by the poorly endowed.[6]

(d) The powerful will, too, takes the form of morality, but not for morality's sake: it wishes to use it as a means. The will to kindness does not inhere in the nature of things; rather it develops only in social formations, "as a consequence of the fact that a greater whole is concerned to preserve itself against another whole." Seeing the will "from the standpoint of morality" enables us to understand "morality as a doctrine concerning the power relations" under which the phenomenon that we call "life" arises.

The exegesis of phenomena as will to power must assume an entirely different character when these phenomena—ranging from the inorganic through the organic to consciousness itself (which is here regarded as the mere manifestation of an organic function)—are mere natural events that are not aware of themselves or knowable *"ab intra"* by us.

(2) *Nietzsche's metaphysical construction.* (a) *The inorganic world:* What kind of causality lies within inanimate nature? Within these dead elements that we view *ab extra* and try to comprehend by means of subsumption under natural laws and other expressions of regularity, what exists intrinsically and apart from the observer? This old question has been answered repeatedly, but always in an imaginative fashion. Here, too, Nietzsche applies his usual exegesis: If "we believe in the causality of the will, then we must experimentally consider the supposition that there is no other causality; then everything is mechanical occurrence insofar as any force is active in it—even the power and activity of the will."

As the ultimate realities of the inorganic world, there remain, not

---

[6] Cf. *supra,* p. 304.

things, "but rather dynamic quanta, related by attraction to all other dynamic quanta," whose essence consists in their *acting upon* one another. But activity originates through the will to power. "The alleged natural laws are formulae for relations of power." But what is this will to power that we cannot see, experience, or verify empirically? It is "not a being, not a becoming, but a pathos—the most elementary fact and the sole source of becoming and acting."

If the will to power is the ultimate reality, Nietzsche still cannot but think of it as analogous to the will that we experience within ourselves. If everything is simply will, then will must be able to act as will. But how *does* it act? "Naturally will can only act upon will and not upon matter." Will can only prove effective when it perceives another will and is perceived by it: "Inorganic entities can only effect each other . . . through action at a distance; hence 'knowledge' is necessarily presupposed in all efficacy: What is at a distance must be perceived." Accordingly, Nietzsche asserts: "The chemical world is governed by the keenest perception of differences in force."

The perceptual cognitions of the inorganic are not separated into the perceptions, representations, feelings, and thoughts of the will to power. This separation first takes place at the organic level, and inexactness and the possibility of error are the result. That is why perception of force-values and power relations is absolutely exact only within the inorganic world: "There the truth prevails." "Indeterminacy and illusion begin with the organic world."

Consequently Nietzsche finds that, from such a standpoint, the inorganic world looms "higher" than the organic: "The realm where there is no error stands higher: the inorganic is unindividualized spirituality," i.e., it is the will to power that is completely harmonious and identical with itself, undivided, always clearly present and truthful. While organic life is a special case, "the inorganic world standing in the background is, as the supreme synthesis of forces, the highest and most venerable. Error and perspectival limitations are absent from it." Nietzsche views the inorganic with enthusiasm: "The dead world, endlessly moved and infallible, force against force! But within the perceived world all is false and presumptuous." The inorganic is not the opposite of the organic, but the matrix; it is the rule, while the organic is the exception.

(b) *The organic world:* Over against the "unindividualized spirituality" of the inorganic stands the organic as a process of individuation achieved first of all through the constructions and exegeses by which individual living beings create their own worlds: "The whole of the organic world is a closely woven fabric of beings enclosed in small

fictitious worlds . . . their external worlds. . . . Its capacity for creation (formation, fabrication, invention) is basic." "For the sake of
self-preservation, each organic creature has its egoistic angle of vision. It
may only think as far as is conducive to its conservation."

In the second place, this fabricated world that is common to all organic
creatures is made possible by *memory,* which is prior to all consciousness: "What distinguishes the organic from the inorganic is the fact that
it accumulates experiences, as a result of which it is never again the same
as before. . . ." "I assume that memory and a sort of spirit are present in
all the organic: the apparatus is so delicate that to us it scarcely seems to
exist." In every single perceptual judgment the whole previous history of
the organism is active. "In the organic kingdom there is no such thing as
forgetting, but there is a kind of digestion of what has been experienced."

As Nietzsche dwells on the nature of the organic, it increases in
importance (in contrast to the above depreciation of the organic derived
from his esteem of the inorganic): "I am deeply impressed by the
powerful organic principle, especially in view of the ease with which it
incorporates inorganic materials. I do not see how such purposiveness
can be explained simply in terms of progressive development. I would
sooner believe that there are eternal organic beings"; "the organic has
not arisen."

But that which produces and enhances vital organization is neither
intention, nor purpose, nor accident. Rather, Nietzsche's metaphysical
exposition shows "that the appearance of such purposiveness (infinitely
superior to that of all human art) is simply the consequence of the *will to
power* that is operative within all events; that increase in strength produces modes of organization that give the impression of purposiveness;
and that the apparent purposes are not intended. Rather, as soon as the
stronger gains control over the weaker and forces it to labor for its sake,
the order of rank thus achieved must create the illusion of a means-
end relationship."

The will to power does not give rise to an eternally static realm of
forms, but transmutes all forms within the flux of incessant becoming.
Nietzsche inquires about the direction of this process. In opposition to
the supposedly self-evident view that life is proceeding toward higher
forms and that life per se is always higher than lifeless matter, he believes
that, "on the contrary, it is demonstrable that the whole process declines,
right down to man. Man, especially the wisest, as the greatest aberration
of nature and self-contradiction (the being that suffers most): nature
sinks to this point. The organic as degeneration."

He sees the organic as a series of constantly changing realizations of the will to power without any single direction. Even man, as an organic existence, is a specialization of the will to power and consequently a form that in any case is destined to perish. "Man is a surviving total organism proceeding in one single line." From the fact that he still exists, it follows that a distinct system of interpretations—which he is—has not changed. But what is to come next? "Our 'dissatisfaction,' our 'ideal,'. . . is perhaps the consequence of this bit of interpretation that is incorporated in us, i.e., of our perspectival viewpoint. Perhaps organic life will eventually be destroyed as a result of it. . . . There can be no doubt that the downfall of organic life (even in its highest form), as much as the downfall of the individual, is destined."

(c) *Consciousness:* Nietzsche calls the form and life of man his *body*. This is not merely the anatomical corpus, and certainly not the cadaver, but the unconscious, all-encompassing vital functions in their entirety. He finds that in comparison with this body "all consciousness [is] poor and narrow." The spirit cannot even come close to performing what the body has to perform. "How little attains to consciousness in us! . . . Consciousness is a mere instrument, and in view of the many great things accomplished without consciousness, it is not the most necessary. . . . There is perhaps no organ that is so poorly developed. . . . It was, after all, the last organ to appear. . . . Everything conscious is of merely secondary importance. . . . We should keep in mind that the spiritual is the sign-language of the *body.*"

The body is not merely the visible form but the living eventuation of the self-individualizing, encompassing whole of the will to power: "The human body, within which every organic being incorporates and relives all of the past and through and beyond which an enormous stream appears to flow—this body is more astonishing than the old-fashioned soul." Belief in the body is rightly a stronger belief than belief in the spirit. The body is the "great reason" which uses the "little reason" merely as an instrument.[7]

---

[7] When Nietzsche says that "the phenomenon of the body is the richer, clearer, and more comprehensible phenomenon"; that it is "methodically prior"; that it is essential to proceed from the body and to use it as a guide since it permits more precise observation; or that, when one uses the body as a guide, an enormous multiplicity is revealed and that the "richer phenomenon should be used as a guide to the understanding of the poorer"; it is not clear what in the end is meant by "body." For after saying this, he repeatedly takes it as the living corpus, which is the object of biology, and as a result its encompassing character is lost. Use of the body as a guide then turns out to be a merely methodical demand, which Nietzsche has observed only in a very general way. For example, he learns, by proceeding "from the body and from physiology," "how the unity of the subject is properly represented, viz., as supreme regent in a society . . . that depends on the subjects and on the

The general purport of these thoughts is a disparagement of consciousness, which, in Nietzsche's view, is nothing in and by itself. In reply to those who overestimate it, he alleges that consciousness hobbles along behind, observes only a little at one time, and, even then, pauses for other things; that it only scratches the surface, is a mere on-looker of the inner as well as the outer world—and not even this until it has arranged them both to suit itself. Furthermore, the conscious is merely symptomatic of a richer world of extra-conscious real occurrence; it is only an end-product, devoid of causal efficacy, as a result of which all conscious sequence is completely atomistic.

But what is this real occurrence which consciousness serves merely as a tool? Will to power again: "Every thought, feeling, and volition . . . is a total state resulting from the momentary power-relations of *all* the drives that enter into our constitution." "That which we call consciousness is only a means and an instrument through which a struggle—not a subject—undertakes to preserve itself." "Actually we do not see the struggle, for this takes place behind the scenes."

Now the question is how consciousness could have originated at all. It must be understood in terms of the service it renders to the will to power. Nietzsche explains it in terms of a situation brought about by need. Need forces men to understand each other quickly and accurately. There is no mutual understanding without consciousness. "The refinement and strength of consciousness always appears to stand in relation to human *capacity for communication* and this latter, in turn, in relation to the *need for communication*." Consciousness is the net which holds men together: "The development of speech and the development of consciousness go hand in hand."

In view of this origin, Nietzsche finds it to be a special property of consciousness *not* to be a special property of the single individual as such. Consciousness belongs "not really to the individual existence of men" and is, on the contrary, "only well developed in connection with its usefulness to the community and the herd." Being "non-individual," it is "the lowest common denominator" of man—"a mere means to communication," rather than the "complete sensorium and highest instance."

Since consciousness has no basis within itself and is merely a product

---

conditions of division of labor and social stratification . . . so that the struggle is expressed even in commanding and obeying. . . ." At this point he simply repeats, without further elaboration, the old idea that "the visible organic life and the invisible creative way of thinking and governing the soul present a parallelism." But, as a statement of a cognitive method, this thought is dubious, and Nietzsche has in fact not derived from it a more accurate understanding, but only an inclination to allow a biological way of speaking constantly to pass for insight.

of need, it is much too prone to err: "The degeneration of life is essentially conditioned by the extraordinary fallibility of consciousness." "All genuine activity is unconscious"; "we must seek the full life where there is the least possible awareness of it."

Then again, Nietzsche finds consciousness to be replete with essential and enigmatic significance. It is "a process that deepens and internalizes itself" or that constantly comes closer to the biological center. What consciousness somehow achieves when I reach out my arm is unintelligible; here knowledge and action lie in two different realms. "On the other hand, Napoleon carries through the plan of a campaign. In this case everything is *known* . . . because everything must be commanded; but still this presupposes subordinates to interpret the universal and adapt it to the necessity of the moment."

But the following statements sound like an appeal to consciousness: "Nature is dumb, and insofar as we are all nature, we are all dumb. Even dumbness has a pretty name, for it is called necessity. Let us come to the assistance of necessity!"

A Critical Characterization of the Metaphysics of the Will to Power. If one explores the many ways in which Nietzsche seeks to conceive of the will to power as the essence of all things, he arrives at the following over-all view: The *form* of Nietzsche's thought is that of a *hypothesis* specifying *the basis presumed to underlie things*. All phenomena are explained in terms of the unity from which they derive: everything is "nothing but," "merely," or "only," will to power in its modifications. What is regarded as itself the underlying basis of things is only arrived at by absolutizing a something that quite commonly appears within the world. The many sense-verifications in empirical observation are fused with an interpretative construct as absolutizing thinking applies them to being itself in a manner that is no longer empirically verifiable or controllable.

When Nietzsche does in fact embrace this metaphysical way of thinking, there can be no doubt that it is at loggerheads with both his starting-point and his aim.

In the first place, he is aware that the will to power which underlies all events is "unknown" [8]: to have a name is one thing, to be known is another. Exegesis *within* the world by means of conceptual fixation differs essentially from exegesis *of* the world as a whole. The latter settles nothing, derives nothing, but simply reads the cipher of the One. Hence,

[8] Cf. *supra*, p. 294.

in the second place, he knows that instead of devising a hypothesis about the being that underlies things, he is in search of that "by which all things can recognize their kinship with it."[9]

If we hold fast to Nietzsche's real starting-point, then, concerning what he expresses in his increasingly metaphysical and dogmatic thesis, we must ask what it signifies as a cipher, to what extent everything can recognize itself as akin through it, and what sort of actual and even essential things there might be that are not represented by it.

The conception of the world as the will to power gives a clear conscience to the struggle per se if everything is involved with and transformed into instruments of warfare. This world-view supplies the context within which the exultation of power reaches its highest affirmation. It constantly encourages and propels the will to fight. All the de facto power and lust for battle found in human existence not only acknowledges kinship with it but derives from it a heightened sense of importance.

Still everything depends upon what will to power affirms itself and what it claims to be. The qualitative differences and the rank-order of the different kinds of wills to power and of the various forms which power can assume decide the value of a concrete lust for battle. Although Nietzsche's metaphysics itself brings this out, ambiguity soon appears in relation to the question of who may feel such kinship and in what way he may feel it. For sometimes kinship may be enjoyed indiscriminately by all existence while, at other times, such enjoyment depends upon rank.

It confirms the thesis of this metaphysics that its acceptance must be conceived as an act of the will to power. As understood by Nietzsche, it is a suitable world-view for strong supporters of the counter-movement directed against nihilism.

The limits of this metaphysical thesis could be precisely demarcated only by showing just what would not recognize kinship with it. Nietzsche's exegesis does not illustrate, with complete thoroughness, the principle of relationship with everything that exists. To be sure, it takes into account the part played in human creation by the will to power and recognizes the possibility that all things may sink to the level of mere means to this will. However, the exegesis misses something within the original being of human Existenz that has nothing to do with will to power and is, in fact, only discoverable apart from it. The will to power is unrelated to the self-being that acknowledges responsibility for itself, to the independent point that is unconditioned and exists only in relation to transcendence, to communication as loving struggle that neither wills

[9] Cf. supra, p. 294.

nor exerts power, and to the truly free and open horizon. To be sure, Nietzsche's metaphysics unveils the perversions of these types of essential being, but their true substance remains untouched.

The essential point here is that this metaphysics of radical immanence undertakes to read the ciphers of being as will to power *apart from transcendence.* He who knows himself to exist in relation to transcendence cannot see himself as having any kinship within its confines. Existence reveals a being that struggles against the possibility of this metaphysics (although the struggle for power is alien to its nature) and that refuses to be encompassed by this exegesis. It accepts Nietzsche's endeavor to illumine specific aspects of the world in a realistic manner, but it turns away when he thereby attempts to apprehend being itself.

A further limit to this metaphysics appears in the exegesis of the *inorganic* and *organic* realms since, at these levels, the kinship can be acknowledged *only by us* who look on. What is involved here is a mere matter of analogies to the power-will and to power-relationships, devoid of cognitive value and incapable of exhibiting any genuine kinship.

In connection with this demarcation of the limits of the will to power, what is essential and characteristic of the entire course of Nietzsche's thought is that *limitations are observed by Nietzsche himself.* A doctrine in which he can entirely acquiesce never occurs to him, and he holds every view in check by opposing it to other views. *The doctrine of the will to power is not his definitive metaphysics, but a thought-experiment performed within the more extensive whole of his investigation of being.* His discontent with this metaphysics is shown by the fact that it contrasts with and supplements his account of *life* and by the further fact that it is overshadowed by his doctrine of *eternal recurrence,* which, in its turn, proves to be merely relative.

Thus the truth for Nietzsche does not relate to such objectives as, at an earlier date, occupied the rationalistic thoughts of the dogmatic metaphysicians. Rationalistic truth appears in conceptual constructs. But these are by no means paramount to Nietzsche; he does not think that they provide the final truth about being itself, even though from time to time he seems to succumb to his own thought-experiment, as it assumes dogmatic form.

Nietzsche's genuine philosophizing first comes to the fore when that level is reached at which every doctrine without exception can become relative. To force one's way into this region, one must break through every confining enclosure and defend the enigmatic character of existence against whatever dogmatic world-view threatens to destroy it.

The World as Pure Immanence

All metaphysical thought from Parmenides through Plato and Christianity to Kant accepted and elaborated upon *the theory of two worlds:* Underlying our world of the finite and perishable, of becoming, and of the temporal and illusory is a world of being in itself, timeless, unending, eternal, and true. In religious terms: There is a God.

Whatever the terms in which the contrast is stated, Nietzsche's resistance is invariably aroused when the beyond is opposed to the here and now, the unseen to the seen, the true world to the merely apparent, or a blissful world to this world of woe. To him this contrast is mere exegesis, as is, in fact, *all* ontological knowledge. In contending with the two-world theory, he is concerned to repudiate, not exegesis as such, but rather a very specific exegetical principle. Exegeses are not of equal value; some take precedence over others.

Nietzsche's Reasons for Repudiating the Theory of Two Worlds. The true world, no matter how it is conceived, is in fact *only the apparent world all over again.* The duplication is superfluous if the other world is unknown and indescribable except through repetition of categories and contents taken from the world we know. He does not reject the possibility of countless worlds in addition to this one in which and as which we are. But these worlds would in no way concern us, while the assertion that the other world is the only true one affects our entire *Existenz.*

The meaning of the two-world theory is shown by the motives from which it springs: When the world confronts men with accident, uncertainty, and sudden shock, they regard it as evil and are afraid. When realistic measures prove incapable of coping with what frightens them, they struggle against it by devising an objectively futile but subjectively comforting exegesis of events: The event was brought about by a person (the Godhead), and men can make a covenant with Him and thus forestall evil. Or again, men may avail themselves of the other account of evil: things only *seem* to be evil, though, in the long run, they are for the best—or perhaps our misfortunes are well-deserved punishments. In any case, this interpretation enables men to resign themselves to evil in such a way that their fear of it and their active efforts really to master it are reduced. Men also fear transitoriness and even change as such; but they comfort themselves by devising another realm of being that, although unknown, is permanent and stable. They fear their own passions (the lust for power, for carnal pleasures, and so forth) and allow them to disappear from the actual world in order to equate liberation from them with authentic being. Always such an exegesis is a flight from this world to another that in truth is nothing. "Instinctive weariness with life has created the other world."

Once the other world is asserted, it maintains itself by new entice-ments: being unknown it attracts us with hopes of adventure and encour-ages unfounded presumptions. Just because the familiar world of the here and now is already known to us, we pass up the opportunity to investigate it further. We easily think that all will probably be well in so different a world, and we hope that we ourselves will be different. We are led to believe that even the present world could be otherwise, and in this way necessity and fate are annulled. Because the other world is the true world, it appears to issue a moral appeal to regard this present world as untruthful, dishonest, counterfeit, and inessential.

The result of such dualism is the defamation of the world and of life. It is just this world within which men have to live and adjust themselves that is discredited. The "true" world "is the great doubter and de-preciator of the *world that we are:* it has been the most dangerous assassin of life."

Nietzsche has not always simply denied the idea of a true world, especially when it originated as an exegesis produced by the strength of the will to power. This is brought out by his constantly self-contradictory relation to Plato: Plato as an artist prefers appearance to being. The artist sees the real value of a thing in the shadowy remains which it leaves him. As he sees it, the less reality, the more value. But Plato goes beyond this in boldness and flexibility when he says: The more ideal, the more being. He prefers the unreal to the existent and calls it genuine being. This true world is in fact accessible to the wise man who dwells in it and *is it.* It amounts to saying: I, Plato, *am* the truth. The idea of the true world, coming from this source, in which, in place of fearfulness and escapism, the mighty power of the creative person is evident, later undergoes a change: In Christianity this world is presently unattainable, but promised to the sinner who repents. In time it becomes a mere *thought* which can be neither attained nor promised, though even as a thought it continues to console men and place them under obligation. It is the old sun, seen through the fog of skepticism as "pale, northern, and Königsbergian." Finally, *as absolutely unknown* and robbed of its ca-pacity to console and command, it surrenders its last vestige of signifi-cance to positivism (agnosticism). The time for its abolition has come. But the abolition which Nietzsche brought about does not mean that now the phenomenal world remains for us, for it has been abolished along with the true world, and the horizon is now open to the world of Nietzsche.

Pure Immanence as Becoming, Life, and Nature. Just what is left after both worlds have been abolished? Nietzsche speaks of (1) *becoming,* (2) *life,* and (3) *nature,* meaning thereby that only the wholly unsettled and essentially unthinkable truly is. He refers to it as the true and the actual, but since to speak of it is to reify it, he must either falsify it as he speaks of it or allow it to disappear.

(1) For the "being" of the philosophers, who have only imaginings to show for the things which they conceived of as existing permanently, Nietzsche substitutes *becoming* as that which alone actually is. Hence permanence does not have value—it does not even exist. Rather Nietzsche enters a plea for the "value of the briefest and most ephemeral, for the seductive gold glistening on the belly of the serpent *vita*—." This must not be taken to mean that we should surrender ourselves to the accidental occurrences of the moment ("If you believed more strongly in life, you would less readily submit to the instant. . . . You are too poor within to be able to wait"). On the contrary, it means that that which ventures, sacrifices itself, and vanishes is the only actual, genuine, and valuable form of being. To comprehend being in this sense, one must take it seriously for what it is. A "beyond" would make this impossible. To locate the essence of life outside of life in the "beyond"—in nothing—is to remove from life all that is essential to it: *"non alia sed haec sempiterna."* This new eternity of being that Nietzsche encountered in becoming will appear in the next chapter as "eternal recurrence."

(2) Objecting to everything rigid, abstract, and merely supposed, and to the deflection toward the nothing of an alien "beyond," Nietzsche pleads the case for *life.* On the one hand, "life" is the word which he uses to refer to existence insofar as it can be subsumed in the categories of biology; on the other hand, it is the sign with which he refers to that ultimate being which we, and we alone, genuinely are. Life, thus affirmed as unconditioned, can never be other than ambiguous. Its meaning is no sooner expressed than it shifts from the *encompassing of authentic being* to the *determinacy of a particular existence* viewed as the subject-matter of biology. Even the affirmation can be conveyed only by means of constant negations directed against those forms of life which *fall short of authentic life.* On the whole this is what is meant when he says: "Is life a duty then? Nonsense!" Life as mere existence need not possess value; it can, in fact, become downright dubious. When Nietzsche sees life that is ugly and repugnant, when he "dislikes monsters" and "bears a grudge

against will-o'-the-wisps" and "all that comes from the swamp," he seems to ask: "Is life then a swamp?" And still he is hostile "to all who seek to cast suspicion on the value of life." Here all depends upon distinguishing between mere life and authentic life. This he does for instance by contrasting rising and declining life and by recognizing various other orders of rank—though always by appealing to the possibilities of *Existenz* rather than by exhibiting objective states of affairs. Still the claim to *Existenz* that repeatedly emerges from his sayings is not relevant at this point, for reliable contact with *Existenz* is not possible when one conceives of life as pure immanence. On the contrary, this concept of life leads inevitably to linguistic tergiversations ending in a biological sort of knowledge which in this case is altogether spurious.

For this reason Nietzsche repeatedly turns away from such dogmatic finalities. It is precisely the boundless ambiguity permeating all the phenomena of life that he then affirms directly: "Perhaps this is the most powerful magic that life possesses: a gold-embroidered veil of charming possibilities covers it, promising, resisting, modest, mocking, compassionate, seductive. Yes, life is a woman!" (*vita femina*). Such ambiguity can indeed awaken mistrust: "Trust in life is gone. . . . It is love for a woman who causes us to doubt her"; but still this mistrust is amalgamated with the unconditional affirmation of life that dominates Nietzsche's thinking, of a life no longer existing as a thought but as a Dionysian state exuberantly evoked in the "Dancing Songs" of *Zarathustra*.

Death belongs to life: "Let us guard against saying that death is opposed to life." His comments on death derive from his philosophy of a life devoid of transcendence, characterized as it is by the way death appears to him. Men are confronted by death and they react to it, and Nietzsche has to interpret this exclusively in terms of life. Life is to him the *signum* of a creative *Existenz* that receives its meaning from creation but, at the same time, is conceived (often exclusively) as a biological object to be investigated by sound scientific research. In any case it is meant to be merely vital and thus devoid of transcendence. Hence he regards death and the realm of the dead as actually nothing at all.

But throughout the whole of the Occident, he encounters fear [10] of the after-death—an attitude radically different from his own—the historical

---

[10] Translations of *Angst* in contemporary existentialist literature are anything but scarce. L. B. Lefebre, in a small glossary in P. A. Schilpp's *The Philosophy of Karl Jaspers* (p. xvi), uses the term "anguish" in preference to the term "dread" which, as he says, relates more closely to Sartre's concept. Werner Brock, in *Existence and Being* (p. 44), uses "dread" for *Angst* and "fear" for *Furcht* and emphasizes that the latter alone is object-directed. R. W. Bretall, the anthologist of Kierkegaard,

origins of which he knows through the study of the mystery religions, Egyptian escatology, Judaism, and Christianity. To this attitude his philosophy of life is fundamentally opposed: death is "final,". . . "the after-death is no concern of ours." Death removes all fear of anything that might follow it. Conversely, knowledge of the pure nothingness of death provides good grounds for avoiding fear of anything that life still has in store for us: "Death is close enough to keep us from being afraid of life."

Death is either a *natural* and unavoidable occurrence, or it can be deliberately brought about through *suicide*. One must adjust to both: to the certainty of the one and possibility of the other.

Natural death, the end that comes sometime or other without my assistance, is not frightful to Nietzsche. What he means by life is by no means a wanting-to-live-forever and being-unable-to-die, but rather a rising above life for the sake of life: "The more fully and energetically one lives, the sooner he is ready to surrender life for a single good experience." Viewed as an end, death itself is really an expression of life. One can attain mastery over death and life through the way in which he conceives of them: "One should make a festival of his own death, if only from sheer spite against life: against this woman who wishes to abandon us—us!"

Thus from the certainty of the creative fullness of life, Nietzsche turns scornfully against every form of fear of death. In the first place, this appears as a generally shared fear that "is perhaps older than pain and pleasure." It is the will to live endlessly, the desire merely to be alive, which, being devoid of energy, is not real life. In the second place, this fear appears as a "European sickness" which derives from a horror of what comes after death. One who succumbs to it is held captive by the fear of hell.

Nietzsche is one of a series of thinkers who wish to overcome every form of fear of death because it is existentially ruinous and a sign of an *Existenz* lacking in self-reliance. These thinkers wish to conquer both the fear that is rooted in an empty greediness for life and the fear that concerns various sufferings and punishments to be experienced in the

---

insists in private conversation that *Angst* should surely be translated "anxiety." However the translators are inclined to believe that what Nietzsche meant nearly a hundred years ago is probably best conveyed by the word "fear": unaffected by later existentialist interpretations of *Angst,* he is simply referring to the universally experienced emotion, the fear of death. That he has the noun invariably followed by the preposition *vor* seems to indicate the object-directedness of the state in question. A precedent for this is to be found in *Christianity and Fear* by Oscar Pfister, as translated by W. H. Johnson.—Trs.

hereafter. Liberation from it is the condition and consequence not only of the full life in Nietzsche's sense but also of the existential truthfulness of the rapture which, as Kierkegaard has illumined it, is made possible by transcendence. But it is characteristic of Nietzsche's philosophy of life that it can lead to the following deviation:

Since fear of death is always a sign of an insipid existence, Nietzsche can oppose it by endorsing even the typical failure to dwell upon death and the general thoughtlessness about it—as though death simply did not occur. Since death is the only certainty of the future, Nietzsche finds it "most remarkable that this one thing which is sure and common to all should have almost no influence over mankind." But this does not lead him to remind and arouse us. Quite the contrary: "I am happy to see," he writes, "that men simply refuse to entertain thoughts of death! I should like to do something to make the thought of life still a hundred times more valuable to them."

In Nietzsche's view, ascendency over death is properly actualized above all in suicide. Throughout his whole life he praised, as truly worthy of man, voluntary (rational) death as opposed to involuntary (natural) death. "We must transform the stupid fact of physiology into a moral necessity." Natural death is "death under the most contemptible circumstances, an unfree death, death at the wrong time, the death of a coward. From sheer love of life we should will death to be otherwise: free, conscious, without surprise, and non-accidental."

Why does this passion for the greatness of man in suicide express itself through Nietzsche—as it did through the ancient tradition, especially the philosophy of the Stoics? Nietzsche too distinguishes the essence of man, his innermost self-being, from his body and its mere existence, the "heart and core" from the "wretched stuff of the shell." In natural death, the body "is the withering, often ill and stupid gaoler, the master who decides the point at which his aristocratic prisoner is to die. Natural death is nature's suicide, that is to say, it is the annihilation of the rational being by the irrational." Nietzsche transcends life to a more-than-life, from the standpoint of which life can be judged, affirmed, and denied, but he does this in such a way that this innermost essence of man—his more-than-life—is itself still thought of as life, as pure immanence, and not as *Existenz* confronting transcendence. Since there is nothing outside of it, life, thus understood, is not merely empowered but required to pronounce true judgment on the whole of its existence and its possibilities. This judgment is to evaluate the significance of life, i.e., to determine whether or not it is "creative."

But then again, narrowing the scope of the judgment, he deals with sickness insofar as it makes creation impossible: "He who is sick is a parasite within society. There are states in which it is indecent to live any longer. Continuing to vegetate in cowardly dependence upon the practitioners of medical science when life has lost all meaning and all justification should be held in utmost contempt by society. The doctors in turn would have to be the mediators of this contempt. . . ."

This miserable state of long drawn-out illness leading to death, as well as any kind of empty though protracted life, is contrasted with suicide as a "consummatory death": "The consummator dies his death victoriously, surrounded by those who hope and vow. . . . To die in this manner is best of all, the second best is to die in battle. . . . But hateful to the fighter as well as to the victor is your grinning death that sneaks up like a thief. . . . Let your spirit and your virtue shine forth even in your death like an evening glow on the earth, or your dying will have come off poorly."

This attitude is intended to conquer natural death by turning it into a free act. Death is to be transformed into an act of *life,* i.e., an act of the more-than-life that oversees and controls life. From this it should follow that if all existence were completely successful, no one would die a natural death any more, but all would die the "free death," "at the right time": "The eminently wise authorization and regulation of death belongs to the still entirely unthinkable and immoral sounding morality of the future, whose dawning must give unspeakable happiness to those who witness it."

The decisive question concerning free death is: When is the "right time"? Nietzsche considers two possibilities. First of all, he thinks of those whose existence from the very beginning was never "the right kind of life": "If one has never lived at the right time, how could he die at the right time? Would that he had never been born!" Nietzsche would have death preached to the "superfluous" and to the "many-too-many." To such men he says: "When one does away with himself, he does the most estimable thing there is; as a result he almost deserves to live. . . . The others no longer have to endure the sight of him." But who could find such words meaningful, and how could such a person be identified? Paradoxically, these words are *entirely clear* to anyone who *can* assimilate them and yet *entirely senseless* when understood, for *he who understands them deserves to live.* It is precisely the man of high rank who, in a moment of logical confusion, could be driven to suicide by this command while one of lower rank, for whom alone it is intended, would be totally unmoved by it.

In the second place, Nietzsche considers those who have lived well.

When is the "right time" for them? When their creative activity has come to an end; when it is "the right time for termination and succession"; when they are sufficiently advanced to make it impossible to live "meaningful and creative lives." If the time of death is actually to be determined, it should be stated in the most general and indeterminate fashion. If the matter were settled by argument, application to a specific case would lead to the following result: Either it is not yet the right time, or it always is the right time, depending upon my evaluation of myself, or that of the one who views my present life with sympathy or antipathy, as the case may be. Or again the question of the "right time" could be stated in terms of an external and brutalizing objective criterion. Or finally the demand that one freely decide upon the instant of his death could be subject to the demand that he so live as to be capable of making the decision: "So to live as to have the will to death when the right time arrives!" This is indeed a command that reaches down to a most profound level, but at the same time it is entirely indefinite, and it excludes all possibility of determination and communication in such a way that, as a command, it either vanishes or is transformed, even while it is being uttered.

This command confronts man with an impossible task. The *absence of transcendence* in his philosophy of life places in man's hand all the possibilities of being as though they were entirely subject to his control and capable of being realized through his creative efforts. But man is not and never can be like a God who surveys everything. Still, profound knowledge may offer various possibilities of action to an exception estranged from the world who withdraws from sight by mysteriously eluding all generally applicable descriptive terms. What is here touched upon is a secret of human nobility, a possibility of magnificent independence, something that could amount to the incommunicable claim that a heroic soul makes on himself—in his loneliness and unobtrusive distantiation from the vulgarity of those who judge him either admiringly or accusingly. But it is impossible to make clear, through reverent illumination, the mystery that could speak through this possibility ("Die at the right time!"), whether it is mentioned, taught, or commanded. When viewed in the light of historical reality, it turns into its opposite.

The position that Nietzsche explicitly takes toward death is a necessary consequence of the deliberate omission of transcendence from his philosophy. This omission appears in two forms:

As long as he thinks in this way, death can never preserve its profundity. Man's awareness of his finitude and the possibility of his becoming resigned to and standing firm in the face of the riddle, must be mistakenly regarded by Nietzsche as possible "only in a religious sense," "for then, as is proper, the higher reason (of God) gives its command to which lower reason has to submit. Apart from the religious way of thinking, natural death is unworthy of glorification." Nietzsche's attitude stands opposed "to the miserable, atrocious comedy that Christianity has made of the hour of death." At the very least, he believes "that the act of dying is not as significant as the reverence generally accorded it would indicate," and, viewing the mere physiological process from the narrow standpoint of the unaffected observer, he can say: "There is no greater banality among men than death."

That death, as a mere occurrence that man is able to deal with, has lost the profundity which it can have only in relation to transcendence, has, in the second place, a connection with the fact that within Nietzsche's philosophizing the dead are not present as dead. No metaphysical recollection penetrates his being, and there is no immortality (in place of which appears an "eternal recurrence" without recollection).[11] The great men of the past stand before his eyes in broad daylight and, as it were, without transparency. It is as though the whole mythical ground of existential being that is bound up with the dead were lost in this philosophy of life that does not go beyond the rapture of creativeness. As a result of the absolutizing of life, death as such is reduced to a matter of no importance.

(3) In opposition to transcendence of every description, to God and morality, to the "denaturalization of morality" and the "denaturalization" that would accept the good, the beautiful, and the true for their own sakes, Nietzsche demands the *"reinstatement of nature,"* the "recognition of a nature-morality," and "purely naturalistic values in the place of moral values."

In contrast to the view of Rousseau which is easily confused with this, Nietzsche does not actually mean "return to nature," but an ascent "into the elevated, free and even fearful nature and naturalness, which deals and dares to deal with great tasks. . . . To express it through example: Napoleon was an instance of a return to nature as I see it." But there is no such thing as a *"return* to nature," "for there never yet has been a natural humanity. . . . Man attains to nature only after a long struggle; he never returns." This nature is nothing other than "the frightful basic text *homo natura";* it is a question of transferring man back into nature.

But it is almost impossible to discover, from the philosophical lan-

---

[11] The "Isle of Tombs" (*Zarathustra,* Part II, Chap. 11) is not a case to the contrary, for there an entirely different meaning of this simile prevails.

guage employed by the ancients—as well as by Nietzsche—what nature really is. Sometimes "nature" is taken to mean the subject-matter of the natural sciences, i.e., the forces that can be governed by man, but at other times it refers to the essence of man himself and to absolute being.

Nietzsche does recognize the misuse of the word "nature" of which he himself is guilty whenever he demands that nature be reinstated: "So you wish to live in accordance with nature," he says to the Stoics. A being such as nature "is indifferent beyond measure . . . , at once fruitful and barren and uncertain. If you regard this indifference itself as power, how can you live in accordance with it? . . . And suppose your imperative: 'Live in accordance with nature' signifies basically the same thing as 'live in accordance with life,' then how could you do otherwise? Why make a principle of that which you yourself are and must be?" It is as though he refutes his own statements when he says of the "natural": "Evil has always produced the most striking effects! And nature is evil! Let us then be natural. This is the kind of reasoning employed by those who wish to create a sensation." Even during his youth, after viewing a storm, he expressed his acceptance of nature's tremendous superiority to human good and evil: "I experienced an incomparable rapture. . . . What did I care about man and his agitated willing! What did I care about the eternal 'You ought,' and 'You ought not'! How different was the lightning, the storm, the hail: unrestrained forces devoid of anything ethical!" (to von Gersdorff, Apr. 7, '66). But later on he speaks disparagingly of this "pleasure at the sight of nature's grandiose indifference to good and evil" as a sort of nature-experience on the part of a "nihilistic artist."

When Nietzsche views the "grandiose model," "man in nature—the weakest, subtlest being—making himself master and placing the more stupid forces under his yoke," and then demands "that henceforth man should stand out from man as today he already . . . stands in front of the other nature," one is inclined to ask: "What then is man himself? Is he perhaps nature become master of nature?" But Nietzsche is more concerned with the "overcoming of nature by great men," and only the distinction between man's innermost self and his nature would make possible the criterion that he sets up in order to determine "the extent to which one can say Yea! to his own nature."

"Naturalization" points to something that is nullified by the contradictions that arise from the very way in which it is stated. It is a question whether the means provided by pure immanence permit even this immanence to be grasped. But such pure immanence is what Nietzsche is after.

The Self-Destruction of Nietzsche's Thoughts about the World. Whether the world-process be viewed as becoming or life or [12] nature, this process of being is to Nietzsche a process of interpreting and being interpreted. That he applies the expression "apparent world" to the worlds that the creative activities of interpreters have actualized even after he has repudiated the distinction between the actual and the apparent world ("the question is whether there could not be many ways of creating such an apparent world") constitutes for him an unavoidable contradiction, for on his own showing the apparent world is the true one. That he himself cannot escape from the snare that his way of expressing these distinctions provides testifies to an insuperable difficulty. He himself made this obvious:

If, on the one hand, our intellect is so constructed that it must place everything in a perspective (i.e., exegetically create its own world) for the sake of the preservation of the species and if, on the other hand, it is capable of recognizing such perspectival seeing for what it is, then the intellect must at one and the same time *believe that its reality is the only one* and also *recognize that this belief is a perspectival limitation.* "But when a belief is viewed with this insight, it is no longer belief; *qua* belief it is vitiated."

Nietzsche here clearly refers to his own method of world-exegesis. But his attitude toward it is self-contradictory. At times he sees in it the possibility of soaring-above-life and discovering our true inner strength capable of mastering the antinomy,[13] but at other times he is ready to repudiate this destructive knowledge of the cognitive process as a logical impossibility: "We must not entertain the self-contradictory notion that our intellect is at one and the same time a belief (*Glaube*) and an explicit awareness that it is merely a belief." To be sure, the basic distinction between the true and the illusory (identified by him with that between reality and appearance) which he must constantly employ forces him to interpret our intellect in the self-contradictory fashion which he here repudiates by applying for once—and by way of exception—the law of contradiction as the final test of the truth of his assertions concerning an intellect that is both exegesis and knowledge of its own exegetical nature. Hence when he concludes: "Let us get rid of the thing-in-itself and, along with it, one of the most obscure concepts of all, that of appearance," he is in no position to do this, notwithstanding his convincing rejection of the particular existential formulations that slander the world

---

[12] Reading *oder for der.*—Trs.
[13] Cf. p. 197 ff. in the chapter entitled "Truth".

and life when they express themselves through some form of the two-world theory while evading the world in their oblique flight into the beyond. Nietzsche is impelled by a source of clarity and breadth of world-understanding that seems at times to show itself for an instant, only to become entangled and futile.

What, in Nietzsche's meditations on truth, was an expressive circle constantly giving rise to new movements of thought, finally becomes, in his thoughts of the world, an annulment of a metaphysics now become dogmatic: that of the will to power, as a militant exegesis temporarily believed. Here the contradictions become incapacitating, for there is a dead finality about them that prevents them from giving rise to anything new. At most we can hope for an emancipation from *this* metaphysics insofar as it purports to be more than one possible specific metaphor designed to raise the question of the extent to which we can sense a relationship to it and the point at which the relationship ceases.

In criticizing the two-world theory, Nietzsche only dealt with its formulation as a crude rationalistic dualism that does indeed end in an empty beyond or in nothingness. In thinking in this fashion, he had to dispense with all those ways of using the categories "reality and appearance," "truth and illusion," "being and existence," which permit them— apart from any assumption about the world outside of the present one— to express such existential tenets as the transparency of things and the cipher-nature (*Chiffresein*) of the world. During these periods of his thinking, he took no cognizance of all those interpretations of world-being, gained in meditative probing, in which (in accordance with his own demands) no concession is made to what does not show itself to be present here and now and which yet avoid a narrowing of world-being to particular categories or to that which can be grasped in determinate knowledge: in them, no "other world" reflects a deceptive dream, and their relation to absolute transcendence (God) supports, within this world, the self-being of those who entertain them in their thoughts.

6

BOUNDARIES AND SOURCES

Man does not inquire concerning the *nature* of existence without at the same time asking about the *value* of existence. Unlike the beings that live passively and uncritically within the world, man—and man alone—is capable of asking whether he cares to live or not, whether life is worthwhile or not, or whether existence is better than non-existence. Existence, thus arraigned and interrogated, so to speak, is either condemned or justified as the case may be. Justification, when the existence of a divine creator is presupposed, amounts to a justification of God (theodicy), but the question arises on the atheistic view of being as well as on any other. Subjectively it appears as a question about one's own affirmation or negation of life, objectively it concerns the meaning and value of the world.

Nietzsche raises in an original fashion the ancient question of theodicy, most profoundly expressed during antiquity in the *Prometheus* of Aeschylus and in the *Book of Job* and rationally argued by Leibniz in more recent times. From the question about meaning and value his philosophizing gains its overwhelming impetus, and from the way in which he affirms being, or rather from his *thinking of the affirmation*—synonymous for him with being itself—it attains fulfillment.

The question of the value and meaning of existence is unlike any other question: man does not seem to become really serious until he faces it. Nietzsche is astonished by the fact that it is rarely asked and even more astonished by the observation that man's desire for knowledge can proceed without it. The youthful Nietzsche is amazed at the scientific man who behaves "as though existence were other than hopeless and questionable; . . . every step should make him think: *Why? Whither? Whence?* But his soul grows ardent over the task of counting the filaments of a flower." Once the question has been raised, existence is deprived of its veil and appears desolate to the scrutinizing eye: it is

333

"nothing but an uninterpreted has-been, a thing that lives by denying, consuming, and contradicting itself." One who views the whole in this way seeks solace and support in his despair. But reflective thinking only increases the despair by making it more and more clear that mankind has no goals, so that all human life seems inundated by a sense of aimlessness. When the question of ultimate meaning and value arises, life no doubt gains seriousness through the possibility of an *Existenz* that can now be truly grasped, but at the same time it loses its unquestioned security. The substantial self-realization of man, as he thus clearly views the whole of existence, depends upon his refusing to return to the constrictive and naïve security previously provided by concealment and gaining original existential certitude instead. With this in mind Nietzsche—at once objectifying and simplifying—can say that "to measure life's value and ascertain the reason for its existence" is "perhaps the most important goal of mankind," and he can predict that, "when the highest intellect appears," "it will be capable of determining once and for all the worth or worthlessness of life."

The question of the value of existence is also seen to be unlike other questions because of the way in which it actually *precludes* any answer. Logical considerations show Nietzsche that an answer is impossible when value judgments assume an objectifying form. That is why he rejects such value judgments concerning life, existence, and the world as a whole:

In order to be capable of pronouncing judgment, one would have to occupy a standpoint from which he could survey the whole. "One would have to have a position outside of life . . . to be permitted even to touch the problem of life's value." But since our place is in life, we are incapable of occupying that imaginary position. Moreover the whole as such has no standard except its own, it has no value at all, either positive or negative, "because there is nothing by which it could be measured and in relation to which the word 'value' could have any meaning. It is not possible to measure the total value of the world."

Furthermore, one would have "to know life like someone, like many, like all those who have lived it" in order to be able to judge.

Thus the basic error involved in any evaluation of the whole lies in the fact that it derives the measure for the entire world from some particular within the world. It is "naïveté to equate desire or spirituality or morality or anything specific within the sphere of consciousness with the highest value and perhaps even seek to justify the world through it."

From these basic objections it can be seen that "all estimates of the value of life are false," and that "all judgments pronounced on the value of life" must be "illogical and therefore incorrect."

Nietzsche nevertheless constantly accompanies this insight by the sort of *value judgment whose impossibility has been revealed.* Here he proceeds in two directions: He passionately desires life, and then again he asks: Why should I still love life? He even confesses: "I do not wish to have life back *again* . . . What makes me endure the moment? The prospect of the superman who *affirms* life. I myself have tried to affirm it—alas!"

The fact that insight into the impossibility of an answer does not prevent the answer from being made and that something within man compels the answer, in spite of the logical impossibility involved in the question, points to the basis of both question and answer that *lies deeper than any insight.* Affirmation and negation of existence are not expressions of proved or provable knowledge but acts of life itself. Nietzsche thus arrives at the basis of his philosophizing by calling in question the question concerning the value of life, the fact that the question is asked, and the very way in which it is answered. Instead of still raising the question concerning the value of existence, he questions the value of the question and the value of affirming and negating life; and he does so in order to arrive at the sources where the inviolable, unquestionably unbiased affirmation of existence will be revealed.

In the course of his philosophizing, Nietzsche first reaches a seemingly simple solution by taking the question and the negative answer merely as a sign of declining life. Zarathustra, perplexed, speaks as follows: "Something unknown is around me and looks thoughtful. What! You are still alive, Zarathustra? Why? What for? Through what? Whither? Where? How? Is it not foolish to be still alive?" But then he immediately adds: "Oh, my friends, it is the evening which thus asks through me. Forgive me my sadness." What is thus seen as the weakness of a mood becomes symptomatic of a certain kind of life when the latter, from its own prevailing situation, pronounces such value judgments about the whole: "Condemnation of life on the part of the living is in the end but the symptom of a certain kind of life," it is "the mark of the vanquished," the sick, and the decadent. To the objection that the wisest of all ages have judged life in a similar manner and that even Socrates, when dying, said that to live means to be sick for a long time, Nietzsche replies by asking: "What does that *prove?* What does that indicate? . . . These wisest of all ages . . . could it be that they no longer were firm of foot?" Since "actual evaluation of life" depends thus "on the generally prevailing moods," Nietzsche demands "highest judgment of life only through highest energy of life. . . . The feeble, the spiritually poor must not make judgments about life." He even turns against the very *question* concerning the value of life because it reveals a "preoccupation through suffering." Against this, Nietzsche at once asserts and exhorts: "Brave and creative men never conceive of joy and grief as ultimate questions of value. . . . One must have the *will* for both. . . . The fact that metaphysicians place the problems of joy and grief in the foreground is an expression of tiredness and sickness."

Little would have been gained, of course, had Nietzsche's philosophizing stopped at this point. Something particular in the world, a viewpoint for discovering biological facts, would have become the criterion for experience at the boundary. But Nietzsche's philosophizing does not run aground on the doctrine of decadence but proceeds to more profound sources. The basic question, meaningless in the realm of verifiable insight and reduced to a symptom and eliminated when viewed objectively from a biological or even a medical standpoint, is resumed again beyond the limits of reason where it assumes its true seriousness for Nietzsche.

Nietzsche's *critique of reason* [1] signifies, first, that being is not synonymous with rational being and, second, that we cannot reach being through reason. But if reason is not being and cannot reach being, is being accessible at all? Nietzsche's thoughts always seemed to terminate in a void. Whether we considered his concept of truth, his concept of man, or his vision of history, we were led into contradictions or to pale symbols or words that indicated a direction but remained abstract. His "great politics," despite its wealth of views, was, on the whole, not a specific procedure, for it ended in undefined "creation"; his metaphysical doctrine of the will to power temporarily granted an absolute status to something particular within the world, contrary to his own awareness of the erroneousness of this method. We heard positivistic and naturalistic utterances which no longer expressed anything at all just when the finding of philosophical fulfillment was imperative (always he scorned positivism in all its forms). Nothing of an affirmative and challenging philosophy heard up to this point was self-sufficient; that from which he lived must be sought elsewhere. Now we see the decisive transition in this philosophizing: Nietzsche discovers what is of genuine consequence precisely when reason seems to terminate in a void. Even his thoughts, which as mere thoughts would vanish, derive vitality from that which seems to remain mute to reason. But how does this being attain fulfillment in actuality rather than in dogmatic doctrines and definite demands, which Nietzsche again subjects to doubt? He finds it beyond all reason in

---

[1] Cf. pp. 211 ff. in the chapter on "Truth."

the being revealed to him through his own actual self. From this the call becomes audible to him; it gives direction to his attitudes and actions and is the beginning and the end of the course of his thought. Nietzsche's "void" only persists as long as we forget his concept of being or fail to establish any relation to it.

Nietzsche's philosophizing finally discovers being precisely at the point at which reason gives no answer and proves to be not a source but only one of the media for communicating being. This positivity, which is not limited to anything that can be methodically known, pervades his entire work and can now be demonstrated:

The decisive affirmation, not possible on the basis of knowledge or insight, springs from our essence (*Wesen*). Affirmation becomes actualized as something which Nietzsche calls a *"state"* (*Zustand*).[2] Psychologically we can designate it as mood, ethically as attitude; but it is the encompassing (*das Umgreifende*) and as such more than any psychologically investigable state or any attitude that, on this basis, can be construed in an ethical sense. It is the existence (*Dasein*) of *Existenz* which as such never really becomes an object; it is the disclosure of being which experiences its own self and never *is* except through this self-experience. It does not experience anything foreign; on the contrary, it experiences that which truly *is* only through itself. It is basis, source, and boundary of all our self-awareness and therewith of our affirmation and negation of existence.

Nietzsche, using the term "state" for the encompassing, considers it the *"source* of thought"; *thought* "expresses in signs something of our total state."

Thought cannot compel the revelation of the essence of self-awareness since after all thought originates with it. And neither can "the ultimate value of existence be the result of insight," for this value is itself "a state and a presupposition of cognizance."

Since the states are numerous, Nietzsche can assume positive or negative attitudes with regard to the various possibilities. He can reject them: "We distrust all those enraptured and extreme states which make us believe that we 'are grasping the truth with our hands.' " He objects to "any repose in contemplative states" and to any striving for an extra-

---

[2] The expression is misleading since one immediately thinks of psychic or even psychopathological states. But if one says: experience, mood, emotion, feeling of truth, self-awareness, attunement, constitution, feeling, intuition, etc., clarity is not increased, and the apparent exactitude on a higher level only proves deceptive. Perhaps just because of its bluntness, the word "state" is suited to provide a language-sign for this "encompassing" that defies precise designation. The fact that Nietzsche chose this word and used it almost as a *terminus* is sufficient justification.

human, divine form of existence that actually amounts to ecstasy or deep sleep. He can regard as a gain the states which in themselves bring to light the source of being: "the states of the soul as the loftiest attainments gained so far"; but he considers no state as absolute: "We must not desire just *one* state." He can feel proud "that the multiplicity of his inner states is extraordinary" and that, while producing a philosophical work, he is able to recognize the task of "gaining from the various experienced *sublime states* the basis for the different chapters and their materials— the regulator of the expression, the delivery, and the pathos prevailing in each chapter—and thus a reflection of my ideal. . . ."

This gives rise to the assertion that it is impossible to discover through study what a philosopher is; one must simply know it, in fact, through the immediacy of one's own "philosophical states." *Philosophy* is nothing but the "expression of an extraordinarily lofty state of the soul," and the love for philosophy is "love of a state, a spiritual or sensual *feeling of completion:* an affirmation and approval from an overwhelming feeling of creative power." The order of states coincides with the order of problems: "In the end there is an order of states of the soul that corresponds to the order of problems; and the greatest problems mercilessly repel anyone who dares to approach them without being destined for their solution through the height and power of his spiritual nature."

A state becomes perspicuous through *communication*. Thought and image express the primary, self-sustaining, and merely interpreting states of consciousness of being.

Communication may be accomplished by way of forms of *thought* which would be valueless as rational knowledge but which, speaking from their very source, proclaim irreplaceable truth to those whose own being is open to it. Using at this point a criterion which ultimately defies rational expression, we can separate Nietzsche's doctrines into two kinds: those that are the true language of the primary state of being or of the contact with being and those that, in the manner of pre-Kantian dogmatic metaphysics, enter the paths of objectivity and presume to provide knowledge of reality.

Communication may also take the form of *images* that express the affirmation of being mythically, with or without some admixture of conceptuality. Nature and landscape, the elements, and life become articulate. Apotheosis, narration, symbolic formulations, and the song say the same as the thought; but they do so in a directly stirring manner, while only thought can give weight and cohesion to this poetic form of communication.

The Source of Awareness of Being: The "States"

Thoughts which do not communicate with compelling force what can be known about things in this world—unless they are mere mental pastimes—issue from a basis which extends beyond them and gives them direction and substance. Such thoughts do not signify anything that can be regarded as detached and objective: anyone who comprehends must grasp what these thoughts inspire from an inner source.

Nietzsche speaks *out of his states,* and none of his thoughts touches a reader who does not unconsciously enter the state in which it was thought by Nietzsche. But the states themselves cannot suitably become objects since they are the unfathomable source from which all objective thinking and decisive acting springs. Hence Nietzsche's insight that one cannot look upon any of these states as *a goal;* and hence his demand: "First principle of my morality: one must *not strive for any state,* neither for one's happiness, nor one's peace, nor one's control over himself." The states come into focus, however, in philosophical thinking: Nietzsche does speak *about* states, and he does characterize them directly rather than indirectly; he does present them and project their ideal. What this presentation intends can nevertheless be only an appeal to their possibility and thus only indirect. That is why it is obvious that the states implied by Nietzsche could not be mere moods or experiences. They are rather the transcending and pervading essence, the source of life-governing impulses: within them and through their movement, *Existenz* becomes conscious of itself and of being. But since this presentation must avail itself of psychological means, there exists always a tendency to allow the states to turn, falsely, into merely psychic conditions. The germ of this misunderstanding is in Nietzsche himself, and we must be clearly aware of it if the misunderstanding is not to increase as a result of an abbreviated survey of the states as he interprets them in his own philosophical way. The following is an attempt at such a survey:

First Group: The urge to continue higher, further; the impulse to the endless movement of overcoming.

This movement signifies initially the state of negation of all ties. Nietzsche's ideal of a free spirit is a separation from everything: "He accepts as the most desirable state the free, fearless soaring above men, mores, laws, and the conventional evaluation of things." This state of complete detachment demands that "we do not remain attached to one person, not even the most dearly beloved—every person is a prison— . . . that we do not remain attached to a fatherland, . . . that we do not remain attached to a compassion, . . . and do not remain so attached to our own virtues that we become entirely victimized by some special aspect of our self. . . ."

But this state, which proceeding thus, dissolves *Existenz* and tears away from any historicity, which as repose would be nothing and as movement would only fulfill itself through incessant negation, is fulfilled in a new form. Nietzsche speaks of the "mysterious pathos, this yearning for an ever-increased widening of distance within the soul itself, of bringing forth ever higher, rare, more distant, more extended, more embracing states." The movement itself is transformed into the positivity of boundless overcoming: "And if you now lack ladders, you must be able to climb even on top of your own head. . . . It is necessary to *look away* from one's self and to look at *much* . . . up, until even your own stars are below you! Indeed! To look down on myself and even on my stars: that . . . is what remained for me as my last summit!"

This primary, existential movement is "something free, divine, and most akin to the dance, to abandonment." In the dance-song to the mistral, the movement fuses with the wind. But let nobody believe, says Nietzsche, "that some day he will jump unawares into a bold state for which this dance-song may be a simile: I am farthest from being innately endowed with such a bold and unrestrained gaiety."

This movement becomes articulate through Zarathustra as something identical with being itself: "My great wing-rustling yearning . . . often tore me forth and up and away . . . out into distant futures. . . . Where all becoming seemed like the dance and the mischievousness of gods, and the world turned loose and unrestrained and fleeing back into itself: as so many gods eternally fleeing from each other and seeking each other again, as the blissful self-contradiction. . . ."

Whatever form the movement may have, as *mere* movement it seems to dissolve man. So far it does not reveal anything of a tangible nature. In its negation it is infinite, and only in this respect does it possess a positive nature. Only as attitudes of dignity, of heroism, and of the Dionysian soul does Nietzsche project states of a more definite substance of humanly bound existence.

Second Group: basic attitudes. Nietzsche's writings abound in characterizations of human activity. At the same time he is continually at loggerheads with the traditional and presumably widespread moral code that is generally taken to be clearly indefeasible; he is forever feuding with "virtue," with the "spirit of gravity," with untruthfulness and spiritual poverty. But he combats "morality" not for the sake of mere life but in the interest of a higher morality. Motivated by basic attitudes of possible *Existenz,* he develops his own ethos chiefly in the following three directions:

(a) *Nobility* (*Vornehmheit*) is founded on an unshakable, "silent," autonomous being, for noble being simply *"is":* The aristocrats are the "truthful ones who do not have to pretend." Since they exist on a self-reliant basis, they need not doubt themselves: "Acting and judging *instinctively* goes with good manners; self-erosion and self-dissolution are ignoble."

In his public relations the man of nobility does not present himself, rather he represents. He has "the pathos of distance." Hence it is noble to "find pleasure in forms," "to be distrustful of all kinds of self-abandonment"; it is "the slow gesture and the slow stance." The man of nobility in this world is "necessarily put to the task of putting up a front."

Further characteristics of nobility are also rooted in autonomous being. To be noble is to be steadfast and, hence, to "bear poverty and want as well as illness . . . , shun little honors . . . , be able to remain silent.[3] Enduring prolonged hostilities: the disposition against easy reconciliation."

Noble being can risk exposure to the ill will of others. Hence nobility is a "lack of distrust" which, to be sure, may imperil and ruin one's own existence and so contains precisely that "on which successful people love to dwell with superiority and derision." But noble being rejects the criteria of existence and success. It rather holds that "it is nobler to put oneself in the wrong than to insist on being in the right, especially if one *is* in the right. Of course, one must be rich enough for this." The noble person will not put anyone to shame.

Furthermore, since the strength of the noble person can bear it, it is noble not to evade the demands of others in a worried or calculating manner. The person of nobility "gladly assumes the obligation to be grateful" and does "not anxiously evade opportunities to obligate himself."

It is noble to affirm, to love, and to associate with him whom I can affirm and love. The noble person "cannot live without venerating." He is unable to say No before having said Yes; when nothing at all is left that he can love, then he holds to the principle: "Where one can no longer love, one should pass by."

---

[3] Certainly not silence because of emptiness, clumsiness, or slyness. In this connection the following is more to the point: "Those who remain silent are nearly always lacking in delicacy and courtesy of the heart; silence is objection, and swallowing down necessarily produces a bad character."

The being of a noble soul is, as being, reliable; for it is not the type "that is capable of the highest flight but the one that, rising little and descending little, dwells always in a freer and more illuminated air and height." One can say of it: "Not the strength, but the permanence of lofty feelings constitutes the noble man." The noble person need not fear himself or anticipate anything shameful of himself.

The noble soul possesses "fundamental certainty concerning himself, something that can neither be sought nor found nor, perhaps, be lost. The noble soul respects himself." On the other hand, "it is noble to be ashamed of the things one possesses because we alone possess them."

The noble person has fullness and substance within himself and hence "the capacity for indolence" and the "conviction that, while following a craft of some kind or other may not be disgraceful, it certainly is degrading." He does not look upon "industry in the bourgeois sense" as the highest virtue, no matter how greatly he may respect and emphasize it.

The fact that nobility, to Nietzsche, always involves (*but does not consist in*) an actual sociological and psychological condition, and thus appears to characterize mere reality, cannot deceive us about the original thrust of his appeal to *Existenz:* namely the expression of an unquestioned attitude that is an affirmed and self-affirming state.

(b) *Heroic existence.* Since Nietzsche regards human existence per se not as final but as something to be overcome, man, who can only *prepare* and provide a transition, has to perish. Man can know this necessity and absorb it within his will. That is why Nietzsche speaks of "heroic greatness" as the "sole state of those who prepare." Within themselves they have a "striving for perishing absolutely which enables them to tolerate themselves." "Heroism is the good will to self-destruction."

The foundation of the heroic, however, is not simply the desire to perish but the *One Goal* on which everything rests: "Heroism—that is the attitude of a man who strives for a goal compared to which he is of no account whatever." "Seeing *one* cause and finding in it the sole motive for action—the criterion of all other activities—characterizes the hero" but, Nietzsche adds, "also the fanatic. . . ." What is heroic is not the urge to sacrifice which desires nothingness and whose cause consists in words, but the sacrificial courage that wills being and whose cause is substantial: "Heroism is a question of sacrifice, in fact of daily and hourly sacrifice, and *much more* than that: the entire soul must be full of One Cause, compared to which life and happiness are of no consequence" (to Rée, draft, letters to his sister, p. 505).

The hero not only considers himself of no account at all in comparison with his cause, but the cause, being the only one, must annihilate him in accordance with the course of existence: "My self-made ideal demands this and that virtue of me, that is to say my destruction in consequence of my virtue; that is heroism"; hence "being heroic causes one to meet his greatest grief and his highest hope at one and the same time."

These defining attributes of the heroic are insufficient; they could easily be confused, and they remain genuine only as long as they belong to a thoroughly independent *self-being:* "Being heroic consists in doing great things (or *refraining,* in a grand manner, from doing a thing) without the feeling of participating in a contest *with* others or *before* others. The hero always carries solitude with him, wherever he may go, as well as the sacred, inaccessible boundary region." "Most idealists at once propagandize their ideal as though they could have no right to it until *everyone* accepts it"; but the hero proceeds differently: "Genuine heroism consists in not fighting under the banner of sacrifice, devotion, and unselfishness, in fact in *not fighting at all.* . . . That is the way *I* am; that's the way I want it to be—to hell with you!"

The heroic man is not one to become pathetic ("becoming pathetic means going backward a step"). What distinguishes him is the fact that he "is ashamed of pathos."

Heroism is basically characterised by *danger,* and the basic impulse of heroic existence is the *will* to live dangerously because one has to. "The secret of harvesting the greatest abundance from existence is: live dangerously!" Zarathustra loves the tightrope walker because he "has made danger his profession." It is the constant danger which heroism takes upon itself that constitutes genuine *freedom:* "For what is freedom? Having the will to individual responsibility. Maintaining the distance that separates us. Becoming more indifferent to distress, hardship, deprivation, even to life itself. . . . One would have to seek the highest type of free men where the highest resistance is constantly overcome . . . : the great danger makes them into something that deserves respect." This necessity of danger holds true also for precisely that which *appears* most remote from risk, viz., for science: "I have heard them whistle a tune about the serene happiness of knowledge—but I did not find it, indeed, I now despise it. I no longer desire any knowledge without danger." In contrast to the disinterestedness of any type of knowledge, Nietzsche experienced the threatening aspect of knowing. Only when the basic desire to know is borne, not by knowledge as a mere occupation but as the revelation of being, does it become imperative to have courage: *sapere aude!* The greatest danger of life, of which thoughtless people are unaware, begins for Nietzsche only with genuine knowledge: "You are totally ignorant of what you experience, you run through life a drunk and now and then fall down some stairs. But still, thanks to your drunkenness, you don't break your limbs in your fall. . . . For us, life is more dangerous:

we are made of glass—woe if we are *hit!* And all is lost if we *fall!*" Science has value for him only as a factor that increases life's danger: "I want to bring about a situation where a *heroic mood* is required to devote oneself to science." "How much truth can a spirit *bear,* how much truth can he risk? This became for me more and more the real criterion . . . . Error is cowardice. . . . Until now one has always made a point of forbidding only the truth."

Nietzsche's own heroic self-assurance developed in the solitude surrounding him. His loneliness was made all the more difficult to bear since the very nature of his task called for communication: that of so comprehending the catastrophe as to present a destiny capable of making possible a counter-movement against nihilism. When the "hero to whom this task is given" waits for someone "to meet him with even one thousandth of the suffering and passion," for someone to divine his state, he will finally learn *"not* to wait any longer, but . . . to be affable and modest and to tolerate everybody and everything from that time forth—in brief, *to bear just a little more. . . .*"

But heroism as such is not necessarily supreme for Nietzsche: "With regard to 'the hero,' I do not think as well of him as you do. At any rate: he is the most acceptable form of human existence, especially if one has no other choice" (to H. v. Stein, 12, '82).

(c) Nietzsche sees *the Dionysian soul* in the person who, in the most complete self-abandonment, approaches and is capable of absorbing everything; the one who, by transforming himself instead of conquering the other, becomes everything that appears actual to him and who attracts everything essential, giving himself to it without losing himself. Nietzsche depicts this soul chiefly in two passages: as the "genius of the heart," [4] and in *Zarathustra* where we read: "The soul which has the longest ladder and can descend most deeply . . . the most extensive soul that can run and stray and roam farthest within itself; the most necessary one that from sheer joy throws itself into accident; the soul in being that immerses itself in becoming; the possessing soul that strives toward willing and desiring; the one that flees from itself and overtakes itself in the widest circle; the wisest soul that is most sweetly persuaded by folly; the self-loving one in which all things have their coming and going and their ebbing and rising tide. . . ." The essence of this soul is "the ease of metamorphosis, the inability *not* to react." The Dionysian man "possesses superlative understanding and divining instinct just as he also possesses superlative skill in communication."

---

[4] Cf. p. 22, above.

What Nietzsche hits upon in this Dionysian soul (especially as the genius of the heart) is the boundless devotion of clairvoyant love to the deepest in man, i.e., to man's existential possibility as it continues to emerge even when this love is obstructed. This affirmation of man refuses simply to accept man's existence in any and every possible form out of shallow humanity, but discovers in its hidden source what is worthy of affirmation, lures it hence, and fosters its growth.

To Nietzsche the basic ethical attitudes—of nobility, of heroism, of the Dionysian soul—are expressions of a being that is constant in them, that prepares and reveals itself. The perfected state however would be that of genuine awareness of being.

Third Group: types of awareness of being: These states can be made manifest only through indirect language, through image and simile. The various ways in which Nietzsche attempts this makes one doubt that he always has the same thing in mind. It appears that during the course of his development his experience of the source of being was transformed. Consequently three stages can be discerned: (1) *contemplative vision,* (2) *mystical oneness with being,* and (3) *Dionysian intoxication:*

(1) *In contemplative vision* the truthful man experiences what he himself is and what being is as "the great enlightenment about existence": "Something inexpressible, of which happiness and truth are mere idol-like copies, comes over him, the earth loses its weight, the events and forces of the earth becomes dreamlike. . . . The visionary feels as though he were just awakening. . . ." He arrives "in the pure air of alps and ice, where beclouding and veiling no longer exist and where the basic constitution of things is expressed roughly and rigidly but with unmistakable clarity!" Here one's view extends "over the immense hieroglyphics of existence, over the petrified doctrine of becoming." Man is transformed: "The soul, thinking of it, grows lonely and boundless; . . . its state . . . this new and enigmatic agitation without excitement" . . . spreads over existence "as a glowing, red-colored light inundating the world." It is as though one tried to resist this tremendous experience through which alone he becomes truly human. Apparently all our efforts serve merely to help us escape from our real task. "Every moment of life has a message for us, but we do not want to listen to this spirit's voice . . . , therefore we hate the stillness and benumb ourselves." Haste is general because everyone flees from himself and rids his thoughts of remembrance and deepening self-awareness with vehement gestures and loud noises because he fears them. Then, when the moment of awakening comes to us, we are too weak to endure it for long. Since, however, we do not have enough strength of our own even to awaken

during those fleeting moments, we search for those who can elevate us to a genuine human existence. These are the "true men, the no-longer animals, the philosophers, artists, and saints."

The philosophical state thus delineated by Nietzsche contains the germ of his later awareness of being. But while the latter is eventually communicated from the source of personal experience, at this point Nietzsche is still the thinker who immerses himself in the thinking of the great philosophers; hence he speaks descriptively, verbosely, striking deeply in individual statements, although it seems as if the truth eluded him like a romantic phantasm. Insofar as the states are described as purely contemplative and as knowledge of being, they are not really what Nietzsche subsequently considers the ultimate revelation of being: "Anyone who stops with objectivity and contemplation as the highest state—does not know enough."

(2) The transformed Nietzsche of the Zarathustra period experienced and presented new states of a *mystical union of being* and uttered them in song. The pertinent sections in *Zarathustra* are "At noon": "Still! Still! Did not the world just now grow perfect? . . . . What happened to me: hark! Did time perchance fly off? I do not fall? Hark! I did not fall into the well of eternity;" further: "Homecoming," "The Seven Seals," "The Drunken Song."

The world's perfection stands revealed. The Yes, which has absorbed all that is, is experienced. It is the love of being in its infinitude:

Oh, man! hark well!
What secret doth deep midnight spell?
"Asleep, asleep,
Now I'm returned from dream's deep well:
The world is deep.
And deeper than the day can tell.
Deep is its woe,
Joy—deeper yet than heart's distress:
Woe speaketh: Go!
But every joy wants timelessness,
—wants deepest, deepest timelessness."

(3) The *"Dionysian"* is for Nietzsche a third stage of experiencing being. It has a multiple meaning.[5] What Nietzsche has in mind is "a highest state of affirmation of exsitence from which even the greatest pain

---

[5] Cf. concerning the Dionysian soul, p. 344, Dionysus as mythical substance, pp. 374 ff.

cannot be excluded: the tragic-Dionysian state." It is "the affirmation of life itself including its strangest and hardest problems, the will to life that rejoices in its own inexhaustibility even as it sacrifices its highest types . . . in order *to be* the eternal joy of becoming itself,—the joy that includes the joy in destruction." Through this state man becomes "the transmuter of existence when he learns to transmute himself." Several examples will illustrate the manner of interpretation employed by Nietzsche to delineate this Dionysian state:

In the Dionysian state, the higher men attain the zenith of their lives: "The spirit then abides and is at home in the senses just as the senses abide and are at home in the spirit. . . . With such perfect and well-formed men, even the most sensual acts are finally transfigured through an intoxication of highest spirituality via a simile; they experience a sort of deification of their bodies and are farthest removed from a philosophy of asceticism." Nietzsche believed that to the Greeks this intoxication was the expression of true perfection: "From that height of joy where man feels himself, and feels himself entirely as a deified form and self-justification of nature, down to the joy of healthy farmers and healthy half-human animals—this whole long and enormous light and color-scale of happiness is what the Greeks called . . . Dionysus. . . ." Nietzsche mentions the following states as those "by which we *transfigure* and enrich things . . . until they reflect our own fullness and joy in life": "The sex urge, intoxication, meal-time, spring, victory over the enemy, derision, an act of daring, cruelty, the ecstasy of religious feeling. Three elements particularly—the sex urge, intoxication, and cruelty—all belong to the oldest festive joy of man."

As Nietzsche envisages the Dionysian state, he tries to unite the most sensual and the most spiritual elements. At one moment he seems to reach the most sublime heights; in the next he allows everything to descend to elemental intoxication. But even the uncompromising affirmations of the elemental reveal something of a desperate attempt to transcend. Nietzsche constantly seems to lose what just before appeared as the most genuine comprehension of being. He so relaxes the reins of his thinking that all distinctions vanish, as they do for the mystics—but in a radically different medium.

So long as the sensual is merely a natural event, it is not transfigured. Only in the *simile-intoxication* does it become for Nietzsche a cypher of being. However, these Nietzschean formulations, at moments seemingly given over to the purely sensual, have their limitations because the source from which this transfiguration of the sensual, in the simile-intoxication of highest spirituality derives, is not decisively kept in view. It

is as though life's exultation as such, even when detached from spiritualization within a transcendentally interpreted historicity, could have this
character of a highest symbol.

Through the "states" in their totality—the movement of ceaseless
overcoming, the noble being, the heroic existence, the Dionysian soul,
and finally, the mystical perfection of an awareness of being—the circle
is completed. For Nietzsche, this comprises the primary and encompassing absolute awareness of *Existenz;* from it proceeds all genuine
thinking, communicating, acting and behaving, as well as the type of
world-being and the affirmation of existence. However, this absolute
consciousness itself cannot in turn, like something merely existing in the
world, be conditioned by something that is merely there for its sake and
only is a part of the whole. Here, in the face of the source of existential
being, all questioning and knowing ceases. A survey of these Nietzschean
states reveals that they have the following characteristics in common:

Each of them issues an appeal from which scarcely anyone can escape:
each possibility, be it the boundless striving toward the heights, nobility,
heroism, the receptivity of the open soul, or the transfiguration of existence, strikes what is responsive within ourselves.

But only the *form* of Nietzsche's presentation is strong. The purity of
the primary impulse from which the appeal proceeds increases with the
paucity of content in its presentation.

The circle has a peculiarly *limited* nature that is characteristic of
Nietzsche. The explicit development of this absolute awareness is devoid
of love, and the "Dionysian soul," which may be interpreted as love,
takes its place. Wherever Nietzsche does speak of love—in the consuming thinking of the truth,[6] in *amor fati,*[7] in the unhistorical affirmation of
existence, and in such sentences as "All great love desires more than
love"—he fails to illumine it as a personally experienced source. Lacking
also are irony and humor. In fact humor is almost completely absent in
Nietzsche's nature; he was capable of a grim sort of humor without the
soul of humor; he uses irony as a keen weapon, but it has no role in the
illumination of the source where it has its proper protective and impelling
function. There is no place for anxiety and conscience, inescapably so
since Nietzsche denies their value and their truth. In grandiose illumination, Nietzsche brings into focus the absolute awareness of *Existenz* that
is self-sufficient and heroically independent; and so he utters the im-

[6] Cf. p. 295.
[7] Cf. p. 367 ff.

mortal truth concerning the human condition. But this turns into a paradoxical autonomous being without God, a depth of godlessness whose independence, contrary to its very meaning, seems to surrender itself to particular causalities in the world by way of literalness of deviating formulas.

The Affirmation of the Concept of Being

Strictly speaking, "states" cannot be presented because any presentation must make use of means which inevitably hit upon something specific in the world rather than upon the encompassing nature of the states (*das Umgreifende der Zustände*). It is essential that they be communicated indirectly, through *thought* and *simile,* rather than directly. Thought and simile assume a new character that requires philosophic illumination when, instead of being directed upon objects in the world, they are used to refer to the ground of being.

Abstract thinking as practiced by Nietzsche is the first kind of communication of essentials to require clarification. This thinking, directed toward being itself and seemingly losing any foothold in the world, is the kind of philosophizing he has in mind when he confesses: "To many people, abstract thinking is a toil, but to me, on good days, it is a feast and an intoxication." The abstractions involved in this thinking are by no means *empty* abstractions, for they are permeated by the other—by being itself: "He whose thoughts have even *once* crossed the bridge leading to mysticism does not escape without a stigma attached to all his thoughts." For Nietzsche's conception of being, the following statement concerning the origin of such mysticism is equally valid: "When skepticism mates with longing, mysticism is born." Hence Nietzsche expresses his own philosophical course in the terse formula: "The new sense of power: the mystical state and the clearest, keenest rationality as a path to it."

Such thinking is compelled to unfold *the thinker's own nature* within his knowledge about being: "One looks for the image of the world in the philosophy that makes us feel most free; i.e., the one in which our most powerful urge feels free in its activity. This is probably also true in my case!" Nietzsche's metaphysical ideas are to him expressions of the substance of the states of his noble being, and it is through them that he gains an understanding of these states; for others these same ideas are to become quickening forces that will bring these "states," along with their possessors, into existence. This is true basically of all essential ideas of Nietzsche, and true *a fortiori* of those that overwhelmed and possessed him: he conceives of being as "becoming" and as "eternal recurrence" and reacts to it with *"amor fati."*

Becoming. The idea of becoming is identical with Nietzsche's abstract, indemonstrable, and, to him, unquestionably self-evident and basic concept of being. A static being that merely exists is unthinkable for him. "We must *never* admit that anything just is." To do so is an illusion which, by purporting to offer something permanent and superior, depreciates the incessant becoming that alone constitutes true being. Becoming has no goal to terminate in: it is not mere appearance; and, when taken in its entirety, it is beyond evaluation. It, and it alone, really *is*.

From beginning to end Heraclitus, as the philosopher of becoming, is *the* philosopher to Nietzsche. Never does he write anything derogatory of him. Even in his first account of the philosophy of Heraclitus, he presents, in effect, his own conception of becoming and, therewith, of the strife of opposites that underlies the constant movement as well as his thoughts about necessity, justice, and the innocence of becoming.

Philosophically, Nietzsche's view of becoming must be understood as a way of thinking in which all determinateness is transcended and in which space itself and all forms of objective being are absorbed by time, while time becomes synonymous with being itself so that it alone is left, as it were. This would seem to be the end of his transcending, for here the actuality of temporality becomes absolute.

But though Nietzsche's philosophizing is immersed in "becoming," he does not stop with it, but again lays hold of *being* (1) as the *intelligible necessity of life* within existence, (2) in his transcending philosophy that aims at *being* per se and (3) by virtue of his *existential attitude.*

(1) *The inconceivability of becoming and the vital necessity of being.* Nietzsche does not suppose that knowledge of being culminates in the doctrine of sovereign becoming. He does not learn from this latter what being is; rather, he is compelled to dissolve every conceivable form of being into the formless ground as he transcends it. Becoming is not accessible to the human understanding (*Verstand*), for its thinking is bound to define all being as static and enduring: "Our intellect is not designed to comprehend becoming; it strives to prove that all things are fixed and unchanging." But if I am only capable of thinking of what in some sense attains being, it must follow that "knowledge and becoming are mutually exclusive." Thought finds the character of a world in becoming to be "impossible to formulate," "false," and "self-contradictory."

If knowledge is never knowledge of becoming but only of what is in being (with the latter merely a necessary assumption if we are to be capable of thinking and drawing inferences), then, according to Nietzsche, everything in being is fictitious. Life—a kind of becoming— *creates* for itself the illusion of things in being. Its prerequisite is a will to intelligibility. No life can be lived without a horizon, so to speak, within which not becoming but determinate and enduring being appears as the very condition of life; for life is impossible without the fictitious assumption of things in being. Becoming, regarded as being, cannot provide the horizon for any living thing. Life quite properly believes in being, and were it to believe in becoming instead, it would perish. That is why Nietzsche can speak of the philosophy of becoming as a doctrine that he considers "true, but deadly." "The ultimate truth of the flux of things resists incorporation; our organs (adapted to life) are disposed to error."

2. *The transcending restitution of being in the philosophy of becoming:* Becoming, despite its inconceivability, is being itself. On the other hand, *being for us* is the interpretation which life (the will to power) has invariably created as its own condition. A comprehensive doctrine of becoming cannot be developed intellectually, for all intellectual determination involves interpretation that would lay hold of existing being. To Nietzsche the thinking that relates to being is merely a tool of ever-changing life creating its own necessary horizon, however unintelligible life as change may be.

But what if the philosopher nevertheless insists upon comprehending becoming as the true essence of being? If life cannot be satisfied by a view of becoming and cannot renounce cognition of being without dying as a result of it, is this true also of *philosophizing* which, after all, is a *form of life?*

The answer to this is, first, that, on Nietzsche's view of becoming, being is indeed restored again—this time as the cycle of *eternal recurrence:* "The fact that everything recurs is the closest approach of the world of becoming to that of being." And Nietzsche knows how this thought originated in his own vital philosophizing: "To *imprint* the character of being upon becoming—that is the *highest will to power.*"

But in the second place, this being which, for philosophically transcending thinking, proceeds from becoming, must be radically distinguished from the being which derives from the will to power as it firmly establishes what is intelligible for it and, in so doing, provides a knowledge of things in this world. This is absolute being disappearing as an object of thought; it is *eternity* as the source and boundary of all objectivity and all existence.

During the course of his philosophizing Nietzsche became aware of what being actually meant to him: being that, not having become, *is no mere becoming* or *any particular being* within the world. He expresses this when he speaks of eternal recurrence: *"The cycle* did not become, it is the primary law. All becoming is within the cycle." Insofar as "the will to power" is the metaphysical sign of being, this not-having-become is also valid for it. "That which is responsible for the fact that such a thing as development exists at all cannot be discovered by an investigation of development: one should not try to understand it as becoming—much less as having become. . . . The *will to power* cannot have become."

3. *The existential meaning of the overcoming of endless becoming:* What is involved here is not merely an intellectual process that, in philosophizing, returns from sovereign becoming to being, but a radical change of Nietzsche's existential attitude:

When the present age with its complete dissolution of principles and its relativizing of all being and all values becomes the "image of universal existence" and when, as a consequence, the negation of life, born of aversion to the senseless futility of mere becoming, begins to threaten, Nietzsche seizes upon his thought, so to speak, as a means to salvation. "I set *eternal recurrence* against the paralyzing sense of universal dissolution and incompletion."

When indifference to one's own existence arises as a result of the vision of aimless becoming and the dissipation of being into the boundless, then the obsession with becoming turns into the yea-saying assimilation of the present: the basic thought of *amor fati.*

Eternal Recurrence. Nietzsche's idea of eternal recurrence is philosophically as essential as it is questionable: to him it was most overpowering, while probably no one since then has taken it seriously. Although it is the decisive point in his philosophizing, attempts to assimilate Nietzsche have usually sought to avoid it.

Stated simply, the doctrine is to the effect that being is not an endless becoming of novelties, for everything recurs in extraordinarily great periods of time (the "great year of becoming"). All that is has existed countless times and will return countless times. "Everything has returned: Sirius and the spider and your thoughts in this hour and this your thought that everything returns," "this moonlight between the trees, and likewise this moment and I myself." It is expressed in a simile: "The river flows forever back into itself, and you, being the same, enter forever the same river;" or: "The eternal hour-glass of existence is turned over again and again." Zarathustra's animals echo the doctrine in these words:

"Everything goes, everything comes back: the wheel of being rolls eternally. Everything dies, everything blossoms again; the year of being runs on eternally. . . . Being begins in every moment; around each Here rolls the sphere There. The center is everywhere. Crooked is the path of eternity."

But one would be mistaken, were he to believe that he held the philosophical substance of the doctrine in this simple image. The slickness of the doctrine destroys its meaning. Hence Zarathustra calls the animals who recite the doctrine "hurdy-gurdies" and scolds them: "Have you already turned it into a hurdy-gurdy song?"

If any understanding is to be reached, all thoughts uttered by Nietzsche about eternal recurrence must necessarily be taken together. Then a *physically* conceived doctrine of the cosmos emerges, though it cannot have been intended as such; for we have here most emphatically to do with *transcending* to a kind of being that is essentially *different* from all merely physical and mechanical beings within the world. This idea is further elaborated upon not so much because of its objective content, as though it concerned an object of scientific investigation, but because it is meant to be *"of the gravest importance"* for man's self-awareness: he who understands it properly and can endure it, thereby proves his strength: the idea will effect a selection and become a means to the future elevation of human nature.

When we deal analytically and critically with this idea, we encounter on its *physical* side a form of scientific argument that in this case cannot but fail. Its *metaphysical* meaning proves to be a version of dogmatic metaphysics of the pre-Kantian variety, while its existential significance simply expresses godlessness. At the same time, critical contemplation of the *truth* of this idea discovers within Nietzsche's thinking the substance of a transcending process which became to him the proper form of an awareness of being that he also attained elsewhere.

Hence we must not overlook the wavering in his idea of recurrence. It may appear as a precise doctrine with a definite content, only to become an indeterminate symbol of faith; or it may first be presented as scientifically demonstrable, only to reappear as something giving non-cognitive meaning to *Existenz*.

We should envisage one by one the steps in Nietzsche's thinking that lead to the formulation of this thought. *The doctrine:*

1. *Supporting arguments:* Nietzsche argues from three presuppositions. The first one depends upon *present evidence for the incessant becoming* and transformation of things: the present situation is by no means final; everything is in flux. In the second place, the *endlessness* as

well as the absoluteness *of time* is presupposed: "Change is a part of being, and consequently temporality likewise." "Space, like matter, is a subjective form, but time is not." In the third place, he asserts the *finiteness of space* and the *limitation of energy*. The last two postulates defy understanding and cannot be demonstrated. Nietzsche occasionally attempts to demonstrate them by showing the inconceivability of the opposite: "An indeterminate type of energy is quite unthinkable for us." "We must not think of the world as unlimited energy, for as such it is unthinkable—we reject the notion of unlimited energy as irreconcilable with the notion of 'energy.' " Herewith he touches on problems that are elucidated in Kant's doctrine of antinomies; but he does not perceive them clearly, and as a result he does not take into consideration Kant's conclusion that it is impossible, by using the principle of contradiction or by any other method, to make valid and definite assertions concerning the whole. (He does, however, express this insight in some other connections.) On the basis of his unproved assumptions Nietzsche then concludes:

a. "Endless new becoming is impossible: it is contradictory, for it would presuppose a constantly *growing* energy; but *from what* should it grow!" If energy does not grow, only two possibilities remain: in the end there must be either a static and permanent equilibrium or eternal recurrence. To exclude the first possibility is to grant that "the principle of the persistence of energy requires eternal recurrence."

b. Since energy is limited, "the number of situations, changes, combinations, and developments of this energy, though of course immense and practically immeasurable, is in any case definite and limited." But since time is *limitless,* "all possible developments must have previously existed. Consequently the present development must be a repetition, as much as the one which gave rise to it. . . . Everything has been in existence innumerable times."

c. Since all possible states of affairs once existed, those states whose previous existence would preclude the present transitory state of affairs must be impossible. This implies that a final state, an equilibrium, a persistence and fixation of being, is impossible; for if a final equilibrium had existed for only one moment, then this state would have continued. Given infinite time, a state of repose, if at all possible, would in fact have occurred. But the fact that "a state of equilibrium was never reached proves that it is not possible." If one assumes, on the other hand, that there once existed a state absolutely like the present one, then this assumption—unlike the assumption of an equilibrium occurring at some time—is not disproved by the present state of things.

Nietzsche thought it possible to prove this doctrine physically and mathematically. In 1882 he intended to provide himself with the necessary scientific background through renewed studies at a university. But since this course was not decisive for the philosophical significance of his idea, he did not pursue it. In the posthumous fragments pertaining to this issue, Nietzsche used arguments requiring a type of logic (involving the law of contradiction and "conceivability") in which he himself actually did not believe. Adapting himself to the scientific atmosphere of his time, he briefly entertained the wish to present as an inescapable conclusion of science what was now to him the fundament of genuine knowledge of being.[8]

2. *The physical doctrine nullified as the idea transcends:* The doctrine seems to be mechanistic: it appears to be modeled upon the conceived cycle of particular events in the world and then transferred to the world as a whole. But Nietzsche uses even this model as an *objection* to the mechanistic cycle, since particular processes within the world never show an exact repetition of any given thing: "Is not the existence of *any difference at all,* rather than perfect repetitiveness, in the surrounding world enough to impugn the idea of a uniform cycle of existence?" But if the cycle does not mechanically bring about the recurrence of the same state, then at least the total state of all forces must recur. But however that may be, it "cannot possibly be demonstrated that anything just like it has ever existed. It seems that the total state forms the characteristics anew, down to the last details, so that two different total states cannot have anything in common." What is decisive, however, is Nietzsche's radical differentiation between the cyclical recurrence of the state of the entire world and all possible mechanical cycles within the world. He views recurrence as a world development in which "the most *general* form of existence" would *not yet be a mechanical world:* the rise of the mechanical world would at first be a lawless play within the whole, a play that finally gains consistency, so that our mechanical laws would not be eternal but would have originated as exceptions and accidents. "It seems that we require some arbitrariness, a real irregularity, a primordial stupidity that is not even suitable for mechanics." The regularity that we

---

[8] In this physical-mechanical form, the idea is not characteristic of Nietzsche alone. Identical arguments can be found, just before him, in Blanqui and Le Bon (Bernoulli, *Overbeck and Nietzsche,* I, pp. 381 ff.). In general formulation as the cycle of happenings, it appeared historically again and again through millennia (cf. Andler, 4, pp. 255–259, cf. also 6, pp. 60–76). Concerning the problem: Abel Rey, *Le Retour éternel et la Philosophie de la Physique,* 1927 (quoted according to Andler); Paul Mongré, *Sant Ilario,* Leipzig, 1897, pp. 349 ff. Concerning a simple mathematical refutation of the "proof" for eternal recurrence, cf. Simmel, *Schopenhauer und Nietzsche,* Leipzig, 1907, p. 250, note.

see would not be a primary law, it would merely be an arbitrariness that had become the rule. But eternal recurrence (the circle) would have to pertain to "the most general form of existence" and not to anything like a particular mechanical happening within it.

Expressed in general terms: eternal recurrence, since it pertains to the *totality* of being, cannot be regarded as applicable to any specific form of existence. Nietzsche therefore sets it apart: "Let us beware of thinking of the law of this cycle as having developed in false analogy to the cyclical movements within the circle. It is not that there was chaos in the beginning . . . and a firm circular movement of all forces in the end: on the contrary, everything is eternal, and nothing has become. If there was a chaos of forces, then it too, like everything else, was eternal and returned in each circle." Hence the cycle of return is not like actual or thinkable cycles within the world: it is indeterminable while the latter are of a determinate nature. Nor is the *primary law* of the cycle like the laws of nature: it cannot be imagined as a model and is indefinable, while the laws of nature are the valid rules of happenings *within* the world. Furthermore the necessity of recurrence has a character different from any lawful necessity within the world: "Let us believe in the absolute necessity of the whole but beware of maintaining, with respect to any law, even though it be a primitive mechanical law derived from experience, that such a law is dominant in this whole and is an eternal property." Neither can a telic law appear within the necessity of recurrence: "The chaos of the whole as the exclusion of any purposeful activity is no contradiction to the thought of the cycle: the latter is simply a *non-rational necessity*." As a consequence, Nietzsche believes that the world "follows a necessary course, not because it is governed by laws, but because the laws are absent absolutely, and each force attains its final consequence at every moment."

What is most general and hence wholly incomprehensible—the totality of eternal recurrence—must not be derived from the observation of any being, organic or mechanical, from the idea of lawfulness, or from the geometric form of the circle. But all of these can momentarily provide similes as means of expression, depending on what is to be said in a given situation. Thus, for instance, the mechanics of inorganic matter provides the simile when it is a question of expressing the radical possibility of identical repetition without historicity (*Geschichtlichkeit*): inorganic matter "has learned nothing and is always without a past! If it were otherwise, there could never be a repetition—for something would always arise out of . . . a new past." When, on the other hand, the whole is seen as a history that remembers and transforms, then we read: "Don't you know that? In each act that you perform, the history of all happening is repeated and abbreviated."

His insistence that the ring of recurrence, with its primary law and its necessity, is not to be confused with the cycles within the world enables Nietzsche to use categories (such as necessity and law) to transcend— i.e., to pass *beyond* these categories into the mystery of being. But he does this in such a way that directly thereafter he inclines toward the conception of an actual world as the "most general form of existence" and thus substitutes a world hypothesis for the philosophical transcend- ence attainable through formal transcending. Lacking sufficient logical clarity concerning the method of his actual philosophizing, Nietzsche is apt to forget what he really wants and, under the influence of contempo- rary science, to attempt to rest his doctrine upon a mathematico-physical proof. Still, transcending continues to be the philosophically moving force underlying his ideas.

3. *The moment of the thought.* The source of Nietzsche's thought is not a playful intellectual reflection, but the experience of being in a moment that itself received decisive metaphysical significance from the very thought to which it gave rise.

Nietzsche emphatically clung to this moment of conception: "The thought of eternal recurrence . . . belongs in August of the year 1881. . . . On that day I walked through the forest by the lake of Silvaplana; I stopped near a mighty, pyramidally heaped block not far from Surlei. Then the thought came to me." And again: "Immortal is the moment when I begot the idea of recurrence. Because of this moment, I can bear recurrence." What sets this moment apart is obviously the occurrence of an extraordinary notion.

When we inquire into the unique experience that places such emphasis on this moment, a psychological investigation is futile. For it makes no difference whether or not Nietzsche's abnormal states included the well- known *déjà vu:* the conviction that everything present, down to the smallest detail, has been experienced in exactly the same way once before. Certain ways in which Nietzsche demonstrates the thought seem to point in this direction: "And this slow spider creeping in the moon- light, and this moonlight itself, and you and I in the gateway, whispering together, whispering of things eternal—must not all of us have been there before? Did I ever hear a dog howl like that? . . . Yes, when I was a child, in remotest childhood—then I heard a dog howl like that. . . ." An inference drawn from the indubitable recurrence of any given moment would be formally valid for all existence: "If even *one* moment of the world were to return,—said *lightning*—then all would have to return."

Of decisive importance is only *that* significance which the moment attains through its philosophical substance. If the moment is at once *revelation of being* and, in this sense, eternity, then recurrence is merely a symbol for this eternity. Nietzsche knew, by way of transcending, of the eradication of time as the revelation of being in (the flash of) the moment: He has Zarathustra say "at the hour of full noon": "Quiet! Quiet! Did the world not become perfect just now? . . . Did I not fall—hark!—into the well of eternity?" This noon is "noon and eternity."

Noon symbolizes to Nietzsche the world-historical moment that signifies the begetting of the thought: "Throughout every ring of human existence, there is always an hour when the mightiest thought, that of eternal recurrence of all things, occurs first to one, then to many, and then to all." Of this moment it is said: "The sun of knowledge once again is at *noon:* and the serpent of eternity lies coiled in its light; it is *your* time, you brothers of noontide!"

During the "moment" of the thought, existential historicity, which is always eternity within time, becomes for Nietzsche interwoven with a historicity of all being which, in an eternal cycle, again and again reaches its climax in the moment of this philosophical thought by comprehending itself. Nietzsche himself, qua thinker, is at this point not merely the historical *Existenz* of an individual, and not merely the one who creates decisively for the history of a whole people and of all humanity, but he is, as it were, the entire axis of all being, the circular movement of which has in him attained once again the point that "is the high noon when man stands in the middle of the course between man and superman." That is why the significance of this thought is without equal for Nietzsche; no other thought can compare in importance with it. He says to the stranger: "Let me tell you of a thought that has risen before me like a star and is eager to shine down on you and on everyone, as light is wont to do." He believes that the *effect* of this thought must be tremendous. The structure of *Zarathustra* was tacitly already oriented to it, so that its effect might be proclaimed symbolically: this thought, like no other, is dangerous for the one thinking it. Hence Zarathustra must first run the risk himself—he must have the courage to think what he already knows—and experience profound personal crises as he, under the impact of the thought, undergoes a complete transformation that will make him mature and ready to proclaim it and, consequently, be destroyed. Nietzsche communicated this thought, in soft whispers, with all the symptoms of terror, and like a secret, to Lou Salomé and Overbeck.[9]

We can follow the two directions in which Nietzsche envisaged the effect of the thought: on the one hand, there is his conception of the *existential* significance of the thought for the individual and, on the other, his notion of its *historical* significance for the course of humanity as a whole.

4. *The existential impact of the thought:* What happens if the idea is true and is seen to be so, or if at least—which amounts to the same thing so far as man is concerned—it is believed to be true?

To Nietzsche the first effect is *paralyzing* shock: "Alas, man eternally returns! little man eternally returns. . . . Even the greatest are far too small—that was my disgust with man! An eternal recurrence even of the smallest!—that was my disgust with all existence!" One may gag on such an idea: "Existence, just as it is, without meaning and goal, but inevitably recurring, without finale into nothingness. . . . This is the most extreme form of nihilism: nothingness (senselessness) forever!"

But this extreme can change into its opposite: Complete, despairing negation of existence can become a no less complete affirmation:

Instead of being crushed, the believer will be *transformed:* "If this idea were to gain power over you, it would completely transform you . . . ; and in all your acts the most important question would be: Would you will this same thing another time and even countless other times?" The task now is "so to live that you must wish to live again." This is like a new ethical imperative, which demands that I measure everything I feel, will, do, and am by one standard: whether I accomplish it in such a way that I should like to do it repeatedly in the same way or, in other words, whether I can will that this same existence occur time and again. This imperative is a mere form, capable of receiving a limitless number of contents. Perhaps each one can experience the eternally desirable only in his own special way and never as something universally valid: "Let him strive who experiences striving as the highest feeling; let him rest who experiences rest as the highest feeling; let him obey who experiences subordination, compliance, and obedience as the highest feelings. But let him be well aware of what *for him* is the highest feeling and not be scrupulous about the means! Eternity is at stake!" This imperative does not demand definite types of action, ways of behavior, and modes of living; it even leaves room for the most radical contrasts and for judgments that mutually exclude each other as contrary with respect to value.

[9] Lou Andreas-Salomé, *Friedrich Nietzsche,* p. 222. Bernoulli, *Nietzsche und Overbeck,* II, 216 ff.

The imperative demands only this one thing: "Let us impress the image of eternity upon our lives!"

If this affirmation, turning as it does from despairing negation, is successful even for a single moment, it becomes, according to Nietzsche, an affirmation of everything, including the undesirable and painful. For since *everything is connected with everything else* in existence, to be induced to affirm life because of even one single moment is to affirm the conditions of that moment and even life in its entirety: "Did you ever say Yes to any joy? Oh, my friends, then you also said Yes to *all* woe. All things are linked together. . . . If you ever desired One Time twice, . . . then you desired *everything* again!" "Sanctioning one thing means approval of everything." "All joy wants eternity of all things."

Insofar as affirmation of existence depends on a single moment being lived in such a way that the person involved wishes to experience it again and again throughout eternity, such a person is "saved," in Nietzsche's eyes, even when he experiences only this single moment. Hence Zarathustra is glad when the most desperate man he meets, "the ugliest man," can, because of one moment, say to life: "All right, once again!"

But the living being can by no means always practice the affirmation of everything as it is. In this world one must have such "protective instincts as disdain, revulsion, and indifference," even though they are bound to make him lonely. But it is "in this loneliness" that Nietzsche is directly touched, and here he can say: "Where I feel everything as necessarily connected, I experience every being as divine."

Implied in this affirmation of all being is the idea that, within the process of becoming, something "is *attained* in every single one of its moments," "and always the same thing." But this something cannot be expressed as a generality, as transcendence, as truth, or even as anything capable of being defined. Inexhaustible in its endless definable aspects, it is pure immanence. Only by an appeal through allusions can a feeling for it be induced. In each case, the one who says Yes reveals his own nature in his affirmation. "Spinoza gained such an affirmative position, insofar as every moment had a *logical* necessity: his fundamental instinct for logic made him victorious." But this is only one among the possible ways of affirming: *Every fundamental characteristic* in the course of events becomes a source of affirmation when an individual experiences it as *his* fundamental characteristic.

But if "every moment of becoming is justified (or escapes evaluation—and this amounts to the same thing)," then it follows that "the present is not to be justified for the sake of the future nor the past for the sake of the present."

To Nietzsche the highest affirmation of life which the thought of eternal recurrence calls forth (when it does not destroy instead) has a liberating and *redeeming* character: In obedience to the imperative that I live so that I must wish to live again, the love of life first provides the authentic courage that "even slays death" when it commands: *"This* was life? All right! Once again!"

In the second place, the thought of eternal recurrence leads through affirmation to an attitude of tolerance: it gives "weight to one's inner life without causing it to become malicious and fanatically opposed to those who hold other ideas." Whatever any single individual may think of as a way to cultivate the love for his own life, "any other person will have to acknowledge it and acquire a new and great tolerance for it." And even if we who affirm must be united in our hostility toward those who seek to cast suspicion on the value of life, still "our hostility itself must become a means to our joy!" When the individual has gained his affirmation through the thought of recurrence, *all existence returns to him as though seen anew.*

In the third place, the redeeming affirmation turns into knowledge of immortality. Nietzsche sees the affirmation of life even in the desire for immortality itself: If the evening glow of parting shines into your happiness, "heed this sign: it signifies that you love life and yourself and, in fact, life as you have experienced it so far—and that you are striving for its eternalization. But know this too!—that transitoriness again and again sings its brief song and that on hearing the first stanza one almost dies of longing at the thought that it might be over forever." But the thought of eternal recurrence makes it certain that "between the last moment of consciousness and the first ray of the new life there lies 'no time.' It is over like a stroke of lightning, whether living creatures measure it in billions of years or even find it quite immeasurable." Everything in existence partakes of this immortality. Nietzsche's basic attitude contrasts with the doctrine of the transitoriness of all things and the consequent demand that nothing be given much importance: "On the contrary, to me everything past is eternal:—the sea washes it up again."

In the fourth place, the Yes of eternal recurrence celebrates its decisive triumph in its redemption of all that is past. Previously it was different, for the will, being only an irate spectator of the entire past, was powerless against anything over and done with. "What causes its wrath is the fact that time does not run backwards; 'that which was'—that is the name of the boulder it cannot roll." Everything past is fragment and accident. Since retroactive willing is out of the question, man, looking backwards in despair, conceived of willing—and hence of life itself—as punishment.

But now, given the thought of eternal recurrence, he can know that "all 'it was' remains a fragment, riddle, horrible accident until the creative will says of it: But I willed it that way." For the creative will in its historicity does not merely take possession of the entire past from which it comes, but in addition it wills that the past return as the future: within the cycle of things, I again bring forth the past that brought me forth as the future in which it returns. The graves are opened. Whatever was, has not merely been.

But, without Nietzsche's being aware of it, an antinomy arises—as always happens in the course of any thinking that transcends. It takes the form of asserting both that the will expresses the freedom to *bring forth what is yet to come,* and that the will itself is after all the cycle that *simply repeats what has been.* The result is that, if this type of philosophizing is genuine, the statements cannot but nullify each other: Assertions to the effect that when the total situation returns the *particulars are non-identical,* are opposed by claims "that we are identical with ourselves in every great year, in every aspect, in the greatest *as well as in the smallest."* A statement like the following seems sufficiently tenable: "But the knot of causes in which I am entangled returns; it will create me again! I myself am among the causes of eternal recurrence." But this is no sooner uttered than it is nullified by another: "I shall return, but not to a new or better or similar life: I shall eternally return to this self-same identical life. . . ." The *inevitably predetermined* becoming within the ring of eternal recurrence and the *freedom to live* under the new imperative in such a way that I will *want* to relive this life forever seem to exclude one another. But this willing of a "must" expresses affirmative and creative awareness of freedom which, in this particular form, is characteristic of Nietzsche but which belongs to any transcending doctrine of freedom as a kind of antinomic expression (found in Augustine, Luther, and Kant as well).

5. *The historical effect:* Nietzsche expects the most tremendous transformation. From the moment of the appearance of this thought, "every color must change, and there will be a different history." "It is the time of the great noon, of the most frightful illumination." What will happen?

While it was obvious to the young Nietzsche that men, looking back over their lives, were agreed that they would not wish to live them over again, he later discovered an important distinction: Those who cannot bear the idea will die off as a result of it, but those who derive an unreserved affirmation of life from it will be *driven upward.* This idea is an instrument of *selective breeding.* "Ecstatic nihilism"—as the longing for the end, made complete through the unbearable thought of recurrence—becomes the hammer that will smash degenerate races. "Only he who considers his existence worthy of being eternally repeated will be left." But even if "the nature of the unbelievers condemns them to eventual extinction," this extinction can occur in the "gentlest" manner: the doctrine is charitable toward them, "it has no hells and no threats. He who does not believe is conscious of a fleeting life." At any rate, the thought of the eternal recurrence of the same thing in its proper place in the cycle is itself the decisive impulse compelling men upward and beyond themselves.

But this effect is by no means unequivocal, for while the capacity to bear our immortality may have appeared to be the highest possible accomplishment, one may also ask: "Perhaps the noblest natures perish from it? Perhaps the basest ones accept it?" "The doctrine of recurrence will first smile appealingly at the rabble, who are indifferent and without much inner need. The most ordinary instinct for life will first give its assent." Nietzsche considers this falsifying effect as temporary: "A great truth wins over the noblest men *at the very last.*"

Hoping to give his doctrine historical effectiveness, Nietzsche issues the following imperative: "Let us guard against teaching such a doctrine like a religion that springs up suddenly! It must enter slowly. . . . The mightiest thought requires many thousands of years—for a long, long time it must be small and impotent!" He does not want "thirty years of bally-hoo with drums and fifes and thirty years of gravedigger's labor." "I certainly intend to *fight off* the credulous and enthusiastic ones. I intend to defend my thoughts in advance. It is to be the religion of the freest, most serene, and most sublime souls—a lovely meadow-land between gilded ice and pure sky!"

But still we see from the following that Nietzsche could view as questionable and hold in abeyance even the thought that was most essential to him: "Perhaps it is not true—may others wrestle with it!"

Summary and the question: God or cycle? Eternal recurrence is, in the first place, a *physico-cosmological hypothesis.* Nietzsche, as its author, succumbs to the charm of its presumptive harmony with the convincingly demonstrable knowledge of science. As a result he loses the philosophical substance of the thought without succeeding scientifically.

In the second place, eternal recurrence is inseparable from the belief in its demonstrable reality; but in this respect it seems empty. For apart from any recollection of former modes of existence, this recurrence would be but a matter of indifference: Having existed innumerable times in exactly the same way is no better than existing only *one* time if existence at one particular time is never related to others though recollection, anticipation, or transformation.

Why did Nietzsche nevertheless place such tremendous emphasis on this idea? His answer is that it *finalizes the "death of God"* and, in addition, *amounts to an overcoming of nothingness.*

Nietzsche's view that *this present world* is all there is, that actuality exists here only, and that any "other world" is worse than nothing because it tends to depreciate the real world compels him to seek a substitute for the deity. This is not to be merely a surrogate required because of an unfortunate loss; it must be superior to what has been lost. Eternal recurrence, which satisfies this requirement, must emerge victorious in the direct contest with the idea of God.

Apropos of the logical consequences of *a belief in God,* Nietzsche sees two possibilities. First, it appears that "God is superfluous unless He *wills something*" although his intentions would be needed only if the world as such were distinct from being. Since, in the becoming of all things, "an accidental repetition of the same throw of the dice is more likely than absolute lack of sameness," the non-recurrence of the same "could be explained *only* through some purposive design. Consequently those who would like to impose upon the world the capacity for *eternal novelty* must arrive at the idea that the world intentionally evades a goal and is even capable of artificially avoiding a cycle." Such purposive willing, however, would be identical with the deity, for he alone would be in the position to prevent the cycle. Hence, "whoever does not believe in the *cyclical process* of the universe must believe in an *arbitrary God.*" But since this latter belief has practically run its course and, furthermore, is incompatible with genuine philosophizing, only the truth of the cyclical world-process remains, and this truth is pre-eminent over the deity.

But there is a second possibility: If the God believed in did *not will* anything, then the belief in him as *"a total consciousness* of becoming . . . would lead to acceptance of events from the viewpoint of a being who felt all, knew all, and yet willed nothing." But "a suffering God who sees everything, a universal sensorium and world spirit, would be *the most valid objection to being."*

Thus eternal recurrence—regarded as the only possibility if there is no God—is to Nietzsche the only means by which the world can escape all defamation: this thought accelerates the self-realization of the world and heightens man's rank in it, increases the indemonstrable and absolute affirmation to its limit, and renders superfluous the deity and all other beings that might appear as extraneous and in opposition to this world.

That is why Nietzsche can say of eternal recurrence: "This idea contains more than all the religions that despise this life as something fleeting." It is the "religion of religions."

While this thought appears empty to us when it is expressed objectively and without transcendence, it still concerns us when we follow Nietzsche's development of it in its entirety:

Eternal recurrence is first of all a way of expressing basic *existential* experiences: It should induce me to exert myself to the utmost in my life's activities so that I may attain to the highest that is possible for me. What once comes into existence is eternal; what I do now is my eternal being; what I am eternally is decided in time.

Furthermore, recurrence expresses absorption (*Aufgehobensein*) of *all things within being itself:* nowhere is there a beginning, nowhere an end—the world is always perfect, always complete, always beginning, middle, and end. Everything is redeemed. Time and annihilation of time become one and the same. Eternity is in every moment when love seizes all beings and elevates them to the perfection of imperishability.

The highest intensification of activity and the deepest devotion to being thus appear to meet in this thought. In it Nietzsche experiences both a freedom of *Existenz* that presses onward and upward and a loving unification of being. In this primal affirmation he sees the source and goal of any theodicy revealed and confirmed, realized and justified. Here Nietzsche touches the boundaries of existence in a manner so genuinely original for him that it is bound to appeal to us as well, if only for this reason.

Still this thought, taken as merely rational, cannot move us at all through what it immediately conveys. To us it is unsuitable as a means of expressing basic human experiences. The gravity attributed to the present moment through the idea that what transpires within it is decisive for all eternity is not diminished but actually increased by the thought that is *contrary* to eternal recurrence: the judgment that nothing that is past will ever recur and that what has happened has happened irrevocably; what occurs now can be understood as *Existenz* only in relation to transcendence. Because of the irreversibility of time and the unrepeatability of temporal existence, *Existenz* in its relation to transcendence, precisely because it never returns, can mean either eternal fulfillment or final and irreparable loss. When we say with reference to Nietzsche that his thought is without transcendence, we are right only with respect to the way in which *we* can conceive of it but not about the way in which *he* experienced it. Through it, Nietzsche, as it were, enters an atmosphere that is inaccessible to us; it is as though he left us and sank into a void.

That we nevertheless maintain some philosophical bond with him in this void is due to the expressed meanings which make his thought a link in the great chain of ethical and mythical thinking. A merely objective presentation that excludes these significant implications would divest it of the import which it had for Nietzsche.

Even in *one word* this meaning is constantly present: Nietzsche does not say "endless recurrence" but *"eternal* recurrence." What does "eternal" mean?

Kierkegaard distinguishes three ways of conceiving the moment in relation to eternity: If the moment is *not essential,* then eternity appears from the rear, as *the past* (just as the path of a man who walks without direction and goal appears only behind him, as the distance covered). If the moment *is essential,* but merely as a decision, then *the future* is eternity. But if the moment itself *is eternity,* then eternity is *"the future returning as the past."* This last concept is, for Kierkegaard, the *Christian* one: "The concept around which all Christianity revolves . . . is the fullness of time; it is however the moment as eternity, and yet this eternity is at once the future and the past." [10] If we regard Kierkegaard as an authority and accept his formula in its close approximation to Nietzsche's thought, we may well wonder whether Nietzsche, with his quite un-Christian thought of recurrence, did not preserve a remnant of *Christian* substance in his "eternal" recurrence—though altered almost beyond recognition. In that case, Nietzsche failed to carry through the extremely radical break which he intended: Though he aimed at a godless philosophy of unhistorical transcendence, what in the end he tacitly accepted as fulfillment was something quite different, composed of the substance of that which he had rejected.

Or was it a Greek thought that he renewed? He did in fact consider his philosophizing a recapturing of pre-Socratic Greek sources. But having known and rejected Pythagorean thought during his youth, he acknowledged no historical lineage of his own thought but experienced it as radically *new.*

Since the thought of recurrence, as Nietzsche views it, is rooted neither in the Christian nor in the Greek world and is thus devoid of history, it may be said to have been forcibly fashioned out of a state of historical forlornness—out of nothingness, so to speak—and to be all-inclusive only in its historical nullity. It might be considered as Nietzsche's means of catching man, as it were, after his total rejection of all traditional matters of belief, with a view to keeping humanity going and—what is even more

---

[10] Kierkegaard's Works transl. by Schrempf. V, 87.

important—forcing it upwards. Nietzsche's creation of the concept of recurrence is inseparable from his formulation of the concept that dominates his universal-historical awareness of his own time—that of catastrophe: Now that the cycle of Christian meanings and all values have turned into a series of ghostlike forms devoid of substance, we are witnessing the most radical change that mankind has ever experienced, and a new source must manifest itself. But grandiose as it may be, such a universal-historical thought is still quite empty: it is easily used to serve a negative approach. The thought of possibilities, however, is no substitute for a forecast of the future or even an evaluation of the present. It is into the complete emptiness of this nothing—an emptiness which he had not merely conceived of but actually experienced with a profound sense of shock—that Nietzsche cast his thought concerning man's elevation. But instead of allowing this actually fathomless thought to attain clarity, in which case it would become unsuitable, he gives it meanings that fulfill it but are not exclusively or even necessarily connected with it. This is signified by the fact that he speaks of "eternal" recurrence and, with his unquestioned sureness of feeling for the meaning of words, permits the word "eternal" to carry overtones that are not explicitly thought.

Amor Fati. Nietzsche uses the expression *amor fati* to refer to an affirmation of being that is at the same time an affirmation of my own conation. When I am neither dissipated in a general affirmation of all being nor compressed within a single individual who clings anxiously to and wills nothing beyond himself, I have returned from both extremes to the present historicity of my existence in this actual world and am, precisely through this historicity, at one with being itself.

Nietzsche's thinking proceeded along these lines when, as an eighteen-year-old student, he considered the relation of free will to the totality of events in connection with the concept of fate and, as a result, came to view "free will as nothing but the highest potency of fate." While freedom of will implies "for the individual the principle of separation from the whole," "fate again places man in organic connection with the total development. . . . Absolute freedom of the will without fate would make man into God," the mere "fatalistic principle [would turn him] into an automaton."

When, only a few years later, Nietzsche probed more deeply and went beyond such schematic antitheses, he came to regard being thrown back upon one's own historicity in the existence of this very moment as the basic truth of *Existenz:* When, in confronting unlimited becoming, we are overcome by the inexplicable fact "that, although we had endless time in which to make our appearances, we are living at this particular moment" and when we realize that we possess only "this shortlived today" in which to show "why and to what end we came into being at just this time," then we are all the more decisively encouraged "to live according to our own standard and law"; we want "to function as the actual helmsmen of this existence and not permit our *Existenz* to appear as a thoughtless accident." But the world aims at so misleading us that we cannot see what is to be done. It diverts us from ourselves: "Certainly all human systems are so arranged that a continuous intellectual distraction prevents life from being *felt.*" But once it has become conscious of its *Existenz* in this moment, of its "curious existence in this specific Now," life can no longer find its significance in complete assimilation to some general class or other. Whatever one may offer the soul as its essence, "she will say to herself: 'You are not all this.' No one can build the bridge on which you in particular will have to cross the river of life—no one but you yourself. Of course there are countless paths and bridges and demigods ready to carry you over the river; but only at the price of your own self. . . . In all the world there is one specific way that no one but you can take. Whither does it lead? Do not ask, walk it." As soon as one says "I want to remain myself," he discovers that "it is a frightful resolve . . . ; now he must descend to the depths of existence."

The being within becoming that the older Nietzsche expressed in terms of the eternity of recurrence, is here still seen as the demand for this descent: "In becoming, everything is hollow, illusory, flat. . . . The riddle which man must solve can be solved only through being, a being that is just what it is and cannot perish. Man is now beginning to gauge the depth of his fusion with becoming and with being." Being, however, can be reached only through a loving embrace of truly present existence, through *amor fati* which finds the way from the stream of mere becoming to the historicity of the presently fulfilled *Existenz* and seizes being within becoming.

In *amor fati* the seemingly incompatible meet: intensified activity aiming at future fulfillments joins loving acceptance of whatever happens. But conceptual expression of this fusion is possible only through paradoxes. A merely rational distinction becomes specious, for it misses the point. The profound significance of *amor fati* is not even reached by the statement: "Before fate strikes us, we should guide it . . . , but once it has struck us, we should try to love it," for this is temporally to separate a unity. At the same time the insight, thus expressed, that I cannot and must not promote fate as though it were something that I know and can set up as a goal, is existentially correct. On the other hand, the formulation furnished by basing *amor fati* on mere subordination of one's destiny to the totality of events is not definitive either: to say "that *all* that a man does exerts an infinitely great influence on everything that is to come" and that "the fateful aspect of his nature cannot be separated from the fateful aspect of all that was and will be" can but mean that "fate is an edifying thought for one who comprehends that he is a part of it" (while also correctly pointing out that it is dependent even on me). Nevertheless, *amor fati* implies more than such antitheses express: as the affirmation of *necessity* itself, it amounts to the unity of becoming and being in the destiny of the individual within his world, the unity of his volition and his acceptance. In it the ethos of the authentic activity of the individual becomes one with his experience of events in being. Everything depends on Nietzsche's interpretation of necessity.

The necessity in question is not the category of necessity that applies to causal processes subsumed under natural laws and pertaining to mechanism. It is such causal necessity that Nietzsche has in mind when he turns against the "deification of necessity" and when he says, in opposition to the presumed over-all necessity of human history: "I do not teach *resignation* to *necessity*—since one would first have to *know* it as necessary. . . ." With respect to the tendency to consider this category as absolute, Nietzsche consequently speaks even of the "eradication of the concept of necessity."

Fatum, for Nietzsche, is *that* necessity which, not being a category, is neither a law of nature nor a law of purpose, neither calculable compulsion nor intention. It includes accident and law, chaos and purpose. The doctrine of eternal recurrence involves this sort of necessity in its claim that if everything that happens happens necessarily, then it is apparent that I myself am a link in the chain of necessity—am myself a part of fate. (Even the thought of eternal recurrence is, after all, the most powerful and effective force within the course of this recurrence.) Because it acknowledges the necessity of fate, *amor fati* is no passive submission to a presumably recognized necessity but rather "enjoyment of all types of uncertainty and experimentation" as the expression of free activity.

Only when the true necessity of a fate that transcends any definite category has gained recognition, can the constantly repeated and consistently interpreted *amor fati* that complements it develop: "Not merely to bear necessity, much less deny it—all idealism is mendacity in the face of necessity—but to love it. . . ." "Yes! I shall henceforth love only what is necessary! Yes! let *amor fati* be my last love!" "I want to learn more and more to see necessity in things as the beautiful . . . *amor fati:* this be henceforth my love!" What Nietzsche desires first of all, he will soon express as his *essence:* "Necessity does not hurt me; *amor fati* is my innermost nature."

The essential attitude attained here is also expressed through the affirmation of eternal recurrence: "Highest state attainable by a philosopher: having a Dionysian attitude toward existence—my formula for this is *amor fati.*"

Even though Nietzsche considers his doctrine as the "completion of fatalism," such fatalism by no means involves the type of compulsion implied in the category of necessity conceived of as natural law, the law of duty, or any other intelligible order. Fate not only resists all attempts to understand it, but it even becomes contradictory when expressed: "Highest fatalism, yet identical with accident and creation (no repetition of things but their future creation)." Identity of opposites is the transcending expression of the essence of being that cannot be categorized. Consequently, Nietzsche's fatalism, like the Christian lack of free will before God, does not express passivity but rather the impetus to authentic noble activity that can transcend any *recognizable* necessity in the world because it faces a necessity of a different kind. Consequently Nietzsche actually hailed it like the deity:

> Oh night, oh silence, oh deadly still noise! . . .
> I see a sign,—
> from farthest regions
> a stellar shape sinks slowly sparkling toward me . . .
> Highest star of being!
> With eternal shapes engraved!
> You come to me?—
> Shield of necessity!
> Highest star of being
> —by no wish attained,
> by No never sullied,
> eternal Yes of being,
> eternally am I your Yes:
> for I love you, oh eternity!

The Mythical Elements in Nietzsche's Nature

Man cannot be moved by values that are foreign to his basic nature. That is why Nietzsche—unlike Hegel, Schelling, and Bachofen—never understood the depths of the myths, just as he—unlike Kierkegaard—

never penetrated the profundities of Christian theology. Consequently he neither really brought forth nor renewed nor even appropriated any myths—with the seeming exception of Dionysus. Still from another point of view this want constitutes his strength.

Nietzsche condemns the acceptance of myths insofar as they remain mere garments that cannot assume substance. The assumption that mankind might be in need of a myth is not to be considered a reason for wishing to create a new one to replace one that is known to have expired. Such false mythologizing deliberately attempts to will the existence of just the sort of thing that, when authentic, cannot be willed. This turns life into a play-acting of the sort that Nietzsche so relentlessly attacked as the affliction of his time. God and the gods cannot be created, they must be experienced. Their being has to be known through ciphers and symbols. Nietzsche remained honest: In traditional myths and symbols that others, to judge from their conduct, claimed to accept, he could hear no language capable of truly penetrating to his *Existenz*. Instead of seeking another myth he pursued the ultimate through his philosophizing. Hence he received his stimulation not from myths or theology but rather from historical actuality which he saw as the historically primal source of philosophizing: he sought to base his own thinking upon a renewal of the fundamental form in which the pre-Socratic philosophers—Heraclitus in particular—had interpreted being.

The fact that he used an abundance of symbols, especially in *Zarathustra,* must not mislead us. These do not have the weight of symbols that are really believed; they represent a less formal language and, in their intention and effect, never anything more. In his youth, Nietzsche as a classical philologist often spoke of myths, but in later life he seldom so much as used the word.

Still, although he never mentions an intentional creation or replacement of myths, he sees with increasing clarity a new, virtually mythical reality: the dynamic presence of landscape and weather, of nature and life, and of the entire infra-human world.

The Mythical Aspect of Nature. The landscape furnishes the background for Nietzsche's thinking; to see his background even once is to be overwhelmed by it. The way in which it speaks to the reader in endless variations of expression and unnoticeably becomes one with him constitutes a universally understood language which keeps Nietzsche's essential nature inviolate—his nobility, his purity, his fate. Here is the most ready access to Nietzsche's magic and to the atmosphere which is the condition of all understanding. In his world, nature and the elements do not appear merely as visual pictures or audible music but as a type of reality that speaks for itself directly and cannot properly be represented.

The way in which landscape and nature speak to Nietzsche reveals a sharp break between the earlier pictorial manner, which observes and paints visually, e.g., *"et in Arcadia ego,"* and the later manner which in effect identifies with the landscape. In the beginning it is only a feeling of being overwhelmed by a nature that stands over against him as objective and independent; later it is as though nature and man's fate, sensual corporeality and true being, become fused. Not until his last decade does the world become transparent and nature assume a mythical guise. As he comes to suffer from the empirically given, he can also discover in it genuine reality, and he is quite capable of doing so in a manner at once visionary and concrete. Not only does he experience an intensified expression of the visible world, but he hears the language of being through nature.

This language can be heard above all in his poetry and in *Zarathustra*. We can come close to it by recalling the *biographical* data: Through daily wanderings he comes to live in the landscape. His sensitivity to climate and weather allows him to feel, painfully or refreshingly, and down to the very depth of his own essential mood and energy, every nuance of the locality and of the time of the day and the year. He expends "much effort and zeal" in order to experience the landscape in depth: "The beauty of nature, like all other beauty, is sufficiently jealous to demand that one serve her exclusively." Nature, as he looks upon her, is a constant world that remains close to him throughout all his disappointments and loneliness. He continually refers to its presence to him throughout his letters and notes. It furnishes him with a language that is pure because of its freedom from romanticism, theology, and mythology: "And to what end is nature suited but to give me the signs with which to speak to souls?" Nietzsche exudes the profound happiness that derives from satisfaction taken in the existence of nature; it is as though he found security and consolation in it. His whole physical self shares in his way of becoming aware of being through it.

Nietzsche's delight in being united with nature can compensate for his loss of communication with men, but the will to communicate is, so to speak, infused into his oneness with the landscape. At first, to be sure, the muteness of nature is still "beautiful and frightful" "in its great silence." But soon a different note is heard when Zarathustra addresses the clear sky before sunrise: "We have been friends from the start. . . . We do not talk to each other because we know too many things: we face each other in silence, we communicate our knowledge through smiles." Finally the torture of his loneliness penetrates nature, questioning without expecting an answer, and sensing its proximity without seeing it: "Oh heavens above me . . . are you watching me? Do you harken to my whimsical soul? . . . when will you drink my soul back into you?" The question sounds infinitely forlorn, but still, being a question, it sounds expectant when his soul sings, into the darkness of the Venetian night, the song that ends: "Was anybody listening to her?"

As Nietzsche envisages the source of his love for *great* nature, it springs from the fact "that there are no *great men* to occupy our minds." For him nature is not the end; something different from the immediate nature myth of youthful vitality lives in him. He wants more than all great nature: "Our intention must be to permeate nature with the essence of man. . . . We want to take what we need from her in order to dream our way beyond man. Something that is more grandiose than storm and mountains and ocean is yet to arise—."

If we should ask which nature, what elemental happenings, and what type of landscape appeal to Nietzsche and how they appeal to him, we find it impossible to arrange the data systematically. But still a survey of random examples reveals, at least externally, what we have to go on, even though it can only be understood through systematic reading of the texts:

The times of the day almost to the nuances of the hour. Noon, for example, becomes the moment in which time is eliminated, eternity is experienced, and perfection is attained. Midnight, akin to midday, is the time of the "drunken song"; the depth of being, eternity, is revealed.

The *elements:* the beloved, pure sky, the detested clouds, the winter sky, the sky before sunrise, the sun in the morning and in the evening, the wind, the thawing wind, the storm, the quietness, fire and flame.

Types of landscapes: mountain ranges, snow, glaciers, ocean, lakes, desert; the south as an ever-different, more remote and never quite present south; "the African aspect."

Numerous *single scenes of nature:* pines, overhanging at the coast, upright in higher regions; the fig tree; the waves of the surf; meadows; the solitary flight of a butterfly high at the rocky shores of a lake; buffalo, chamois, bull; a sail on the water; a rowboat on the lake and the golden oar in the evening sun.

Nature is one with the *vitality of his own body* as he hikes, climbs mountains, dances, and—in his dreams—flies; he experiences it while lying in the sun like a lizard (to Overbeck, Aug. 1, '81). His basic thoughts come to him while he is in contact with nature; he is accustomed "to think while walking, jumping, climbing, and dancing in the open, preferably in lonely mountains or close by the ocean, where even the paths become pensive."

Nietzsche has *landscapes and cities that are his,* that belong to him, so to speak. The *Upper Engadine* heads the list: "My landscape, so remote from life, so metaphysical" (to Fuchs, Apr. 14, '88). "In many a region of nature we rediscover ourselves, with a sort of pleasant shudder. . . . Here where Italy and Finland have formed an alliance . . . to me this is intimate and familiar, related by blood, in fact even more." "The air too full of smells, the way I like it" (to Overbeck, July 11, '79). *Sils-Maria,* "this eternally heroic idyl" (to Gast, July 8, '81), this "amazing mixture of things gentle, grandiose, and mysterious!" (to Gast, July 25, '84), is the place where he really felt at home with his philosophy. There he lived, with "a mountain range for company, but not a dead one, one with eyes (that is, with lakes)."

A description addressed to Gast (Oct. 10, '86) expresses the incomparable mood of Nietzsche at the Riviera, 400 meters above the sea: "Picture for yourself an island of the Greek archipelago, strewn at random with forests and mountains, which through some accident swam up to the mainland one day and cannot go back again. Without doubt there is something *Greek* about it; on the other hand something pirate-like, sudden, covert, dangerous; finally, at a lonely turn, a piece of *tropical* pine forest which takes one away from Europe, something Brasilian, as my table-companion, who has traveled repeatedly around the world, told me. I never lay around so much, in true Robinson insularity and forgetfulness; occasionally I let large fires flare up before me. To watch the restless flame with its white-gray smoke rise toward the cloudless sky—heather all around and the sort of October blissfulness that has a way with a hundred kinds of yellow. . . ."

To him three cities were especially dear: Venice, Genoa, and Turin; with their atmospheres, their unique locations, and their *genius loci,* they seemed very much like landscapes to him. He had a decided aversion to Rome.

Dionysus. The strength of what is mythically real and omnipresent to Nietzsche lies in its simplicity and obviousness. It is that in his works which speaks the truth without ostentation and without the intentional use of symbols. On the other hand emphatic symbolism, like the Dionysus symbol, becomes questionable and almost obtrusive. Still is it important for Nietzsche—contrary to his generally prevailing instincts—to choose in the name, Dionysus, a traditional mythical figure through which he could unite the *totality* of being. The symbol is intended to present him with what he cannot and will not lay hold of through a metaphysically constructed system of thought.

For him, being is life, will to power, and eternal recurrence—thought-complexes that have separate sources and are nearly independent of one another. They are unified by the fact that they relate to the *one historical moment* in which, after "God is dead," the nihilistic movement is to meet its counter-movement through Nietzsche. All his philosophical thoughts about being are intended to present the *Weltanschauung* of the future master race that is to overcome nihilism through the energy and the nobility of its life.

Their *unity* lies also in Nietzsche's *vision of the totality of the world,* within which he summarizes everything he has ever thought concerning being. Here his metaphysics and his mysticism, becoming, life, and nature come together: "What does the world mean to me? . . . A monster of energy, without beginning and without end . . . which changes without exhausting itself, . . . bounded by 'nothingness,' . . . not infinitely extended, . . . a sea of energies storming and flowing within themselves, . . . eternally receding, with immense years of *recurrence,* with an ebb and flow of its formations, pushing forth from the simplest to the most complex, from the most rigid and unfeeling forth into the . . . wildest and most self-contradictory, and then returning home from abundance to simplicity, from the play of contradictions back to the joy of harmony, self-affirming in this sameness of its courses and years, self-blessing . . . as a becoming that knows no satiation . . . no fatigue: this my Dionysian world of eternally-creating-itself, of eternally-destroying-itself, . . . this my 'Beyond God and Evil,' without goal, unless the happiness of the circle contains a goal, and without will, unless a ring returning to itself has good will. Do you want a name for this world? . . . This world is the *will to power*—and nothing else! And you yourselves, too, are this will to power—and nothing else!"

It follows from Nietzsche's basic position, according to which there really is no whole and can be none, that the unity of a world-vision within which eternal recurrence, the will to power, and Dionysian life are fused together, must qua unity, be symbolic rather than ideal. And it follows equally that the whole is not conceived on the basis of a principle but is felt as a mood generated with sweeping rhetoric through an abundance of motives.

To be sure, Nietzsche did somehow form an idea of a whole which, as it were, provided security and justification: "An emancipated spirit will stand in the midst of the All with a joyous and trusting fatalism, sustained by his *faith* that only the particular is reprehensible and that everything is redeemed and affirmed within the whole. He no longer denies." Thus Nietzsche, the herald of heroism and enemy of all creeds of redemption, can still accept this ancient philosophical thought of "redemption" as well as a belief in the *one whole* within which everything balances out and is in order. He himself arrives at his own idea of reconciliation—or rather at a mood of wholeness—even though he had previously viewed the "ideal of a harmonious total development" as in *conflict* with his heroic ideal, regarded this contrast as "desirable," to be sure, but disdainfully referred to the ideal of harmony as "merely an ideal for good people."

Still, it is the opposite basic attitude which consistently pervades Nietzsche's thought—an attitude which recognizes and insists that "there is no All." To him it is essential "that one get rid of the All, of oneness." Why? "Because one could not help accepting it as superlative and giving it the name 'God.' The All must be fragmentized. . . . What was once given to the Unknown and the whole must be reserved for what is ours and lies near at hand." Only insofar as Nietzsche involuntarily creates for himself a substitute for God can the totality—even momentarily—assume validity within a harmonious world vision, and then only as the myth of a mon-atheism, so to speak.

It was in the figure of Dionysus that Nietzsche, in spite of his basic philosophical position, objectified his systematically desired myth. By fusing all conceptual ingredients within it, he hoped to summarize all of his philosophizing. It is as though he tried to vindicate, with respect to the most inaccessible things, the statement that "the more abstract the truth you wish to teach, the greater the necessity of seducing the senses into accepting it." However numerous the traits that remind us of the ancient myth,[11] Nietzsche neither intended nor brought about an understanding of it; it was rather a matter of consciously choosing a symbol suitable for his own philosophizing. Hence his Dionysus is something completely different from the old myth, something that does not take real shape.

Dionysus is primarily the symbol of intoxication in which "existence celebrates its own transfiguration": "This mysterious symbol originated . . . when the Greek body and the Greek soul 'were in bloom.' . . . Here is a criterion by which everything that has developed since is found to be too short, too poor, too narrow: let one merely utter the word 'Dionysus' before the best of more recent names and things, for instance before Goethe, before Beethoven, before Shakespeare, or before

---

[11] Concerning the antique god, cf. Walter F. Otto, *Dionysus*, Frankfurt, 1933.

Raphael, and at once we feel our best things and moments judged. Dionysus is a judge!"

Dionysus is also intended as a contrast to *Christ,* the tragic life versus life under the cross: "Dionysus against the Crucified." This contrast is not "a difference of opinion concerning martyrdom itself—it simply has another meaning. . . . The problem concerns the meaning of suffering and whether it has a Christian or a tragic meaning. In the first case, suffering is supposed to lead to a holy existence; in the latter case, being is considered holy enough to justify even an immensity of suffering. The tragic man affirms even the harshest suffering: for this he is strong and whole enough, and quite capable of deifying; the Christian man will deny even the happiest lot on earth. . . . The God on the cross is a curse on life and a sign to seek release from it; Dionysus cut into pieces is a prophecy of life: it will be eternally reborn and return home from destruction."

Before the blurred figure of this god Nietzsche's indefinite vision ends—as had his thinking—"with a theodicy, i.e., with an absolute affirmation of the world, but precisely for the reasons that previously had led to a denial."

His Dionysus, however, never appears as a god to whom one would pray or who could give rise to a cult. In the last analysis he is a *"god who philosophizes."* He (the "experimenter-god") has all the characteristics of the new philosopher whom Nietzsche views as on the way or feels himself to be: "experimenting" and the "great ambiguous one." Nietzsche is aware of the strange newness of such a symbol: "The very fact that Dionysus is a philosopher and that even the gods philosophize seems a novelty to me that is not altogether natural." Nietzsche's self-identification with Dionysus is still concealed when he says: "I, the last disciple and initiate of the God Dionysus." In the first stage of madness it becomes a *fait accompli.*

Beyond this, the symbol of Dionysus repeats what is already contained in a more pregnant and articulate form in Nietzsche's philosophizing, e.g., "with the name Dionysus, becoming is actively apprehended and subjectively experienced as the raging lust of the creator who, at the same time, knows the fury of the destroyer." The aspect of challenge, but certainly not of finality, present in the naturalistic deviation of the conceptual formulations, seems to reappear in various transformations in the manner in which the mythical figure is expressed. While the basis and language of modern philosophizing has been enriched, through imperceptible appropriation, by Nietzsche's original nature-mysticism, no one has adopted his Dionysus as a symbol or, for that matter, any of the affirmatively defined and *ipso facto* narrowly delimited, metaphysical hypostatizations that he formulated, including the superman and eternal recurrence.

Book Three

NIETZSCHE'S WAY OF THINKING, VIEWED WITHIN THE ENTIRETY OF HIS *EXISTENZ*

Examination of Nietzsche's *life* has shown us how it manifested a truth through virtually constant self-sacrifice: Presentation of his *basic thoughts* threw light upon the unlimited scope of his thinking, the annulment of all fixed positions through objective self-contradiction, including those that he seemingly accepted as final, and the implausible whimsicalness of the few doctrines that almost became his dogmas. It is now our task to apprehend his truth when it is placed within *the whole of his Existenz*. But this is to pose a problem that must in the end prove insoluble—or, in other words, a problem that every generation must solve for itself.

Anyone who expects to view Nietzsche as a static historical figure whose significance is perspicuous and unchanging is bound to be disappointed. To present his thoughts in terms of the devastating and all-consuming dialectic that derives from the critique that he originated and developed is to make him more inexhaustible than he probably was; to interpret his words literally, clinging to specific and definite dogmatic statements, is to make him narrower than he was. Neither procedure brings out the full effect of what, haunted by a drive that was probably never fully realized, he truly undertook to be.

We are confronted by a riddle: When, under Nietzsche's own guidance, we approach his writings uncritically, everything seems to vanish; and yet, after a period of satiety and disenchantment, the magic of his thinking reasserts itself. The riddle is this, that Nietzsche's truth, contained in no doctrine and enshrined in no permanent ideal, gains a purer and more decisive power when the captivating charm of the first impression, strengthened by the enigmatic directness of isolated statements, has ceased to attract us.

Nietzsche is not merely the source of new reflections and the creator of a new language, but, in view of the whole course of his life and his thought, an event. What Nietzsche signifies—beyond all his fundamental principles and apart from his expression of the crisis of his own age— could be said, with the definiteness required by the history of philosophy, only by one who accepts the content of an encompassing history of philosophy that surveys all mankind. For us it must suffice to see that the fact of his existence signifies a historical ground that has become to us, as his heirs, an inescapable claim on our integrity as well as a condition of our actuality, and, consequently, of our genuine participation in his philosophizing. What applies to everything great that enters existence by a leap, so to speak, applies here: Nietzsche's source is unprecedented and incalculable.

Again following his lead, we shall now take the first route to a solution of the problem concerning the entirety of his way of thinking, viewed as a manifestation of his philosophical nature.

1

HOW NIETZSCHE UNDERSTANDS HIMSELF AND HIS OWN THOUGHT

When knowledge, abandoning the firm ground that it occupies when it deals directly with specific things, turns philosophically to the question of being itself, then the source, the process, and the communication and self-awareness of thinking must be different from what is required in both daily and scientific commerce with the objects that words and concepts appear to place before us in unquestioned clarity.

Self-consciousness of thought, as awareness of method, is a stage in all scientific knowledge, but, as self-understanding, it becomes an essential stage in philosophizing. The latter cannot rest satisfied with the control which scientific knowledge imposes upon itself when it tests its assertions by means of factual data. Rather, philosophizing tests itself by measuring itself against the possible *Existenz* of the thinker and thus attains self-understanding. Such thinking is accomplished through a self-related struggle of the whole man.

What such *self-understanding* really is remains a secret of philosophizing, lying beyond the grasp of the cognitive methods that serve it. One can only see how it expresses itself and place it in relation to the entire body of thought of the philosopher in question. When one speaks directly of this self-understanding, it is easier to say what it is not than what it is. For when the obscure self-being of the philosophizing person wishes to know what he is, misunderstanding is easily possible in connection (1) with the psychological *observation* of his existence, and (2) with endless *self-reflection.*

(1) When Nietzsche acknowledges that he has "few good intentions towards self-observation," he means that he is not a psychologist in the sense of an empirical investigator who merely observes, seeking to grasp his facts experimentally, casuistically, and statistically, with a view to

causal explanation; rather his psychology consists in a philosophical illumination of *Existenz*. The psychology that practices self-observation differs from that which illumines *Existenz* through self-understanding: self-observation relates to empirical existence (including one's own); self-understanding relates to possible *Existenz*. Certain aspects of my existence, with their endless special ramifications, are indeed knowable through observation, and it is reasonable to concern oneself with them insofar as technical aids are applicable (thus Nietzsche observes the dependence of his psychic states upon diet and climate) and phenomena are discoverable in or to which possible *Existenz* speaks (extensive parts of his psychological work are of this nature: illuminations that appeal to *Existenz,* even when they deal with facts). But it is fatuous for the observer to gyrate around the empirical factuality of his own existence as though, by applying self-observation psychologically, he might therein find himself as *Existenz*.

(2) When I attempt to understand myself through self-reflection rather than through observation of my existence, then in the mirror of possibilities I see myself in a movement that can cause everything that I can possibly think of myself to appear in a different or even opposite form. The more honest I remain while reflecting, the more boundless the possibilities will become.

> Between a hundred mirrors
> False to yourself . . .
> Self-knower!
> Self-murderer.

The kind of self-understanding that constitutes a fulfilling rather than a disintegrating philosophizing does not arise until one makes the unaccountable leap from possibility to actuality, becomes aware of the source, and attains a certainty that has no fixed determinate content and does not consist in knowledge of a thing or of a self. The fact that the philosophy that fulfills can only be honest when it has hazarded the infinitely disintegrating illumination of the possible is what gives such self-reflection its meaning. But to persist in it would be to destroy one's own self-being as well as one's philosophizing.

Thus Nietzsche opposes self-observation and self-reflection (although he practices both) with a view to limiting them and finding the proper way to the kind of self-understanding that has its roots and its goal elsewhere. He almost invariably disparages mere self-observation. Its range is limited: "One can usually perceive no more of himself than the breastworks. The real fortress is inaccessible and even invisible to him. . . ." Man is denied access to himself in the form of self-knowledge: "Each is the farthest from himself." "Every day I am astonished: I do not know myself." In addition, self-reflection as a means of knowing one's self is dangerous. When it takes the form of destructive thought viewing its possibilities in the "hundred mirrors" of a skeptical illumination of *Existenz,* thereby debasing the latter to the level of a supposed psychological knowledge, the result is the "self-knower—self-murderer." For authentic philosophic knowledge (in connection with which Nietzsche often calls himself the "psychologist"), sustained self-observation and self-reflection are ruinous: "We psychologists of the future . . . we are instruments of knowledge who would like to have the complete naïveté and precision of an instrument. Consequently we must not . . . know ourselves." Hence his declaration: "I have never been very good at thinking of and about myself. . . . I suppose it goes against my grain to believe something definite about myself. . . ." Again: "It seems to me that one closes the gates of knowledge in his own face as soon as he interests himself in his own personal case."

In contrast to the misunderstood ways of psychological self-observation and endless self-reflection stands *self-understanding* as illumination through the *inner activity* of philosophizing. This involves *not* merely *my individual existence* (subjectivity), and *not* merely affairs that concern *men generally* (objectivity), but *Existenz* which is inherent in both. *Existenz* is the self-being that I alone *am,* in that I am in the world, have to deal with many things, and live within the whole. Self-understanding relates to the individual who, as possible *Existenz,* is what he is through the manner in which being shows itself to him. Thus, within self-being, self-understanding touches upon something *general* or something exceptional but still generally essential. Nietzsche's thinking is, in large part, a self-understanding by way of specific contents which, as such, he again understands within the whole. As a young man he wrote: "I am trying to discover in what respect my misery is general, and I shun any opportunity to become personal" (to Rohde, May, '74). And in later life he is consistently concerned with this: "At every moment I am governed by the thought that my history is not merely personal and that I am serving many people when I live and develop and go on record in this way."

Thus Nietzsche's self-understanding is bound up with his thinking, not as a product but as a creative process. It is not something incidental that makes us wonder, in passing, how the author thought about himself; rather it is so essential that it supports the whole structure. When one is not caught up in the process of Nietzsche's self-understanding, his thoughts bog down in the misleading univocality of their momentary expressions. It is for this reason that the study of all those autobiographical and self-critical pronouncements that interpret his own works is an essential approach to his philosophizing.

In our presentation of Nietzsche's life and basic thoughts, his self-understanding provided a background that occasionally became thematic.[1] But conscious self-understanding, achieved in his last reflections upon what he speculatively did and was, must be explicitly clarified in its own proper context. His specific accounts, in writings and sketches, of his own comprehension of his understanding in its entirety provide him with a free standpoint in relation to himself and his work that raises him and all that he stands for above the special contents of his thought. His self-understanding transcends any and every specific content and, in relation to his own philosophizing, constitutes an increase of clarity within a whole that never quite reaches its goal. For either he understands himself as universal, i.e., as an individual representing mankind, in which case his self-understanding never attains the systematic wholeness of knowledge since everything universal came to seem dubious to him; or he understands himself as an exception and, in the nature of the case, is unable to make his own exceptional nature generally understandable.

His conscious self-understanding concerns, first, *his life as the basis of his knowledge;* second, the *logical form* of his thinking; third, the *possibility of communicating his thought;* and fourth, the *meaning of his whole existence.*

Life and Knowledge

That the source of philosophical knowledge is not to be found in thinking about mere objects or in investigating mere facts but rather in *the unity of thought and life,* so that thinking grows out of the provocation and agitation of *the whole man,*—all this constitutes for Nietzsche's self-consciousness the real character of his truth: "I have always composed my writings with my whole body and life"; "All truths are bloody truths to me." "I do not simply present mental processes, I only speak of *experienced* things."

Nietzsche understands truly knowledgeable thinking as that which takes place within the subjectivity of a life that enters existence and the world, and that itself *is* all of this. "We belong to the character of the

---

[1] In connection with his self-understanding of his spiritual development, see pp. 44 ff.; of his loneliness, pp. 91 ff.; of his historical significance, p. 244 and pp. 357 ff.; and of his immoralism, p. 153.

world. . . . We have no access to it except through ourselves." I participate in existence and in the world through my own subjectivity, through the interpretative being of my own life, and through all the various ways in which I *am*. But man is by no means equally close to his own being or to being as such in all the ways or states that he *is* and all that he does and thinks. Hence the way to actuality—thinking with the "whole body and life"—is at the same time the way to the complete man who, as such, becomes really aware of the character of the world. Such a one "conceives reality *as it is*, . . . is not estranged from or transported out of it . . . for he is reality itself." Knowledge would be complete if the knowing individual were himself all that is and could recognize the all as his own being. Such a one says Yes to being insofar as he says Yes to himself and vice versa because both are the same to him: "If a basic characteristic which lies at the foundation of every event were experienced by an individual as basic to him, it would inevitably drive that individual triumphantly to approve of every last moment of existence." Conversely, man knows himself through his knowledge of things, and "man will first have knowledge of himself when his knowledge of all things has been completed. For things are simply the boundaries of man."

Life and Knowledge as Unified Though Distinct. Many of Nietzsche's utterances give the impression that he sets himself apart from life, intending to gain knowledge as a spectator. This would mean to have experiences first, and then to view them from a standpoint external to life. This is what he has in mind when, as early as 1867, he commends the capacity "to possess even in pain and sorrow the *glance of a Gorgon* that . . . instantly turns everything into stone." The knower comes to himself and his insight as he attains noonday peace after the stormy morning of life: "He wants nothing, his heart stands still, only his eyes live—it is *a death with waking eyes*. Then one sees much that he never saw before." But since he is a living being he must again abandon this cognitive state: "Finally the wind starts up in the trees, noontime has passed, life snatches him on again—life with its unseeing eyes."

This separation between life that does not know and knowledge that does not live would mean that while each disturbs the other, blind life must be lived for the sake of the materials that cognition requires. In the interest of knowledge, life must proceed without impediment. Anyone who constantly observes himself becomes thereby incapable of living, and hence unable to gain the vital experience of being which genuine knowledge requires as its foundation. Hence one must not wish to see at the wrong moment: "So long as one is experiencing something, he must close his eyes, yield to it wholly, and not indulge in observation at the same time." "Even if one is accustomed to practice contemplation of his own activities, it is necessary for him to close his inner eyes while those activities are in progress. Furthermore, if he is to experience and comprehend average thought, he must know how to think with his mental eyes closed when he converses with average men. Such closing of the eyes is a palpable act that can be accomplished at will." Thus Nietzsche wishes to have experiences, not in order to unite with them, but for the sake of knowing what *is*.

In such reflections it appears that Nietzsche regards his living and experiencing as a process to be accepted passively, his own acts serving merely to eliminate possible disturbances so that events can be solidified in subsequent knowledge. But within his quest for self-understanding this transitory point of view is soon absorbed within his cognitive *activity,* viewed as "experimenting" (*Versuchen*). Even the supposedly merely contemplative knowing of passively accepted experiences is really an active discrimination: in contrast to the falsifiers of their own experiences he addresses the following demand to himself: "We intend to scrutinize our own experiences as rigorously as any scientific experiment." He transforms life itself in its entirety into a series of tests: "We ourselves wish to be our own experiments and our own experimental animals." The thought "that life can be an experiment of the knower" is his great liberator. As a result knowledge becomes "a world of dangers and victories." "Indeed, to become wise one must will to have certain experiences—rush into their jaws, so to speak." This is of course extremely dangerous; many a 'wise one' was devoured in the process." He unreservedly asserts that he sees his experiments as limitless transformations of his own experiences under deliberate guidance: "To see things as they are! The means: to be able to view them through a hundred eyes, and through many persons!" While the *impersonal ones* experience nothing at all in their neutrality, having no eyes for actual phenomena, and while the *powerful natures* in their tyranny remain false since they see only themselves, measure everything by themselves, and inject them selves into all things, Nietzsche chooses to follow the third way: to be personally present in countless forms. *"New* creatures have to develop themselves"; in order to become just, one must "have traversed *many* individuals" using "all of them as functions." "To be *one* man does not suffice." "One must know how to *lose* himself from time to time—and then to find himself again. . . ." "He who wishes to participate in everything that is good must know how to be small at times." Of those who suppose that they know men, he asks: "Have you experienced history within yourselves? Shocks, earthquakes, prolonged grief, and sudden bliss? Have you shared the follies of great and little fools? Have you actually endured the madness and the woe of good people? And the woe and special kind of happiness of the worst to boot? . . ." Everything becomes an experiment, and nothing serves as a solid ground upon which reliable knowledge could rest.

When we thus discover that Nietzsche views his life and experience as a kind of experiment, we have to ask whether he retains his existential seriousness and whether everything, taken as a mere means to knowledge, does not vanish into thin air, leaving knowledge itself without foundation. Those who have been in agreement with Nietzsche about the dissolution of every unambiguous account of enduring being, insofar as it takes the form of philosophical certainty concerning the intrinsic nature of things, may well be shocked when all forms of life are debased to the level of mere experiments and thus seemingly robbed of their grave decisiveness.

The answer is that, while Nietzsche regards a surrender to possibilities as the condition of cognitive scope, his truth is attained through the seriousness of the possible. What he actually lived through is in fact inextricably interwoven with what he experienced as merely possible, and both actuality and possibility remain true for him to the extent to which the passionate consuming earnestness of the actual speaks within the realm of the possible. It is precisely his thought-experiments with the possible to which he refers when he distinguishes his thinking from that of others: "While you know these things as thoughts, your thoughts are not your experiences but the echoes of those of other people. They are like the shaking of your room when a wagon goes by. But I am sitting in the wagon, and often I myself *am* the wagon." Thus Nietzsche as knower becomes the man whose experience has the full earnestness of an experiment with the possible through which he attempts to become one with the process of being itself, while at the same time cognizing this experience philosophically. Often he no longer experiences simultaneously as he cognizes. Then he can say: "It is a long time since I experienced the grounds of my opinions." But on other occasions, to experience and to know is one and the same act. Still experience is for him no longer a substance certain of itself, and cognition is never a permanent and unchanging knowledge. Consequently he is not always sure of himself. He deliberately runs the risk of the possible, of the disintegrating experience of mere experimenting, and of the fusion of the genuine and the false; he exposes himself to this danger to an extent that to most people either remains unknown or proves fatal. With a right that is his alone he can say of himself: "Unhesitating use of dangerous means; perversity and plurality of character recognized as an advantage and exploited. My deep indifference to myself. . . . I manipulate my character. . . ." However this dangerous sovereignty that threatens to annihilate his *Existenz* in its historical fulfillment is to be regarded as simply an exceptional *Existenz* of the possible that sacrifices its actuality. Nietzsche's experimenting constitutes his unity with the world as he understands it; his possibility is itself actuality, his experimentation is the mode of his historically existing decision. In viewing his intellectual life as experimentation, he attains the unity of life and knowledge that is peculiar to him.

Thinking by Means of Real Dialectic. Life and knowledge, which, as Nietzsche understands himself and his task, become one within the process of experimentation, are in constant movement. This movement, though not deliberate to begin with, becomes conscious and voluntary. Since it is both thought and life, he is constantly involved in it. He takes up his position with the directness of a vital force and in a tone of absolute assertion. It is as though he has just arrived at the sole authentic truth. Then the process of doubting and the transition to the opposite pole is carried out with the same vigor. The fact that he does not follow the traditional method of thinking dialectically by means of hasty surveys (which would amount to no more than a circular arrangement of the husks of the conceivable within a large and vacuous medium), but rather must *actually live through the various positions with his whole being* is what we mean by *"real dialectic."* In this process the oppositions and contradictions are *real*. They are not subordinate from the outset to a known synthesis; rather they terminate in a synthesis that is existentially open. "A thinker of this kind does not need anyone to contradict him: he is capable of doing that himself."

According to Nietzsche's self-understanding, this real dialectic may be characterized as follows: (1) the movement is not an arbitrary and undirected process; it is self-related. Nietzsche calls it *"overcoming (Überwindung)."* (2) Due to its connection with the possible *Existenz* which inspires life, this thinking is *substantial* and quite distinct from intellectual arbitrariness. (3) It is *constructive* in its purpose, though by its very nature it is in constant danger of sinking into negation. (4) It has *direction but no terminus,* and the ground that is lost is never regained; its substantiality consists simply in its being-on-the-way.

(1) In the indissoluble unity of possibility and actuality within Nietz-

sche's *Existenz* as an exception, his self-understanding discovers the *"overcoming"* that is achieved both within his life and within the cognitions that are life to him. He understands his "experimenting" in terms of the task to be performed by his knowledge as it penetrates to the sources within the whole. Such knowing requires familiarity with all possibilities so that it may overcome each specific possibility. But since a merely conceived possibility does not take on a life of its own and remains outside of actual experience, Nietzsche must always identify himself with that of which he speaks. But what becomes for others an exclusive reality to cleave to, turns for Nietzsche into a mere moment in the movement of his vividly illuminating process of thought. Since he is potentially anything, he is actually nothing: he can adhere to no specific position. Real dialectic incessantly forces new experiences upon him in the course of his merciless self-overcoming. When he calls this self-overcoming his "strongest characteristic," he knows that it springs from a danger that is peculiar to his life and his thought: "I need it most of all—I am always on the brink of an abyss."

The significance of this overcoming for Nietzsche is that it always involves an attack, a calling-in-question, an experimental negation, while that which is rejected must previously, however, have been directly experienced, real, and even identical with his own being. That is why he investigates the full extent of those things that he finds to be very real possibilities. He inveighs against those who try "to acquire *one* kind of disposition and *one* kind of view to serve in all of life's situations" and against the uniformity that is referred to as "being of a dignified philosophic disposition." He believes that for enrichment of knowledge it may be better to hearken to the soft voices of the different situations in life: "These bring their own views with them. Thus one participates cognitively in many lives and natures when he refuses to treat himself as *one* permanently fixated individual." As opposed to those who remain unenlightened and impervious to enlightenment as a result of not having successively entertained numerous persuasions, Nietzsche expresses his way and his goal as follows: "To have circled the whole periphery of the modern soul, to have sat in every one of its nooks—that is my torment and my delight." Thus he understands everything that he contests as belonging to his present or former self. This applies to what he honors and believes; it applies above all to what he regards as the real destiny and impending downfall of man: nihilism and decadence. He confesses that he is "the first consistent nihilist in Europe, the one who has already lived nihilism through to the very end." Or again: "At once a *decadent* and a *beginning.* . . . I am both." "Viewing healthier concepts and values with a sick person's vision and, on the other hand again, viewing the stealthy work of the decadence-instinct from the fullness and self-assurance of a rich life—that was what I practiced at greatest length. It was my true experience."

This is then *the meaning of "overcoming": that he never yielded* once and for all *to any possible experience,* whether negative or positive, *but rather ventured to take up all positions* in order to master them through dialectical negation: "Shake me together with all the tears and all the misery of mankind, and I must always rise to the top, like oil on water," and "whatever I may create and however much I may love it,—soon I must oppose it and my love."

In dealing with himself he consciously adopts the technique of "withstanding all his natural inclinations to see whether there may not also be something of the opposite inclination" in him. "Why do I silence my passions? . . . Others express their whole souls in passions, but I express my soul through suppressed and vanquished passion." Hence the search for truth involves "striving against and disputing with what is agreeable to my innermost feeling." For "I would have perished as a result of any single one of my affects. I have always played each one off against the others."

(2) Only because throughout his whole life—wherever he is and whatever he does—real dialectic at once assumes the form of thinking, while his thinking becomes the indwelling reality of his nature, is he able to call his thinking "substantial" and say of it: "When thinking is your fate, you should pay divine homage to it and sacrifice to it what is best and dearest to you." He does not mean just any kind of thinking, but precisely this necessity that makes a philosopher of him, *the thinking that is a constant substantial movement of his whole nature.* Since he must himself have participated in everything that he intends to overcome, there is no effective way to overcome thoughts that, being merely intellectual, are without substance. Hence he refuses to be identified with the "Don Juan of Cognition," who, because of his constant movement, is superficially like himself. But this does not prevent him from momentarily assuming his guise and experiencing his mode of life: "He lacks love for the things which he knows, but he has spirit and appetite and takes pleasure in the hunt and the intrigue which knowledge involves . . . until nothing remains to be hunted but the most agonizing effects of knowing. . . ."

(3) Dialectical knowledge guided by self-being can *never merely deny. The No is the path to a new Yes.* Thus, for example, Nietzsche demands that we "overcome everything Christian by what is more than Christian and not merely rid ourselves of it." To one who violently

overcomes himself through mere negation he calls: "You have overcome yourself. But why do you present yourself to me simply as the vanquished? I am looking for the victorious. . . ." To be a victor is to win a Yes from which a No would proceed as a mere consequence. For him, "self-overcoming has meaning merely as a means to the development of ruling power." But how the Yes proceeds from the No is expressed simply as the secret of the creator: "I went in search of the sources; I became a stranger to all kinds of veneration. . . . But the desire to venerate within me—mysteriously began to sprout. From this grew up the tree in whose shadow I sit—the tree of the future." Zarathustra's first discourse provides a picture of the real dialectic of *Existenz*. He sees the "three metamorphoses of the spirit" proceed from the *bearing* of the heaviest burdens, through a *release* from such fetters by means of a sacred negation, to the attainment of the right to possess new values, i.e., to *creation* and sacred affirmation.

Whether *dialectical denial* is merely contemplated or actually carried out, it *derives its meaning solely from* its function in *a constructive movement*. In the historical connection between the steps, and in the preservation of the past, this amounts to the following: "Become more and more the one you are—creator of yourself! . . . In this way you retain your recollections of your good moments and discover their connection, the golden chain of your self." But when, in the process of constant self-overcoming, everything whatsoever—including this path of free knowledge itself—becomes equally questionable ("Accursed one! You have even seen through the life of the lonely and the free, and again . . . you have barred the way to it through your knowledge"), the philosophic task still remains: "I wish to place in order everything that I deny and to recite the song to its very end." A connection is revealed here which could be regarded as the very essence of knowledge of the possibilities of being. But such intellectual objectivization is merely one of the transitional perspectives with which Nietzsche would never have been content. In his eyes real dialectic remained a source and a destiny.

(4) But overcoming and self-overcoming—this penetration of all possibilities—*appears to have no goal*. In what will this path end—this dialectic that is experienced as real, kept in motion as it is by the constant sacrifice of what is one's own? If the last overcoming (thus, for example, of the higher men in the fourth book of *Zarathustra*) is mere movement impelled by the most extreme requirements of truthfulness, without a clearly conceived ideal, without creation and actualization of man himself, and hence without reconciliation and without any decision other than denial, then it would appear to be simply a matter of

constant self-crucifixion terminating in nothingness. But where Nietzsche cannot confront us with a visible ideal, he finds the positive meaning of overcoming *in the way* itself: *he affirms endlessness.*

Very different was Nietzsche's view as a young man: he then thought that closed horizons were indispensable to a full life: "This is a universal law: Living beings can become healthy, strong, and fruitful only within a horizon. For a powerful nature the horizon is closed and complete." But later on he reversed his appraisal of himself as he looked back on his writings; he found that he harbored "a fondness for open horizons and a certain prudent caution with regard to convictions." The truth is that in his conscious willing and thinking the drive towards the infinite recurs again and again; with increasing clarity he sees himself in the face of the inevitability and immense danger of the infinite which he—being an exception—must embrace unreservedly and not merely in moments of possibility:

He feels himself to be "a bird intent upon distant shores." A new homesickness consumes him: "the homesickness of the homeless." "Distance increases along with the force of his spiritual vision; . . . his world becomes deeper, and ever new stars, ever new riddles and images come within the scope of his vision."

Nietzsche also experiences the horror of confronting the danger lurking "in the horizon of the infinite": "We have abandoned the land and gone aboard ship! We have demolished the bridges behind us—more than that, the land behind us! Now little ship! Take care. . . . Woe to you if you become homesick for the land, as though more freedom had existed there—when there is no more 'land' !" "Your eye, how frightful to have it look on me, infinity!"

It is the way itself, merely as such, that remains. Nietzsche often paraphrases it. In the "Consolations of a Desperate Progress" he states: "And in addition we cannot return to the old; we have burned the ships; there is nothing left but to take courage. . . ." And in *The Wanderer:* "He who has even to a slight degree attained to the freedom of reason can only feel like a wanderer on earth." This way is further dealt with in the section "Forwards," in "We Air-Travelers of the Spirit," and in "We Argonauts of the Ideal."

The path of this real dialectic within an unlimited horizon must, as something universally knowable, grow increasingly narrow and incalculable. As a process of overcoming, it must be determined by an unknowable self-being which alone can bring it to fulfillment instead of nothingness. It is this that constitutes its incomprehensible singularity. So far as

Nietzsche's self-understanding is concerned, its possibility becomes questionable even to himself: "I can still stand upon the narrowest step in life, but who would I be if I were to teach you this art? Do you wish to see a rope-dancer?"

Nietzsche's Conception of Logical Forms

The way each philosophy understands itself is indicated first of all by its conception of logic. Philosophizing knows both what it does and how it does it; it knows this with a clarity that derives from its method.

Nietzsche's thinking, far from being a merely intellectualistic activity of drawing logical conclusions about an object, assumes the form of an articulation and expression of thoughts that originate in real dialectic. In this kind of thinking propositions taken in isolation are dubious, while taken together they are inconsistent. In the real dialectic of a kind of thinking that is vibrantly pursued and vividly experienced one can hear the utterances of an objective dialectic, i.e., of a thought-movement that is dissolved or intensified by contradiction. Such objective dialectic is made possible by the ambiguity and flexibility of all that is thinkable.

Although Nietzsche, in his unfailing veracity, gave himself over entirely to the dialectic and applied it to each of his thoughts, he never methodically formulated the process as such. The very vehemence of his own precipitate ideas and his self-consuming life as a thinker who found rest from tension only in rare moments of mystical experience was enough to prevent him from doing that. He was also hindered by a failure to achieve conscious mastery of philosophical methods. Actually he never developed logical self-understanding, though he occasionally made attempts at it. Still he was cognizant of the basic question underlying the very possibility of philosophical thought: the question concerning logical forms. He has this in mind when he speaks of opposition and contradiction, of the whole, and of system.

Opposition and Contradiction. As a young man Nietzsche tried out the metaphysical thought: "If contradiction is . . . true being, and if becoming belongs to appearance, then profound understanding of the world consists in understanding contradiction." Long before this he had discovered a riddle: "When I was twelve years old I thought to myself . . . God—Devil. I concluded that if God were to be able to think of himself, he would be forced to think of his opposite. . . ."

The question arises: Do oppositions and contradictions inhere in being itself, or are they merely modes of appearance devoid of real existence?

Is becoming an ultimate reality that resolves all opposition and overcomes all contradictoriness, or are contradictions the reality which the appearance of becoming merely obscures? Nietzsche did not think with any consistency beyond these beginnings, but again and again he touched upon this perennial problem of philosophy in which logic and metaphysics meet.

When, for example, he finds that "philosophical problems now have the same form that they had two thousand years ago [and one is bound to ask, for example], how anything can derive from its opposite (e.g., the rational from the irrational) . . . ," it soon occurs to him that "one may ask whether there are any opposites at all, and then ask whether the popularly accepted value-conflicts are not perhaps mere surface evaluations." Thus in his thought and judgment he defends himself "against all clumsy four-square oppositions": "Only in the market-place do they pin you down with the question: Yes or No?"

When Nietzsche comments in this fashion, he seems suddenly to penetrate for an instant to the underlying ground. But he generally is simply concerned with particular aperçus that show him that truth is not to be found in crude antitheses and alternatives: because the opposites are bound up with each other, truth and true being can only arise through contradiction. It is even possible that "the value of good things . . . consists precisely in their being deceptively related to, tied together and hooked up with, and possibly even essentially the same as the evil things that appear as their opposites," and "that the highest man . . . is the one who most fully represents the antithetical nature of existence. . . . Normal average men . . . come to grief as soon as . . . the tension of the antitheses increases. . . ." Thus he can say: "The wisest man would be the richest in contradictions . . . interspersed with great moments of grandiose harmony."

From this encompassing grasp of being as being in contradiction and opposition, neither of which exists per se, he derives the form of philosophy as dialectic and the form of the free resourceful life as real dialectic. The No is at the same time a Yes. Zarathustra, "this most affirmative of all spirits, contradicts with every word. All oppositions are brought together within him in a new unity. The highest and the lowest forces emerge from one and the same fount with deathless certainty." Consequently he considers it a mark of "mediocrity" in man "when he does not recognize the necessity of the *reverse sides of things;* that he struggles against evil conditions as though it were possible for man to escape them; and that he will not accept the one with the other. . . ."

He extols the German way (manifest in Leibniz, Goethe, Bismarck) "of living unhesitatingly in the midst of antitheses, supported by that supple strength which guards against persuasions and doctrines by playing the one against the other while preserving one's own freedom." Freedom from the fixity that results from exclusion of opposites, seen as the strength to endure opposition and contradiction, does not merely lead to a tolerance for the other's contradiction, but it enables the free man even to desire and invoke contradiction. Such freedom requires the process of real dialectic: "You must have the desire to be consumed in your own flame. . . . You are going the way of the creator: you will to make a God of your seven devils!"

It is clear that in Nietzsche's experience with contradictoriness no conscious method and no thorough and abiding understanding of his own thinking ever developed. He does not distinguish clearly between sophistry and dialectic, or between the purport of a union of opposites and that of a distinction between them. He does not develop the multi-dimensional logic of opposition and contradiction. He becomes clear-sighted by fits and starts as it were, and fails to clarify further what he sees. But he actually carries out what he logically perceives only on occasions. His logical self-understanding touches upon, but does not completely illumine, that which formally constitutes the nucleus of his philosophizing.

The Whole. Nietzsche's consciousness of the inner connection of his entire being and thought as they develop in time is originally not logical in nature: "We grow like trees—not in one place, but everywhere, not in a single direction but up as well as out, in as well as down. It is no longer open to us to do one specific thing or even to be anything wholly specific. . . ."

As a result, he first imposes upon himself (in connection with *knowledge*) the logical requirement of wholeness: "Neither truth nor error may be found in the specific. . . ." Every thought, however, *is* specific. It therefore follows that the truth-claims of a thought can not be absolutely valid. He rejects the "original sin of philosophers": the corrupting of propositions by taking them absolutely and unconditionally. Thus Schopenhauer's "will" became "pernicious through the philosophical madness of generalization when he asserted that all things in nature have will." One cannot even "paint *the* picture of life," for "the result is always pictures *from one life merely.*" The whole never becomes an object; it remains a task for Nietzsche and dissolves upon logical reflection into a mere "all": "This one says that all the world is idea, will, war, love, or hate. My brethren, I tell you that each of these, taken individually, is false and all of them, taken together, are true."

In the second place, it becomes evident to Nietzsche (in connection with evaluation) that the whole is inestimable.[2] The horizon provided by the idea of the whole requires that in evaluating events one "attain to a view sufficiently lofty to enable him to see how everything actually proceeds just as it should and how every kind of imperfection belongs and contributes to what is pre-eminently desirable." Even the misunderstandings in the usual view of the world would require sanctions within any perfectionistic conception; the negated aspects of existence would have to be conceived as desirable and not merely necessary.

Nietzsche's thinking touches upon the predicament that is logically fundamental, namely, that only the specific can be thought and evaluated while only the approach to the whole yields true knowledge and evaluation. But such formulations fail to satisfy the self-elucidating demand for reconciliation of all actuality within the whole. He thereby loses sight of the cleavage between a conceivable whole in which all contradictions are resolved and the finiteness of *Existenz* that must choose between contradictories. Without realizing it, he is for a while stranded on the ancient idea of reconciliation within the whole. But what within the movement of thought can be regarded as a whole is not what one can become through concrete decision. Reconciliation, if there is such a thing, occurs only within transcendence, not in a conceived whole or a final deed. Between the totality of a knowledge that embraces all contradictions and the singularity of a decisively acting *Existenz,* there will always be the final contradiction with respect to time. I cannot resolve to accept the existence of contradiction within me as though I myself could be the whole, without existentially dissolving into nothing.

But here too Nietzsche's actual philosophizing is incomparably stronger than his logical astuteness. To be sure, he is occasionally capable of doing, without premeditation, what he inveighs against in philosophers who are strongly attracted by the thought of a reconciliation within the whole. But apart from these moments, he quite decisively takes his stand on finitude. When he says: "I am one thing, but my writings are another," he appears to have a substantial feeling for the wide gap between *Existenz* and the knowability of the whole. And above all, he is distinctly aware that "there is no whole" and that "there is no total process (conceived as a system) at all." He doesn't even undertake

[2] Cf. pp. 334 ff.

to systematize the whole of his thoughts; rather he excludes this possibility in favor of the inconclusive openness of the endless. The demand of *Existenz* gains the upper hand over every sort of tranquil acquiescence in what is known.

The System. Philosophies exist in the form of systems. Nietzsche views them as necessarily polymorphic creations. The systems of the pre-Socratics "have one point in common that is entirely irrefutable, a personal mood. . . . In any case, this way of viewing human things was once extant, and it is possible." "The various philosophical systems are to be regarded as educative methods of the spirit. They have best developed an especial spiritual strength with their one-sided demand that we view things just so and not otherwise." Systems are not arbitrary; they grow in their own proper soil: "The warring of systems is a warring of quite specific instincts (forms of vitality, of decline, of social classes, and of races)."

But Nietzsche does not follow the way of these systems. He regards himself as at the farthest remove from those philosophers "who live in custom-built and well-accredited houses of knowledge." He has the "power and motility necessary to remain in an uncompleted system, with a free and unlimited view," and he needs no dogmatic world.

He finds that systems originate in "the basic prejudice that order, perspicuity, and system must inhere in the true being of things, while, on the other hand, disorder . . . can make its appearance only in a false or imperfectly known world. . . ." Certain kinds of men are inclined to be prejudiced in this way, e.g., the "schematic heads to whom a constellation of ideas is truer when it can be inserted in a previously designed table of categories" or those who are impelled toward some rigid belief because they suffer from uncertainty. Veracity leads Nietzsche to reject system: "The will to system represents a lack of integrity." Its development requires "the histrionics of the systematists: in their desire to round out a system . . . they must attempt to let their weaker characteristics assume the role and the style of the stronger ones: they wish to represent complete and uniformly strong natures." Consequently "it is a kind of fraud when a thinker today promulgates a whole of knowledge, a system . . . ," and "I am not narrow-minded enough for a system—not even my own system."

That Nietzsche nevertheless presses for a system must have another meaning. It could be a logico-technical one: "It is sufficient if we reach agreement about a whole on the basis of methodological presuppositions. . . ." This meaning was never elaborated. Or again the system could be—in contrast to those of dishonest systematizers—that of a being who thinks of the whole even though he dislikes the schematic and is a friend of uncertainty. Nietzsche is this being: he whose sense for the whole is so decisive cannot entirely dispense with all forms of system. We have now to see how this appears to him.

In the first place his thinking is governed by the *aphoristic form*.

Nietzsche's procedure [3] is aphoristic; it seems to have remained essentially the same throughout his entire life. Impressions came to him while he walked; during his last decade he spent many morning and afternoon hours in the open hastily jotting down memoranda to be painstakingly transcribed in his notebooks upon his return home. Thus there arose an unusual number of fragments made up of thoughts that received their form even as they came to him. From such materials are derived the topical essays that appear in the books of aphorisms as well as his plans for the great systematic work of his last years. Quite as much material as he published remained to be published posthumously just as it stood. Since all his publications are either aphorisms or essays, and since these latter, when compared with the idea of the whole, are also plainly aphoristic, actually the entire literary output of his thought has retained an aphoristic form.

This aphoristic form was chosen deliberately. Of course he was forced by his illness to content himself for long years with the polishing and trimming of aphorisms for publication. And he laments the fact that for the reader "the basis for misunderstanding is often close at hand; the brevity and the accursed telegraphic style to which my head and eyes compel me is the reason" (to Gast, Nov. 5, '71). But he turned this to advantage: since modern men open their hearts and souls only when travel releases them from the demands of their professions, those whose job it is to alter generally held views have to address themselves to travelers. This consideration gives rise to "an especial form of communication: long drawn-out systems of thought conflict with the very nature of a journey. . . . There should be books that one does not read right through but opens frequently." This view is never repeated, but later on he finds other reasons: "What is said briefly can be the harvest of much long-sustained thinking." Contrary to appearances, it can be a constituent part of a whole. "Do you really suppose that it must be a patchwork just because it is—and must be—presented to you in patches?" The aphoristic form is even necessary for the communication of certain essentials: "Can a thing fail to be understood solely because it is

---

[3] On this see August Horneffer, *Nietzsche als Moralist und Schriftsteller*, Jena. 1906, pp. 58 ff.; Ernst Horneffer, *Nietzsches letztes Schaffen*, Jena, 1907.

glimpsed only during flight? . . . There are, to say the least, truths
. . . which one seizes suddenly or not at all. . . ." Hence "the deepest
and most inexhaustible books will always have some of the aphoristic
and startling character of Pascal's *Pensées*." Right up to the end Nietzsche favored this form: "The aphorism and the maxim, in the use of
which I am the first among German masters, are the forms of 'eternity.'
My ambition is to say in ten sentences what everyone else takes a whole
book to say—or rather, what the others do *not* say in a book. . . ."

Nevertheless when he wrote this, he had for some time had his mind on
a comprehensive work of a non-aphoristic nature. However, his numerous plans are not outlines of a system, but rather of a presentation; as
time passes they are not methodically developed into a thorough systematic formulation with each step indicated in the sketches, for the plans
themselves have a pluralistic and aphoristic character. Furthermore, a
constructive system concerning the whole of things would certainly be
nonsensical from his point of view: he may indeed make some systematic
sketches for himself but they have to remain his tools; they cannot
express the whole of his thought.

In contradistinction to a systematic presentation as well as to a systematic world-view in the style of previous metaphysicians, the interconnected whole of his thought is "more than has ever gone by the name of
philosophy" (to Overbeck, Aug. 20, '84). (Had he had sufficient time and
not been ill, he could have achieved both, but only as a function of his
thought as a whole, and not as a definitive formulation.) What constitutes
the whole in Nietzsche's work is the comprehensive character (*der
zusammengreifende Zug*) which includes and preserves moments which,
taken singly, would be deprived of their meaning, viz., great politics,
systematic ontological construction, and mystical intuition. Thus his
thought is only an analogue of previous systems. The organic totality of
his thought is implicit; it is not a theme or an object, but it develops as
the interconnectedness that pervades the whole. When one attempts to
bring out the system (our presentation of his basic thoughts made several
starts in that direction), his efforts come to grief on the infinity of the
task. At best what is brought out may perhaps be something more or even
something new in the form of a whole that now can be known, but it also
will always be something less because one must forget, neglect, and
exclude. What Nietzsche himself occasionally selected from his life as a
thinker for inclusion in narrowly circumscribed works—for instance,
when through polemical thrusts and aphoristic principles he presented
the "vestibules" of his philosophy—was no longer a whole.

For Nietzsche the whole consists in passing through all the ways of
mastering the truth. In reflection and contemplation, in experience and

mystical rapture, he always passes from one possibility to another. Like Kierkegaard, he reads the "primordial script of human existential relations." Truth of every kind, so long as it is existential—even in its spurious and irrelevant forms—comes within his purview. This movement, however, continues for decades. Nietzsche's truth is not to be found at any one stage. It is not at the end, not at the beginning, and not at any single level; it inheres in the movement as a whole—a movement within which every phase has its place and its own indispensable and unique significance.

This cohesive energy of the whole that appears only within the movement is not as such expressed in Hegelian fashion through a systematic work. The robust envisagement of particular situations, the construction of specific connections, the thought-experiments relating to all that is possible—all these matters without exception are fused together and unified within the movement as a whole.

Hence it is impossible to arrive at Nietzsche's system through synthesis. The system remains always in an ever-renewed germinal state. But his most profound insights, with their extensive ramifications, are not always in evidence: What Nietzsche says cannot be read on one single level, for the steps are at various removes from what underlies and supports the movement. His lack of a consciously developed method accounts for what is limited, unjust, and even banal; it makes possible the occasionally absolutistic, exclusivistic, and dogmatic ways of speaking. His psychological unmasking, always striking, sometimes strikes with deadly effect. But, thanks to Nietzsche's innate sureness and methodical consciousness, the very manner in which his self-analysis proceeds reveals these flaws. His self-corrective method corresponds to the way in which his statements limit, qualify, and interpret each other. It must be admitted that the substance of his philosophizing is not equally present in all the countless things that he jotted down. Only in his better moments could he visualize with plastic totality the task that his work as a whole was meant to perform. That the particular isolates itself and comes glaringly into prominence is due to the strength of its substance; that it does not persist is due to the strength of the systematically effective, immanent dialectic, which Nietzsche clearly stated during his moments of highest awareness.

The Possibility of Communication

Throughout his entire life Nietzsche was aware that his loneliness was a basic trait.[4] Our discussion of truth in transcending breakthrough

---

[4] *Vide* pp. 85 ff.

revealed incommunicability and silence as an essential boundary.[5] In understanding his own philosophizing, he reflected upon no problems as often as those relating to *what* is communicable, *how* it can be communicated, what *underlies* incommunicability, and what *conclusions* follow from this.

The Necessity of Communication. That being true and being communicable belong together Nietzsche expressed in the simple statement: "Alone one is always in the wrong; the truth begins with two." He experienced this when he found not only that the public failed to respond, but also that not one single person appeared to understand what he was driving at. Peter Gast became a substitute for the understanding that he found wanting. When he believed that he and Gast had "ever so many good things in common," he wrote as follows of his profound happiness: "You can scarcely realize how comforting the thought of our mutual understanding is to me, for one who is *alone* with his thoughts is accounted a fool, and often he is such to himself; but *two* is the beginning of 'wisdom,' confidence, valor, and mental health" (to Gast, Apr. 10, '81).

Such satisfaction turned out to be evanescent, however, and the dubiousness of all communication loomed larger and larger before him. This provided the impetus to his self-understanding: "Our skepticism concerning the communicability of things of the heart is profound. . . ." It depends upon the others: "One cannot communicate at will . . . he must find someone with whom communication is possible" (to his sister, May 20, '85). It also depends upon himself, but "I am the most secretive of all secretive natures." That such statements appear repeatedly does not show resignation, but rather a passionate urge to communicate the truth in its purity. Even when aware of the impossibility of conveying his deepest thoughts, Zarathustra, affirming at least the semblance of communicability, can say to the vainly talking animals: "It comforts me so to hear your chattering. . . . How wonderful that there are words and sounds, for are not words and sounds rainbows and illusory bridges between the eternally separated? . . . This illusion deceives most pleasantly those who are most similar; for the smallest gap is the most difficult to bridge. Speech is a lovely kind of tomfoolery! . . ."

The Reason for Incommunicability. Nietzsche recognizes the reason why the essential—the truth itself—is incommunicable: Only that which can be said can be communicated; only the intelligible can be said, but

[5] *Vide* pp. 220 ff.

what is intelligible is always interpretative. Hence he is convinced that "only something hard and fast, simplified, and capable of being made precise can be communicated"; i.e., it must be "fixed up." What is said, as such, has already ceased to be true. Anything communicated retains its truth only when the determinacy involved is overcome. But he himself developed very determinate symbols and dogmas as a part of his philosophy. Like all his other expressions, these latter must be taken up into the movement, not as final conclusions, but as truths to be qualified and revised—except, of course, when these statements convey simply a dimming and narrowing of Nietzsche's view, the drastic expression of some formulation of the moment or some occasional intolerant judgment, the sketchy outline of a doctrine that threatens to overshadow everything further, or glaring highlights so arranged that they reveal one thing, only to conceal something else the more decisively. Thus the reader is impelled by Nietzsche himself, in approaching the increasingly rigid doctrines of his last decade, not to overlook the critical probing to which occasionally the superman, eternal recurrence, and the will to power are subjected. He regards his own doctrine as merely an attempt at a new exegesis. And since the path of exegesis and of overcoming through new exegesis never comes to an end, "the world once more becomes *endless* insofar as we do not reject the possibility that it contains endless interpretations. Again a great shuddering overtakes us. . . ." This is the real endlessness of Nietzsche, within which the communicability of the truth to oneself or to others is impossible, insofar as it is meant to be unequivocal even in its essentials.

As a result of his awareness of the presence of truth and the fulfillment of infinity as the source, he cannot but become chronically discontented with his thoughts when they are viewed in connection with the source from which they come: "Ah, what then are you, you my written and painted thoughts! . . . A few of you are, I fear, ready to become truths. . . . We immortalizers of the things which can be written—what can we actually paint? Alas, only that which is about to wither. . . ."

For anyone who does not comprehend the situation that arises because of actual incommunicability, the consequences of the above are profound. The inflexibility of an explicitly stated conviction to which such a person clings turns the tables by making him thoroughly false: inasmuch as all his apparent communications are spurious and devoid of authenticity, he is actually incommunicado. He has lost his plasticity, he is "hard, unknowledgeable, unteachable, devoid of gentleness, eternally suspicious, and precipitate in judgment. He seizes every possible means of maintaining his opinion, for he cannot understand at all that there are bound to be other opinions." He is not capable of conveying anything, and his incapacity is due precisely to the fact that he behaves as though univocal truth has been found and can be communicated. But the apparent impossibility of communicating what lies *at* the source does not exclude the possibility of all communication *from* the source. Nietzsche's efforts and his self-understanding proceed together towards a true communicability which can no longer have the express intention of conveying the dogmatic finality of one single truth.

Indirect Communication. It may appear as an extraneous technique when a speaker does not simply say right out what is true for him but reaches the other by arousing his attention in an ambiguous manner that forces him to arrive at it for himself. When an explicit statement, represented as absolutely valid just as it stands, proves to be false, the question remains whether it says something indirectly, so that truth still encounters truth through the medium of this communication. Nietzsche comments on this indirect approach when he reminds us of the frequent *"exhortatio indirecta"* in his *The Dawn:* "In comparison, direct admonition and incitation have something so precocious about them" (to Gast, Aug., '81). Every truth asserted straight out is prophesy, which Nietzsche rejects: "Do I speak as one who has had a revelation? If so, despise me and do not listen to me." By now he finds expressive extremes suspicious and says of his earlier writings: "Carrying things to extremes betrays . . . the tenacity with which one seeks to hold fast to a delusion." He is shocked by the "common characteristic" of these assertive and demanding writings: "They speak the language of fanaticism. Almost always when they deal with those who think otherwise, that same cruel sort of slander . . . becomes evident, . . . hateful shibboleths, as a result of which I could not have continued to read these writings to the end, had I been somewhat less well acquainted with their author."

When Nietzsche took up the problem of indirect communication with critical intent, it occurred to him, in relation to his work *Human, All-Too-Human,* that the form of indirectness might consist in having a character speak instead of speaking himself. A portrait of the "free spirit" should be painted and one should have the daring "to allow this spirit to speak for himself, and even to attribute a book to him." This idea of speaking in pseudonyms was considered but not carried out; it seldom appears in the posthumous materials and letters. When, after *Zarathustra,* he completed his *Beyond Good and Evil,* he experienced "the difficulty of finding a vantage point from which to speak. . . . Here the previously prepared type, 'free spirit,' was most helpful to me" (to Gast, July 20, '86). Even Zarathustra is not Nietzsche: "Never believe that my son Zarathustra expresses *my* opinions. He is a part of my preparations and my *entr'actes*" (to his sister, April, '85). Finally, instead of letting various figures speak for him, he decides to speak himself: "Resolved: I will speak instead of Zarathustra." The nature of the situation leads Nietzsche to the same problem that Kierkegaard consciously dealt with at length by means of his pseudonyms and his illumination of "indirect communication"; Nietzsche, however, only occasionally touches upon it. For the most part, he actually feels himself to be identical with the "free spirit" and with Zarathustra—even though at times he seeks to overcome them.

The Necessity and Truth of the Mask. If what is true is not directly given, then the mask is part and parcel of existence—not the mask that is intended merely to deceive, but rather the protective mask that can be penetrated only by those whose vision is sufficiently authentic to hit upon the truth. Indirectness is no longer a technique of communication; it is the truth of being, manifest in existence and conveyed in speech. The mask involves both the common lie and the authentic truth; as a mask a *work* offers changeability through ambiguity and foreground.

Nietzsche's basic attitude taught him "to be silent at the right time and that he must learn to speak in order to be silent in the right way. Also that a man with hidden depths needs an external appearance both for his own sake and for the sake of other people: it is necessary if he is to recover from himself, and also if others are to be able to live with him." Now he knows that "everything deep loves masks. . . . There are events of such a tender nature that one does well to obscure them by crudities and make them unrecognizable. . . . Every profound spirit needs a mask, and what is more, such an one is constantly enveloped and concealed by a mask, thanks to the false—i.e., shallow—interpretation imposed upon all his words, steps, and signs of life." Gaiety is such a mask: "There is something in us that is very fragile. . . . Does it not seem that we are gay because we are terribly sad? . . . We smile among ourselves about those who cultivate a taste for melancholy, . . . for we are not happy enough to afford their gentle sadness. . . . We have a kind of knowledge of which we are afraid and with which we do not wish to be left alone. . . . Remain bravely at our side, mocking frivolity. . . . Let us pray to the mask as to our last deity and savior."

Nietzsche distinguishes the mask, of which he approves, from histrionics, in which all genuineness is lost: "In the play-actor we recognize the Dionysian man, . . . a Dionysian who is acted out." "Even in the mouth of a most convincing actor, a profound thought, a simile, indeed every word sounds weakened and desecrated. . . . What once struck us as the most profound world-revelation now seems to us like an objectionable masquerade."

Playacting in the sense of playing the fool (the Harlequin or jester) can itself become an affair of masks, though with the ambiguity of being the fool and playing the fool—an ambiguity that cannot be resolved by the one who acts out what he is: "From time to time we have to relax by . . . laughing at or weeping over ourselves. We must discover the hero as well as the fool who is hidden away in our passion for knowledge. . . . For this purpose nothing is so helpful as the *cockscomb:* we need every bit of wanton, dancing, mocking art if we are not to lose our freedom from things. . . . How, for this purpose, could we do without art or the fool?" The inseparability of being and appearance, of genuineness and foolishness is not only expressed for the artist, for whom "the Harlequin and God are neighbors," but expressed again as Nietzsche looks into the depths of being and says: "I measure the value of men by their need to comprehend the God as inseparable from the Satyr."

Nietzsche seems most contradictory when he deals with questions concerning tomfoolery as a mask. Jesters, buffoons, clowns, and cynics repeatedly appear in significant ambiguity, being sometimes identified and sometimes contrasted with himself:

The *jester* appears as an uncanny *double of Zarathustra* (see the *Prologue*)—very close to him, but still sharply contrasted as the one who fails to discover the authentic truth. When Zarathustra wishes truly to "overcome" man, the impudent jester is content to think that he can "over-*leap*" him. Zarathustra, himself ineffective in dealing with the masses, watches the "solemn jester" take his place; and he repudiates these "higher men" when he calls to them: "Oh you bunch of buffoons, you jesters."

Apropos of *Socrates,* whom he is forever attacking, Nietzsche says: "Wherever authority is still considered a matter of good taste, and where commands are used instead of arguments, the dialectician is a kind of clown: people laugh at him and fail to take him seriously. Socrates was the clown who made people take him seriously." But again Nietzsche appears to feel close to this same Socrates when he writes: "I seem to feel that Socrates was deep (his irony consisted primarily in having to appear superficial in order to get along with men at all)." But the following rejection sounds decisive: "Everything about Socrates is exaggerated, eccentric, caricature. He is a buffoon having the instincts of Voltaire in him."

Cynicism is recognized, but clearly not in a sense that is close to Nietzsche's own make-up: "Cynicism is the only form in which ordinary people have any contact with honesty." But then he encounters it on another level as something more like himself: "There are free, audacious spirits who wish to conceal . . . the fact that their proud hearts are incurably broken (Hamlet's cynicism, the case of Galiani); and at times foolishness itself is used to mask a wretched, all-too-certain knowledge."

Shakespeare in *Julius Caesar* "twice introduced a poet and twice heaped abysmal contempt upon him. . . . Brutus himself lost patience when the poet made his appearance, . . . as a creature who seemed to be puffed up with possibilities of greatness—including moral greatness— but who seldom attained even to common honesty in his philosophy of life and action. Brutus shouts: 'I'll know his humor when he knows his time: Away with the jingling fool!' [6] Imagine this projected back into the soul of the poet who wrote it." "I know of no more heart-rending reading than Shakespeare. What must a man have suffered to feel such a need to be a clown! Do we understand Hamlet? It is not doubt, it is certainty that brings on madness. . . . But this requires depth. To feel thus, one must be deep, an abyss, a philosopher. . . . We *are afraid* of the truth. . . ."

When we take all these things together, we are able to see the true significance of his later interpretations of himself. He says of his books: "Here and there they attain to the highest that can be attained on earth—cynicism. . . ." And he says of himself: "I do not choose to be a saint, . . . but rather a clown. . . . Perhaps I am a clown. . . . But still . . . the truth speaks through me." To Avenarius [7] he writes of himself: It "belongs among my proofs of strength to be to a certain extent a clown, a satyr, or, if you prefer, a 'feuilletonist'—or at least to be *able* to be one, as I was in connection with the *Wagner Case*. That the deepest spirit must also be the most frivolous is very nearly the formula of my philosophy." Overbeck said of the insane Nietzsche whom he found in Turin: "On the whole he expressed himself most frequently about the profession he attributed to himself, that of being the jester of the new eternities."

Such words as the above must remain ambiguous. The mask in itself

[6] *Julius Caesar,* Act IV, Scene 3. The original reads: "I'll know his humor when he knows his time:/ What should the wars do with these jigging fools?/ Companion, hence!"—Trs.
[7] Ferdinand Avenarius, poet and esthete, brother of Richard, the German positivist. Founded *Kunstwart,* an art journal, in 1887.—Trs.

and the clown are acknowledged as his own and still repudiated as his opposite. Sometimes it is the nothingness hiding nothing, the histrionics of the fraudulent, enacting itself before itself and others. Then the mask is entirely alien to him, an object of a horror mixed with hostility because he has allowed himself to be so profoundly deceived by it. But then again it is the protection sought when, in despair, one does not want to know what he knows: "Uncertain among a hundred recollections . . . strangled by his own noose." Finally it is the possibility of existence that seems to express the most profound truth and yet lacks it; it is that which looks upon the being of not being and, with an inverted sort of truthfulness, paradoxically lays hold of being by allowing it to become appearance. In any case Nietzsche regards "respect for the mask" as a sign of "refined humanity."

The necessity of being masked throws its shadow on the meaning of a work: No thoughts that go into a work can convey the truth itself. The lack of authenticity in everything determinate results in the ambiguity of the authentic; incommunicability produces the loneliness that hides behind masks. The work of a thinker who has allowed this boundary-experience to permeate his very being is identifiable, as it were, by stigmata: "The writings of a hermit always seem to contain an echo of the desert; in his strongest words one hears a new and more dangerous kind of silence. . . . Whenever one . . . alone with his soul . . . in his cave—whether it is a labyrinth or a gold-mine—becomes a cave-bear or a treasure-seeker, his very concepts will take on a peculiar twilight color and the smell of mould as well as of depth—something unsharable . . . . The hermit does not believe that any philosopher has ever published his authentic and final views in books. . . . Indeed he will doubt that a philosopher could have final and authentic views at all: Perhaps all his caves conceal deeper caves and beyond all his grounds lurks the groundless. . . . Every philosophy is a foreground-philosophy. . . . Every philosophy conceals another philosophy."

The experience of living on the edge of an abyss receives a very ambiguous formulation in the kind of work that Nietzsche takes his to be. When he sees "the supreme form of spirituality" found in modern Europe in "ingenious buffoonery," it appears that this signifies nothing less than the dissolution of Europe's spiritual substance: the loss of the feeling for "a unified stylistic coloration," "the many-colored suit of the clown," and virtuosity in "every kind of style." But it seems to be precisely this that he claims for his own style: "Thanks to the fact that the variety of my inner states is extraordinary, many possible styles are open to me—the most varied art of style that any man has ever had at his disposal. . . . Every style that actually communicates an inner state is good. . . . Good style per se is sheer folly, mere idealism. . . ." One can distinguish the virtuoso in all stylistic forms from the creative thinker who uses all possible styles, and fraudulent masquerading from the masked appearance of genuine wealth. But while Nietzsche at times emphasizes this distinction most decisively, at other times he seemingly leaves it unexpressed.

Simile and Song. Communication is not limited to thought and exegesis. Simile and song, which at first provided a means of communication between Nietzsche and his own dark and mysterious depths, became the most genuine and final communication in connection with his understanding of himself through his work. His poems belong to his philosophizing, not as the garb of thoughts that could also be quite differently expressed, but as the definitive fulfillment of his philosophic progression. Not that they emerge as the end-product of his thoughts; they arise from the source directly out of pregnant *silence.*

Genuine awareness of being senses the horror of silence: "Now all is silent! The sea lies . . . there; it cannot speak. The heavens . . . cannot speak. The little reefs and cliffs . . . —none of them can speak. This frightful silence that suddenly comes upon us is beautiful and horrible. . . . Nature, I pity you because you must be silent. . . . Ah, . . . the heart: it is alarmed . . . it too cannot speak. . . . Speech, even thought, becomes hateful to me; do I not hear behind every word the laughter of error, imagination, and illusion? Oh sea! Oh evening! You are evil teachers! You teach man to cease to be man! . . . Should he become as you now are, . . . monstrous, resting content with himself? Elevated above himself?"

Openness of being—deliverance from silence—is found, according to Nietzsche, in simile when "enhancement of life increases man's power to communicate," as happens to Zarathustra when he returns home to his cave: "Here all things come caressing and flattering to your discourse, for they wish to ride on your back. On every simile you ride here to every truth. Here words and word-shrines of all being open up for me: All being desires here to become articulate, and all becoming here desires to learn to speak through me." To be sure, we hear the disparaging statements: Truth is "a mobile host of metaphors"; truths are "illusions . . . metaphors that are worn out"; "he who is given to rigorous thinking does not care for the images of the poets"; and "with images and similes one persuades but does not prove; that is why men of science fight shy of images and similes." But on the other hand, wherever being per se is spoken of through similes, something superior to science appears ("a fool who wishes to learn from them"). What Nietzsche says of himself is here applicable: "The most remarkable thing is the involuntary occurrence of the image and the simile; one no longer has any idea what is image and what is simile. Everything appears as the nearest, most correct, and simplest expression. . . ." This creative height is irrecoverable: "Pay heed to every hour in which your spirit is ready to speak in similes." Of course, Zarathustra is also capable of saying: "I am ashamed of the fact that I must continue to be a poet" ("that I speak in similes"); but at this point he is referring to the very opposite of present vision and future actuality.

Song is even better than simile. What remains when all else ceases is "that I must sing again,—this is the comfort and the way to recovery that I discovered for myself." At the end of *The Gay Science* Nietzsche writes that "the spirits of my book [assail] me:" "We can no longer bear it. . . . Who sings us a song, a morning-song . . . ?" In the later preface to a new edition of *The Birth of Tragedy* he confesses concerning himself: "It should have *sung*—this 'new soul'—and not have spoken!" And he admits: "Thus I read the thinkers and sing their melodies after them. I know that a soulful longing moves behind the cold words; I hear its singing, for my own soul sings when it is moved."

Polemics. Nietzsche employs polemics because vigorous attack increases his chances of reaching other people. When one is attacked he is compelled to listen, and only then does he become fully conscious of his own truth. Nietzsche's self-understanding makes the meaning of his polemics clear. It is not essentially a matter of a real struggle to dispose of the vacuities of deception and perversion, of hollowness and artificiality (although even this may play a role); what is involved is a struggle with the *best*. "I only attack causes that are victorious. . . . I only attack causes when I have no allies and stand alone . . . I never attack persons; I use a person only as a strong magnifying glass with which to disclose some general critical situation." He wants to respect those whom he forces to oppose him. As he sees it, the greatness of Wagner is indicated precisely by the fact that he struggled against him throughout his whole life. He only attacks a man of rank; he calls for an opponent who is his own equal, and he does not do battle with the vulgar. Something can be extraordinary and still false; Nietzsche does not deplore it, for it manifests the greatness of some actuality within existence. Truth in communicable form must emerge—but by means of a struggle. Without it the truth would not be brought to conscious awareness and actualized. Communication through struggle is itself a kind of truth that by its very nature is incapable of being simply spoken, set down, and permanently fixated.

Since what is attacked is not to be annihilated but affirmed, the battlefield is basically Nietzsche himself, his opponents are forms that he assumes, and the communicable truth is not an immutable certitude independent of the opponents, but simply the impetus to every form of communication, one of which is struggle.

What Nietzsche Is to Himself

Nietzsche's view of himself as a whole could never have been unambiguous. When we bring together all his utterances, we find at once the decisiveness of his self-certainty and the constant dubiety in which he places himself.

Self-certainty appears in his consciousness of his task. The task is not an enterprise that he assumes as a result of reflection; it is identical with his very nature and becomes representative of all men in an historical instant, without allowing him to become a prophet and founder.

From a very early period on, he was conscious of a task that remained indefinite until, after 1880, it grew into an inexorable and exclusive service devoted to an obligation now recognized. As early as 1872 he wrote to Rohde: "A frightful earnestness grips me whenever I hear anything said about it (*The Birth of Tragedy*) because I perceive in such voices a hint of the future of what I have planned. This life is going to be very difficult" (Jan. 22, '72). The way became clearer as he realized in 1877 that his professorship would have to be terminated: "I know and feel that there must be a higher destiny for me than is expressed to me in my so respectable position in Basel" (to Frau M. Gaumgartner, Aug. 30, '77). Later he came to understand what was happening to him: "I did not understand myself, but the urge was like a command. It seems that our remote, irrevocable destiny disposes of us." "The choice of men and things, the rejection of the most agreeable and often of the most venerated—this frightens us, as though an accident, a caprice, broke forth from us, sometimes with volcanic force. But it is *the higher reason of our future task*."

Since 1880, what impresses his whole being into its services is constantly present. It is "that hidden and imperial something, to which we can give no name until it finally proves to be our task." From that time on he is constantly haunted by the fear of "not being able to cope with" his frightful task. "Whether or not I shall succeed in bringing my huge task to completion depends upon circumstances regulated not by me but by 'the nature of things' " (to his sister, Nov. 29, '81). "This path is so dangerous! I dare not call to myself, like a night-wanderer."

But the nature of this task becomes to him one with that of the task of mankind in this world-historical instant. In his youth he wrote: "My task: to grasp the inner connection and necessity of every true culture, the protective and remedial measures of this culture, and its relation to the genius of the people. . . ." In the middle period he states vaguely: "Goal of the free spirit: future of mankind." And at the end we hear: "My task is to make preparations for an instant of the highest possible self-awareness of mankind, a *great midday,* when men will look back and look ahead and when they . . . for the first time will pose the entire question of the Why and the Whereto?"

But at the same time, what Nietzsche really *is* in the fulfillment of his task seems questionable to him right up to the end. To be sure, he is certain, *historically* at least, "of being a capital event in the crisis of value-judgments." From a higher point of view, he sees himself as the source of the great politics of the future, a world-historical being at the turning-point—he *is* in fact himself the turning of world history since he is the first to realize and assimilate it. "And if I do not succeed to such an extent that people render their highest vows in my name for thousands of years, then, in my estimation, I shall have accomplished nothing" (to Overbeck, May 21, '84). He is the transvaluator of values and consequently the lawgiver of the future, for he creates a counter-movement to the nihilism of the turning-point. *Metaphysically* he sees himself as standing at a reversal, not merely of human history, but of the course of world events in its entirety: In thinking of eternal recurrence, he constitutes the point at which all worldly being reverses itself; [8] through him existence discovers itself in self-knowledge. But his awareness of being a momentous fact is accompanied by the torment of being human as well as by jubilation. The kind of man he is, as he represents this crisis, is expressed seldom though aptly in a series of similes:

It may sound as though he wished ironically to belittle the source of his transvaluation when he says: "And I myself, my foolish friends!— What *am* I then, if I am not that subject for dispute: a taste!"

The repudiation of the meaning of his existence together with an awareness of the epochal significance of his torment are expressed metaphorically: "I often see my entire self as the scribble-scrawl drawn on a sheet of paper by an unknown power testing a new pen" (to Gast, Aug., '81). Or again: "How much, since 1876, have I been in many

[8] Cf. pp. 357 ff.

respects, both physical and mental, more a battlefield than a man!" (to Gast, July 25, '82).

He compares his own tireless movement which consumes his very existence with a *flame*, a *light*, a *fire-brand*, and a stroke of *lightning:* "My life is a burning and a consuming. . . ." "I wish to be considered a firebrand and a threat to all dry souls. . . ." "I want to disappear in a dark thunderstorm and be both man and lightning-flash when my last moments arrive." And, above all, we have the following noble expression of his nature:

> Yes, I know from whence I came!
> Discontented as a flame,
> Upon myself I live and glow.
> All I grasp like lightning flashes,
> All I leave behind is ashes:
> Flame I am—that much I know!

2

HOW NIETZSCHE IS TO BE UNDERSTOOD

Whenever we think that we see where Nietzsche stands, we soon find that he is first here, then there, then gone. He is neither here nor there; always he seems to vanish. A capacity for assuming different guises is basic to his nature. Nietzsche's demand: "Above all, do not mistake me" is apposite and true: "I grant that people tend to mistake me; and by the same token I should consider it a great service if some other person would identify me and prevent these confusions."

Nietzsche's protean variability manifests itself not only in all that he says, but in his whole appearance. Just as Socrates and the Sophists were indistinguishable to the crowd, so the truth that cannot be understood by every individual in precisely the same way is invariably subject to confusion with its opposite.

But Nietzsche's variability is not such that, after seeing through each momentary appearance, one could encounter his true and immutable self. The enigma and the difficulty is precisely this, that the endless variability of his appearance seems to spring from his innermost being. Apart from his inexpugnable ambiguity and many-sidedness he simply would not be himself.

We shall begin by examining the typical ways of criticizing Nietzsche and find that, although no one of them can succeed in actually comprehending him, they do prepare us for a potential comprehension when we come to realize *why* they failed.

Ways of Criticizing Nietzsche

Every presentation, by its very nature, must pass judgment upon what it presents, though the judgment may be vague as well as unintentional and indirect. But deliberate criticism that aims at judgment must use the following procedures:

1. *Logical Criticism.* To proceed logically is to show that Nietzsche's pronouncements are *self-contradictory*.

A merely external difficulty arises from the fact that in different contexts Nietzsche uses the very same words to mean entirely different and even opposite things (for example, "illusion," "mask," "truth," "being," "people," "will," and almost all essential words appear as *termini* only temporarily). Furthermore he almost never corrects himself, as he seldom even notices the difficulty. In spite of this, his instinct for the truth makes him, throughout various contexts, assume the positions that are pertinent and suitable within the whole of his thinking. Verbal contradictions are to be ignored, since they are not true contradictions.

The important question concerns the significance of the inexpugnable contradictoriness of all Nietzsche's writings. Does he simply write down anything that occurs to him? Do his thoughts merely express a chaotic multiplicity of moods? Or are the contradictories governed by a necessity, and do the various moods belong together and reveal their unity only in accordance with a law that manifests itself within the whole?

One simply rejects these questions when he approaches Nietzsche with the assumption that he is only properly understood when he is seen to be consistent, and that whatever is self-contradictory is to be excluded as erroneous. He who makes this assumption must do one of two things: Either he finally rejects Nietzsche as inconsequential since he thinks in contradictions from beginning to end, though often without consciously relating the contradictories to each other; or he arbitrarily singles out what Nietzsche himself regarded as an isolated train of thought and then, having excluded what is incompatible because contradictory to it, he purports to criticize the single dogmatic position which remains.

Our proper task, however (undertaken in the presentation of Nietzsche's fundamental thoughts) is to see, first of all, what Nietzsche could *not* have meant by his contradictions, viz., the one to the exclusion of the other. After this it is necessary to bring together that which unites the contradictories, even though he did not point it out (we must, in other words, examine the statements that seem to have been annulled through contradiction, with a view to arriving at the significant thoughts expressed through the contradictoriness itself). Finally we must separate the genuine contradictions that will not yield even to an erroneously unrestrained dialectic that aims at total reconciliation.

The questions that arise are not adequately answered by Nietzsche himself. Here more than anywhere else it becomes clear that he only occasionally deals directly with logical methods. He never realizes that he is wanting in the sort of philosophical training that comes through a painstaking study of the great thinkers. It is understandable that such things remain inessential to him since he himself stands with ever increasing decisiveness at the sources of philosophizing. His own originality permits him to take his professional inadequacies lightly by ignoring them. But his lack of restraint with regard to contradictoriness, accompanied by a tendency to allow his understanding (*Verstand*) to indulge in undialectical forms of thought—forms which he in turn scorns—constitutes a serious formal flaw in his entire work and an obstacle to an understanding of him.

Consequently he repeatedly descends to what he himself regards as false objectifications, fixations, absolutizations, naturalizations; then in other connections he annuls them all without referring to them explicitly. The reader who cannot supply the context himself (i.e., who sees only, and without connection, what Nietzsche actually is doing) cannot, if he is honest, avoid being confused by the discrepancies, contradictions, and products of mere caprice that arise everywhere. Repeated confirmation has strengthened my basic conviction that Nietzsche's thinking receives its philosophic organization, not through conscious method, but rather through an unmatched instinct for truthfulness. Apart from this conviction he would sink to the level of an inspired aphorist, and his philosophizing would have little value. But even if it is possible to illumine the positive implications of his necessary contradictoriness, it is undeniable that there remains a considerable residue of contradictoriness that cannot be regarded as necessary.

A logical analysis should demarcate the cognitive field in which it is possible to express the truth under consideration unambiguously and without contradiction, and then proceed to illumine the philosophic area in which an expression, to communicate the truth, must necessarily become ambiguous or move dialectically in contradictories.

Examples of contradictions that Nietzsche himself grasps and demonstrates are afforded by his twofold evaluation of what appears as the same: Pessimism and skepticism have both positive and negative value, depending upon whether they are to be understood as resulting from strength or weakness; there are two kinds of sympathy and two kinds of decadence; the longing for being (will to eternity) and the longing for becoming (will to destruction) are both ambiguous.

An inherent difficulty is due to the fact that the contradictories cannot simply be conceived as antitheses which, in their movement, change into each other on one single level, as it were, for they also move vertically from one level to another with a resultant antithetical involvement.

Within this second movement there is a further distinction: at times a movement deriving from an earlier level remains to be united with its opposite (e.g., masters and slaves appear as essentially different, although when, at a higher level, the whole of mankind reaches its consummation, the two groups are seen to belong together and to be positively justified). But at other times, what is indispensable to the movement may eventually have to be excluded since no such union with its opposite is possible (e.g., whatever is inauthentic, weak, and fixated and thus lacks the force necessary to endure and has no inner resources). In this case the alternative, being existential rather than logical, would lead to clarity of decision concerning being and not-being, rather than to a rational reconciliation.

He who, in confronting the task of logico-dialectical thinking, persists in discovering hard and fast formulae and strict unwavering dichotomies simply cannot understand Nietzsche. He does not experience the immanent dialectic of things which Nietzsche obeys without always realizing it (but which receives due expression through him nevertheless, since it inheres in the cause he represents), nor does he develop his own nature by actively assimilating the movements of which Nietzsche was aware. He can only dogmatize in a misleading fashion—something to which Nietzsche admittedly comes close as a result of his apodictic way of expressing himself. He is bound to consider as fixed and final formulae what to Nietzsche were only steps and to pervert these formulae by turning them into jargon, demagogic means of persuasion, or sensationalistic journalese.

Due to Nietzsche's lack of method, what is often experienced at the very beginning constantly recurs: one runs into the wall of the seemingly onesided and undialectical—the gross so-be-it and so-ought-it-to-be. One only discovers Nietzsche's immense depth by *studying* him philosophically (and this always involves an inner striving for intellectual growth). But in order to keep this depth in sight one must again and again overcome the rationally onesided formulations of the understanding which he himself recognized in his own thinking but failed to check.

The lack of methodical philosophizing that appears on the very surface of his thought accounts for the seemingly easy availability of Nietzsche's conceptual formulations. And it also explains why his thoughts are at once extensively disseminated and eminently capable of being misunderstood. Nietzsche's true philosophy, however, is understood as rarely as is that of all other philosophers.

2. *Criticism of Contents.* In the second place, criticism can deal with what is asserted and point out errors of fact. It is true that Nietzsche

expresses his unconditional affirmation of genuine science, when, for example, because of his "belief in the supreme utility of science and the knower," he demands "more respect for the knower," or when he demands that "we must become the best learners and discoverers of everything in the world that follows law and is necessitated" if we are to become what we are: the creators of ourselves. But still he experienced his own lack of knowledge and scientific method as a vexatious restriction: "I am so unschooled! And I really need to know so very much!" (to Overbeck, Sept., '81). And on another occasion: "Badly needing to learn something and knowing full well where to find exactly what I personally have to learn, I must allow my life to pass away in the manner required by my miserable organs, my head and my eyes!" (to Gast, March 30, '81). Repeatedly he wanted to resume his studies at universities, but was forced to content himself with the reading of books about the natural sciences and cultural history.

This deficiency, forced upon him by protracted invalidism, was of little consequence for his truly philosophical thinking. Besides, when he spoke of things relating to scientific methodology and conveyed ideas that needed to be expressed in a methodical fashion, his penetrating insight often enabled him to derive extraordinary conclusions from a handful of data (even in dealing with problems of physics). And we may add that his knowledge was restricted only when measured by the scope of the subject-matter that he wrote about.

Still when we study Nietzsche, we must keep the limitations of his knowledge in mind. By busying himself during his youth with the languages and texts of antiquity, he had acquired an extensive experience with philology as a scientific method and had absorbed a wealth of ideas about human actuality. What was missing, as he himself felt, was a fundamental knowledge of the matters of fact that are open to causal investigation—as well as knowledge of law, theology, and critically investigated world history.

That Nietzsche was not always inclined to acknowledge the deficiencies emphasized in the above appears in certain self-assured statements of his later years: "It is even worse with my ignorance, which I make no effort to conceal from myself. There are times when I am ashamed of it but, to be frank, other times when I am ashamed of my shame. Perhaps we contemporary philosophers, as a whole, have an adverse regard for knowledge. . . . Our task is and remains above all that of not becoming confused about ourselves. We differ from scholars, although it is not to be denied that, in addition to other things, we are also scholarly."

It goes without saying that when Nietzsche writes of things that can be investigated within the world—the findings of biology, sociology, physics, etc.,—the reader should not accept his pronouncements uncritically. Nietzsche's own inclinations drive him to use the form of methodical knowledge whenever possible. But Nietzsche must be appealed to against Nietzsche when his snap judgments lead the reader to take seriously what was intended as merely experimental. Only knowledge of biology serves to put Nietzsche's naturalistic conceptualizations to rights, and only precise and methodical sociological insights are suitable as tests of his sociological conclusions.

3. *Existential Criticism.* Finally, criticism may undertake to interpret Nietzsche's *Existenz* as this is disclosed in his books, his letters, and the course of his life. To be sure, *Existenz* is not an object that can be known, and existential interpretation (interpretation being one kind of criticism) is not an expression of knowledge about another person. It expresses, rather, the communicative attitude of the interpreter, and this attitude depends as fully upon the interpreter's own capacities and deficiencies as upon the true being of the one under consideration.

While this kind of criticism could not claim to be universally valid, it would still be most essential if, when pursued with the deepest earnestness, it could yield a decisively univocal conclusion. That in this case such criticism must fail constitutes Nietzsche's uncanny incomprehensibility. In the process of dealing critically with his *Existenz* one encounters partial truths, univocalities that are not to be taken seriously, and possibilities that never become plausible. If one does not become so blind as to lose sight of the real Nietzsche and finally even proclaim him a hopeless incorporation of nothingness, then one sees in him the exceptional individual who constantly calls everything, including himself, in question.

We must examine and counteract several kinds of existential criticism, proceeding always in such a way as not to lose sight of the fact that it is Nietzsche's manner of appearing that makes possible such wholly or partly irrelevant interpretations. They are not completely arbitrary or accidental. Nietzsche can be viewed only from the loftiest standpoint, for he can only live and think when inspired by the most sublime vision of the task he has in mind. When the presence of this task becomes uncertain or veiled for him, then existential criticism expressed in psychological terms turns into mere obtrusive illusion. Nietzsche lives and moves in a realm of the extreme that would not suffer even a moment's neglect. That is why his abysmal questionability is always present. In the end, all kinds of existential criticism turn out to be untrue. Were this not the case and were a denial of Nietzsche's *Existenz* to result from calling him in question, then anyone who accepted this denial would find his nature to be unsound and would no longer need to study him philosophically.

To start with, we shall examine a particular criticism of Nietzsche's *Existenz* in order to show that in spite of its plausibility it is untrue. Next we shall design constructs relating to the whole of his *Existenz* with a view to showing how even these fall short of the whole man.

Nietzsche is reproached for his *individualism* and *distance from the people* (*Volksfremdheit*). His works are full of glorifications of the great individual and contempt for the many-too-many—the masses. But reliance upon words is deceptive.

It is true that expressions such as the following appear unambiguously to support the unlimited absoluteness of the individual: "Selflessness is worthless." "One must stand firmly upon his own feet." "Sanctify the ego." The "creating, willing, evaluating ego" is "the measure and value of things." "Will to be a self!" But these are to be set over against the following: His "ponderous, serious, granite ego" says to itself: "What do I matter!" And with respect to man, we read that "we are buds on a single tree; . . . the individual per se is a delusion. . . . You must put an end to feeling your self as such a phantastic ego!"

Actually Nietzsche is not an individualist, and neither is he lost within the whole of things. The dichotomy along with the question which it generates is inapplicable to him; it is not even implied by the statements quoted above. His "individualism" is devotion to causes, and he esteems himself only insofar as the necessity of being gains expression through him. An individual existence that revolves around itself is always foreign and contemptible to him, though he is still confident that matters of paramount importance can only come into existence through authentic selves.

Accordingly his countless disparaging statements about the masses do not represent a distance from the people rooted in his lack of *Existenz*. That he often says "people" when he really means *masses* is simply a matter of verbal usage that need not mislead us. The substance of the true people, i.e., the people in the true sense of the word, is not only not foreign to him, but it is the constant object of a longing that will not permit itself to be deceived or turned aside. He suffers deeply because our "people have no cultural unity." "How can the great productive spirit stand being among a people whose unity of experience has vanished?" To him "the alien nature (*das Unvolkstümliche*) of the culture of the neo-Renaissance is a frightful fact."

Thus Nietzsche's individualism and his distance from the people can be attested by countless isolated statements and contested through others. It is a matter of realizing in what respect he does *not* have the attitude for which he is reproached and that he in particular truly wishes to live in what is generally referred to as "the whole" or "the people." He attacks, in its appearance, not its source, what had been so grossly perverted in the language of his day. He does not reject its true actuality and constant possibility, but the secondary source of its perverse transformation into a spurious reality, i.e., an unreality. Consequently his formulations have a curious tendency to reverse themselves:

His "distance from the people" is his will to the people whom he regards as authentic: "A people is worthy only insofar as it can press the stamp of eternity upon its experiences." "A people is characterized not so much by its great men as by the way in which it accords them recognition and honor." To him the people consists in the minority of the masters who, because of their creative natures, are called upon to frame laws, as well as in the scale (*Stufenbau*) of capacities that emerge because of the inequality of men and that should condition and affirm one another.[1] Having believed during his youth, only later to renounce and finally cry out in despair, he seeks his people in the distant future. He sees that not only those who lead—those who are careful not to go *too* far ahead, i.e., those who as fuglemen remain near the people and in touch with the realities that must be faced—are bound up with the people, but also those who rush ahead by trying out possibilities and revealing things that have not yet become effective within the whole. A people that, being more than a mere mass devoted to the moment, is really a people and that consequently possesses and lives by the most extensive recollections and future possibilities, can bring forth these far-roaming ones: adventurous representatives of the people's spirit, heroes of lonely questions and discoveries, experimenters, actualizers and projectors of true humanity, testers and inexorable unveilers. The people makes them possible, and —when it takes notice of them at all—tolerates them and stands in awe of them, but is slow to follow them. Perhaps long after they are dead they will be emulated as the truly alive, though not without modification and frequent misunderstanding. Nietzsche is indeed bound up with his people and its substance. Only this self-identification enables us to understand how the relentless and, to the superficial observer, merely hostile criticism of the appearance of things German in his time could actually be self-criticism.

The reproach of individualism and distance from the people is only

---

[1] Cf. also pp. 271–272 (chapter on Great Politics) concerning Nietzsche's conception of the inevitable and necessary *Stufenbau* of the human society.—Trs.

one of many which, if expanded to apply to Nietzsche's whole *Existenz,* would assert that his thinking and even his entire being is devoid of substance. But it is well to experiment with the possibility of relentless critical construction; in this way the objection is carried to its extreme limit, and one is forced to make a decision on the basis of one's own existential experience in studying Nietzsche:

Nietzsche's thinking stops short at nothing: "In the presence of any individual there are a hundred reasons for being considerate, but I do not see why one should not force his honesty to its outermost limits when he writes." But such honesty allows him to experiment with and express whatever occurs to him. He is no longer aware of limitations or restrained by antitheses, and he displays a lack of respect for greatness (Kant becomes the Chinaman of Königsberg; Schiller, the Moral-Trumpeter of Säckingen, etc.),[2] so that his ideas of spiritual substances and of men become distorted. The growing intensity of expression, the increase in strident value judgments, in self-assurance, and in demands for the eccentric are bound to dupe or repel.

Early in his career he knew "of two very high things: measure and the mean"; he often expressed his rejection of the fanatical. But it becomes possible for him to reject measure, though with a feeling of awe in confronting a fate that he did not choose: "Measure is foreign to us—we may as well admit it to ourselves. What provides our titillation is precisely the endless, the unmeasured. . . ." What he calls "modern existence" seems to him "like unalloyed hybris. . . . *Hybris* is our entire attitude to God, that is to say, to any alleged spider of purpose and morality hiding behind the ensnaring net of causality. . . . *Hybris* expresses our attitude to ourselves, for we experiment on ourselves as we would not permit anyone to experiment on a beast. . . . What do we still care about 'salvation' of the soul! In the end we cure ourselves: being ill is instructive. . . ." Finally he sounds triumphant: "We immoralists—we are today the only power that needs no allies. We will gain power and victory even without the truth. The enchantment that fights for us . . . is the magic of extremes, the seduction that goes all the way. We immoralists—we are the most extreme."

The question is whether these experiments with the immoderate derive from an approval of immoderation, the possibility of which is existentially rooted in the whole of his thinking. Such an interpretation relates to the role imposed on the exceptional man: When, from a new source he

---

[2] The allusion is to the somewhat shallow, neo-Romantic epic poem, *Der Trompeter von Säckingen* by J. V. v. Scheffel, perhaps better known as the author of historical novels and student songs.—Trs.

comes into existence in an old world and is the only one to detect the sham and falsehood concealed by the seemingly self-evident and generally unquestioned import of all its aspects, he tries desperately to communicate what he sees. Stifled by fear of being ignored or misunderstood, he raises his voice to a strident pitch and assumes an immoderately aggressive attitude. All this is but a symptom of his defenselessness and fatal vulnerability in the darkness of the world. Nietzsche appears as the representative of one kind of fanaticism after another, although his nature, his frame of mind, and his goal are far removed from fanaticism. He cannot attain the detached wisdom and steadfast circumspection possible to the non-revolutionary spirit. Since he conceals nothing and gives of himself freely, his own profound wisdom—like that of Prometheus—becomes *hybris*. His immoderation expresses the impossible task with which he lives.

At the same time, an interpretation that fails to recognize that an exceptional nature must inevitably alienate others can give a very different account of the origin of his immoderation: Now it appears that Nietzsche's existence is not animated by a temperate love that observes limits. Just as his spiritual climate is chilly and the very glow of his passion can be frigid ("I am light: Ah that I were night! . . . But I live in my own light and drink back the flames which burst from within me"), and just as the atmosphere of his vitality appears to find no erotic expression, so it seems that the constant presence of love can never take concrete historical form as a basis for his *Existenz*.

But when the firm ground of living historical actuality no longer seems to speak, everything of human value and every single human being become thoroughly dubious in Nietzsche's eyes. Then immoderation actually spells the ruin of all determinate being. When his shocking strictures and judgments eradicate the moderation that he previously willed, his timid reserve seems to vanish. To be sure, he surrenders himself unreservedly to his dialectic by living through it instead of simply thinking it through. But the dead earnestness which permeates his being can make him appear to consume and efface himself existentially.

This earnestness grows out of his contact with the actual world. However, he becomes increasingly estranged from it as he proceeds in thought to the involuntary unworldliness of an existence that becomes little more than imaginary. It is as though his experience is entirely for the sake of knowledge; he seems to see the present as well as the future in a visionary fashion, without ever identifying himself with the historical reality around him. This may be regarded as symbolized by the "principle" that he stated as a student after he had belonged to a fraternity for two semesters: "In doing this, I violated my own principle of devoting myself to things and to men only long enough to become acquainted with them" (to Mushacke, Aug., '65). What is confusing here is that Nietzsche never contents himself with mere esthetic observation and enjoyment but, instead, suffers to the point of despair, without finding a firm anchorage: He can never identify himself with another human being, with a profession, or with his fatherland. He is entirely at one only with his work.

When one examines such constructions as the above and then discovers how much Nietzsche really knows of just that of which the constructions, strictly applied, would show him to be ignorant—the fullness of historical *Existenz*—then paradoxical questions arise: Could it be that the existential deficiency of his being gives rise to a new and, to us, unfamiliar *Existenz* devoted to mankind as a whole? Is it possible that the standpoint to which he banished himself affords him a perspective and a medium for insights that are of incomparable value to the rest of us? Perhaps these insights touch so clearly and decisively upon existential possibilities precisely because they relate to an *Existenz* that is not granted to the one who illumines them—the existential exception whose awareness of this fact springs from another level. In this case, Nietzsche's greatness consists in an awareness of nothingness which enables him to speak more clearly and passionately of the other—of being—and to know it better than those who perhaps share in it without even being sure of it and consequently remain inarticulate. Then his banishment from reality and his passion for the truth would seem to be interrelated. In particular, the significance of communication with one's neighbor, i.e., with friends, comrades in arms, fellow-workers and one's own people, would become clear to Nietzsche as a result of his being deprived of everything.

One must devise these constructions in order to entertain such possibilities and see whether or not they are credible. The sudden emptiness that can overtake one in the study of Nietzsche when he falsely expects more than Nietzsche himself is able to give—namely, positive fulfillment instead of incitement, challenge, and skeptical questioning—may occasionally make such constructions appear quite convincing. But, taken by themselves, they are untenable: Purporting to show that Nietzsche is devoid of *Existenz,* they present a phantastic *Existenz* of empty possibility. Whenever they show something to be objectionable in his nature, it soon turns out that he himself represented its opposite. No one has ever been so keenly aware of and so deeply concerned to advocate moderation and circumspection as the immoderate Nietzsche; no one has ever had so adequate a conception of communication and incommunicability; no one has been more uncompromising in relentlessly carrying out his task. No one could more sharply call in question the life of knowledge than he who yet wished to sacrifice his life for knowledge. His immoderation, like everything that is questionable, represents fate and not a fixed position voluntarily assumed. When he proceeds to the boundary where the fullness of being is lacking, he characterizes himself truly as a buffoon. In opposition to his seeming lack of love stands his terrible and indefinite statement: "No great love seeks love—it seeks something more," as well as the reversal that seems to call everything in question: "What does anyone know of love when he has not despised precisely that which he has loved?" All that he says must be considered, not only in context, but within the whole of his thought.

But at the same time the whole is not actually available to us. Any attempt to arrive at a comprehensive and final account of Nietzsche shows a foolish and heedless presumption; never does he emerge *in propria persona* as a figure of unquestionable self-sufficiency. Every construction must inevitably founder on Nietzsche's reality, which becomes the more enigmatic, the more we attempt to know its many facets in detail. While any attempted imitation of Nietzsche's questionable doctrines will soon come to nothing and be condemned as a result of its discoverable logical structure, all of Nietzsche's thoughts are fused into something greater. He remains a historical anomaly who, in spite of all that is astonishing, oblique, and misleading, recovers himself and rewards those who seriously immerse themselves in his thinking.

There are philosophers whose statements are increasingly seen to be interrelated as one arrives at a better understanding of them, so that in the end a complete whole resting upon firm ground appears. There are others who stimulate and allure, only to let their victims fall into a void that offers nothing. And there are true philosophers who offer neither firm ground nor a void but a depth that discloses an endless space; they carry one forward indefinitely without leaving him in the lurch. Everything seems to appear in Nietzsche: when a concept suddenly becomes flat and stale, the foundation gives way and the end appears; his nothingness, an empty horizon infinitely extended, causes us to lose all ground; he attains the rank of speculative philosophic creation only by fits and starts. But he has a rank of his own and a new way of philosophizing.

None of the critiques discussed reaches Nietzsche's true substance: every one merely shows how difficult and exacting is the task of really approaching this philosopher. Refuting his arguments, pointing out factual errors, and questioning his *Existenz* through speculative constructions are all insufficient: always something irrefutable that is actually—though indirectly—illumined by criticism reasserts itself. When criticism is at an end, the task of interpreting Nietzsche must be undertaken again and again. In order finally to arrive at a comprehensive view and, through it, sense the active power of his philosophizing, we shall begin by considering Nietzsche's regnant position, namely, *the will to pure this-worldliness* (academicians call it the "standpoint of immanence"; his detractors refer to it as his "godlessness"; while he himself, knowing of the present historical turning-point, applies the formula: "God is dead"). Next we shall take up *his new way of philosophizing;* and finally we shall consider *the possibility of assimilating what he has to say.*

The Will to Pure This-Worldliness

Nietzsche's basic thoughts on transvaluation seem to have but a single source: The downfall of all that once counted as valuable results from the fact that God is dead. Consequently, what was once the object of faith has become illusory, and disclosure of the illusion reveals the immanent catastrophe. Faith (*Glaube*) in God, once the source of the way that led historically to a gradual lowering of man's rank, has now, after the loss of faith, become the indirect source of the present catastrophe.

But Nietzsche's thought turns to the authentic being of man that finally, after the catastrophe, should be sufficiently free from the illusions of religious faith to become stronger than ever before. He regards the death of God as a frightful event, but he wills godlessness nevertheless. Because he strives for the highest level of humanity that can ever be actualized, he undertakes to develop in thought the will to pure this-worldliness.

To him this is not a matter of one basic principle (*Grundgedanke*) among others: it is his governing propensity; it is, as it were, the principle of principles—the one to which all the others are subservient. It has been emphasized in every chapter and must now be viewed and interpreted in connection with the whole.

How Nietzsche Posits Godlessness. Believing in the existence of God amounts, as Nietzsche sees it, to defamation of the world [3] and the fullness of actual life and to an escapism that would abandon the world and the arduous tasks that it imposes. But we are called upon to do and to realize all that is possible here and now. The possible has its source and its limit in the creative will alone. Zarathustra demands that all imagin-

---

[3] Cf. pp. 320 ff.

ing should stop within these limits: "God is a supposition; I want your suppositions to go no further than your creative wills. . . . I want them to be limited by what is thinkable. . . . Neither the realm of the inconceivable nor of the unreasonable shall be your home." Thus God was the greatest danger and had to die. As a "delusion and product of human artifice," he became the greatest objection to existence. But this illusion not only distracts men from what can actually be achieved; his existence would actually be unbearable for creative man: "If there were gods, then how could I bear not to be a god? *Ergo,* there are no gods."

If the regnant directive in Nietzsche's thought is the attainment in actuality of the highest and best that is possible for man without God, nevertheless, Nietzsche, in spite of himself and without being aware of it, shows decisively that the limited existence of man cannot fulfill itself without transcendence. The negation of transcendence brings about its own reappearance. It appears to thought in falsifying constructions of substitutes and to the authentic self in a still uncomprehended shattering confrontation of true transcendence in opposition to false. Nietzsche's nobility and honesty, in a time of apparently universal godlessness, produce in him the restive form of godlessness that, so far as we are able to discover, issues in the most extreme falsity of thought as well as the most genuine confrontation with transcendence. Both alternatives need to be examined more closely.

A Substitute for Transcendence and How it Fails. A man is only himself when he lives in relation to transcendence. Transcendence is the manner of appearance in existence through which alone man can confront the nature of being and of himself. The necessity is inescapable: when one disowns it, some surrogate is bound to appear. Nietzsche chooses to live without God since his honesty requires him to believe that life with God involves self-deception. But just as his actual loss of communication with men gave rise to the association with his invented friend Zarathustra, so his denial of God had to give rise to a surrogate. We shall see how this came about.

His metaphysical doctrine tells us what that being per se, conceived as nothing but pure this-worldliness, actually is: Being is *the eternal recurrence of all things.* The insight into this recurrence, with its consequences for our awareness of being, our conduct, and our experience, has taken the place of belief in God. Being is *will to power;* all that occurs is nothing but a mode of the will to power which in its endless appearances furnishes the sole propulsion of becoming. Being is *life;* it is designated by the mythical symbol, Dionysus. The meaning of being is *the super-man:* "The beauty of the superman came to me like shade: what do I now care about—the gods!"

In each case, being is no longer the transcendence of God; instead it is the immanence that I can discover, investigate, and produce. Nietzsche wishes to prove eternal recurrence physically, to observe the will to power and life empirically, and to bring the superman into existence. But his metaphysics never really relates to determinate, specific beings within the world. Thus the referent of his thought, insofar as it is not to be confused with any determinate object within the world, actually amounts to transcendence, although verbally it refers to absolutized immanence. The being that Nietzsche has in mind can only be observed and conceived in actual specific objects within the world. Hence the constant transformation of transcending total immanence into the known immanence of particularity pertaining only to specific mundane things. This comes about because, having previously identified the essence of being meta-physically with an absolutized specific world-being, he can always return to the latter. Thus his meaning is constantly changing from transcending thinking to discursive thinking within the world as he shifts from one method of thinking to another:

(1) Being, as the endless becoming of life and the will to power in the circle of recurrence, is reached by a series of leaps: from occurrences experienced as near and actual to distant possibilities of occurrence in general, and from these latter to the becoming of the natural world in its entirety. *These leaps,* always made within the world, *take the place of the leap to transcendence.* Already they transcend, for they no longer arrive at compelling empirical knowledge of things in the world. But such transcending leaps over all specific things to the totality of immanent existence, instead of proceeding from the self-being of *Existenz* to transcendence. Instead of seeking, within the realm of what the understanding cannot grasp, the eternal presence of transcendence through historically decisive, actualizing self-being with respect to it, the individual, caught up in endless becoming within a presumably intelligible whole, becomes important only because he eternally recurs, manifests a degree of power, and represents true life. Since this transcending is not merely a perversion, but actually involves a process that is genuine, he is often, in his mood, dimly aware of its true sense, although his thoughts about it end in mere objectivization.

(2) Such transcending makes no use of the distinction between the *objectively discoverable* truth that is capable of providing effective means

to planned activity within the world and the *illuminating* truth that arouses impulses without definitely pointing out the way to the calculating understanding and reads ciphers without conceptualizing being. But the thought that illuminates is not a kind of knowledge that can be applied: the latter, because of its unavoidable narrowness, is in and by itself without sufficient force to provide a basis for a consciousness of being. When, as a result of confusion, the two change places, the possibility arises that the thinker will be enchanted by non-existent tasks that could be pursued only in a state of self-deception.

For example, a fantastic type of human being is to be created to take the place of transcendence. The superman becomes an ideal product of planned breeding to be carried out on earth; his superiority to the gods consists after all in the fact that he is a possible product of human contrivance: "Can you create a god? Then be quiet about all gods! But you are quite capable of creating the superman." If there were gods, there would be nothing to create. But as it is: "Again and again I am driven to man—by my ardent will to create. Just so is the hammer driven to the stone." But how? Through thoughts that I cause others to think, or through breeding humans as animals are bred, with a view to the selection of certain highly esteemed, useful, and easily recognized characteristics. In any case man can only really conceive of a finite purpose, and he never knows what the results of his activity will be. He may of course place himself above men by assuming the role of a creator-god; but this is sheer illusion.

While for an instant the superman appears to offer something in the nature of a task, the substance of the purely worldly impulse substituting here for divine transcendence in the end becomes increasingly indefinite and disappears into a void: "Up to now there have been a thousand tasks, for there have been a thousand peoples. . . . The *one* goal is missing. Humanity is still without a goal." The deity may well have a goal for humanity; but no man can know it and properly take it as his task. The final result of the sort of thinking that is intended to substitute for transcendence is indulgence in merely imaginary situations that leave the impression of being a future reality of the highest order; but being nothing but vain illusions, they do not constitute transcendence.

The setting up of impossible tasks causes man to forget his finitude and his limits by requiring of him what no man, but only an omnipresent God, could accomplish. For example, when Nietzsche presumes to teach that one should "die at the right time," [4] he is speaking as though man

---

[4] Cf. pp. 324 ff.

could not only hazard his life and sacrifice it for a cause or for other persons, but could even survey and evaluate his whole existence and know when to bring about his own death.

(3) Confusion of the truth that can be investigated objectively with that which can only be elucidated, or confusion of the always relative knowledge of particular things in the world with transcending, results in ambiguity whenever transcending is expressed by means of the concepts of physical science or of psychology and sociology. Nietzsche commits this error repeatedly in using biology, psychology, and sociology as media of inspirational appeal and illuminating cipher-writing. So, for example, next to the passionate "excelsior" which his guiding types of higher men signify, we find neutralizing tendencies in the form of an insipid recognition of *homo natura,* and next to an appeal to overcome the psychological appears psychological leveling. The perverse confusion of fact-finding psychology with hortatory elucidation of *Existenz* derives in the end from a will to pure immanence that cannot but transcend constantly in spite of a determination to reject every kind of transcending and to avoid *Existenz* as well as transcendence.

Concepts that remain immanent are either determinate and effective concepts of things in the world, or they refer to the whole of being and become indeterminate and ineffective, except when they cause those who are deceived by them to act in ways that—when they are not downright destructive—bring about very different results from those intended. The ersatz concepts which Nietzsche uses to deny transcendence succeed in muting transcendence but become empty of worldly knowledge as well. Everything that human beings can think comes either from knowledge of actually existing particulars that can be pointed out, or from the language of a transcendence that relates to the *Existenz* of a self which can no more be pointed out than can transcendence. What makes Nietzsche's positions empty is that, while he intends to remain within the world, he abandons the objects of worldly knowledge.

It can hardly be denied that at critical points something like tedium can overcome the reader, who is disenchanted when all terminates in speechless symbols, and when an empty becoming, an empty movement, an empty creation, and an empty future appear to have the last inane word.

But this appearance is not the final truth. When Nietzsche is called an "anti-Christian" and charged with atheism, we must remember that his atheism is neither a categorical denial of God's existence nor the indifference of an ungodly man whose disbelief consists in a disinclination to search for Him. Even the way in which Nietzsche establishes for his generation the fact that "God is dead" is an expression of his profound shock. Just as his immorality is intended to promote the destruction of a deceptive and superficial current morality by an authentic ethos, so his "godlessness" seeks to suppress the leveling and apathetic lie of pretended belief in God in favor of a genuine commitment to being. And when, in his godlessness, the inexorable drive to elevation of his humanity becomes operative and the honesty that he demands turns into a radical negation of all belief in God, even then Nietzsche shows a remarkable proximity to Christianity: "It is still the best bit of ideal life that I have ever come to know: from my childhood on I have followed it into many nooks, and I believe that in my heart I have never been vicious against it" (to Gast, July 21, '81).

Such things as the above indicate that, in spite of Nietzsche's attempt to avoid transcendence by rejecting belief in God and substituting pure this-worldliness, he remains strongly inclined to transcend.

Nietzsche's Transcending. The surest sign of his transcending is the absolute universality of his negativism—as opposed to the position of all positivists, naturalists, and materialists who, with complete and unshakable self-confidence, confine themselves to those palpable objects which they take to constitute genuine being. Positivism is treated with scorn, though many of its formulae appear in his writings. The source from which his thought springs is not the usual godlessness that is content to investigate empirical objects within the world, formulate hypotheses about them, and then invent some superstitious view or other to explain what being is; the source is his boundless discontent in confronting every form of being that appears to him. Quite possibly everything that Nietzsche denies has been denied before, but only singularly, with all the rest remaining to be naïvely affirmed, or without endangering the denier existentially because of the secret safety of some obvious existent standing in the background. In Nietzsche's case, on the other hand, dissatisfaction gives rise to such a passionate and self-sacrificing impulse to deny that it seems to come from the source that impelled the great religious leaders and prophets.

Nietzsche's transcending appears as a nihilism which he admittedly followed out to the end. This, which he regards as the creative nihilism of the strong, is contrasted with the uncreative and merely destructive nihilism of the weak: "Each forceful and fruitful movement of humanity has created some nihilistic movement."

He finds the nihilism he rejects in great historical phenomena and in modern decadence. He calls Brahmanism, Buddhism, and Christianity nihilistic religions "because they have all glorified Nothing—the very opposite of life—as the goal, the *summum bonum,* or as 'God.' " This passive nihilism of weakness, in which all values war upon the others, is decomposition; "everything that comforts, heals, quiets, benumbs," comes to the fore "in various kinds of disguise, religious or moral, political or esthetic." Weakness is also the "nihilism after the Petersburg model (i.e., belief in unbelief right up to the point of martyrdom)." It "always shows first of all the need for a belief, a support, a backbone, a prop." Nihilism is a phenomenon of decline. The destruction of the nihilists becomes self-destruction: They are "instinctively driven to undertake activities that make deadly enemies of the powerful ones": There is a residue of a transformed power-will left to them "in that they *force* the powerful to be their executioners. This is Buddhism in its European form: acting negatively after all existence has lost its sense."

When set over against such possibilities, Nietzsche's nihilism proves to be a form of transcending that is much too ambiguous to be easily understood. Being is to reveal itself to him in the nihilism that transcends. But to the onlooker this does not seem to happen: he has overcome nihilism, but in the form decreed by temporal existence, which means that it constantly reappears and has to be defeated all over again. His increasingly dogmatic statements (e.g., his unsuccessful attempt to find substitutes for transcendence) can appear as an unbeliever's will to believe. Nietzsche's leap to doctrines is not a leap to tradition (as in Dostoevski or Kierkegaard) but to self-made beliefs and self-devised symbols (superman, eternal recurrence, Dionysus, etc.) that are wholly lacking in historically convincing atmosphere. Hence when one considers only the dogmas, Nietzsche can appear to be a thinker who is unable to live with his own conclusions: He seems to use his admittedly nihilistic position to force an escape from the conclusions that he originally intended to overcome. He now seems to have nothing at all and to grasp the illusion of being in the emptiness of an immanence that is merely imaginary. His forced belief, born of despair, appears to cling to something fictitious. But still it only looks this way when one isolates the positivist aspects of his doctrine instead of considering the whole. His nihilistic transcending does not attain to peace within being. Hence his godlessness is the increasing agitation of a search for God that perhaps no longer understands itself.

Nietzsche expresses his godlessness in a manner that conveys his unspeakable torment: Having to renounce God means that "you will never again pray, . . . never again find peace in boundless trust. You deny yourself the opportunity to come to rest before a final wisdom, a final goodness, and a final power, and to throw off the harness of your thoughts. . . . Man of renunciation, do you really choose to deny yourself all this? Who will give you the strength to do so? No one ever had *this* much strength!" Nietzsche's insight, his nature, and his exhortation are such that he could not but wish that he might be mistaken: "Right up to the end, those who somehow managed to have a god for a companion never experienced what I know as 'loneliness.' Today my life consists in the wish that all things could be quite different from the way I see them to be, and that someone could cause my 'truths' to become incredible" (to Overbeck, July 2, '85). He saw the abyss clearly and took its measure with magnificent honesty: "A profound man has to have friends, unless he still has his god. But I have neither god nor friends!" (to his sister, July 8, '86). But although terrified, he does not retreat. We can thus understand what he considers true human courage to be: "Do you have courage? . . . Not courage before witnesses but the courage of the hermit and the eagle which is no longer witnessed even by a god!"

It is not surprising that we can finally discover direct expressions of his contact with transcendence. Even his thinking allows for the resurrection of the god that he must deny, when he says, for example: "Actually it is only the moralistic god that has been refuted." He decisively leaves room for the divine, though he speaks of gods and the godly rather than of the One God: "How many new gods are still possible! To me, in whom the religious (i.e., god-building) instinct occasionally comes to life at the wrong time: how very differently, how variously has the divine revealed itself on each occasion. . . . So many strange things passed me by in those timeless instants that drop into life, . . . I would not doubt that there are many kinds of gods." But quite as decisive is the movement that places the whole burden on man: "It seems important to me that one get rid of the All, of Oneness—of the Unconditioned. One could not help accepting it as superlative and giving it the name 'God,' . . . What once was given to the unknown and the whole must be reserved for what is ours and lies near at hand."

If this "near" always seems inadequate, Nietzsche can in the end accept as essential the act of transcending every present situation (though the interrogative form of his expression amounts to a surrender): "Can it be that the whole is composed of nothing but discontented parts that have only desirabilities in mind? Is the whole course of things perhaps simply the 'Away from here! Away from actuality!'—eternal dissatisfaction itself? Is desirability perhaps the moving force itself? Is it—*deus?*"

Only in one connection do we find Nietzsche somewhat at rest in transcendence. He instinctively created for himself a new landscape-mythology of pure immanence.[5] Nature provided refuge for his nobility and, through a cipher-language, confronted his godlessness with the final identification of his being and the being of things. Here we have a mythical spiritualization of nature on the part of a man whose loneliness is absolute; it is the landscape per se, apart from any human being other than the one who hearkens to it, that here becomes mythical. If this myth amounts to an expression of his lack of capacity for human communication, then the question that arises concerning the boundary of Nietzsche's nature may be stated: "Are godlessness and incapacity for communication intimately related to each other?" Actually there is a meaningful connection between his philosophical and poetic expressions. But in any case one would be drawing a false inference to the whole man from what is surely a regnant trend in his thought, were one to say: "God is dead to him because he never loved anyone unconditionally; his radical godlessness stands in existential relation to his radical incommunicability." On the contrary, his passionate longing for communication never permits the complete disappearance of his indefinite deity: his godlessness is the agitation that penetrates to the innermost being of his *Existenz*. His *Existenz* and his thinking are too extensive to be so easily captured. But at any rate the fact that the idea of a unity between godlessness and incommunicability (false as it is when absolutized) can be entertained even for a moment is a sign of the interpretative possibilities offered by the thought of substitutes for the deity.

Philosophizing in a Godless World. The godlessness that Nietzsche represented is not to be regarded as simply true or false. There is no proof that God exists, and the godless have no proof that He does not exist. Likewise one can neither prove nor disprove that man is merely a kind of animal: man is always at liberty to feel that he is an animal when he is capable of it. In questions of this kind, arguments settle nothing; at best they clarify matters. When we are dealing with what lies beyond the limits of universally valid knowledge (*das allgemeingültige Wissbare*), the truth is what has been actualized. Its existential seriousness is undeniable, whether we meet it in Nietzsche or anywhere at all in its process of actualization. Godlessness is a force in the world. What Nietzsche saw and expressed was just such a reality, and he promoted its subsequent growth to an incalculable extent. This kind of godlessness is not the tedious inanition of nothingness; it is a demonic passion. Nietzsche

[5] See pp. 371 ff.

created an utterly magnificent expression of this godlessness in all its incomprehensible manysidedness.

Although no compelling insight shared by all rational beings can force a universally valid decision of the issue dividing the faithful from the godless, still truthfulness requires us to observe the actuality of existing godlessness and the effects of its power. Philosophizing must continue to live with this actuality to preserve its honesty. If there is any truth in the transcendence of the self as the basis of philosophizing, then this truth exists only when it holds its own during critical questioning by the other—by godlessness—and recognizes not merely the actuality and strength of this other but also its courageous willingness to sacrifice, its readiness to throw life itself into the balance, and its rousing force.

A supreme existential necessity for each individual is the decision whether to live for oneself in godlessness or to live in relation to the godhead; a decision dependent, not upon verbal formulation of knowledge about oneself but upon one's inner attitude and evaluation of things, one's daring, and one's experience of being.

Philosophizing recognizes its own insufficiency. It is unsure of itself in the absence of the other: the *revealed religion* that forever eludes it, that constantly calls it in question, and that of itself it can neither emulate nor understand. The godlessness that Nietzsche grasped in its entirety is no less critical of philosophy. In its claim to exclusive possession of the truth, godlessness is related to revealed religion which for its own reasons it wishes to destroy. Philosophizing based upon self-being is not opposed to the actuality of either revealed religion or godlessness; it is concerned to illumine itself through them, to raise questions, and to allow itself to be questioned. It is distinct from godlessness in that it recognizes—or at least is not concerned to destroy—revealed religion even when it disowns it; it is distinct from revealed religion in that it does not wish to wage a war of extermination against godlessness. Philosophizing, as a physically powerless psychic actuality, can only appeal to the rationality of autonomous human beings, awakening and stimulating them by quietly handing on the heritage of millenniums. The visibly growing powers of revealed religion and godlessness may tolerate it, promote it, or reject it and force it into hiding. Philosophy is devoid of coercive force: when it uses argument, it can merely point out the implications of explicit religious dogmas or godless assertions; existentially it can reveal the abysses and possibilities. By its very nature it possesses boundless openness and readiness, but it completes itself through confrontation with revealed religion and godlessness, both of which at decisive points in the process of communication become taciturn and withdraw. Horror at this actual breaking off of communication on the part of men—who, being men and not mere forces of nature, are capable of communicating—is one of the strongest impulses to the sort of philosophizing that wishes to awaken all the powers within man and bring them to fruition. Philosophizing as such leads neither towards nor away from God; it has its source in a transcendent relatedness of self-being. It is human actuality that attempts to elicit that from which it actually lives from the depths of reason and *Existenz,* and this in a secret-manifest dialogue carried on through thousands of years.

Nietzsche himself pitilessly exposes the conclusions to be drawn from his godless premises: Christianity and every form of belief in God are unmasked. Everything that man does occurs within the context supplied by a world-exegesis which in every one of its transformations turns out to be just another illusion. Every illusion is an appearance employed by a will to power. Even his own exegesis of the world as the will to power is the exegesis supplied by a will to power. From this it follows that nothing is true and everything is permitted. The power-will insists on being effective, and the most irresistible effect lies, not in any truth, but in the magic of the extreme. There is no restriction by unconditional commands and no limit but that of actual power. The struggle is for its own sake. But within the rubric provided by this metaphysics of power, ambiguity is general, and only nihilism stands out as the constantly present actuality to be overcome.

What thus appears may seem arbitrary and lawless by nature. But at the same time it is the actuality of the power of our own creative law, a victory for power without transcendence, a law that is the law of this power. Unbridled desire is found in the masses, creative force in the superior ruling class. The former group obeys instinctively; the latter group commands because it has the capacity and the power. The one group has to have illusions because it is too weak to affirm its own true self; the other group protects and even creates illusions for its slaves. While rejecting such illusions for itself, it replaces, with sovereign superiority, the supposed illusion of transcendence with those interpretations that, ironically enough, constitute the innerworldly illusion of this will to power.

What Nietzsche has thus conveyed in endless variations with such suggestive power effectively expresses a living being who shrinks from nothing. His kind of philosophizing draws its strength from its readiness to go the whole way and to abide by whatever conclusions are required. Because he follows out this path, one may identify him with it and regard him as the great historical representative of godlessness. But because he is also something more (i.e., because in his shrinking-from-nothing he transcends and does not actually bind himself to his form of godlessness), he is the philosopher who not only *is* but also *philosophizes about* godlessness. That is why, on the one hand, he investigates the nature of the man who takes himself to be only a kind of animal, while, at the same time, he rejects and goes beyond positivism, naturalism, biologism, and pragmatism. When the *philosophizing on the boundary* that Nietzsche performs is placed within a scientistic frame of reference, it at once sinks to the level of biological, naturalistic, and purposive things and events within the world and is *transformed into unphilosophy*. This reversal, followed by a return to philosophy, constantly takes place in his own thinking: it amounts to an experience with a genuine godlessness that cannot endure itself.

One cannot say that without God there would be no more philosophizing, but only that there would be none without transcendence. That is why the reception accorded Nietzsche's views by an unquestioning and stale godlessness and a sophistry that greedily seeks verbal weapons would, without fail, tend toward a straightforward acceptance of his nihilistic immanence and would be recognizable as unphilosophical in that—Nietzsche to the contrary—the shrinking-from-nothing would inevitably be limited in expression but unlimited in practice.

Nietzsche, whose reversion to the unphilosophical (made possible by the fact that only the unphilosophical remains as content) is so commonly misunderstood, can be used by just those powers that he most vigorously opposed: *resentment* that turns its powerlessness to account when it traduces the world and men; *violence* that confuses the thought of the will to power as the basis for rank with the justification of every kind of brutality; *hostility to the spirit* that glorifies life as a mere vital process; *mendacity* that uses Nietzsche's conception of illusion as truth to vindicate every lie; *unconcerned nonentity* that denies everything in order to be able to affirm that its own existence is natural.

Because at the boundary of philosophizing Nietzsche turned toward unphilosophy, risking all in thought, he arrived at the terrible expression of existential godlessness and indicated the other truth before which philosophizing stands. Thus in thought he assumed many positions that proved to be dead ends. To put it otherwise: On the overladen tree of Nietzsche's thought many blooms wither without bearing fruit.

But still his godlessness possesses the greatness of the permanently invincible:

Nietzsche did not consider truth to subsist timelessly—as either the being or the non-being of God. The truth that spoke through him when he transcended was never intended to be permanently possessed in the form in which it was expressed. In this he is invincible.

He saw, in a visionary fashion, the existence of godlessness as the power that might well control the earth. The undeniable existence of this power which, after his time, only continued to increase shows him again as invincible.

If in his radical boundary-experience he erred because of his failure to cope with transcendence, it was a magnificent error, thanks to the earnestness of the experience and the force of his expression. And it was also a necessary and permanently fruitful error since it indirectly points to the truth with compelling power. Man does not grasp truth in its purity. Just as light exists for us only because there is darkness, so we find truth only when we successfully combat the corresponding error. For the third time Nietzsche appears as invincible.

However dominant a role godlessness may play in Nietzsche's thinking, it is not representative of the whole of his thought. For he also works out what is incompatible with this possibility of existence—and does so deliberately. This formulation, though regnant, is after all but one special way of stating his meaning, and his new philosophy turns out to lie deeper.

The New Philosophizing

Nietzsche's godlessness is the most extreme expression of his *total* break with traditional historical substance insofar as the language of this latter lays claim to universal validity. All human ideals seem to him to have come to nothing: He wishes to reject morality and surrender reason and humanity. He views truth as a universal lie; previous philosophy as an established deception; Christianity as the triumph of the misfits and the failures, the weak and the impotent; there is nothing holy or valid that he does not condemn. Or so it seems. Compared with the breaks made by previous thinkers, all of which were particular and limited, since a clear and unquestioned criterion of validity was always left intact, Nietzsche's break is a *ne plus ultra*. He has so thoroughly thought through all its consequences that one can scarcely take a further step in the same direction. The pessimistic analyses and dire predictions of eventual decline that have appeared since his time merely repeat the statements of Nietzsche, who saw Europe press onward towards inevitable catastrophe. His vision, in its magnificence and its depressing ominousness, was original and true, although, when expressed by others at a later date, it usually became meretricious. Nietzsche was essentially different from these latter ones because, being profoundly shaken, he pledged his whole life as a thinker to an approach to the future that would not involve the decline of man. No specific saying of his can be as essential as the terrible seriousness of his life when he broke with everything. The impulse underlying this heroic break derived, not from a will to break, but from a will to affirm.

Here one must ask how Nietzsche grasps and expresses the Yes in its positivity.

The superman, the will to power, life, and eternal recurrence are apt to bowl us over, so to speak, when their positivity is made explicit. Still, these positions, as developed by Nietzsche, prove to have many meanings: Although in their immediate objectivity they are disillusioning, they do have stimulating inner depths that are lost to sight as soon as they are expressed in so many words. It is as though Nietzsche, in proceeding to a metaphysics whose immediate contents no longer concern us, illuminates the existential in mere flashes and not with a sustained light capable of revealing being in peaceful clarity. Hence we have attempted to present more than the factual contents and the immediately present objectivities (shown even in their emptiness when this was necessary), for such things do not by any means answer the challenge posed by the question; above all it was our intention to bring out as many of his concealed meanings as possible. Often this was achieved through reference to occasional scattered sentences which convey more than the fixed positions themselves.

It is not the flat determinacy of the immanent that provides the positivity upon which Nietzsche lays hold, but the indeterminate boundlessness that appears within an endless horizon. But as all ties are loosened and all limiting horizons are transgressed, his thought loses itself in nothingness.

Finally, when he seeks the positive in images and figures, he arrives for the most part at futile symbols that, notwithstanding their eloquence and visionary penetration, lack the compelling force of mythical ciphers.

When, after the break and the loss of all solid ground, Nietzsche finds himself entirely at sea, he clings to eternal recurrence and other dogmatic doctrines like a drowning man saved by an ice floe that is bound to melt away. When he presses on into the boundless, it is as though he wants to fly in a vacuum. In availing himself of symbols, he seems to lay hold upon lifeless masks. No one of these ways is successful.

At the same time they are not entirely futile, for it seems that on all of them the *historicity of Existenz* (*Geschichtlichkeit der Existenz*) continues to provide his incitement and goal. He wills a substance that is not thought but the master of all thought. Whether or not this becomes manifest in an illuminating manner depends upon the thought, for the source can only express itself ambiguously. It appears as though Nietzsche's philosophizing touches upon *Existenz* in its historicity almost unconsciously without grasping it decisively and as though he urges us to return to our own historicity both from the limited determinacy of thought and from endless indeterminacy. But again it often appears as' though Nietzsche no longer thinks on the basis of historicity.

The will to truthful historical *Existenz* impelled Nietzsche to melt everything down in order to arrive at the new source. Wherever he unmasked by overturning façades, exposing untruths, and undermining empty but generally accepted tenets, he was the storm that cleared the air. His magnificent demolition of customary "morality" was demanded by the situation: it opened up a way for a philosophy of *Existenz*. For as long as life was based on self-evident truths simply taken for granted but never truly and unconditionally accepted, philosophizing remained one harmless business among others, and its "themes" continued to be chosen as a result of fortuitous circumstances. Only after a life thus founded had been renounced, did it become possible to philosophize from the whole of the being of *Existenz*.

When we compare Nietzsche's attitude with the attitudes that prevailed during the period of the French Revolution, it becomes clear that, on the one hand, his break was more radical while, on the other, he never lost his will to tradition, in whatever transformation the latter might appear. It is not only that he always regarded the pre-Socratic Greeks as an unattainable high point and model for humanity (a substitute for the Christian New Testament, as it were); he never even considered the possibility of simply forgetting historical tradition and trying to start all over again from the nothing of a new barbarism. His entire work is permeated by his preoccupation with the greatness of the past—even when he rejects it.

Nietzsche's new philosophizing—in spite of the decisiveness with which it was proclaimed, the excitement which it aroused, and the inexorability of its sustained attack on everything permanent—does not attain a complete and final form. This unprecedented struggle of all his feeling, experiencing, and willing expresses itself in the form of thoughts that never reach their goal.

Absolute Negativity. In the course of his factual dialectic, Nietzsche even permits contradictions to increase in depth. In philosophizing such as this, everything has to reverse itself: honesty calls itself to account, the godlessness that he willed fails to overcome the god-building instinct, the will to reject all prophecy still tolerates the prophecy of the absurd, Dionysus stands over against the Crucified, and both can become Nietzsche.

If nothing definite remains as the doctrine concerning the whole that Nietzsche intended, then what is decisive in his philosophizing cannot be any definite thought-content—even though this content be the most prominent and effective in all his works. We must discover the significance of the fact that whatever he says is invariably called in question, and that all his thoughts—as a result of intention and not caprice— appear to annul themselves through contradictions.

Above all Nietzsche wants scope for his thoughts and, therein, the substance of being, genuine and unveiled. He proceeds by overcoming every form of being, every value, every fixation of essence within the world: "My writings speak only of my overcomings." He makes the extraordinary claim to attain authentic being by clinging to nothing that is fixed and final.

Overcoming is carried out through "suspicion" and "betrayal." *Suspicion* is the attitude that allows nothing to remain unquestioned. Not that things must be doubted and then reinstated when the doubt is refuted but that they must be transformed if they are to participate in being. Nietzsche believes that "no one has ever looked into the world with so deep a suspicion," and he describes his writings as "a study in suspicion." "So much mistrust," he says "so much philosophy." *Betrayal* is not the faithlessness of a dishonorable leaving in the lurch, but the surrender of historical substances that have become empty as a result of a necessity that is not yet understood; it is the possibility of arriving at the source of something radically different at the risk of *Existenz* itself. At an early age he writes: "Driven by the spirit," we stride "from opinion to opinion, through the change of parties, as noble betrayers of everything that can be betrayed at all."

But what begins as the unmasking of many things becomes to him an indication of the illusoriness of existence in its entirety and of this illusoriness as the sole reality. An endless dialectic permits no rest at any point and provides nothing fixed to cling to. So long as one remains on the path of unmasking, the distinction between true and false remains. But when the overcoming is no longer unmasking for the sake of truth but absolutely universal annulment of everything actual, the distinction between those things that can be betrayed and those that are bound to maintain themselves becomes untenable, for everything is subject to betrayal. Whatever Nietzsche thinks is changed into the mere possibility that it momentarily becomes. But what he himself really wants is related to traditional transcendence through the fact that he goes beyond every tangible form in the world, every position and every goal; it is different from this transcendence simply through the fact that, in the end, nothing at all seems to remain.

Never do we reach a halt when we are thinking Nietzsche's thoughts with him. Whenever we hope to lay hold upon the final truth—to capture *the* truth—he forces us to continue. Again and again it seems that in the end nothing remains. Absolute negativity—whether it appears in mistrust and suspicion, in overcoming, or in contradiction and persistence in contradictoriness—is like a passion for nothing, although it contains the will that ventures everything in its search for the genuine being that cannot attain definite form. This will is intent upon bringing forth the truth from those depths at which it cannot be grasped without contradiction, bringing to expression and fruition what is veiled by the determinacy of thought, and returning to the historicity of one's own *Existenz* in its source.

An indication of this is the will to say Yes that penetrates all of Nietzsche's work. While this reaches its highest point in the idea of eternal recurrence and *amor fati,* it is constantly present to some extent as an indicator of his negation of nothingness. It is with this in mind that Zarathustra can say: "How much has already succeeded! How rich the earth is in good little things that are complete, in things that have turned out well!" Instead of leading by way of a gamut of denials to the final nothing, his thinking leads via a gamut of countless small affirmations to the final Yes.

Experimenting. Absolute negativity includes the kind of philosophizing that limits all of its positive acts to attempts (*Versuchen*).[6] To this philosophy of the "dangerous perhaps," everything, viewed in relation to the last horizon of the unending, becomes merely preliminary. Thus there is nothing that is not attempted: "Such an experimental philosophy (*Experimental-Philosophie*) as the one I live by anticipates by way of experiment even the possibility of a fundamental nihilism, which is not to say that it ends . . . in negation."

Philosophizing that proceeds experimentally thinks of and experiences possibilities and remains master of all thought instead of being mastered by it. Without sinking into skepticism, it wishes, through sovereign manly skepticism, to prepare the actuality of historical *Existenz* and of the deed that, far from consisting of mere thinking of the truth, becomes that truth

[6] Cf. pp. 388 ff.

compared to which all conceptualized truths remain mere experiments and possibilities.

Here is the difference between the idea of Nietzsche's experimental thought and the lawless irresponsibility of the arbitrary and capricious. Nietzsche with his experimental philosophizing does not struggle as one who wishes to confront some worldly doctrine with a newly formulated doctrine: it is not a matter of dogma against dogma or of one definite *Weltanschauung* against another. He does not decisively introduce a palpable faith into the world in order to defend it and extend its scope or, perhaps, to test the fruitfulness of an accepted error in the struggle. As Nietzsche proceeds in almost all situations of his life—suffering, renouncing, and withdrawing, trying out possibilities in thought until in the end nothing remains—so he proceeds while philosophizing: as his own ambiguous description would have it, he is the "spirit of experimentation." But his experimenting, instead of being irresponsible, has a profound basis: the struggle takes place at a wholly different level from the struggle of existence within the world (which also employs dogmatically asserted and developed truths); he is engaged in the struggle of substance against nothingness. This struggle takes place everywhere at a level at which existence has no definite battle-fronts; it is the profound, decisive struggle in the soul of each individual and in the soul of the people. It is the internal, invisible, and inaudible struggle for whose existential meaning Nietzsche provides such weapons as probing questions, misapprehensibilities, and opportunities for testing. His message is communicated by way of an appeal never to stop at any insight—not even at Nietzsche's philosophizing itself—as though it had been once and for all delivered to us as a true and final *Weltanschauung*.

Nietzsche as a Sacrifice. Philosophizing that has no upshot and proceeds as did the historically earlier enthusiastic search for God, sees itself condemned to loneliness and abandonment, for, measured by the usual life of the average man, such philosophizing is unnatural: "A philosophy that does not propose to make one happier and more virtuous but, instead, gives one to understand that he will probably come to grief in its service, i.e., become lonesome in his own time . . . and have to put up with various kinds of mistrust and hate . . . , such a philosophy will not easily gain anyone's favor: one would have to be born for it, and I have not yet found anyone who was. . . ."

Unlimited negativity and experimenting could be carried out as an irresponsible activity of the understanding in its dealings with all things insofar as they constitute the world outside of one's own existence. But what negativity and experimentation actually are, and what is shown by them—not accidentally but really—can be seen only when a man springs with his whole being, as it were, into this abyss and, as a representative, does what would destroy everything if all did it. But that means to be a sacrifice.

First of all Nietzsche appears as a sacrifice within what he knows to be the *moment of a crucial historical turning point.* No longer can he enter into the actuality of his time *in propria persona;* he has to be excluded from the world in order to see, from the outside so to speak, what he experiences of it. But further, since he actually has to live and think during his own time, his thoughts also appear in a guise that is unsuitable to him. He is thus easily confused with what he is not because he continues to adhere to the attitudes and ways of thinking of his own time (and is himself what he struggles against, e.g., a positivist or a Wagnerian) and because, having lost all communal ties in his growing loneliness, he now loses all moderation. We have here the philosophizing of one who risked his own self in the greatest crisis of the Occident to experience in loneliness and transmit to us in fragments what only a man who founders is able to see.

In the second place, Nietzsche appears as a sacrifice when, as Everyman, he takes *the eternal negativity of the finite* upon himself through pitiless identification with it. While, for the others, finitude creates the ground of the possibility of self-being within contemporary limits and upon presently concrete grounds, so that they experience the ciphers of existence in their historical peculiarity, Nietzsche wins his historicity in union, not with finitude, but with negativity. It is like an extension of humanity, normally bound and actual only because it is bound, beyond itself in a self-consuming process that leaves no residue.

His insanity, senselessly brutal as an empirical fact, appears as a mythical symbol of his sacrifice. This once again makes him appear in a confusing light because, as a result of it, he lost all restraint and broke down completely. Nietzsche's originality first assumed a radical form when distortion through loneliness as well as illness took effect so that the outermost possibilities of his philosophizing appear unimaginable, even apart from the biological processes leading to insanity. Thus his insanity can be included in the sacrifice that his whole life and thought represent.

The sacrifice also appears in his works: These cannot attain the fixed and final form that all the great systems possess—including the critical philosophizing of Kant. What Nietzsche's thinking accomplishes is accomplished unwittingly, in spite of his consciousness that reflects without ceasing. The thought as such is not mastered: because he ventures everything, it runs into error and even caprice. In spite of its boundless overcoming, in spite of its skepticism and critical dissolution, his thinking is uncritical in the Kantian sense—it constantly deviates into dogmatic assertions that are not controlled but only repeatedly overcome as the movement proceeds. He must assert a great deal to have his assertions turn at once into their opposites; it is as though a fanaticism of thought were constantly changing into another fanaticism of thought as a result of which all fanaticism is placed at the level of mere attempting that annuls itself. Since he commits errors that he knows to be such, no one can look to him for support as he might look to a critical philosopher. There results an ineradicable confusion with regard to Nietzsche's thinking that is based upon the innermost part of this work and expresses a sacrifice rather than a historically fulfilled self-actualization within the world.

By being the kind of sacrifice that he is, Nietzsche makes the highest possible claim, but in such a way that no one can go with him on his way. As a philosophical *Existenz,* he resembles the fire that he understands himself to be. His existential authenticity reveals itself in the way in which the flame within him consumes everything, leaving no incombustible remnant of existence and individual will, as his *Existenz* disappears in incommunicable concealment.

But to know that Nietzsche sacrifices himself in this way is not equivalent to comprehending him: he is not to be subsumed under any known type of human existence. The word "sacrifice" expresses merely the incomprehensibility that characterizes the being of an exception—not the kind that, simply as an exception, leaves us indifferent but the kind that arouses our concern as it touches our innermost self.

The Openness of What Nietzsche Is and Does. If in the end anyone should wish to be told in a few words what Nietzsche really is, instead of experiencing it himself through interacting with Nietzsche's thought, so that he may pass it on in easily repeated propositions, he may be told the following:

It is the beginning of all untruth to wish to pronounce and hear final judgments where being per se is concerned. Only within the world—in the knowledge of determinate objects, in working for distinct purposes, in acting so as to promote definite goals—is communicable decision and definiteness not only possible but even necessary as a condition of all meaningful activity. But such activity itself must be encompassed by an awareness of the being of *Existenz,* for this is the foremost bearer of all expressible meaning. Such awareness of being attains clarity through agitated communication with the original thinkers—those who are not final and complete—and, at the same time, through a movement of thought that never comes to rest in any proposition. The thoughts thus entertained are the medium of the basic assurances from which the definiteness of contemporary intention, activity, and knowledge first develops.

From Nietzsche we may learn of a new philosophizing that never becomes a thoroughly finished conceptual whole: what he was and wanted to be remains open. He is like an eternal beginning because it is not his own work but man in the process of becoming that is central to the task he seizes upon. But at the same time we find here a philosophy that exists only in Nietzsche and cannot be transmitted, one that speaks without disclosing the way and that *is* without being a model.

Appropriating Nietzsche

Although the works and letters that have come down to us from Nietzsche are multifarious, still his philosophizing would seem to be somehow concealed. For those of us who cannot and dare not follow him, this kind of philosophizing at least enables us to feel the source from which the life that is possible for us today must eventually be thoroughly transformed. Here is the point from which we may proceed to demonstrate the uniqueness of a possible appropriation of Nietzsche.

This appropriation was not realized when Nietzsche, with his wealth of astonishing aperçus and his consummate linguistic felicity, was approached from an esthetic point of view and hailed with unrestrained enthusiasm as a creative genius. That was the approach of those who, in the end, allowed form and measure to decide: Enraptured during their youth, then annoyed and disgusted with incessant contradiction, immoderation, misinformation (especially during his last years), with the exaggerated and verbose figures, with the dogmatism that seemed to become blind, and with the derailments (*Entgleisungen*) that occasionally became ridiculous—these people experienced the typical disillusionment of those who no longer see what is essential: in the end nothing remained but a few trivial accomplishments of the critic, the language-creating author, the exceptional aphorist, essayist, and poet. All valid meaning disappeared when the assimilation limited itself to edification through beauty and delight in language, and ingenious sensation.

Unless I deliberately allow the possible impetus of Nietzsche to become effective within me, he is taken esthetically and not assimilated with philosophic earnestness. And it is futile to accept him in part and reject him in part—whether this involves the esthetic, the logical, the systematic, or anything else. What counts is not constant preoccupation with

Nietzsche's work, but the desire to make contact with the source. But this is to be achieved within the medium of the whole and not in connection with specific thoughts, esthetic experiences, or critical truths.

Since Nietzsche does not present us with a self-completing phenomenon but a self-consuming one that constructs no world and really leaves nothing behind—nothing but pure impetus devoid of a form that we could take hold of—he comes to us as an assignment in self-transforming assimilation. In carrying out this assignment we must, without fail, reveal our own natures, whether we do this by a self-unveiling or a self-generating process. Then the excitement generated by the drastic and the radical ceases, and the strawfire of empty inspiration is no longer confused with the quiet impulse that operates inexorably. Nietzsche becomes an educator. But he becomes this only to the extent to which we master his seductive deceptions.

Being Deceived by Nietzsche. The Athenians were enraged by Socrates' questions and inquiries into possibilities: Anyone who believed that he possessed the truth, incapsulated in commonplace propositions or new catchwords, was reduced to a state of confusion. It remained possible either to excoriate the troublemaker and finally put him to death, or to diminish the bewildering confusion that Socrates had initially increased by participating in the profound Socratic exaltation of mankind.

The reader is affected in the same way by Nietzsche when his way of reading permits the entire Nietzsche to ask and speak. The same confusion follows—but also the possibility of the true earnestness that, by going beyond the fixation of any statement, really reacts to the demands that lie hidden in Nietzsche. The weight of possible *Existenz* imposed upon mere existence and the burden of the real mental labor that, driven by existential possibilities, must be performed, first furnish the ground for a true relation to Nietzsche.

Failure will result not only from complacent rejection of Nietzsche but also from an intensive preoccupation with him if confusion gains the upper hand and gives rise to misunderstanding and misuse of his thinking in such a way that he provokes boundless sophistry instead of awakening *Existenz*. For, objectively considered, the thoughts of Nietzsche can easily become the medium of a sophistry that applies his sayings in a contradictory fashion according to the uses and caprices of the moment, without participating in the sense of the movement (something that reveals itself through first insisting upon and then quickly forgetting the absolute validity of whatever happens to have been last asserted); and they can, on the other hand, become the medium of an awakening

Existenz that takes firm hold of its own historicity. Nietzsche's external closeness to and immense internal distance from the sophists is the reason why he is forever being confused with them. This can be brought out in various ways:

Nietzsche's philosophy is productive of "moods" (*Stimmungen*), and it ends in moods rather than in positions. These are clear and immune to perversion only as long as they are confirmed by his whole thought-movement, even as they generate and preserve it in turn. But when they are detached and allowed to become moods merely, then they can be used as arbitrary and ambiguous coverings for all kinds of banality, uninspired caprice, and unbridled instinctivity. They are suited for just that which Nietzsche opposed: play-acting, striving for effects, and stunning thoughtlessness.

As immoralist he rejects determinate morality because he wills something superior to it; he dissolves bonds because he seeks that by which all bonds are encompassed. (His statements can always be applied to something inferior. For example, a licentiousness which disregards any law purports to call him as a witness, using him to vindicate its own ethical chaos.) Nietzsche affirms lying, the will to power, godlessness, and bestiality; always his formulae are capable of giving a good conscience to mendacity within the world, to the brutal power-will and the factual existence of power, to the movement of godlessness, and to a simplistic affirmation of intoxication and everything that is merely instinctive. What Nietzsche wants, however, is just the opposite: the lie that is the authentic truth (i.e., is more than what is commonly presumed to be the truth); being that is worthless when devoid of power or the power that derives its rank from the worth of its substance; the godlessness that makes possible the higher men (who are to be more truthful, sober, creative, and moral than those who believe in God); a nature that from the fullness of its *Existenz* and the strictness of its discipline is at once master of all nature and far removed from all unnatural craving, wishing, and prevaricating.

Nietzsche tries out all possibilities. Experiments directed toward *Existenz* can easily be turned away from it and perverted into the irresponsible enjoyment of the manifold aspects of existence, experience, and all that can be imagined. The study of Nietzsche can lead to the indulgence of a laissez-faire attitude and to the complacency that permits one to think something through with vivid emotion and then, becoming indifferent, do nothing at all about it. It can make one too indifferent to contradictions to experience them as a goad, a language, and a task. When nihilists employ at will the turns of speech, the drastic assertions, and the extreme positions of Nietzsche, remote as their natures may be from his, their verbal formulations seem to show a similarity that approaches identity. The depths of possibility in Nietzsche's negativity can obscure one's own nothingness by arousing excitement over the nothingness of nihilism, until the illusionary dreams with their deafening noise, to which Nietzsche seems to furnish the text, come and blot out the insufferable.

One can observe this distressing misunderstanding in the ways in which Nietzsche has been treated. It sometimes seems as though Nietzsche deliberately seduces the reader, twists him around, robs him of himself, carries him to the point of intoxication and fanaticism, deprives him of his wits or merely incites him, and makes him more clever only to expose him when he thinks he is saying the same thing that Nietzsche says: "Not every word belongs in every mouth." Nietzsche knew about all these deceptions and misunderstandings, and he foresaw them with a sense of shock; but still there were times when he willed them: "To these men of today I will not be a light—not even in name. These—I will blind: Lightning flash of my wisdom, put out their eyes!"

In dealing with Nietzsche, concern for *Existenz* requires many things: One must enter into communication with him (and thus improve one's own capacity for communication within the actual world) instead of succumbing to sophistry. One must share in the authenticity and truthfulness of his movement instead of accepting a possible sophistical maneuver in the service of limited objectives—aggrandisement of one's personal power-will and personal existence, for example. Again, one must gain insight into the means and necessities of Nietzsche's philosophical thought-process instead of allowing oneself to be constantly surprised by all manner of suggestions. One must attain existence in the service of transcendence, instead of simply remaining in the service of the mere existence of one's just-happening-to-be-that-way, by transcending all possibilities into nothing (dramatically undertaken). Finally one must preserve the freedom of genuine movement and not oppose it by submitting to a doctrine which the understanding accepts as absolute only to exchange it later for its opposite.

The Philosophic Educator. All great philosophers are our educators. From our association with them arises our awareness of being, involving, as it does, such varied factors as our impulsions, evaluations, and goals, our modifications and states, and our self-overcomings. Philosophers are incapable of providing the sort of knowledge that consists in information about things in the world; they are misused when we unquestioningly take their opinions and judgments as valid statements to be learned and then applied in everyday life as though they were correct maxims of the understanding or self-evident articles of faith. The special and irreplaceable value of philosophers derives from their capacity to lead to the source in which we confirm ourselves in philosophizing. For self-becoming—insofar as it takes place in thought and thus in inner activity and thereby affects and develops the self—comes about, not through a quick leap that results from direct insight, but as a result of consorting with those who have followed the human way and have pointed it out through thinking.

The latest philosopher who, acting upon the sources and limits of man, could effect this to almost the entire extent of the possibilities of being is Nietzsche. As the one who is closest to us in time, he is the most understandable, even though, the modes and possibilities of our world being what they are, he has been more readily misunderstood than anyone, as has been shown. The fact that cheap intoxication as well as lifelong seeking and more complete awareness can draw sustenance from him shows how he differs from all his predecessors. Externally this is reflected by the number of copies of his chief works printed—a number that far surpasses that of the works of any previous philosopher.

Nietzsche's way of educating is also determined by the moment of the turning point within the history of the Occident: He is the educator who has no doctrines or imperatives and no fixed and final criteria, and he is not a model to be imitated by others. He educates by questioning us and thus testing our capacity to stand up to him. This occurs entirely through a movement. We have new experiences as we go along with him. Possibilities of human existence open up, the construction, in thought, of our own humanity is brought about, possible evaluations are attempted, and a heightening of value-sensitivity results. We are carried to the boundaries and thus to the source of an independent awareness of being. However, this does not occur as a result of clear guidance within the whole but through a claim on us: we are to use his thoughts to *educate ourselves*. Nothing comes to us in finished form but what we attain by our own struggles.

Such self-education comes about through a study of Nietzsche characterized by an *earnestness* that derives from a stirring experience and the patience to engage in careful integrative *thinking:*

The earnestness declares itself in the way Nietzsche is received: what is required is not an intellectual game but "a thinking feeling," not a passive viewing but an experiment with the possibilities of one's own passion. Through self-education I am to draw out of myself what actually is to be found there. Nietzsche wishes to arouse in us what cannot be won simply through formal discipline but arises through a constant struggle with oneself as an ordering of the passions in obedience to the ground of being. Precisely that which cannot be attained through unambiguous precepts can truly develop only through increased philosophical sensibility. It must develop clearly, in converse with Nietzsche, through the constant exposure of one's own being, as it were, to the purgatory of truth.

When all that is said turns into its opposite, and, in the movement towards pure possibility, everything is at once true and false, there is no remedy apart from the painful effort and power of *thinking*. Only strenuous self-education makes it possible, within the widely dispersed stream of the magical, endlessly ramified spirit of Nietzsche, to avoid arbitrariness by laying hold upon what actually goes together. It is just Nietzsche's lack of a systematic procedure that best insures the education of the thoughtful reader by forcing him to discover for himself the interrelations of whatever he encounters. When the urge to be first involved and then disengaged causes one to lose himself, self-education, nourished by the mental intoxication which he produces, will seek the way to a solution by ordering the whole on the basis of historical *Existenz*. It is precisely through the kind of shortwinded thinking that his specific utterances at first arouse that Nietzsche, thanks to the interconnectedness of his thoughts, can most decisively ward off shortwindedness. Indirectly he leads us to think calmly within the wide perspective that he achieves himself and requires of others.

Especially the thinking in *contradictions* is to be brought to conscious awareness and made effective through self-education. In reading Hegel, the danger is that the conciliatory equalization of all dialectic will conceal the sharpness of the breaks and leaps in existence as well as the existential Either/Or. In reading Nietzsche, one is in danger of becoming indifferent to contradictions and of misusing their possibilities.

He who believes that he possesses the truth without inner tension and opposition is defenseless against these thoughts. Equally so is anyone who expects to master them and carry them out to dialectical completion. He who uses the oppositions and contradictions to deceive others for his own purposes is untruthful. Only practice in grasping the contradictory, while employing a sort of thinking that is guided by the continuity of the substance, can bring out the truth for us without destroying our defenses. We must see how the dialectic of the movement is everywhere grounded in things themselves, so that ascent within the movement and sophistry are both possible.

To achieve self-education by thinking Nietzsche's thoughts with him is therefore only possible by means of the integrative thinking that we bring with us to the task. Thus it is quite natural that Nietzsche was seldom comprehended while he was publishing his volumes one by one, and that for the most part he was necessarily misunderstood when he was heard at all: since the true meaning of his thoughts does not reside in them individually but as a whole, they could not become properly effective until after the appearance of the posthumous materials. It is through an appropriation, accomplished by self-education in thinking, that we are drawn into the movement. There is no repose to be found in Nietzsche: no final truths and no articles of faith. On the surface, the way may lead nowhere and still be significant and effective as a way. Nietzsche is the agitator and preserver of the unrest that activates the strides to which our impulses for truthfulness and desire for genuine self-being urge us. Thus it is typical of education through Nietzsche that one seems to fall through the "positive" and rise through the "negative."

By virtue of this movement, Nietzsche teaches endless *expansion:* he provides orientation on the way into the boundless, shows us how to think in antitheses and to entertain the possibility of contradictory evaluations, exhibits ineradicable contradictoriness as well as dialectical connections, and still draws no final conclusion for formative knowing. It is quite possible that he who has not dared to expose himself to the dangers of studying Nietzsche and the resulting practice in experimenting can, in the present historical instant, not stand really free in the widest horizon of possibility. With only a superficial knowledge of Nietzsche, one will sink to either doctrinaire *narrowness* or to *sophistry,* or, more probably, to both at once.

Narrowness is the fate of the one who succumbs to isolated formulae, radical thoughts, and determinate positions—in cheap flight from the dizziness produced by the process. Such a one has not allowed Nietzsche to become effective as his teacher. Even those who hold fast to outmoded dogmas are closer to the truth than those who turn Nietzsche's thoughts into dogmas.

Sophistry results for anyone who views the emancipation through Nietzsche as irresponsibility. The sophist wishes to be like Nietzsche, but he lacks the requisite strength, right, and calling. What Nietzsche did could, without sophistry, be existentially realized as truth in our age only by *one* who represents all.

Narrowness and sophistry belong together since the sophist is accustomed arbitrarily to lay hold upon and traffic in narrow doctrinaire statements. In studying Nietzsche, we learn to master completely the constant inclination to fall prey to the wording of utterances; we are trained to overcome the crudeness of arguing with isolated propositions and of subsuming and labeling the great in spirit. This is accomplished because we come to see the possibility of both narrowness and sophistry, we fully experience them as possibilities, and we conquer them by knowing them well.

In order to awaken the entire power of the existential source, education through Nietzsche leads into an area so huge that we tend to become giddy. This education is like a *training in ambiguities:* the ambiguous is grasped *positively* as the medium of genuine, decisive self-being that escapes ambiguity through *Existenz,* though it must submit to endless reflection when it is expressed; it is grasped *negatively* as the medium of possible sophistry that, more or less at random, makes use of the possibilities in emotive acceptance and rejection and in an instinctive purposiveness dictated by the situation and the drives for existence that happen to be operative. Such an education, both inescapable and dangerous in our age, means that, without Nietzsche, no one can have authentic knowledge of existence and be truthful in philosophizing; but neither can anyone simply stay with Nietzsche and find fulfillment in him.

What this signifies for the *Existenz* of the individual is simply the attitude demanded by Nietzsche: "Only he who changes continues to be related to me." "Only through alteration can one be unalterably mine." This amounts to saying that understanding Nietzsche is not passive acceptance but active self-development of a sort that can never be completed once and for all. Being able to change oneself means readiness for the always possible crisis in which one's own being is dissolved and born again. Being "related" to the other as one changes himself means above all being in communication with every possible self-being, including even one so far removed as to be an "exception." Such education excludes every change in the self that implies forever becoming different and always being something new. For it is intended to promote transformation from the authentic source of *Existenz* to the authentic goal of true kinship in self-being.

The uniqueness of a philosophical education provided by this man who belongs to the present age and represents its changes signifies the following: Unlike the great philosophers of previous times he is not to be accepted for himself as though in him we could seize all that is thinkable by being at home with the totality of being and by laying hold of certainty as expressed in the inviolable laws of mankind. Rather he is to be properly understood only when systematic logical schooling has already been gained elsewhere and when perseverance and precise thinking are brought to the task along with a capacity for dialectical thought. But on the other hand, it is perhaps also true that the singularly great philosophers of the past today can only be understood through Nietzsche, apart from whom they turn much too easily into fossilized legacies of doctrinal articles. Everything depends upon assimilating Nietzsche through an improved philosophizing and rediscovering the old as we compare it with Nietzsche, instead of losing what we have already acquired.

One is profoundly touched by Nietzsche the educator because, as he points to the future, he arouses a unique impulse which, although devoid of any specific purpose, derives from an unquestionable source and remains absolutely valid for those who share in his thinking.

Reactions to the Exception. If instead of creating for himself an atmosphere of real substantial being, Nietzsche appears to present the enchantment of his purity as a spirituality devoid of vitality, if his fire fails to warm and merely consumes, if the nobility of his glance seems to remain empty like "death with waking eyes," if he who has lived in all corners of the modern soul and is still nowhere at home seems to lead into bottomless vacancy—all these things are but paradoxical expressions denoting the exceptional being whom we keep at a distance even while his communications touch us to the quick; i.e., we approach him without uniting with him or caring to do so.

The question is: Considering the possibility of universality and of communication, how does one react to Nietzsche as the exception in whom both are abandoned at the sacrifice of his own life? To the man who is *not* an exception, what is the meaning of the thinking of the one who leaves the world to become as lonely as Nietzsche was and whose final reality appears to be only his thinking?

Our question can also be stated in another way: Is the dissolving power of the thinking and experimenting that would lead everyone who repeats it to the nothingness of irresponsibility actually his essence, or is it really the other way around, namely that Nietzsche, because he took upon himself the universal dissolution of our world, provides the only possible starting point and motive power leading to the indissoluble truth and to the being of man?

To philosophize with Nietzsche is an exercise in possibility. One who is not an exception can do this authentically only on the basis of his historically *existential obligations.* It cannot be a matter of imitating Nietzsche—of casting off all real ties in order to build on nothing. The point is rather to win the free space of the possible that includes all ties in order to awaken, within *Existenz,* the depths of genuine freedom.

Because everything remains open to him, because he cannot pass on anything as a permanent possession but can only assist with preliminaries, Nietzsche presents to each individual the task of winning his ground through relation to transcendence in existential historicity. Nietzsche's convulsive thinking, proceeding always from the transcendence that he denies, prepares us for the transcendence that he does not reveal and for the historicity of *Existenz* to which he never directly refers.

But no readiness remains genuine when it simply leaves Nietzsche where he is and fails to become seriously involved with him. That the rigorous concentration which provides the dangerous experience of the possible creates the medium in which I, in my place, become what I am, constitutes Nietzsche's unspoken challenge. While he turns disciples away and insists that his path is not for everyone, he describes the goal of his philosophizing as follows: "Every philosophy must be able to do what I require, viz., concentrate a man—but at present none can."

Perhaps it is just the one who rejects the proffered ground (eternal recurrence, the metaphysics of the will to power, the superman) whom Nietzsche can best force back to the ground from which he draws his life. Only insofar as we approach him from our own substance can he speak to us without promoting misunderstanding. What he truly *is* will in the end be decided by what others bring with them as they approach him.

But no one will complete this kind of assimilation. For the reader will again and again be repelled when he finds himself unable to take up into the whole what he reads, or he will pervert it by understanding it in too univocal and detached a manner. In this relation to the greatness of the exception which always remains unavoidably ambiguous, Nietzsche can disappear as it were; but a deep-rooted love holds fast to him—one that can lose its object except for an indeterminate tender nobility of Nietzsche's being that remains when everything said appears suddenly to become nothing; it is at once the unweighable and the unmistakable in *Existenz* and transcendence that, unheard by others, speaks to each one who has once become aware of it.

To philosophize with Nietzsche means to be constantly taking issue with him. In the fire of his thought, one's own existence can become purified to the point of awareness of genuine self-being when tested by the boundless honesty and danger of Nietzsche's critical questioning. Such self-being can only be experienced as something that passes, not into existence, and not into objectivity or subjectivity of world-being, but rather into transcendence. Nietzsche does not lead one to this at once—he tries rather to free one from it. But the earnestness of the total surrender that Nietzsche achieves is—in spite of his rejection of transcendence—like an unintended simile and archetype that expresses the profound experience of being consumed through transcendence. One grows shy in the presence of this incomprehensible one who is transparent to the source but not to us.

APPENDICES

CHRONOLOGICAL TABLE I

10/15/1844	Born in Röcken (near Lützen), the son of a clergyman.
1849	Death of father.
1850	Family moves to Naumburg.
1858–1864	Attends Schulpforta.
1860–1863	Literary Society Germania.
1864–1865	Bonn (two semesters of philology and theology). *Burschenschaft* Frankonia.
1865–1867	Leipzig (four semesters of philology). Student of Ritschl. Friendship with Rohde.
1867–1868	Military service in Naumburg.
1868–1869	Leipzig. Fall of 1868: acquaintance with R. Wagner.
1869–1879	Professor in Basel.
1869	Acquaintance with J. Burckhardt.
1869–1872	Visits with R. Wagner in Tribschen near Lucerne. August to October, 1870: volunteer nurse in the war. October: in Basel again. Acquaintance with Overbeck.
May, 1872	Laying of cornerstone in Bayreuth.
1875	Acquaintance with Köselitz (Peter Gast).
August, 1876	First festival plays in Bayreuth. Acquaintance with Rée.
1876–1877	Year's leave of absence. Sorrento: Malvida von Meysenbug. Last conversation with R. Wagner.
1878	End of relationship between Wagner and Nietzsche; January: *Parsifal* sent to Nietzsche; May: *Human, All-Too-Human* sent to Wagner.
May, 1879	Resignation because of illness.
1879–1889	Retired professor; *"fugitivus errans":* from 1883–88 in Nice during the winter, in Sils-Maria during the summer, in different places during transition periods, among them Venice as the most beloved city. Personal discovery of Turin in 1888.
1879	Wiesen. St. Moritz. Naumburg.

460

1880	Naumburg. Riva. Venice. Marienbad. Naumburg. Stresa. Genoa.
1881	Genoa. Recoaro. Sils-Maria. Genoa (Nietzsche hears Bizet's *Carmen*).
1882	Genoa. Messina. Rome. Lucerne. Basel. Naumburg. Tautenburg. Naumburg. Leipzig. Rapallo. May to November 1882: relationship with Lou Salomé.
1883	Rapallo. Genoa. Rome. Sils-Maria. Genoa. Nice. February, 1883: death of R. Wagner.
1884	Nice. Venice. Sils-Maria. Zurich. Mentone. Nice. August, 1884: H. v. Stein's visit in Sils-Maria.
1885	Nice. Venice. Sils-Maria. Naumburg. Leipzig. Nice.
1886	Nice. Venice. Leipzig (last meeting with Erwin Rohde). Sils-Maria. Ruta. Nice.
1887	Nice. Canobbio. Zurich. Chur. Sils-Maria. Venice. Nice.
1888	Nice. Turin. Sils-Maria. Turin. Brandes' lectures on Nietzsche at the University of Copenhagen.
1889	Turin. Since January insane. In the institutes of Basel and Jena.
1890	In Naumburg with his mother.
1897	Death of mother, under his sister's care in Weimar.
1900	Died August 25, 1900.

CHRONOLOGICAL TABLE II: ORIGIN OF THE WORKS AND THE WRITINGS IN THE POSTHUMOUS MATERIAL

(Cf. the notes in *Works* I, XI ff. and pertinent supplementary reports)

Works (Time of first publication in parentheses)		*Posthumous Material*
1858–1868		Writings of his youth
1866–1877	*Philologika*	Writings on the Greeks:
1869–1872		Vol. IX. *Concerning the Future of Our Educational Institutions*
1870–1871	*The Birth of Tragedy* (Jan., 1872)	
1872–1875		Writings Vol. X, containing: *Philosophy during the Tragic Age of the Greeks*
1873	*Untimely Meditations I: David Strauss* (Aug., 1873)	*Concerning Truth and Falsehood from an Extra-Moral Point of View*
1873–1874	*Untimely Meditations II: Of the Advantage and Disadvantage of History for Life* (Feb., 1874)	
1874	*Untimely Meditations III: Schopenhauer as Educator* (1874)	
1875		*We Philologists*
1875–1876	*Untimely Meditations IV: Richard Wagner in Bayreuth* (1876)	
1875–1881		Vol. XI: from the period of *Human, All-Too-Human and The Dawn*

462

1876–1878	*Human, All-Too-Human* (May, 1878)	
1878–1879	*Mixed Opinions and Maxims* (Mar., 1879)	
1879	*The Wanderer and His Shadow* (Dec., 1879)	
1881–1886		Vol. XII: from the period of *The Gay Science* and *Thus Spake Zarathustra*
1880–1881	*The Gay Science I–IV*	
1881–1882	*The Dawn* (Jul., 1881) (Sept., 1882)	
Feb., 1883	*Thus Spake Zarathustra I* (May, 1883)	
Jun.–Jul., 1883	*Thus Spake Zarathustra II* (1883)	
Jan., 1884	*Thus Spake Zarathustra III* (1884)	
1884–1885	*Thus Spake Zarathustra IV* (1892)	
1883–1888		Vols. XIII–XVI. Contains: *The Will to Power*
1885–1886	*Beyond Good and Evil* (1886)	
1886	*Prefaces* (1887) *The Gay Science V* (1887)	
1887	*Toward a Genealogy of Morals* (Nov., 1887)	
1888	*The Wagner Case* (1888) *Twilight of the Idols* (Jan., 1889) *The Antichrist* (1902) *Nietzsche contra Wagner* (1901) *Ecce Homo* (1908)	
1884 ff.	*Dionysus Dithyrambs*	

BIBLIOGRAPHY
Works

The Complete Edition (*Gesamtausgabe*) prepared by Nietzsche's sister, in the form of the small octavo edition of 16 volumes (in pages and lines identical with the large octavo edition), is the easiest to work with; our quotations are from this edition. Of the new and inexpensive printings, Kröner's pocket edition must be given preference because of its completeness and because the volumes can be purchased separately. Only the posthumous material is represented by selections.

In addition one must use: *Philologika,* 1866–1877, found only in the large octavo edition, vols. 17–19, Leipzig, 1910–13 (edited by Holzer, Crusius, and Nestle); *Jugendschriften* (Youthful Writings), 1858–1868, in vol. I of the *Musarion* edition, published as a separate volume, Munich, 1923 (now doubled in content in the new historical-critical edition of the *Nietzsche-Archiv*); and *Gedichte und Sprüche* (Poems and Maxims), as a complete edition and dispersed, Leipzig, 1898, C. G. Naumann (most but not all found in the *Gesamtausgabe;* their place in the various volumes indicated in vol. 8, p. 449).

Nietzsche's *Compositions: Hymnus an das Leben. Für Chor und Orchester* (Hymn to Life. For Chorus and Orchestra), 1887. *Hymnus an die Freundschaft. Chor mit Klavier vierhändig* (Hymn to Friendship. Chorus with Piano for Four Hands), 1874. *Manfred. Meditation für Klavier vierhändig* (Manfred. Meditation for Piano for Four Hands), 1872. *Siebzehn Klavierlieder* (Seventeen Songs for the Piano) as well as a series of *Klavierstücke* (Pieces for the Piano).

Miscellanea: Friedrich Nietzsches Randbemerkungen zu Bizets Carmen (Friedrich Nietzsche's Marginal Notes to Bizet's Carmen), edited by Hugo Daffner, Regensburg. *Nietzsches Randbemerkungen zu Guyau* (Nietzsche's Marginal Notes to Guyau), appendix to the German translation of *Sittlichkeit ohne Pflicht* (Morality without Duty), Leipzig, 1909.

The Nietzsche-Archive is preparing a *Complete Historical-Critical Edition* of the works and letters. So far three volumes of the *Youthful Writings* have appeared (Munich, 1933–34). The edition is to bring the whole posthumous material as well as all extant letters into chronological sequence. If realized as planned, it will be the basis for future studies of Nietzsche.

To understand existing editions of the posthumous materials and the way in which Nietzsche's manuscripts were written, one must note, not only the supplementary reports and prefaces of the editions, but, above all, August Horneffer's *Nietzsche als Moralist und Schriftsteller* (Nietzsche as Moralist and Writer), Jena, 1906, and Ernst Horneffer's *Nietzsches letztes Schaffen* (Nietzsche's Final Creative Activity), Jena, 1907.

Indispensable for any work with Nietzsche is the *Nietzsche-Register* by Richard Oehler, Leipzig, 1926. The volume and page numbers of this register refer to the above-mentioned Complete Edition (large or small octavo format). Not included in this excellent register are the *Youthful Writings*, the *Philologika*, and the *Letters*. One cannot expect perfection of a register. Anyone working for himself must expand it for his own purposes. This one is restricted to the key-words, listing only what belongs to them in a literal sense rather than according to subject matter. It often fails to provide a survey when the extensive materials relating to a key-word are subdivided. Especially extensive are the passages dealing in a very revealing manner with the posthumous materials. The words and contents of Nietzsche's later philosophy do not come off very well in the first volume of this work. In connection with some key-words, only part of Nietzsche's works seems to have been examined. But these defects mean little in view of the fact that we have here a guide that saves us much of the time that we would otherwise spend searching. This register was later appended to the *Musarion* edition, being expanded to two volumes of greater completeness by including the *Youthful Writings* and the *Philologika*. The *Musarion* edition is of value only because of this expanded register. This "monumental edition" is cumbersome to work with because of the size of its volumes.

Letters

Friedrich Nietzsches Gesammelte Briefe (Friedrich Nietzsche's Collected Letters), Leipzig, Inselverlag. Vol. I: to Pinder, Krug, Deussen, v. Gersdorff, Fuchs, and others; 3rd ed., 1902. Vol. II: Nietzsche's correspondence with E. Rohde; 2nd ed., 1903. Vol. III: correspondence with Ritschl, Burckhardt, Taine, Keller, H. v. Stein, Brandes, H. v. Bülow, v. Senger, M. v. Meysenbug; 2nd ed., 1905. Vol. IV: Nietzsche's letters to Peter Gast, 2nd ed., 1908. Vol. V (in two parts): Nietzsche's letters to his mother and his sister; 2nd ed., 1909. Also *Nietzsches Briefwechsel mit Franz Overbeck* (Nietzsche's Correspondence with Franz Overbeck), Inselverlag, Leipzig, 1916; various passages omitted here were published in Podach's writings.

In addition, miscellaneous letters: to Lou in Lou Andreas-Salomé, *Friedrich Nietzsche*, Vienna, 1894; to Strindberg in Karl Strecker, *Nietzsche und Strindberg*, Munich, 1921; to Hillebrand in O. Crusius, *Friedrich Nietzsche und Karl Hillebrand. Unveröffentlichte Briefe* (Unpublished Letters). *Süddeutsche Monatshefte* VI, 2, 1909, pp. 129–142; to Krug in *Zwölf Briefe Nietzsches an einen Jugendfreund* (*Gustav Krug*) (Twelve Letters by Nietzsche to a Friend of his Youth), *Süddeutsche Monatshefte*, Vol. 27, August, 1930; facsimile of last letter to Burckhardt (Jan. 6, 1889) in Podach, *Nietzsches Zusammenbruch* (Nietzsche's Collapse), Heidelberg, 1930; to A. Heusler in: *Zwei ungedruckte Schriftstücke Nietzsches* (*Briefe an Andreas Heusler*, Dec., 1888) [Two Unpublished Writings by Nietzsche (Letters to Andreas Heusler, Dec., 1888)], *Schweizer Monatshefte für Politik und*

Kultur, vol. 2, Zurich, April, 1922; to publishers in: *Friedrich Nietzsche, Briefe aus dem Jahre 1880* (Letters from the year 1880) (especially to the publisher C. G. Naumann and to Meta von Salis-Marschlins), *Die neue Rundschau* XVIII, pp. 1367 ff., Berlin, 1907; the last letter to H. v. Bülow in Andler, vol. IV, p. 530, footnote.

Editorial Requirements

Since Nietzsche's sister, beginning in the nineties, made Nietzsche's works accessible through editions of the posthumous materials, and since inexpensive printings of his works and of selections from the letters and the posthumous materials have satisfied the needs of the reading public, the one great task that remains is that of creating new editions to serve as the basis for the new study of Nietzsche that certainly must be undertaken now that it is possible.

To study Nietzsche properly, one must participate in the movement of his thought or, in other words, in the inner movement of his being. Never allowing oneself to be captivated by single aphorisms or even separate treatises, one must pursue every turn, follow him into every corner, and experience every overcoming with him. Consequently the possibility of penetrating to Nietzsche's depths depends to an uncommon degree on the way in which his writings are arranged in print. Completeness of presentation and suitable organization of what Nietzsche has said will convey what no amount of tedious exposition could ever make clear. Future editions should meet the following requirements:

1. As a basis for further studies, all the material without remainder must be brought together within three groups. It is to be hoped that the new edition of Nietzsche's writings that appears in the meantime will fulfill the first two of the following requirements:

a. The works published by Nietzsche himself are now readily accessible in their entirety, and no difficulty exists on that point. But the fact that the equally important posthumous material has been published only provisionally, and in arrangements provided by the editors (with the partial exception of *The Will to Power*), gives rise to a difficulty that will never be completely removed. The proper way to proceed will always have to be decided on the basis of the manuscripts themselves, and it will probably differ from case to case. But what is needed is obvious: Everything that is at all intelligible must be printed faithfully and without additions, in chronological order if possible, or—whenever dating is impossible—in the precise sequence in which the notes happen to appear in the notebooks. Only the material itself can show us what is and what is not possible. The order in which Nietzsche recorded his thoughts is essential, and insofar as it can be discovered at all, it must be preserved. In the past, philologists like Rohde may have regarded such demands as nonsensical, but if they did, it was because they underestimated the significance of Nietzsche's thinking.

At any rate, very considerable changes must be made in the printed posthumous materials, arranged, as they were, on the basis of subject matter, with a view to making them as readable as possible. It seems to me that even the separation of *The Will to Power* from the posthumous material reproduced in the thirteenth and fourteenth volumes, as well as the arrangements within the volumes themselves, fails to produce the intended clarification. The arrangements that Nietzsche had in mind must be printed as he noted them down. At the same time, the pursuance of any particular one is to be avoided since the reason for choosing it would lie with the editor rather than with Nietzsche.

Illegibility would appear to make a facsimile publication of the posthumous materials purposeless. But whatever can be read with certainty should be reprinted, in spite of its disorder, with a view to preserving a chronological sequence, even though this sequence must often be interrupted because information is lacking or verification is impossible. Only thus can we obtain the true and direct picture of Nietzsche's thinking that is indispensable for a starting point. A few volumes more or less should not matter.

The separation of works and posthumous materials that his sister undertook seems to make sense. New editions of his works will be of little significance—except when words and statements have actually been suppressed (as, according to Hofmiller, the word "idiot" was deleted from *The Antichrist*). It is to be hoped that a new edition of the posthumous material will furnish a substantially improved basis for the study of Nietzsche.

b. All letters and drafts of letters should be printed in chronological sequence. In addition, all ascertainable facts contributing to an understanding of the letters should be gathered and presented in footnotes, without interpretations and criticisms.

Nothing less than a comprehensive edition can make it possible for the student not only to have the relevant facts always before him, but also to penetrate to Nietzsche's innermost experience of life. The way the available correspondence is now presented separates what belongs together chronologically and makes it inevitable that something will be overlooked.

c. All the reports and evaluations by Nietzsche's contemporaries that derive from direct contact with him should be collected. Many incidental statements that appear separately are of considerable interest when taken together. The criterion to be used in selecting materials for publication is their significance within the concrete experience of Nietzsche. Only what derived from such experience—and not what his contemporaries thought of his writings—is of interest to us.

2. By promoting completeness, these three extensive editions would provide the basis for supplementary editions devoted to the task of giving proper organization to the materials. Such work is indispensable if we are to explore various objective and personal relations in a manner hardly feasible within the Complete Edition. Only suitable arrangement can provide completeness with respect to the materials under consideration. Such completeness is not to be found in the arbitrarily arranged editions now available; it appears neither in the autobiographical writings, nor in those dealing with the Nietzsche-Wagner relationship, nor anywhere else.

a. All that refers to Nietzsche's relations to individuals should be brought together and properly documented: not only the letters but verifiable facts along with everything in Nietzsche's works that bears directly upon them (especially in connection with Wagner).

b. All obtainable statements concerning the illnesses of Nietzsche's whole life should be collected in one work (something more important than any pathographies): all that Nietzsche says about illnesses in his letters, all that others have to say, and all that proves relevant from definite ascertainable points of view. The goal should be simply the collection of available documents without prejudice and without diagnosis (except of course for the diagnoses of those physicians who treated him during his lifetime). The greatest possible exactness in connection with chronological order is essential.

c. While a refined sensitivity to the factual and an ability to apply the philological method (as well as, in the second case, some medical and psychiatric experience) should enable the above to be carried out with a high degree of accuracy, a third way of ordering the materials requires, in addition, the ability to create for oneself the thoughts of another: Only objective arrangement, on the basis of Nietzsche's publications and the posthumous materials, of the thoughts that belong together can penetrate to the mansions and the highways at present hidden under the immense heap of ruins that constitutes the posthumous materials. This procedure will reach its goal of organizing Nietzsche's thoughts to the extent to which philosophical understanding—without eliminating anything and without doing violence to the text—can so arrange Nietzsche's thoughts as to reveal their immanent dialectic. Similar thoughts would be brought together in such a way as to manifest their complex variations and their relations to other thoughts; contradictions would become evident; gaps would become noticeable. This arrangement can only be accomplished (1) as a result of a work that considers everything that Nietzsche has thought, (2) on the basis of viewpoints proceeding from Nietzsche's own thinking and consciously moving with him, and (3) with a view to providing the kind of organization that, remaining truthful, will preserve the fragmentary and dispersed ingredients both as a measure of the understanding so far attained and as a starting point for the work of future students.

Only Nietzsche offers so strange a problem. It is not a matter of using some of the rubble to produce a system and neglecting the rest, but of giving shape to the whole that Nietzsche envisaged. But given the impossibility of ever rounding out this whole, we should not be so narrow as to require that Hegelian methods be employed for the sake of bringing everything together within a single dialectical scheme.

One must play a mosaic game with Nietzsche's statements, as it were. This game is endless when it proceeds arbitrarily or tendentiously. But years of work on Nietzsche give rise to the conviction that, so far as the subject-matter is concerned, this mosaic game is neither arbitrary nor endless when it brings out the relationships intrinsic to the whole—or to whatever part one is considering—in such a way that the shortcomings of various arbitrary arrangements are readily seen. What is required can be accomplished only through cooperative and mutually corrective efforts extending over a long period of time (my work is intended as a step on this path). Nothing can be gained by facile classifications and other schemes imposed from above, for these, in their rational univocality and systematic unilaterality, are as ruinous to Nietzsche as they are indolent.

d. While it is often appropriate to select all the writings that bear upon a given topic or problem, selections that purport to extract the best from a whole, while always of dubious merit, are more untrustworthy in Nietzsche's case than in that of any other great thinker. Understanding is not a matter of esthetically enjoying what erroneously purports to be a total picture. It requires first of all the rethinking of particular thought-relationships in many different ways in order to reach the last possible boundary through a knowledge of all the deviations, and thereby to arrive at the source of the entire conceptual scheme. In the second place, understanding calls for biographical study: exploring (for example) the ramifications of a friendship down to the concrete particulars and details in order to come close to the actuality that renders the unmistakable existential language audible.

Writings about Nietzsche

The most complete bibliography, Friedrich Würzbach's *Nietzsche, Ein Gesamtüberblick über die bisherige Nietzsche-Literatur* (Nietzsche: a Complete Survey of the Present Literature about Nietzsche) is to be found in *Literarische Berichte aus dem Gebiete der Philosophie* (Literary Reports from the Field of Philosophy), ed. by Arthur Hoffmann, Erfurt, K. Stenger; numbers 19, 20, 26.

Our footnotes on pages 32, 37, 38, 59, 65, 71, 80–81, 90 provide a supplement to the following list which contains only a few writings:

1. For a *complete presentation* see Charles Andler's six-volume *Nietzsche. Sa vie et sa pensée*, Paris, 1920–1931: 1. Les précurseurs de Nietzsche, 2. La jeunesse de Nietzsche, 3. Le pessimisme estétique de Nietzsche, 4. La maturité de Nietzsche jusqu'a sa mort, 5. Nietzsche et le transformisme intellectualiste, 6. La dernière philosophie de Nietzsche. By surveying the material in an elegant, judicious, and knowledgeable manner, these six volumes provide an excellent orientation. Andler's approach is literary and historical rather than philosophical; objectively and without being captivated by Nietzsche, he subjects Nietzsche's life and work to a historical analysis along the lines of traditional philosophic categories. This work is valuable for its scope and freedom of view, its sustained effort to determine the source and effect of Nietzsche's thoughts, and for its pervading honesty. Furthermore, it is the only comprehensive presentation in existence. But for all that, there is no disguising the philosophical naïveté that enables Andler to view the writer and poet—even the thinker—on the niveau of mere discussion of ideas rather than that of the genuine philosopher.

2. *Comprehensive views:* Lou Andreas-Salomé, *Friedrich Nietzsche in seinen Werken* (Friedrich Nietzsche in His Works), Vienna: 1894. Alois Riehl, *Friedrich Nietzsche, der Künstler und Denker* (Friedrich Nietzsche, the Artist and Thinker), 3rd ed., Stuttgart, 1901. Karl Joel, *Nietzsche und die Romantik* (Nietzsche and Romanticism), Jena, 1905. E. Bertram, *Nietzsche,* Berlin, 1918. Karl Justus Obenauer, *Friedrich Nietzsche, der ecstatische Nihilist* (Friedrich Nietzsche, the Ecstatic Nihilist). Jena, 1924. Ludwig Klages, *Die psychologischen Errungenschaften Nietzsches* (The Psychological Achievements of Nietzsche), 2nd ed., Leipzig, 1930. Alfred Baeumler, *Nietzsche, der Philosoph und Politiker* (Nietzsche, the Philosopher and Politician), Leipzig, 1931. Reclam. Josef Hofmiller, "Nietzsche," *Süddeutsche Monatshefte,* XXIX, pp. 73 ff., 1931. Kontroverse Hofmiller-Baeumler (The

Hofmiller-Baeumler Controversy), *Süddeutsche Monatshefte*, 28 (1930–31), pp. 536, 607 ff., 685 ff., 758 ff. Of these the most important are by Bertram, Klages, and Baeumler.

3. *Specific problems:* Max Scheler, "Das Ressentiment im Aufbau der Moralen" (Resentment in the Structure of Morals) in: *Abhandlungen und Aufsätze* (Treatises and Essays), vol. 1; and "Versuche einer Philosophie des Lebens" (Attempts concerning a Philosophy of Life), vol. 2. A. Baeumler, *Bachofen und Nietzsche*, published by *Neue Schweizer Rundschau*, Zurich, 1919; and Baeumler in: *Bachofen, Orient und Occident, Einleitung*, 1926, pp. 241–255. Friedrich Metz, *Nietzsche, der Gesetzgeber* (Nietzsche, the Lawgiver), Leipzig, 1930.

The following also deserve mention: Julius Zeitler, *Nietzsches Ästhetik*, Leipzig, 1900. Nicolai v. Bubnoff, *Friedrich Nietzsches Kulturphilosophie und Umwertungslehre* (Nietzsche's Philosophy of Culture and Doctrine of Revaluation), Leipzig, 1924. Werner Brock, *Nietzsches Idee der Kultur* (Nietzsche's Idea of Culture), Bonn, 1930. Erika Emmerich, *Wahrheit und Wahrhaftigkeit in der Philosophie Nietzsches* (Truth and Truthfulness in Nietzsche's Philosophy), Halle, 1933 (diss. Bonn). Erich Hocks, *Das Verhältnis der Erkenntnis zur Unendlichkeit der Welt bei Nietzsche* (The Relation between Knowledge and the Infinity of the World in Nietzsche), Leipzig, 1914. Karl Löwith, *Nietzsches Philosophie der ewigen Wiederkunft des Gleichen* (Nietzsche's Philosophy of the Eternal Recurrence of the Same), Berlin, 1935. Ernst Howald, *Friedrich Nietzsche und die klassische Philologie* (Friedrich Nietzsche and Classical Philology), Gotha, 1920. Gustav Naumann, *Zarathustra-Kommentar; vier Teile* (Zarathustra Commentary, Four Parts), Leipzig, 1899–1901.

4. *Invective:* Every great spirit is characterized in part by the way in which he is reviled. The unbiased reader must know how an author has been abused if he is, first of all, to test his ability to refute the critics or to resolve the problems under discussion, second, to become aware of the sort of facts which only hate can reveal, and third, to face up to the question as to what it is within the abused person himself that makes such abuse possible. I mention as examples: Ludwig Stein, *Friedrich Nietzsches Weltanschauung und ihre Gefahren* (Friedrich Nietzsche's *Weltanschauung* and its *Dangers*), Berlin, 1893. Johannes Schlaf, *Der Fall Nietzsche, eine Überwindung* (The Nietzsche Case, Something Overcome), Leipzig, 1907. Gustav Büscher, *Nietzsches wirkliches Gesicht* (The Real Face of Neitzsche), Zurich, A. Rudolf, 1928.

INDEX

Absolutization, of categories of world exegesis 244; of creation 160; of single world-being 316

Activity, active, in *amor fati* 368 f.; creative 274, 277, 280 f.; in experimenting 288 ff.; inner 139, 190 f., 453; justice 205; of life 297; negation of N. 247; new after 1887 98; as philosophizing 385; in spiritual development of N. since 1880 91 ff., 103, since 1887 97 f.; in studying N. 420, 452 ff.; of N. in world of reality 77

Actuality, union of thought and life as way to actuality and to whole man 387

Affirmation, of being 346, 360, 367 ff., 374 f., 377; decisive affirmation from essence ("state") 337 f.; N.'s great affirmation after 1880 93 f., 104; of illusion (as illusion) 200; as active justice 206; in complete knowledge 387; of man 126 f., 345; and negation of existence as vital activity 335; negation simultaneously as affirmation 396; through negation 359, 392 f.; N.'s thinking of 333 ff.; N.'s way to 45 f.; N.'s will to 442, 445

Age, of N. 65 f., 140 ff., 176 f., 210, 231 ff., 237 ff., 240 ff., 250, 258 ff., 271, 276, 278; N. and his age 97 f., 352, 367, 447 (see also world 1–1 history); N. misunderstood by his age 23, 244, 344

"All is well" 206

Ambiguity, in N.'s appearance 422 ff., 427 f.; clarifying N.'s ambiguity 418 ff.; education in ambiguity through N. 456; of exegesis, see exegesis; of a formula 227; of the great among men 35; of "healthy" and

"sick" 111 f.; inexplicable 227; of life 332; of the mask 406 ff.; in N.'s metaphysics of power 300, 309, 317; in portrait of N. 35 ff.; in N.'s self 417 ff., 450 ff., 456; in N.'s self-understanding 412 ff.; in N.'s transcending 430 ff., 434 ff.; necessary ambiguity of truth 18 f., 20 f.

Amor fati 348, 350, 352, 367 ff., 445; and N.'s awareness of destiny 55 f., 159

Animal, man as the "still not fixated animal" 130

Antiquity, Greek 30 (see also Greeks); N. and myths of 376; philosophy of 165 (see also pre-Socratic); power relationships in 300; science in 173 f.

Anxiety 348

Aphorism 3, 4 f., 103, 400

Appearance, concepts of "appearance" and "thing-in-itself" 329 f.; and the mask 407; of the will to power 308 ff.; the world as 185 f. (see also world)

Appropriation of N., limits of 318, 365 f., 377 f., 422 ff.; of N. as a task 6, 449 ff. (see also assimilation)

Ariadne 225 ff.

Aristocracy, aristocratic, the aristocratic man 133 (see also nobility, noble)

Art, N.'s interpretation of 310 f.

Assimilation, incompleteness of 458 (see also appropriation)

Athena 164

Autobiographical pronouncements of N. 386

Autonomous being (see also self-being), without God 349; of the individual 282 f.; as nobility 341 f.; of the thinker in his conception of being 348 f.

Genius, "genius of the heart" 22, 344
Glance, "glance of the Gorgon" 387
Goal, N.'s 252, 283, 363 ff., 375, 413,
442 f., 458; N.'s awareness of his
goal 44 ff.; of humanity 245, 276,
334, 432; of the knower 226; the One
goal 342, 432; the question concerning 157 f., 167 f., 224, 350; in N.'s
self-understanding 393 f.
God, "God is dead" 121, 135, 167, 210,
242 ff., 269 f., 276, 364, 375,
429 ff.; or cycle 363 ff.; freedom without 157 f.; or hybris 160; the "new
masters" in place of 269 ff.; morality
without 139 ff., 158; self-being without 160 f., 276; self-deification 88,
160, 377; "God's shadow" after His
death 247, 293
Godlessness, godless, and morality
139 f.; and philosophizing 437 f.;
N.'s philosophy of 363 ff., 429 ff.;
the superman in a godless world 167;
and will to truth 209 f.; and vision of
a whole 375
Greatness, great, creation of 121; and
honesty 202; N.'s longing for great
people (of highest rank) 86; great
men in N.'s historical consciousness
35; philosophy as "legislation for
greatness" 183; realization of greatness sought in cooperation with
Wagner 66 ff.; and the superior man
162 ff.; and the superman 162, 167 f.
Greeks (see also antiquity) 32, 46, 60,
134, 164, 200, 208 f., 235 f., 240 f.,
304 f., 347, 366, 374, 376, 443 (see
also index of names)

Handwriting, of N. 38 f.
Happiness, truth and 195, 226, 342 f.
Health, of N. 111 ff.; N.'s certainty concerning his existential health 115;
existential and medical 111 ff., 306 f.;
the "great health" 115; concept or
formula of "normal health" 111 f.;
will to health 115
Heir, contemporary man as heir of past
239
Heroism, hero, heroic, N.'s heroism
81 f., 344; heroic existence (a
"state") 342 ff.; hero and "super-
hero" 165
Historical consciousness, its infinitude
276; its limits and ambiguity 277;
its mode of knowledge 245 f.; its importance in N.'s philosophizing 280 f.,
429 ff. (see also world-history, age,
moment); of N. with respect to the
present as turning point of history
231 f., 240 ff., 244 ff., 250 ff., 258 ff.;
and N.'s task 247, 268 ff.

Historicity, N.'s affirmation of genuine
historicity 239 f.; and *amor fati*
367 ff.; communication in concrete
historicity 82; and N. as exception
426 ff.; N.'s experience of existential
historicity with the historicity of the
whole in the idea of eternal recurrence 356 f.; and law 141, 149; N.'s
philosophizing toward historicity of
Existenz 442 f.; and the rational
121 ff.; truth of *Existenz* in concrete
historicity 227; historicity of values
154
History, historical 231 ff., 236 ff.; N.'s
evaluation of 234 f.; in "excess"
238 f.; historical justice 207; as actual
events and universally valid knowledge 236 f.; of life and the universe
239; N.'s thoughts and views concerning history 232 ff.; the "unhistorical" as antidote for excess of history
237
Histrionics, foreign to N.'s nature 36;
of the "ideal" 165; and truth of
the mask 406 f.
Homo natura 290, 327, 433
Honesty, N.'s 430, 434; and cynicism
408; as the "new virtue" 202
Horizon, N.'s way to infinite horizon
31, 394, 442
Humanity, human, its decline through
knowledge 223 f.; goal of 432; man
as more than human 56; within the
whole world process 232, 239, 245
Hybris 160, 425 f.

Idea (see also thought), existential effect of 359 f.; of eternal recurrence
in its uniqueness 354 ff., 362 ff., 369
Ideal, idealism, idealists, idealism 369,
idealists 190, 343; existential nature
of N.'s ideal 121, 338, 342 f., 376;
N.'s ideal of man 126, 162 ff., 165;
philosophy of the ideal 212 f., 290 f.
Identity 212
Illness, N.'s 29, 88 ff., 447; N.'s attitude to 108 ff.; N.'s concept of "illness" 111 ff., 130 f., 306, 325, 335 f.,
425; diagnosis of N.'s illness 89 ff.,
100 f., 104; N.'s insight into 110 ff.;
N.'s existential interpretation of
111 ff.; "view of the ill": experience
of illness as source of concepts of
health and value 392; illness and
work 101 ff.; its source in organic
world 312
Illusion, as being itself 187; necessary
198; of things in being 350 f.; truth
as illusion 185 ff.; universal and specific 190 f.; the world as 204

understanding 386 ff.; total 237; "tragic finale of knowledge" 223 f.; unity and separation of life and 387 ff.; of the whole and the task of science 197 f.

Labyrinth 225 f.
Landscape 103 f., 372 f.; mythical aspect of 437; types favored by N. 373
Language, as medium of self-deception 133; nature as language 371 f. (see also poetry, simile, song, symbol, thought)
Laughter, as expression of philosophical truth 220
Law, of conformity or consent 233, 273; creative law and lawlessness 439; encompassing 151, 159, 281; and encompassing necessity 369 f.; in existential historical reality 149, 151; lawfulness in general 141, 143; N. as lawgiver 22, 413; lawgivers, legislation 183, 251, 273 ff.; moral 139 f., 143; of nature 289, 293; the "primary law" (cycle) 352; in science 172; telic 356
Leap, from experienced occurrences to transcendence 431
Library, N.'s library 31
Life, ambiguity of 322; ascending and descending 301, 307 f., 335; as being itself and as existence 321 ff. (see also man); chronological tables of N.'s life 460–61; cognitive 184 ff.; creative 157 ff., 208; dangerous life ("live dangerously") 258, 297, 343 f. (see also danger); and death 322 ff.; Dionysian 344 ff., 349 f.; as the encompassing 184 ff., 375 f.; in exegesis 294; as "experimenting" 388 f.; life's forces as source and danger of truth 192 ff.; destroyed through historical science 238; as justice 207 f.; and knowledge 222 ff., 298, 343; destroyed through morality 145; mere life without moral purpose 157; rank orders of 145, 191, 208; self-controlled effective life within concrete reality 199; self-limitation of 188, 351; in N.'s self-understanding 386 ff.; the signum of creative *Existenz* 322 ff.; source material for N.'s life 27 f., 386; soaring above 198, 329; surveys of N.'s life 27 ff.; relationship of N.'s life to his thought 12 f.; as tragic 346 f., 377; transformations in N.'s life, see transformations; as a trial 296 f.; "life of truth" 190 ff., 217 f.; value of 333 ff.; and the will to power 294 ff.

Limit (see also boundary), awareness of limits of theory of knowledge 187, 189 ff.; of comprehension and experience 226 f.; of doubt 227; lack of limits in N.'s thinking 425; of thought 189 f. (see also circle)
Logic, logical, N.'s "logic" 107 f., 212 f., 310; N.'s lack of logical clarity 357; N.'s conception of logic 395 ff.; N.'s logical consciousness 217 ff.; and logical N.-criticism 418 ff. (see also categories, circle, contradiction, dialectic); and logicians and "logical optimism" 214; philosophical 217
Loneliness, of the autonomous being 283; N.'s increasing loneliness 70 ff.; inherent in N.'s nature 87 (see also mask); from existential inadequacy 81 f. (see also communication, love); N.'s knowledge and avowal of 56, 74 f., 84 ff., 225 f., 372, 436, 437; "great politics" from a position of loneliness (separation) 251 f.; possibilities of psychological and existential illumination of N.'s loneliness 81 ff.; N.'s loneliness as a form of sacrifice 446 ff.; N.'s self-understanding of his loneliness 86 f., 225 f.; as a "state" 402; as result of his task 83 (see also exception)
Love, N. and love 82 f., 224 f., 348, 426, 428; and *amor fati* 367 ff.; for authentic life 361; of being 346; blind and clear-sighted 207, 345; cognition and 86 (see also knowledge); justice and 206 f.; knowledge and 224 f.; N.'s love for man 345, and discontent with man 125 ff., 165 f.; for nature 373 f.; for real life 297

Magic, "magic of the extreme" 161, 425, 439
Main, N.'s plan for and renewed work on his philosophical "main edifice" 1884 and 1887 50 f., 104 f.; main parts of presentation of N.'s philosophy 13 ff.
Man 125 ff.; and animal ("man the beast") 129 f., 239; in his awareness of existence 231 ff.; as boundary of existence 129 ff., 239; N.'s conception of man 162 ff.; N.'s concern over man 56, 67, 125 f., 192, 249 ff., 267 ff.; as his own creator 139 ff.; the Dionysian man 344 f.; goal of N.'s philosophizing "to concentrate a man" 458; the heroic man (as "transition") 342 f.; and history 231 ff., 236 ff.; way to complete man through knowledge 386; idea of more-than-man 56; nature of 127 ff.; and nature

INDEX OF NAMES

KARL JASPERS was born in Germany in 1883, studied medicine, received the degree of M. D. in 1909, published a major text on psychopathology in 1913, and by 1921 was applying these insights on human behavior to the field of philosophy as a professor at Heidelberg University. He was removed from his post by the Nazis in 1937 and reinstated in 1945. Since 1948 he has been professor of philosophy at the University of Basel, Switzerland. He is the most distinguished exponent of the philosophy of *Existenz*.

CHARLES F. WALLRAFF and FREDERICK J. SCHMITZ are heads of the departments of Philosophy and German respectively at the University of Arizona. Professor Wallraff was a student of Jaspers in Heidelberg in 1935, at about the time this book was published. He is a graduate of the University of California at Berkeley, a former teacher at Colorado and Olivet colleges, and the author of PHILOSOPHICAL THEORY AND PSYCHOLOGICAL FACT. Professor Schmitz, a native German, studied in Germany and received his B. A., M. A., and Ph. D., degrees from the University of California. He is the author of LESSINGS STELLUNG IN DER ENTFALTUNG DES INDIVIDUALISMUS and THE CRISES IN THE LIVES OF LESSING AND HAMANN.